Frommer's®

D1487945

Egypt
1st Edition

by Matthew Carrington

WITHDRAWN

Here's what the critics say about Frommer's:

"Amazingly easy to use. Very portable, very complete."
—*Booklist*

"Detailed, accurate, and easy-to-read information for all price ranges."
—*Glamour Magazine*

"Hotel information is close to encyclopedic."
—*Des Moines Sunday Register*

"Frommer's Guides have a way of giving you a real feel for a place."
—*Knight Ridder Newspapers*

WILEY

Wiley Publishing, Inc.

About the Author

Matthew Carrington has lived and worked in the Middle East as an editor, writer, and, most recently, photographer, for the last 10 years. He has done spells as an editor at the American University Press in Cairo, as publications director at the American Research Center in Egypt, and as editor of *The Cairo Times*. He also devoted a year to founding Egypt's most frequently censored English-language publication, *Cairo Magazine*. Work has taken him to Lebanon, Syria, Tunisia, Egypt, and Iraq, and his writing and pictures have appeared (amongst other places) in *The Guardian, The Globe and Mail,* and *The Pittsburgh Tribune-Review.*

Published by:

Wiley Publishing, Inc.

111 River St.
Hoboken, NJ 07030-5774

ISBN 978-0-470-25929-0
Editor: Anuja Madar
Production Editor: Katie Robinson
Cartographer: Roberta Stockwell
Photo Editor: Richard Fox
Production by Wiley Indianapolis Composition Services

Front cover photo: Cairo, Memphis: alabaster sphinx, close-up of head
Back cover photo: Men outside tents in souq area of Islamic Cairo

For information on our other products and services or to obtain technical support, please contact our Customer Care Department within the U.S. at 800/762-2974, outside the U.S. at 317/572-3993 or fax 317/572-4002.

Wiley also publishes its books in a variety of electronic formats. Some content that appears in print may not be available in electronic formats.

Manufactured in the United States of America

5   4   3   2   1

Contents

5 Cairo 72

6 Alexandria & the North Coast 127

7 The Sinai Peninsula 156

8 The Red Sea Coast 186

9 Upper Egypt 215

10 The Western Desert 254

Appendix A: Egypt in Depth   292

Appendix B: Useful Terms & Phrases   318

Index   327

List of Maps

Acknowledgments

This guide would never have been finished without the generous support of many people. I particularly want to acknowledge the patience and warmth of countless Egyptian small-business owners who unquestioningly toured this hurried stranger through their restaurants and hotels, cafes, stores, and offices, letting me bounce on the beds, sniff under the sinks, and ask intrusive questions about their business practices. You guys are what make Egypt a great place to be a tourist.

A partial list of people to whom I owe specific thanks: Nancy Albert, Sa'ad Ali, Abdullah Baghri, Eman Morsi, Ahmed Moussa, Paul Schemm, Amr Shannon, Ahmad Aboul Wafa, Tara Todras-Whitehill, Peter Wirth, and Abu Zahra.

And finally, to my wife Veronica Coulter, without whose research, forbearance, patience, imagination, and hot chocolate this would never have been finished: Thank you.

Any omissions and errors remain entirely my fault and responsibility.

An Invitation to the Reader

In researching this book, we discovered many wonderful places—hotels, restaurants, shops, and more. We're sure you'll find others. Please tell us about them, so we can share the information with your fellow travelers in upcoming editions. If you were disappointed with a recommendation, we'd love to know that, too. Please write to:

Frommer's Egypt, 1st Edition
Wiley Publishing, Inc. • 111 River St. • Hoboken, NJ 07030-5774

An Additional Note

Please be advised that travel information is subject to change at any time—and this is especially true of prices. We therefore suggest that you write or call ahead for confirmation when making your travel plans. The authors, editors, and publisher cannot be held responsible for the experiences of readers while traveling. Your safety is important to us, however, so we encourage you to stay alert and be aware of your surroundings. Keep a close eye on cameras, purses, and wallets, all favorite targets of thieves and pickpockets.

Other Great Guides for Your Trip:

Frommer's Morocco
Frommer's Israel

Frommer's Star Ratings, Icons & Abbreviations

Every hotel, restaurant, and attraction listing in this guide has been ranked for quality, value, service, amenities, and special features using a **star-rating system.** In country, state, and regional guides, we also rate towns and regions to help you narrow down your choices and budget your time accordingly. Hotels and restaurants are rated on a scale of zero (recommended) to three stars (exceptional). Attractions, shopping, nightlife, towns, and regions are rated according to the following scale: zero stars (recommended), one star (highly recommended), two stars (very highly recommended), and three stars (must-see).

In addition to the star-rating system, we also use **eight feature icons** that point you to the great deals, in-the-know advice, and unique experiences that separate travelers from tourists. Throughout the book, look for:

Finds	Special finds—those places only insiders know about
Fun Fact	Fun facts—details that make travelers more informed and their trips more fun
Kids	Best bets for kids and advice for the whole family
Moments	Special moments—those experiences that memories are made of
Overrated	Places or experiences not worth your time or money
Tips	Insider tips—great ways to save time and money
Value	Great values—where to get the best deals
Warning	Warning—traveler's advisories are usually in effect

The following **abbreviations** are used for credit cards:

AE	American Express	DISC	Discover	V	Visa
DC	Diners Club	MC	MasterCard		

Frommers.com

Now that you have this guidebook to help you plan a great trip, visit our website at **www. frommers.com** for additional travel information on more than 4,000 destinations. We update features regularly to give you instant access to the most current trip-planning information available. At Frommers.com, you'll find scoops on the best airfares, lodging rates, and car rental bargains. You can even book your travel online through our reliable travel booking partners. Other popular features include:

- Online updates of our most popular guidebooks
- Vacation sweepstakes and contest giveaways
- Newsletters highlighting the hottest travel trends
- Podcasts, interactive maps, and up-to-the-minute events listings
- Opinionated blog entries by Arthur Frommer himself
- Online travel message boards with featured travel discussions

The Best of Egypt

Egypt is such a big and varied country that it's hard to know where to even start describing its best, most intense, and most satisfying places and moments. Every time I'm in the country, I think I've found the best of Egypt, and every time I go back, I find something new that convinces me afresh that this time, finally, I've got them. Egypt offers everything, and more, from sunrise in the desert on the edge of the Great Sand Sea, to sunset over the granite mountains of the Sinai where they meet the shimmering azure of the Red Sea, to trailing my fingers in the cool waters of the Nile from the back of a *faluca* after a day of exploring underground tombs. Below are some highly subjective "best of" lists that I invite you to use in building your own Egypt adventure. I am certain that as you try out some of the places and activities that I have savored over the years, you'll find your own way to appreciate and experience them, and to make the story of Egypt your own.

1 The Best Purely Egyptian Experiences

- **The Call to Prayer from the Citadel** (Fatimid Cairo): As the sun sets over Fatimid Cairo, dozens of mosques send out their calls to prayer. With flocks of pigeons circling in the golden light and the last sun of the day picking out the highlights of the domes below, the ancient chanting surrounds you and takes you to centuries past. See p. 95.

- **Cairo Tower** (Cairo): From this tower in the middle of the city, your view encompasses everything from the Great Pyramid in Giza all the way to the Moqattam Hills on the other side of the valley. For just a moment, it feels as though you can actually get your head around this extraordinarily complex, vibrant city. See p. 82.

- **A Cold Beer at the Cap d'Or** (Alexandria): No visit to Alexandria is complete without a stop at this back-street pub, which retains the ambience of an era that has now all but slipped away. Look around at the fading posters, and watch the regulars come and go. See p. 148.

- **Tea at the Old Cataract Hotel** (Aswan): If it was good enough for Winston Churchill and Agatha Christie, it's good enough for me. This is a great place to catch the sunset; the sun turns the dunes on the other side of the famous First Cataract of the Nile to a reddish gold, and the *falucas* drift back and forth. See p. 251.

- **Sunrise at the Summit of Jebel Moussa** (Mt. Sinai; St. Catherine): This is where Moses is said to have received the tablets containing the Ten Commandments. The view across the rugged red mountains of the Sinai as the sun rises is unforgettable. See p. 171.

- **Tea at Fishawy's** (Cairo): What could be more Egyptian than drinking sweet tea among the spices, gewgaws, and crowds of a densely packed souk? Watch the crowds of people from all over the world, and haggle with merchants who will stop by with everything from saffron to sunhats. See p. 121.

- **Palm Sunday in Coptic Cairo** (Cairo): Celebrate Easter with one of the oldest Christian communities in the world. Children and families crowd the ancient church-lined street giving out crosses and little figures made of local palm leaves. See p. 100.

2 The Best of Ancient Egypt

- **The Pyramids in Giza** (Giza): There's no way to come to Egypt and not visit the pyramids. They are as vast and imposing as they were when they were built more than 4 millennia ago, and their impact has not been dimmed by the crowds of tourists and touts. See p. 82.
- **Valley of the Kings** (Luxor): Since it was first excavated at the beginning of the 20th century, this steep-sided valley on the west bank in Luxor has long been drawing tourists to its underground complex of richly decorated tombs. There is now a whole industry built on these visitors, and rightly so—it's a must-see. See p. 229.
- **Sound and Light Show at Karnak Temple** (Luxor): Justly famous for its massive hypostyle hall, this vast temple complex reveals a whole new side of itself at night. Follow the narration through the ancient courtyards, and try to snap a picture of the dramatic lighting effects. See p. 224.

- **Medinet Habu** (West Bank): This often overlooked temple has it all: big walls, glorious gory hieroglyphs, and a great rural setting—and with far less hassle than you get almost everywhere else in Upper Egypt. See p. 226.
- **Temple of Amun** (Siwa): This small, remote temple in the distant western desert oasis is plain and not very well preserved compared to the sites of Luxor and the Giza Plateau, but it does have unparalleled mystique. See p. 261.
- **Saqqara:** The setting makes this site even more special than its historical significance. Like the pyramids in Giza, it sits on the edge of the desert looking down at the river valley. Whereas the megalopolis of Cairo sits at the foot of the monument at Giza, Saqqara is surrounded by greenery and looks like it might have many millennia ago. See p. 123.

3 The Best Islamic Sites

- **Al Azhar Mosque** (Cairo): This mosque has undergone a number of changes since it was built in A.D. 972 and has been the centerpiece of the Islamic world's most prestigious university since A.D. 988. See p. 93.
- **Bab Zuweila** (Cairo): This huge gate, which rises out of the thick-packed confusion of a local souk, was one of the original entrances to the Fatimid city of Qahira (Cairo). Its colossal

shoulders bear witness to the architectural and military power of the 11th-century founders of this dynasty. See p. 93.
- **The Madrasa of Sultan Hassan** (Cairo): This massive example of Mamluke self-aggrandizement casts a massive shadow over the rundown neighborhood that surrounds it. Yet, from inside, the 14th-century domes and courtyards are gracefully

proportioned and somehow human in scale. See p. 97.

- **Mohamed Ali Mosque** (Cairo): Its high Ottoman dome gives this mosque a tremendous sense of calm and space, and the view across old Cairo from the courtyard is second to none. See p. 95.

- **Mosque of Ibn Tulun** (Cairo): Unique, Iraqi-style decorations set this 9th-century mosque apart from others in the city. The enormous courtyard is a reminder that there was once a time when you could build a mosque big enough to hold every man in the surrounding area. See p. 98.

4 The Best Shopping Experiences

- **Aswan Souk:** Even though it's rapidly becoming more touristy, this rambling, sprawled-out souk retains all the vibrancy you would expect of a millennia-old crossroads on the trading routes between Africa and the Mediterranean world. See p. 253.

- **Egypt Craft Center** (8–27 Yehia Ibrahim St., Zamalek, Cairo; ✆ 02/27365123): Here you have low-hassle access to a range of folk crafts from around Egypt. This is a particularly good place to pick up pottery from the Fayum or handmade scarves from Upper Egypt. Proceeds go to support community development nongovernmental organizations (NGOs).

- **Khan al Khalili** (Cairo): This centuries-old souk in the heart of old Cairo is a must for anyone who has the shopping bug or just wants to experience the real hustle and bustle of an Arab city. Take cash, and be prepared to haggle. This is the best place in town to buy novelty T-shirts, souvenirs with your name printed in hieroglyphics, and those little bottles of colored sand that have pictures of camels in them. See p. 96.

- **Khan Msr Toulon** (Tulun Bey Street, Cairo; ✆ 02/33652227): This French-run store, located just across the street from the mosque of the same name (but spelled differently), has a not-at-all-surprising sense of style. Shelves are stuffed with interesting handicrafts, furniture, and glassware from Cairo and beyond.

- **Nomad** (14 Saraya Al Gezira, Cairo; ✆ 02/27361917): Check out the main branch of this store for a great selection of handicrafts from all over Egypt, including hand-woven Bedouin blankets, silver jewelry, and embroidered pillow slips. Prices are fixed, and staff are friendly and helpful.

- **Siwa Souk:** For an end-of-the-world shopping experience, the central square in Siwa is hard to beat. It wasn't long ago that all the goods brought here were bartered for in this marketplace, and many of the locally made handicrafts on sale here are impossible to find anywhere else. See p. 265 and p. 266.

- **Souk el Fustat** (Cairo): This is a little shopping mall just outside the northern entrance to Coptic Cairo that's aimed squarely at the discerning foreign buyer. Check out the beautiful handmade copies of Mamluke and Fatimid lamps sold here by Hassan and Mohamed. See p. 119.

5 The Best High-End Hotels

- **Adrere Amella** (Siwa; ✆ 02/2735 1924; www.adrereamellal.net): Gorgeous local scenery meets gorgeous local architecture in this high-end, high-concept, all-inclusive ecolodge. Bask by the pool, eat local foods, and pamper yourself in the palatial bathroom, all with an ecofriendly peace of mind.

- **Four Seasons Hotel Alexandria** (399 Al Geish Rd., Alexandria; ✆ 03/5818000; www.fourseasons.com): The only criticism you could make of this re-creation of a classic Alexandria hotel is that it's just a little too perfect.

- **Four Seasons Hotel Cairo at the First Residence** (35 Giza St., Giza, Cairo; ✆ 02/35731212; www.fourseasons.com): It says it all that the only hotel in Cairo that competes with the Four Seasons (below) is another Four Seasons. The First Residence is a little out of the center, but it makes up for it by having the greenest view of any hotel in the city—it looks out across the Giza Zoo.

- **Four Seasons Nile Plaza** (1089 Corniche el Nile, Cairo; ✆ 02/27917000; www.fourseasons.com): It's hard to get any more central or stylish than the smoothly modern Four Seasons Plaza. From the cutting-edge collection of Egyptian art on the walls to the beautifully designed pool and dining facilities, you can rest assured that nobody's staying anywhere nicer tonight.

- **Hotel Al Moudira** (West Bank, Luxor; ✆ 095/2551440; www.moudira.com): This is a lovingly put together boutique hotel on the edge of the desert. The individually designed and decorated rooms are spread through a splendidly understated garden, and the pool is a tranquil work of art. The food, though, tops it all.

- **Mena House Oberoi** (Pyramids Road, Giza, Cairo; ✆ 02/33773222; www.oberoimenahouse.com): Beautiful period furniture in an authentic 19th-century setting, Oberoi service standards, and the best Indian food in town—oh, and did I mention the view of the pyramids on the Giza Plateau from your room?

6 The Best Midrange Hotels

- **Bab Inshal** (Midan el Souq, Siwa; ✆ 046/4601499): You can't get much closer to the ruins of the old city than the Bab Inshal—it's literally built into the ancient walls. Combine this with gorgeous, traditionally constructed rooms and fantastic food in the rooftop restaurant, and you've got your desert base sorted out.

- **Cosmopolitan** (21 26th of July St., Cairo; ✆ 02/25752323): Take a step back about 50 years to a quieter, cleaner Cairo, a Cairo where the brass handles on the lifts gleamed unobtrusively and the wooden banisters were polished to a mirror finish. It's still here, faded in places and needing some modern plumbing in others, but basically intact.

- **The Badawiya** (Gama Abdel Nasser St., Farafra; ✆ 092/7510060; www.badawiya.com): Accommodation in the middle of nowhere doesn't get much better than this. Big rooms made out of local sandstone, deliciously comfortable beds, and endlessly friendly and accommodating staff make this a desert home away from home.

- **Shali Lodge** (El Seboukha St., Siwa; ✆ 046/4601299): Tucked out of sight amongst the palm trees, this comfortable little hotel combines the smooth lines of traditional Siwan architecture with the best of casual, warm, and efficient Bedouin service. Kicking back in the pool in the heat of the day and watching the palm trees wave gently in the breeze is pretty close to heaven.

- **Sheraton Luxor** (Khalid Ibn el Walid St., Luxor; ✆ **095/2274544;** www.starwoodhotels.com): This big, secluded hotel at the southern end of Luxor delivers resort-style accommodation and quick, efficient service at a midrange price. Watch the Nile roll slowly past from the riverside pool, or relax in comfort with a beer on the terrace.

- **St. Joseph Hotel Luxor** (Khalid Ibn el Walid St., Luxor; ✆ **095/ 2381707**): Friendly service, comfy rooms, and a view of the Nile from the rooftop bar make this widely copied expat favorite the best value for the money in Luxor. Toss in a good location, with restaurants and bars within walking distance of the front door, and you have champagne accommodations on a beer budget.

- **Talisman** (39 Talat Harb St., Cairo; ✆ **02/23939431**): If you want to get away from the cookie-cutter chains and see the real Cairo, but you don't feel ready to kip with the backpacker crowd, head to this downtown boutique hotel in a renovated 19th-century flat. Every room is different, and the hallways are an antiques collector's dream.

7 The Best Budget Hotels

- **El Karm Ecolodge** (Sheikh Awad, St. Catherine, Sinai; ✆ **010/1324693**): This is the only budget hotel that's a destination as well. Classic Nabatean-style rockwork combines gracefully with simple architecture here in the middle of the Sinai. This is a clean, quiet getaway for those willing to rough it a little.

- **Dolphin Camp** (Mashraba, Dahab; ✆ **069/3640081;** www.dolphin camp.net): Grass huts, a sea breeze, and a laid-back attitude are what make Dolphin Camp the place to go hang, hang, and then hang some more. If you feel like splurging, they have rooms with air-conditioning, but if you want to stretch the budget into another week of, well, hanging, then take a hut and let nature keep you cool.

- **El Salam** (101 Corniche el Nil, Aswan; ✆ **097/2302651**): This deceptively large hotel is quiet and takes you back to basics. Compromise the rooms without the en suite, and get a big balcony with a stunning view up and down the Nile. If you remembered to go to duty-free at the airport, it's the perfect place to put your feet up and toast the end of the day.

- **Mina Palace** (Corniche el Nile, Luxor; ✆ **095/2372074**): Who says you get what you pay for? This is a $10-a-night hotel with a $300 view across the Nile. Plus, it has a killer location across the street from the gory-yet-fascinating Museum of Mummification and is halfway between Luxor Temple and the must-see Luxor Museum.

- **Nakhil** (Gezirat al Baraat, West Bank, Luxor; ✆ **095/2313922**): This is a lovely little getaway in the back of the tranquil West Bank. The Nakhil has mid-level rooms for a bottom-end price. About the only thing it lacks, in fact, is the noise and hassle of the East Bank.

- **Nefertiti Hotel** (Al Sahabi St., Luxor; ✆ **095/2372386;** www. nefertitihotel.com): Jammed into the heart of Luxor's tourist souk, the Nefertiti is a travel agent, social hub, pool hall, and Internet cafe all rolled into one affordable package. Oh, yeah, and some comfy rooms and hot showers are thrown in there as well.

- **Union Hotel** (164 26th of July St., Alexandria; ✆ **03/4807771**): This has long been the preferred hideaway of expats on a weekend pass and archaeologists passing through town on their way to work. The Union plays out the classic budget formula: clean sheets, hot water, and a friendly, honest staff. And if you lean way out from your balcony, you can even see the sea.

8 The Best Restaurants

- **Abu Sid** (Off 26th of July St., Zamalek, Cairo; ✆ **02/27359640**): Reservations are required at this upscale eatery, and when you get to the table, traditional Egyptian cuisine never tasted so good. Get down to the classics in an intimate atmosphere decorated with icons of Egyptian culture from the golden days of music and film.

- **Bab Inshal** (Midan el Souq, Siwa; ✆ **046/4601499**): This place is about atmosphere as much as the food. The rooftop restaurant at the Bab Inshal is backed into the ruins of the ancient city of Shali in the center of the oasis. The menu of Siwan dishes was developed by a French chef and is at once bold and satisfyingly simple. This restaurant serves the best Egyptian breakfast in the country.

- **Fish Market** (El Geish Road, Alexandria; ✆ **03/4805114**): Down-market atmosphere and upmarket food make this the best place to settle into a traditional Alexandrian meal of shrimp and grilled fish. Head down here around sunset to take advantage of the best harbor view in town.

- **La Scala** (Abu Tig Marina, Gouna; ✆ **065/3541145**): Look in the window, and you're going to see a basic diner with a long open kitchen and simple decor. Get down to business with the food, though, and you're going to have the best steak and grilled vegetables on the Red Sea coast.

- **Mogul Room** (Pyramids Road, Giza, Cairo; ✆ **02/33773222**): It's a long drive from Downtown Cairo, but the Mogul Room would be worth it even if it was another hour. The food is the best Indian meal in town, and the location—the lush, 19th-century Mena House Oberoi and the pyramids—adds additional spice to the meal.

- **Moudira Hotel Dining Room** (West Bank, Luxor; ✆ **095/2551440**): Classically elegant tables amidst the garden of Al Moudira's central courtyard makes for one of the loveliest and most sophisticated restaurant settings in Egypt, and the food lives up to the architectural billing.

- **Tandoori** (Naama Bay, King of Bahrain Street, Dahab; ✆ **069/3600700**): From the street, the only indication that this place even exists is the scent of spices that wafts through the doors of the Camel Hotel. Inside you'll find the best north Indian cuisine on the coast at a price that won't make a dent in your wallet.

9 The Best Christian Cultural Sites

- **Al Bagawat Cemetery** (Kharga): One of the largest ancient Christian cemeteries in the world, al Bagawat in the Western Desert is still comprised of more than 200 domed mausoleums, some of which contain exceptional wall paintings depicting biblical scenes. See p. 289.

- **Church of St. George** (Cairo): This small, domed, Greek Orthodox church in Coptic Cairo is built on top of the ruins of the Roman Fortress of Babylon. With the lights low and the lines of candles flickering beside the altar, this is one of the most atmospheric spots in all of Cairo. See p. 100.

- **Monastery of St. Anthony** (Red Sea): Set in the middle of the magnificently stark scenery of the remote Red Sea coast, this ancient monastery was built on the site near Anthony's cave where his followers established a camp. The chapel where they buried him is decorated with some of the richest Coptic art in the world. See p. 210.

- **Monastery of St. Paul** (Red Sea): This is a high-walled compound, fortified against attacks by local Bedouins, that is still a functioning monastery not far from the Monastery of St. Anthony. St. Paul is said to have been fed every day by a crow that brought him bread. See p. 210.

- **Monastery of St. Simeon** (Aswan): This monastery is still massive and imposing despite having been abandoned for centuries. It stands like an abandoned fortress on the edge of the desert on the west bank of the Nile at Aswan. See p. 246.

- **St. Catherine's Monastery** (Sinai): The oldest continually working Christian monastery in the world, St. Catherine's is uniquely steeped in tradition. It's also rich in religious art, having neglected to take part in the 8th- and 9th-century destruction of iconographic art. See p. 171.

10 The Best Resorts

- **Four Seasons Resort Sharm el Sheikh** (1 Four Seasons Blvd., Sharm el Sheikh; ℭ **069/3603555;** www. fourseasons.com): Perfect from the moment you ride through the front gate until the time you leave, the Four Seasons in Sharm sets the standard for service and restrained-but-lavish architecture.

- **Le Méridien Dahab Resort** (Dahab; ℭ **069/3640425;** www.starwood hotels.com): In addition to boasting top-notch facilities in a striking location, this stylish new resort impresses from the moment you walk into the lobby with its bold mix of colors and textures and innovative use of light and shadow.

- **Mövenpick Quseir** (Sirena Beach, El Quadim Bay, Quseir; ℭ **065/ 3332100;** www.moevenpick-hotels. com): This low-key, family-friendly resort hugs the coastline, blending with the local scenery and making a perfect setting for a romantic getaway—even if you have to take the kids along.

- **Oberoi Sahl Hashish** (Sahl Hashish; ℭ **065/3440777;** www.oberoihotels. com): With standard rooms that would pass muster as junior suites anywhere else, bathrooms that could do double duty as a spa, and the best massage facility on the Red Sea coast, the Oberoi at Sahl Hashish is guaranteed to put a smile on your face even as it wipes away the lines from around your eyes.

- **The Palace at Port Ghalib** (Port Ghalib, Marsa Alam; ℭ **02/ 27351962;** www.discoverportghalib. com): Sun International's debut on the Red Sea coast is set in a complete, purpose-built village on the edge of a full-size lagoon. The hotel is as top end as it gets, with imposing architecture, splendid dining, and everything from diving and beach parties to desert safaris.

- **Sheraton Soma Bay** (Soma Bay, Safaga; © **065/3545845**; www. sheraton-somabay.com): A hypostyle lobby and a beach that seems to go on forever make this expansive resort a great place for an active vacation or just lolling about in the sand. Fun architecture, great food, and unparalleled facilities mean a good time whichever way you decide to go.

11 The Best Diving Spots

- **Giftun Island** (off Hurghada): The coral reefs around this big, sandy island are second to none for color and variety. There are at least a dozen places to dive around the edge of the island, and with a good guide you can usually get away from the crowds and have a reef to yourself. See p. 204.
- **Panorama Reef** (Hurghada): This is a long block of vibrant colored coral that offers the possibility of seeing eagle rays, turtles, and even white-tipped and hammerhead sharks. See p. 199.
- **Ras Mohamed National Park** (Sinai): Where the deep waters of the Gulf of Aquaba meet the warm shallow waters of the Gulf of Suez at the southern tip of the Sinai Peninsula, this thin finger of a reef houses some of the richest and most colorful coral and fish populations in the world. See p. 180.
- **Seven Pillars** (Soma Bay): As easy for beginners as it is rewarding for experts, the Seven Pillars site off the Sheraton Soma Bay beach has a resident Napoleon fish. It's named for the coral pillars that rise from a depth of 12m (39 ft.) almost to the surface and play host to scores of puffer, lizard, and lion fish. See p. 199.
- **Straits of Tiran** (Sharm el Sheikh): The warm waters off Sharm el Sheikh offer the possibility of some of the most dramatic drift dives in the world through Jackson, Woodhouse, and Gordon reefs, and dozens of other sites. See p. 179.
- **The Wreck of the SS** *Dunraven* (Sharm el Sheikh): This late-19th-century wreck of a spice ship from Bombay is a popular dive from Sharm el Sheikh. The upside-down hull is broken open, and it's possible to enter the wreck and look at the old boilers. See p. 179.
- **The Wreck of the** *Thistlegorm* (Sharm el Sheikh): Thirty meters (98 ft.) below the surface, between the Red Resort City of Hurghada and the Ras Mohamed National Park, lies this World War II cargo vessel. Check out the vintage motorbikes as well as a pair of locomotives that were flung away from the wreck by the force of the explosions that sunk it. See p. 204.

12 The Best Museums

- **Aswan Museum:** This tiny museum on the southern end of Elephantine Island in Aswan lost most of its best pieces to the new Nubian Museum and, hence, doesn't receive many visitors now. But its 19th-century building, the residence of the architect of the Aswan Dam, Sir William Wilcocks, is a museum itself and deserves a visit. See p. 245.
- **Egyptian Museum** (Cairo): With a history that goes back to the very

beginning of the archaeological exploration of Europe, the collection of antiquities held by the Egyptian Museum is one of the richest and most varied in the world. From Tutankhamun's tomb to the Fayum portraits, there is no way to come to Egypt and miss this one. See p. 89.

- **Luxor Museum:** It may be smaller than the Egyptian Museum in Cairo, but the Luxor Museum is better lit, better organized, and better documented. Housing an impressive display of ancient Egyptian artifacts, it's not something that you should miss if you're in town. See p. 223.

- **Mummification Museum** (Luxor): It sounds lurid, and it is, but it's also well laid out and holds some impressive items. Kids will particularly enjoy the displays of mummies and the tools used to embalm them. See p. 225.

- **The Museum at St. Catherine's Monastery:** This monastery's collection of ancient manuscripts is second in size only to the Vatican's. A few of these are on display, as well as some impressive early icons, truly jaw-dropping golden reliquaries, and examples of devotional embroidery. See p. 172.

- **Nubian Museum** (Aswan): This is a long-overdue monument to the land of Nubia, flooded by the construction of the Aswan High Dam in the early 1970s. The museum tries to re-create the lost culture and leads the visitor through the history of the land all the way to its rather abrupt modern truncation. See p. 246.

2

Planning Your Trip to Egypt

Egypt is a big, diverse country that encompasses some of the most verdant and fertile farmland in the world, stretching across thousands of miles of the most forbidding and remote desert on Earth and bordering on two seas. As culturally diverse and exciting as it is topographically varied, Egypt offers visitors a chance to explore 6,000 years of history, while a burgeoning outdoor-adventure industry gives you a chance to explore the empty expanse of the desert on camels, sandboard down mountainous dunes, sailboard, or just lie on the beach and enjoy the pristine azure of the Red Sea.

Egypt sits on the northeast corner of Africa, and though it is generally lumped in with the Middle East, it remains, technically at least, an African country. To the west, it shares a long desert border with Libya, and to the south it borders on Sudan. To the east there is a short land border with the Gaza Strip, controlled by the Palestinian Authority. With a total area of around 1 million square kilometers (386,000 sq. miles), it is about three times the size of New Mexico, but the vast majority of the 80 million people who live in Egypt are squeezed into a narrow, densely populated strip of fertile land close to the Nile.

Despite an economy that has rebounded in the last few years, Egypt remains mired in the problems all too familiar to states dominated by their armies. Corruption is endemic, administrative and political incompetence the norm, and heavy-handed security forces maintain political stability by means well outside what even Egyptian law permits. In spite of being beset by a myriad of problems, however, Egyptians remain a remarkably cheerful and open people with an admirable *joie de vivre.*

For the most part, tourism in Egypt is concentrated around Cairo, Luxor, and Aswan in Upper Egypt, and around two new centers—Sharm el Sheikh and Hurghada—that have been built in the last 25 years to serve the sun-and-fun industry on the coast of the Red Sea. Alexandria and the oases of the Western Desert, despite having as much (in some ways much more) to offer, remain secondary destinations.

Egypt is an easy country to get around, and services are generally quite economically priced, so spur-of-the-moment travel is quite practicable. Buying bus and plane tickets, making hotel reservations, and simply finding your way about a country with shaky infrastructure and almost nonexistent English-language signage can be time-consuming, however; for this reason, it's probably a good idea to take advantage of your travel agent for help booking some basic items before you go. At the same time, midrange and upper-range hotels in Egypt are set up to deal with block bookings from abroad much more efficiently than they can accommodate walk-ins, and your travel agent, or the companies listed here, in the "Packages for the Independent Traveler" (p. 40) section, will have access to substantially reduced prices on resorts and some adventure-travel services. However you choose to mix the ad hoc with the preplanned, this chapter will provide you with the resources that you need to make your Egyptian trip a hassle-free and pleasant adventure.

1 Regions in Brief

Cairo & Environs The capital of Egypt is a massive, densely populated city of around 13 million people. Crammed with historic mosques, great museums, and must-see sights, Cairo is, by the same token, probably not a place that you want to spend more than a few days. The air is polluted, the infrastructure on the point of collapse, and the roads edge closer to gridlock with every week.

The pyramids of the Giza Plateau, maybe the most famous works of public architecture on Earth and the only one of the original Seven Wonders of the World still extant, lie on the western outskirts of the city. A short drive into the countryside to the south lie the necropolis of Saqqara and the remnants of the ancient capital of Memphis, as well as the sites of Dashur and Abu Sir.

Beyond Giza and Saqqara, but still an easy day trip from the city, the oasis of Fayum offers a unique cultural and shopping experience.

Trains run north and south from Cairo, and it is the hub for both air and bus transport all over Egypt. Almost all travel agents have offices here, and the head offices of all the airlines that service Egypt are here as well.

North Coast Egypt's Mediterranean coast has long been a world apart from the interior of Egypt, and did not become important until it was invaded by Alexander the Great (for whom Alexandria is named) in 331 B.C. Until the exodus that followed the army's takeover of the government in the 1950s, Alexandria was the center of a thriving and cosmopolitan Mediterranean society. Evidence of this past can still be seen in the stunning Roman mosaics that have been unearthed near the train station, the densely interwoven cosmogony of the Kom al Shuqafa catacombs, and even the gleaming wood and brass of the old coffee shops around Midan Saad Zahgloul.

Recently the coast to the east and west of Alex, as the city is affectionately known, has experienced something of a resurgence as a summer getaway for upper-class Cairenes escaping the muggy July and August heat of the capital. Holiday villas now blight miles of once-pristine white beach, and you have to go a long way these days to find an open spot of sand. Most foreigners, however, visit the north coast for the diving. From World War II submarines and planes to the ruins of what just might be Cleopatra's Palace, there is a world of underwater treasures to be explored.

Upper Egypt From the Valley of the Kings and Tutankhamun tomb to Karnak Temple, Abu Simbel, and the Colossus of Memnon, Upper Egypt has become synonymous with ancient Egyptian treasures. Luxor, close to the ancient capital of Thebes, and Aswan are the two cities of Upper Egypt that serve the tourists who flock here in the hundreds of thousands to tour the Pharaonic monuments around these otherwise unremarkable little cities.

Upper Egypt is also home to Nubia, which has a culture, history, and way of life all its own. Coming from Cairo to Aswan, you will immediately notice the change in atmosphere. Gone is the hustle and bustle of the big city, replaced by a laid-back attitude that takes the days as they come and seems to match the monuments themselves for timeless tranquility. With fewer must-see sights, Aswan is the place to unwind—go for a sunset sail on the Nile and wander the souk in search of local handicrafts.

Sinai Peninsula Fought over in the 1960s and 1970s, Sinai did not come into its own as a tourist destination until the 1980s. The first to note its potential were the occupying Israeli forces, but after their withdrawal in 1982, Egyptians and foreigners began to flock to the deserted,

The Regions in Brief

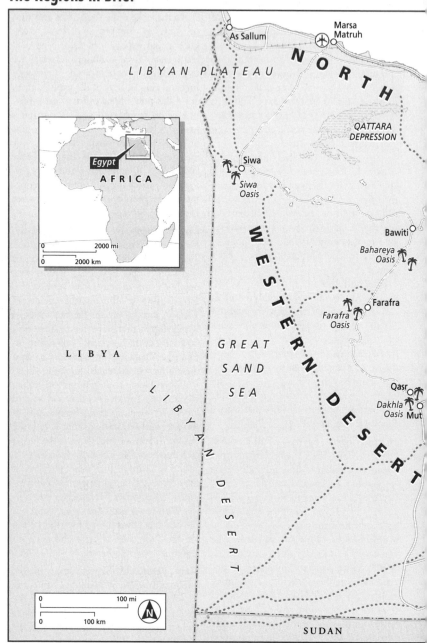

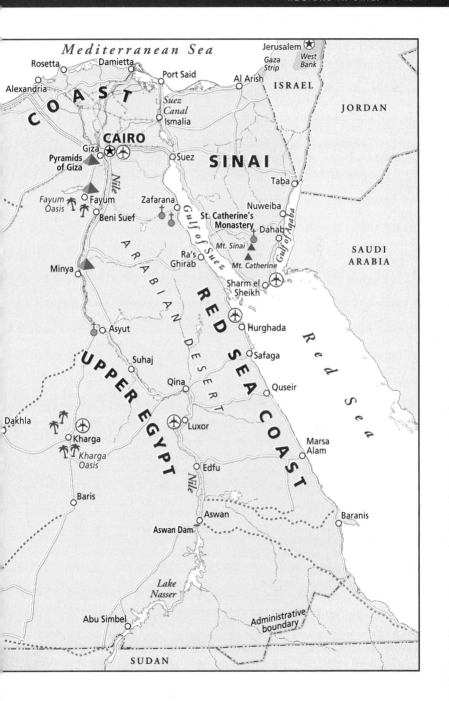

palm-lined beaches and miles of pristine coral on the Sinai's eastern coast. Twenty-five years later, the main center of Sharm el Sheikh is a thriving, and still growing, city, and the coast is lined with literally hundreds of resorts. According to government statistics, 80% of all housing in Sharm is in the form of hotels, and only 3% is used by the original local population.

All this development has come at an environmental cost—tables and chairs have supplanted palm trees as the dominant beach fauna, and in many places the coral has been severely damaged. Substantial efforts are now being made by both international donors and local non-governmental organizations (NGOs) to preserve what's left.

With all the hotels and the saturation level of advertising showing beaches and coral, it's easy to forget that the Sinai Peninsula has some of the most stunning desert scenery you can imagine, a must-see 6th-century monastery, and a spectacularly remote Pharaonic site.

Red Sea Coast　The stretch of coastline from Marsa Allam up to Gouna is the new boomtown of Egyptian tourism, a spectacular desert coastline now being developed with a series of plush (and some not-so-plush) resorts. Long the preserve of divers intrepid enough to brave a 12- to 18-hour bus ride to camp on a beach, the wrecks and marine life are now accessible to those of us whose ideas of hardship are having to wave down a waiter or carry our own towels.

Around Hurghada, where much of the development first started, many of the resorts are all-inclusive and have slid down-market. In recent years, the town has been held up by development experts and businessmen as an example of how

not to do it in the future. Lax planning and cut-throat pricing have resulted in a frankly ugly, disorganized mess of a town, at once overbuilt and half-finished.

Less frequently cited, however, are the positive examples on either side of Hurghada—Soma Bay, Gouna, and Sahl Hashish all combine first-class resorts with stunning beaches and great diving.

Western Desert & the Oases of the New Valley　The vast stretch of desert to the west of Cairo, Luxor, and Aswan is a rough oblong bordered by Libya to the west and the Nile Valley to the east, with the top and bottom defined by the Mediterranean and Sudan, respectively. In prehistoric times, this desert was alternately savanna and submerged by water, and the fossilized traces of both aquatic and land-based life lay scattered about underfoot almost everywhere you look. At the same time, rock paintings showing life of early man abound in certain areas, with some of the richest finds in this regard in the deep south around the Gilf Kebir (made famous by the 1996 movie *The English Patient*).

There are five main oases in the desert—Siwa in the north and, heading south, Bahareya, Farafra, Dakhla, and Kharga. Each of these communities—which were isolated from the outside world until the 1970s, when the first asphalt roads connected them with the Nile Valley—has its own character and is the stepping-off point for expeditions into the surrounding desert. Spend a night in the White Desert amongst the outlandish white outcroppings, explore the ancient mud-brick town of Qasr, or search out the names of the first European explorers carved on the side of a Roman temple on the edge of the Great Sand Sea.

2　Visitor Information & Maps

The **Egyptian Ministry of Tourism** has a colorful website (www.egypt.travel) with a fair bit of information (if you can

navigate your way through the animation). The ministry also maintains offices in New York, 630 Fifth Ave., Ste. 1706,

New York, NY 10111 (𝄞 212/332-2570 or 212/956-6439); Chicago, 645 N. Michigan Ave., Ste. 829, Chicago, IL 60611 (𝄞 312/280-4666 or 312/280-4788); Los Angeles, 8383 Wilshire Blvd., Ste. 215, Beverly Hills, CA 90211 (𝄞 323/653-8815 or 323/653-8961); Montreal, 1253 McGill College Ave., Ste. 250, Montreal H3B2Y5 (𝄞 514/861-4420 or 514/861-8071); and London, Egyptian House, 170 Piccadilly, London W1V9DD (𝄞 171/493-5282 or 171/408-0295).

The Ministry of Tourism offices in Egypt vary wildly in usefulness from the completely pointless (Luxor, for example) to the extremely helpful (in Aswan and Bahareya). Addresses and contact information have been listed in the relevant chapters throughout this book.

There are quite a few good online sources for information about Egypt:

- **www.arabist.net** is a political blog written by journalists with experience in Egypt and North Africa, and is a lot more trenchant than anything else produced locally.
- **www.egy.com** is one of my personal favorites, an idiosyncratic site devoted to the research of Samir Rafaat, author of two books on Cairo's historic buildings. Full of fascinating historical snippets that Rafaat digs up from the archives, his articles will have you seeing Cairo in a whole new way.
- **www.egyptvoyager.com** is one of those sites that never seems to be finished, but it does have a series of panoramic photos of Cairo that can be used to preview museums, buildings, and even shopping areas to decide whether you want them on your itinerary.
- **www.travelblog.org/Africa/Egypt** and **www.travelpod.com/travel-blog-country/Egypt/tpod.html** have up-to-date individual accounts of travel in Egypt. Quality varies, of course, but there's usually something fun and informative here.
- **www.touregypt.net** is run by an organization that calls itself the Association of Egyptian Travel Businesses on the Internet. Hectic and badly written, the site nevertheless has articles on just about everything and a large amount of useful information.

In Egypt, the best place to go for maps is the **American University in Cairo Bookstore** (p. 117).

3 Entry Requirements

PASSPORTS

Your passport must have a minimum of 2 months' validity beyond your departure date in order for you to enter Egypt. Everyone older than 16 is required to have his own passport.

For information on how to get a passport, go to "Passports" in the "Fast Facts" section of this chapter—the websites listed provide downloadable passport applications as well as the current processing fees. For an up-to-date, country-by-country listing of passport requirements around the world, go to the "Foreign Entry Requirement" Web page of the U.S. State Department at **http://travel.state.gov**.

VISAS

Most Western visitors to Egypt are required to have a visa. The main exceptions to this rule are travelers who have a National Identity Card issued by Belgium, France, Germany, Italy, or Portugal. Visas can be acquired at the nearest Egyptian Embassy or at the point of entry (note that if you are traveling on a National Identity Card, as noted above, and want to get your visa at the point of entry, you need to bring a passport photo with you). A 30-day tourist visa costs $15/£7.50 (Egyptian pounds not accepted).

Tourists traveling directly to the Sinai Peninsula by air have two options: the standard 30-day visa that is valid for all of Egypt, or a free 14-day visa valid only for the Sinai tourist zone (which includes St. Catherine). The 30-day visa is easily extended for a small fee and can also be acquired (for a surcharge) after entry through travel agents in Sinai if you enter on the 14-day visa and then decide to visit the rest of the country.

Officially it is recommended that you obtain a visa before you travel, but most regular visitors to Egypt who arrive by air find it quicker and easier to pick up a visa on arrival at the airport.

Travelers who arrive overland should obtain their visas before arrival. Coming through Taba, there may be problems obtaining the 30-day visa without the help (and extra expense) of a travel agent.

Visa requirements can change without notice, and you should check the latest requirements as far in advance as possible in order to allow time to obtain a visa in your home country should that be necessary.

Americans can check http://travel.state.gov/travel/cis_pa_tw/cis/cis_1108.html.

Canadians can check www.voyage.gc.ca/dest/report-en.asp?country=79000#4.

British tourists can check www.fco.gov.uk/knowbeforeyougo.

MEDICAL REQUIREMENTS

For information on medical requirements and recommendations, see "Health," p. 26.

CUSTOMS

For information on what you can bring into and take out of Egypt, go to **"Customs"** in the **"Fast Facts"** section of this chapter.

4 When to Go

WEATHER

Egypt is best visited in the fall (Sept–Nov) and spring (Feb–Apr). The weather is relatively chilly (see chart) December through January, except in the south, where the winter is very pleasant. The summer is the only time to be avoided for climatic reasons. Cairo is hot, muggy, and filthy for most of June through August, and most residents take their vacations during this period, if possible. Upper Egypt and even the Red Sea coast can also be uncomfortably hot during the summer.

Average Monthly High & Low Temperature (°F & °C)

		Jan	Feb	Mar	Apr	May	June	July	Aug	Sept	Oct	Nov	Dec
Cairo	Temp (°F)	64/18	68/20	73/54	82/59	90/64	93/70	93/72	91/72	90/70	84/64	75/57	66/52
	Temp (°C)	18/9	20/10	23/12	28/15	32/18	34/21	34/22	33/22	32/21	29/18	24/14	18/11
Luxor/	Temp (°F)	73/42	78/44	84/57	95/60	103/69	105/72	104/74	106/74	101/71	95/64	85/54	77/46
Aswan	Temp (°C)	23/5	25/7	29/11	35/16	39/21	41/23	41/24	41/24	39/22	35/18	30/12	25/8
Fayum	Temp (°F)	55/41	75/45	73/47	83/52	95/61	97/66	100/72	100/55	95/68	86/61	81/52	55/48
	Temp (°C)	13/5	24/7	23/8	28/11	35/16	36/19	38/22	38/13	35/20	30/16	27/11	13/9
Kharga	Temp (°F)	74/43	79/46	82/52	88/59	102/70	104/75	106/75	106/77	100/71	90/66	84/52	75/48
	Temp (°C)	24/6	26/8	28/11	31/15	39/21	40/24	41/24	41/25	38/22	32/19	29/11	24/9
Dakhla	Temp (°F)	74/40	79/43	83/50	88/71	84/64	102/70	106/72	106/75	100/68	73/63	82/48	75/46
	Temp (°C)	23/4	26/6	29/10	31/22	29/18	39/21	41/22	41/24	38/20	23/17	28/9	24/8
Siwa	Temp (°F)	68/39	72/48	72/49	81/53	95/63	100/68	100/73	100/73	97/70	86/61	77/50	70/48
	Temp (°C)	20/4	22/7	22/10	27/12	35/17	38/20	38/23	38/23	36/21	30/16	25/10	21/9
Red Sea/	Temp (°F)	75/56	78/57	77/57	84/64	91/75	99/80	101/80	100/80	93/79	86/73	82/66	73/61
Sinai	Temp (°C)	24/13	26/14	25/14	29/18	33/24	37/27	38/27	38/27	34/26	30/23	28/19	23/16

High and low seasons follow a combination of weather patterns and school holidays. Thus, summer in Upper Egypt is low season because of the heat (despite the summer holidays), and winter is high season, with the market peaking around Christmas, New Year's, and Easter. The same is true for Cairo and the Red Sea, though with less dramatic fluctuations. Winter is low season in Alexandria and along the north coast, but temperatures are relatively cool and the wind picks up. During the summer, with Egyptian schools on holiday and the unpleasant Cairo climate in stark contrast to the moderate warmth of the Mediterranean, the high season takes the north coast with a vengeance.

To avoid the crowds, go against the seasons, but be prepared for some serious heat if you're headed for Upper Egypt during the summer. Luxor in August is not for the faint of heart, and venturing out to the sights without a fairly serious sunblock, an extravagantly brimmed sun hat, and a couple of liters of water is simply unwise. Personally, I would try to stay at the margins of the high season and visit around the first 2 weeks of November or June. The same goes for Cairo, the Red Sea coast, and the Sinai.

The main thing to watch on the north coast is the Egyptian school schedules. Once the Egyptian schools and universities let out, cities and beaches on the Mediterranean become very noisy and crowded, and Western tourists, women in particular, will find themselves subject to substantial unwelcome attention. For this reason, I would advise visiting Alexandria in March and April or October and November.

HOLIDAYS

Egypt is a country that takes a lot of holidays, both secular and religious. Public holidays in Egypt are a mix of secular celebrations of the achievements of the post-1952 state and religious holidays. Islamic religious holidays can be a little hard to pin down sometimes, because they occur according to a lunar calendar; by religious reckoning, they happen on the same day every year, but according to the modern Gregorian calendar, the dates move about 11 days earlier every year. Further complicating matters is that for the beginning of the key month of Ramadan to be officially declared, the new moon must be spotted.

Government offices (including visa extensions) and many public services (like banks) are closed for secular holidays such as July 26 or October 10. Most general services, including money-change offices and major tourist sights, operate as normal, however.

Religious holidays carry more social significance and provide you with fascinating opportunities as well as potentially insurmountable obstacles. Ramadan, the month of fasting that precedes Eid el Fitr, is a great example. On the one hand, it's a fascinating time to be in Egypt: the streets are decorated and, once the sun goes down, the streets of poorer neighborhoods are filled with parties and celebrations that go on most of the night. On the other hand, the already-brief Egyptian working day is substantially shortened during Ramadan, which means that getting the most minor arrangements made or changed can quickly become a frustrating and pointless exercise.

All the holidays listed wreak havoc on public services. Restaurants and tourist facilities largely remain open, but government offices close and many stores also close or open late. Here are the highpoints of the annual holiday schedule in Egypt:

- **Coptic and Orthodox Christmas,** January 7: Unlike Western Christians, the Eastern church celebrates the birth of Christ on January 7. This day has only recently been made a national holiday.

A Day to Stay Inside & Read

Eid al Adha, which follows the end of the annual pilgrimage to Mecca and commemorates Ibrahim's willingness to sacrifice his own son to God, is celebrated over 4 days during which everyone who can afford it slaughters sheep, goats, and cows. A third of the meat is distributed to the poor and a third to family and friends, with the remaining third going to those who paid for the animals. In the days leading up to the feast, the roads into major cities are jammed with trucks full of livestock.

The first day of Eid is marked by early morning prayers. When the men return from the mosque, the animals are killed in the street, in the stairwells of apartment complexes, and in parking lots. In accordance with Muslim tradition, the animals must bleed to death, and the mess, often not cleaned up for days, is extraordinary and can be overwhelming. There is generally no problem going out and participating in the celebrations if you feel like it—participants, including children who dip hands and feet in the pools of blood, are usually very happy to pose for macabre pictures. However, the sight of animals dying slowly in often unsanitary conditions may be disturbing for many, and I would advise spending the day well away from it all. This would be a good day to visit the nearest major tourist site or stay in your hotel room with a good guidebook.

- **Muharram,** approximately January 10: This is the beginning of the Islamic year (the first month of which is named Muharram).
- **Moulid El Nabi,** approximately March 20: The birthday of the Prophet Mohamed is celebrated with special sweets such as the sesame-seed-based *sensemeya.*
- **Sham El Nessim/Easter,** April 9: This celebration of spring cuts across social and religious lines in Egypt, and on this day everybody who can collect a meal in a basket and get out of the house goes for a picnic. The name of the holiday simply means "smell the breeze" in Arabic.
- **Sinai Liberation Day,** April 25: This commemorates the day that the Sinai Peninsula was returned to Egypt by the Israelis under the terms of the American-brokered Camp David Accords.
- **Labor Day,** May 1: Paying lip service to the socialist propaganda of yesteryear, the Egyptian government still celebrates May Day.
- **National Day,** July 23: This commemorates the occurrences of 1952 that brought Gamal Abdel Nasser and his group of Free Officers to power.
- **Ramadan,** approximately September 2 to October 2: A month in which Muslims all over the world are enjoined to abstain from food, drink, and sex between sunup and sundown. The major meal of the day becomes *iftar* (literally, breakfast), which is consumed with great enthusiasm the moment the sun goes down.
- **Eid al Fitr,** approximately October 2: Egyptians spend these 3 days celebrating the end of Ramadan with street celebrations and special sweets. "*Al fitr*" means breaking the fast. Eid is originally 1 day only (the day when fasting stops), but in Egypt it lasts for 3 days during which traditional Egyptian sweets such as *kahk* and *ghouraiyyeba* are baked.
- **Armed Forces Day,** October 6: This commemorates the crossing of the

Suez Canal by Egyptian forces in 1973.

• **Eid al Adha,** approximately December 8: Commemorating the completion of the Haj and the return of the pilgrims from Mecca as well as Ibrahim's willingness to sacrifice his only son, Eid al Adha celebrations may be a little too colorful for comfort (see box, "A Day to Stay Inside & Read"). Most stores, most banks, and all public offices are closed for this holiday. Restaurants, however, remain open.

5 Getting There

BY PLANE

CAIRO   Cairo International Airport (CAI) is the main international hub for Egypt. EgyptAir, which has a virtual domestic monopoly, uses it as its hub for internal flights (often meaning that relatively short distances must be covered with long flights to Cairo and then back out to the final destination). There are two other airports in Cairo, but they are both used exclusively for private internal and government flights.

Many major European and Middle Eastern airlines have regular flights into Cairo International. These include Air France, Alitalia, Austrian Air, British Airways, Czech Airlines, Emirates, Gulf Air, Iberia, KLM Royal Dutch Airlines, Kuwait Airlines, Lufthansa, Malaysian Airlines, Maley, Olympic Airlines, Royal Jordanian, Saudi Arabian, Swiss International, Singapore Airlines, Qatar Airways, and Turkish Airlines. EgyptAir, the Egyptian national carrier, also operates flights to most major European hubs and has a daily direct flight to New York.

SHARM EL SHEIKH (SSH)   Sharm el Sheikh International Airport (SSH) now receives international flights directly from all over the world from major airlines including Alitalia, Austrian Air, British Airways, LOT Polish Airlines, Royal Jordanian, and Swiss International, as well as many low-cost operators such as Air One, Condor, Eurofly, and Transavia. This is a good port of entry to the Sinai. Dahab, St. Catherine, and Taba are a few hours' drive from Sharm, and EgyptAir flights are cheap and reasonably reliable. Very rarely this airport is also referred to by its Israeli name Ophira.

ALEXANDRIA BURG AL ARAB (HBE)   Farther outside Alexandria than Al Nozha, but with more-modern facilities and a longer runway, this airport is serviced by EgyptAir, Emirates, and Lufthansa/United Airlines. There is a shuttle from the airport into the middle of Alexandria, but though flights from Cairo are cheap (around LE300/$55/£28 for a return flight), any of the express trains from Ramsis are a more pleasant way to get there and, at around 2½ hours, quicker when you take into account the transfer time.

ALEXANDRIA AL NOZHA (ALY)   Closer to the city than the newer Burg al Arab facilities, Al Nozha has an unnervingly short runway and is only used by EgyptAir. Unless you're a fan of exciting landings, you're better off on the train from Ramsis. Airfare from Cairo is the same as for Burg al Arab.

LUXOR INTERNATIONAL (LXR)   This airport is serviced mainly by internal EgyptAir flights and international low-cost charter carriers such as My Air, TNT, and Transavia (which runs popular direct flights to Amsterdam). Flying time from Cairo is about an hour, making this an excellent alternative to the tedious and sometimes uncomfortable 12-hour train trip from Cairo. Return airfare from Cairo is around LE1,000 ($180/£93).

ASWAN AL DARAW (ASW) This small but surprisingly new little airport is serviced by EgyptAir. Annoyingly, many flights from Cairo require a 2- to 3-hour layover in Luxor (which is more than the flying time) and a change of planes. If you're going to fly, check that the flight is direct. Return airfare from Cairo is around LE1,400 ($253/£130).

ABU SIMBEL (ABS) This airport is exclusively for EgyptAir tourist flights. Flying rather than driving makes sense, as there's nothing to see en route, and waiting for the convoy can be pretty tedious.

HURGHADA (HRG) This small, modern airport effectively serves Gouna, Hurghada, Makadi Bay, Soma Bay, Safaga, and Quseir. It is served direct from Europe by low-cost operators such as Condor, Thomas Cook, and Transasavia, as well as internally by EgyptAir. Airfare from Cairo is around LE750 ($136/£69), and will save you a tedious and unpleasant bus trip.

MARSA ALLAM (RMF) EgyptAir was flying to Marsa Allam twice weekly (Sun and Wed) at the time of writing. However, demand is sure to increase dramatically in this area, and the number of flights should as well. Price for a return ticket is around LE1,200 ($218/£109).

MARSA MATRUH (MUH) There is only service here during the summer, when EgyptAir usually has a few flights a week.

TABA (TCP) This airport is currently only being used by direct charters from European hubs.

KHARGA (UVL) This airport services one EgyptAir flight a week, on Sundays. Ticket price is LE400 ($73/£37). You may have a problem booking a seat—this is officially a government flight, but the EgyptAir office in Kharga can do it. If you run into problems in Cairo, phone Mahmoud Shokri at the Kharga office (✆ 092/7921695).

FLYING TO CAIRO FOR LESS: TIPS FOR GETTING THE BEST AIRFARE

- Passengers who can book their ticket either **long in advance or at the last minute,** or who **fly midweek** or **at less-trafficked hours** may pay a fraction of the full fare. If your schedule is flexible, say so, and ask if you can secure a cheaper fare by changing your flight plans.

- Search **the Internet** for cheap fares. The most popular online travel agencies are **Travelocity.com** (www.travelocity.co.uk); **Expedia.com** (www.expedia.co.uk and www.expedia.ca); and **Orbitz.com**. In the U.K., go to **Travelsupermarket** (✆ 0845/345-5708; www.travelsupermarket.com), a flight search engine that offers flight comparisons for the budget airlines whose seats often end up in bucket-shop sales. Other websites for booking airline tickets online include **Cheapflights.com, SmarterTravel.com, Priceline.com,** and **Opodo** (www.opodo.co.uk). Meta search sites (which find and then direct you to airline and hotel websites for booking) include **Sidestep.com** and **Kayak.com**—the latter includes fares for budget carriers such as Jet Blue and Spirit as well as the major airlines. **Lastminute.com** is a great source for last-minute flights and getaways. In addition, most **airlines** offer online-only fares that even their phone agents know nothing about. British travelers should check **Flights International** (✆ 0800/0187050; www.flights-international.com) for deals on flights all over the world.

- A number of low-cost airlines in Europe are now well known for their cheap flights to Egypt. Expect crowded planes, little leg room, and low, low prices. Dutch-based **Transavia** (✆ 20/4060406; http://en.transavia.com/en) has taken a lot of business away from major airlines with its cut-rate flights to Sharm el Sheikh and Luxor from Amsterdam.

- Keep an eye on local newspapers for **promotional specials** or **fare wars,** when airlines lower prices on their most popular routes.

- Try to book a ticket **in the ticket's country of origin.** If you're planning a one-way flight from Johannesburg to New York, a South Africa–based travel agent will probably have the lowest fares. For foreign travelers on multi-leg trips, book in the country of the first leg; for example, book New York–Chicago–Montreal–New York in the U.S.

- **Consolidators,** also known as bucket shops, are wholesale brokers in the airline-ticket game. Consolidators buy deeply discounted tickets ("distressed" inventories of unsold seats) from airlines and sell them to online ticket agencies, travel agents, tour operators, corporations, and, to a lesser degree, the general public. Consolidators advertise in Sunday newspaper travel sections (often in small ads with tiny type), both in the U.S. and the U.K. They can be great sources for cheap international tickets. On the downside, bucket-shop tickets are often rigged with restrictions, such as stiff cancellation penalties (as high as 50% to 75% of the ticket price). And keep in mind that most of what you see advertised is of limited availability. Several reliable consolidators are worldwide and available online. **STA Travel** (www.statravel.com) has been the world's leading consolidator for students since purchasing Council Travel, but its fares are competitive for travelers of all ages. **Flights.com** (© 800/ **TRAV-800** [872-8800]; www.flights.com) has excellent fares worldwide, particularly to Europe. It also has

"local" websites in 12 countries. **Fly-Cheap** (© **800/FLY-CHEAP** [359-2432]; www.1800flycheap.com) has especially good fares to sunny destinations. **Air Tickets Direct** (© **800/ 778-3447;** www.airticketsdirect.com) is based in Montreal and also books trips to places that U.S. travel agents won't touch, such as Cuba.

- Join **frequent-flier clubs.** Frequent-flier membership doesn't cost a cent, but it does entitle you to free tickets or upgrades when you amass the airline's required number of frequent-flier points. You don't even have to fly to earn points; **frequent-flier credit cards** can earn you thousands of miles for doing your everyday shopping. But keep in mind that award seats are limited, seats on popular routes are hard to snag, and more and more major airlines are cutting their expiration periods for mileage points—so check your airline's frequent-flier program so you don't lose your miles before you use them. *Inside tip:* Award seats are offered almost a year in advance, but seats also open up at the last minute, so if your travel plans are flexible, you may strike gold. To play the frequent-flier game to your best advantage, consult the community bulletin boards on **FlyerTalk** (www.flyertalk.com). Or go to Randy Petersen's **Inside Flyer** (www.insideflyer.com); Petersen and friends review all the programs in detail and post regular updates on changes in policies and trends.

LONG-HAUL FLIGHTS: HOW TO STAY COMFORTABLE

- Your choice of airline and airplane will definitely affect your legroom. Find more details about U.S. airlines at **www.seatguru.com**. For international airlines, the research firm Skytrax has posted a list of average seat pitches at **www.airlinequality.com**.

- Emergency-exit seats and bulkhead seats typically have the most legroom. Emergency-exit seats are usually left unassigned until the day of a flight (to ensure that able-bodied people fill the seats); it's worth getting to the ticket counter early to snag one of these spots for a long flight. Many passengers find that bulkhead seating (the row facing the wall at the front of the cabin) offers more legroom, but keep in mind that bulkhead seats have no storage space on the floor in front of you.
- To have two seats for yourself in a three-seat row, try for an aisle seat in a center section toward the back of coach. If you're traveling with a companion, book an aisle and a window seat. Middle seats are usually booked last, so chances are good you'll end up with three seats to yourselves. And in the event that a third passenger is assigned the middle seat, he will probably be more than happy to trade for a window or an aisle.
- Ask about entertainment options. Many airlines offer seatback video systems where you get to choose your movies or play video games—but only on some of their planes. (Boeing 777s are your best bet.)
- To sleep, avoid the last row of any section or the row in front of an emergency exit, as these seats are the least likely to recline. Avoid seats near highly trafficked toilet areas. Avoid seats in the back of many jets—these can be narrower than those in the rest of coach. Or reserve a window seat so you can rest your head and avoid being bumped in the aisle.
- Get up, walk around, and stretch every 60 to 90 minutes to keep your blood flowing. This helps prevent **deep vein thrombosis,** or "economy-class syndrome.".
- Drink water before, during, and after your flight to combat the lack of humidity in airplane cabins. Avoid alcohol, which will dehydrate you.
- If you're flying with kids, don't forget to carry on toys, books, pacifiers, and snacks, as well as chewing gum to help them relieve ear pressure buildup during ascent and descent.

6 General Travel Resources

MONEY & COSTS

It's always advisable to bring money in a variety of forms on a vacation: a mix of cash, credit cards, and traveler's checks. American and Canadian dollars, pounds sterling, and euros are all easily exchanged in Egypt, and Cairo International Airport has a number of 24-hour banks that give the same rates as in town. It's easy to exchange enough on arrival to cover tips and the cost of transport into town.

ATMs, once a rarity in Egypt, are now common in large cities and tourist destinations. While they offer good rates of exchange, some networks also charge hefty transaction fees. Check with your bank before leaving home.

Unlike exchange bureaus in many countries, most of the exchange offices (maktab sarafa) in Egypt offer competitive rates. They also offer longer hours and quicker service.

Hotels, however, offer bad rates of exchange and should be avoided except in emergencies.

There has been no black market for hard currencies in Egypt for several years and therefore no advantage to changing on the street.

CURRENCY

You will find Egypt cheap compared to any Western country. Like most third-world countries, however, Western goods

The Egyptian Pound, the U.S. Dollar, the Euro & the British Pound

Egyptian Pound (LE)	US$	Euro €	UK£
1.00	0.18	0.13	0.09
5.00	0.90	0.63	0.46
10.00	1.80	1.30	0.90
25.00	4.52	3.15	2.28
50.00	9.04	6.29	4.55
100.00	18.00	13.00	9.00
250.00	45.19	31.47	22.77
500.00	90.37	62.94	45.54
1,000.00	180.75	125.89	91.08
2,500.00	451.87	314.72	227.70

are available in major centers, but usually at prices that are well beyond the reach of most of the working population. In fact, you will find various services, including midrange and upper-range accommodation, priced in "hard currency" (U.S. dollars or euros, generally) rather than Egyptian pounds (LE), therefore, the Egyptian pound pricing for some accommodations is for reference only.

ATMs

The easiest and best way to get cash away from home is from an ATM (automated teller machine), sometimes referred to as a "cash machine" or a "cashpoint." The **Cirrus** (© **800/424-7787;** www.master card.com) and **PLUS** (© **800/843-7587;** www.visa.com) networks span the globe and are easy to access in all major tourist spots in Egypt. Go to your bankcard's website to find ATM locations at your destination. Be sure you know your daily withdrawal limit before you depart. *Note:* Many banks impose a fee every time you use a card at another bank's ATM, and that fee can be higher for international transactions (up to $5 or more) than for domestic ones (where they're rarely more than $2). In addition, the bank from which you withdraw cash may charge its own fee. For international withdrawal fees, ask your bank.

Note: Banks that are members of the **Global ATM Alliance** charge no transaction fees for cash withdrawals at other Alliance member ATMs; these include Bank of America, Scotiabank (Canada, Caribbean, and Mexico), Barclays (U.K. and parts of Africa), Deutsche Bank (Germany, Poland, Spain, and Italy), and BNP Paribas (France).

CREDIT CARDS

Credit cards are another safe way to carry money. They also provide a convenient record of all your expenses, and they generally offer relatively good exchange rates. You can withdraw cash from your credit cards at banks or ATMs, but high fees make credit-card cash advances a pricey way to get cash. Keep in mind that you'll pay interest from the moment of your withdrawal, even if you pay your monthly bills on time. Also, note that many banks now assess a 1% to 3% "transaction fee" on *all* charges you incur abroad (whether you're using the local currency or your native currency).

Most mid- and high-end tourist hotels will accept major credit cards, with Visa

What Things Cost in Egypt	LE	US$	UK£
Taxi from Cairo airport to Downtown	40.00–60.00	7.23–10.84	3.64–7.55
Roundtrip airfare from Cairo to Luxor	1,000.00	180.75	91.08
Double room (expensive)	1,380.00	250.00	126.00
Double room (moderate)	442.60	80.00	40.00
Double room (inexpensive)	80.00	14.46	10.00
Dinner for one, without wine (expensive)	100.00	18.00	9.11
Dinner for one, without wine (moderate)	50.00	9.00	4.55
Dinner for one, without wine (inexpensive)	20.00	3.61	1.82
Local taxi ride	4.00–8.00	0.72–1.45	0.36–0.73
Can of Coca-Cola	2.00–4.00	0.36–0.72	.018–0.36
Cup of coffee	2.00–8.00	0.36–1.45	0.18–0.73
Bottled beer (Stella)	8.00–16.00	1.45–2.90	0.73–1.46
Liter (¼ gal.) of petrol	1.50	0.27	0.14
Admission to sites/museums	10.00–50.00	1.80–9.00	0.90–4.55

and MasterCard having the widest acceptance in Egypt. American Express is less commonly accepted but still useful in higher-end facilities. Diner's Club is rarely accepted in Egypt. The majority of restaurants and shops remain cash-only.

TRAVELER'S CHECKS

Most banks and many change offices will cash traveler's checks, albeit at a less advantageous rate than cash. Midrange and upper-range tourist hotels also generally provide facilities for cashing traveler's checks and make it possible to settle your bill with them.

You can buy traveler's checks at most banks. They are offered in denominations of $20, $50, $100, $500, and sometimes $1,000. Generally, you'll pay a service charge ranging from 1% to 4%.

The most popular traveler's checks are offered by **American Express** (© **800/807-6233** or © **800/221-7282** for card holders—this number accepts collect calls, offers service in several foreign languages, and exempts Amex gold and platinum cardholders from the 1% fee); **Visa** (© **800/732-1322**)—AAA members can obtain Visa checks for a $9.95 fee (for checks up to $1,500) at most AAA offices or by calling © **866/339-3378**; and **MasterCard** (© **800/223-9920**).

Be sure to keep a record of the traveler's check serial numbers separate from your checks in case they are stolen or lost. You'll get a refund faster if you know the numbers.

American Express, Thomas Cook, Visa, and **MasterCard** offer **foreign currency traveler's checks,** useful if you're traveling to one country or to the euro zone; they're accepted at locations where dollar checks may not be.

Another option is the new prepaid traveler's check cards, reloadable cards that work much like debit cards but aren't linked to your checking account. The **American Express Travelers Cheque Card,** for example, requires a minimum deposit, sets a maximum balance, and has a one-time issuance fee of $15. You can withdraw money from an ATM (for a fee of $2.50 per transaction, not including bank fees), and the funds can be purchased in dollars, euros, or pounds. If you lose the card, your available funds will be refunded within 24 hours.

TRAVEL INSURANCE

Egypt is a large, fascinating country and is full of people who are willing to help make your vacation go smoothly (and help out as much as they can when it doesn't). Don't let this cloud the fact, however, that Egypt's public infrastructure is badly underdeveloped, where it exists at all. When arrangements go off the rails or an emergency situation develops, you'll find yourself paying out of your own pocket to make things right again. For many people, a comprehensive travel insurance package makes sense in Egypt.

The cost of travel insurance varies widely, depending on the destination, the cost and length of your trip, your age and health, and the type of trip you're taking, but expect to pay between 5% and 8% of the vacation itself. You can get estimates from various providers through **Insure MyTrip.com.** Enter your trip cost and dates, your age, and other information, for prices from more than a dozen companies.

U.K. citizens and their families who make more than one trip abroad per year may find an annual travel insurance policy works out cheaper. Check **www.money supermarket.com**, which compares prices across a wide range of providers for single-and multi-trip policies.

Most big travel agents offer their own insurance and will probably try to sell you their package when you book a holiday. Think before you sign. **Britain's Consumers' Association** recommends that you insist on seeing the policy and reading the fine print before buying travel insurance. **The Association of British Insurers** (✆ 020/7600-3333; www.abi. org.uk) gives advice by phone and publishes *Holiday Insurance,* a free guide to policy provisions and prices. You might also shop around for better deals: Try **Columbus Direct** (✆ 0870/033-9988; www.columbusdirect.net).

TRIP-CANCELLATION INSURANCE

Independent travelers in Egypt will find themselves working around all kinds of obstacles to get where they're going. Many people, therefore, opt for an insurance package that includes trip-interruption and trip-cancellation insurance. Trip-cancellation insurance will help retrieve your money if you have to back out of a trip or depart early, or if your travel supplier goes bankrupt. Trip-cancellation insurance traditionally covers such events as sickness, natural disasters, and State Department advisories. The latest news in trip-cancellation insurance is the availability of **expanded hurricane coverage** and the **"any-reason"** cancellation coverage—which costs more but covers cancellations made for any reason. You won't get back 100% of your prepaid trip cost, but you'll be refunded a substantial portion. **TravelSafe** (✆ 888/885-7233; www.travelsafe.com) offers both types of coverage. Expedia also offers any-reason cancellation coverage for its air-hotel packages.

For details, contact one of the following recommended insurers: **Access America** (✆ 866/807-3982; www.access america.com), **Travel Guard International** (✆ 800/826-4919; www.travel guard.com), **Travel Insured International** (✆ 800/243-3174; www.travel insured.com), or **Travelex Insurance Services** (✆ 888/457-4602; www.travelex-insurance.com).

MEDICAL INSURANCE

For travel overseas, most U.S. health plans (including Medicare and Medicaid) do not provide coverage, and the ones that do often require you to pay for services upfront and reimburse you only after you return home.

Between unhygienic food and the traffic, leaving aside a whole range of potentially risky vacation activities such as diving and go-karts, Egypt is not a place where you want to gamble with your medical coverage. State-supplied medical care is to be avoided in all but the most immediately life-threatening situations. Anyone traveling in Egypt should be prepared to cover the cost of the best private treatment available in country (which, it should be noted, is extremely cheap compared to the United States), as well as medical evacuation to Europe should that become necessary.

For most people, particularly those traveling to remote or high-risk areas where emergency evacuation might be necessary, this means purchasing travel medical insurance. If you require additional medical insurance, try **MEDEX Assistance** (© 410/453-6300; www.medexassist.com) or **Travel Assistance International** (© 800/821-2828; www.travelassistance.com; for general information on services, call the company's **Worldwide Assistance Services, Inc.,** at © 800/777-8710).

Canadians should check with their provincial health plan offices, or call **Health Canada** (© 866/225-0709; www.hc-sc.gc.ca) to find out the extent of their coverage and what documentation and receipts they must take home in case they are treated overseas.

LOST-LUGGAGE INSURANCE

Lost luggage is not uncommon flying into Cairo, but the bags always arrive eventually. The main problem is poor service from local airline representatives, which may mean some frustrating time on the phone and perhaps having to waste valuable holiday time going back to the airport to retrieve your bags. The concierge at your hotel should be able to deal with this issue.

A more serious problem, though only for tourists routed through Paris's Charles de Gaulle Airport or Milan's Malpensa International Airport, is the recurring thefts from checked baggage. If you have a connection through Charles de Gaulle or Malpensa, do not leave anything of value in your checked bags; cameras, jewelry, and computer equipment should be packed only in carry-on luggage.

On international flights (including U.S. portions of international trips), baggage coverage is limited to approximately $9.07 per pound, up to approximately $635 per checked bag. If you plan to check items more valuable than what's covered by the standard liability, see if your homeowner's policy covers your valuables, get baggage insurance as part of your comprehensive travel-insurance package, or buy Travel Guard's BagTrak product.

If your luggage is lost, immediately file a lost-luggage claim at the airport, detailing the luggage contents. Most airlines require that you report delayed, damaged, or lost baggage within 4 hours of arrival. Though airlines are required to deliver luggage, once found, directly to your house or destination free of charge, branch offices in Cairo have proved reluctant to honor this, and persuading them to keep this commitment may require some persistence and pressure.

HEALTH
STAYING HEALTHY

Public health standards are low in Egypt, with little government investment in programs to improve it. Eating in restaurants that do not regularly serve foreign clientele or drinking water that has not come from a well-sealed bottle is asking for a bout of traveler's diarrhea or worse (including cholera and hepatitis). Most problems are easily avoided by following a few simple rules:

- **Only drink bottled water.** If the water doesn't taste right, even if it was unsealed in front of you, send it back and get another.
- **Eat in restaurants with a high volume of foreigners** whenever possible, particularly expats. Word gets around quickly when someone gets sick.
- **Avoid the muddy banks** of the Nile and other waterways. Schistosomiasis, or bilharzia, a parasitic disease caused by flatworms that live close to shore, remains a problem in Egypt.

General Availability of Healthcare

Contact the **International Association for Medical Assistance to Travelers** (IAMAT) (© **716/754-4883** or, in Canada, 416/652-0137; www.iamat.org) for tips on travel and health concerns in the countries you're visiting, and for lists of local, English-speaking doctors. The U.S. **Centers for Disease Control and Prevention** (© **800/311-3435;** www. cdc.gov) provides up-to-date information on health hazards by region or country and offers tips on food safety. **Travel Health Online** (www.tripprep.com), sponsored by a consortium of travel medicine practitioners, may also offer helpful advice on traveling abroad. You can find listings of reliable medical clinics overseas at the **International Society of Travel Medicine** (www.istm.org).

COMMON AILMENTS

TROPICAL ILLNESSES There is a very limited risk of *P. falciparum* and *P. vivax* malaria in the oasis of Fayum during the summer months (June–Oct). It has been a decade since any indigenous case was reported, but you should still use a good insect repellant and a mosquito net at night if you are visiting the oasis during these months. Antimalarial medications are not recommended by the World Health Organization for tourists planning to visit Fayum.

Egypt's first confirmed case of the H5N1 strain of avian flu was back in March 2006. By July 2007, there had been 37 more cases and 15 fatalities. These outbreaks will occur periodically as long as Egypt's standards of public hygiene remain low and people and livestock intermix freely. Travelers should check the news and the websites of the World Health Organization (www.who. int/countries/egy/en) and the Centers for Disease Control and Prevention (wwwn. cdc.gov/travel/destinationEgypt.aspx) for updates before traveling. Note that in the event of a serious outbreak, acquiring Western medical supplies in Egypt would be extremely difficult.

DIETARY RED FLAGS Tap water in Egypt is not potable and should be avoided. Only drink bottled water from a sealed bottle, and if you have doubts about the contents, get another one. This is not usually a problem, as upmarket and tourist restaurants will automatically provide bottled water. In private homes, you may be offered glasses of tap water. Particularly outside a big city, in any kind of rural settings, these are best politely refused.

Fresh fruit juice from the street-side juice shops are a judgment call but generally best avoided. Sniff the air inside the shop and make your choice.

Green salads are best avoided as well, even in high-end hotels. Not only are they often washed in contaminated water, but they can contain bacteria because of agricultural practices. Also avoid fruit that you have not peeled yourself, and chicken and eggs that have not been thoroughly cooked.

BUGS, BITES & OTHER WILDLIFE CONCERNS There is rabies in Egypt and care should be exercised not only with wildlife, but semi-domestic animals such as cats and dogs.

The deserts of Egypt contain a variety of poisonous insects and snakes. Take care when hiking; wear closed-toe shoes, and don't go reaching into nooks and crannies. Turn over rocks with a stick and watch where you're putting your feet. Choose your guide with care, and make sure that he has received at least basic first-aid training and knows what to do in the event of emergencies.

Mosquitoes and a variety of other biting insects may not be life-threatening, but they can certainly spoil the fun. Five-star resorts spray heavily for insects and keep rooms pristine. If you are staying in midrange or budget-range accommodations, I recommend having some good bug repellant handy, as well as a can of insecticide. It's best to bring the repellant with you, but there are a variety of lethal sprays available on the local market, including Raid.

RESPIRATORY ILLNESSES Air quality is a serious problem in Egypt—in Cairo, in particular. Some government sources say that the situation has improved in recent years, but levels of lead and particulate in the capital still often exceed even relatively lax domestic standards and are frequently several times the amounts considered safe under international standards. Tourists with asthma or other respiratory problems should limit the amount of time they spend in Cairo.

SUN/ELEMENTS/EXTREME WEATHER EXPOSURE Heat stroke and excessive sun are both potential problems in Egypt, particularly during the summer months. You should be prepared with sunblock, a good sun hat, and a way to replace electrolytes lost to sweating, such as oral rehydration salts, which are available over the counter at almost any Egyptian pharmacy for around LE1 (18¢/9p) a dose.

AIDS Figures differ on the number of HIV/AIDS cases in Egypt. UNAIDS estimated there to be about 5,300 people living with HIV in Egypt in 2006. It seems likely that the number of cases is underreported, however, given the social stigma associated with AIDS, the low awareness of preventive measures among IV-drug users and other high-risk groups, and the difficulty involved in obtaining anonymous testing. Condoms are readily available in pharmacies.

WHAT TO DO IF YOU GET SICK AWAY FROM HOME
Check "Fast Facts," p. 48, for the best **medical clinics** and **hospitals** in Cairo, but keep in mind that even here, service is well below Western standards.

At any hospital in Egypt, you will be expected to pay upfront and in cash for any treatment. Keep this in mind in the event of an emergency—arriving at the clinic with your wallet is very important.

Medicare and Medicaid do not provide coverage for medical costs outside the U.S. Before leaving home, find out what medical services your health insurance covers. To protect yourself, consider buying medical travel insurance (see "Medical Insurance," under "Travel Insurance," above).

Very few health insurance plans pay for medical evacuation back to the U.S. (which can cost $10,000 and up). A number of companies offer medical evacuation services anywhere in the world. If you're ever hospitalized more than 150 miles from home, **MedjetAssist** (© **800/527-7478;** www.medjetassistance.com) will pick you up and fly you to the hospital of your choice virtually anywhere in the world in a medically equipped and staffed aircraft 24 hours day, 7 days a week. Annual memberships are $225 individual, $350 family; you can also purchase short-term memberships.

U.K. nationals will need a **European Health Insurance Card (EHIC)** to receive free or reduced-cost health benefits during a visit to a European Economic Area (EEA) country (European Union countries, plus Iceland, Liechtenstein, and Norway) or Switzerland. The European Health Insurance Card replaces the E111 form, which is no longer valid. For advice, ask at your local post office or see www.dh.gov.uk/travellers.

If you suffer from a chronic illness, consult your doctor before your departure. Pack **prescription medications** in your carry-on luggage, and carry them in their original containers with pharmacy labels—otherwise they won't make it through airport security. Carry the generic name of prescription medicines in case a local pharmacist is unfamiliar with the brand name. Try to avoid buying prescription drugs in Egypt (even if they are dramatically cheaper than back home), as the quality control of drug production is not guaranteed.

SAFETY
STAYING SAFE

One of the enormous advantages that Egypt offers visitors is that it is generally very safe when it comes to petty crime. Independent travelers and groups alike can wander at will, exploring deserted temples and crowded tourist sites without worrying about anything other than being overcharged for souvenirs and taxi rides. On the other hand, there is the potential for problems with home-grown terrorist attacks. It has been a number of years since there's been an incident in Upper Egypt, but the same is not true for the Sinai and Cairo. There were a series of shootings and bombings targeting the tourism industry in Cairo and on the Sinai Peninsula in 2005 and 2006. The government now overstates the problem in Cairo and Upper Egypt for political reasons, but it is quite possibly understating them in the

medium to long term on the Sinai Peninsula. The politically and economically repressive conditions that gave rise to the 2005 and 2006 attacks have not been ameliorated, and the heavy-handed security response will probably prove counterproductive.

In terms of street crime and random violence, Egypt is a remarkably safe country. Although there is potential for violence, it takes a lot of provocation and occurs in areas and situations that tourists are unlikely to encounter.

Women in particular, however, will find themselves subject to a high level of verbal harassment in public areas. In more crowded areas, this will escalate to groping, and in less crowded areas to self-exposure. For more information, see "Women Travelers" under "Specialized Travel Resources," below.

For both men and women, personal safety is based on the usual rules. Keep away from street fights—absent a professional civil police force, these can turn nasty quickly and tempers can run pretty hot in Egypt. It is highly unlikely for a foreigner to be consciously targeted, but collateral damage is always a possibility. Avoid badly lit, deserted places after dark. Most heavily touristed areas are fine at all times of day and night.

The threat to personal safety from political instability is low. Cairo has seen sporadic, usually low-key, demonstrations by various pro-democracy and reform groups in recent years, and these are best avoided. The government routinely deploys plainclothes operatives to harass and intimidate, and there is a very real risk to locals and foreigners alike of being assaulted by the police in the vicinity of these demonstrations. Women perceived as being involved in the demonstration are particularly at risk, as security forces have been known to sexually assault female participants as a way of discouraging further participation.

In any dealing with the police in Egypt, keep in mind that this is not the kind of coherent, professional organization that you expect in the West. Officer and management positions are assigned by social class and connection, and lower positions are not paid a living wage. Corruption is rife. If you find yourself on the wrong side of the law, do not hesitate to buy yourself out of trouble either directly or through the mediation of a lawyer. At its most basic, this will involve paying a few pounds to a traffic cop for parking your car in a no-parking zone (which is most of Cairo). For more serious problems, your focus will be getting out of the country (with the assistance of your embassy's consular section, if needed).

That said, law enforcement agencies will generally work hard to accommodate foreigners when they have a problem. Don't expect any actual police work in the event of a theft or accident, but they should be able to provide a friendly face, a glass of tea, and pro-forma services such as a police report for insurance purposes.

Drugs such as a hashish and cannabis are officially illegal, and penalties, at least in theory, are harsh. Signs at the airport warn of severe penalties for drug possession and trafficking in Egypt. In practice, the situation is a little murkier. Though it is generally only Egyptian nationals and non-tourist foreigners who get into serious trouble for drug offenses, any kind of involvement in illegalities can leave you open to blackmail and a host of other best-avoided entanglements.

The traffic is perhaps the greatest routine threat to personal safety in Egypt. Extreme care should be exercised in crossing the road and in driving. Highways are particularly dangerous, and unless you have high confidence in your driving ability, you should hire a driver from a reputable firm. Avoid driving outside the city at night.

Many governments maintain advisory pages online that provide useful, up-to-date information on everything from the potential for political instability to the latest outbreaks of avian flu. See "Travel Warnings" in the "Online Traveler's Toolbox" later in this chapter. Registration with your country's embassy in Cairo can also help consular officials warn you of problems and contact you in the event of a situation back home.

DEALING WITH DISCRIMINATION

Egypt remains, unfortunately, a society in which racism and sexism is both prevalent and acceptable.

Egyptians are particularly biased toward other Africans, whom they regard as inferior both socially and economically. African-American visitors, even holding their U.S. passport in their hands and speaking English, will probably find problems getting past security at some restaurants and hotels, and African-American women have reported higher-than-average levels of sexual harassment.

Asians, or people who look Asian, will find a different set of problems. Over the last 10 years, an increasing number of economic migrants from China have drawn the attention of Egyptian authorities. Generally the attitude of people in the street will tend more toward parochial curiosity than outright discrimination, but police will tend to be suspicious of independent travelers, and tourists may be subject to random document checks and searches.

There is also a degree of anti-Western feeling in Egypt, which has been substantially increased by the 2004 invasion of Iraq and subsequent "War on Terror." On the whole, however, individual Egyptians recognize the difference between government policies and the intentions of citizens, and it is unlikely that resentments will be visited on individual travelers.

Similarly, though there is a high degree of acceptance of anti-Semitism in Egypt, it is rare for it to be visited on individual Jewish people.

Clothing, not surprisingly, is a major factor in how you will find yourself being treated in Egypt. When possible, smart-casual clothes are best: dress pants and long-sleeved shirts for men, long skirts or loose pants and long sleeves for women. This, of course, isn't always practical while traveling, but men should avoid shorts and tank tops, and women will experience elevated levels of harassment in direct proportion to the amount of skin they bare.

This also applies, though to a lesser degree, in the big resort towns such as Sharm el Sheikh or Hurghada. Resorts with private beaches have rigidly enforced rules regarding local access and staff who are accustomed to Western clothing habits, but the same only applies to a limited degree on the streets outside the resort walls. Here you will be under the assumption that Westerners are rich but morally lax. This will only be intensified by low-cut shirts, shorts, or tight pants.

7 Specialized Travel Resources

TRAVELERS WITH DISABILITIES

Most disabilities shouldn't stop anyone from traveling. There are more options and resources out there than ever before, but Egypt poses a number of challenges.

Cairo is emblematic of the difficulties that you will face: high curbs, a complete absence of ramps, and broken pavements. The situation is best in the high-traffic tourist areas. Many hotels in Luxor and Sharm el Sheikh, for example, now offer a few wheelchair-accessible rooms, and an increasing number of dive centers are equipped to deal with less-mobile customers.

Organizations that offer a vast range of resources and assistance to disabled travelers include **MossRehab** (© 800/CALL-MOSS [225-5667]; www.moss resourcenet.org); the **American Foundation for the Blind (AFB)** (© 800/232-5463; www.afb.org); and **SATH** (Society for Accessible Travel & Hospitality; © 212/447-7284; www.sath.org). **AirAmbulanceCard.com** is now partnered with SATH and allows you to preselect top-notch hospitals in case of an emergency.

Access-Able Travel Source (© 303/232-2979; www.access-able.com) offers a comprehensive database on travel agents from around the world with experience in accessible travel; destination-specific access information; and links to such resources as service animals, equipment rentals, and access guides.

Many travel agencies offer customized tours and itineraries for travelers with disabilities. Among them are **Flying Wheels Travel** (© 507/451-5005; www.flying wheelstravel.com) and **Accessible Journeys** (© 800/846-4537 or 610/521-0339; www.disabilitytravel.com).

Flying with Disability (www.flying-with-disability.org) is a comprehensive information source on airplane travel. **Avis Rent a Car** (© 888/879-4273) has an Avis Access program that offers services for customers with special travel needs. These include specially outfitted vehicles with swivel seats, spinner knobs, and hand controls; mobility scooter rentals; and accessible bus service. Be sure to reserve well in advance.

Also check out the quarterly magazine *Emerging Horizons* (www.emerging horizons.com), available by subscription ($16.95/year U.S.; $21.95/year outside U.S).

The "Accessible Travel" link at **Mobility-Advisor.com** (www.mobility-advisor.com) offers a variety of travel resources to disabled persons.

British travelers should contact **Holiday Care** (© 0845-124-9971 U.K. only; www.holidaycare.org.uk) to access a wide range of travel information and resources for disabled and elderly people.

GAY & LESBIAN TRAVELERS

Egyptians have a somewhat schizophrenic attitude toward homosexuality. On the one hand, homosexuality is considered deviant and gay men are discriminated against; on the other hand, sexual relations between men are often ignored as harmless.

The upside of the situation is that gay men can enjoy a variety of casual sexual encounters with relative ease. The downside is that, once identified as a homosexual, a visitor may experience discrimination and face problems with the police.

Lesbians, meanwhile, have no public profile as a group, and there is no "scene" as such. Because of this, couples can hold hands in public—this is what friends do in Egypt—but any further display of affection is not recommended.

You should also be aware that the security services actively work against the gay community. Cases of entrapment followed by detention and torture are regularly documented by human rights groups such as Human Rights Watch. Websites such as www.gayegypt.com are routinely monitored by the security services, and chat groups are used to set up fake meetings.

Gay Egypt (www.gayegypt.com) details cruising locations in many of Egypt's main cities. Much of the information appears to be dated, but it should still provide some useful leads as well as still-relevant warnings of the dangers. The site **www.arab-gay.com** has an active travel section, and the more journalistically inclined **Gay Middle East** has an interesting Egypt section (www.gaymiddleeast.com/country/Egypt).

The International Gay and Lesbian Travel Association (IGLTA) (© 800/448-8550 or 954/776-2626; www.iglta.org) is the trade association for the gay and lesbian travel industry, and offers an online directory of gay- and lesbian-friendly travel businesses and tour operators.

Many agencies offer tours and travel itineraries specifically for gay and lesbian travelers. **Above and Beyond Tours** (© 800/397-2681; www.abovebeyond tours.com) are gay Australia tour specialists. San Francisco–based **Now, Voyager** (© 800/255-6951; www.nowvoyager.com) offers worldwide trips and cruises, and **Olivia** (© 800/631-6277; www.olivia.com) offers lesbian cruises and resort vacations.

Gay.com Travel (© 800/929-2268 or 415/644-8044; www.gay.com/travel or www.outandabout.com), is an excellent online successor to the popular *Out & About* print magazine. It provides regularly updated information about gay-owned, gay-oriented, and gay-friendly lodging, dining, sightseeing, nightlife, and shopping establishments in every important destination worldwide. British travelers should click on the "Travel" link at **www.uk.gay.com** for advice and gay-friendly trip ideas.

The Canadian website **GayTraveler** (**www.gaytraveler.ca**) offers ideas and advice for gay travel all over the world.

The following travel guides are available at many bookstores, or you can order them from any online bookseller: *Spartacus International Gay Guide,* 35th Edition (Bruno Gmünder Verlag; www.spartacusworld.com/gayguide); *Odysseus: The International Gay Travel Planner,* 17th Edition (www.odyusa.com); and the *Damron* guides (www.damron.com), with separate, annual books for gay men and lesbians.

SENIOR TRAVEL

The idea of student discounts is now well rooted in Egypt, but the idea of similar discounts for seniors is unfortunately not. Egyptians are, however, on the whole more respectful to their elders, but expect respect rather than discounts.

Members of **AARP**, 601 E St. NW, Washington, DC 20049 (© **888/687-2277;** www.aarp.org), get discounts on hotels, airfares, and car rentals. AARP offers members a wide range of benefits, including *AARP: The Magazine* and a monthly newsletter. Anyone over 50 can join.

Many reliable agencies and organizations target the 50-plus market. **Elderhostel** (© **800/454-5768;** www.elder hostel.org) arranges worldwide study programs for those age 55 and over. **ElderTreks** (© **800/741-7956** or 416/558-5000 outside North America; www.eldertreks.com) offers small-group tours to off-the-beaten-path or adventure-travel locations, restricted to travelers 50 and older.

Recommended publications offering travel resources and discounts for seniors include: the quarterly magazine *Travel 50 & Beyond* (www.travel50andbeyond.com) and the bestselling paperback *Unbelievably Good Deals and Great Adventures That You Absolutely Can't Get Unless You're Over 50 2007–2008* McGraw-Hill), by Joann Rattner Heilman.

FAMILY TRAVEL

Egyptian society is very family oriented. Children of all ages are gladly accepted in virtually every context, and it is quite common for restaurant and hotel staff to whisk toddlers away for playtime, leaving parents to enjoy their meal. That said, Egypt has less specifically child-oriented activities than other countries, and equipment in parks and zoos do not live up to Western safety standards.

To locate accommodations, restaurants, and attractions that are particularly kid-friendly, refer to the "Kids" icon throughout this guide.

Recommended family travel websites include **Family Travel Forum** (www.familytravelforum.com), a comprehensive site that offers customized trip planning; **Family Travel Network** (www.familytravelnetwork.com), an online magazine providing travel tips; **TravelWithYourKids.com** (www.travelwith yourkids.com), a comprehensive site written by parents for parents, offering sound advice for long-distance and international travel with children.

Also see *Frommer's 500 Places to Take Your Kids Before They Grow Up* (Wiley Publishing, Inc.).

WOMEN TRAVELERS

Women traveling alone in Egypt face some challenges, and it's important to get the cultural cues correct in order to minimize the hassle and potential problems.

First, recognize that simply by being an unaccompanied woman, you are perceived as potentially available. Second, realize that though Egypt is a highly controlled and repressive society, the West is viewed as free and easy, particularly with regard to matters of sexual relations. Western women are frequently portrayed in the media as promiscuous, and they figure large in the Egyptian-male imagination as the answer to their stifled dreams.

The result is that you will be on the receiving end of a range of comments and invitations in the street, and you may find yourself being crowded and groped in markets and other tight spots. Reports of taxi drivers exposing themselves are not uncommon. Following some simple guidelines can help reduce the problem, if not eliminate it entirely.

Most important, **dress conservatively.** Bare arms and legs will indicate that you are the loose Westerner of their imagination, and you will find the level of harassment increasing commensurately. Tight jeans and tops are better than shorts and a tank top, but not by much. Best to stick to loose pants or sensible, ankle- or mid-calf-length skirts and frumpy long-sleeved tops.

Avoid eye contact. As much as revealing clothing, this is seen as another signal that you are interested. Unfortunately, so is laughing. Allowing a man to put his hand on you, a liberty that an uninterested Egyptian woman would never allow—whether on your hand, forearm, or shoulder—will also indicate to him that you are open to further advances.

Turn the conversation, any conversation, to your family or his family. Ask questions about his children, and invent a husband and several children if you want to avoid being propositioned.

Finally, **don't accept food or drink from strangers when alone.** Cases of women being drugged and assaulted are not common, but they certainly happen. The most common place for them to happen is on the train and in taxis.

Check out the award-winning website **Journeywoman** (www.journeywoman. com), a "real life" women's travel-information network where you can sign up for a free e-mail newsletter and get advice on everything from etiquette and dress to safety. The travel guide *Safety and Security for Women Who Travel* by Sheila Swan and Peter Laufer (Travelers' Tales Guides), offering common-sense tips on safe travel, was updated in 2004.

AFRICAN-AMERICAN TRAVELERS

As detailed in "Dealing with Discrimination" (p. 30), African-American travelers may experience difficulties in Egypt.

Black Travel Online (www.blacktravel online.com) posts news on upcoming events and includes links to articles and travel-booking sites. **Soul of America** (www.soulofamerica.com) is a comprehensive website, with travel tips, event and family-reunion postings, and sections on historically black beach resorts and active vacations.

Agencies and organizations that provide resources for black travelers include: **Rodgers Travel** (𝄞 800/825-1775; www.rodgerstravel.com); the **African American Association of Innkeepers International** (𝄞 877/422-5777; www. africanamericaninns.com); and **Henderson Travel & Tours** (𝄞 800/327-2309 or 301/650-5700; www.hendersontravel. com), which has specialized in trips to Africa since 1957.

Go Girl: The Black Woman's Guide to Travel & Adventure (Eighth Mountain Press) is a compilation of travel essays by writers including Jill Nelson and Audre Lorde. *The African-American Travel Guide* by Wayne C. Robinson (Hunter Publishing; www.hunterpublishing.com) was published in 1997, so it may be somewhat dated. *Travel and Enjoy Magazine* (𝄞 866/266-6211; www.travelandenjoy. com) is a travel magazine and guide. The well-done *Pathfinders Magazine* (𝄞 877/977-PATH; www.pathfinders travel.com) includes articles on everything from Rio de Janeiro to Ghana to upcoming ski, diving, golf, and tennis trips.

STUDENT TRAVEL

The **International Student Travel Confederation** (ISTC) (www.istc.org) was formed in 1949 to make travel around the world more affordable for students. Check out its website for comprehensive travel services information and details on how to get an **International Student Identity Card** (ISIC), which qualifies students for substantial savings on rail passes, plane tickets, entrance fees, and more. It also provides students with basic health and life insurance and a 24-hour helpline. The card is valid for a maximum of 18 months. You can apply for the card online or in person at **STA Travel** (© **800/781-4040** in North America; www.statravel.com), the biggest student travel agency in the world; check out the website to locate STA Travel offices worldwide. If you're no longer a student but are still under 26, you can get an **International Youth Travel Card (IYTC)** from the same people, which entitles you to some discounts. **Travel CUTS** (© **800/592-2887;** www.travel cuts.com) offers similar services for both Canadians and U.S. residents. Irish students may prefer to turn to **USIT** (© **01/602-1904;** www.usit.ie), an Ireland-based specialist in student, youth, and independent travel.

SINGLE TRAVELERS

On package vacations, single travelers are often hit with a "single supplement" to the base price. To avoid it, you can agree to room with other single travelers or find a compatible roommate before you go, from one of the many roommate-locator agencies.

Canadian-based **Connecting Single Travel Companions** (© **604/886-9099;** www.cstn.org) runs personal ads on its website from single travelers looking for companions; it also offers useful links to other sites.

TravelChums (© **212/787-2621;** www.travelchums.com) is another Internet-only travel-companion matching service with elements of an online personals-type site, hosted by the respected New York–based Shaw Guides travel service.

Many tour companies offer singles-only trips. **Singles Travel Company** (© **888/286-8687;** www.singlestravel company.com) offers budget-oriented singles-only escorted tours to places like Italy, Belize, and Egypt. **All Singles**

Travel (© **800/717 3231;** www.allsingles travel.com) arranges Egypt tours with good hotels and possible extensions to see Israel as well. **Backroads** (© **800/462-2848;** www.backroads.com) offers "Singles + Solos" active-travel trips to destinations worldwide.

For more information, check out Eleanor Berman's classic *Traveling Solo: Advice and Ideas for More Than 250 Great Vacations,* 5th Edition (Globe Pequot), updated in 2005.

VEGETARIAN TRAVEL

Vegetarian options are becoming more common in Egyptian restaurants, but the best bet remains ordering a variety of appetizers. Between stuffed vine leaves and hummus, yogurts and cheeses, and fresh bread, a good restaurant can provide a well-balanced and filling meal. Make sure you ask before ordering the stuffed vine leaves—these are sometimes cooked with a small amount of meat inside.

One potential boon to vegetarian travelers is that the Christian community in Egypt maintains a rigorous fasting calendar. Unlike the Muslims, who abstain from food or drink during daylight hours, the Coptic community eschews meat and dairy products during their fasts. Enquire after "fasting foods" at restaurants and bakeries.

Happy Cow's Vegetarian Guide to Restaurants & Health Food Stores (www.happycow.net) has a restaurant guide with more than 6,000 restaurants in 100 countries, though at the time of writing, it has only one, outdated, listing for Cairo. Hopefully, this will expand with reader contributions. **VegDining. com** (www.vegdining.com) also lists vegetarian restaurants (with profiles) around the world. **Vegetarian Vacations** (www. vegetarian-vacations.com) offers vegetarian tours and itineraries.

8 Sustainable Tourism/Ecotourism

Until a few years ago, scant attention was paid in Egypt to the environmental impact of the millions of tourists who visit every year.

This has started to change, as foreign donors have pressed the government on the consequences of environmental degradation caused by massive development along the Red Sea coast.

Egypt has established 21 protected areas, and foreign donors, including the European Union, have contributed large amounts of capital to develop them on behalf of future generations of Egyptians.

The best known of these protected areas are St. Catherine protected area (p. 171), Ras Mohamed National Park (p. 199), and the Wadi Rayan protectorate (p. 125). Read more about the protected areas at the **Egyptian Environmental Affairs Agency (EEAA)** website (www.eeaa.gov.eg/protectorates).

A number of resorts on the Sinai Peninsula, down the Red Sea coast between Gouna and Marsa Allam, and even in Cairo have begun to participate in environmental certification programs designed to assess their environmental footprint and maximize their sustainability. One of the more common ones is **Green Globe 21** (www.ec3global.com/products-programs/green-globe). The program is named for the U.N. environmental **Agenda 21** program (www.un.org/esa/sustdev/documents/agenda21/index.htm). You can contribute to making tourism greener by learning about the program and asking about it when you make your booking: Make it clear that your tourist dollars prefer to flow to sustainable enterprises.

Additionally, a number of local Egyptian NGOs have emerged that work on raising awareness of environmental issues and train tourism workers in ways that they can preserve the natural capital on which their jobs depend.

The **Hurghada Environmental Protection and Conservation Association (HEPCA)** is focused on marine issues along the coast. Read more about their efforts to protect marine life, coral, and wrecks at www.hepca.com.

Red Sea Rangers is an organization based on the Red Sea coast that aims to protect the marine environment over 700 km (435 miles) of coastline. It has an interesting and informative website at www.redseaparks.net.

Environmental Quality International (www.eqi.com.eg) is a private consulting firm that has done an enormous amount in the isolated desert oasis of Siwa, including the development of an ecolodge (p. 261).

There are a number of locations in the Red Sea where it's possible to swim with wild dolphins. For information about the ethics of swimming with dolphins and other outdoor activities, visit the **Whale and Dolphin Conservation Society** (www.wdcs.org) and **Tread Lightly** (www.treadlightly.org).

Apart from staying in low-consumption facilities, you can also look at carbon offsetting as a way of reducing the overall impact of your vacation. Each time you take a flight or drive a car, CO_2 is released into the atmosphere. You can help neutralize this danger to our planet through *carbon offsetting* (paying someone to reduce your CO_2 emissions by the same amount you've added). Carbon offsets can be purchased in the U.S. from companies such as **Carbonfund.org** (www.carbonfund.org) and **TerraPass** (www.terrapass.org), and from **Climate Care** (www.climatecare.org) in the U.K.

Although one could argue that any vacation that includes an airplane flight can't be truly "green," you can go on holiday and still contribute positively to the environment. You can offset carbon emissions from your flight in other ways.

Frommers.com: The Complete Travel Resource

Planning a trip or just returned? Head to **Frommers.com,** voted Best Travel Site by *PC Magazine.* We think you'll find our site indispensable before, during, and after your travels—with expert advice and tips; independent reviews of hotels, restaurants, attractions, and preferred shopping and nightlife venues; vacation giveaways; and an online booking tool. We publish the complete contents of over 135 travel guides in our **Destinations** section, covering over 4,000 places worldwide. Each weekday, we publish original articles that report on **Deals and News** via our free **Frommers.com Newsletters.** What's more, **Arthur Frommer** himself blogs 5 days a week, with cutting opinions about the state of travel in the modern world. We're betting you'll find our **Events** listings an invaluable resource; it's an up-to-the-minute roster of what's happening in cities everywhere—including concerts, festivals, lectures, and more. We've also added weekly **podcasts, interactive maps,** and hundreds of new images across the site. Finally, don't forget to visit our **Message Boards,** where you can join in conversations with thousands of fellow Frommer's travelers and post your trip report once you return.

Choose forward-looking companies that embrace responsible development practices, helping preserve destinations for the future by working alongside local people. An increasing number of sustainable tourism initiatives can help you plan a family trip and leave as small a "footprint" as possible on the places you visit.

Responsible Travel (www.responsible travel.com) contains a great source of sustainable travel ideas run by a spokesperson for responsible tourism in the travel industry. **Sustainable Travel International** (www.sustainabletravelinternational.org) promotes responsible tourism practices and issues an annual *Green Gear & Gift Guide.*

You can find eco-friendly travel tips, statistics, and touring companies and associations—listed by destination under "Travel Choice"—at the International Ecotourism Society (TIES) website (www. ecotourism.org). Also check out **Conservation International** (www.conservation. org), which, with *National Geographic Traveler,* annually presents **World Legacy Awards** (www.wlaward.org) to those travel tour operators, businesses, organizations, and places that have made a significant contribution to sustainable tourism. **Ecotravel.com** (www.ecotravel.com) is part online magazine and part ecodirectory, letting you search for touring companies in several categories (water-based, land-based, spiritually oriented, and so on).

In the U.K., **Tourism Concern** (www.tourismconcern.org.uk) works to reduce social and environmental problems connected to tourism and find ways of improving tourism so that local benefits are increased.

The **Association of British Travel Agents (ABTA)** (www.abtamembers.org/ responsibletourism) acts as a focal point for the U.K. travel industry and is one of the leading groups spearheading responsible tourism.

The **Association of Independent Tour Operators (AITO)** (www.aito.co. uk) is a group of interesting specialist operators leading the field in making holidays sustainable.

9 Staying Connected

TELEPHONES
To call Egypt:

1. Dial the international access code: 011 from the U.S. or Canada; 00 from the U.K., Ireland, or New Zealand; or 0011 from Australia.
2. Dial the country code, 2.
3. Dial the city code and then the number.

To make international calls: To make international calls from Egypt, first dial 00 and then the country code (U.S. or Canada 1, U.K. 44, Ireland 353, Australia 61, New Zealand 64). Next, dial the area code and number. For example, if you wanted to call the British Embassy in Washington, D.C., you would dial 00-1-202-588-7800.

For directory assistance: The once-disastrous state of directory assistance in Egypt has undergone a miraculous transformation in recent years. Now you can dial 140 and get English-speaking directory assistance for inside Egypt that is accurate and up to date. The same service exists online at www.140online.com, but the numbers are less likely to be up to date. For business phone numbers and addresses, try www.yellowpages.com.eg. For international directory assistance, dial 144.

For operator assistance: If you need operator assistance in making a call, dial 120 if you're trying to make an international call and 140 if you want to call a number in Egypt.

Toll-free numbers: Toll free numbers start with 0800 in Egypt. There is a partial and hard-to-search list of them on the Telecom Egypt site (www.telecomegypt.com.eg/English/Home_FindNumber_aNumSearchFreePhone.asp). Calling an 800 number in the States from Egypt is not toll-free; in fact, it costs the same as an overseas call.

In 2007, Cairo phone numbers (city code 02) were changed from 7 to 8 digits. The rule of thumb is, on the west side of the Nile (Giza, Mohandiseen, Agouza, Dokki, and so on), add a 3. On the east side of the river, and in the middle of the river (downtown, Heliopolis, Maadi, Garden City, Zamalek, and Manial), add a 2.

Meanwhile, mobile numbers are all 10 digits and do not need an area code.

CELLPHONES

The three letters that define much of the world's wireless capabilities are **GSM** (Global System for Mobile Communications), a big, seamless network that makes for easy cross-border cellphone use throughout Europe and dozens of other countries worldwide. In the U.S., T-Mobile and Cingular Wireless use this quasi-universal system; in Canada, Microcell and some Rogers customers are GSM; and all Europeans and most Australians use GSM. GSM phones function with a removable plastic SIM card, encoded with your phone number and account information. If your cellphone is on a GSM system, and you have a world-capable multiband phone such as many Sony Ericsson, Motorola, or Samsung models, you can make and receive calls across civilized areas around much of the globe. Just call your wireless operator and ask for international roaming to be activated on your account. Unfortunately, per-minute charges can be high—usually $1 to $1.50 in Western Europe and up to $5 in places such as Russia and Indonesia.

For many people, **renting** a phone is a good idea. In Egypt, you will need to buy or rent a handset, buy a phone number, and purchase a prepaid phone credit. Many five-star hotels' business centers rent phones, too. The Conrad and the Four Seasons, for example, will supply you with a handset for around LE125 a day ($23/£12). With a perfectly functional, low-end handset running LE300 to LE600 ($55–$109/£28–£56) on the local market, however, it makes sense just to buy if you're going to need it for more than a couple of days.

SIM cards and phone numbers can be purchased for about LE125 ($23/£12) from almost any store advertising the products of one of the three local mobile service providers: Mobinil, Vodafone, and Etisalat. You will have to give them a copy of your passport and fill out a form.

Prepaid credit, available where you buy your SIM card and phone number, comes in various denominations from LE10 to LE100, and you pay the face value of the card plus about 15%. I usually get the guys in the store to deal with the complicated business of entering the code rather than struggle with the automated voice system in Arabic. Outgoing calls are about LE0.15 (3¢/1p), and incoming calls are free.

North Americans can rent a phone before leaving home from **InTouch USA** (✆ **800/872-7626;** www.intouchglobal. com) or **RoadPost** (✆ **888/290-1606** or 905/272-5665; www.roadpost.com). InTouch will also, for free, advise you on whether your existing phone will work overseas; simply call ✆ **703/222-7161** between 9am and 4pm EST, or go to **http://intouchglobal.com/travel.htm**.

INTERNET/E-MAIL
WITHOUT YOUR OWN COMPUTER
Internet access in most of Egypt is cheap and easy, with even the smallest and most out-of-the-way villages sporting at least rudimentary Internet capacity. You may have to elbow game-playing kids out of the way, but you'll be able to check the news and collect your messages.

For specific recommendations, see "Fast Facts" and/or "Tourist Information" in the appropriate destination chapter.

It is also worth noting that a 2006 amendment to the local Ministry of Tourism hotel rating system requires that all four- and five-star facilities provide Internet access.

WITH YOUR OWN COMPUTER
For travelers with Wi-Fi–equipped laptops, life is good in Egypt. In Cairo, almost every cafe and quite a few fast-food outlets feature free wireless Internet, and those that don't are usually within range of one that does. Additionally, in Luxor and Sharm el Sheikh, two major mobile service providers, Vodafone and Mobinil, are competing to provide Wi-Fi coverage throughout town. At the time of writing, service was iffy—free beta roll-outs that offered low bandwidth and patchy coverage—but look for it to improve. *One word of caution:* Privacy provisions appear to be quite lax on these networks. If you're concerned about your browsing being monitored or your e-mails being read, read the fine print before you log on.

The big hotel chains have also jumped on the Wi-Fi bandwagon in Egypt, but for the time being they are not offering it for free. The irony of charging LE165 ($30/£15) a day for Internet access when it's available for free just across the street in a cafe or at their three-star competition is lost on them.

For a list of hotspots in Egypt, check out the database at **www.jiwire.com**. Truly determined Wi-Fi hunters, however, won't be satisfied with anything less than a pocket-size "Wi-Fi spy." Available at Western gadget stores for $20 to $200, depending on features, these handy little devices can sniff out and analyze surrounding wireless networks.

If your laptop is not Wi-Fi equipped, there is cheap and good dial-up access throughout the country that you can access from your hotel room. Most hotels and Internet cafes will also let you plug into their network through the Ethernet port on your laptop.

At the time of writing, Terminal One of the Cairo International Airport was equipped with free Wi-Fi service and Terminal Two had a Wi-Fi system with pay cards (available in the terminal).

Electricity supply is 220 volts in Egypt, and plugs are European style, with two round prongs. Adapters are readily available.

Ethernet patch cables are easy to find (and are generally supplied by hotels with in-room high-speed Internet), but replacement power cords, even for very common laptop models, are not.

CENSORSHIP

The Internet is not widely censored in Egypt, though access to some sites that are critical of the government have been blocked. A greater concern for some will be the monitoring of certain sites (such as www.gayegypt.com) and the use of chat rooms to set up gay men for unpleasant encounters with the police.

10 Packages for the Independent Traveler

Package tours are simply a way to buy the airfare, accommodations, and other elements of your trip (such as car rentals, airport transfers, and sometimes even activities) at the same time and often at discounted prices. In Egypt, they are also one of the best ways to save money. Most tourist hotels in Egypt are oriented toward travel-agency and group bookings. Walk-ins will often be charged double or triple what customers who have booked as part of a package are paying.

One good source of package deals is the airlines themselves. Most major airlines offer air/land packages, including **American Airlines Vacations** (© 800/ 321-2121; www.aavacations.com), **Delta Vacations** (© 800/654-6559; www.delta vacations.com), **Continental Airlines Vacations** (© 800/301-3800; www. covacations.com), and **United Vacations** (© 888/854-3899; www.unitedvacations. com). Several big **online travel agencies**—Expedia, Travelocity, Orbitz, and Lastminute.com—also do a brisk business in packages to Egypt.

Thomas Cook (© 0870/7505711; www.thomascook.com) is one of the biggest operators in the Egyptian package market, and it has well-trained staff in strategically placed offices around the country. (I'm a fan of its Luxor office.) In-country services booked through them tend to be higher-end than some of the local agents, but in the end you get what you pay for.

Thomson Holidays (© 0870/ 1650079; www.thomson.co.uk) is a British package dealer that specializes in keeping prices down and does a huge volume of business in Egypt. In addition to providing airfare and accommodations packages at substantially low prices, Thomson sells day and multi-day packages for everything from monument sightseeing to Red Sea snorkeling through representatives who can be found at the travel desks in the lobbies of most high-traffic tourist hotels in Cairo, Luxor, and Sharm El Sheikh.

Travel packages are also listed in the travel section of your local Sunday newspaper. Or check ads in national travel magazines such as *Arthur Frommer's Budget Travel Magazine, Travel + Leisure, National Geographic Traveler,* and *Condé Nast Traveler.*

11 Escorted General-Interest Tours

Escorted tours are structured group tours with a group leader. The price usually includes everything from airfare, hotels, and meals to tours, admission costs, and local transportation.

Despite the fact that escorted tours require big deposits and predetermine hotels, restaurants, and itineraries, many people derive security and peace of mind from the structure they offer. Escorted tours—whether they're navigated by bus, motor coach, train, or boat—let travelers sit back and enjoy the trip without having to drive or worry about details. They take you to the maximum number of sights in the minimum amount of time with the least amount of hassle. They're particularly convenient for people with limited mobility and they can be a great way to make new friends.

On the downside, you'll have little opportunity for serendipitous interactions with locals. The tours can be jam-packed with activities, leaving little room for individual sightseeing, whim, or adventure—plus they often focus on the heavily touristed sites, so you miss out on many a lesser-known gem.

Egypt Magic (© **888/575-6941** or 352/402-0412; www.egyptmagic.com) has a variety of 1- and 2-week Egyptian packages. Its accommodation choices are solid and its itineraries are reasonable. The Egypt Adventure tour, which costs $1,700 to $2,100 depending on the season, doesn't include a cruise, but it sees Upper Egypt sites by car and includes good flexibility for travelers to do their own thing, with or without their guide.

British-based **Insight Vacations** (www. insightvacations.com) has economically priced tours that hit all of Egypt's must-see sites. Its 17-day Grand Tour of Egypt runs about $3,000 (£1,528) and covers Alexandria, Cairo, Upper Egypt (including a cruise), and a visit to St. Catherine's monastery on the Sinai Peninsula.

American luxury travel company **Abercrombie & Kent** (© **800/554-7016;** www.abercrombiekent.com) is at the high end of the scale, with an 11-day Highlights of Egypt tour running around $4,000 to $6,000, with accommodations and food to match.

12 Getting Around Egypt

THROUGH TRAVEL AGENTS

Booking tickets for transport inside Egypt is very straightforward. Plane tickets can be booked online, and bus and train tickets can be purchased at the appropriate stations. The downside is that, mainly because of traffic congestion, it's very time consuming. Simply getting to the train station to buy your tickets can set you back 1 or 2 hours, and then you have to fight through the crowds. For this reason, I recommend using a travel agent to make the arrangements. Expect to pay a premium, of course, for this service. In the case of train tickets (which pay no commissions to agents), it will help if you have other business to do with that agent—book your pyramid tour and your van rental at the same time as you ask for your train tickets.

There are literally thousands of travel agents in Egypt, and the main squares in tourist destinations are crowded with musty offices where papers are piled on top of broken computers. It is very much a caveat emptor market.

The **Travco** office in Zamalek, 13 Mahmoud Azmi St. (© **02/27362042** or 02/27354493; www.travco-eg.com), has an excellent reputation, as does **Guardian Travel,** 5a Maruteia St., Giza (© **02/37404747;** www.guardiantravel.com). You can also try **Garden City Travel,** 20 Maamal Al-Sokar, Garden City (© **02/27940663;** www.gardencitytravel.net).

BY AIR

Getting around Egypt means covering substantial distances from one tourist center to the next. Though there is reliable bus service between most places and excellent train service to a few, the best way to get around is by air.

EgyptAir has a virtual monopoly on internal flights. (There are a few charters operating inside the country, but standards are low and they offer no advantages over the state carrier.) The planes aren't always the cleanest, and the flying style will make you nostalgic for the international airline that brought you to Cairo, but they're usually reliable. If you plan to read or sleep, bring earplugs; EgyptAir's domestic flights run a constant stream of ads and music videos, and the volume is turned up to maximum for the benefit of the hard of hearing.

Tickets can be booked with any travel agent or at an EgyptAir travel office (where service is friendly but always frustratingly slow), but booking online at www.egyptair.com beats both these options hands down. It's quick, easy, and cheap.

BY BUS

Buses are how the majority of Egyptians get around the country. You can get almost anywhere on the bus, and the service is reliable and relatively safe.

Service is divided up geographically between a number of older companies including West Delta, East Delta, Upper Egypt, and Pullman. High-volume destinations such as Dahab, Sharm el Sheikh, Hurghada, and Luxor are served by Super Jet, which is just slightly more expensive and has newer buses with air-conditioning and toilets.

Two things to check on before setting out on a bus journey are videos and air-conditioning. If there is going to be a video, take earplugs—there are no earphones, and the sound is played at maximum volume over speakers. Air-conditioning is also usually turned up too high, and even in the height of summer you may find yourself wishing for a jacket.

The newly built Turgoman bus station in the middle of Cairo services all destinations in Egypt.

BY CAR

There are two ways to see Egypt by car: hiring a car with a driver or hiring a car that you drive yourself. I recommend the former, simply because it's the low-hassle option, with the driver taking care of most of the problems associated with driving yourself.

Driving yourself is a viable option if you have quick reflexes and nerves of steel, and it will probably work out to be cheaper and more flexible if you're driving from town to town. On the other hand, for getting around Cairo, I recommend taking taxis or hiring a driver. Between congestion and lack of parking, your own car is more of a burden than anything else.

The most important thing to consider is that the standard of driving in Egypt, particularly on highways, is appallingly bad. Locals think nothing of passing on blind corners or coming up on the crest of a hill. Opposing traffic is simply expected to make room by pulling off the road. Signaling follows a different protocol; for example, a driver on the highway with the left turn signal flashing may be indicating to you that it's safe to pass, or that he plans to turn left, or that he forgot to turn off his indicator. Note that Egyptians drive on the right, in theory at least.

Speed limits vary between 50kmph (31 mph) inside towns to between 90 and 110kmph (56–68 mph) on highways. Congestion means that you'll rarely get over 20kmph (12 mph) in the city, but highway limits are routinely ignored.

Petrol, though getting to be more expensive, is still extremely cheap by Western standards—between LE1.20 and LE1.50 per liter (22¢–27¢/11p–14p) for regular and premium gas. Expect to tip the attendant LE1 (18¢/9p) for a fill up and the person who cleans your windshield another LE1 (18¢/9p).

Gas stations are not hard to find, though they tend to be widely spaced out in the desert, so it's wise to fill up the tank at every opportunity—you never know when any particular station is going to run out and leave you wondering whether you can make it to the next one.

There are a few toll roads in Egypt. Going to Ain Sukhna, for example, to Fayum or Alexandria will cost you LE2 (36¢/18p). More of a hassle are the security checkpoints, where you may be asked to hand over your documents and answer a few questions.

Note that foreigners were not being allowed to drive the Nile Valley road between Luxor and Cairo at the time of writing.

The main campus branch of the American University in Cairo Bookstore (p. 117) has a selection of road maps to Egypt.

BY TRAIN

There is a functional north–south railway backbone in Egypt, so travel by train between Aswan in the south and Alexandria in the north is a pleasant and practical way of seeing the country and getting to where you're going. With the exception of the three-times-a-week service to Marsa Matruh, there is no useful service outside this corridor.

Most trains leave from the main downtown station in Ramsis Square. Tickets are sold here, and they have a useful information office.

Note that tourists are not officially allowed to travel on non-tourist-class trains to Upper Egypt. This only becomes a problem if you accidentally board the wrong train (in which case you're probably looking at an uncomfortable taxi ride back from the first stop to the station to try again).

The difference in cleanliness and comfort level make it worth traveling first class. Note, however, that the air-conditioning is usually cranked to maximum in both first and second class. Bring a sweater or a scarf for train travel, even in the summer.

On shorter trips, there is usually a snack and hot-drink trolley. The system is that you pay at the end of the trip for everything you've had—if the attendant demands payment on the spot, he's probably trying to scam you.

Reserved seating is the norm in first and second class between major centers, but double booking has been known to happen. When it does, conflict-averse conductors tend to flee, leaving it to the passengers to sort out where to sit.

13 Tips on Accommodations

Accommodations in Egypt run the gamut from flea-pit to palatial, and an enormous number of choices exist throughout the country. Despite the numbers, however, value for money can be a little hard to find.

At the palatial end of the market, there has been a huge, and often slapdash, investment in holiday resort-style facilities—big glitzy hotels designed to live up to a not-always-realistic idea of what luxury-loving Westerners want when they come on holiday. At the low end, the emphasis has been on delivering the cheapest beds to backpackers, with little thought to cleanliness, let alone quality. There is relatively little midrange quality to be had, and while second-rate resorts abound, few hotels deliver either a first-rate resort experience or a truly Egyptian sense of place and culture.

That said, every city has its gems, and with careful perusal of this guide, you can now visit most parts of the country and be well accommodated on a variety of budgets.

Egyptian hotels are rated by the Ministry of Tourism on the basis of a star system. The rankings are complicated and obscure, and they're based on size, facilities, and service; they aren't very useful in deciding which hotel to stay at.

At the two-star end of the spectrum (don't consider anything less), you are guaranteed a hotel with 30 rooms or more. At the four- and five-star end, you are guaranteed a large hotel with two dining rooms, at least one bar, a swimming pool, elevators, and Internet access. You are not, however, guaranteed decent service or good food in any of them.

At the upper end of the market, foreign-run chains dominate and offer substantially better service than their scarce domestic competition. Prices in these hotels are quoted and charged in dollars (only Egyptians pay in local currency at a substantial discount, usually around 50%), and all services in the hotel (including meals and drinks) are taxed at about 24.5% (see "Taxes" under "Fast Facts," later). Rack rates in these hotels run around $100 (£51/LE550) to $500 (£255/LE2,750) per night for a double. *Note:* Most tourist-class hotels (and all international chains) in Egypt only accept payment in "hard currency." As you go downmarket, you'll notice increasing flexibility on this point, but if you only have local currency, check before you check in. Prices in LE are provided for comparison only.

At the middle and lower end of the market, however, prices—which range from $20 to $80 (£10–£41/LE110–LE440) for a midrange facility—usually include taxes and often breakfast as well. This is a good negotiating point. If you're quoted a price that doesn't include taxes, try for one that does, and tell them to throw in breakfast, too. Here are the major chains in Egypt:

- **Accor/Sofitel** specializes in blandly renovated heritage properties such as the Old Winter Palace in Luxor, the Cataract in Aswan, and the Cecil in Alexandria. These hotels are generally overpriced for the level of service.
- **Four Seasons** has four hotels (two in Cairo, one in Alexandria, and one in Sharm el Sheikh), and is possibly the best chain in Egypt. Its hotels are well designed and well run with an emphasis on seamless, understated service.
- **Hyatt**'s Cairo property goes all out to impress with its cavernous, glitzy lobby but follows up with characterless, overpriced rooms. The chain's Sinai resorts, however, are top-notch. The Hyatt in Sharm el Sheikh, embracing a little water park that tumbles down to the Red Sea, is one of my favorite hotels in the area.
- **Marriott**'s Egypt hotels are generic, cookie-cutter properties for the most part, but they make up for lack of character with professional service and above-average food. The exception is the Cairo Marriott, which has some character but below-average food.
- The **Méridien** hotels in Egypt rise considerably above their Accor siblings, and feature some of the most stylish decor in the country. If snappy color schemes matter to you, forget

the Four Seasons and head to the Méridien.

- Once you get outside Cairo, **Mövenpick**'s facilities are usually the best in town. This certainly holds true for its resorts in Quseir and Aswan.

- **Oberoi** competes with the Four Seasons in terms of price, and wins hands down on location with a hotel next to the pyramids in Giza and one on a long, lovely sweep of beach south of Hurghada. Unless you like Indian food, the menu tends to be mediocre, but everything else is perfect.

- **Pyramisa** is a chain to avoid. Some of the facilities look great on paper, and some (like the Isis Island resort in Aswan) are fun, but facilities are second rate, and the food can be truly bad.

SURFING FOR HOTELS

In addition to the online travel booking sites **Travelocity, Expedia, Orbitz, Priceline,** and **Hotwire,** you can book hotels through **Hotels.com, Quikbook** (www.quikbook.com), and **Travelaxe** (www.travelaxe.net).

HotelChatter.com is a daily webzine offering smart coverage and critiques of hotels worldwide. Go to **TripAdvisor.com** or **HotelShark.com** for helpful independent consumer reviews of hotels and resort properties.

It's a good idea to **get a confirmation number** and **make a printout** of any online booking transaction.

SAVING ON YOUR HOTEL ROOM

The **rack rate** is the maximum rate that a hotel charges for a room. Hardly anybody pays this price, however, except in high season or on holidays. To lower the cost of your room:

- **Ask about special rates or other discounts.** You may qualify for corporate, student, military, senior, frequent flier, trade union, or other discounts.

- **Dial direct.** When booking a room in a chain hotel, you'll often get a better deal by calling the individual hotel's reservation desk rather than the chain's main number.

- **Book online.** Many hotels offer Internet-only discounts, or supply rooms to Priceline, Hotwire, or Expedia at rates much lower than the ones you can get through the hotel itself.

- **Remember the law of supply and demand.** You can save big on hotel rooms by traveling in a destination's off season or shoulder seasons, when rates typically drop, even at luxury properties.

- **Look into group or long-stay discounts.** If you come as part of a large group, you should be able to negotiate a bargain rate. Likewise, if you're planning a long stay (at least 5 days), you might qualify for a discount. As a general rule, expect 1 night free after a 7-night stay.

- **Sidestep excess surcharges and hidden costs.** Many hotels have adopted the unpleasant practice of nickel-and-diming their guests with opaque surcharges. When you book a room, ask what is included in the room rate and what is extra. Avoid dialing direct from hotel phones, which can have exorbitant rates. And don't be tempted by the room's minibar offerings: Most hotels charge through the nose for water, soda, and snacks. Finally, ask about local taxes and service charges, which can increase the cost of a room by 15% or more.

- Consider the pros and cons of **all-inclusive** resorts and hotels. The term *all-inclusive* means different things at different hotels. Many all-inclusive hotels include three meals daily, sports equipment, spa entry, and other amenities; others may include most alcoholic drinks. In general, you'll save money going the all-inclusive way—as long as you use the facilities provided. The downside is that your choices are limited and you're stuck eating and playing in one place for the duration of your vacation.

- Carefully consider your hotel's meal plan. If you enjoy eating out and sampling the local cuisine, it makes sense to choose a **Continental Plan (CP),** which includes breakfast only, or a **European Plan (EP),** which doesn't include any meals and allows you maximum flexibility. If you're more interested in saving money, opt for a **Modified American Plan (MAP),** which includes breakfast and one meal, or the **American Plan (AP),** which includes three meals. If you must choose a MAP, see if you can get a free lunch at your hotel if you decide to do dinner out.

- **Book an efficiency.** A room with a kitchenette allows you to shop for groceries and cook your own meals. This is a big money saver, especially for families on long stays.

- **Consider enrolling in hotel chains' frequent-stay programs,** which are upping the ante lately to win the loyalty of repeat customers. Frequent guests can now accumulate points or credits to earn free hotel nights, airline miles, in-room amenities, merchandise, tickets to concerts and events, discounts on sporting facilities—and even credit toward stock in the participating hotel, in the case of the Jameson Inn hotel group. Perks are awarded not only by many chain hotels and motels (Hilton HHonors, Marriott Rewards, Wyndham ByRequest, to name a few), but individual inns and B&Bs. Many chain hotels partner with other hotel chains, car-rental firms, airlines, and credit card companies to give consumers additional incentive to do repeat business.

LANDING THE BEST ROOM

Somebody has to get the best room in the house—it might as well be you. You can start by joining the hotel's frequent-guest program, which may make you eligible for upgrades. A hotel-branded credit card usually gives its owner silver or gold status in frequent-guest programs for free. Always ask about a corner room. They're often larger and quieter, with more windows and light, and they often cost the same as standard rooms. When you make your reservation, ask if the hotel is renovating; if it is, request a room away from the construction. Ask about nonsmoking rooms and rooms with views. Be sure to request your choice of twin, queen-, or king-size beds. If you're a light sleeper, ask for a quiet room away from vending or ice machines, elevators, restaurants, bars, and discos. Ask for a room that has been recently renovated or refurbished.

If you aren't happy with your room when you arrive, ask for another one. Most lodgings will be willing to accommodate you.

In resort areas, particularly in warm climates, ask the following questions before you book a room:

- What's the view like? Cost-conscious travelers may be willing to pay less for a back room facing the parking lot, especially if they don't plan to spend much time in their room.

- Does the room have air-conditioning or ceiling fans? Do the windows open? If they do, and the nighttime entertainment takes place alfresco, you may want to find out when show time is over.

- What's included in the price? Your room may be moderately priced, but if you're charged for beach chairs, towels, sports equipment, and other amenities, you could end up spending more than you bargained for.

- How far is the room from the beach and other amenities? If it's far, is there

transportation to and from the beach, and is it free?

14 Tips on Dining

I have divided restaurants throughout the book into four categories. Very Expensive meals are LE150 ($27/£14) or more, Expensive meals are LE100 ($18/£9.25) or more, Moderate meals are between LE50 to LE80 ($9.10–$15/£4.65–£7.40), and Inexpensive meals range from LE25 to LE50 ($4.55–$9.10/£2.30–£4.65).

MEAL TIMES

Egyptians are enthusiastic about their meals and are ready to tuck into food at almost anytime of the day. Formal meal times, however, tend to be later than we are used to in the West, with the main meal of the day happening in the middle of the afternoon or sometimes being put off until after work (around 3 or 4pm), and dinner times as late as 9 or 10pm.

During the month of Ramadan, of course, this changes entirely, with a light *sohour* meal eaten just before sunrise (which makes it either a late dinner or an early breakfast) and the enormous *iftar* (literally "breakfast") happening just after sundown.

TIPPING

Most restaurants will automatically add a 12% service charge to the bill, but most people will leave another 5% to 8% in cash on the understanding that the staff probably never sees the service charge.

LOCAL DISHES

Breakfast is usually a selection of flatbread and eggs, often with a side dish of *fuul* (simmered fava beans).

Lunch is usually the main meal of the day, in which meat is served. Families often sit down together immediately after work (which ends a lot earlier in the day than in the West but may be supplemented by a return to the office or shop in the evening) around 3 or 4pm for plates of *kosherie* (a mix of macaroni, lentils, rice, fried onions, chickpeas, and spicy tomato sauce), *molakheya* (sauce of Jew's mallow) and chicken or rabbit, and *fateer* (a flat pastry that can be served either savory or sweet). For more on Egyptian food, see p. 311.

LOCAL BEER & WINE

Just a few years ago, Egypt produced a single brand of beer, which, though inconsistent in taste and alcohol content, was drinkable. The wine was unpalatable, and the hard liquor was downright dangerous. These days, thanks to the privatization of the state alcohol monopoly and the purchase of the country's largest single producer by Dutch beer producer Heineken, there are several drinkable beers and a choice of presentable locally made wines. The most popular of these include **Stella; Saqqara,** a light lager, indistinguishable from Stella by most drinkers; and **Meister** and **Meister Max,** an attempt to make a darker beer (Meister Max sacrifices taste for alcohol content).

Beers cost from LE6 ($1.09/55p) at a store up to LE30 ($5.45/£2.80) in a five-star hotel.

Grand Marquis, Cape Bay, and Sheherezad are the best of the local wines and cost about LE65 to LE80 ($12–$15/£6–£7.40) retail and LE100 to LE200 ($18–$36/£9.25–£19) in a restaurant or hotel.

FAST FACTS: Egypt

American Express Cairo: 33 Nabil El Waqad St., Ard El Golf, Heliopolis (© **02/24130293/4/5** or 02/26909129; fax 02/26909131), and 15 Kasr El Nil St. (© **02/25747991/2**; fax 02/25747997). Alexandria: 14 May St., Madenat El Sayadla, Semouha (© **03/4241050**, 4290800, or 4282021; fax 03/4241020). Luxor: Winter Palace Hotel (© **095/2378333**; fax 095/2372862). Aswan: Kornish El Nil Street (© **097/2306983**; fax 097/2302909).

Area Codes Cairo: 02. Alexandria: 03. Aswan: 097. Luxor: 095. Fayum: 084. Hurghada 062. Marsa Matruh: 046. Siwa, Baherya, Farafra, Dakhla, and Kharga: 092.

ATM Networks See "Money," p. 22.

Business Hours You have to accept that, in Egypt, businesses are open when they're open. Posted hours should be considered guidelines, not hard and fast rules, and you should expect most places to open a little late, and sometimes close a little early as well. Banks are open from 9am to 2pm, and quite frequently in the evening from 5 to 7pm. Stores generally open between 9 or 10am and stay open until between 7 and 10pm. Small grocery stores are open the longest hours, and you can expect to find a box of milk or a pack of cigarettes easily at midnight. Restaurants tend to stay open from midmorning until late at night.

Car Rentals See "Getting Around" in the appropriate destination chapter.

Currency See "Money," p. 22.

Customs What You Can Bring into Egypt   Egypt imposes large import duties on electronics, including cameras, stereos, and laptop computers. There is no problem bringing in items for personal use, but if you're traveling with diving equipment, a laptop, or extensive video or photographic equipment, you may find yourself required to register them upon entry. This will actually reduce your hassle on exit, as it makes it easy to prove that you haven't sold anything during your visit.

Only LE5,000 ($909/£463) can be brought into (or taken out of) the country, which shouldn't be an issue given the ease with which you can exchange money inside the country and the bad rate of exchange outside of Egypt. Foreign currencies to a value of $10,000 can be brought in.

Duty-free allowance on arrival is:

1. 200 cigarettes, 25 cigars, or 200 grams of tobacco
2. One liter of alcoholic beverages
3. A reasonable quantity of perfume and 1 liter of eau de cologne
4. Noncommercial articles up to a value of LE100 ($18/£9.25)
5. Personal items such as hair dryers and razors

Interestingly, these allowances are made "irrespective of age." Prohibited items include birds (live, stuffed, or frozen), Viagra, antiques, narcotics, cotton, and "items offensive to Islam."

What You Can Take Home from Egypt: You cannot export more than LE5,000 ($909/£463) or an equivalent of more than $10,000 in any foreign currency. You are also not allowed to take out drugs, food, silver, or gold bought on the local market (these last two have an exception for "very small quantities for personal use"). Note that at the time of writing there was a blanket ban on bringing any kind of bird back from Egypt to the United States.

U.S. Citizens: For specifics on what you can bring back and the corresponding fees, download the invaluable free pamphlet *Know Before You Go* online at www.cbp.gov. (Click on "Travel," and then click on "Know Before You Go! Online Brochure.") Or, contact the U.S. Customs & Border Protection (CBP), 1300 Pennsylvania Ave. NW, Washington, DC 20229 (© **877/287-8667**) and request the pamphlet.

Canadian Citizens: For a clear summary of Canadian rules, write for the booklet *I Declare,* issued by the **Canada Border Services Agency** (© **800/ 461-9999** in Canada, or 204/983-3500; **www.cbsa-asfc.gc.ca**).

U.K. Citizens: For information, contact **HM Customs & Excise** at © **0845/010- 9000** (from outside the U.K., 020/8929-0152), or consult its website at **www. hmce.gov.uk**.

Australian Citizens: A helpful brochure available from Australian consulates or Customs offices is *Know Before You Go.* For more information, call the **Australian Customs Service** at © **1300/363-263,** or log on to **www.customs.gov.au**.

New Zealand Citizens: Most questions are answered in a free pamphlet available at New Zealand consulates and Customs offices: *New Zealand Customs Guide for Travellers, Notice no. 4.* For more information, contact **New Zealand Customs,** The Customhouse, 17–21 Whitmore St., Box 2218, Wellington (© **04/473-6099** or 0800/428-786; **www.customs.govt.nz**).

Driving Rules See "Getting Around," p. 41.

Drugstores There is no shortage of drugstores (*saydeleya* in Arabic) in Egypt, and they're found in every neighborhood selling everything from shampoo to antibiotics. Most of their products are available over the counter. Pharmacists are also relatively well trained in Egypt and are commonly used for a wide range of medical advice. Additionally, many drugstores will deliver.

Seif Pharmacy is a well-regarded local business with branches all over Cairo. If they don't have what you need, they can tell you which store has it and have it delivered if you want. Branches include: Kasr el Aini Street, downtown (© 02/27942678); Manial el Rouda, Manial (© 02/23624505); Degla Street, Mohandiseen (© 02/37489923); El Koba Street, Heliopolis (© 02/24507185); and Midan el Mahata, Maadi (© 02/3593846).

Electricity Electrical current is 220 volts in Egypt. Plugs are European-style, with two prongs. There are very few grounded circuits in Egypt, so it is particularly important that you turn off the power to appliances such as washing machines before touching them. Adapters are readily available for two-pronged North American plugs.

Embassies & Consulates U.S. Embassy, 8 Kamal El Din Salah St., Garden City, Cairo (© 02/27973300; consularcairo@state.gov); British Embassy, 7 Ahmed Ragab St., Garden City, Cairo (© 02/27940852; info@britishembassy.org.eg); Canadian Embassy, 26 Kamel el Shenawy, Garden City, Cairo (© 02/27918700; cairo@dfait-maeci.gc.ca); Australian Embassy, 11th Floor of the World Trade Center, Corniche el Nile, Boulac, Cairo (© 02/25740444; cairo.austremb@dfat.gov.au).

Emergencies For the police, dial ℂ122; fire, 180; or ambulance, 123.

Etiquette & Customs **Appropriate Attire:** Egyptians place a lot of stock in dressing well in informal situations, and a good pair of slacks and a few long-sleeved shirts should come with you on your holiday. For women, loose-fitting long-sleeved shirts and trousers or long skirts are the best choice. In mosques, you will be expected to take off your shoes, and women will be expected to cover their heads. Unless you expect to visit a lot of mosques, the issue of lace-ups versus slip-ons isn't very important, but you should have socks without holes. Women should carry a light scarf.

Gestures: Meeting and greeting are important ceremonies in Egypt. Shake hands, introduce yourself, and take a moment to get to know people, even if you don't expect to see them ever again. Your left hand is left out of social occasions, for the most part, and once the introductions are out of the way and everyone is sitting down, be careful to keep your feet pointed at (or, better, firmly planted on) the floor. The soles of your shoes are unclean, and it is offensive to point them or even show them. Platonic same-sex friends often hold hands in the street, but it is quite daring for men and women to do so. Cheek-kissing and hugging are de rigueur displays of respect and warmth between men and women, but any kind of public displays of affection are highly inappropriate between couples.

There are few gestures that will cause offense by misinterpretation, but pointing at someone with your finger is disrespectful. Generally Arabs have a richer gesture vocabulary than Westerners and are far more familiar with our signs than we are with theirs.

Avoiding Offense: Egyptians are easy-going and socially skillful, making genuine offense difficult to cause in the first place and easily worked through if it does happen. Religion can be a touchy subject but can be discussed as long as you keep in mind that Sunnis are as used to being members of the socially dominant religion as Christians, Jews, or Hindus are in their countries, and, as such, make the same basic assumptions of universal superiority and correctness as many members of other religions do. Muslims generally see more in common between Judaism, Christianity, and Islam than they do to divide them. Politics can also be discussed, but keep in mind that the Egyptian government doesn't look favorably on its citizens when they criticize the state, and you can inadvertently put people in an uncomfortable position when discussing internal matters. On the other hand, if you're talking international politics, expect a heated argument if you set out to defend positions contrary to the accepted wisdom.

Punctuality is a loose concept in Egypt. It is fine to be 30 minutes late for a social engagement, but on the other hand, Egyptians try to make a point of being on time for foreigners.

Obscenity, whether casual or pointed in either English or Arabic, is inappropriate until you know people well. The same goes for passing comment on women (odd, considering the casual and habitual level of harassment) and absent acquaintances.

Eating & Drinking: A small gift is always appreciated when visiting someone's home. A small bouquet of flowers or a box of sweets are generally appropriate gifts. It goes without saying that in a Muslim country, showing up at someone's house for dinner with a bottle of wine will produce much laughter or an awkward silence.

Business Etiquette: Unlike social appointments, business meetings are held as close to the set time as possible. Handshaking and exchanging business cards are the norm. Expect water, tea, coffee, and sweets to be served. Also expect a lot of smoking.

Photography: Photographing anything official, from the traffic policeman to government buildings and even bridges, will usually prompt an official warning and in many cases some kind of attempt to seize your film and camera. Disorganized and ineffective security arrangements, on the other hand, generally mean you can get away with it if you're willing to ignore the shouting and walk away quickly. Actual military installations are where you should draw the line, and in no circumstances should you take an obvious photo of a military officer.

Further Reading:
- *The Global Etiquette Guide to Africa and the Middle East* (Wiley Publishing, Inc.)
- *Kiss, Bow or Shake Hands: How to Do Business in 60 Countries* (Adams Media)
- *Culture Shock! A Survival Guide to Customs and Etiquette* (Marshall Cavendish Corporation)

Holidays Islamic feast days and religious holidays follow the lunar calendar, and so the exact dates on which they fall may vary by a day or two; they will fall back 11 days each year against the Gregorian calendar used in the West. Holidays for 2009 are Islamic New Year (approximately Jan 1); Mulid an Nabi, birthday of the Prophet Mohamed (approximately Mar 10); Sinai Liberation Day (Apr 25); Shem an Nessim/Easter (Apr 27); Labor Day (May 1); Revolution Day (July 23); Ramadan (approximately Aug 26th–Sept 23); Eid el Fitr (approximately Oct 23–25); Armed Forces Day (Oct 6); Eid al Adha (approximately Nov 30–Dec 1); Victory Day (Dec 23); Islamic New Year (approximately Dec 19).

Hospitals The following hospitals provide an ambulance service: Al Salam Hospital, 3 Syria St., Mohandiseen (✆ 02/33030502 reception, or 02/33034780 ambulance); Al Shorouk Hospital, 5 Bahr el Ghazal St., Mohandiseen (✆ 02/33044891 or 02/33044901 reception, 02/33459941 or 02/33044901 ext 103 or 105 ambulance); Nile Badrawi Hospital, Nile Corniche, Maadi (✆ 02/25240022 reception, or 02/25240212 ambulance); New Kasr el Aini Teaching Hospital, Kasr el Aini Street, Garden City (✆ 02/23654060 or 02/23654061 reception, 02/23654045 or 02/23654101 ambulance). For medical helicopter service (with a doctor and nurse), call ✆ 02/24184531 or 02/24184537 24 hours.

Internet Access Most cafes have free Wi-Fi access, and small Internet cafes abound. In Cairo, Zamalek and Mohandiseen are the most wired-up neighborhoods. Most smaller centers feature hole-in-the-wall Internet shops where you can check your e-mail for LE2 to LE10 (35¢–$1.80/20p–90p) per hour.

Language English is widely understood around Cairo and in tourist hotels and restaurants throughout the country, but off the beaten track and in smaller towns it is relatively rare to find functional English speakers. *A Pocket Dictionary of the Spoken Arabic of Cairo* (AUC Press) is an excellent and convenient linguistic companion to exploring Egypt.

Laundromats Self-service laundromats are extremely rare in Egypt. Instead, you will find small laundry shops, usually tucked away on a side street. The service is cheap but can be slow (reckon on a 24-hour turnaround unless you can get a specific commitment to be quicker). Shrinkage is not usually a problem, but broken buttons from overly enthusiastic ironing is common.

Legal Aid Tourists who find themselves in legal entanglements should immediately contact the consular department of their embassy in Cairo for advice. Although there is often little that embassy staff can do directly to help, they will provide references for lawyers and can help to ensure that legal procedures are followed.

Liquor Laws Egyptian liquor laws are obscure and unevenly applied. Most bars and stores frequented by foreigners, however, have well-posted policies of not serving or selling to anyone under 18. Local beer, wine, and hard liquor can be purchased at Drinkies chain outlets and a dwindling number of independently operated outlets. Drinkies also delivers (© **19330**).

Lost & Found Be sure to tell all of your credit card companies the minute you discover your wallet has been lost or stolen, and file a report at the nearest police precinct. Your credit card company or insurer may require a police report number or record of the loss. Most credit card companies have an emergency toll-free number to call if your card is lost or stolen; they may be able to wire you a cash advance immediately or deliver an emergency credit card in a day or two.

To report lost or stolen credit cards in Egypt, call: Visa (© 410/581-9994), Mastercard (© 636/722-7111), or American Express (© 19327).

If you need emergency cash over the weekend, when all banks and American Express offices are closed, you can have money wired to you via **Western Union** (© **800/325-6000**; www.westernunion.com).

Mail Egyptian post offices are not swift, but they are a reliable way of sending postcards and letters home. A card will cost LE1.50 (25¢/15p) to destinations in the U.S., Canada, Australia, and England. Envelopes of 50 grams or less will cost LE3.5 to LE5.5 (60¢–$1/30p–50p) depending on the destination.

Medical Clinics **Shaalan Surgicenter,** 10 Abd el Hamid Lotfi St., Mohandiseen. Outpatient clinic (around the corner), 11 al Anaab St., Mohandiseen, open 9am to 10pm daily except Friday. Clinic © 02/37605180, 02/37482577, 0122263606, or 0101050571. Surgery 02/37603920 or 02/33387648. **Degla Medical Center,** 4 St. 2003, Degla, Maadi (© 02/5213156 or 02/2523157), open 9am to 10pm daily except Friday.

Newspapers and Magazines The newsstands on 26th of July Street and bookstores in Cairo (p. 117) stock a variety of international magazines and newspapers. Expect daily newspapers to be 1 day late, and save 50% on weekly magazines by buying them one week late from independent newsstands.

Local Media There are a variety of English-language newspapers and magazines in Egypt, but none of them are very good. You are better off reading about Egypt in the international media.

Newspapers: *Al Ahram Weekly* (http://weekly.ahram.org.eg) is the major English-language publication in Egypt, at least measured by print run, but it is closely associated with the government, and its thin coverage of domestic issues rarely strays off the government message. *The Egyptian Gazette* (www.algomhuria.net.eg/gazette/1) is a thin daily newspaper also closely associated with the government. Widely distributed in tourist hotels throughout the country, it is sometimes worth a laugh for its disastrously badly translated crime pages. *The Daily News* (www.egyptdailynews.com) is the closest thing to an independent English-language newspaper in Egypt and the best bet for local news coverage. The *News* comes bundled with the *International Herald Tribune.*

Magazines: *Egypt Today* (www.egypttoday.com) is the biggest English-language magazine in Egypt. Close editorial identification with the government undermines the credibility of its political coverage, but lifestyle features and listings are good enough if you can find a complimentary copy. The same company produces *Travel Today, Business Today,* and *Horus* (the not-very-good EgyptAir in-flight magazine). *Business Monthly* is the publication of the American Chamber of Commerce in Cairo (www.amcham.org.eg) and is the best business-focused publication available. *Community Times* has lifestyle coverage of interest to expats.

Other publications with titles such as *Enigma, Ego,* and *Teen Stuff* cover fashion and youth issues for a young local audience.

Passports Allow plenty of time before your trip to apply for a passport; processing normally takes 3 weeks but can take longer during busy periods (especially spring). And keep in mind that if you need a passport in a hurry, you'll pay a higher processing fee.

For Residents of Australia: You can pick up an application from your local post office or any branch of Passports Australia, but you must schedule an interview at the passport office to present your application materials. Call the **Australian Passport Information Service** at ✆ **131-232,** or visit the government website at www.passports.gov.au.

For Residents of Canada: Passport applications are available at travel agencies throughout Canada or from the central **Passport Office,** Department of Foreign Affairs and International Trade, Ottawa, ON K1A 0G3 (✆ **800/567-6868;** www.ppt.gc.ca).

For Residents of Ireland: You can apply for a 10-year passport at the **Passport Office,** Setanta Centre, Molesworth Street, Dublin 2 (✆ **01/671-1633;** www.irlgov.ie/iveagh). Those under age 18 and over 65 must apply for a 3-year passport. You can also apply at 1A South Mall, Cork (✆ **021/272-525**) or at most main post offices.

For Residents of New Zealand: You can pick up a passport application at any New Zealand Passports Office or download it from the website. Contact the **Passports Office** at ✆ **0800/225-050** in New Zealand or 04/474-8100, or log on to www.passports.govt.nz.

For Residents of the United Kingdom: To pick up an application for a standard 10-year passport (5-year passport for children under 16), visit your nearest passport office, major post office, or travel agency or contact the **United Kingdom Passport Service** at © **0870/521-0410** or search its website at www.ukpa.gov.uk.

For Residents of the United States: Whether you're applying in person or by mail, you can download passport applications from the U.S. State Department website at **http://travel.state.gov**. To find your regional passport office, either check the U.S. State Department website or call the **National Passport Information Center** toll-free number (© **877/487-2778**) for automated information.

Restrooms The best bet for restrooms in Egypt is to head for the nearest tourist-class hotel. If there's nothing in sight, the next best option is a Western-style fast-food operation or a cafe. In my experience, McDonald's and Costa Coffee have the best, followed by Pizza Hut, Hardees, and KFC.

Safety See "Health" and "Safety," earlier in this chapter.

Smoking Egyptians smoke everywhere. Quite a few tourist facilities are now establishing nonsmoking zones, but this is unheard of in the rest of the country, so feel free to light up in the bank, at the doctor's office, or in the elevator.

Taxes Tourist services are generally taxed at about 22%, which is often referred to as the "plus plus" because it is made up of "plus" 10% tax and "plus" 12% service. The exact makeup of the "plus plus" varies between municipalities, and in some places is now "plus plus plus."

Time Zone Egypt is GMT+2, which means GMT+3 when daylight saving time (DST) is in effect. DST comes into effect in the last week of April and ceases to be in effect in the last week of September.

Tipping The general rule for tipping in Egypt is simple: When in doubt, tip. Tip drivers (except for taxi drivers, whom you pay by the ride), waiters, bellhops, and guides. Tip anyone who performs a service for you (shows you to your seat on a train or opens an extra door at the museum), and tip those who haven't done anything directly but ask for it anyway (often the case with street sweepers). How much depends on circumstances and service—a bellhop in a $400-per-night hotel who gives good services should be slipped LE50 ($9.10/£4.60) or more, while waiters should receive a percentage of the bill that reflects the quality of the service. Being provided extra access at monuments or museums is worth LE5 (90¢/45p) at most, on the other hand. Bathroom attendants are well served with LE1 (20¢/9p), as are street sweepers and anyone else looking for a handout.

Useful Phone Numbers U.S. Department of State Travel Advisory (© **202/647-5225** manned 24 hours), U.S. Passport Agency (© **202/647-0518**), U.S. Centers for Disease Control International Traveler's Hotline (© **404/332-4559**).

Water Tap water in Egypt is not generally suitable for drinking. Bottled water costs about LE1 to LE2 (18¢–36¢/9p–19p).

3

Suggested Egypt Itineraries

Egypt is a deceptively large country. The intensely populated Nile Valley, while it holds the vast majority of the population and contains all the best-known sites, actually only constitutes a tiny fraction of the overall landmass. Seeing the whole country is a huge undertaking, and even hitting the high points can mean traveling significant distances in a limited amount of time. For this reason, it's important to plan ahead and develop a workable itinerary that takes into account not only what you want to see, but the inevitable hassles of arranging transport.

Almost all transport routes run north-south in Egypt, so for planning purposes it makes sense to divide the country into three major zones, from west to east: the New Valley and surrounding deserts (which contain the oases of Siwa, Bahareya, Farafra, Dakhla, and Kharga), as well as Marsa Matrouh on the north coast as the transportation gateway to Siwa; the Nile Valley, which contains Alexandria, Cairo, Luxor, and Aswan, and, thus, most of the Pharaonic antiquities; and the Red Sea coast, where most of the truly spectacular diving as well as the fun-in-the-sun resorts are located.

The itineraries here lay out fairly detailed suggestions about how you can go about making the most of your time in specific zones (Cairo, for example, or Cairo and Alexandria). They are intended to be used either individually or as modules that you can link together in whatever order you wish.

1 Cairo in 3 Days

Chances are that you arrived the night before Day 1, so you should be ready to dive right in. With only 3 days, you're not going to be able to cover everything, and you'll have to make some choices as you go.

Day ❶: Exploring Cairo's Neighborhoods

After a good breakfast, head to **Khan al Khalili** via taxi by around 10am. You want to catch the stores as they open and before the other tourists crowd in and start driving the prices up. A late morning tea or coffee at **Fishawy's** (p. 121) will keep you going until lunch at the **Naguib Mahfouz Café** (p. 113). As you refuel, make a choice: If you've had it with the hustle and bustle, catch a taxi to **Coptic Cairo** and retreat to the relative calm of the **Coptic Museum** (p. 100) and the **Ben Ezra Synagogue** (p. 100). If you're just hitting your stride with the whole souk experience, take a walk down to **Bab Zuweila,** and from there to the Tentmakers' souk. Check out some of the monuments of **Islamic Cairo** on your way to the **Madrassa of Sultan Hassan** and the **Mosque of Al Rifai** (p. 97). Try to be back in Zamalek by the late afternoon for a long elevator ride up the **Cairo Tower** (p. 82). This is great place to get your bearings—look at where you've been for the day and where you're going tomorrow. If you like a sundowner with your sundown, try the view from **Mojito** (p. 121) instead: you can't see quite as far, but the menu's a lot more tempting. For your first dinner in Cairo, try **Abu Sid's** (p. 110) in Zamalek.

Day ❷: Pharaonic Sites & More

You can't be in Cairo and not see the **pyramids,** so that should be the first thing you do today. A bus tour from Thomas Cook or Travco is not a bad idea, but you could also just grab a cab off the street (or have your concierge arrange a car for the day) and head out there after breakfast. For lunch, you have two good choices and a fallback. You could take a sandwich from Maison Thomas if you're in Zamalek, or a Cilantro or Beano's outlet if you're not, or (if you have a driver who knows where it is) you could go to Andrea's. Fallback is either the Pizza Hut by the exit from the pyramids or the Mena House Oberoi, depending on your budget.

The afternoon presents a couple of options: If you're game for more Pharaonic sites, head upriver for Saqqara, Memphis, and Dashour (whether you can actually get all of these in depends on how quickly you're willing to go through the sites). If you're not into seeing pyramids but want to see a little of the countryside around the city, head in the other direction to the **Camel Market,** or head back into town and do whichever choice you passed up in the afternoon of Day 1.

In the evening, take a *faluca* from the docks below the Four Seasons and spend an hour or two enjoying the sunset. If you're headed back to Zamalek for the night, try **Bodega** for dinner, otherwise a 10-minute walk through Garden City can get you a quiet meal at **Taboula.**

Day ❸: Cairo Museums

Head to the **Egyptian Museum** (p. 89) first thing in the morning and get your fill of statues, paintings, and mummies. Downtown, your best choice for lunch is **Felfella's;** you can walk there from the museum in about 15 minutes, but keep in mind that you are almost guaranteed to pick up a couple of helpful touts (*khertee* in street Arabic) on the way. They're probably not dangerous, but know that any purchases you make under their helpful supervision will cost you at least 40% more than if you made them alone. If you do have a hankering for papyrus—a staple lure of the touting community—avoid the shops that line the streets here, and buy from one of the street vendors (they're generally a lot more pleasant to deal with).

If the prospect of more dirt and heat in the afternoon makes you groan, take a taxi over to Zamalek and make an afternoon of the **Islamic Ceramics Museum** (p. 82), a little shopping at **Nomad,** and some refreshments on the Marriott Terrace (though I don't recommend the food). If you're up for a little more action, however, head up to the **Ibn Tulun Mosque** (p. 98) and the **Gayer-Anderson Museum** (p. 96). Consider making the **Citadel** (p. 95) your final stop of the day. You won't have much time for the museums, but late afternoon and dusk from the forecourt of the **Mohamed Ali Mosque,** with the view over Fatimid Cairo, is stunning. The route back to Downtown and Zamalek takes you past **Khan al Khalili,** which just after dark is a shopping wonderland of souvenir possibilities.

Cairo & Alexandria in 3 to 5 Days

❶ Exploring Cairo's Neighborhoods
❷ Pharonic Sites & More
❸ Cairo Museums
❹ Intro to Alexandria
❺ Alexandria Museums

---

2 Cairo & Alexandria in 5 Days

Days ❶, ❷ & ❸
See days 1, 2, and 3 in "Cairo in 3 Days," above.

Day ❹: Intro to Alex
Catch one of the morning trains to Alexandria from **Ramses Station.** On summer weekend (Thurs and Fri) mornings, it's essential to have bought the tickets at least 1 day in advance. Upon arrival in Alexandria, buy your return tickets to Cairo if you haven't already got them; then walk from the station to **Kom el Dikka** and check out the **Villa of the Birds** (p. 138). If you got a really early start, you'll have plenty of time to walk down through Attarine past the junk stores, pausing for a cup of coffee at one of Alexandria's old coffee shops before lunch at **Trianon** in Saad Zagloul Square. After lunch, head over to **Pompey's Pillar** (p. 138) and the catacombs at **Kom al Shaqqafa** (p. 135).

Dinner is going to be fish (what else?) at the **Fish Market** or **Abou Ashraf,** depending on your idea of what makes a good view. After dinner, a brief roam from Saad Zagloul Square to Cap d'Or for a beer can be fun. If you've only got the 1 night in the city, I recommend using one of the hotels close to Saad Zagloul. The **Salamlik** and the **Helnan Palestine** (p. 140) are possibilities, but you won't enjoy the racetrack commute up and down the 8-lane, seaside thoroughfare that they necessitate.

Day ❺: Alexandria Museums

I never go anywhere in the morning in Alexandria without a couple of coffees and a pastry from one of the cafes in Saad Zagloul Square. Spend the morning browsing through the excellent **Graeco-Roman Museum** (p. 137) and, if you have the time, the **Cavafy Museum** (p. 137), before heading out to the **Greek Maritime Club** (p. 146) for lunch. After lunch, it's just a 2-minute walk up to the **Qaitbey Fort** (p. 139).

Your schedule will now depend on what time you are heading back to Cairo. If you have a couple more hours, consider a loop that takes you to the **Bibliotheca Alexandrina** (p. 135) for a look at the mosaics in the basement, then to the **Royal Jewelry Museum** (p. 139)—assuming that it has finally reopened—before heading back to the train station. When considering this, keep in mind that until about 6 or even 7pm, the streets between the museum and the station will be jammed, and the final taxi ride could take upward of 30 minutes.

3 Luxor: 3 Days of Ancient Egypt

Because of the sun—which is strong even in the depths of winter—the rule of thumb in Luxor is to see the major outdoor monuments as early as possible during the day.

Day ❶: Intro to Luxor

Karnak Temple (p. 224) is best seen first thing in the morning. Take a break halfway through the morning by the sacred pool. Lunch at the **Oasis Café,** and then wander the excellent **Luxor Museum** (p. 223) in the early afternoon, followed up with the close-by **Mummification Museum** (p. 225). Stroll down to **Luxor Temple** (p. 223) at dusk as the big lights come on and the day starts to cool. Dine on some of the best Egyptian food in Egypt at **Sofra** (p. 240).

Day ❷: Tombs & Temples

This morning it's the **Valley of the Kings** (p. 229). Take plenty of water and a snack. If you've got time, hit the **Mortuary Temple of Hatshepsut** (p. 227) before lunch on top of the **Nile Valley Hotel** (p. 236). If you're not tombed and templed out, and the heat's not too bad, head back to the desert for a second round with the **Valley of the Queens** (p. 230) for the afternoon, rounded out by sunset at **Medinet Habu.** Dinner at the **El Moudira** would be a nice way to round out the evening. Even if you have

a driver, make sure he only takes you back to the boat dock so that you can enjoy the nighttime crossing of the Nile; the road trip back to the east bank is dreary and long. If at lunch you decide that you've had it with the heat, dust, and dead folk, then make like Howard Carter and head for the garden of the **Old Winter Palace** (p. 233) for afternoon tea. You can always head back to **Medinet Habu** in the evening if you feel like it.

Day ❸: Exploring the West Bank

A balloon ride is a great way to see where you've been and where you might be going. There's also still plenty left on the West Bank to keep you well occupied for the morning once you set down. I recommend squeezing in both the **Ramesseum** and the **Valley of the Nobles** (p. 230) before giving up and heading to **El Kababgy** (p. 239) for lunch. After lunch you can either play catch-up and do a museum such as the **Luxor Museum** or the **Mummification Museum,** or do a little shopping until it's time to go to the train station or airport.

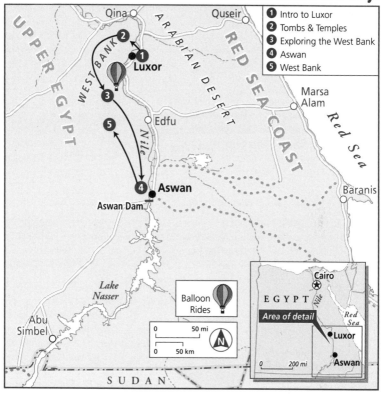

Luxor & Aswan in 3 to 5 Days

❶ Intro to Luxor
❷ Tombs & Temples
❸ Exploring the West Bank
❹ Aswan
❺ West Bank

Balloon
Rides

EGYPT

Area of detail

---

4 Luxor & Aswan: 5 Days of Ancient Egypt

Days ❶, ❷ & ❸

See days 1, 2, and 3 in "Luxor: 3 Days of Ancient Egypt," above. **Optional Day 4:** If you're particularly keen on seeing Abu Simbel, take the early morning flight there instead of doing Philae. You can then head to Philae after dinner for the sound-and-light show.

Day ❹: Aswan

Aswan may be relatively close to Luxor, but it is very different. Take a moment to shift gears and appreciate that the pace of life is a lot slower here. Head south to the **Philae** (p. 249) temple complex first thing before the day starts to heat up. If you're going to check out the **High Dam,**

do so on the way back from the temples, but a better way to spend your hour before lunch would be to stop by the **Unfinished Obelisk.** Lunch in the air-conditioned comfort of the **Mövenpick,** and spend the heat of the afternoon at the **Nubian Museum** (p. 246). After that, head down to the old **Aswan Museum** (p. 245) at the southern end of Elephantine Island. The gardens around the museum are a great place to see out the day. Around sunset, catch a *faluca*, disembarking on the Corniche close to the **Blue Moon** for a simple fish dinner. Spend the evening doing a little shopping in the souk.

Day ❺: West Bank

Start the day with an after-breakfast boat ride to the West Bank and a hike up to the **Tombs of the Nobles** (p. 247). If you've got the gas, hike over to the abandoned **Monastery of St. Simeon** (p. 246); if not, take a boat to the jetty. After lunch, while away the heat of the afternoon lolling in the shade of **Kitchener Island** (p. 246), and then, if you have time before your plane or train, head over to the **Panorama Bar** (p. 250) for an unparalleled view up and down the river and a couple of pre-trip drinks.

5 Western Desert/4-Day Desert Safari

The details of desert safari programs are best worked out with your guide, who will have specific locations to recommend and favorite spots to camp. The itinerary below is a very general framework to give you an idea of how long it might take you to see the desert.

Day ❶: Cairo to Bahareya

Make sure you book your hotel before leaving Cairo so that there'll be a friendly face to meet you; your accommodation will also be able to arrange transport, and offer advice and directions as needed. Arriving in the oases around noon, try to sneak in a visit to the **Golden Mummies** (p. 270) before lunch at your hotel (or try out the landmark **Bayoumi's Popular Restaurant**, but be aware that the bathrooms are not nice, and you might prefer to use the facilities back at your hotel). After lunch, do the **tombs of Banentiu** and **Zed-Amunefankh** (p. 270 and p. 271). End the day with a trip to a **hot spring** before dinner.

Day ❷: Duo of Deserts

After breakfast, head south with your guide to the **Black Desert** for lunch. Take in the **Tomb of Amenhotep** or **Temple of Alexander the Great** on your way out of town. In the afternoon, head down to the **White Desert,** perhaps via **Crystal Mountain** or the **Twin Peaks,** for the sunset and an evening meal amidst the spectacular white inselbergs. Wrap up tight in the camel's-hair blankets; that sand that was burning your toes during the day retains almost no heat once the sun is set, and the desert night can get pretty chilly.

Day ❸: Arrive in Farafra

Check into the **Badawiya Hotel** (p. 276) for a hot shower and some lunch. Visit the **Palm Groves** and **Ain Romana** in the afternoon. Look up **Badr** at his museum on the way back to the hotel. After dinner, a nice soak in **Bir Sitta** will take care of the knots and bruises that you picked up yesterday.

Day ❹: Shop, Eat & Play

First thing in the morning, head up the hill behind the **Badawiya** to the **Al Haya/Farafra Development Association** store to do a little shopping. Head back to **Bahareya** by road midmorning. Try lunch at **Bayoumi's Popular Restaurant** (p. 273) for a real taste of the oasis, and then climb **Black Mountain** before a short afternoon nap so that you can stay up late and track down **Abdel Sadek el Badramany** at the **Concert Bar** for some Bedouin music.

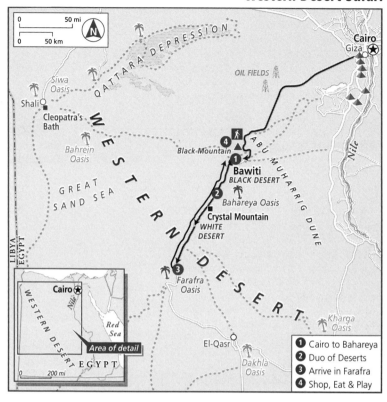

Map legend:
1 Cairo to Bahareya
2 Duo of Deserts
3 Arrive in Farafra
4 Shop, Eat & Play

6 Sinai Peninsula

The Sinai is big, and if you try to move around much, you'll find yourself spending a lot of time waiting for buses or sitting in taxis. My advice is to figure out what you want and stay in the place that provides that for as long as your schedule will allow. If you need a laid-back resort atmosphere, then head to Dahab. If high-end resorts and nightclubs are more your speed, Sharm el Sheikh or Taba Heights will fill the bill. Unless you're going to stay a long time, and exhaust the diving possibilities of one area and have to move on, it's really not worth chasing your tail up and down that long hot coast looking for something better than what you've got.

Warning: Sinai roads, particularly on public holidays, can be lethal. Something about unpoliced blind corners brings out the very worst in Egyptian drivers, and the results speak for themselves. You'll see wrecked cars and buses close to the edge of the road, and the odds are that you'll also come across recent accidents on the road itself. It is, therefore, imperative that you have transport that you trust. If you drive yourself, be aware that no laws apply to, and even the laws of physics are rarely respected by, the other drivers: Don't ever think that just because it's a blind corner or a blind hill somebody's going to think once, let alone twice, about passing. This isn't a place that you want to be driving tired or under the influence. If you have a car with a driver, insist on seatbelts, and do not hesitate to tell him how to drive. Somebody has to have common sense, and it's your life on the line as well as his. Finally, I personally avoid public minibuses; they rarely have any safety equipment at all, and the drivers have generally been scraped off the very bottom of the barrel.

2 DAYS FOR ST. CATHERINE

Day ❶

Take the bus, or drive, early in the morning from Cairo to St. Catherine. Arriving early in the afternoon, check in and have lunch at the **Monastery Guest House** (p. 174). If you're feeling energetic, try a walk to one of the sites nearby, such as **Wadi Ferrah** and **Wadi Shrayj** to see the Nabatean and Byzantine ruins, and maybe spot an ibex. Check to make sure that you don't need to go into the village to buy fresh flashlight batteries before heading back to the Guesthouse for an early dinner. This is a good opportunity to see who else is there, get to know some of your fellow travelers, and, crucially, find out what time the sunrise is going to be the next day.

Day ❷

Well before the crack of dawn—you should be on your feet and moving about 2½ hours before the sun comes up—head up **Mount Moussa.** Pause at the foot of the mountain in the dark to get your bearings and appreciate the peculiar beauty of the scene: the line of sleepy pilgrims trudging up the slopes above you is traced by the small golden dots of their flashlights. You'll be back down in time for breakfast at the Guest House and be at the door of the Monastery at 9am. If you're one of the first through the door, you'll get just a moment of seeing it without the crowds who are pressing in behind you. Grab a quick lunch at the Guesthouse, check out, and head for the coast or back to Cairo.

4 DAYS ON THE SINAI: ST. CATHERINE AND DAHAB

Days ❶ & ❷

Follow "2 Days for St. Catherine," above; this itinerary picks up where Day 2 leaves off.

Day ❷: Unwind & Plan Ahead

You've booked ahead at **Castle Zaman** (p. 161), so you're expected as you roll up to the front gate. Spend a few hours lounging by the pool and sipping cold drinks while dinner cooks. Eat fairly early—around dusk—because you have about an hour's drive to get you down to your hotel in **Dahab.** (Obviously, this only works if you've hired a car.) Thumb through the "Active Vacation Planner" (p. 65), and decide what to do tomorrow.

Day ❸: Active Outdoors

Spend time today doing whatever activities you decided on last night. On a recent trip, I rented snorkel equipment from one of the many little stalls on the main street and stuffed it in my bag next to the packed lunch from my hotel. I hopped in the back of a jeep—after a 10-minute discussion on prices—for the 15-minute drive out to the **Blue Hole** (p. 165) for a long, lazy afternoon of alternately swimming with the fish and looking at the coral and lying about at one of the informal cafes chatting with slackers and hippies from every corner of the world. For dinner, try the seafood at **Lakhbatita.**

Sinai Peninsula

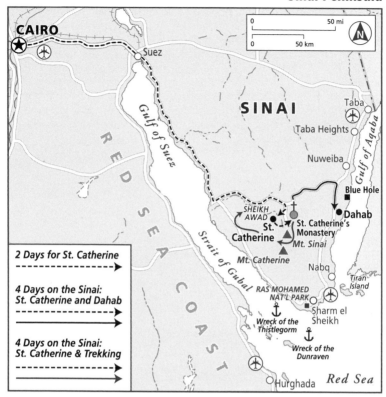

CAIRO

Suez

SINAI

Taba

Taba Heights

Nuweiba

Blue Hole

SHEIKH AWAD

St. Catherine's Monastery

St. Catherine

Mt. Sinai

Dahab

Mt. Catherine

Nabq

Tiran Island

RAS MOHAMED NAT'L PARK

Wreck of the Thistlegorm

Sharm el Sheikh

Wreck of the Dunraven

Hurghada

Red Sea

RED SEA COAST

Gulf of Suez

Gulf of Aqaba

Strait of Gubal

0   50 mi

0   50 km

2 Days for St. Catherine
- - - - - - - - - - - - - - - →

4 Days on the Sinai:
St. Catherine and Dahab
- - - - - - - - - - - - - - - →

4 Days on the Sinai:
St. Catherine & Trekking
- - - - - - - - - - - - - - - →

Day ❹: Relax, Rinse & Repeat

After a late breakfast, I recommend hiring a bike and heading down to Dahab City for a bit of fun with the wind. After all that lolling about yesterday, you might want a bit of adrenalin, so you can try **kitesurfing**. If not, hang at your hotel, watch the waves, and do a little snorkeling.

In the late afternoon, load into a taxi and head to the airport in Sharm el Sheikh for your return to Cairo.

4 DAYS ON THE SINAI: ST. CATHERINE & TREKKING
Days ❶ & ❷

Follow "2 Days for St. Catherine," above; this itinerary picks up where Day 2 leaves off.

Day ❷: Al Karm

Meet up with your guide (see "Active Vacation Planner," p. 65), and walk from St. Catherine to **Al Karm Ecolodge** (p. 174). It's about 15km (9 miles) and will take you around 3 hours, getting you there well before dark (vital if you've elected to do this without a guide). Enjoy the sunset light on the mountains around Al Karm with tea and biscuits (the wise will have packed snacks with them). Dinner will be something tasty and filling concocted by Jamal and his associates.

Day ❸: Trekking Sheikh Awad

This is a full day of trekking around the rugged valleys and hills of the Sheikh Awad area. You can consult the St. Catherine section (p. 170) for ideas, but the staff at Al Karm or your guide will have a much fuller menu, along with helpful ideas tailored to your fitness level and interests. Keep your eyes open for wildlife, but you'll probably see more people than animals. Trekking on the Sinai can actually be quite a sociable activity: You'll certainly have hours of alone time, but inevitably you'll run across shy-but-friendly shepherds and farmers.

Day ❹: Heading Back to Cairo
You have time after breakfast for another walk in the area before you head back to Cairo in the early afternoon, making sure that you arrive before dark. The traffic between the tunnel under the Suez Canal and Cairo itself, especially on a Saturday evening or at the end of any public holiday, is something to avoid after dark.

4

Active Vacation Planner

Until fairly recently, the tourism industry in Egypt has been heavily focused on shuttling people into and out of Luxor. Diving is about the only well-established activity for tourists in Egypt other than lying on a beach or digging holes in the West Bank of the Nile Valley. This, however, is changing. Desert trekking, be it with jeeps or camels, is becoming popular in the Western Desert and slowly becoming possible on the Sinai Peninsula. Wind sports, however, are likely to be the next big thing on the Sinai, where clement weather, steady winds, and great preexisting accommodations and restaurants are already in place.

1 Activities A to Z

DIVING

For experts and beginners alike, Egypt offers some of the best diving in the world. Not only is there unparalleled sea life in the Red Sea, including some of the most spectacular corals anywhere and sea life that ranges from massive schools of fish to sharks, but the North Coast offers the opportunity to dive Greco-Roman archaeological remains, as well as 18th-century naval wrecks and the remains of vessels sunk in World War II. Expect to pay between LE330 and LE468 ($60–$85/£31–£43) per day for boat dives, including lunch and tanks.

NORTH COAST

Master Divers International, Amreya, Alexandria (© **03/4485882,** 03/4485883, or 03/4485884; fax 03/4482963; www.alexandria-wreckdivers.com), is the most professional company currently operating on the North Coast. They can run trips on any of the sites on the coast; they even have experience diving in the Siwa oasis.

MARSA ALAM

Oasis Diving Center (© **010/5052855;** www.oasis-marsaalam.com) is right on top of a prime reef-side dive spot and an easy ride to world-class sites Elphinstone, Abu Dabab, Dolphin House, and more than two dozen others. Stay on-site at the **Oasis Dive Resort** (p. 192), or take advantage of the high-end resorts between there and the airport, only 20km (12 miles) away.

The **Orca Dive Club, Abu Dabab** (© **012/2337950** or 012/6650240; fax 065/3555851; www.orca-diveclub-abudabab.com) is one of a string of Orca centers up and down the coast. This one is located right on the beach at Abu Dabab, across the road from the **Abu Dabab Dive Lodge** (p. 189). They have another center farther south at Hamata, which is also worth considering (check the Abu Dabab website for a link).

Pioneer Divers has four centers in the Marsa Allam area, all within an hour of 15 to 20 dive sites and each close to accommodations. The center on the grounds of the

---

Tips Taking a Dive

If this is your first experience diving, remember that not all dive centers are created equal. This is particularly true in a country such as Egypt, where national regulations are loosely enforced and easy to circumvent. It is essential, therefore, that wherever you choose to dive is registered and certified by the American-based **Professional Association of Diving Instructors (PADI)**—all the companies listed in this guide are PADI certified. A good way to find more centers near your destination is to visit the PADI website (www.padi.com).

You can also do a few simple checks on your own at the dive center if you have doubts. Ask to have a look around. A dive center with nothing to hide will have no problem giving you a tour of its equipment and compressor room. Everything should look neat and well organized. Equipment should be clean and well cared for. The compressor used to fill the bottles is vital and should not be close to any source of potential contamination. If you have any doubts, hold a clean white T-shirt over the air outlet while the compressor is running; if there's any residue left on the shirt, think twice about breathing from tanks that have been filled there.

Kahramana Resort (p. 190), for example, is within 15 to 30 minutes by speedboat of both Elphinstone and Abu Dabab. The center close to Shagra Ecolodge Village, meanwhile, has reasonably priced all-inclusive accommodations. Visit the website (www.redsea-divingsafari.com), or call its Cairo office, 53 el Hussein St., Dokki (© **02/33379942** or 02/33371833; 02/37494219), to decide which works best for you.

QUSEIR

Excellent shore diving on nearby reefs makes Quseir a great place for a relaxed dive vacation. The wreck of the Salem Express is also close enough to dive, and a car ride puts the southern highlights Elphinstone and Dolphin House within range, too.

Subex, Sirena Beach (© **065/3332100;** fax 065/3332124; www.subex.org), is one of the nicest facilities on the coast. Tucked into one end of a small bay with the **Mövenpick Resort el Quseir** (p. 196, p. 212), it has a lovely veranda bar and lunch spot, and the reef is an easy beach dive. Though it's not the budget option when it comes to diving the Red Sea, it's good quality and value for money.

SAFAGA

Better known than the more recently opened southern extremities of the Red Sea coast, Safaga remains one of the premier dive destinations in the world. The wreck of the **Salem Express** is within easy day-diving radius of the town, as well as some of the coast's most spectacular coral and undersea life at sites such as Panorama Reef and Abu Kefan. It's also possible to book longer dive safaris that will take you overnight to sites such as **Thistlegorm** and **Ras Mohamed National Park.** Accommodations in the area range from the very basic and fairly cheap to a couple of the nicest resorts on the coast.

The **Dune Diving Center** (© **065/3253075;** www.duneredsea.com) is a well-established dive center in the older part of town that's popular with French divers. Unlike most centers on the coast, Dune is a free-standing business away from any hotel, but they can recommend local accommodations, and daily prices include hotel transfer. Dune is an easy walk to the **Yasmin** (p. 201) and the Nemo Hotel (which runs its own, competing, dive outfit), and a short drive from the Menaville. The Soma Bay resorts are a little farther, but no more than a 15-minute drive.

The **Nemo Diving Center** (© 010/3648708 or 010/1137707; www.nemodive.com) is run by a Belgian-Dutch partnership and has been in operation for the last 4 years. They also run the **Nemo Hotel** (p. 201), which makes the arrangements for accommodations quick and easy.

HURGHADA

Hurghada may be a failure as a town, but it's the best-established center for diving on the Red Sea. It abounds with good-quality, professional dive centers, both in the hotels and operating independently.

Ilios, Steingenber Al Dau (© 065/3465442; fax 065/3465410; ilios@steigenberger aldau.com), is a real five-star operation, with the plush comforts of the Steigenberger at its disposal. If you have to be right in Hurghada, you may as well splurge.

The Hurghada branch of **Subex,** Dahar (© 06/53547593; fax 065/3547651; www.subex.org), is well known on the coast. It's not the cheapest, but you're in good hands.

Dive Buddy, Sakkala (© 012/3214820; fax 065/3442233; divebuddyredsea@ yahoo.com), is a lot smaller than the big hotel-based centers and has a cozier, more casual atmosphere.

GOUNA

With better facilities, better food, and an all-around friendlier atmosphere than Hurghada, all within range of the same dive sites, I don't know why anyone goes anywhere else. Go to Gouna, or spend your holiday in Hurghada wishing you had. If Orca's all booked up, try the Dive Center at the Sheraton Miramar.

Orca Dive Club El Gouna, Abu Tig Marina (© 012/2480460; fax 065/3580171; www.orca-diveclub-elgouna.com), is located in the Turtles hotel near Abu Tig Marina. Stay at the hotel, and you'll be a 5-minute walk from the boats and surrounded on every side by good eats and good bars.

If your accommodations tastes are a little more upmarket than the Abu Tig Marina, **TGI Diving** (© 065/3545606 ext 19; www.tgidiving.com) is located on its own little island right in front of the Sheraton Miramar.

SHARM EL SHEIKH

Sharm el Sheikh started as a divers' destination, and there's no shortage here of highly competent centers. The short list here provides a starting point, but it's definitely not exclusive.

The **Camel Dive Club,** Naama Bay (© 069/3600700; fax 069/3600601; www. cameldive.com), is a one-stop shop for diving in Sharm. It's the best value for money in a midrange hotel; it has a great bar and some of the best food in the city.

Emperor Divers, Rosetta Hotel, Naama Bay (© 069/3601734; fax 065/3450537; www.emperordivers.com), is a big, well-established company with several centers in Sharm, as well as on the Red Sea coast. The comprehensive website allows you to pick up last-minute deals.

Diving World Red Sea, Travco Marina, Sharm al Maya (© 069/3660065; www. divingworldredsea.com), is one of the bigger Egyptian dive businesses. It started in Hurghada and now has centers up and down the coast. It's not the most intimate of outfits, but prices are good and service should be reasonable.

DAHAB

Good diving and a great laid-back attitude characterize this funky alternative to the glitz and gloss of Sharm and the sprawling mess of Hurghada. Despite its mellow style, however, Dahab is serious about its diving and its professional standards. There are lots of PADI-certified, high-quality dive businesses to choose from.

Desert Divers, Masbat (© **069/3640500;** www.desert-divers.com), is a great, locally owned and run business in Dahab that's becoming a center for free diving and yoga. It pioneered the idea of "camel dive safaris," where you trek up the coast with camels to do the shore dive.

Big Blue's (© **069/3640045** or 010/1945466; www.bigbluedahab.com) logo says it all: It's time to chill out and dive. Big Blue is a brand-new dive center right next to the water, which means a great combination of uptight standards and chilled-out diving.

The dive center at the **Nessima Resort,** Mashraba (© **069/3640320;** fax 069/ 3640321; www.nesima-resort.com), not only has a first-class reputation, but is conveniently located in one of the nicest places to stay and eat in the middle of Dahab. It's not the budget option, but it's certainly comfy.

SAFARIS AND TREKKING

The romance of the open desert, combined with spectacular and varied scenery, is turning the Western Desert of Egypt, virtually unknown 20 years ago outside a small circle of explorers, into a major tourist destination. The Sinai Peninsula, which offers a different, and perhaps even more hostile, environment, is a little behind the curve in this regard, but more and more tourists are reaping the rewards of taking the path a little less traveled.

With the tourists have come two developments. First, the inevitable expansion of outfits offering guiding and safaris is swamping the market with inexperienced guides looking to cash in on the rush. Second, well-organized efforts are being made to organize and train guides, and to clean up and maintain the natural beauty on which the industry is based.

If you've never been in the desert, it's hard to imagine how easily you can get lost or stuck. And with temperatures that can run to 120°F (50°C), you can get into serious trouble. Remember when you book a guide that you're trusting him—his driving, his navigation, his judgment, and his equipment—with your life. Apart from this, you're also trusting him to cook decent meals, respect your privacy, and not cut his costs by jamming you in with another group or by neglecting his equipment.

If you have a good company or guide, pricing is going to be pretty much "get what you pay for." A good 4×4 with a guide/driver and some food and bedding should cost around LE600 to LE700 ($109–$127/£56–£65) for 24 hours. The simple fact is that if you're getting a cheaper price, corners are being cut—maybe on the vehicle (bad idea), maybe on the driver's pay (also a bad idea—imagine being stuck in the desert with a bad-tempered driver), or on your food (yet another bad idea). Look at it this way: Even the basic Land Cruisers favored by most guides will take three passengers comfortably, and four isn't bad, so at the still safe and comfortable low end of desert safaris, you're looking at around LE150 ($27/£14) for food, lodging, and transport through some of the most difficult, not to mention beautiful, landscape in the world.

The recommendations below may be divided by oases, but by definition these guides all have a scope of expertise that runs well beyond the narrow boundaries of their town or immediate home area. You'll be able to find cheaper guides, but you won't find better.

CAIRO-BASED COMPANIES

The **Shannon Desert Tribe,** Maadi (✆ **010/1778188** or 012/8188; ashannon@ internetegypt.com), is run by the legendary Amr Shannon, who seems to be laying off desert guiding and heading into early retirement. If you can get him to take you into the desert, however, it's your lucky day. If he's too busy, follow his recommendations on alternatives.

Badawiya Expedition Travel, Maadi (✆ **02/25260994;** fax 02/25287273; www. badawiya.com), was originally based in Farafra, where it remains heavily involved in training and development, but it now runs safaris through the Western Desert. Badawiya offers pretty complete packages and can even arrange your visa and pick you up at the airport if you need.

Pan Arab Tours, El Nozha St. (✆ **02/24184409** or 02/24184419; fax 02/ 22913506), is another big, Cairo-based operator with experience running safaris from the North Coast all the way to the Sudanese border. The same company owns and operates the **Desert Lodge** in Bahareya, the natural stepping-off point for safaris into the far reaches of the southern desert.

SIWA

Abdullah Baghri (✆ **01/11180680;** shali55@hotmail.com) is the doyen of Siwa guides and an all-around pleasant and helpful guy who speaks great English. Like Amr Shannon in Cairo, Abdullah is well established with an A-list clientele, so he may not be able help you directly, but his judgment on who can take his place is to be trusted.

Omar Abu Zahara (✆ **010/6118139;** fax 046/4600761; omar.abuzahra@hotmail. com) is another excellent Siwa guide who not only knows the desert around the depression but is careful and attentive to the needs of his customers. He speaks only very basic English, but he has an assistant and cook who can translate just fine.

BAHAREYA

White Desert Tours (✆ **02/38472322** or 01/23212179; www.whitedeserttours.com) is run by an Arabic-speaking German transplant to the oasis, Peter Wirth, who also runs the International Health Center (known locally as Peter's Hotel). Peter uses the best local guides to put together excellent safaris that range from simple tours of local sites to more elaborate trips out to Dakhla and beyond. He can also arrange pickup in Cairo.

The diminutive and rather gruff **Badri Khozam,** Bawiti (✆ **012/7313908;** www.desert-safari-home.com), has been running tours and safaris around Bahareya for about as long as anyone can remember. He can be found at his Desert Safari Home (p. 271). His English is very good.

Mohamed Kosa (✆ **012/2248570**) is tall and a little forbidding when you first meet him, but his face splits with one of the widest smiles in the oasis. He is one of the best known and most competent deep-desert guides around, and his basic English is sufficient.

FARAFRA

If you're in Farafra, you're probably already hooked up with **Badawiya Expedition Travel.** If you're not but want to be, just head over to the Badawiya Hotel (p. 276), and they'll fix you up.

Ahmed Abed (✆ **010/3064733;** sahara_farafra@yahoo.com) is a third generation guide who moonlights as an English teacher, so his ability to communicate information about the landscape and animals that you see is unparalleled.

DAKHLA

Dakhla is the southernmost of the big oases, and the natural jumping-off point for trips down to the Gilf Kebir (p. 275). While **Pan Arab Tours** (see "Cairo-Based Companies," above) is the big player in Dakhla Oasis, running the Desert Lodge, there are a couple of other people whom you could consider as well.

Abdel Hamid runs the **Dohous Bedouin Camp** (© 092/7850480; www.dakhla bedouins.com) as a base for desert excursions by jeep or camel. The camels live just behind the camp, so you can even check them out and choose your favorites before making up your mind.

Hatem Mohamed Shafik, who runs the **Bir Gebel Hotel and Camp** (© 092/ 7726600 or 012/1068227; fax 092/7727122; elgabalcamp@hotmail.com), also organizes local safaris. There's not going to be anything elaborate about the affair, but for a few nights in the desert close to the oasis at a decent price, you'll be in good hands.

SINAI

Sparsely populated but impressive and ruggedly beautiful, the Sinai Peninsula used to be pretty inaccessible without your own 4×4 and a thick Rolodex of contacts. Fortunately, a couple of companies are making it a lot easier to get out and see this fascinating part of Egypt. Prices tend to be marginally higher on the Sinai than in the Western Desert. Both the companies below are open and upfront about their pricing policies, however, and can be trusted to present you with an honest, take-it-or-leave-it price.

The St. Catherine–based **Away Away Sinai** (© 012/2270443; www.awayaway-sinai.net) doesn't only book guides who have been trained as part of a European Union project to improve the tourist infrastructure, but can arrange transport in the central Sinai and even reserve rooms with the sometimes elusive Jamal at Al Karm Ecolodge.

Desert Divers (© 069/3640500; www.desert-divers.com) in Dahab arranges trips that run the gamut from overnights between Dahab and St. Catherine with jeeps to a 2-week trans-Sinai camel trek. Bedouin owned and run, well established, and experienced, this is a company that can access the best of local knowledge while providing excellent service.

SAND BOARDS, DIRT BIKES & QUADS

There's one thought that goes through the head of a skier or a boarder when they first see a really big sand dune, but all too often there's nothing they can do about it. Packing your board along for your desert safari just isn't something that most people think about. Fortunately, there are now a small number of boards to be rented in Egypt.

Quad safaris, on the other hand, are a dime a dozen. On the whole, they offer a low-value combination of nonexistent safety standards and boring drive-in-a-line driving. KTM (below) is the exception.

The **Desert Adventure Company,** Amreya (© 03/4485883 or 03/4485882; fax 03/4482963; www.saharaadventurecompany.com), are the same guys who can take you surfing off Alexandria and also deal in the sandy variety of surfing.

KTM Egypt, Naama Bay (© 010/1794907; www.ktmegypt.com), may be a little pricier than most places, but it also offers top-flight KTM bikes (ranging from little 50cc kiddy bikes to full-on 600cc desert-eating monsters), quads and buggies, well-trained instructors, and full-on European spec safety equipment. The practice track at its elaborate facilities, on the edge of the desert outside Naama Bay in Sharm el Sheikh, is long and twisty and features one very imposing jump.

For biking the Western Desert, try Franco Picco's (if you ▮▮▮ an Internet search for this well-known Italian rally biker before ▮▮ bikes) outfit based at the **International Health Center** (℃ 02/38▮ 3212179; www.whitedeserttours.com) in Bahareya. At around LE1,265 ▮ per person, per day (all-inclusive, mind you), it's not cheap, but there can b▮ ter way to thrill than a few days of blasting over sand dunes on long-range 6▮ Yamahas. Tours are tailor made, with a four-person, 3-day minimum.

SURFING: KITE, WIND & WATER

Both kitesurfing and windsurfing are quite new to Egypt, but they fit naturally with the long, windy coastlines of both the Red Sea and Sinai Peninsula. For a while, it looked like the failed beach-resort industry along the western coastline of the Sinai might be revived by the sport, but so far the enthusiasm of tourists for the relentless wind there seems to have been insufficient to overcome their distaste for the terrible hotels. For now, the three main centers of the sport are Safaga, Gouna, and Dahab.

Surfing, meanwhile, hasn't really caught on, perhaps because the North Coast—about the only place in the country that gets any real waves—has been developed primarily to serve a domestic market. There is one company (Sahara Desert Company, below), though, that might be able to make your African surfing dreams happen.

SAFAGA

A combination of friendly pleasant staff, excellent up-to-date equipment, and great wind and sea conditions make the **Club Nathalie Portman,** at the Menaville Hotel on outskirts of the old town (℃ **012/1170793;** www.fun-kite.com), Gouna's only competition for windsurfing.

DAHAB

The **Harry Nass Center** (℃ **069/3640559;** fax 069/3640559; www.harry-nass.com) in Dahab City is a one-stop shop for anyone (beginners to experts) looking to spend some time on the lagoon.

GOUNA

Mangroovy Beach, a little to the north of town, offers first-class facilities on a beach that combines a long, shallow walkout for beginners and some big waves farther out for experts, all within a 5-minute *tok-tok* ride of Gouna's great hotels, bars, and restaurants. A number of companies there teach and rent equipment, including **Kitepower** (www.kitepower-elgouna.com) and **Red Sea Zone** (℃ **01/02955209;** www.redsea zone.com).

NORTH COAST

If you've got a hankering to hang ten while you're in Egypt, contact the boys at **Sahara Desert Company** in Amreya, Alexandria (℃ **03/4485883** or 03/4485882; fax 03/ 4482963; www.saharaadventurecompany.com).

don't know the name, do
you get on one of his
472322 or 012/
($230/£117)
no bet-
0cc

Cairo

When the historian and explorer Hero-- -d this city in 500 B.C., some of the pyramids were already 2,000 years old, but it wasn't until more than 1,000 years later that Cairo—Al Qahira (The Victorious) in Arabic—was founded. The view of the valley from the Moqatam Hills was a little different back then—a little quieter, a little cleaner, and certainly a lot less crowded—and today the city sprawls almost 13km (8 miles) wide and is bursting at the seams with around 18 million people, making it one of the most populous cities in Africa. The last 2,000 years have seen occupation by the Romans, Syrians, Turks, North Africans, Gulf Arabs, French, and British, and each has left their own distinctive imprint on the city.

Built around A.D. 969, Cairo was originally a royal enclosure for the leaders of the new Fatimid occupation, who took over the country from the Syrian Umayyad rulers. They needed a safe place to live, so they built what amounted to a gated community close to the existing capital of Fustat. Administration of the country, meanwhile, continued to be carried out in Fustat (see "Old Cairo," later), and it wasn't until a century later that Cairo took over these functions under threat of invasion by European Crusader forces.

Since then, Cairo has spread out, taking over the space previously occupied by older cities such as Fustat, and crossed the Nile to fill the valley all the way up to the once isolated Giza plateau, where the three famous pyramids tower over their surroundings. Sitting on the very edge of a vast desert, the site chosen by the ancient Egyptians for these monumental works of engineering lies right on the line between the verdant green farmland of the Nile Valley and a desert that reaches westward thousands of miles across Libya, Algeria, and Morocco.

It is only in the last 20 years that the city has begun to overcome this formidable obstacle to its expansion. Faced with overcrowding and the gradual collapse of neglected water, sewer, and electricity services, more and more of Cairo's residents are opting to move to new suburbs built in the desert. Serviced by massive water pipes and new electricity grids, these satellite developments offer escape from the increasingly unhealthy environment of what is becoming the new Old Cairo.

Despite this, the Cairo that is bound by the Nile Valley is a fascinating place to visit. From 5,000-year-old pyramids and temples to British colonial architecture, Cairo is an adventure in historical discovery.

Peopled by the ever-sociable Cairenes, this city is usually very safe, and though it may seem intimidating, dense, and crowded, it is one of the warmest and most welcoming places in the world.

1 Orientation

ARRIVING

BY PLANE   All flights arrive at **Cairo International Airport** (www.cairo-airport.com; airport code CAI), about 24km (15 miles) from the city center. At the time of writing, the light was glimmering at the end of the tunnel on a massive renovation and expansion project underwritten by the World Bank, and getting into and out of the country has been a bit of a trial involving long bus rides and even longer lines. The government signed up the managers of the Frankfurt Airport to take over running the new facilities in 2007, however, and the airport is expected to run more smoothly under their direction than it did under the old management.

There are a number of bank kiosks inside the entrance terminals for changing money and buying visas (p. 15). These banks offer the same exchange rate as banks and offices in town, and it makes sense to change money here at the same time as you buy your visa. Unlike the banks in town, however (which are usually very honest), these guys will sometimes try to jigger the exchange-rate calculations or shortchange you. Don't take any guff. Do your own calculations (on the teller's calculator if necessary), and calmly request everything that you are owed on the basis of the posted rates until you have it. You will find that dragging out the process of handing over small bills is one of the most common tactics used to try to eke a little extra cash out of a transaction. Have patience, but be firm until all your money is handed over.

BY BUS   Arriving in Cairo by commercial bus is a lot easier than it used to be, and is very likely to be presented to you as an option if you are in Sharm el Sheik or Marsa Alam (having arrived by charter flight direct to one of these coastal resort towns) and want to visit the pyramids and the Egyptian Museum. Buses run the length and breadth of the country frequently and fairly reliably, and, despite the appallingly bad driving habits of locals, they may offer an appealing way of seeing the countryside and meeting people. However, if you're traveling from a city with an airport, you may want to consider the following: Distances in Egypt can be quite long, and the price of a long, cramped bus ride can (a bit illogically) be comparable to the cost of a short and convenient internal flight. Many women have reported unpleasant incidents of harassment on these buses, particularly at night. Buses often carry unauthorized passengers in the luggage compartments below the seats, where they usually escape unnoticed at the frequent security checkpoints. Whether this is a real problem is

---

Renewing Your Visa

If you think that you're going to need more than the 30 days that the airport visa gives you in the country, it's best to get it extended before you leave Cairo. The office is in Tahrir Square, across from the Egyptian Museum in the mighty Soviet-inspired edifice known as the Mugama. Standing outside looking up at the dark Orwellian bulk of the place, you might think that you're in for a horrendous experience. On the contrary, if you show up by 9am before the place gets busy, and remember to get two passport photos at the little shop in the lobby before following the signs upstairs, you can be out and on your way before you've had time to say "1984."

questionable, but on the Sinai, there have been a number of bombings since 2005, so it's something to keep in mind.

Of course, you may have no choice but to take the bus (if you're coming from the oases, for example). If this is the case, make sure to take food and water with you, as well as plenty of reading material and earplugs. Smoke, bathroom, and eating breaks tend to be frequent, but roadside food in Egypt is not the best. Many buses offer a movie during the trip, but it will be in Arabic and probably quite loud. Also note that in the winter, buses crossing the desert can get quite chilly inside, so pack a blanket or at least an extra sweater.

Coming into Cairo by bus, you're likely to stop at a number of places as you enter the city. Unless you have a firm grip on the city's layout—which can be pretty tricky after dark—stay on the bus until the final stop at the new **Turgoman Bus Terminal** in Shobra. This is quite centrally located, so both downtown and Zamalek are a less than a LE10 ($1.80/90p) taxi ride away. Though Cairo is astonishingly safe (in terms of petty crime at least—traffic is another matter entirely), the area around the bus station isn't a great place to walk with a bag—it's crowded, it lacks sidewalks, and there's a lot of car and bus traffic.

BY TRAIN   Trains are my favorite way to travel Egypt (though, depending on how much time you have, they may not be the best way to get to where you need to go). If you're headed to Upper Egypt on a tight schedule, you're probably better off flying (p. 73). Trains conveniently depart from the heart of downtown and usually leave (if not arrive) right on time, making train travel to nearby destinations such as Alexandria just as convenient and quick as flying—and it's cheaper and more environmentally friendly. The most appealing part of train travel, however, is that it offers an experience. The ride may not be the smoothest, but the views of village life and rural Egypt are fascinating.

There are two main train stations in Cairo, and you should consult your hotel or travel agent as to which one is most convenient for your arrival. Odds are, however, that it's going to be the main **Ramsis Square** (© **02/25790767**), a British-built station in the middle of Downtown, or the more modern and, consequently, less interesting **Giza** station, which is a good distance from most of the hotels and sites.

While both stations appear to be in total unmitigated chaos, they actually work reasonably well. On arrival, follow the flow of passengers to the parking lot in front of the building. If you're coming into Ramsis from Luxor or Aswan, this will probably mean having to go through a short tunnel underneath the tracks and into the main building; the exit is from the main terminal building and not the side building where the trains arrive.

Feel free to ask men in uniforms for directions; officers (who carry sidearms, not AK-47s) often speak a little English and will be more forthcoming.

Ignore the entreaties of the touts, who will insist that they have the cheapest cars and the best hotels. These are baldfaced lies—you will probably pay about double the going rate for your ride (LE15 [$2.70/£1.35] instead of LE5–LE7 [90¢–$1.25/45p–65p] for a quick ride to Zamalek or Downtown) and have to deal with more aggressive negotiating. The one advantage these touts offer is that they'll carry your bags through the swirl of humanity on the platform; something you may want to consider.

Regular taxis (see "The 30-Second Taxi Survival Guide," below) swirl through the parking lot outside, and if you flag one down while it's moving, it should take you where you're going at more or less the going rate.

Tips Buying Train Tickets

There are three different places to buy tickets in Ramsis, depending on where you're headed. One thing remains the same, however: Queuing means nothing here, and you have to be prepared to defend your turn with your elbows. Also keep in mind that the ticket sellers are frequently dishonest with the prices, so if you have any doubt about the price of your ticket, find out the correct price for your train from the helpful folks at the Tourist Information office by the main entrance before you head to the wickets.

If you're headed north to Alexandria, the ticket office is in the back-right corner of the main hall of Ramsis Station. (Put your back to the trains and look a little to your right—over in the corner, there is a line of ticket windows.)

If you're taking a sleeper train south to Luxor or Aswan, the office is directly ahead of you if you're in the main hall with your back to the trains.

Finally, if you're headed south to Luxor or Aswan in a seat, you have to head through the main hall (leaving the trains to your right), and through to a second set of platforms that are outside and behind the main hall. Turn sharply left when you get there, and you'll see a tunnel underneath the tracks. Go through the tunnel, turning right at the end. The ticket offices for Upper Egypt are about 20m (65 ft.) ahead of you on the left.

BY CAR   Arriving in Cairo by car is exciting—probably too exciting for the comfort of most travelers. Unless you are already experienced with driving in the Third World, I suggest you hire a car with a good driver. It is also strongly recommended that you be off the highways by dark. They are not for the fainthearted during the day, and they're downright dangerous at night.

The excellent *Cairo Guide Maps* (American University in Cairo Press), available at both branches of the American University in Cairo Bookstore and Diwan (p. 117), will help once you've penetrated the confusing sprawl of highways and sideways that surround the perimeter districts of Misr Gedida, Maadi, and Shobra al Kheima.

GETTING INTO TOWN

The best way to get into town from the airport (a distance of around 15–20km/10–14 miles, depending on which neighborhood you're going to) is by car. A large number of private companies offer their services from the airport, with prices ranging from around LE70 ($13/£6.34) for a compact car to LE150 to LE200 ($27–$36/£14–£19) for a ride in a shiny, late-model Mercedes. Depending on the time of day and whether there's a football game at one of the stadiums along the way, the ride can take from 15 minutes to an hour. The battered black-and-whites hanging around the exit present a cheaper option and will, with a little bit of discussion, usually run you into town for around LE50 to LE60 ($9–$11/£4.60–£5.55). If, in the future, there is a yellow taxi stand at the airport, this will probably be the best option. Yellow cabs are about the same price as black-and-whites, though they're newer, more comfortable, and run on a bona fide meter system that takes much of the hassle out of the trip.

There are also buses that run into town from the airport. Look for the **Cairo Airport Shuttle Bus** (© 02/22653937) kiosk inside the terminal or their red-and-white buses parked outside the terminal, and ask for your destination. Fares range from LE25 ($4.50/£2.30) per person to nearby Heliopolis to LE35 to LE40

Tips The 30-Second Taxi Survival Guide

There's no better way to get around Cairo than the venerable black-and-white Ladas and Fiats that cruise the streets, flashing their headlights and honking at potential customers. Easy to find and economically priced, they can provide both functional transport and fun social encounters. The flip side is that the meters haven't worked for years, and many drivers are looking to take tourists for the wrong sort of ride. Fortunately, you can keep things easy and pleasant by following a few simple rules:

- To **engage a taxi,** just tell the driver your destination by telling him—through the always-open driver's-side window—the neighborhood you're headed to. He'll either wave you in or wave you off. In a few cases, he'll ask you how much you're going to pay, which leads to the next rule.
- **Don't negotiate the fare.** Cairenes know from experience how much any given trip is worth. They pay on arrival, plus extra for traffic congestion, and everyone's happy. If you let on that you don't have a clue, get ready for endless hassles and price gouging. If the driver asks about the fare, find another cab or accept paying at least double the going rate.
- **Know the fare before you start.** Ask a local or consult my fare table (p. 79). Pay on arrival, and walk away from demands for more. If you have doubts about how the process is going, get your driver to stop on a busy one-way street, pay him, and walk back the way you've come. The other drivers will soon ensure that your unruly cabby is on his way.
- **Always have the exact fare handy.** Extracting change from an unwilling driver is like pulling teeth from the proverbial chicken, and even honest and cooperative drivers carry very little change.
- A rule for **single women: Always sit in the back.** Sitting in the front seat is considered an unambiguous sexual invitation. Dress conservatively and either ignore attempts to strike up conversation or be prepared to turn it quickly to family: asking about children and wives and telling him about your husband (fictional or nonfictional) establishes your respectability.

These rules only apply to the taxis that cruise the streets. The black-and-whites waiting outside the door of the five-star hotels tend to charge several times the normal fares. They also tend to be a little cleaner and newer than the others, and the drivers might speak a little more English and be more familiar with the tourist sites. With these, negotiate what you are willing to pay before heading out. This also applies to the taxis waiting around the airport.

($6.35–$7.25/£3.25–£3.70) to downtown, Zamalek, and Mohandiseen. In theory, the buses leave the airport every 30 minutes, but if you hold people in Cairo to promises like this, your vacation will quickly be ruined by frustration and annoyance. In practice, expect the bus to leave within a reasonable amount of time (less than an hour) and take between 20 minutes to an hour to get to your destination, depending on the traffic.

VISITOR INFORMATION

Ministry of Tourism information offices in Cairo are a hit-or-miss affair. Some are quite helpful, while others are a waste of time. (By contrast, these offices are generally excellent in the smaller towns and cities.) I find the office in Ramsis Station, main hall, next to the sleeping-car office (© **02/25790767**), to be the most useful office in Cairo, but the Adly Street office, 5 Adly St. (© **02/23913454**), may be helpful as well. I wouldn't go out of your way to get to either. Your time in Cairo is better spent with a trip to one of the bookstores listed in the "Shopping" section (p. 116) to buy a few maps and a book or two. Because the airport is undergoing renovation, it's not clear where the tourism offices will be located, but there will be one in each of the terminals.

I've found that hotel concierges in Egypt tend to be the best sources of the kind of information that you would normally expect from tourist information offices. Note that you don't have to be staying there to get help: Just call any of the big hotels listed in this guide and ask for the concierge desk.

SAFETY

Though it's easy to take advantage of the personal safety offered by Cairo, it doesn't mean you should ignore the usual danger signs. Women walking alone should be particularly careful in crowds and avoid straying far from the well-lit areas after dark. I would also avoid the City of the Dead without a guide (and certainly after dark), the area to the west of Khan Al Khalili after dark, and the sprawling slums on the outskirts of the city.

CITY LAYOUT
THE NEIGHBORHOODS IN BRIEF

Zamalek Until the 19th century, this island in the middle of the Nile was little more than a sandbar. Zamalek became a favored residential district under the British, who barred Egyptians from living here. A few of the stately villas built during this time survived, and though overshadowed by cement high-rise apartment blocks and shorn of their gardens, they retain undeniable shades of their original charm. Zamalek remains an upmarket district and is home to many expats and foreigner-friendly restaurants and businesses with some English-speaking staff.

This is also a good area for restaurants and hotels. Better value for money can be found downtown, but for many, Zamalek offers a hard-to-beat combination of modern amenities and relatively functional infrastructure.

Zamalek is conveniently located almost exactly halfway between The Citadel, Islamic Cairo, and the pyramids and Sphinx in Giza. The Egyptian Museum and other downtown attractions are 10 to 20 minutes away by taxi.

Mohandiseen The name literally means "engineers," echoing Nasserist hopes of raising up a corps of technocrats who could push Egypt into the First World. Though these dreams remain sadly unrealized, the layout of Mohandiseen's streets is more logical than anywhere else in Cairo, with many leafy, quiet, residential side streets and a few decent restaurants.

Garden City This was the administrative center of British rule, and a number of embassies, including the British and American, are still located here. Like Zamalek, the area has suffered from shoddy, unplanned building over the last half-century, but like Zamalek, it retains a few examples of its former grace. It's an interesting place for an afternoon stroll.

Downtown Literally *wust al balad,* or "middle of the town," in Arabic (also the name of one of the most popular local bands), this area loosely reflects the European expansion of Islamic Cairo westward to the banks of the Nile. It may be a little hopeful to call it "Paris on the Nile," but it's stuffed with grand old buildings, many of them built by turn-of-the-century Italian stonemasons who came to Egypt masquerading as architects. Very few of the buildings have seen any maintenance since Gamal Abdel Nasser's time (partly because of some ill-advised rent-control measures that keep rents today at 1960s levels), and many are now being deliberately destroyed to make way for the kind of shoddy buildings that have blighted much of the rest of the city.

Islamic Cairo Misleadingly named (it doesn't seem to be any more Islamic than any other part of the city), this is the oldest part of the city, built originally in A.D. 969 as a walled, secure environment for the leaders of the Fatimid dynasty. Though it has had a number of wide, straight streets punched through it at various times in its long history, much of this area remains a densely packed network of twisting, turning alleys and little streets that you can only explore on foot. Some will find it too dense and too hectic, but for me, Islamic Cairo is the city at its best, and an afternoon exploring it never fails to put me in a good mood. A good point of entry is the old Midan Opera. Al Azhar Street runs up through Ataba to Khan al Khalili, and commercial areas on either side of it are vibrant, friendly, and fun.

2 Getting Around

Ideally, you should move between neighborhoods at times of low traffic (before 8am or 11am–1pm) and within them at all others. This, of course, is impossible all the time, but it's a helpful rule of thumb when planning your day.

BY TAXI

The black-and-whites are the basic staple of transport for middle-class Egyptians, tourists, and anyone who has to transport a TV or a dishwasher from the souk. They are ubiquitous and have become so numerous that the government stopped handing out new taxi licenses several years ago, the result being an aging fleet choking the city.

The meters that they sport on the dashboard are so outdated that they're useless and universally ignored (except for the odd enterprising individual who will attempt to scam an inexperienced victim by playing with the decimal point and claiming to be owed exorbitant sums of money).

There is no system, per se, for fares; everyone simply knows what the rates are to and from various points. You tell the driver where you want to go (usually leaning forward and shouting the neighborhood through the open passenger window as he rattles past), and if he consents to go there, he waves you in and off you go. Upon arrival, you ante up the fare and wander off, unless the driver senses that you're not in the know, and then a whole raucous opera is played out with red-faced demands for sky-high fares.

There are clearly two ways to deal with this as a tourist: Either negotiate the fare to begin with, or go local and just tell the driver where you're going and pay when you get there. In either case, use the rate table below as a point of reference. These fares

Taxi Fares (in Egyptian Pounds) in Cairo

	Heliopolis	Airport	Mohandiseen	Downtown	Zamalek
Heliopolis	3–5	10	30	20	25
Airport	10	X	70	60	65
Mohandiseen	25	50	5	7	5
Downtown	20	50	7	5	5–6
Zamalek	25	50	5	5	3
Giza	40	70	15	10–15	20–25
Garden City	30	50	7	5	5–6
Khan al Khalili	25	40	15	5–6	7
Ramsis Station	25	40	12	5	5–6
Pyramids	70	100	30	50	50

	Giza	Garden City	Khan al Khalili	Ramsis Station
Heliopolis	50	30	25	20
Airport	70	60	40	50
Mohandiseen	15	7	15	12
Downtown	10–15	5	5–6	5
Zamalek	20–25	5–6	10–12	5–6
Giza	5–10	10–20	40	40
Garden City	10–20	3	7–10	7
Khan al Khalili	20–40	7–10	X	7
Ramsis Station	20–40	5	5	X
Pyramids	20–25	30–40	60	50

are generous and marginally more than an expat would pay (and certainly in excess of what the locals are handing over for their rides), but they should give you a fair idea of what to expect. Whatever objections the driver may raise will be purely tactical and aimed at extracting a little extra cash from your pocket.

I also highly recommend the new system of yellow cabs, but they are becoming harder and harder to find. Introduced with great flourish back in March 2006, they were supposed to bring the Cairo taxi fleet up to the standards of neighbors in Jordan and Syria. Indications at the time of writing, however, were that the whole plan is falling victim to a depressingly familiar pattern of bad maintenance and incompetent management. That said, if you can find one, take it. They are only marginally more expensive than the black-and-whites but substantially more comfortable.

There is supposed to be a taxi stand in Tahrir Square close to the massive, Soviet-era Mugama building and another in Mohandiseen on Gamat al Daawl al Arabia (across from the restaurants Raucha and Kandahar), but the drivers at both these spots will turn down fares to nearby locations, preferring to sit idle and wait for the more lucrative rides to Maadi and the airport. If you want to go to Zamalek or Mohandiseen from these spots, you're going to have to tell them that you want to go to the airport and then "change your mind" once the cab is a little way from the stand. Worst-case scenario is a driver who decides to terminate the ride, in which case you can pick up the next black-and-white that comes along. All that has ever happened to me with this stunt is a somewhat sullen driver.

ON FOOT

At first glance, Cairo looks chaotic and terribly crowded with cars, donkeys, buses, and people, but it's actually a surprisingly walkable city for the reasonably fit. Safety is a very minor concern in Cairo, with random violent crime virtually unheard of and pickpocketing rare. What is fairly common, however, is general hassling. In a car or on a bus, you'll be cut off from the street, but walking through town there will be a lot of people who want to talk to you and get a tip. Downtown, particularly around the museum area, and out by the pyramids in Giza, this takes the form of touts (*khertee* in the local street Arabic) who will use any ploy to strike up a conversation and then try to entice you into a range of commercial transactions, all of which are designed to fleece you. As you leave the areas frequented by tourists, however, you'll run into more and more people who simply want to talk to you and be seen talking to you. This can be fun, but it can also get tiresome, and you can simply smile and wave as you keep walking. If you're feeling antisocial, stay away from elementary schools in the afternoon—you risk being mobbed by exuberant 8-year-olds, all of whom need to shake your hand and ask after your health.

For exploring beyond the limit of the maps in this guide, I highly recommend *Cairo: The Practical Guide Maps* (AUC Press), which was originally published as an addition to *Cairo: The Practical Guide* (which, while once excellent, has not been properly kept up to date). Both are available at the AUC bookstores and Diwan (see "Books" under "Shopping," later in this chapter), and can also be found at the bookstores in major hotels. And though it might sound extreme, I also recommend a compass if you're going to wander into areas such as Moski or Ataba, where the alleys are frequently covered and always densely packed.

BY CAR

There is little point in using a car to explore within Cairo. With traffic congestion that verges on gridlock at certain times of the day and a disastrous parking situation, a private vehicle is more likely to be a 3,000-pound albatross around your neck than a convenience. A driver changes the picture a little and solves most of the parking problems, but I still recommend cabs or the Metro.

For the sites around the outskirts of the city, such as Saqqara, Birqash, and even the pyramids in Giza, a car with a driver is the best way to go. A reliable driver is a great source of information, and having a fixed price for all your transport from the beginning of the day can save an enormous amount of hassle. It may cost a little more, but the peace of mind is worth it. For information on hiring a car for the day, see "Day Trips" later in this chapter.

BY METRO

The Metro is a rare example of functional transportation in Cairo. It's crowded—extremely crowded during rush hour—but trains run about every 10 to 15 minutes and are tolerably clean, though during the summer months they can become quite malodorous. Women can decide whether to take advantage of the women-only cars, which are usually the first two in the train (after 6pm, the second car usually becomes general seating). Traveling alone, women may find themselves the object of unwanted attention in the mixed cars. On the other hand, unveiled women report increasing levels of religious harassment in the women's car, with "modestly" attired Muslim women praying loudly, making comments about their "immodest" fellow passengers, or even

Cairo Metro

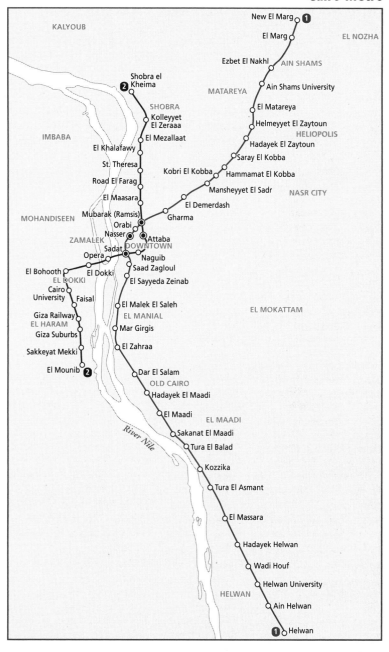

overtly proselytizing. The line between a cultural experience and an annoyance is a matter of individual tolerance.

There are currently two Metro lines in operation, and a third is under construction (which probably means that it will be under construction for a long time). There are several particularly useful stations on the Marg-Helwan line including Sadat (directly underneath Midan Tahrir, beside the Egyptian Museum), Mubarak (next to the Ramsis train station), and Mar Girgis (next to Coptic Cairo).

Tickets cost LE0.50 (9¢/5p) for nine stops and are for sale inside all stations. You will need the ticket not only to get onto the platform, but to exit at the other end as well, so keep your ticket for the duration of the trip. Trains run from about 6am to midnight.

3 What to See & Do

ZAMALEK

Cairo Tower   This is the tall, thin communications tower that you'll see when heading to and from downtown on the 6th of October Bridge. The concrete sheathing on the outside of the 187m (614 ft.) edifice is said to represent the lotus flower. It took the Nasser government 5 years to build, starting in 1956, and they say it was meant to show that Egypt was capable of building the Aswan High Dam (which was ultimately only completed with Russian assistance in 1970). There is an elevator to the top, and on a clear day the view of the city is spectacular. Try going just before sunset to get the full range of light. There is also a restaurant and some toilets, neither of which I would recommend.

Admission LE70 ($13/£6.50). Daily 8am–midnight.

Islamic Ceramics Museum 🏶   Located a couple of minutes' walk from the Cairo Marriott (p. 102) in a nicely restored palace, the Islamic Ceramics Museum contains a stunning collection of ceramic pots, plates, and bowls from the 9th to the 18th centuries. It is also worth visiting simply for the building, which was originally a small palace for Prince Amr Ibrahim in the 19th century and was seized by the government in 1953. Designed by a Turkish architect, it is a graceful and balanced building, especially in contrast to some of the old colonial piles you'll see if you take the time to stroll around Zamalek or Garden City.

The documentation is uninformative, but most of the pieces in the museum speak for themselves. The atmosphere of the usually half-deserted old palace still makes it a great place to relax after a hectic day in Islamic Cairo. **Note:** Non-flash photography is permitted free of charge, but officially you need to get permission from the (rarely present) director. In practice, just ask at the door, and there'll usually be no problem.

16 Gezira St. 🕾 **02/27373298** or 02/27373296. Free Admission. Daily 9:30am–1:30pm.

GIZA

THE PYRAMIDS

The question of how the ancient Egyptians, without any of the powerful modern building equipment that we've taken for granted for several centuries, managed to build some of the biggest, most enduring, and perfectly engineered structures ever, is a toughie, so I encourage you, as I have, to consult Miroslav Verner's *The Pyramids* (AUC Press). The truth is that nobody has come up with a watertight answer yet. There are plenty of theories around, and they run the gamut from the truly ridiculous

Fun Fact **Off the Mark**

The Pyramid of Khufu in Giza is so precisely laid out that a mere 2cm (1 inch) error in the height of the southeast corner was enough to puzzle Egyptologists. The explanation, it seems, is that when the ancient engineers leveled the site by covering it with water, the prevailing north wind on the plateau was enough to press the water up a little and throw off their calculations.

alien-intervention spiels of the "pyramidiot" crowd to some that are eminently reasonable, but in the end they all still fall just short of complete.

Leaving aside the possibility of help from above, the theories fall into two obvious categories: First, that the ancient Egyptians built ramps up the side of the pyramids, and second, that they used some kind of lever device to lift up the blocks.

Back in the 5th century B.C., the Greek traveler and historian Herodotus recorded the entirely plausible explanation that the blocks had been lifted up one course at a time with "machines made of short pieces of timber." Herodotus was notoriously slack in details (he also wrote that the stone for the pyramids had been brought from Arabia when there was a perfectly good limestone quarry just up the river near Saqqara, and that the number of leeks that the pyramid builders received for their troubles was recorded on the side of the monuments), but in this case he seems to make sense, and many people have followed up with theories about what sort of elaborate machines might have been used for the task.

The problem with the lifting machine theories is that there is very little evidence to actually support the theory. The Egyptians recorded just about everything else, from harvests to battles to parties in elaborately detailed wall paintings, but not these "machines made of short pieces of timber." Aside from this, consider on the one hand that some of the individual blocks used in the smallest of the Giza Plateau pyramids, the Pyramid of Menkaura, weighed around 220 tons. A compact car weighs around a ton, so we're talking about 200 cars being shifted in a single go. These would have been quite some timbers.

The other group of theories circles around the idea of ramps. This too makes good sense. The ancient Egyptians were clearly adept at sliding these massive blocks of limestone out of their quarries and down to the Nile, so why not up ramps built onto the side of the pyramid? As each course was added, the ramp would simply have to be made a little higher and a little steeper.

But stand back a little and squint at a pyramid. If you're lucky enough to be in Giza, have a good look at the Pyramid of Khufu. It's 137m (almost 450 ft.) high now, but when it was first built it was 146m (almost 480 ft.). Imagine the size of the ramp needed to get to the top—building it would have been a feat greater than building the pyramid itself. This, of course, isn't an objection in and of itself, but the problem with size is simply that there's no evidence of the material. By one estimate, the ramp would have required more than 4 million cubic meters of material (more than 140 million cubic ft.). A hole that big doesn't just fill up with sand and disappear, and a pile like that doesn't just blow away, yet there is no evidence of either. Another problem plagues the ramp-theorists, however. We know approximately how long they took to build, and we have a pretty accurate idea (thanks to ultrasound investigations) of how much

Cairo

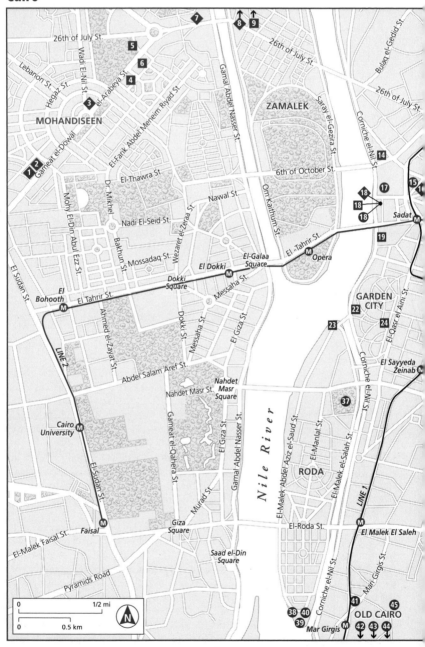

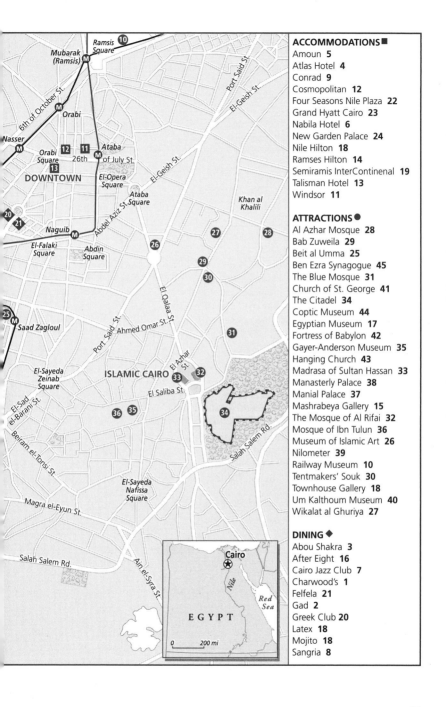

ACCOMMODATIONS ■
Amoun **5**
Atlas Hotel **4**
Conrad **9**
Cosmopolitan **12**
Four Seasons Nile Plaza **22**
Grand Hyatt Cairo **23**
Nabila Hotel **6**
New Garden Palace **24**
Nile Hilton **18**
Ramses Hilton **14**
Semiramis InterContinenal **19**
Talisman Hotel **13**
Windsor **11**

ATTRACTIONS ●
Al Azhar Mosque **28**
Bab Zuweila **29**
Beit al Umma **25**
Ben Ezra Synagogue **45**
The Blue Mosque **31**
Church of St. George **41**
The Citadel **34**
Coptic Museum **44**
Egyptian Museum **17**
Fortress of Babylon **42**
Gayer-Anderson Museum **35**
Hanging Church **43**
Madrasa of Sultan Hassan **33**
Manasterly Palace **38**
Manial Palace **37**
Mashrabeya Gallery **15**
The Mosque of Al Rifai **32**
Mosque of Ibn Tulun **36**
Nilometer **39**
Railway Museum **10**
Tentmakers' Souk **30**
Townhouse Gallery **18**
Um Kalthoum Museum **40**
Wikalat al Ghuriya **27**

DINING ◆
Abou Shakra **3**
After Eight **16**
Cairo Jazz Club **7**
Charwood's **1**
Felfela **21**
Gad **2**
Greek Club **20**
Latex **18**
Mojito **18**
Sangria **8**

Fun Fact **The Height of the Matter**

The Great Pyramid, as the Pyramid of Khufu is also known, was 146m (479 ft.) high until stripped of its gleaming white casing of limestone. Now it is "only" 137m (449 ft.) high. Napoleon, who actually spent a night alone in its dank depths, is reported to have announced that if it were dismantled and taken back to France, a 2m-high (6.5-ft.) wall could be built around the entire country with the stone in this enormous monument.

---

material they contain. We can therefore calculate how quickly the material would have had to flow up the ramp in order for the whole thing to work out. Many ramps that could have plausibly been built—including some of the ingeniously efficient spiral ramps that would have hugged the outside of the structure—fail this critical test by simply being too narrow to allow the stone to be slid up in sufficient quantities in the time allowed.

At the end of the day, then, we're left not much further ahead than Herodotus. It seems highly possible that, in fact, both theories contain the essential elements of a complete solution: that the ancient Egyptians used a combination of machinery made of wooden levers, rollers, and papyrus ropes and inclined ramps to get those blocks of stone to the top of their manmade mountains. Whether the details of how they did it will ever be fully worked out, however, remains an open question.

The Pyramids *Kids* It's a cliché, but there's really no sight like them. For sheer, dominating bulk, the pyramids on Giza have got pretty well everywhere else in the world beat. It used to be that you came upon them slowly, riding on horseback across the green fields that separated the plateau from the city. Nowadays, urban sprawl laps at the very feet of the Sphinx himself, and by the time you see the pyramids, they're right on top of you. It's a moment that you'll never forget.

The Great Pyramid of Khufu is the first one you come to. The entrance is on the north face, and once inside, you face a long and uncomfortable scramble to the Great Gallery, which is some 47m (154 ft.) long and 8.5m (28 ft.) high. Don't even think about going in if you suffer from the slightest bit of claustrophobia—the passages are narrow and the spaces are tight, and in the heat of the summer stuffed with tourists, the inside of this place is guaranteed to set you off. Other than the thrill of where you are, there is little to see inside the pyramid. Do note, however, the extraordinary stone masonry involved in fitting the building blocks together, and take a pause to consider the skill involved in positioning the massive slabs of limestone and granite that make up the walls and roof.

Around the back of Khufu's pyramid, on the south side, is the strangely shaped **Solar Barque Museum,** which houses a boat that was disassembled and buried near the pyramid in a sealed pit as part of the interment rites for the deceased Pharaoh. Another one was discovered, but left in place, in 1985. When excavators found the boat, it had been carefully stored as 1,224 separate pieces, which had to be carefully fit together in precisely the right fashion before being put on display. The result is a breathtakingly graceful vessel with a high, curved prow and a narrow entry.

The medium-size **Pyramid of Khafre** is a lot easier to visit than its bigger neighbor—both because it's smaller (not that the corridors are any wider, but they are

The Giza Pyramids

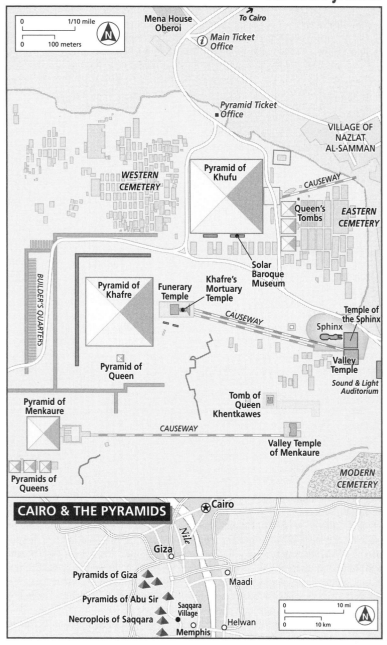

0 ——— 1/10 mile
0 ——— 100 meters
N

Mena House Oberoi

To Cairo

(i) Main Ticket Office

Pyramid Ticket
■ Office

VILLAGE OF
NAZLAT
AL-SAMMAN

*WESTERN
CEMETERY*

Pyramid of
Khufu

CAUSEWAY

Queen's
Tombs

*EASTERN
CEMETERY*

Solar
Baroque
Museum

BUILDER'S QUARTERS

Pyramid of
Khafre

Funerary
Temple

Khafre's
Mortuary
Temple

CAUSEWAY

Temple of
the Sphinx

Sphinx

Valley
Temple

Pyramid of
Queen

*Sound & Light
Auditorium*

Tomb of
Queen
Khentkawes

Pyramid of
Menkaure

CAUSEWAY

Valley Temple
of Menkaure

*MODERN
CEMETERY*

Pyramids of
Queens

CAIRO & THE PYRAMIDS

✪ Cairo

Nile

Giza

Pyramids of Giza

Maadi

Pyramids of Abu Sir

Saqqara
Village

Necroplois of Saqqara

Memphis

Helwan

0 ——— 10 mi
0 ——— 10 km
N

Just the Facts

The three pyramids in Giza are the oldest and biggest tourist sites ever, and they've been attracting visitors since before Greek historian Herodotus named the biggest of the three as one of the Seven Wonders of the World. The pyramids were built on the western edge of the Nile Valley, by 4th-dynasty rulers between about 2589 and 2530 B.C., and given their age, they have survived remarkably well; the most noticeable damage has been the loss of most of the gleaming white limestone casings, which has changed the dimensions of the biggest pyramid, Khufu, giving it a saw-toothed profile when viewed up close. The medium-size pyramid was built for Khafre, the son of Khufu, and the smallest was for Menkaura, who succeeded Khafre.

shorter) and because there are generally fewer people—which is something to consider when you're fighting for tickets or simply trying to have a relaxed day on the plateau. Have a good look at its peak as you approach, and check out the remnants of its white limestone casing. Inside, you can still see Khafre's granite sarcophagus.

The **Pyramid of Menkaura,** the smallest on the plateau, was the target of some 12th-century vandalism when Salah el Din's son, Othman Ibn Yusuf, attempted to have it dismantled and removed. You can see the dent his workers made in the north face. This is the sum of their achievements after about 8 months of work, testimony to the solidity and sheer bulk of even the least imposing of these structures.

After you've seen the three pyramids, the **Sphinx** is about all that's left before lunch. Legends and stories have attached themselves by the dozen to the battered half cat, half human figure on the southern edge of the site, close to the bottom of the causeway up to the Pyramid of Khafre. The bottom line seems to be that it was carved from the bedrock at about the same time as the pyramid, and that its features were those of Khafre himself. Napoleon, despite rumors to the contrary, did not remove the nose—it seems to have been chipped off at least 500 years before the diminutive Frenchman was born.

Take a full morning to see this site, and try to leave before the midday heat sets in. Take plenty of water with you, and think about retiring to the Mena House Oberoi for a light lunch when you're finished. In fact, this hotel is a great place from which to admire the pyramids without the stress and hassle of actually going in. In the summer, this is best done from the pool.

The business of selling tickets and getting around the plateau, even after so many years, is still not perfected. Changes are ongoing, and it's all still a bit ad hoc. Start with the general admission ticket at the kiosk at the main gate (on the road that turns past the Mena House Oberoi). You will need an additional ticket for each pyramid, and sometimes there is a limit imposed on admission to the pyramids of Khufu and Khafre of 300 tickets per pyramid per day—150 at 8:30am and the rest at 1pm. When this is the case, you have to be prepared for a bit of pushing and shoving. The best way to avoid the scene is to take a bus tour (below).

In addition to the limit on the number of tickets, the usual situation is that only one of the two smaller pyramids is open at any given time to accommodate ongoing restoration work inside them. To find out about either of these conditions, call the Pyramids Tourist Information Office (✆ **02/33838823**), located across from the Mena House Oberoi near the main gate to the plateau.

Note: The pyramids in Giza have the highest density of con artists and touts of any site in the country. Before you even make it to the gate, you'll be surrounded by eager young men who insist that you will not be allowed in without a guide (don't worry, you will be), or that you need a horse to get around (you don't). Once inside, the offers will keep coming, many of them from uniformed policemen who will offer a variety of favors in return for cash. They may be irritating, but they are not dangerous and can safely be ignored. If you do opt for a horse or camel ride, agree on the price first, and do not pay until you get where you're going—pay upfront, and your horse will "go lame" within a couple of feet, necessitating another steed and another payment. Incidents of theft are also not uncommon; don't hand anyone your camera to get your picture taken—you may find yourself having to buy it back.

Downtown/Garden City. Admission LE40 ($7.25/£3.70) for the site; LE100 ($18/£9.25) Pyramid of Khufu; LE20 ($3.60/£1.85) Pyramid of Khafre; LE20 ($3.60/£1.85) Pyramid of Menkaura; LE40 ($7.25/£3.70) Museum of the Solar Barque. Students with valid card get 50% off. Site Oct–Apr daily 8am–4pm, May–Sept 8am–5pm; all pyramids and museum Oct–Apr daily 9am–4pm, May–Sept 9am–5pm.

Beit al Umma   This is the house of Sa'ad Zaghloul, a key Egyptian nationalist in the early 20th century. Zaghloul led the Wafd party, had a brief stint as prime minister in 1924, and represented the possibility of a peaceful transition from the British occupation to civilian government after World War I. The modesty of the Zaghloul residence contrasts sharply with the extravagant ostentation in which subsequent military rulers of the country lived. The house is maintained in a calm and reverential atmosphere, with the same carpets, furnishings, and everyday items that were here when Zaghloul lived here. If you visit the office, note the arrangement of the desk in relation to the window; Zaghloul had a (well-founded) fear of being attacked and had his furniture arranged so that he could keep an eye on every avenue of approach.

2 Saad Zagloul St., Mounira. ✆ 02/27945399. Admission LE10 ($1.80/95p); students half-price. Daily 10am–5pm.

Egyptian Museum ★★   Egypt's national collection of archaeological treasures has been housed in the same place since 1902. Though its current home is in a slightly outlandish, neoclassical building on the edge of Tahrir Square in downtown, a new national museum in Giza is in the works (at the time of writing, there was no sign of new construction, however). Ideally, you should visit the museum repeatedly—there are 120,000 or so pieces in the collection. Since numerous visits aren't usually possible, I recommend buying a good guidebook; *The Illustrated Guide to the Egyptian*

⌐Tips Take a Break, Take the Bus

I am no fan of the organized bus tour, but unless you have someone to drive you out to the pyramids, fight for the tickets, and keep away the touts, it's actually the best way to see the site. The front desk of almost any hotel in town sells the tours, which usually include doorstep service. Thomas Cook has an excellent reputation, but most companies offer the same thing: an air-conditioned bus, tickets, and a guide. About the only thing that you want to look out for when booking your tour is the tacked-on "tour of the papyrus factory" or "visit to the carpet workshop," during which you'll find yourself herded through an overpriced tourist store in Giza and pressured to buy by a "guide" who gets a healthy cut of whatever you spend.

Museum in Cairo, published in Egypt by the American University Press and available from its bookstore on the other side of the square, is excellent. Also, either find one area of interest to focus on after you've taken a general tour (or skip the tour entirely— the acoustics in the old building are pretty bad, and if you're in a large group, you're not going to hear much anyway), or just wander until you find yourself lost in some obscure backroom full of dusty but marvelous treasures.

The ground floor is dominated by massive sculptures, while the upper floor has the smaller pieces. On a recent visit, I found myself focusing on the **Greco-Roman collection,** which occupies a corner of the second floor and includes the Fayum portraits, a collection of a dozen or so hauntingly beautiful death portraits that were painted on coffins by artists in the first few centuries A.D. During other visits, I've spent time in the **Daily Life in Egypt** section, which has fascinating artifacts from spoons to furniture, and the **Tutankhamen exhibit,** which features the treasures unearthed by Howard Carter in 1922. Another favorite includes the **animal mummy room,** which has the best documentation in the museum.

Allow a half-day to do the museum in a reasonably relaxed manner, and bring a bottle of water with you, because there is no cafe inside the museum (but there are decent toilets). There's a cafe on the outside of the main building, but it's nothing of great interest. You must check your camera at the main gate before going in, and make sure the attendant gives you the right bag on the way out (mistakes happen). Don't bother trying to smuggle your camera in; you have to pass through an X-ray check just inside the main building. The museum can get quite full and noisy on holidays, as Egyptians will visit for fun, and if you're traveling alone, you'll certainly be approached frequently for chats.

Midan Tahrir. ✆ **02/5782448** or 02/5782452. www.egyptianmuseum.gov.eg. Admission LE50 ($9.10/£4.60) adults, LE10 ($1.80/95p) children; extra LE100 ($18/£9.25) to see the mummies.

Faluca **Ride** 🐫🐫 You shouldn't leave Cairo without taking a sunset or evening cruise on the Nile in one of these traditional lateen-rigged sailboats. The best place to start your cruise is the docks between the Four Seasons and the Hyatt Regency, which are shared by several companies with two or three boats apiece. There's not much to differentiate the companies, but you may be able to gain a little ground by playing one off the other in the price negotiations. Once onboard, more or less anything goes, so feel free to bring a pizza and some beer for a lovely new perspective on dinner in Cairo. The owner of the dock and the boats are from Cairo, but the pilots are usually from Upper Egypt; they will probably appreciate sharing whatever you have onboard, and are usually good for a chat and a whole new perspective on life in the big city.

LE50–LE60 ($9.10–$11/£4.60–£5.55) an hour plus an extra LE10 ($1.80/95p) to the pilot. Cash only.

Manasterly Palace This lovely mid-19th-century building on the southern tip of Roda Island is now run by the Ministry of Culture and usually only open for concerts. It is, in fact, the remnants of a much larger facility that lost much of its garden space to

---

⌒ *Fun Fact* **Hi, My Name is . . .**

It was the Greeks, not the Egyptians, who named the Sphinx. In Arabic, he is known as Abu al Holl, or "Father of Terror."

Sound and Light Show

The keyword here is *cheesy*. This over-the-top light show (**℗ 03/23852880** or 02/33857861; www.soundandlight.com.eg; admission LE60/$11/£5.55), ostensibly narrated by the Sphinx, is historically uninformative and giggle-worthy for the most part. The upside is that you get to be out on the plateau after dark. The downside is that they turn the volume up too high, and the sound system isn't really that great. Unless you are a huge fan of this kind of thing, or have an ironic sense of humor, I would advise saving your sound and light budget for Karnak (p. 225).

There are three shows a night, each in a different language. Showtimes in the winter (Oct–Apr) are 6:30, 7:30, and 8:30pm. In the summer (May–Sept), shows are at 8:30, 9:30, and 10:30pm. The logic behind the language schedule has always escaped me, and I would recommend double-checking the information below before trekking out to Giza.

Note: If your curiosity's been peaked, but you're not willing to ante up the cost of entry, you can get a pretty good view of the proceedings from just outside the exit from the plateau over by the Sphinx.

	First Show	Second Show	Third Show
Sunday	German	French	Russian
Monday	English	French	Spanish
Tuesday	English	Italian	French
Wednesday	English	French	German
Thursday	Japanese	English	Arabic
Friday	English	French	No show
Saturday	English	Spanish	Italian

the sewage treatment plant that the government decided to build on the grounds. The setting alone is worth a visit, however, and if you happen to have an evening free, it's worth checking to see what's on. During the day, the grounds around the palace offer a nice view downriver to Dahab Island and are an excellent place for a picnic lunch between checking out the Nilometer and visiting the Um Kalthoum Museum (below). ℗ 02/23631537. www.manasterly.com.

Manial Palace ✦   Originally built in the late 19th century as a royal park, the palace itself was added to this space and renovated in the 1920s. It occupies a large walled plot of land on Roda Island, which is just about a half-mile south of the tip of Zamalek (or more properly Gezira, where the massive Sofitel tower stands). The grounds are heavily wooded, and the site consists of a series of buildings reached by paths that wind through an artfully untended forest. In spite of its relaxed charm, it doesn't attract many tourists, so it's a wonderfully quiet and atmospheric place to visit.

I usually avoid the display of hunting trophies in the Hunting Hall, a 1960s add-on near the entrance, and head into the **gardens** themselves. For me, the two most interesting parts of the palace are the completely over-the-top **palace building,** set in the center of the grounds, and the **museum,** tucked away toward the back. The palace exterior is unexciting, but the interior is a pastiche of Islamic decoration and architecture set to the theme of barely restrained opulence. The museum is devoted to a collection of antiques that Prince Mohamed Ali assembled between 1914, when the British deposed King Faruq, and 1952, when he fled the country after Nasser's military takeover.

A few years ago, the ceiling of the opulent throne room (a separate building from the palace) collapsed, and at the time of writing, had not yet reopened. The complex has been undergoing renovations for a number of years, so you may not be able to access all parts of the palace or all the museum rooms.

Roda Island. ℭ 02/23687495. Admission LE20 ($3.60/£1.85) adults, LE10 ($1.80/95p) students. Daily 9am–4pm.

Nilometer   At the southern tip of Roda Island, between the Manasterly Palace and the Um Kalthoum Museum, this well was used to measure the height of the Nile through the course of its annual fluctuations. Taxes could be calibrated from knowing the height of the floods, and the timing of the opening and closing of irrigation and drainage canals around the delta could be determined. Entering at the top, you can walk almost to the bottom by way of a narrow staircase cut into the side. The top is enclosed in an attractive 19th-century dome. The grounds around the Nilometer are relaxed and pleasant, with a view south up the river toward Dahab and, usually, a cool breeze off the water.

Roda Island. Admission LE11 ($2/£1). Daily 9am–5pm.

Railway Museum 🕭𝒊𝒹𝑠   Cairo is full of dusty little museums tucked away in unlikely spots. This one is tacked onto the back of the Ramsis train station and is an absolute must-see for train buffs or for those who love old museums of any sort. The star of the collection is a magnificently opulent 19th-century engine built for Mohamed Said Pasha, which you can walk into, but the two floors of the museum are stuffed with enough model trains, planes, and bridges to keep your inner (and actual) 12-year-old happy for a couple of hours.

Ramsis Station. ℭ 02/5763793. Admission LE20 ($3.60/£1.85). Sat–Thurs 9am–2:30pm.

Um Kalthoum Museum   This small museum is dedicated to the singer Um Kalthoum, who, more than 3 decades after her death, remains a cultural icon and symbol of Egyptian nationalism. Born in 1904, she was the daughter of an imam (a position at a mosque roughly equivalent to a parish priest) in a small rural village in the Delta. During the 1940s, '50s, and '60s, she was known throughout the Arab world and her 5- to 6-hour concerts, broadcast on the first Thursday of the month, were claimed to clear the streets of Cairo as people made their way home and to cafes to listen. She died in 1975, but you will still hear her music being played around Cairo. Her death prompted a massive reaction, and it is claimed that millions attended her funeral. You'll recognize her on posters throughout Egypt as a substantial lady wearing sunglasses (she had an eye problem) and holding a white handkerchief. The museum plays recordings of her works, and reverentially displays ephemera such as her diamond-studded sunglasses and her diplomatic passport.

Roda Island. Admission LE2 (35¢/20p). Daily 9am–5pm.

ISLAMIC CAIRO

Islamic Cairo is an ill-defined area covering, roughly, the densely packed neighborhoods between Khan al Khalili and Midan Ataba, and the neighborhood of Gamaleya to the north and Sayed Zeinab to the south. It is the setting for a number of Nobel-laureate Naguib Mahfouz's works, and reading *Midaq Alley* or the *Cairo Trilogy* can give you a good head start on understanding the area (all Mahfouz's works are available at the American University in Cairo bookstores and Diwan, see p. 117).

Though it is an older section of the city, much of the core being within the 10th-century Fatimid walls of Qahira, Islamic Cairo doesn't seem to be especially Islamic. What it is notable for, however, is the density of its old buildings and the number of its people. This is Cairo certainly as I imagined it before I had been to Egypt: a constant jostling of busy, friendly people packing alleyways lined with stalls selling everything from nightdresses, rope, and fish to pots and pans, buckets, and stools. The place is alive with the sound of people living outdoors—greetings yelled across the heads of others, wares advertised, and scores being settled—and the air is thick with the smells of cooking and livestock. Islamic Cairo is a place that vibrates with life, a place that you experience with all your senses, and no visit to Egypt is complete without a wander through these ancient streets.

Al Azhar Mosque   Completed in A.D. 972 (at the same time as the then-new city of Cairo), this mosque has since undergone many renovations, restorations, and additions. And though it may not be the most architecturally interesting mosque in the city, it's certainly the most politically significant. Since A.D. 988, it has also been the center of the most prestigious university in the Islamic world. The mosque itself is at the center of a sprawling and diverse campus more or less invisible to the casual observer because of the way it's woven into the fabric of the neighborhood. There are nine other campuses around Egypt, and the total student body, which includes many international students, is more than 100,000. Moving with the times, at least in form, it now teaches a fairly full curriculum of modern courses (including medicine), as well as the more traditional theological studies. It also has a women's annex.

Visitors should be particularly aware of religious sensitivities here. Women should wear clothing that covers the arms, legs, and shoulders, and should cover their heads with a veil. Scarves and *burqas* are available at the entrance for those who aren't carrying something with them, and both men and women need to remove their shoes at the entrance. The mosque has been the focal point of periodic anti-government demonstrations in the past, and visitors should particularly avoid Friday prayers here.

Inside is a mix of the original architecture and subsequent additions. For example, the central courtyard that you see as you enter is to the original dimensions, but the roundels and arches were added as part of a 12th-century renovation. Inside, the Kufic lettering around the mihrab is original, but much of the decorative stucco work was added in the early 14th century.

There are usually a number of fairly well-mannered students relaxing in the mosque reading or chatting with friends, and you may find yourself being offered guiding service. As with almost everywhere in Egypt, expect to be hit up for a tip at the end of the tour. I would give LE5 (90¢/45p) if the tour has been interesting and worthwhile; LE2 (36¢/19p) would be quite sufficient if you just want to get rid of them.

Admission is officially free, but the men who take care of the shoes near the entrance tend to be firm in their demands for *bakshish*. Preemptively give a couple of pounds to avoid any hassles.

Bab Zuweila   Part of the original Fatimid fortifications, this massive gate surmounted on either side by the minarets of the Al-Muayyad Mosque was one of three main portals to the city. Painstakingly restored with USAID funding in 2001, it's the centerpiece of a plan to revive the area around the gate and is well worth a visit as part of a walk from Al Azhar Mosque (p. 93) to the Tentmakers' Souk (p. 99). Over the years, the gate has been used as a venue for dancing, a cure for toothaches (driving a

---

Bakshish: The Art of Giving

Everywhere you go in Egypt, you're going to be asked for money, and you're life is going to improve immeasurably once you get comfortable with handing out a steady stream of small change to anyone who asks you for it. The guy who carries your bags to the car, the janitor who switches on the lights at the back of the museum, and the old guy at the mosque who takes care of your shoes while you walk around the building—they should all get a couple of LE discreetly slipped into the palms of their hands. The closest equivalent in the West is a tip—a little extra payment for a little extra service—but here it's a simple expression of appreciation that another person's there should you need anything (even if you don't need it right now).

---

nail into the wood of the doors could apparently work magical wonders), and an execution ground (the last heads were displayed here at the beginning of the 19th century).

If you don't have time for a complete tour, at least walk through the gate, looking up as you pass between its massive doors. Local belief has it that the spirit of a certain Ottoman Sheikh Al Mitwali lives in the doorway, and it is possible that the model boat that hangs there is to provide him with transport to Mecca.

The tiny museum upstairs, which displays everyday items found during the excavation of the street around the door itself, is well worth a visit, particularly because the ticket includes access to the roof. From up here, you can get a much better idea of the layout of the neighborhood than you can from the crowded street below. You are also sure to notice the rickety wood structures on top of nearby buildings. These are pigeon coops, built to house the flocks of pet pigeons that you'll sometimes see circling at sunset.

Consider continuing past the Tentmakers' Souk toward The Citadel (p. 95), the Madrasa Sultan Hassan, and the Mosque of Al Rifai (p. 97) to the decidedly scruffy neighborhood of Darb al Ahmar, which was an open field in the 11th century when the wall and gate were first constructed.

Admission LE20 ($3.65/£1.85) adults, LE10 ($1.80/95p) students. Daily 9am–5pm.

The Blue Mosque   This is not Cairo's easiest site to find, partly because it's known by several different names. It is worth the effort, though, if you like tiles. The mosque takes the "Blue" name for a wall of multicolored Turkish tiles that was installed during a mid-17th-century renovation by an Ottoman officer, who brought in the decoration from Istanbul and Damascus. The mosque is also known by the officer's name—Ibrahim Agha Mustahfizan. The formal name of the place, however, is Mosque of Aqsunqur, who was the original builder back in 1346.

There are three tombs in the Blue Mosque, one each for Aqsunqur, Mustahfizan, and Aqsunqur's brother-in-law, who sat on the throne 5 months after his 6th birthday before being killed by his brothers.

Apart from the tiles, the biggest reason to visit the mosque is the minaret. The 80-plus-step climb is a little scary—the steep swirl of a staircase isn't in the best of shape, and the lights are pretty bad—but the view from the top over the old town all the way up to The Citadel is fantastic. I also enjoy the fact that it really is tucked into a part of the city that few tourists venture into. This is not a tour-bus accessible area, and you can easily be the only person standing in the modest central courtyard.

Starting on the northwest side of The Citadel, walk north on Sharia Bab al Wazir (which runs away from the base of The Citadel) past the first major intersection and another five streets to the right (big and small) before the mosque appears on your right. It takes me about 10 minutes to walk.

Bab al Wazir Street. Free admission, but an LE10 ($1.80/95p) tip to the guard is suggested.

The Citadel   The manner in which The Citadel dominates the skyline of Cairo is largely due to the efforts of an Iraqi Kurd named Salah el Din. Salah entered Egypt around 1163 with an army sent by Syrian ruler Nur el Din. By 1171, he had made himself ruler of the country and set about modernizing the defenses of Cairo. The cornerstone of his plans was the magnificent, and virtually impregnable, walled compound that he built on the eastern edge of the city. It was completed in 1183, when Salah left Egypt to fight the crusaders. By the time he had expelled them from Jerusalem in 1187, Salah was well known, and rightfully feared, in Europe as Saladin.

The Citadel is perhaps most famously associated with another great leader, Mohamed Ali, who ruled Egypt in the early 19th century. You can still see the alleyway below The Citadel where his soldiers slaughtered almost the entire nobility of Egypt one night in an after-dinner ambush.

The compound is quite large and contains a number of museums and mosques. It was still a military facility until fairly recently, and though the museums aren't to Western standards, the aura and atmosphere of the place, not to mention the view over the city, make this an afternoon or morning well spent.

The **Mohamed Ali Mosque** is my favorite mosque in Cairo because of its huge, typically Ottoman dome, which will be familiar to anyone who has visited Istanbul. It's usually not very crowded, and because it sits on the edge of the escarpment over Cairo, it has an unusual amount of light and fresh air. The view from the courtyard over Cairo is the best in the city, and if you time your visit properly (I recommend sunset), you can hear the call to prayer rising up from the various mosques around town.

The **Coach Museum** houses a small but well-preserved collection of ornate coaches used by the royal family and ranking government figures from before 1952. At **Gawhara Palace,** get a taste of how the other half lived by touring one of Mohamed Ali's palaces. It is, I have to say, pretty musty, and the re-created throne-room scene is mediocre at best. I wouldn't travel up to The Citadel just for the Gawhara, but if you're already here, it doesn't hurt to have a look.

The **Military Museum** is a musty old place full of moth-eaten dioramas and misspelled placards, but the collection of colonial uniforms and weaponry from the 1970s will interest war buffs. I have never fully understood the positive reviews the **Police Museum** gets. There are some interesting displays, but you get the feeling that all the best stuff ended up in somebody's house. The best that can be said for it, in my opinion, is that the damp smell and the peeling plaster will give you a good idea of what the inside of a real police station in Egypt is like.

✆ **02/25123109** or 02/25121735. Admission for entire compound LE40 ($7.25/£3.70) adults, LE20 ($3.60/£1.85) students. Daily 9am–4pm.

Friday Market   If Khan al Khalili's tourist-oriented souk is giving you that "been there done that" feeling, get up early and head near The Citadel (p. 95) to the neighborhood of Hafif, and check out the famous Souk el Gomaa (Friday Market). This sprawling, chaotic market is about as far from the tourist scene as you're likely to get in Cairo. Though there is a vestigial scattering of stalls during the week, with a core of all-week venues specializing in plumbing and building materials, the main day is Friday, and by midmorning the whole place is extremely crowded. It's hard to define what's for sale here, but you'll find everything from old doorknobs, used batteries, dismembered dolls, camel meat, canaries, snakes, and chickens to bolts of cloth, clocks, *gallebeyas,* shoes, and mobile phones (mostly used, but some new).

Note: I know several resident expats who have taken one look at this dirty, sprawling market and gotten back into their cars with a shudder. This is not a tourist area, and foreigners will find themselves the subject of quite a bit of attention. Women should not consider going to the Friday Market without a couple of confident, and preferably burly, male friends. As with most of Cairo, there is no serious risk of violent crime, but pickpocketing is certainly possible. The area under the bridge where the dog cages are is probably best avoided by non-Arabic speakers, and the areas in which the market sprawls into the nearby cemetery are also strictly for the adventurous.

Free admission. Fri 6–11am.

Gayer-Anderson Museum 🕿🕿
This was the residence of British army officer and doctor R. G. Gayer-Anderson between 1935 and 1942. Gayer-Andersen joined and renovated two adjacent 16th-century buildings and collected their present contents, which include contemporary books and art as well as more apropos 16th- and 17th-century furniture and some antique curios, such as a 13th-century sundial. By the time he left, the place was a massive and fascinating warren of restored rooms, courtyards, and balconies stuffed with a museum-ready collection. Before heading back to England, he signed the whole lot over to the Egyptian government, which has been operating the house as a museum ever since.

A must-see for most, it will be of particular interest to James Bond fans, who might recognize it from *The Spy Who Loved Me,* in which Roger Moore huffs and puffs his way somewhat implausibly through the house in pursuit of some villainous SMERSH-type baddies.

The museum is next to the Ibn Tulun mosque, and it makes sense to visit them both at the same time. It is easy, in fact, to spend a full morning exploring these two buildings and a little bit of the neighborhood nearby. There is excellent shopping to be had at Khan Misr Toulon across the street from the mosque, but there is nowhere to eat.

For a detailed look at the museum, I recommend the excellent Nicholas Warner *Guide to the Gayer-Anderson Museum, Cairo* (Press of the Supreme Council of Antiquities) and R. G. "John" Gayer-Anderson Pasha's *Legends of the House of the Cretan Woman* (American University in Cairo Press). Warner's guide is available at the museum, but you may have to ask for it.

Ibn Tulun Street. Admission LE30 ($5.45/£2.75).

Khan al Khalili
Bustling doesn't begin to describe this souk, located in a dense network of twisting alleys. Every corner is jam-packed with stores and stalls that sell everything from Nefertiti busts to spices. This souk has been a center for craftsmen and trade since it was built in 1382 by Amir Jarkas al Khalili. The former Fatimid cemetery site was a place where caravans of traveling merchants could rest and engage in trade, and though in recent years it has focused mainly on the tourist trade, it retains much of its character and feel of a genuine Arab souk.

That said, it's hard to recommend actually shopping in the Khan if you're serious about getting something specific. Prices are higher than in other less-touristed parts of town, and quality is not always the best. On the other hand, this is the place to get a genuine

Egyptian shopping experience. The crowds are dense, and the pressure to buy can be intense. You will be serially accosted by dealers in everything from *shisha* pipes to tea.

A couple of things to remember: First, keep your wallet somewhere safe; the only confirmed incident of pickpocketing that I know of happened here. Second, the black basalt carvings that they insist are real aren't. Third, have fun. You may find bargains or get ripped off, but as long as you have a sense of humor, you're in for a great time.

Allow for several hours of wandering the narrow alleys and exploring the different sections. Don't be afraid to wander beyond the main tourist areas into the spice souk or the narrower, darker areas toward the back—in fact, I positively recommend it. Except for the odd pickpocket, the whole area is very safe.

Free admission. Daily midmorning until late at night.

Madrasa of Sultan Hassan & the Mosque of Al Rifai These two massive and outwardly similar buildings are located directly below The Citadel and within a few meters of each other, so it's best to consider them as one site. They are monumental examples of Mamluke architecture and engineering, and should be high on your list of things to see.

Madrasa of Sultan Hassan, named for al Nasir Hassan, who sat on the throne between 1347 and 1361 (with a break during his teens, when he was confined by an amir to the harem), was built in turbulent political times. Hassan's effective reign lasted until he was imprisoned in a military revolt and never seen again. His *madrasa* (school) and tomb took 4 years to build, and was more than twice the size of anything else being built at the time. Funding was made possible, ironically, by the bubonic plague that swept through Cairo in 1348, swelling the state treasury with the estates of its victims.

The massive building faced some engineering challenges: The western minaret collapsed before the whole project was finished, killing hundreds of people. The eastern minaret stayed up for 3 centuries before it collapsed, bringing about the collapse of the building's dome.

It didn't take very long after the place was finished for the military to put it to use, with its roof getting turned into an artillery platform from which to lob projectiles at The Citadel. While damage from the return fire was apparently evident in the 17th century, it seems to have been patched up since then.

The Madrasa of Sultan Hassan is a lovely place to visit any time of day, and it is particularly pleasant in the morning, when the light comes through the mausoleum windows. The entrance is dramatic and rather eerie, with a dark, twisting hallway decorated with stalactites leading to the main building. The main building is composed of four *liwans* (open halls) around a central courtyard, and a mausoleum is attached to the western *liwan*. The four Sunni schools each had a *madrasa* in one of the *liwans*,

---

(Fun Fact) Back to School

The *madrasa,* a state religious school, was introduced after the fall of the Fatimids in the 12th century and the return of Sunni government to Egypt under the Ayyubid dynasty. The four bays, or *liwans,* that you see in the courtyard represent the equal hand shown by the government to the four schools of Sunni religious thought named for four early Islamic religious thinkers Malik, Abu Hanifa, Ibn Hanbal, and al Shafa'i.

where students and teachers lived and studied. The mausoleum was designed as Sultan Hassan's final resting place, but his body was never found after the 1361 revolt that deposed him. Take time to sit in one of the *liwans,* looking up at the incredibly high arches and the lamps hanging on long chains swinging in the breeze.

The Mosque of Al Rifai was built 500 years after the neighboring *madrasa,* and was completed in 1912 in mock-Mamluke style. It's more straightforward architecturally than the *madrasa* and tomb next door, but the massive enclosed dome makes for a spectacular sense of space. The main point of interest for many here is the tomb of an important Sufi, Sheikh Ali Al Rifai, who is celebrated during an annual *moulid* (local festival for holy figures). The mosque also contains the tombs of several members of the Egyptian royal family (including Fuad I and Faruq) and of Mohamed Reza Pahlavi, the last Shah of Iran.

The entrance is at The Citadel side of the enclosure, facing onto the traffic circle. Admission LE30 ($5.45/£2.75) for foreigners. There are toilets down the stairs from the ticket kiosk, on your left as you enter the garden. The main section of Al Rifai tends to be closed to foreigners during prayers.

Mosque of Ibn Tulun *☞* This huge and magnificent mosque and enclosure is almost all that remains of a 9th-century city built here by an enterprising upstart named Ahmad Ibn Tulun. Ibn Tulun was the son of a Turkish slave who served in the military and amassed enough military power to establish a city on empty land near Fustat, which was then the capital of Egypt. The mosque has been subjected to a heavy-handed government restoration in the last few years, but it remains one of my favorite places to visit in the city. Lacking the spectacular interior spaces of Sultan Hassan or the view of Mohamed Ali, Ibn Tulun's innovative Iraqi-influenced architecture and massive courtyard have a power and space that the others lack.

The whole building survived relatively unscathed from the destructive process of addition and renovation that most other major mosques have suffered over the century, at least until the late 20th century, when a heavy-handed Ministry of Culture renovation "cleaned away" a good deal of material that they deemed stylistically inappropriate.

There is a 2km (about 1¼ mile) Koranic inscription on sycamore wood that runs around the entire mosque. Some of this wood is said to have been salvaged from Noah's ark.

Although the distinctive square minaret was closed when I last visited, you may be able to walk up. It's not too high, and the view is nice. The roof may also be open for visitors, so just ask. (It may cost you a bit more in *bakshish* [about LE5/90¢/45p].)

Ibn Tulun Street. Free admission, but the men who tend the shoes at the front entrance usually insist that foreigners wear cloth slip-ons over their shoes rather than remove them. They then ask for money. LE5 (90¢/45p) is quite sufficient, but they may try for more.

Museum of Islamic Art *☞☞* Still in the middle of a seemingly endless renovation, the Museum of Islamic Art promises, when it eventually reopens, to be an absolute must-see. The square-shouldered 19th-century edifice that houses the museum is impressive in its own right, but the incredibly rich and eclectic collection of Islamic decorative items is the main draw. If you don't have any experience with the history of Islamic art, it's going to be an eye-opener. Responding to the Quranic injunction against representing God with a broad abandonment of figurative art as a whole, artists in Islamic countries developed intricate epigraphic and geometric designs that they then applied to everything from stone to glass. The collection includes finely decorated lamps, worked stone fountains and domestic fixtures, and wooden *mashrabeya* screens.

Before it closed for renovation, the main problem with the museum was that (like all too many Egyptian museums) the documentation and signage was appalling. Much work in the renovation has been done to address this, and there are hopeful signs that when the facility reopens, this spectacular collection may be displayed in the way it deserves.

Port Saied Street. (© 02/23901520 or 02/23909930. Closed to public at time of writing.

Tentmakers' Souk (Kheimeya)   Just across from Bab Zuweila is a short covered souk known in Arabic as *Sharia al Kheimeya,* or "Street of the Tentmakers." This may not sound like much of a shopping opportunity (after all, who wants to pack a tent home?), but the same vibrant embroidery used for centuries to decorate celebratory tents now finds its way onto everything from quilts to cushions. Much of the work is done in the little shops that line the streets, so you can watch the complicated geometry of the traditional designs slowly taking shape as you decide what to buy. If you have a few weeks, you could place a special order for a particular pattern in colors of your own choosing. Prices are definitely negotiable, but expect to pay LE50 ($9.10/£4.60) for small pillow covers and up to LE3,000 ($545/£278) for elaborately worked bedspreads and wall hangings.

Darb al Ahmar. Free admission.

Wikalat al Ghuriya   This Mamluke commercial building (it was built in 1504) isn't the easiest of places to find, but having been restored, it rewards a little effort with a glimpse of the past. Some will argue that it's a little sterile given the noisy and enthusiastic buying and selling in the shops and workshops that it once housed, but it certainly makes a change from the sad, moldering piles that fill most of the streets in the area. The lovely central courtyard is worth a daylight visit, despite the somewhat drear "cultural artifact" displays that the Ministry of Culture uses it for. What I really recommend, though, is coming to see the Sufi dancers, the famous Whirling Dervishes, on Wednesday or Saturday evenings. The show starts at 8pm, and make sure that you're on time—the doors close at 8:30pm.

Admission LE10 ($1.80/95p) adults, LE5 (90¢/45p) students. Sat–Thurs 9am–5pm.

Turning to God

You're going to see it billed as "whirling dervishes" or "Sufi dancing," and when you do, grab the opportunity: This is one practice that has survived commercialization and retains, even performed in odd costumes on a cruise boat in the middle of the Nile, a powerful and unique aura of spirituality. The "dance" is actually a type of *zikr,* a religious act of "remembering" God. These *zikr* take many different forms in the celebrations and rituals of the various Sufi sects, and whirling—which is literally turning away the world and toward God—is the specific form given to it by an originally Turkish sect called the Mevlevi. The traditional garb for the performance is a white gown, which swirls out and rises as the worshipper whirls around, and a long black cloak. Many of the cheesy "folklore shows" foisted on unsuspecting cruise-boat passengers include some whirling, and the odds are that it's going to be good—this is one skill that you cannot learn to fake (try it yourself afterward if you don't believe me). The best place to catch the real thing, however, is at the Ghuriya in Islamic Cairo (below).

OLD CAIRO

Also known as Coptic Cairo, this is a rich and fascinating area on the site of Fustat, the capital of Egypt until 1169. The area contains a number of sites, several connected by picturesque cobbled streets, and requires at least half a day if you want to see and appreciate them all. Old Cairo is the easiest of Cairo's sites to access. Simply board a southbound (toward Helwan) Metro at Sadat Station in Tahrir Square to Mar Girgis Station (three stops); tickets cost LE50 ($9.10/£4.60).

Ben Ezra Synagogue 𝆑 This simple and graceful little temple behind the Church of St. George is the oldest synagogue in Egypt. Though the site itself has been holy to the Jews as long as they've been in Egypt—it is said to be where Moses was found in the reeds—the structure there today was originally built as the Church of St. Michael the Archangel in the 4th century and did not become a synagogue until the 9th century (after St. Michael's was closed during the reign of Khalif al Hakim, the insane Fatimid ruler who, among other things, banned sleeping at night and making women's shoes). The building was restored in the 12th century by Abraham Ben Ezra, who was rabbi of Jerusalem, and extensively rebuilt in the 1890s. During the rebuilding process a huge cache of documents was found in a *geniza* (hiding place). More a disposal method than an archive (old scrolls and documents were placed there for fear of discarding something with the word of God written on it), this collection of around 250,000 pieces of paper includes contracts, receipts, and ordinary correspondence that have allowed researchers to reconstruct daily life in Fustat. Restored again in the 1980s, Ben Ezra is in great condition today and definitely warrants a visit.

Coptic Cairo. Free admission. Daily 8am–4pm.

Church of St. George One of the most atmospheric churches in Cairo, this round Greek Orthodox church is actually a reconstruction of a 7th-century church that almost burned to the ground in the 19th century. It is built on top of the north tower of the old Roman fortress of Babylon and within the grounds of the Monastery of St. George. If you can, it is well worth descending underneath the church to see the Roman foundations there. For decades, these were full of water, until a huge USAID-funded project started in the 1990s allowed the drainage of built-up ground water and made it possible to see the original Roman stonework. There is a nice relief of St. George on the second landing as you climb the stairs to the church, and underneath (though still above the Roman foundations) there are small chapels and displays that are worth visiting if they're open.

Coptic Cairo.

Coptic Museum 𝆑𝆑 The Coptic Museum, which opened originally back in 1910, has just emerged from an extensive refurbishment The result is a far better organized, presented, and documented museum, and it's a must-see for anyone interested in the history of Egypt. This is also a museum with a mission—the intent behind the layout is to show how Coptic imagery is deeply embedded in all aspects of Egyptian life, and following the displays you can see the sun discs of ancient deities morph into iconographic halos and the capitals of Pharaonic columns transform into baptismal basins.

One of the museum's most prized holdings is a manuscript collection of the Nag Hammadi library (popularly known as the Gnostic Gospels). Access to the library is restricted, but several folios, scrolls, and a sublime Book of Psalms dating from the 4th century are on display.

In the center of Old Cairo, across from the exit from the Mar Girgis Metro stop. ✆ **02/33628766** or 02/33639742. Admission LE16 ($2.90/£1.50); students half-price. Daily 9am–5pm (ticket office closes at 4pm).

Fortress of Babylon There is unfortunately little left above ground of the massive fortress built by Roman Emperor Trajan (98–117) to protect a strategically important dock facility on the banks of the Nile. Several of the churches of Coptic Cairo are built on the foundations of the fort, and the Coptic Museum lies within its ancient walls. By 640, when the area was conquered by the Arabs, the fort had 40-foot walls and was linked to the Red Sea by a series of canals and interlinked waterways. Until fairly recently, much of the fort's foundations were flooded by rising groundwater, and they have only recently been dried out by a massive USAID-funded archaeological effort. It was unclear at the time of writing how much would ultimately be open to public exploration, but it's well worth taking some time while you're in the area to check it out.

Coptic Cairo.

Hanging Church Named for the manner in which it was built (across the water gate into the old Roman fort of Babylon), this 7th-century (or 9th-century, depending on who you believe) Coptic Church is still in use today. It is known more formally as Church of the Virgin. The facade that you encounter as you enter is 19th century and not particularly attractive, but the original interior of the church is charming. The nave is barrel-vaulted, and the inside of the church echoes with the whispers of visitors. The traditional **marble pulpit** is from the 13th century and is used on Palm Sundays. One of my favorite things in the Hanging Church is the series of **18th-century icons** showing the martyrdom of St. George. Kids, meanwhile, will be interested in the window that's been cut in the floor to give a view of the water below.

There are a couple of nice stalls in the entrance to the church where you can purchase books, postcards, and reproduction icons. Another nice thing about this church is that the young men you encounter who offer to show you around are not only knowledgeable but not interested in a tip (though they will be happy to show you where the donation box is).

Coptic Cairo.

4 Where to Stay

Cairo's accommodations seem to lie at extreme ends of the spectrum. You'll either find cheap backpacker places of dubious cleanliness or high-priced, high-rise, tourist-class hotels that are often heavy on glitz and light on actual deliverables. There are a small number of decently priced, clean, basic hotels, but by focusing on a few key areas, you'll find some good deals.

ZAMALEK
VERY EXPENSIVE
Safir Suite Hotel This is more of an apartment hotel than a suite hotel, offering a quick and easy, but not cheap, solution to those who need a bit more space. Suites are commodious and include a full kitchen, full bathroom, guest toilet, and a substantial living room and dining room. Decor is bland, to say the least, and even with the spectacular Nile view, ambience is about zilch. At the time of writing, the Nile-side pool was still under construction but looked set to be one of the nicest in Cairo.

12 Mohamed Mazhar St. ✆ 02/27370055. Fax 02/27371202. www.safirhotels.com. 100 units. LE2,310 ($420/£210) 1-bedroom suite; LE4,950 ($900/£450) 2-bedroom suite. AE, MC, V. **Amenities:** Pool; 24-hr. room service; laundry service; Wi-Fi. *In room:* TV, kitchen.

EXPENSIVE

Cairo Marriott Hotel   This former palace was built especially for France's Empress Eugenie, who came to Egypt for the opening of the Suez Canal in 1869. The main building has retained much of its 19th-century charm, but there have been several modern renovations, including two somewhat out-of-character towers. The Marriott has a limited business center, but its lush gardens and pool are attractive for those looking for a relaxing vacation. Many of the rooms in the north tower have been renovated in the last year and offer spectacular views of the Nile and the downtown core. Less modern but very comfortable business suites are available in the south tower and feature fold-out desks, high-speed Internet access, and a range of complimentary international newspapers and magazines.

The hotel has several upmarket restaurants, including JW's Steakhouse and the Marriott Terrace. The food at the Terrace is mediocre, but it's a favorite lounging spot for Egypt's TV and movie glitterati and enjoys a steady clientele of those who want to see and be seen.

Overall, this hotel is geared primarily toward an American clientele and manages to balance a relaxed and friendly Egyptian attitude with efficiency.

16 Saray el Gezira. ℭ 02/27283000. Fax 02/27283001. www.marriott.com. 1,009 units. LE1,073 ($195/£98) double; LE1,265 ($230/£115) deluxe pool view. AE, MC, V. **Amenities:** 9 restaurants; 2 bars; casino; pool; fitness center; business center; 24-hr. room service; laundry; bank; Wi-Fi. *In room:* Satellite TV, safe, high-speed Internet (executive rooms).

Flamenco   This Dutch-run hotel doesn't have much to offer in the way of character, but the rooms on the river side of the building have very nice views of the Nile and the houseboats that have been moored along the opposite bank since the 19th century. The food in the upstairs restaurant is nothing to write home about (positively or negatively), but the view of the river is lovely. The rooms are neatly kept and clean, and the place is conveniently located around the corner from a couple of cafes and is an easy walk to a variety of restaurants.

2 El Gezira El Wosta St. ℭ **02/27350815**, 02/27350816, or 02/27350818. Fax 02/827350819. www.flamencohotels. com. 178 units. LE748 ($136/£118) standard double; LE886 ($161/£81) superior double. Breakfast included. AE, DC, MC, V. **Amenities:** 2 restaurants; bar; laundry; safe at reception. *In room:* Satellite TV, minibar (executive rooms), Internet (executive rooms).

Sofitel el Gezirah Cairo 𝒞𝒞   The new Sofitel in a recently renovated tower at the southern end of the island (officially called Gezira) has real style. Normally, I'm not a fan of Egypt's Accor hotels, finding them overpriced and complacent, but this branch exhibits none of these faults. From the elegant lobby to the chic, earth-tone rooms, the interior decor is innovative and fun. The rooms are a little smaller than the competition's, but for me the experience of being in a well-put-together space outweighs the value of an extra square meter or two. Add to this one of the nicest spas in the city, three restaurants, and a bar within a couple of meters of the river, and you have my recommendation for the nicest of Cairo's five-star hotels.

3 el Thawra Council St., Gezira. ℭ **02/27373737**. www.sofitel.com. 433 units. LE1,705 ($310/£160) double; LE3,575 ($650/£325) junior suite; LE6,600 ($1,200/£600) panoramic suite. AE, DC, MC. **Amenities:** 6 restaurants; 2 bars; pool; spa; 24-hr. room service; Wi-Fi. *In room:* TV, minibar, safe.

MODERATE

Horus   Quiet, clean, and in the heart of Zamalek near a variety of restaurants and shops, the Horus is well suited to a longer stay (they will negotiate weekly and

Zamalek

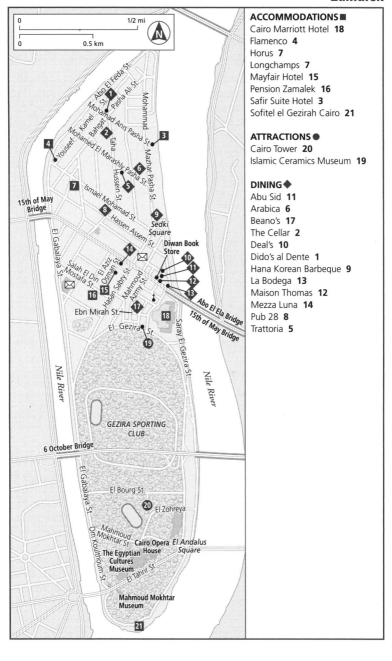

monthly rates). There is no view to speak of and it's a little shabby, but the staff are friendly and helpful, and the hotel has a soothing, if somewhat musty, charm.

21 Ismail Mohamed St. ℂ **02/27360694.** Fax 02/27353182. www.horushousehotel.4t.com. 35 units. LE286 ($52/£26) double. MC, V. **Amenities:** Restaurant. *In room:* A/C, satellite TV.

Longchamps ★★★ Nestled in the heart of Zamalek, this quiet midrange hotel has been family-run since 1953. Investment and reenergized management have brought significant improvements over the last couple of years, however, and the Longchamps now shines in its class, putting many significantly more-expensive hotels to shame. The surprisingly spacious rooms, and even more spacious executive rooms, have been spruced up with the kind of high-quality fittings that you would expect in a more expensive facility; the restaurant has also been completely renovated. The public areas, which are decorated with photos and furniture collected by the owner's family over the last 5 decades, have a comfortable and homey feel to them. About the only thing that this place doesn't have is a view, but at less than half the price of the cheapest Nile-view rooms in town, this is the only area in which the Longchamps comes up short. This is certainly the best value for money in Zamalek, and possibly in Cairo.

21 Ismail Mohamed St. ℂ **02/27352311.** Fax 02/27359644. www.hotellongchamps.com. 22 units. LE374 ($68/£34) double; LE413 ($75/£38) executive double. Rates include breakfast and taxes. MC, V. **Amenities:** Restaurant; bar; laundry; Wi-Fi. *In room:* AC, satellite TV, minifridge.

INEXPENSIVE

Mayfair Hotel *Value* The Mayfair is a very clean, small hotel located on three floors of a converted residential building in the middle of Zamalek; it's probably the best value for money in Cairo's budget range. The place doesn't have any atmosphere—hallways are narrow and utilitarian, decor is sparse, and furnishings say "budget-hotel" loud and clear—but rooms have high ceilings and comfortable beds, and are far enough from a main road to be relatively quiet. Public areas have better lights and a more spacious feel than other hotels in this price range. Breakfast is served year-round on a balcony overlooking the street.

9 Aziz Osman St. ℂ **02/27357315.** Fax 02/27350424. www.mayfaircairo.com. 40 units. LE190 ($35/£18) double with A/C and private bathroom. Rate includes breakfast. MC, V. **Amenities:** Wi-Fi. *In room:* TV, fridge.

Pension Zamalek This simple and small hotel in a quiet area of Zamalek used to be my pick for the best budget accommodation in the city, but a recent price hike has made it as expensive as (or even more than) hotels that have a lot more to offer, such as the Mayfair (above) down the street. Value for money aside, I like this place because it feels a little like a pension in France or Portugal—the hallways are wide and a little gloomy, and the owner is usually parked in the small lobby sitting area watching television. With shared bathrooms and clean rooms, Pension Zamalek remains a good, comfortable choice if the Mayfair is booked.

6 Salah El Din St. ℂ **02/27359318** or 0122110491. Fax 02/27353773. pensionzamalek@msn.com. 20 units. LE250 ($45/£23) double. Rate includes breakfast. Cash only. **Amenities:** TV in lobby. *In room:* No phone.

DOWNTOWN AND GARDEN CITY

Downtown is where the action is; its hustle and bustle and street life are part of what make Cairo a special place—whether you want to stay here is a different question (some people find the sheer press of crowds, the traffic, and the constant din a bit much). The hotels listed below all offer a quiet refuge, and some (like the Four Seasons or the New Garden City) are located well off to the side. Others, like the Talisman or the Cosmopolitan, are right in the thick of the action.

Garden City is a small neighborhood to the south of downtown proper. Built by the British as their administrative center, it now molders in quiet, boring respectability. Other than a number of embassies (including the American, British, and Canadian), it has one restaurant and two or three hotels worth noting.

EXPENSIVE

Conrad ⍟ At the opposite end of the Corniche from the cluster of the Hyatt, Four Seasons, and InterContinental, the Conrad looks across the Nile to Zamalek. Service is prompt and efficient here, and the business center is one of the best and most comprehensive in the city. (If this is a major priority to you, the Four Seasons First Residence over in Giza, p. 109, also deserves consideration.) With its massive, gleaming lobby and swirl of a staircase, the Conrad works hard to make sure you know you're in a five-star hotel—the only problem is that it could be any five-star hotel. What the place lacks in character, however, is made up for by good service; the rooms are clean and well maintained, and the staff are pleasant and well prepared. The Conrad is very reasonably priced when you consider the competition down the Corniche or across the river in Zamalek.

1191 Corniche el Nil. ✆ 02/25808000. Fax 02/25808080. www.conradcairo.com. 617 units. LE1,205 ($219/£109) double; LE1,975 ($359/£180) executive double; LE2,525 ($459/£230) executive suite. **Amenities:** 5 restaurants; 2 bars; spa; fitness center; 24-hr. business center; Wi-Fi. *In room:* TV, safe.

Four Seasons Nile Plaza ⍟ The Four Seasons might fall short of competitors such as the Sofitel (p. 102) when it comes to flashy design, but you'd be hard-pressed to find a better-run hotel, even at this price. The Four Seasons sets out to make you feel recognized and special, and it does it very well. This is a hotel that balances the predictability and comfort of a big chain with the up-close-and-personal, tailored service that comes naturally in smaller facilities. Your airport pickup arrives with moist towels and water, and you can begin check-in and even order room service from the car so that you don't have to wait when you get to the hotel.

Inside, everything is understated and elegant, and the ambience is relaxed and comfortable yet sophisticated. The walls of the second-floor restaurant and bar area are hung with an impressive collection of modern Egyptian art, and there are spectacular flower arrangements everywhere you look. Rooms are large and manage to be homey and elegant at the same time. Like the service, they manage somehow to deliver everything that you need in a relaxed and effortless manner.

1089 Corniche el Nil. ✆ 02/27917000. Fax 02/27916900. www.fourseasons.com. 365 units. LE1,870 ($340/£173) double; LE5,500 ($1,000/£500) Corniche suite. AE, DC, MC, V. **Amenities:** 6 restaurants; 2 bars; 3 pools (including lap pool); spa; fitness center; Wi-Fi. *In room:* TV, safe.

Grand Hyatt Cairo *Overrated* Located directly across the water from the new Sofitel el Gezirah and across the road from the Four Seasons Nile Plaza, the Hyatt's massive curved tower is hard to miss. Inside the lobby, huge pillars and a flight of stairs dominate the space. The view of the river is still pretty good, although (unlike the Sofitel) the design keeps you from getting too close to water, which is a pity. The view only gets better from the higher floors, and on the rare day that Cairo has clear air, you can see all the way to the pyramids in Giza.

In sharp contrast with the Four Seasons—which oddly enough is marginally less expensive for a standard room—the Hyatt feels like a big, impersonal hotel. The rooms, even though they have a spectacular unimpeded view of the river from above, are generic and substantially smaller than over at the Four Seasons. If you want to save a bit of money, I'd opt for the Semiramis InterContinental (below).

Corniche el Nil. © **02/23651234.** Fax 02/23621927. www.cairo.grand.hyatt.com. 716 units. LE1,925 ($350/£175) double; LE2,200 ($400/£200) executive room; LE2750–LE2,888 ($500–$525/£250–£273) suite. Breakfast additional LE83 ($15/£7.50). **Amenities:** 10 restaurants and bars; pool; fitness center; car service; bank; Wi-Fi; movie theater. *In room:* Minibar, safe, Internet.

Nile Hilton   Opened in 1959, this hotel was intended to showcase the new Egypt that then-President Gamal Abdel Nasser, who had led the army to overthrow the monarchy 7 years before, was hoping to create. Subsequent bland renovations have reduced the glories somewhat, and maintenance clearly hasn't kept up with problems, but the Nile Hilton still has echoes of that earlier time when the likes of Frank Sinatra were guests. The public areas around the lobby are somewhat tacky now, but the hallways upstairs retain a 1960s feel that I also enjoy.

To many, the colors and furniture in the rooms will simply seem dated, but I like touches such as the *mashrabeya* screens. I also like the size of the rooms—clearly standards in this regard were higher back in Nasser's day—but poor soundproofing means you can hear traffic from the Corniche. Also, rooms with a back-facing view look across the never-ending construction chaos adjacent to the Egyptian Museum and Midan Tahrir.

The top-floor Rotisserie Belvedere is notable for its decor rather than its food, and though the hotel's location next to the Egyptian Museum may be convenient for some, you're still going to have to get a taxi to get everywhere else.

1113 Corniche El Nil. © **02/25780444.** Fax 02/25780475. www.hilton.com. 431 Units. LE1,210 ($220/£110) city-view double; LE1,293 ($235/£120) Nile-view double. AE, DC, MC, V. **Amenities:** 3 restaurants; 4 bars; pool; tennis courts. *In room:* A/C, TV, minibar, Internet.

Ramses Hilton   The adjective that comes to my mind for the Ramses Hilton has always been *defensible.* A massive, overhung tower block, it looks like it was designed by the same guy who did the Palazzo Vecchio in Florence—but this time he decided to make something seriously big. The lobby reinforces the notion with a confusing design on several different levels. It only makes sense when you get into the rooms, which are modern and pleasant, if wholly lacking in any particular character.

Stuck between two busy roads with a major bus station on the corner and backing onto a somewhat insalubrious neighborhood, the Ramses Hilton's location isn't great, but it's fairly central and certainly easy to catch a taxi from here. This is a place to stay if you get a really good price or everywhere else is full.

1115 Corniche el Nil. © **02/25777444.** Fax 02/25752942. www.hilton.com. 755 units. LE1,073 ($195/£99) double. AE, DC, MC, V. **Amenities:** 5 restaurants; 3 bars; pool; tennis courts. *In room:* A/C, TV, minibar, Internet.

Semiramis InterContinenal   Recently renovated and very conveniently located on the edge of downtown, the Semiramis is a perfectly fine hotel. Service is friendly, if not as smooth as at the Four Seasons, and facilities are commodious. Substantial differences in the price of rooms at the front of the hotel and the back tell the story of the view: At the front, it's as good as the Hyatt, while at the back, well, it's just not that great. Decor is a little more ostentatious than it should be, a reminder that this hotel—like the Cairo Marriott in Zamalek—does a brisk summer business with tourists from the Gulf, but it remains a staple of diplomats coming to Cairo to work at one of the nearby embassies or at the Arab League just across the street.

Corniche el Nil. ② **02/27957171.** Fax 02/27963020. www.ichotelsgroup.com. 727 units. LE946 ($172/£136) double; LE2,090 ($380/£190) deluxe Nile-view double. AE, DC, MC, V. **Amenities:** Casino; pool; gym; sauna. *In room:* A/C, TV, minibar, Internet.

MODERATE

Cosmopolitan *(Finds*   If you want a glimpse of what Cairo was 50 years ago, the Cosmopolitan's decor and furniture has changed little since then. The lobby is a deeply shadowed place, full of *mashrabeya* and armchairs, but the upper floors, serviced by a pair of gleaming antique Schindler elevators, are light and spacious. The rooms are not very big (in fact, it's worth checking out more than one because they vary in size), and some of the bathrooms are downright cramped, though they are generally clean and well maintained. Rooms at the front of the hotel have a view across busy 26th of July Street to the Supreme Court or the ruined, collapsing, 1920s Art Deco Theatre Rivoli. The street life (intense, dirty, and loud) around the hotel is in sharp contrast to the hotel's cool and quiet interior. If you want a reasonably priced refuge in the heart of downtown, the Cosmopolitan offers solid value for money.

21 26th of July St. ② **02/25752323.** 60 units. LE190 ($35/£18) double. Rate includes tax and half-board. MC, V. **Amenities:** 2 restaurants; bar; laundry. *In room:* A/C, fridge.

New Garden Palace   Located on a quiet side street of a quiet neighborhood, it's to be expected that this is going to be a quiet hotel. The building has more character from the outside than from inside, and it's very much a budget facility. Rooms are basic and views are limited, but both rooms and public areas, which include a rooftop bar/restaurant, are clean, and staff are friendly and helpful. The immediate neighborhood is pleasant, and is an easy 10- to 15-minute walk to the Egyptian Museum or the American University; taxis are plentiful and easily available on nearby Kasr el Aini Street for places farther afield.

11 Moderat al Tahrir St. ② **02/27964020.** Fax 02/27963630. 55 units. LE187 ($34/£17) double. Rate includes tax. Cash only. **Amenities:** Restaurant; bar; laundry; Internet. *In room:* A/C, TV, fridge.

Talisman Hotel   This one-of-a-kind hotel in the heart of downtown was founded 4 years ago by French owners who completely renovated the fifth floor of a 70-year-old colonial building. They've brought the place up to modern standards, while retaining the essential character of the building. It still feels like an old house, with long, winding corridors and antique furniture tucked into nooks, and the public areas are furnished with period pieces and wall hangings. Rooms are carefully constructed and have personal touches such as the "hand of Fatima" door handles and old embroidered bedspreads.

39 Talat Harb St. ②/fax **02/23939431.** www.talisman-hotel.com. 24 units. LE649 ($118/£59) double. Rate includes tax and breakfast. Cash only. **Amenities:** Laundry; Wi-Fi. *In room:* A/C, TV, minibar, hairdryer.

Windsor   This downtown fixture has changed little since it opened in the 1930s. Travel posters from the 1950s adorn the walls, and while the claim that the Schindler elevator is one of the oldest operating in the world is hard to verify, it's certainly the oldest in Egypt to still be carrying passengers. The building was originally a khedival bathhouse and served as a British Officers Club during World War II. The heart of the hotel is undoubtedly still the lounge bar on the second floor, with its chairs cut from old barrels and a chandelier of antlers. The vintage reception desk in the lobby, with its original switchboard, however, comes a close second.

Rooms vary considerably, from high ceilinged and spacious to small and quite dank. At the best of times, the whole place is somewhat musty, but if history is your thing, it's going to seem a small price to pay for the sense of time that the hotel conveys. Less forgiving are recent reports that visitors have felt pressured to accept guide services touted by the front desk.

19 Alfi Bey St. © **02/25915277**. www.windsorcairo.com. 50 units. LE220–LE319 ($40–$58/£20–£29) double. Rate includes tax, service, and breakfast. AE, DC, MC, V. **Amenities:** Restaurant/lounge with satellite TV. *In room:* TV.

MOHANDISEEN

There isn't much to attract a tourist to Mohandiseen, but the neighborhood is between Giza and downtown and has good access along the 26th of July corridor in both directions, making it a convenient place to stay. There are a number of midrange hotels here, but nothing either at the higher or lower ends of the scale that are worth considering.

MODERATE

Atlas Hotel   The best thing about the Atlas is its rooftop pool with a restaurant and the bar. The food's mediocre—stick to the basic Egyptian dishes such as *shish tawook*—but the evening light is fantastic. Rooms are standard midrange with basic bathrooms. The carpet and paint haven't been redone as recently as at the Nabila (which is just a few meters up the street), and the levels of maintenance certainly aren't what they should be. Like the Nabila, however, I think that though racks rates are too high, discounts are probably to be had, especially in the winter.

20 Gamat el Dawal el Arabeya. © **02/33466569** or 02/33464175. Fax 02/33476958. 76 units. LE385 ($70/£35) double. Rate includes breakfast and taxes. MC, V. **Amenities:** Restaurant; pool; laundry; Wi-Fi. *In room:* TV, minifridge.

Nabila Hotel   Located on the main thoroughfare of Mohandiseen, the Nabila is very much a standard Egyptian midrange hotel. If you need a pool and a gym, but you're not in the market for a Hilton or a Marriott, this is it. Rooms are clean, if somewhat lightless, and the beds are comfortable. The pool has a shaded area for lounging and keeping an eye on the kids, and though the health club is small and basic, it is also clean and the staff are friendly.

Aiming at slightly downmarket Gulf tourists, the hotel has been recently redecorated in a somewhat tacky way. At the rack rates, this place is overpriced, but I would expect a substantial discount if booking on short notice in the winter here.

The location can only be described as busy, and the hotel is close to a variety of fastfood outlets and one or two decent restaurants. The downside is that the traffic level on the street outside is intimidating, and to get across to the other side you'll probably want to take a taxi down to the next intersection and double back.

4 Gamat el Dawal al Arabia. © **02/33030302**. 220 units. LE550 ($100/£50). MC, V. **Amenities:** Restaurant; bar; pool; health club; business center. *In room:* TV.

INEXPENSIVE

Amoun   A bit of a seedy place at the intersection of two major roads, the Amoun has the advantages of being cheap and close to easy transportation (there's a yellow taxi stand just around the corner). The atmosphere both in the lobby and in the rooms is a bit on the musty and dusty side, and I don't think that women traveling alone would be very comfortable here. That said, the basic rooms are clean enough and larger than expected, the air-conditioning works (though the telephone that I tested did not), and many expats swear by the Korean restaurant in the basement.

Sphinx Square. © **02/34611434**. 40 units. LE220 ($40/£20) double. Rate includes breakfast. Cash only. **Amenities:** Restaurant. *In room:* A/C, TV, no phone.

GIZA/DOKKI/AGOUZA

Four Seasons Hotel Cairo at The First Residence   This is the older of Cairo's two Four Seasons properties, and though the view here is not the greatest (despite its Nile-side location), I really like this hotel for the simple fact that it doesn't feel like one. For example, there is no glitzy lobby: On arrival, instead of checking in at an industrial-size desk in a room the size of a couple of tennis courts, you slip discreetly upstairs to an intimate check-in lounge on the third floor. There are rooms that face the Nile, but the view is obstructed by a tower block; the city-view rooms, which over-look the rambling, jungle-like green space of the old Giza Zoo, are more attractive.

35 Giza St. ✆ 02/35731212. Fax 02/35681616. www.fourseasons.com. 271 units. LEI,870 ($340/£173) standard double; LE2,420 ($440/£224) deluxe double. AE, DC, MC, V. **Amenities:** 3 restaurants; 2 bars; pool; gym; spa; 24-hr. business center; 24-hr. room service. *In room:* TV, minibar, safe, Internet.

Mena House Oberoi ★★★   Apart from the fact that it's historically worth a visit in its own right, the Mena House is a good place to stay for those who are in Cairo to see the Pharaonic sites at Giza and up the valley toward Saqqara, Dahshur, and Mem-phis. Originally built as a hunting lodge next to the pyramids for the Khedive Ismail, it was converted to a hotel in the 1890s. Oberoi took it over in the 1970s and distrib-uted a roomful of 19th-century furnishings throughout the present guest rooms.

The hotel's location is not ideal for venturing into Islamic Cairo, but it cuts an enormous amount of hassle out of getting to Saqqara and Memphis, as well as the Giza pyramids (which can be viewed directly from the hotel). Public areas of the hotel are decorated with dark wood paneling and *mashrabeya*, which evoke a time of more relaxed and elegant tourism. Add to this one of the nicest outdoor pools in the city and easily Cairo's best Indian restaurant, the Mogul Room, and the Mena House makes a pretty good home base for Egypt.

Pyramids Road. ✆ 02/33773222 or 02/33766644. Fax 02/33775411 or 02/3376/7777. www.oberoimenahouse.com. 523 units. LE1,045 ($190/£95) standard double; LE1,650 ($300/£150) deluxe pyramid view; LE3,630 ($660/£330) exec-utive suite. AE, DC, MC, V. **Amenities:** 4 restaurants; 2 bars; pool; golf course; spa; helipad. *In room:* TV, minibar, safe.

Mövenpick Resort Pyramids   This resort is nearly in the shadows of the pyramids (about 2km/1½ miles away) and affords easy access to the Pharaonic sites here and in Saqqara and Memphis. However, the shops, restaurants, and sites in the middle of Cairo are still a 15- to 30-minute taxi ride away.

Mövenpick's aesthetic is known for its Swiss restraint, but that's nowhere to be found in this location's lobby, with shiny floors and masses of brass, which give the space a shopping-mall feel. Rooms, however, are large and spread amongst low build-ings, decorated in light colors, and open onto a garden.

Alexandria Road. ✆ 02/33772555. Fax 02/337750067. 240 units. LE853 ($155/£78) double; LE1,375 ($250/£125) business suite; LE2,200 ($400/£200) family suite. AE, DC, MC, V. **Amenities:** 5 restaurants; 3 bars; pool; 4 tennis courts; health club; playground; racquet ball. *In room:* TV, minibar, safe, Internet.

Pyramisa Suites Hotel   The quality of the Pyramisa hotel may be below the for-eign-run competition, but so are the prices. It wouldn't take much of a discount to make this place a value for money, and it makes up for rough-edged service and bad maintenance by having friendly, helpful staff.

Rooms are large by midrange standards, but not very light due to small windows and a dark color scheme. Because the hotel is located off a main thoroughfare, make sure you get an inward-facing pool-view room, and preferably one on the west side of the building, away from the road. The building seems to ramble on and on, and trying to find your way to the pool, you're likely to pop out beside the bar or the gym and have to retrace your steps to figure out where you went wrong.

60 Giza St. ✆ 02/3337000. Fax 02/33361936. 377 units. LE880 ($160/£80) pool-view double. AE, DC, MC, V. **Amenities:** 3 restaurants; bar; 2 pools; health club; business center; Wi-Fi; Internet. *In room:* TV, minifridge, Internet.

HELIOPOLIS/AIRPORT

JW Marriott　　More like a small resort town than a hotel, the JW Marriott has everything from a water park to a golf course. Located a 10-minute drive from the airport, it's a bit out of the way for the pyramids in Giza and the Saqqara, but it's actually as convenient to Khan al Khalili, The Citadel, and Islamic Cairo as the big downtown and Zamalek hotels. At the end of the day, however, it isn't Cairo sights that drive this hotel's popularity, but quite the opposite: From the extravagant lobby to the acres of greenery and the artificial beach, the intention is to take you away from the city. The rooms are spacious and lushly decorated, as if compensating for a somewhat generic overall look and feel. All of them look out over either the golf course or the water park. If a pause from the chaos and the excitement and something absolutely predictable and familiar is what you need, this is a good base for your Cairo visit.

Ring Road, Mirage City. ✆ 02/24115588. Fax 02/24112266. www.marriott.com. 349 units. LE1,650 ($300/£150) double. AE, DC, MC, V. **Amenities:** 6 restaurants; 3 bars; water park; golf course; gym; spa. *In room:* A/C, TV, minibar, safe, Internet.

Le Méridien Heliopolis　　Conveniently located on the main road between the airport and the center of Cairo, this Méridien is substantially more subdued than the new facility out on Dahab (p. 166) but shares the same lushness of color and decor. The neighborhood is certainly good enough—the president lives just down the street—but makes for a somewhat uninspiring view for the majority of rooms that look outward. My advice is to try to get a garden- or pool-view room. That said, the gardens and pool offer an excellent, calm ambience for relaxing after a day down at the Khan or trekking through Islamic Cairo. The main advantage that this place has going for it is its location: 5 minutes from the airport and 10 minutes (20 in rush hour) from The Citadel, Khan al Khalili, or any of the Islamic Cairo sites.

51 El Uruba St. ✆ 02/22905055. Fax 02/22918591. 283 units. LE1,513 ($275/£140) superior double. AE, DC, MC, V. **Amenities:** 4 restaurants; 3 bars; pool; spa. *In room:* A/C, TV, minibar, safe, Internet.

5 Where to Dine

Cairo has seen an explosion in the number of restaurants serving Western food in recent years. Between a well-paid expat community and economic growth that favors the upper classes, there has been a steady increase in demand and good support for new places that can deliver a decent dining experience. The main eating district is the upmarket island district of Zamalek, where a core of well-established places is regularly supplemented by new trendy eateries (of which a few survive to become part of the established list).

ZAMALEK

VERY EXPENSIVE

Abu Sid ⟨ EGYPTIAN　　Abu Sid is simply the best place in Cairo to sample real Egyptian food. The service can be slow, and the staff has been known to try and move diners to less desirable tables in the middle of the meal to clear space for new arrivals, but there's no arguing with either the food or the funky-yet-traditional decor. For appetizers, try the *fuul* (fava beans stewed in a traditional way) or *wara ainab* (stuffed grape leaves). Though there is a large and varied menu for main dishes that includes a delicious Circassian chicken in walnut sauce, I recommend ordering the above appetizers along with some *koshari,* an odd-looking mix of macaroni, lentils, and chickpeas topped off with hot sauce and fried onions. This quintessential Egyptian street-food dish is delicious when properly prepared, and it's dirt-cheap (and almost as appetizing) at the stalls that line certain downtown streets. The Abu Sid dish is about ten times as expensive, which still only comes to LE22 ($4/£2). After the *koshari,* end the meal with a traditional Egyptian dessert such as *om aly* (a raisin-studded variation of bread pudding) or a honey *fateer* (layers of pastry baked pizza style and drenched in honey).

Off 26th of July Street. C 02/27359640. Appetizers LE10–LE20 ($1.80–$3.60/90p–£1.80); main courses LE40–LE70 ($7.30–$13/£3.70–£6.50). MC, V. Daily 12:30pm–2am.

Trattoria ⭐ ITALIAN   A cool white interior and simple elegance characterize this pricey Italian eatery in the middle of Zamalek. One of a string of good restaurants in Egypt owned by the son of Egyptian movie star Omar Sharif (who can be spotted eating here), Trattoria serves small portions, but the food won't disappoint. Start with spaghetti carbonara (this being one of the very few places in Egypt where you can get safe pork products) and move on to the rich and filling osso buco. If you have space left, the ever-changing dessert selection usually includes something for every palate.

13 Marashly St. C 02/27350470. Reservations recommended. Appetizers LE20–LE30 ($3.60–$5.45/£1.85–£2.75); main courses LE40–LE140 ($7.25–$25/£3.70–£13). MC, V. Daily 1pm–12:30am; Fri they open at 2pm. Last order 11:30pm.

EXPENSIVE

The Cellar AMERICAN/INTERNATIONAL   This is an affluent dive in the middle of Zamalek that's favored by businessmen and well-heeled locals. Dark and low-ceilinged, The Cellar is a little less lively than Pub 28 (below) and a little more expensive. The food's not as good as Pub 28, but I recommend this place on a Thursday night if you're looking for a pub atmosphere and want to be able to hear what your friends are saying. Note that there is usually a minimum charge equivalent to about four beers per person.

22 Dr. Taha Hussein St. C 02/27353752. Main courses LE40–LE70 ($7.25–$13/£3.70–£6.50). Minimum purchase LE80 ($15/£7.40). MC. Daily noon–3am.

Hana Korean Barbeque ⭐ *Finds* KOREAN   As the name implies, you'll find barbecue here, only you get to make it yourself using small charcoal grills built into the table. Large portions of items such as beef and squid are accompanied by rice or noodles. If self-service isn't your thing, it also has an extensive menu of Korean and Asian food that stretches from Western Chinese standards such as egg fried rice and egg drop soup to more obscure dishes such as shark fin soup. Decor is basic, and service, though slow, is very pleasant and helpful. One nice touch here is the half-dozen or so dishes of assorted *kimchi* and appetizers that arrive before your food to tide you over until the entrees arrive. *Note:* Hana closes unusually early for Cairo, so get there by 9pm.

21 Aziz Abaza St. C 02/37382972. Appetizers LE10–LE20 ($1.80–$3.60/90p–£1.85); main courses LE30–LE60 ($5.45–$11/£2.75–£5.55). Cash only. Daily noon–9pm.

La Bodega FRENCH   Located in a renovated portion of the historic Baehler Mansions, La Bodega serves an eclectic mix of French and European food. The decor and atmosphere, particularly in the bistro portion (on the left), is my favorite in Cairo, with a combination of high ceilings, huge windows, and muted murals. The three-and four-course set menus, available at lunch and dinner, are excellent value for money if you've got a big appetite. My favorite dish here is the hearty Tunisian lamb shank with couscous and vegetables. They also serve an excellent steak, though the chef here consistently undercooks the meat, so remember to order at least one level better cooked than you actually want. The salads are large and fresh, and the desserts (with the exception of the gluey and tasteless chocolate mousse) are usually good. Though typically half-empty during the day, Bodega can get quite busy after 7pm, so reservations, particularly for groups of three or more, are a good idea.

157 26th of July St. ⓒ 02/27362188 or 02/27350543. Appetizers LE20–LE50 ($3.60–$9.10/£1.85–£4.60); main courses LE40–LE100 ($7.25–$18/£3.70–£9.25). MC, V. Daily noon–1:30am.

MODERATE

Arabica EGYPTIAN/INTERNATIONAL   This is a pleasant, if slightly worn, lunch spot in an upstairs location overlooking a lively street. For breakfast try out the variations of the traditional *fateer,* a pizza-sized pastry that comes sweet or savory; my favorite is the apple cinnamon. For lunch try the crispy, fried goat cheese salad or a chicken and grilled pepper wrap with a side of fries (the best in town). The restaurant is Wi-Fi equipped, so you can do some work over an espresso or fresh-squeezed fruit juice.

20 El Marashly St. ⓒ 02/27357982. Sandwiches LE10–LE25 ($1.80–$4.55/95p–£2.30); salads LE15–LE25 ($2.70–$4.55/£1.40–£2.30). Cash only. Daily 10am–2am.

Beano's CAFE/SANDWICHES   Another local chain, Beano's has locations all over the city. It's an acceptable lunch option if you're looking for clean, moderately priced hot and cold sandwiches, but where Beano's really shines is breakfast. Its American coffee, served in a personal-size Bodum coffee press, is the best in the city, and if you need a light, healthy breakfast (not an easy thing to find in this city), try the granola-yogurt parfait.

8 El Sheikh el Marsafy St. ⓒ 02/27362388. Sandwiches LE10–LE25 ($1.80–$4.50/95p–£2.30). Alcohol not served. Cash only. Daily 6am–1am.

Deal's (Value) INTERNATIONAL   This is a fun little pub-restaurant across the street from Abu Sid. Frequented by a younger, livelier crowd than you'll find at either Pub 28 or The Cellar (above), this is the place to watch the football game and meet some new friends. The food is surprisingly good, however, and you shouldn't ignore this place when considering where to get a reasonably priced lunch or dinner. The *chili con carne* is a tasty and substantial meal, and the chicken stir-fry with a couple of local Stella beers is one of my favorite comfort-food meals in the city.

1 Said el Bakry St. ⓒ 02/27360502. Main courses LE25–LE35 ($4.55–$6.35/£2.30–£3.25). MC, V. Daily 3pm–3am.

Maison Thomas (★★) PIZZA/SANDWICHES   This simple bistro is my favorite breakfast and lunch spot in the city. Clean and sleekly decorated (thanks to a recent renovation), this is one of a half-dozen branches of a venerable chain that dates back to the early 20th century. Probably best known these days for its pizza delivery (which I highly recommend), Maison Thomas also has great sandwiches, salads, and desserts (all of which are also available for delivery). My recent favorite is the Parisian sandwich, a fresh baguette piled high with ham and cheese. This is the only place in Egypt where I eat the pork, other than the rather pricey Trattoria (above).

157 26th of July St. ⓒ 02/27357057 or 02/27350415. Pizzas and sandwiches LE15–LE45 ($2.70–$8.20/£1.40–4.15). Cash only. Daily 24 hours.

Mezza Luna ITALIAN   Located on a quiet cul-de-sac off 26th of July Street, this small, relatively new (opened 2007), bistro-style restaurant has fresh pasta at very reasonable prices. Service can be iffy, but the decor is pleasant and very clean, with Italian pop music in the background. All the dishes come with garlic bread. The only drawback is that you'll have to have your Italian food without wine, as Mezza Luna has no liquor license.

118 26th of July St. ℂ 02/27352655. Pasta LE8–LE15 ($1.45–$2.70/75p–£1.30). Cash only. Daily 8am–midnight.

Pub 28 INTERNATIONAL   When the heat and dust of Cairo begin to get the best of you, Pub 28's cool, dark interior may be just what you need. Though conveniently located in the center of town, this well-established expat watering hole takes you out of the city with its funky faux-candle light fixtures, wood-paneled walls, heavy wood tables and high chairs, and welcoming ambience. A pleasant combination of good service and reasonable prices explain its enduring popularity among Cairo residents. The menu is a mix of Western and Egyptian, and the food is tasty. Try the *filet au beurre du chef* after a starter of French onion soup, or stay with the Egyptian option and have a *shish tawook* (succulent cubes of chicken and vegetables roasted over a charcoal brazier). Pub 28 stocks both local and imported beers and wines, and a small-but-delicious variety of desserts to close the deal. The only downside is its small size. Get here early or reserve ahead, particularly on Thursday and Friday nights, when it can be packed to capacity and too noisy for easy conversation by 8pm.

28 Shagarat el Dor St. ℂ 02/37359200. Reservations recommended Thurs and Fri nights. Appetizers LE10–LE20 ($1.80–$3.65/95p–£1.85); main courses LE30–LE60 ($5.45–$11/£2.75–£5.55). Cash only. Daily noon–2am.

INEXPENSIVE
Dido's al Dente (Value ITALIAN   As every student at the American University's nearby hostel knows, Dido's is the place for cheap, filling pasta in an informal setting. Squish into the tiny, usually crowded, main room and watch the cooks whip up your pasta in the open kitchen. The location on a quiet side street near the water is relaxed and pleasant, and the food is filling if not exactly gourmet. A downfall: The restaurant doesn't have a liquor license, but you can bring your own if you keep it well hidden.

21 Baghat Ali St. ℂ 02/27359117. Main courses LE10–LE20 ($1.80–$3.60/90p–1.80). Cash only. Alcohol not served. Daily 24 hours.

DOWNTOWN
EXPENSIVE
Naguib Mahfouz Café 🍴🍴   Hidden in the heart of the Khan al Khalili shopping district, this Oberoi-run restaurant is the perfect cool-off place for lunch. I highly recommend making this place a planned stop on your shopping itinerary: the food is excellent, the air-conditioning is efficient, and the washrooms are spotless. Prices may be expensive by Cairo standards, but the Naguib Mahfouz delivers the kind of service and food that you would expect from this first-rate hotel chain. I recommend starting with a fresh fruit juice—maybe mango or tamarind depending on the season—and then having a fairly light lunch, especially if it's hot. Try a sampling of local appetizers such as *tameya,* stuffed grape leaves, and *tahina.* If you're in the mood for something with a little more heft, the kebab is excellent and comes with fresh baked bread.

5 Sekket al-Badistan, Khan al-Khalili. ℂ 590-3788 or 593-2262. Appetizers LE20–LE50 ($3.60–$9.10/£1.85–£4.60); main courses LE50–LE100 ($9.10–$18/£4.60–£9.25). Open daily noon–midnight.

Nile Peking *(Kids* CHINESE   The Nile Peking is one of my favorite places to eat, despite the mediocre food. In this case, it all comes down to location: an old steam-driven yacht that once belonged to King Faruq. The boat's decor is reminiscent of the stage set in an overblown production of Puccini's Chinese fantasy opera *Turandot*, complete with steam puffing extravagantly from the dragon's-head prow. Take your fried-banana and ice cream dessert to the open-air lounge up top as the boat makes its way up and down the Nile.

Corniche el Nil, Msr al Qadima. ⓒ 25323755. Reservations recommended. Set menu LE70–LE110 ($13–$20/ £6.50–£10). Cash only. The boat usually sails at 7:30pm and is back at 9:30pm.

MODERATE

Felfela *(* *Value* EGYPTIAN   This rather enigmatic restaurant has the best moder-ately priced food in downtown Cairo. The decor includes water features, a woven-grass roof, live canaries, and a lot of hanging lamps, while the food is straight-up Egyptian fare. Start with a side plate of *tahina* and a bowl of lentil soup (served with croutons and lemons), and move on to *dawood basha* (meatball stew) or *kebab hella* (stewed lamb). For a real taste of local food, try a pair of grilled *hamama* (pigeons) or *samman* (quail); with a flavor very much like chicken, but substantially smaller, it takes two birds to make a nice light meal. End with a bowl of sweet, cool *om aly*. Felfela serves local wine and beer, but it also does a particularly good *aseer leimoon* (lemonade), which may be a better bet on a hot, dry summer day when you have a few hours of sightseeing still ahead.

15 Hoda Sharawi. ⓒ 02/23922751. Appetizers LE8–LE20 ($1.45–$3.60/74p–1.85); main courses LE20–LE60 ($3.60–$11/£1.85–£5.55). MC, V. Daily 8am–midnight.

Greek Club INTERNATIONAL   Perhaps the quintessential Cairo expat hangout, the Greek Club is a must for anyone who wants a sense of what this city used to be. Once a members-only establishment, the dwindling number of Greeks has forced the doors open to the public. Now the only vestige of its former restrictions is the entrance ticket you have to buy for a few Egyptian pounds at the door. In the winter months, dining and drinking (often more of the latter than the former) takes place in a high-ceilinged, high-windowed room that overlooks the bustling traffic of Midan Tahrir. As the weather heats up, the action moves out onto the open-air terrace at the back of the club.

Food is not complicated and very much average in quality. Start with some *saganaki* (fried cheese) and Greek salad, followed by *shish tawook* or deep-fried cala-mari. I tend to avoid the rubbery shish kebab and any desserts that may be on offer. Local beer and wine is available, and the lemonade is excellent. Stay away from the ouzo unless you want to wake up wondering what happened to your head.

It's worth noting that the opposition Ghad party has its headquarters upstairs in the same building, so if you find the place sealed off by riot police, don't worry—it's not for health violations. Just tell them where you're going, and they should let you through.

28 Mahmoud Bassyouni St., Midan Talat Harb. ⓒ 02/25750822. Appetizers LE10–LE20 ($1.80–$3.60/95p–£1.85); main courses LE20–LE40 ($3.60–$7.25/£1.85–£3.70). Cash only. Daily 8pm–late.

Le Bistro FRENCH   An odd little restaurant on the same street as Felfela (above), Le Bistro is easy to miss because it's located well below street level. Ambience is a lit-tle bit odd, with the blue paint and bright lights giving it the feeling that you're in an aquarium looking out, but it's extremely clean and service is very pleasant. Operated by the same management that does catering for the French cultural center, Le Bistro offers a Cairo take on French fare. Try the chicken in red wine sauce with a side of pasta and grilled vegetables, and order the profiteroles for dessert. Though this isn't Paris, it can be a welcome change.

8 Hoda Sharawy St. ⓒ 02/23927694. Appetizers and salads LE8–LE15 ($1.45–$2.70/75p–£1.40); main courses LE20–LE40 ($3.60–$7.25/£1.85–£3.70). Cash only. Daily 10am–11:30pm.

MOHANDISEEN
EXPENSIVE

Charwood's ⓖⓖ STEAK/PIZZA   I was the first customer on the first day of business for this cozy, upmarket eatery on Mohandiseen's biggest and least attractive street. The place is all about steak, and though they also serve some of the best pizza in town, it's the meat that keeps the customers coming back for more. All the meals start with an excellent mixed salad topped with a light dressing and fresh bread baked daily on the premises. My favorite entree is the tournedos, grilled rare, with a side of mustard sauce and a baked potato; cuts come from the best butchers in town. If red meat's not your thing, they also have excellent grilled shrimp. Dessert selections vary, but all tend to be good. The lemon tart, usually present on the menu, makes an excellent choice, followed by a *café correto*.

53 Gameat El Dowal El Arabia St. ⓒ 02/37490893 or 0121481344. Pizza LE40–LE60 ($7.25–$11/£3.70–£5.55); main courses LE70–LE120 ($13–$22/£6.50–£11). MC, V. Daily 1–10:30pm.

MODERATE

Abou Shakra EGYPTIAN   This is the place for meat-lovers looking to sample real Egyptian fare. If you're hungry, go for the charcoal-grilled kebab and *kofta* plate, which features a full kilo (2¼ pounds) of meat. If you're not quite in full caveman mode, though, go for the grilled pigeon or *ouzi* (grilled lamb). None of the main dishes comes with much on the side, so ask for some grilled vegetables or a rice *tagine*. Since this isn't really a tourist-oriented restaurant, Western stomachs should avoid the salad.

17 Gamat el Dawal al Arabeya. ⓒ 02/33444767 or 02/334419090. Appetizers LE3–LE8 (90¢–$1.45/45p–75p); main courses LE20–LE60 ($3.60–$11/£1.80–£5.40). MC, V. Daily noon–1am.

INEXPENSIVE

Gad ⓥalue EGYPTIAN   This inexpensive chain has outlets all over the city, with the Mohandiseen branch conveniently located on Gamat al Dawal al Arabeya, just past Midan Mustafa Mahmoud. The food and decor are simple, but this place will give you a great feel for the friendly hubbub of Cairo. Sample a typical Egyptian take-away sandwich of pita bread stuffed with *fuul* or deep-fried *tamaya* (chickpea paste).

47A Gamat el Dawal al Arabeya. ⓒ 02/37495206. Sandwiches LE5–LE10 (90¢–$1.80/45p–90p). Cash only. Daily 10am–midnight.

MAADI
EXPENSIVE

Bu Khoa ⓖ THAI   This is not only the best Thai restaurant in town, but one of the best places to eat in Cairo. The decor is nothing special, but the food is first-rate. Start with a spicy chicken salad followed by red or green curry or, one of my favorites, the chicken with basil leaves. Menu items change seasonally, but if you're here at the right time of year, I recommend the deep-fried calamari in coconut batter. Try the fried bananas with honey for dessert. Specials vary and are always worth a try.

151 Rd. 9. ⓒ 02/23580126. Reservations recommended. Appetizers LE6–LE28 ($1.10–$5.10/55p–£2.60); main courses LE28–LE150 ($5.10–$27/£2.60–£14). MC, V. Daily 6–11pm.

6 Outdoor Activities A to Z

GOLF   There are more opportunities than you might expect in and around Cairo to hit the links. Close to the airport, try the **JW Marriott,** Heliopolis (② **02/24115588,** 02/24118258, or 02/24091464 for the pro shop). The most historic course in Cairo is the one attached to **Mena House Oberoi,** Giza (② **02/33833222**), which opened in 1889. This 18-hole, par-68 course abuts the Giza plateau where the pyramids are located. Less romantic but more modern, the **Katameya Heights Golf and Tennis Resort,** Katameya (② **02/27580512** or 02/27580517), has a 27-hole, par-72 course in the middle of a wealthy housing estate on the southeastern edge of the city.

RIDING   There are few better ways to experience the space and atmosphere of the Giza plateau than on horseback, and riding is a popular pastime for visitors and expat residents of Cairo. It used to be that the crowded little village of Nazlet es-Samaan, around the feet of the Sphinx in Giza, was the place to go, and there is still a row of stables there. However, a recently built fence preventing access to the site around the pyramids has reduced the value of this excursion, and the place to go is now farther out on the ring road toward Saqqara. Take the Mounib Bridge south of Roda Island, and go straight on the highway until it ends, a little abruptly, in the desert. Here there will be signs to the **International Equestrian Center** (② **02/33820435** or 02/33820435), which is quite a large stable complex. They have quiet tree-lined driveways and around 100 horses in a series of stables. While they have a number of practice rings for instruction, most of their business is sending riders into the desert, which is just 100m (328 ft.) away. Expect to pay between LE70 and LE100 ($13–$18/£6.50–£9.25) per hour for a good horse and tack.

TENNIS   The two cement courts at the **Nile Hilton,** 1113 Corniche el Nil (② 25780444), are next to the swimming pool and bar, which may give you some ideas of what to do when you're done with your match. Rates are LE77 ($14/£7.15) per hour in the morning and LE88 ($16/£8.15) per hour in the afternoon with a pro; prices are reduced to LE39 ($7.10/£3.60) per hour in the morning and LE44 ($8/£4.05) per hour in the afternoon without a pro. The **Cairo Marriott**'s, 16 Saray el Gezira (② **02/27283000**) popular and well-maintained hard-surface courts are tucked into a discreet corner of the resort's 6-acre garden. Rates vary from LE30 to LE50 ($5.45–$9.10/£2.75–£4.60) per hour, depending on whether you're staying at the hotel. The Marriott's balcony and pool are close by for some post-game refreshment.

7 Shopping

Depending on what you're looking for, you've either come to the end of the Earth or its absolute center. Bedouin handicrafts, antiques, simple silver jewelry, and embroidered cloths are really what it's all about here. Though you can also find some good deals on attractive carpets, they're nothing like what's available in Damascus or Istanbul.

Keep in mind that in Cairo haggling is the norm. Most of places that I recommend below are, by Cairo standards, quite high end and offer fixed prices. In the shops and stalls of Khan al Khalili or Kheimeya, however, there is simply no such thing as a fixed price, and you should expect to be able to take 20% to 25% off the asking price with a little argument.

Expect stores to open around 10am and stay open at least until 7 or 8pm. Many stores still close for lunch between about 1 and 3pm, however.

BOOKS

Anglo American Bookstore   Located in the heart of downtown, the Anglo American is better for nonfiction than fiction, but always a pleasure to browse through. Saturday to Thursday 10am to 5pm. 165 Shar'ia Muhammad Farid. 🕐 **02/33914337.**

American University Cairo Bookstore   Well stocked and well run, the main branch is the best place in Cairo to look for nonfiction (though it has a pretty impressive popular-literature section), including guidebooks and background information on Egypt. It also stocks everything printed by the AUC Press, which includes an impressive list of Egyptian authors in translation (including, of course, Nobel laureate Naguib Mahfouz). When visiting the main branch, enter the AUC campus through the Mohamed Mahmoud entrance (across from McDonald's), and be prepared to leave some form of ID with security at the gate. The **Zamalek Branch,** 16 Mohamed Thakeb St. (🕐 **02/37397045**), is located in considerably smaller quarters underneath the AUC hostel, but is still a good place for general-interest books and guidebooks. Both stores are open Saturday to Thursday 9am to 6pm; the Zamalek branch is also open Friday 1 to 6pm. Main campus, American University in Cairo. 🕐 **02/27975900** or 02/27975370.

Azbekeya Book Market   This is a somewhat sanitized version of what began as an informal, and illegal, used-book market around the fence of the historic (and now very much reduced) Azbekeya gardens. After years of back and forth with the authorities, it was finally moved—not entirely willingly—to its current location in lines of uniform and rather soulless metal kiosks. Getting there can be a bit of an adventure, but well worth it if you want to see a downmarket part of Cairo while picking through a vast collection of books that range from discarded medical texts to moth-eaten leather-bound Rabelais. Bargaining can be pretty tough here, but you should generally see a drop in the asking price of around a quarter to a third.

The best way to get here is to take a cab to Midan Opera in downtown (make it clear that you do not want the place of the same name in Zamalek), and walk over to the western entrance of the Azbekeya Metro station. Walk through the station and out the other side. The entrance to the book section of the market, if you're standing with your back to the direction from which you've come, is in front of you and to the left. Open daily late morning till evening; fewer dealers on Sunday and Friday than during the rest of the week.

Diwan   Diwan may not have the biggest selection of books in the city (that would probably be the main branch of the AUC bookstore), but it certainly has one of the best. It carries not only current nonfiction, but a fair range of light literature and classics as well. It also stocks DVDs of old Egyptian movies with English subtitles. The store is well organized and a pleasure to browse through, and includes a small Wi-Fi–equipped cafe that serves excellent cookies. 159 26th of July St. 🕐 **02/27362598.**

FOOD & LIQUOR

Cairo is dotted with convenience stores *(ba'ala)* where you can pick up an amazing range of items from bottled water to fresh batteries to basic groceries.

Drinkies   This is the retail outlet for the Heineken-owned behemoth Al Ahram Beverage Company, which, protected by massive import duties, makes almost all the alcoholic beverages produced in Egypt. There are outlets all over town, but the most convenient outlet is on 26th of July Street in Zamalek across from the Cairo Marriott. It sells all the beers, wines, and hard liquor that are produced in Egypt (except for

Scheherazade wines, which are a little tricky to find outside restaurants), including Stella, Saqqara, and Meister beers; Omar Khayam, Grand Marquis, and Cape Bay wines; and a line of best-avoided hard liquor, which includes the undrinkable Ould Stag whiskey and some headache-inducing vodka. Its drop-off service (② **19330**) is pretty efficient, but you're going to have to slip something substantial to the concierge to accept the delivery (LE50–LE100/$9.10–$18/£4.60–£9.25). ② **19330.** Main locations: 5 Ibn el Nabih St., Zamalek; 55 Ramsis St., Heliopolis; 162A 26th of July St., Agouza; and 14 Talat Harb St., downtown.

Sekem Organic Food   With poor government regulation and a polluted environment, worries about what kind of chemicals are getting into the food chain are particularly germane in Cairo. Fortunately, Egypt is home to a burgeoning organic food industry, and though most of these products (which are quite expensive by local standards) are produced for export to Europe, enough end up in large local grocery chains (such as Metro). This store stocks a wide range of fruits, biscuits, and juices that can be packed as healthy sightseeing snacks, as well as basic grocery items for those with access to kitchens. 8 Ahmad Sabri St., Zamalek. ② **02/27382724.**

HANDICRAFTS, JEWELRY & DECOR

Akhtoun   Situated in a funky renovated old building behind Al Azhar Mosque, Akhtoun stocks an eclectic variety of furnishings and decor items in original and traditional designs. Cloth wall hangings decorated with calligraphic prints, metalwork lamps and lampshades, fabrics, and prints of old photographs are neatly arranged. There are no antiques here, but the new items are still very nice. Prices are fixed. 3 Mohamed Abdu St. ② **02/25147164.**

Egypt Craft Center   This is one of my favorite places to buy gifts in Egypt, because, apart from carrying top-quality handicrafts, the store is attached to a number of nongovernmental organizations (NGOs), which ensures that the profits from selling the goods go to the people who produced them. This is one of the best places in town to buy the now well-known Fayum pottery, and it's also an excellent source for locally woven cloth, clothes, scarves, and postcards. Prices are reasonable and fixed. 8–27 Yehia Ibrahim St., Zamalek. ② **02/27365123.**

El Ain Gallery   This is the place to come for elaborate high-end jewelry from Azza Fahmy, one of the first modern Egyptian jewelry designers to get international attention. Her work tends to be big, rich, warm, and studded with semiprecious stones, while at the same time recalling traditional Egyptian themes. The store also has furniture, lamps, and some metalwork. 73 el Hussein St., Dokki. ② **02/33381342.**

Kasr El Shook   Located in the middle of Zamalek, Kasr El Shook is a small but tightly packed silver store that sells everything from card holders to *shisha* pipes. Quality is excellent and prices are, with a little haggling, comparable to Khan El Khalili. The owner is an aficionado of classic Egyptian films, so ask him about the retired actors still living in the neighborhood. 11 Brazil St., Zamalek. ② **02/37372111.**

Khan Msr Toulon   Located directly across from the front entrance of the Ibn Tulun Mosque, this French-run store is a great spot to shop for a wide variety of handicrafts from around Egypt including glass, cloth, and furniture. The owner tends to leave town during the hottest months, so hours can be a little restricted during July and August. Tulun Bey Street, directly across from the Ibn Tulun Mosque. ② **02/33652227.**

Nagada This wonderful store brings some of the best handicrafts from around Egypt—including handmade fabrics from Upper Egypt, pottery from the Fayum, and jewelry and clothing from Cairo—into one spot. Daily 9:30am to 6pm. 13 Refa'a St., Dokki. ✆ 02/33748666. www.nagada.net.

Nomad This small, high-end handicraft boutique seems to be expanding into a chain. From its original Zamalek locations, it has now spread to the Nile Hilton and the Grand Hyatt hotels. The Zamalek locations remain my favorites, however. The smaller is located downstairs in the Cairo Marriott's mall, and the main branch is close by on the second floor of an old apartment building. For traditional silver designs and hand-woven crafts, this place is hard to beat. In the larger store, they also have a stock of Bedouin camel's-hair carpets and *kheimeya* embroidery. The atmosphere is relaxed (and air-conditioned) and helpful, and prices are fixed. 14 Saraya Al Gezira. ✆ 02/27361917.

Souk el Fustat This is a great shopping opportunity next to Old Cairo that brings together an excellent selection of the best handicrafts from around the country. It's named for the old city that once occupied the site. Smooth sandstone arches and shaded courtyards make browsing the 40 shops a civil, and even tranquil, experience. Shops offer everything from traditional *khameya* needlework, handmade lanterns (ask for Mohamed Amin—his work is famous), and furniture to Fayum pottery, soap, and rugs. Prices are more or less fixed, so don't expect to find the kind of cut-throat haggling here that you'll be subject to in Khan al Khalili, but there should be a little "wiggle room" in the price, especially if you're buying a number of different items. There is also a little cafeteria that's a great place to take a break on a hot day of sightseeing in Old Cairo. Daily 10am to 10pm. Across the road from the security checkpoint at the northern end of Old Cairo.

SPORTING GOODS

Alfa Market This place is not quite as good as Sports Mall in Mohandiseen (below), but it's definitely more convenient if you're staying in Zamalek. Alfa Market is pretty close to being a full-blown department store. Sporting goods—which range from sneakers to snorkeling gear—are on the top floor, with a whole world of housewares and general groceries on the first two floors. 4 el Malek el Afdal St., Zamalek. ✆ 02/27370801.

Sports Mall If you've just decided that you want to head for the Red Sea but arrived in Egypt without your snorkel and fins, or just want to get into the gym at the hotel, the Sports Mall in Mohandiseen can probably come up with everything that you need. It's definitely the best store in Cairo to shop for everything from tennis rackets to snorkels (which, by the way, you can actually rent at most resorts). 80 Shehab St., Mohandiseen. ✆ 02/33026432.

8 Cairo After Dark

ARTS

Cairo Opera House Built in the late 1980s as a Japanese development project, the new opera house in Zamalek replaced the 19th-century facility downtown that burned down in 1971. The Japanese government paid for an overhaul in 2003 that upgraded the sound system, and the building now hosts visiting international companies and its own Cairo Opera company. Performances are patchy, but it's a fun and reasonably priced night out. Reservations are taken 9 to 11am. Gezira, Zamalek. ✆ 02/27390114.

Mashrabeya Gallery   Located a few minutes' walk from the Townhouse (below), the Mashrabeya takes its name from the traditional woodwork screens on its windows. It's a cozy place with low ceilings and nice lighting. Shows are usually good and feature the work of both local and international artists. 8 Champollion St., Downtown. (C) **02/5784494.**

Townhouse Gallery 🖈🖈   The Townhouse Gallery is the most extensive and exciting gallery in Cairo. Between its main 3-story building and an echoing 650-sq.-m (around 7,000-sq.-ft.) addition across the alley that includes a book and art store, it is larger than any other privately run gallery, and shows feature an amazingly broad range of local and international talent. Saturday to Thursday 10am to 2pm and 6 to 9pm; Friday 6 to 9pm. Hussein el Me'mar Street, Downtown. (C) **02/25768086.** www.thetownhousegallery.com.

BARS & LOUNGES

After Eight 🖈   Tucked down an alley in the heart of downtown, After Eight is a stylish live-music venue for a funky, well-heeled set of expats and locals. It's also the only place I know of in the city that has a suit of armor as a doorman. Built into a renovated ground-floor location in an old building, it's not a small venue, but by 11 or 12 on a Thursday or Friday night, it's usually packed shoulder to shoulder. Definitely a place for dancing and drinking rather than a quiet beer and an intimate chat, After Eight still manages to maintain an upmarket atmosphere. No boisterous late-night tour of Cairo would be complete without stopping by. A minimum charge equivalent to a few local beers applies. 6 Kasr El Nil St. (C) **02/25740855** or 02/25765199.

The Bullseye   There's only one thing that you really need to know about the Bullseye, and it's either going to make the place irresistible or keep you away forever: karaoke, every Wednesday night from about 10pm until late. For the rest of the week the place returns to being a quiet back-street pub with dart boards and reasonably priced beer. 32 Jeddah St., Mohandiseen. (C) **02/37616888.**

Cairo Jazz Club 🖈🖈   Across the river from downtown, the Jazz Club is actually pretty easy to access from Zamalek. Offering a lively combination of DJs and live bands (though actual jazz is quite rare), it has been a staple of the late-night weekend circuit since the late 1990s. Decor is laid back and funky, and the food's pretty good, too. If you're going to eat, though, do it early—this place gets jammed by 9 or 10pm, and though you can still order, it's going to be a long, hungry wait. 197 26th of July St., Agouza. (C) **02/33459939.**

La Bodega 🖈🖈   This is one of my favorite Cairo bars, tucked into the back corner of the bistro side of this popular restaurant. It's one of the only places in town where you can pull up a stool and chat with the bartender, and it's subtly lit and quiet enough for conversation without being eerie. Bodega has a dark-wood bar and hanging drink glasses, solid brass railings, and a comfortable feel. You can also order dinner off the bistro menu and eat it in the bar, or move to a table when your food is ready. 157 26th of July St. (C) **02/27362188** or 02/27350543.

Latex   Situated under the Nile Hilton, Latex is as close as it gets in Cairo to a clubbing scene. It was renovated a few years back with expanses of white plastic, and features local and international DJs and a lot of house music. Like all popular Cairo nightspots, Latex can get very busy Thursday, Friday, and Saturday, and you should expect a bit of a wait on these nights. There's a patchily applied dress code and no-single-men policy, which means that you're best off showing up well-dressed with a member of the fair sex on your arm. 1113 Corniche El Nil, Cairo. (C) **02/25780444.** Minimum LE50 ($9.10/£4.60).

Coffee Culture

What the bar or pub is to Western culture, the *ahwa*, or coffee shop (*ahwa* means coffee in Cairene Arabic), is to Cairo. The *ahwa* is a place to relax at the end of the day or late into the night, meet friends, and watch passing strangers. The staples of the *ahwa* are *shisha* (the water pipe known elsewhere as narghile or hookah), coffee that comes strong and black in little cups, and *shai*, or tea, in glasses rather than cups. *Ahwas* are a ubiquitous presence in Cairo, from the neighborhood dive stuffed into the cranny of an old building to the well-cushioned opulence of a five-star hotel.

There are *ahwas* literally everywhere in Cairo, and I highly recommend taking a moment to stop randomly and grab a cup of coffee or a glass of tea. Watch the TV, read the newspaper, or find yourself in conversation with whoever's in the place that speaks a little English. This is the real Cairo.

One of my favorite places is right next door to the popular downtown Townhouse Art Gallery. This *ahwa* actually features an old car under a tarp that's used to store *shisha* tobacco. Attracting the after-exhibit crowd from the gallery, as well as a full roster of neighborhood locals, this place features a comfortable mix of classes and nationalities. Possibly the most famous *ahwa*, however, is **Fishawy** in Khan al Khalili. It's cramped, busy, and incredibly atmospheric, with high ceilings and enormous mirrors on the walls in which you can watch the whole bustling scene of the busy souk from several angles at once. The tea comes in ancient enamel pots, and you'll have a stream of vendors trying to sell you everything from Chinese Rolexes to incense. At night it's particularly attractive, as the alleys between the shuttered stores echo with the words and laughter of the off-work storekeepers.

Library This place isn't cheap, but it's very quiet and very civilized. Dark wood and rows of books lining the walls give this bar in the Four Seasons First Residence an air of subdued sophistication. Rumor has it that a few years ago this was Angelina Jolie's hangout in Cairo when she was taking a break from filming *Alexandria*. Give it a try, and you'll see why: efficient and discreet service, a relaxing ambience, and first-rate drinks. 35 Giza St., Giza. © 02/35731212.

Mojito Half-restaurant, half-lounge, Mojito is the perfect place to enjoy the Cairo sunset with a cocktail. It's perched on the roof of the Nile Hilton, with a view over bustling Midan Tahrir and downtown Cairo to the Muqatam hills in one direction and over the Nile to the pyramids in the other. Though service is slow enough to rule out any ideas you may have about a quick bite before kicking off somewhere else, the Spanish-themed menu is a pleasant accompaniment to the cocktails. Mojito serves its eponymous Cuban cocktail two-for-one daily between 5 and 7pm. 1113 Corniche el Nil. © 02/25780444.

Sangria Relaxed and funky decor and one of the few truly Nile-side locations in the city combine to make this one of my favorite spots in Cairo. Service can be slow, so this is a place for kicking back with some tasty snacks or a light dinner and a few glasses of sangria. Note that a sometimes restrictive door policy means that you should show up in smart-casual attire. Corniche el Nil, across from the Conrad Hotel. © 02/25796511.

9 The Gay & Lesbian Scene

Homosexuality is not actually illegal in Egypt, but gay men are subject to a significant level of officially sanctioned police harassment, detention, and, at times, abuse. The existence of lesbians, meanwhile, is simply not acknowledged. That said, there is a lively gay scene in Cairo and wide acceptance of recreational homosexual sex. An important point in understanding this peculiar contrast is that, though it is generally not acceptable to be gay—a high degree of homophobia is not merely acceptable but expected here—a man is not necessarily gay simply because he happens to have sex with men. The distinction lies in being either the active partner (not necessarily gay) or the passive partner (to whom the derogatory term *khawal* applies). Throw into this mix the highly repressive social mores concerning sex between unmarried people of the opposite sex, and you have a complicated, but active, situation.

One of the most surprising aspects of Egypt may be that you can expect the police to come on to you. This is particularly true of the tourist police around the pyramids in Giza. Don't be surprised if you're offered a ride on a camel—this will be a precursor to a short jaunt to the more discreet area between the Great Pyramid and the Sphinx. Army guards at embassies and government facilities will also try to attract your attention as you pass, and this is more often than not a sexual overture. Stop for a chat, and find out.

Popular civilian pickup spots include areas around the Kentucky Fried Chicken near Midan Tahrir, the Mubarak Metro station in Midan Ramses (sit on one of the benches by the mosque), Merryland Park in Misr Gedida, Horreya cafe in downtown, the Qasr el Aini Bridge (the one guarded by the large lions between downtown and Zamalek), and the Marriott Terrace. The health club at the Nile Hilton is also known to be quite gay friendly, as well as the Hammam al Nahhasin on Muizz din Allah Street across from Harat al Salihiyah in Khan al Khalili.

10 Day Trips from Cairo

GETTING THERE

BY CAR   The best way to get to sites within a few hours' drive of Cairo is to hire a car and driver for the day. Expect to pay LE250 to LE300 ($45–$55/£23–£28) for a half-day and LE400 to LE500 ($73–$91/£37–£46) for a full day. Long-term local driver Fathy Diab (© **0106525301**), if you can get him, is a great example of someone who knows the sites, speaks enough English to get by, and will take care of you for the day.

In a pinch it's also easy enough to pick up a black-and-white from the street for this purpose; just make sure you pick one that's in good condition and negotiate a price before you go. These could be a little cheaper than the prices above. The front desk of your hotel will also be a good source.

The last resort is the "limousine car" desk in the hotel lobby. The only guarantee you have there is that they will be the most expensive option.

BUS TOUR   Many of the sites listed below (Saqqara, Memphis, and Wadi Natrun) are popular, well visited, and served by well-organized bus tours that are available through the front desks of most tourist-class hotels in the city. If you don't fancy your options there, contact the listed travel agents.

Camel Market   The Birqash camel market, about an hour's drive from town, is best visited on early Friday morning (try to get there before 9am), which is when the business of buying and selling camels takes place. There is a constant stream of photo opportunities, with men yelling and waving their long *shooma* walking sticks and camels bellowing and jostling for space. Most of the animals have arrived via the ancient *dar al arbayeen* (the 40-Day Road) from Sudan. Though there is less action during the week, a stroll amongst the pens looking at the animals, most bearing elaborate brands identifying their owners, and chatting with dealers is also an atmospheric and interesting experience. Plan on taking half a day to venture out and back, and be sure to take the time to enjoy the view of the countryside along the way. The taxi ride there should cost about LE100 ($18/£9.25).

For years, entrance to the market was free, despite what the enterprising lads around the entrance might have said to scam a few LE from you, but recently the ramshackle compound has acquired a uniformed guard with a ticket book. I paid LE5 (90¢/45p) to get in.

Blrqash. LE5 (90¢/45p). Daily dawn–dusk.

Dahshur (the Bent Pyramid) & the North Pyramid 𝄐𝄐   If it's possible to have favorite pyramids, then these are mine. Defining exactly why is a little difficult. This isn't a big tourist site—the tour buses don't stop here, and you're not going to get mobbed by touts as you get out of the car. This is probably a big part of it. The two pyramids here, both of which were built for Sneferu (2613–2598 B.C.), sit a little back from the edge of the valley, and you really get a feel for the desert. The air is clean, hot, and dusty, and the sky goes west forever.

In terms of historical period, these pyramids come after the relatively crude step, or *mastaba,* pyramid at Saqqara, and before the fully developed Great Pyramid of Giza, which accounts for the odd aspect of the **Bent Pyramid,** from which it gets its name: about halfway up, the sides take on a dramatically new angle. The theory is that the builders started at one angle (about 55°), but realized midway that it just wasn't going to work and made a dramatic alteration (to about 44°). When it came to the **North Pyramid,** the builders used a more conservative 43° angle of attack, and made it all the way to the peak without having to make a change. A steep 30m (98-ft.) climb gets you to the entrance of a low-ceilinged 70m (230-ft.) passage that slopes steeply back down into the North Pyramid (if you've got a bad back or suffer from claustrophobia, head back to the car at this point). The high-ceilinged chambers in the depths of the structure are worth the scramble, however.

Dahshur. ℂ 02/33838823. Admission LE20 ($3.65/£1.85). Winter daily 8am–4pm; summer 8am–5pm.

Memphis   Not much is left of this city, despite its early importance as a national, and later provincial, capital. Constructed on the banks of the river around 3100 B.C., the site was not abandoned until the Arab invasion nearly 4,000 years later. The ruins aren't much to look at, but there is a museum featuring a 13m (43-ft.) figure of Ramses II, which is incredibly big, and an alabaster Sphinx in the garden of sculpture. If you're pressed for time, Dahshur and the necropolis at Saqqara are far more impressive, and this should be lower on your priority list.

Memphis. Admission LE25 ($4.55/£2.30). Winter daily 8am–4pm; summer 8am–5pm.

Saqqara 𝄐𝄐   The site of this huge necropolis, which was attached to the ancient city of Memphis, includes a massive step pyramid. Built by a prolific innovator named Imhotep for the 3rd-dynasty king Dsojer (2667–2648 B.C.), the structure represents a number of important developments in engineering without which the later, and now more famous, pyramids in Giza would not have been possible.

The complex also includes a number of other tombs, with spectacular wall paintings and carvings, and the **Serapeum,** where the Apis bulls were interred. These bulls were considered to be the living manifestation of the god Ptah (who you will also see in wall carvings as a man wearing a tight-fitting cap and grasping an ankh), and were mummified and buried with all due ceremony.

Depending on the depth of your interest in Egyptology, you will need between an hour to half a day at the Saqqara site. There is a new **museum** just inside the main entrance. Though documentation is of the same unfortunate standard as most Egyptian facilities, this museum is worth a visit for orientation before you proceed up the hill to the site itself. If you're lucky enough to be here on a day with some clouds, the light on Djoser's pyramid in the hour or so leading up to sunset is spectacular. While you wander the site, you'll inevitably be approached by men who will ask if you want to see some extra tombs or sites. It is generally worth saying yes and paying about LE2 to LE5 (35¢–90¢/20p–45p).

Photography is theoretically restricted inside the tombs, but in practice the guards will accept a couple of pounds to let you do whatever you want, and the only real limit to what you do inside the tombs is your reluctance to damage irreplaceable ancient historical art with your flash or by touch.

Saqqara. (C) **02/33838823.** Admission LE35 ($6.35/£3.24) adults, LE20 ($3.65/£1.85) students. Winter daily 8am–4pm; summer 8am–5pm.

Wadi Natrun   In many ways the historical seat of Coptic Christianity, this little depression on the edge of the Nile Delta is about 100km (60 miles) from the city and makes a great day trip from Cairo. With four thriving monasteries dating from before the Muslim conquest, you can get a real taste here of a now much-ignored period of Egyptian history.

The name of the valley (*wadi* literally means "valley" in Arabic) comes from *natron* (as it is now known), a naturally occurring salt that can be collected here and was used by the ancient Egyptians in the mummification process. By the 6th century, however, the valley was best known as the monastic center of Christian Egypt. It had a thriving community of ascetic Christians and contained some of their most important monuments. As you can imagine, the community has had its ups and its downs since then, but though the current number of monasteries is substantially below the more than 100 that were reported in the 14th century, it has enjoyed a real resurgence over the last 20 years. What you'll find today is a viable, committed Christian community living out forms of worship that were developed at the very beginning of the religion's history.

Always call the Office of the Patriarch ((C) **02/25900218**) before you go to check that the monasteries are open (they close to visitors frequently for religious holidays) and to arrange any necessary permissions. Overnight stays at the monasteries can often be arranged through the Office of the Patriarch as well. For these purposes, Deir al Baramus is the most comfortable and should be your first choice.

Wadi Rayan 🎖🎖   Wadi Rayan is a depression to the south of Fayum Oasis that, though best visited from Fayum, is also very doable in a day from Cairo. Expect the drive out there to take no more than 2 hours (see below).

FAYUM OASIS

This is the closest of the Western Desert oases, and if you want to get a taste of the desert and a feel for the oases, but you don't have time to get out to Bahareya or Siwa, this is a good way to do it. Avoid Fayum City as much as possible—it's dirty and crowded—and stay outside of town at one of the two places listed below. I also recommend picking up a copy of Neil Hewison's *The Fayoum: History and Guide* (available at the AUC bookstore and Diwan) if you want more information than is provided below. You can easily do Fayum in a day from Cairo, but a relaxed visit to the area that includes a shopping trip to Tunis and a visit to Wadi Rayan, as well as a bit of lounging, could warrant an overnight stay.

WHAT TO SEE & DO

Tunis Pottery   The Fayum Oasis has a long tradition of creating pottery, and about 15 years ago, two Swiss potters, Evelyne Porret and Michel Pastore, built the Fayoum Pottery School in the small town of Tunis above the western end of Lake Qaroun to promote local skills. The center has put Tunis on the map and has spawned an industry. The town's narrow, dusty streets are now alive with more than half a dozen studios, each selling items from plates to sculptures. You could easily spend an afternoon wandering from studio to studio. The two must-see locations are the **Fayoum Pottery School** (© 084/6820405; daily 10am–8pm) and the studio of **Ahmed Abu Zeid** (ask for directions at the school, or anywhere in the village).

Wadi Rayan 🌟🌟   Wadi Rayan is a depression in the desert to the southeast of Fayum Oasis (*wadi* literally means "valley" in Arabic) that was made a protected area in 1989. Part of it (see Wadi Hitan, below) was then declared a World Heritage Site in 2005. Wadi Rayan contains a pair of new lakes, which were actually created by a mismanaged government drainage project in the 1970s. Though just a 30-minute drive from Fayum Oasis, the lakes are surrounded on all sides by golden sand dunes and new growth that houses both indigenous and migratory birds; two bird-watching sites have been established on the southeastern side of the lake.

Though it covers around 1,800 sq. km (around 700 sq. miles), two areas are particularly worth visiting in Wadi Rayan. The **waterfalls** aren't of the Niagara variety, but what makes them worth visiting is the desert setting; they're nestled into the thick reeds between the two lakes and face the beach of the lower. They're a great place for a swim, but there tends to be an audience of young local males. Still, it's a good place to stop for a picnic lunch before moving on.

Wadi al Hitan, or "Valley of the Whales," is named for the ancient whale skeletons that were found on the surface of the desert. These spectacular, 40-million-year-old remains are reminders that the entire area was once covered by a giant inland sea. Declared a World Heritage Site in an effort to protect the fossils, the Orientation Center is accessible by car along a rough, unpaved 34km (21-mile) road. Be prepared to hike from there, however.

© 084/6830535. Admission LE17 ($3/£1.50) per person, LE5 (90¢/45p) per car, LE10 ($1.80/95p) per person for overnight camping. Daily 11am–3:30pm.

Waterwheels *Overrated*   The water-driven waterwheels (*al sawaai* in Arabic) used in the Fayum Oasis to lift irrigation water into the old canals are much touted in any promotional literature about the area, but I'm a little more cautious about them. They are unique in Egypt (no other area provides the kind of fast-running streams needed to power them) and historically significant (they were introduced by Roman engineers, and the design has not been significantly altered since). Their setting, however, leaves a lot to be desired, and unless you find the wheels themselves to be interesting, you're going to be disappointed.

The most easily accessible and largest of the wheels still in operation are the four in the center of the city. I would recommend avoiding these, however—the square is garbage-strewn and crowded, and the police are rude and intrusive. There are seven more, however, on the canal named *Bahr Sanussi* that runs north out of the city. You can follow the canal on foot or by car until the houses become less dense, and you'll come upon the wheels after 10 to 20 minutes (depending how often you get lost). They are big, black, and shiny, and their wood axles make a loud groaning noise as they turn. The setting, which is fairly pastoral, is also unfortunately squalid, and your enjoyment will depend largely on your tolerance for mud and being the center of attention among crowds of semi-naked teenage boys who come to frolic in the canal.

WHERE TO STAY

Hotel Auberge Fayoum   Originally built in 1937 for King Farouk, the Auberge was run as a hotel by the Oberoi chain before it drifted into the 1980s and 1990s as an increasingly seedy and run-down independent. Recently reopened under the Helnan group, it hasn't exactly been restored to its former glory (Winston Churchill once stayed here), but it's certainly looking a lot better. It's located on the edge of the lake, flanked on either side by beaches, and the view is lovely. Rooms have little character, and while the dining room, with its wood-beamed ceiling, evokes the prewar hunting lodge feeling, you'll have no doubt that you're staying in a chain hotel.

Karoun Lake. (?) **084/6981300.** www.helnan.com. 70 units. LE605 ($110/£55) double. MC, V. **Amenities:** Restaurant; bar; pool; Wi-Fi. *In room:* Minibar, safe, Internet.

Zad al Musafr Ecolodge   This relaxed little place, built among the palm trees in the fields below the town of Tunis, may be a little rough around the edges for some. Built around a grassy courtyard, most of the rooms are of the "bathroom down the hall" variety, but in this case, the hall is outside, and the bathrooms are rather big and comfortless. The most comfortable accommodations are the four cottage suites, essentially double rooms with their own bathrooms. These are charming and rustic, tucked into the jasmine of the garden, with reed ceilings and plaster walls. Bedclothes are good-quality cotton, and the bathrooms are sufficient.

The pool is small but perfect for a dip in the warmth of the Fayum afternoon. They also have a number of well-fed and nicely behaved horses. Riding is probably the best way to see the area around Tunis and the lake, and it'll cost you about LE35 ($6.35/£3.25) per hour.

The restaurant is, apart from the Helnan, which is a good 20km (12 miles) down the road, the only place to eat on this side of the Fayum. The menu is basic—meat and chicken cooked over a wood grill—but tasty, and reckon on the food taking at least 30 minutes to get to your table.

The lodge is within easy walking distance of the long sandy beach on the edge of the lake and Tunis. The journey to the latter is a short climb up a bath that runs next to a series of private gardens; you'll find yourself in the back of the village and ready to do a tour of the various potters selling their wares.

Tunis. (?) **084/6820180** or **010/6395590.** www.zadalmosaferecolodge.com. 12 units. LE60 ($11/£5.55) double, LE120 ($22/£11) villa. **Amenities:** Restaurant; pool. *In room:* No phone.

Alexandria & the North Coast

Egypt's northern border is a 1,000km (600-mile) stretch of Mediterranean coastline, bracketed between the contentious border between the Sinai and the Gaza strip at the eastern end, and the border with Libya to the west.

This has historically been Egypt's interface with the Western world. The country's own rulers ignored the sea on the whole, seeming to prefer the calmer, and more easily defended, river valley and its wide, fecund delta. The coast was the scene of a number of dramatic invasions, however, and Alexandria, often called "Egypt's second city," still bears the name of the 25-year-old Macedonian who led the most famous and lasting of the early incursions—Alexander the Great. The Ptolemaic dynasty that he left behind ran the country until the Romans took it from them in the 1st century A.D., and it wasn't until the Arab conquest of the 7th century that Egypt's center of political gravity returned again to the vicinity of Cairo.

Fourteen centuries later, it was the French who were invading, passing through Alexandria's decrepit defenses on the way to Cairo, where Napoleon's infantry slaughtered the Mamluke cavalry and effectively put a permanent end to Egypt's independence. Though the French were expelled by the British within a couple of years, at least one aspect of their legacy remains vital to the Egyptian economy.

Napoleon brought with him a team of scientists who busied themselves with everything Egyptian—observing and recording everything that they could get at in the short time that they had the run of the country. In a coastal town 30km (18 miles) east of Alexandria named Rashid, the occupiers were rebuilding a fort when they found a large black stone carved with a decree from a 2nd century B.C. ruler, Ptolemy V. Its contents are unexciting—taxes and temples—but it was written in three different languages (demotic, hieroglyphs, and Greek), and this allowed scholars to decipher previously unreadable inscriptions on the monumental temples and tombs that were being unearthed in Upper Egypt. Today, Europeans and North Americans continue to flood into Egypt to see these monuments and read the inscriptions that would have remained mysterious if not for the rock, which became known as the Rosetta Stone.

Alexandria, which is almost exactly in the center of the coast, is an exciting city with a rich heritage of Roman ruins, including some of the most spectacular mosaics in the world, and European influences to explore. Damietta *(Damiyut)* and Rosetta *(Rashid)* are both worthwhile day trips, and along the coast in the direction of Libya there are the remains of a Ptolemaic temple close to the highway and Alamein, where the dramatic World War II confrontation between the dug-in Allied forces and attacking German tanks took place in 1942. The last town of any significance before Libya, Marsa Matruh has some unique diving opportunities and a lovely beach.

On the north coast, as with much of Egypt, you have to develop the trick of

Northern Egypt

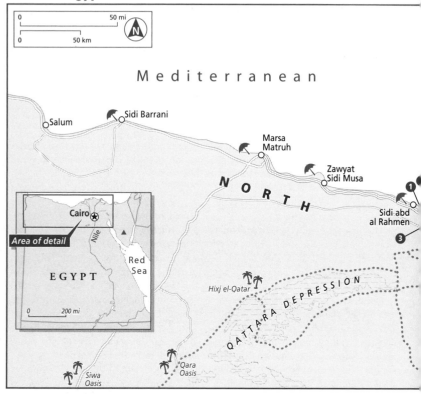

seeing through a thick layer of urban sprawl that has taken place in the last 30 or 40 years, as well as past the decay that has accompanied it. Many miles of once pristine beach both east and west of Alexandria have been obscured by swathes of cheap concrete "holiday village" development, and the city itself has swelled from a population of 1 million in the 1960s to almost 4 times that today, with some of the growth going into new, unplanned neighborhoods and the rest being absorbed into the neglected housing of Alexandria's old quarters. Against this backdrop, the historic treasures of the city and the surrounding towns shine, but you have to know where and how to look to pick them out.

1 Alexandria

Alexandria, named for 25-year-old Alexander the Great, who added the area to his conquests in 332 B.C., has had its fair share of abuse. A small but vibrant and cosmopolitan city in the 19th century and the first half of the 20th, Alex was dealt a heavy blow by the 1952 military takeover led by Gamal Abdel Nasser, which resulted in the mass exodus of the Greek and Jewish communities. Since then, the population of the city has expanded dramatically, and much of its character has been buried under a steady spread of charmless cement buildings thrown up to house new inhabitants.

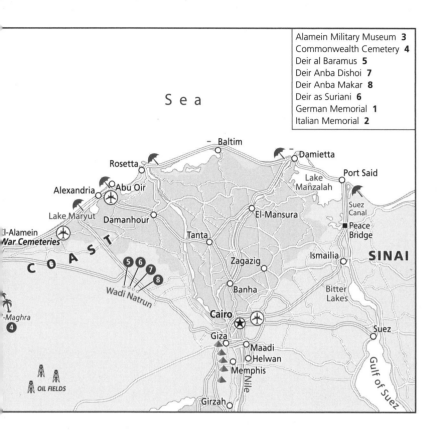

Alamein Military Museum **3**
Commonwealth Cemetery **4**
Deir al Baramus **5**
Deir Anba Dishoi **7**
Deir Anba Makar **8**
Deir as Suriani **6**
German Memorial **1**
Italian Memorial **2**

Pay too much attention to what's wrong with the city, however, and you'll miss its charm. Coffee shops and restaurants such as Trianon, Pastroudis, and Delices have been lovingly maintained over the years, and hotels such as the Metropole offer a step back to a time when the city was small and beautiful.

Perhaps the most amazing thing about Alexandria is not what you can see above ground, but what lies beneath. Even while admiring the remnants of the 19th-century Mediterranean city, it's all too easy to forget that a few meters down lie untouched and unexplored ruins of a Ptolemaic and Roman city. The mosaics that have been unearthed at the Kom el Dikka site, as well as underneath the stunning modern new Bibliotheca Alexandrina, are not to be missed. To get a sense of the city as it was (or was imagined to be) in its glory days, rent famous Egyptian director Youssef Chahine's 1977 *Alexandrie Pourquoi,* or read Lawrence Durrell's wildly romantic tome, "The Alexandria Quartet."

ESSENTIALS
ORIENTATION
Alexandria is a long, narrow city spread out over a 25km (15-mile) strip of coastline, with no part of it much more than 5km (3 miles) from the sea. At the western end of the city lies the harbor, where the famous lighthouse once stood (now the site of the

Alexandria

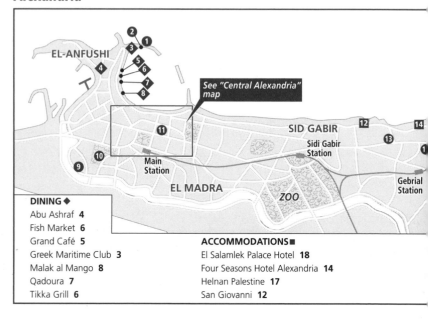

DINING ◆
Abu Ashraf **4**
Fish Market **6**
Grand Café **5**
Greek Maritime Club **3**
Malak al Mango **8**
Qadoura **7**
Tikka Grill **6**

ACCOMMODATIONS ■
El Salamlek Palace Hotel **18**
Four Seasons Hotel Alexandria **14**
Helnan Palestine **17**
San Giovanni **12**

Qaitbey Fort); at the eastern end are the Montaza Gardens, once a royal hunting ground and now the site of the Helnan Palestine and Salamlek hotels. The two are rather unfortunately linked by an enormous road that runs where you would expect the beach to be and cuts the city off from the sea. Known as the Corniche, it represents one of the biggest failures of urban planning in Egypt. It's almost completely unbroken by any traffic lights, and only a few of the promised pedestrian tunnels have been built. Locals, let alone tourists, cross with trepidation. Fortunately, there is little to draw you over—the beaches are narrow, rocky, and, in the summer, crowded.

The most interesting area of the city, which contains almost all the sites worth visiting, is within a 2km (1¼-mile) radius from Saad Zagloul Square. Facing south here, your back to the Corniche and the sea, the eastern harbor is spread out behind you. To your left (east), after about 1km (⅔ mile), is the new Bibliotheca Alexandrina. To your right is the long curve of the harbor that will take you, after 2km (1¼ miles), out to Qaitbey Fort. Ahead of you is the neighborhood of Raml (or more properly *Mahatet al Raml,* which means "Raml Station" and refers to the tram station that you might be able to see just over to the left side of the square), and beyond that (no more than 0.5km/⅓ mile) is Attarine. Connecting the two areas is the north-south Al Nabi Daniel Street, which was once known, 2,000 years ago, as the Street of Soma.

The major street that runs through Attarine is the east-west Horreya Street (granted, it becomes Fouad Street at some point), which used to be called the Canopic Way. Soma and Canopic Way were the two main axes of the grid-patterned Ptolemaic city.

Be careful where you step on either of these streets: The ancient sewers run underneath, and local stories abound of people who have disappeared through holes in the street never to be seen again.

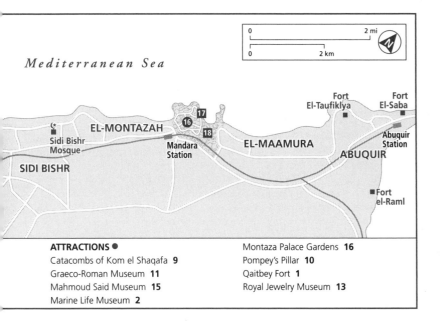

ATTRACTIONS ●

Catacombs of Kom el Shaqafa **9**

Graeco-Roman Museum **11**

Mahmoud Said Museum **15**

Marine Life Museum **2**

Montaza Palace Gardens **16**

Pompey's Pillar **10**

Qaitbey Fort **1**

Royal Jewelry Museum **13**

East of Al Nabi Daniel Street is the neighborhood of Kom el Dikka, which literally means "hill of rubble." If you came from Cairo by train, you likely arrived at the Misr Train Station and came to Raml by taxi, descending over this hill of old, mostly Roman, building materials. If you walk east from Al Nabi Daniel along Horreya, the old Roman site of **Kom el Dikka** will be on your right. You will, however, be around the back and have to walk almost all the way up the hill to the train station to find the entrance. The Graeco-Roman Museum also lies to the east of Al Nabi Daniel.

To the west of Al Nabi Daniel is the antiques shopping district of Attarine, followed by Ahmed Orabi and Tahrir squares. Tahrir Square is generally known as Mansheya Square, and there is a large statue of Mohamed Ali on a horse here.

Long and narrow, Ahmed Orabi Square is around 0.7km (½ mile) southwest from Saad Zagloul Square, but it stands at the edge of another universe. If you go north(ish) on Fransa Street, you'll find yourself embraced by narrow alleys and masses of tightly packed stores and stalls selling, according to the area, just about everything from buttons and cloth to fish and vegetables. As you make your way up this street, you're heading into a neighborhood called Gumrak, which means "customs" and is named for the Customs facilities at the dock, which are close to here. You're heading out onto the western arm of the bay, and you'll ultimately arrive (if you maintain your orientation) at the end of the headland where the Qaitbey Fort is located.

The Kom el Shaqafa Catacombs and Pompey's Pillar lie to the southwest of Ahmed Orabi Square.

GETTING THERE

BY TRAIN There are regular and fairly comfortable trains to Alexandria from downtown Cairo. They take about 2½ to 3½ hours depending on how many stops they make and the usual range of exigencies that afflict everything in Egypt. The

The Lighthouse

From the sea, the Egyptian coastline looks like a flat land, devoid of hills that could be used as landmarks. One can imagine that before the age of coastal towns and GPS, it must have presented navigational challenges. That is, until Ptolemy II built a massive tower on a small island at the entrance to the Alexandria harbor.

One of the fabled Seven Wonders of the World, the Lighthouse of Alexandria was finished around 265 B.C., having been under construction for 15 years. Towering 152m (500 ft.), it was constructed in three sections starting with a square base and ending in a conical peak, which was topped off with a massive statue of Poseidon. Though it didn't acquire its light for another 3 centuries, it would have been visible for miles out to sea, offering pilots a point of reference as they made their way up and down the coast and into the harbor.

Skeptics question the lighthouse's place on the world wonders list (which was compiled in Alexandria), but the tower was undoubtedly ahead of its time. It's still not clear, though, how the light was made to shine (there's a theory that there were oil lamps whose light was shone out to sea by burnished metal reflectors), and there are even indications that it may have been equipped with some kind of telescope.

The lighthouse stood for more than 1,500 years, collapsing after it was heavily damaged by an earthquake in 1303. The island on which it stood is now connected to the shore by a breakwater and is the site of the Qaitbey Fort.

1960s rolling stock isn't as clean as it could be, but the atmosphere and view of the Delta countryside make me a big fan of this journey.

Trains leave Ramsis Station between 6am and 10:30pm. Trains are named either French, Turbina, or Spanish. First-class tickets range from LE35 ($6.35/£3.20) on the French, which stops three times, to LE46 ($8.35/£4.25) for the nonstop Turbina and Spanish trains. Second-class tickets are LE19 to LE29 ($3.45–$5.25/£1.75–£2.70). At the price, there's no point in riding second class, where the seats are narrower, the floor a little grungier, and the air-conditioning not so reliable. Your ticket has a car and seat number on it, and if you feel like having someone carry your bags to your seat, a LE2 (35¢/20p) tip should adequately cover this convenience.

There is a food and beverage cart on the trains, but I would avoid the food and beware the scam in which the waiter demands payment immediately—he should come around 30 minutes or so before arrival and tally up your total. Drinks are around LE2 (35¢/20p) and sandwiches LE5 to LE7 (90¢–$1.25/45p–65p).

BY PLANE   EgyptAir's internal flights go both to the old, convenient Al Nozha Airport and the newer Borg al Arab Airport. Prices are the same (around LE460/$84/£43) round-trip, but while Al Nozha is a short taxi ride into town, Borg Al Arab is about 30 minutes to an hour away via shuttle or taxi. The downside of Nozha is that the facilities are older and the runway very short, resulting in some quite abrupt landings.

BY CAR   Arriving by car from Cairo is very simple, as the main Cairo–Alexandria desert road takes you past Lake Maryut on the south side of Alexandria and feeds into the city's main arteries. Go directly for the Al Misr Train Station or, better, to Saad Zagloul Square and ask at the tourist information office for a map. A number of excellent maps can also be purchased at bookstores around Saad Zagloul Square.

BY BUS   Unfortunately the bus station has recently been moved from its old, and very convenient, location in Sidi Gaber to Al Mawkaf el Gedid, which is near the beginning of the Cairo–Alexandria desert road. Expect to pay LE15 to LE20 ($2.70–$3.60/£1.40–£1.85) for a taxi into town (about 30 min.).

Southbound buses run every hour to Cairo from Alex between 5am and 1:30am. They terminate either at the Turgoman bus station (LE23/$4.20/£2.10) or the airport (LE35/$6.35/£3.25). The first bus to Marsa Matruh leaves at 7am and the last one goes at 1am. The tickets cost LE35 ($6.35/£3.25) for the air-conditioned and toilet- and video-equipped bus. It's about a 3-hour ride. Buses run every 30 minutes to Damiatta for LE10 ($1.80/95p) and to Port Saied from 6am to 8pm at regular intervals for LE25 ($4.55/£2.30). The West Delta office (✆ **03/4809685**) is located on Saad Zagloul Square between the Hotel Sofitel Cecil Alexandria and the tourist information office.

GETTING AROUND

BY TAXI   Other than the color—Alexandria taxis are black-and-yellow instead of black-and-white—taxis work the same way here as in Cairo, though drivers do tend to be a bit more aggressive about demanding exorbitant fees from foreigners. The table below will provide you with some guidance. Amounts are approximate, so don't be afraid to bargain before you get in.

Taxi Fares in/around Alexandria (in Egyptian Pounds)

	Saad Zagloul Square	Qaitbey	Pompey's Pillar
Saad Zagloul Square	X	LE10	LE10
Qaitbey Fort	LE10	X	LE6–LE8
Pompey's Pillar	LE10	LE6–LE8	X
Kom el Shaqafa	LE10	LE6–LE8	LE3
Montaza Gardens	LE20	LE25	LE25

	Kom el Shaqafa	Montaza Gardens
Saad Zagloul Square	LE10	LE20
Qaitbey Fort	LE6–LE8	LE25
Pompey's Pillar	LE3	LE25
Kom el Shaqafa	X	LE25
Montaza Gardens	LE25	X

	Misr Train Station	Four Seasons
Saad Zagloul Square	LE5	LE10
Qaitbey Fort	LE10–LE12	LE20
Pompey's Pillar	LE8–LE10	LE25
Kom el Shaqafa	LE7–LE9	LE25
Montaza Gardens	LE25	LE15

BY TRAM   Alexandria has some beautiful old trams rattling up and down its streets. Unfortunately the whole system is extremely run down, slow, and not very clean. It can also be very crowded. If you're a fan of such things and understand their romance, try a midmorning trip to Pompey's Pillar or, to the east of Raml Station, the Said Mahmoud Museum; otherwise you're better off in a taxi.

The main hub for tourist purposes is at Raml Station, on the edge of Saad Zagloul Square. The most useful line is no. 2, which runs east to west. Tickets are LE0.25 (5¢/2p) and are purchased onboard from the conductor. During busy periods, the front car is reserved for women.

BY FOOT   As long as it's not raining, Alexandria is a fine city for walking. In fact, your feet are probably the best way to navigate the back streets and alleyways around Raml or the souks up Fransa Street. I wouldn't recommend trying to make much distance up and down the Corniche, however—the level of traffic and (in the summer) the level of hassle will quickly overwhelm your sense of fun.

BY CAR   A car is the most comfortable way to see the city while avoiding the hassles of negotiating with taxis. A car with a driver should cost around LE250 to LE350 ($45–$64/£23–£32) inside the city and around LE400 to LE500 ($73–$91/£37–£46) outside the city, while a rental will set you back LE165 to LE275 ($30–$50/£15–£25) per day plus mileage. (Most companies offer 100km/60 miles free and charge LE1/20¢/10p per km after that.) Try **Avis,** Hotel Sofitel Cecil Alexandria lobby, Saad Zagloul Square (© **03/6857400**), or **Francis Brothers Travel** (© **012/3108173;** francisbrostravel@yahoo.com), a small family business run by a pair of brothers, both of whom speak fluent English. They have a small bus and a car that can be used across the north coast as well as the Sinai.

TOURIST INFORMATION

Alexandria is blessed with one of the most efficient and helpful tourist information offices in Egypt, tucked away at the edge of **Saad Zagloul Square** in Raml (© **03/4851556;** daily 8:30am–6pm). It may not look too promising, but the ladies know everything they should about the city, and then some. Stop at the office in **Al Nozha Airport,** to the left as you are about to exit the main doors (© **03/4202021;** daily 9am–5pm), before you head downtown, and anything they can't answer, the main office in Raml probably can. There's an office at the far end of **Al Misr Railway Station,** where the Cairo trains arrive (© **03/4925985;** daily 9am–5pm), but it's less helpful than the main office in Saad Zagloul Square.

MAPS & BOOKS   The small bookstore in the **Hotel Sofitel Cecil lobby,** Saad Zagloul Square (© **03/4877173**), has a small-but-good selection of books about Alexandria and some maps. **Alaa Eldin Bookstore,** 63 Sofia Zagloul St. (© **03/4876186**), is a small store a few steps up the street from Saad Zagloul Square and is crammed with books in Arabic; it's also a good source for maps. The owner speaks English. **Monshat Al Maaref,** 44 Saad Zagloul St. (© **03/4873303**), just off Saad Zagloul Square, stocks English books, including some guidebooks, in the back to the left; the staff are very friendly and helpful. **Al Ahram Bookshop,** 10 Horreya St., Raml (© **03/4848563**), has a small collection of English-language books, including some guidebooks, and maps; the staff speak no perceptible English, however.

VISA EXTENSIONS   Take at least one passport photo and a copy of your passport to the **visa extension office,** 28 Talaat Harb St., which is open 8am to 1pm. The earlier you get there, the better, and don't expect to be able to apply after noon.

E-MAIL & INTERNET   Staying connected in Alexandria is a lot easier than it was even a couple of years ago. Around Saad Zaghloul Square, there is now a thick scattering of Internet cafes. Expect to pay LE5 to LE 10 an hour (90¢–$1.80/45p–90p) for good bandwidth and a clean, decent place. **Pharos Net,** 25 Horreya St. (✆ 03/4976405), which has a dozen PCs with clean, modern furniture and excellent bandwidth. My personal favorite is **MG Net,** 10 Shohoda St. (✆ 03/4806981), which has 12 PCs stuffed into a little corner shop. Staff are friendly, and the bandwidth is excellent.

WHAT TO SEE & DO

Bibliotheca Alexandrina   This is one of those big, well-intentioned projects that nobody really thought through. It is, however, well worth visiting both for the architecture and for the museum in the basement, which contains a sampling of Roman artifacts that were saved from destruction as the foundations of the library were being excavated. The original idea was to re-create the Ptolemaic Library of Alexandria, which is said to have been the biggest and most comprehensive library of its time.

Located on a curve in the main seaside road a couple of kilometers from Saad Zaghloul Square, the Norwegian-designed building is simply spectacular. The front slopes gently into a wide pool of water, with obvious reference to the coastline of Egypt. From the street outside, the water is at eye level and the effect is intense, and a flying pier structure juts out from the second floor.

Inside the **library,** the best perspective is from above, at the level of the entranceway. From here you get a marvelous sense of space, which extends to the stacks, mostly empty due to a combination of censorship and lack of funding. The irony here is that the Bibliotheca is the mirror site for the Internet Archive project, which attempts to download and archive the entire contents of the Internet.

The **Antiquities Museum** in the basement isn't very good—it feels like an afterthought—but it has two exquisite mosaics as well as some lovely Mamluke glass and Coptic icons. The documentation is in broken English and difficult to follow.

The Bibliotheca also hosts traveling international exhibits from time to time, and it's worth checking its website if you're in town for a few days.

Tickets (for everything including the passable planetarium), are purchased at a separate building next to the back of the library. There is also an ATM about 20m (66 ft.) away on the first corner in the direction of Qaitbey.

Chatby. www.bibalex.org. Museum ✆ 03/4839999. Admission LE20 ($3.60/£1.85) adults, LE10 ($1.80/95p) students, LE20 ($3.65/£1.85) with camera. Sun–Thurs 9am–7pm, Fri 1–7pm, Sat 11am–7pm. Library: ✆ 03/489999 ext. 1575. Sat–Thurs 11am–7pm, Fri 3–7pm. Admission LE10 ($1.80/95p).

Catacombs of Kom el Shaqafa *🦎🦎🦎* *Kids*   Perhaps I have a taste for the macabre, but this is one of my favorite Alexandria outings. Part *Lord of the Rings,* part *Indiana Jones,* the catacombs are about 35m (115 ft.) below ground level and reached by a spiral staircase that circles an open central shaft that was once used to lower dead bodies into the tombs below. The story goes that the whole complex was discovered in 1900 when a donkey, working the land above, fell in.

At the bottom of the stairs, you'll find yourself in a funerary complex, with rooms and passages leading off in all directions. It was more formally laid out when it was built in the 2nd century A.D., and many of the interconnecting passages that you see now are the work of grave robbers.

Dive Right In

When people think of diving in Egypt, they think of the Red Sea, but that might be about to change. The seabed around Alexandria is littered with debris from not only the Greco-Roman period, but the late-18th-century Franco-British conflict over control over Egypt and World War II. Most sites along the coast are shallow, with much to see in less than 10m (33 ft.) of water. However, visibility can be a challenge. Consult with local guides (see "Active Vacation Planner," p. 65) on both the best months to dive specific sites and also on what sites are open.

Jars, off the Montaza district of Alexandria, offers, well, dozens of jars—Greco-Roman amphorae, to be precise—as well as other artifacts from this extremely busy port site, including anchors and other debris from ships and the remains of some small work boats that were used around the harbor. Depth is around 7 to 10m (23–33 ft.), and the site is an easy swim from the shore.

The remains of the **Pharos lighthouse** is a boat dive but close to the harbor. A big debris field is all that remains now of one of the Seven Wonders of the World—columns, some broken statuary, and a few pieces of hieroglyph-bearing stones laying about on the bottom of the Mediterranean.

The remains of **Napoleon Bonaparte's fleet,** sunk by ships under Rear-Admiral Horatio Nelson in the 1798 Battle of the Nile, lie in about 10 to 14m (33–46 ft.) of water a few kilometers off Aboukir, a small town to the east of Alexandria. Three boats are known, and one, the French flagship *l'Orient,* is intact enough to be an interesting dive.

There is also at least one reasonably intact World War II airplane and a landing craft off Alexandria, though the history, and even nationality, of these remain an open question.

The recently discovered Greco-Roman cities of **Herakleion, Menouthis,** and **Canopus** also lie submerged off Aboukir. Not only are amphorae, millstones, old wells, and other urban artifacts to be found, but around the site of Herakleion lie intact walls, complete temples, and massive statuary.

The burial tomb chamber is obvious once you're at the bottom of the stairs; it's through the doorway that's flanked by Anubis and Agathodaemon. Stop for a moment before going in to consider the odd mix of Egyptian, Roman, and Greek symbolism here—it's an excellent illustration of the syncretism of Ptolemaic culture. Anubis is the Egyptian god most closely associated with tombs, and he features prominently on royal tombs in Upper Egypt, where he protected the mummified remains of the occupants. But here, instead of the traditional collar around his neck, Anubis wears the uniform of a Roman legionary. The snake-tailed Agathodaemon, meanwhile, is an expat Greek god associated with good food and plenty, which may or may not be a reference to funeral rites that included feasting in the tombs. The chamber is modeled on a temple, with an antechamber and an inner sanctum. *Note:* Even though the statues and carvings have been left unprotected and unsupervised, you shouldn't touch them.

The rest of the catacombs, though less elaborate, are well worth a visit. If you've brought water or a snack, try the **triclinium,** the large room with the benches close to the bottom of the stairs. This was where friends and family of the deceased gathered periodically to feast and pay their respects.

The amount of the water in the lower tombs goes up and down, and there are always limits to how far you can explore. Much of what you can access was added well after the original construction, and access was further improved by later raiders in search of treasure. There is a usually accessible section behind the main tomb where a narrow hallway goes off into a series of little tombs and a wholly separate section known as the **Hall of Caracalla** off to the right (standing with your back to the main stairs).

Note: Officially you are not allowed to take pictures in the catacombs, so tuck your camera into the depths of your bag (no X-ray machine here) and be discreet.

Tawfikeya Street. No phone. Admission LE25 ($4.55/£2.30) adults, LE15 ($2.70/£1.40) students. Daily 8am–5pm (ticket window closes at 4:30pm).

Cavafy Museum ✿ This house of poet C. P. Cavafy has been charmingly reconstructed and offers a relaxing way to spend an hour or so away from the crowds. Cavafy, who was born in Alexandria in 1863 and lived most of his life there until his death in 1933, was much admired by E. M. Forster, who lived several years during World War I in Alexandria and wrote a fabulous guidebook to the city. Cavafy's belongings and books (though the furnishings are authentic period pieces, his actual furniture was sold before the museum was founded in 1991) are housed in his apartment on the second floor of an old apartment building and evoke not only the life of the poet but of the period.

35 Sharm el Sheikh St. ✆ 03/4825205 or 03/4821598. Admission LE20 ($3.60/£1.85) adults, LE10 ($1.80/95p) students. Sun–Tues 10am–3pm, Sat and Thurs 10am–5pm.

The Graeco-Roman Museum ✿✿ This is a great museum, and with around 40,000 items in its collection, dating back as far as the 3rd century B.C., there's a fair bit to see here. Pieces you must see, for their local relevance, include the giant **Apis bull** from the temple that used to exist around Pompey's Pillar and the heads of Serapis. This uniquely Alexandrian god, Serapis, came into being under Ptolemy Soter, a general under Alexander the Great and the man who took over as ruler when the famous leader died. Looking for a figure that the Egyptian population and their Greek rulers could both worship, Ptolemy anthropomorphized the Egyptian Apis as a bull-necked and heavily bearded Greek god.

The feast for those who like mosaics also continues in the museum. There is a splendidly detailed **mosaic portrait of Berenice II,** wife of the 3rd century ruler Ptolemy III. Also among the must-sees are the **3rd century B.C. lanterns** that show the famous lighthouse and a mummified crocodile; **Roman glass and coins,** and a wonderful **stone sarcophagus** that almost everyone thinks is a bathtub on first sight. Plan on spending several hours here.

There is a small gift shop and bookstore where Jean-Yves Empereur's excellent, and short, guide to the museum can be picked up, as well as a pleasant cafe in the courtyard, where you can rest with a cup of tea and write a few postcards.

Mathaf al Romani St. ✆ 03/4865820 or 03/4876434. www.grm.gov.eg. Admission LE16 ($2.90/£1.50) adults, LE8 ($1.45/75p) students, LE10 ($1.80/95p) camera, LE100 ($18/£9.25) video camera. Daily 9am–5pm (museum closes 11:30am–1:30 pm for prayers on Fri).

Kom el Dikka ✿ Until archaeologists from the University of Warsaw began to excavate this site in the 1960s, it looked like what the name suggests—literally a "hill of rubble." Now, after the removal of more than 10,000 cubic meters (340,000 cubic ft.) of earth and the construction of a new building to protect the mosaics, Kom el Dikka is an example of the kind of Roman ruins that likely underlie other sections of modern Alexandria. Though the site is not huge, it comprises a column-lined street, a 3rd century A.D. theater with 13 intact tiers of seats that accommodated an audience of 600, and the remains of a villa with a series of truly lovely mosaics on the floor. The curve and size of the theater is impressive, but the most amazing thing about it is that it was originally covered with a roof. The mosaics, meanwhile, are worth a careful look for their intricately detailed and colorful depictions of local wildlife.

Kom el Dikka is an easy walk from the train station, or a 10-minute taxi ride from either downtown or, from the other direction, the Catacombs of Kom el Shaqafa. The mosaics of the Villa of the Birds are definitely worth the extra ticket.

Ismail Mehanna Street. Admission LE15 ($2.70/£1.40) adults, LE10 ($1.80/95p) students; Villa of the Birds extra LE10 ($1.80/95p). Daily 9am–4:45pm.

Mahmoud Said Museum   A scion of the Egyptian royal family, Mahmoud Said (1897–1964) spent most of his life working as judge, not a painter. It was only when he retired at the age of 50 that he was able to devote himself to art. By then he had absorbed a good deal of cubism and social realism, and these both came through powerfully in his work. He painted scenes from a range of settings around Egypt, from whirling Sufi dancers to prostitutes, in warm, earthy tones. Said was far from a towering artistic talent—his importance lies much more in the way that he used European techniques in rendering Egyptian subjects—but the museum dedicated to him, which is in his columned Italianate villa, is still worth a visit.

6 Mohamed Said Pasha St. (⒞ 03/5821688. Admission LE20 ($3.60/£1.85) adults, LE10 ($1.80/95p) students. Daily 9am–5pm.

Marine Life Museum   I find this kitschy exhibition of stuffed fish and mocked-up sea mammals to be charming and pointless at the same time. One of the great things about it is, of course, that's it's so cheap that if you walk in and decide it's just plain stupid, you can walk away without a worry. Displays include an enormous stuffed (and quite possibly entirely fake) sunfish, a fin whale skeleton, and a diorama of a fishing boat from the perspective of the fish. As long as I have been coming here (I'm a regular visitor), there has been a hugely out-of-scale footprint in the sand on the bottom of the diorama, as though a giant has just walked through.

Under the Qaitbey Fort. No phone. Admission LE1 (20¢/10p). Sat–Thurs 9am–6pm.

Montaza Palace Gardens *(Overrated*   These gardens used to be the grounds of a royal palace and a hunting lodge built in the late 19th century during the reign of Khedive Abbas Hilmy. Though they are attractively laid out and there's a beach that can be used for a small fee, I'm not sure that the gardens are worth a visit on their own merit. In the summer, they're crowded with local youth and in the winter they're chilly and bleak. However, they are a lovely setting for the El-Salamlek Palace Hotel (p. 140), which is a great place for a quiet lunch or a couple of days' stay. There's an admission to the gardens, which is waived if you're staying at either the Helnan or the Salamlek hotels. Avoid the McDonald's in the garden unless you're truly desperate.

Montaza. No phone. Admission LE5 (90¢/45p).

Pompey's Pillar *(Overrated*   For the casual visitor, this site doesn't offer as much as the spectacular Kom el Dikka or the Catacombs of Kom el Shaqafa. The red granite column for which the site is named is admittedly massive—9m (30 ft.) around and 30m (100 ft.) tall—but had nothing to do with the Roman General Pompey (who was killed here in 48 B.C.), and was erected in A.D. 293 for Diocletian. It used to stand in a large temple to Serapis and is now flanked by a pair of sphinxes from Heliopolis. There are some catacombs underneath that are worth the small fee that you'll need to pay the "guard" for a tour. The rest of the site is an unimpressive and rather bleak hillside.

It's an easy walk from here to the Catacombs of Kom el Shaqafa (p, 135), and it's best to do them as a pair. If you're in a hurry, you can actually get a decent view of the column from the road before continuing on to the catacombs. To walk there, just turn right on leaving, and follow the edge of the dig to the first big street. The entrance to the catacombs will be on your left after about 100m (328 ft.).

Amoud el Sawary Street. No phone. Admission LE15 ($2.70/£1.40) adults, LE10 ($1.80/95p) students. Daily 9am–4:45 pm.

Qaitbey Fort ⚓ From almost any place along the Corniche, you can see a short, squat castle perched on the end of the breakwater at the outer rim of the eastern harbor—this is Qaitbey Fort. For fans of military history and kids who like forts, Qaitbey is a great place. Austere and solid inside, you can wander the little rooms and peer across the harbor toward the town through the narrow windows of the upper floors, or check out the massively thick-walled sea side of the fort where they have a few old cannons. There's a small, high-roofed mosque in the center of the fort that you shouldn't miss, more for its simplicity and austerity than any elaborate tile work or architectural flourishes. Unfortunately, Qaitbey lacks any documentation or exhibition of artifacts.

The fort may seem to be in remarkably good condition given its age—it was built between 1477 and 1480 during the reign of the Sultan Qaitbey—but this is due to extensive restoration to repair damage from, among other sources, a British bombardment in 1882.

If you came to Alexandria hoping to see the famous lighthouse (p. 132), this is as close as you're going to get: The fort was built on the site of its foundations about 175 years after it collapsed in an earthquake. Though the lighthouse stood on an island at the entrance to the harbor, the fort lies on a causeway, which was built to provide defense against potential Turkish attacks, that's accessible by foot. Rubble from the old lighthouse was likely used in the construction of the fort, and there's a theory that the large, red, granite pillars incorporated into the outer defenses came from just this source.

The small gift store lacks any souvenirs specific to the fort, and the toilets are all right.

Admission LE20 ($3.60/£1.85) adults, LE10 ($1.80/95p) students. Daily 9am–4pm.

Royal Jewelry Museum At the time of writing, the Royal Jewelry Museum was under renovation and had been since 2003. The best thing about the museum was the villa that housed it, with its painted glass windows and gloriously tiled bathrooms complete with elaborate bathing facilities. The jewelry collection, an odd and charming mix of diamond-studded tools, watches, miniatures, and medals, and some exquisite coffee cups, felt like the stuff that nobody could be bothered to take with them when the revolution came. It's a definite must-see if it's reopened, but it appears that the building has been gutted, and I fear that Egypt has lost yet another treasure from its past.

27 Ahmed Yehia Pasha. ☎ 03/5868348.

WHERE TO STAY

Alexandria has several nice high-end hotels and a couple of really good budget places, but almost nothing in the midrange that I can recommend. Travelers looking for something better than the budget options (which are very basic) should spend their time bargain-hunting and negotiating among the locally-run expensive hotels (The

Metropole, The Windsor Palace, and the San Giovanni, for example) instead of trolling through the overpriced, dreary, and usually unclean midrange options that can be found on the Internet.

VERY EXPENSIVE

El-Salamlek Palace Hotel 🏵🏵   Built in 1892 as a hunting lodge for the mistress of then-Khedive Abbas Helmi II, the Salamlek has survived its conversion to a hotel with remarkable grace. The Salamlek is located at the eastern end of the Corniche, which puts it beyond walking distance to most restaurants and sites. On the other hand, you aren't going to be able to avoid taxi rides in Alexandria anyway, so unless you plan to stay up very late, you might as well take advantage of this pleasant location in the middle of the Montaza Gardens and the hotel's direct view of the sea.

The rooms—actually, most of them are suites—have been fitted with somewhat generic modern furnishings, but at least one of them has a beautiful original wood ceiling. Maintenance isn't what it should be, but the view from the front rooms (across the garden to the Mediterranean) is lovely.

One of the best parts of the Salamlek is the room that used to be the khedive's office, which is now the King Farouq dining room. The ceiling and walls are original, as is the fireplace, and there's a door concealed in the back of the room that was first used as a discreet exit for its intended occupant but is now a service entrance. The bar is actually made out of Farouq's secretary's desk, and in the corner there's a lovely old folding pipe table. Unfortunately, quite a few of the royal portraits that now adorn the lobby and other public areas are second-rate reproductions, but the elevators that slide you soundlessly up to the rooms on the second floor are the real thing.

Montaza Gardens. © 03/5477999. 20 units (14 suites, 6 rooms). LE847 ($154/£78) single; LE10,890 ($1,980/£1,008) 5-room suite. MC, V. **Amenities:** 2 restaurants; bar; health club; Internet. *In room:* TV, minibar, safe.

Four Seasons Hotel Alexandria 🏵🏵   I have my reservations about the location of the new Alexandria Four Seasons (more on this later), but there's no denying that this chain has worked its customary magic here. Though many guests arrive in a shiny, black car, the staff will make you feel like you just stepped out of a limo even if you roll up in a battered taxi with a backpack.

Despite the sweeping and apparently massive facade, the place is actually quite small and has been painstakingly designed to re-create the look and feel of a classic Alex hotel. The rooms have period prints hung on the walls, the wallpaper is striped in shades of sherbet, and the furnishings are highly polished wood. It goes without saying that the difference in the fit and the finish, as well as the overall elegance of execution, between here and the Metropole or Cecil is enormous.

Both the spa and restaurants are what you'd expect from the Four Seasons (actually, in the case of the spa, a little more—it's the most spacious facility of its kind I've seen in Egypt). The only issue I have with this hotel is the location. Because the building fronts an eight-lane thoroughfare, the sound of the sea outside on the terrace or by the pool is almost drowned out by the din of the traffic. The double-glazing on the windows is excellent, mind you, so as long as you stay inside, it's just fine.

399 Al Geish Rd. © 03/5818000. www.fourseasons.com. 118 units. LE1,919 ($350/£178) standard; LE2,467 ($448/£228) sea-view double. AE, DC, MC, V. **Amenities:** 6 restaurants; 3 bars; pool; health club; spa. *In room:* Minibar, safe, CD player, dataport and Wi-Fi Internet access.

Helnan Palestine   An unattractive cement building from the outside, the Helnan Palestine nevertheless has a lovely location on the sweep of the beach in the Montaza

Gardens at the eastern end of the Corniche. Sea-view rooms have a great, unobstructed view (no eight-lane thoroughfare here, thanks to the garden location) out over the Mediterranean, and both the pool and the restaurants look over the cove and the beach. Inside, the public areas and restaurants are a lot more attractive than you might expect from outside, with clean modern lines and nice light. The rooms are medium-size and nothing special, especially considering the price. The main asset here is the view. The hotel is at least 15 minutes by taxi from restaurants (except for a single Chili's outlet just outside the gardens, and the Salamlek's two restaurants 5 minutes' walk across the park) and the nearest sights. That said, it is a quiet location and the service is professional.

El Montaza Palace. ✆ **03/5473500** or 03/5474033. www.helnan.com. 230 units. LE2,343 ($426/£217). AE, MC, V. **Amenities:** 3 restaurants; 2 bars; pool; business center; Wi-Fi. *In room:* Minibar, safe, Internet.

Hotel Sofitel Cecil Alexandria   Built in 1928, the Cecil has unfortunately lost much of its old-world charm to a series of renovations, which have stripped away period fittings and marble and left the rooms with little character. Public areas—the lobby and the Monty bar upstairs—still have original wood paneling, and the elevators and staircase are gleaming originals, too. Located on the corner of Saad Zaghloul Square and facing the sea, the location is hard to beat, with half the rooms having a view of the sea. The rooms, if generic, are large and pleasantly appointed. The atmosphere is a good mix of hustle and bustle, but the staff can be surly and service isn't up to five-star (even Egyptian five-star) standards. The rack rates are ridiculously high, all things considered, and I would only recommend the Cecil if you can get the rooms at a significant discount.

16 Saad Zagloul Square. ✆ **03/4877173** or 03/4855655. www.sofitel.com. 83 units. LE1,447 ($263/£134) standard double; LE1,672 ($304/£155) sea-view double. AE, MC, V. **Amenities:** 2 restaurants; bar. *In room:* Minibar, safe.

EXPENSIVE

Hilton Borg al Arab   Located 50km (31 miles) west of Alexandria, this isn't exactly a downtown hotel. It is, however, the first recommendable beach resort on the highway from Alexandria in the direction of Marsa Matruh. The architecture is fairly typical for the neighborhood—big and built around a very solid-looking central concrete building, with plenty of parking out front for the buses. Inside's not bad, though. Though it feels a bit like an all-inclusive place, the staff are friendly and the lobby is big and spacious.

Most of the rooms are in the main building, but I prefer the ones spread between it and the beach in the chalets. Rooms are not very big, but they have a funky beach getaway ambience to them that I like. The beach is pretty good, with fine sand, a fairly low umbrella density, and water that's an ever-changing turquoise. That said, if you're looking for peace and quiet, this is not going to be your kind of place in the summer months, when it fills up with local tourists. The place is also in need of a renovation, but if you get a good discount from the rack rates, it could be a fun place to spend a few days.

Kilometer 52, Cairo–Marsa Matruh Highway. ✆ **03/3740730.** Fax 03/3740760. www.hiltonworldresorts.com. 227 units. LE980 ($178/£91) double. AE, MC, V. **Amenities:** 4 restaurants; 4 bars; 2 pools (including 1 kids' pool); tennis court; health club; business center. *In room:* Minibar, safe.

Hilton Green Plaza   Located away from the crush of people and cars along the seafront, and just a few minutes from Al Nozha Airport, the Green Plaza is a good option if you're just passing through or are visiting Alexandria in the summer and want to avoid the rowdy mobs of local youth on school holiday. Surrounded by cinemas and shops, this makes a good base from which to see the monuments, and it's an easy 10-minute taxi ride to where the older restaurants and coffee shops are located.

The lobby and public areas are spacious, modern, and well lit. Rooms are large and pleasant, if somewhat generic, which really sums up the ambience of the whole place quite well.

14th of May Bridge Road, Smouha. ✆ **03/4209120.** Fax 03/4209140. www1.hilton.com. 650 units. LE1,045 ($190/£97) double; LE1,375 ($250/£127) executive double. AE, MC, V. **Amenities:** 3 restaurants; bar; pool; health club. *In room:* A/C, TV, minibar, safe, Internet.

Metropole Hotel ⚐ On the other side of Saad Zagloul Square from the Cecil (above), the Metropole, which dates from 1902, offers much of the same period glamour and atmosphere at less than half the price. The lobby, with its high ceiling, gold lead, and neoclassical friezes is smaller than the Cecil's and lacks the dark-wood sobriety, but with period lamps and an original lift, it has its own particular, and very Alexandrian, character. The marble reception desk is short, tucked into a corner as you enter beneath a period chandelier, and as you approach it, you half expect to see Agatha Christie sitting in the corner.

Rooms are large and have also suffered from renovations—in this case, the designers have aimed for just a little too much glitz. Huge curtains, gold frill, and empire-style frippery abound. Fit and finish isn't as good as the Cecil's, but the staff here are friendlier.

52 Saad Zagloul Square. ✆ **03/4861467.** 64 units. LE658 ($120/£61) standard double; LE795 ($145/£74). AE, DC, MC, V. **Amenities:** Restaurant; bar; Wi-Fi. *In room:* A/C, TV, fridge.

San Giovanni This is a nice enough small hotel with some character, a pleasant staff, and a not-so-great location. A few years ago, it had a great location between the road and the sea, but then the road was widened, and the San Giovanni found itself cut off from the sea on one side. It still backs onto a beach, but it's unfortunately not accessible from the hotel. The main drawback of the arrangement is the traffic noise, and if it weren't for the fact that every hotel on the seaside shares the same issue (actually, this place is a little better off than some, in that the surf is loud enough sometimes to drown the traffic), I would hesitate to mention the San Giovanni at all. As it stands, it is only worthwhile at a significant discount from the quoted room rates.

There is a restaurant and a cozy bar, both with a view of the beach (though the view of the ocean is partially blocked by a bridge). Rooms vary in size and some are oddly shaped and have bad light (not helped by the dark trim, red carpets, and heavy curtains), so it's worth checking out one or two before making a decision.

205 Al Geish St. ✆ **03/5647775.** www.sangiovanni.com. 32 units. LE996 ($181/£92) double; LE1,183 ($215/£109) suite. **Amenities:** Restaurant; bar; Wi-Fi. *In room:* Minibar, safe.

The Windsor Palace Hotel ⚐ On the Corniche, a few hundred meters east of Saad Zagloul Square, the Windsor, with its modestly sized but ostentatious lobby and dining room, used to be a haunt of well-to-do Alexandrians. From the lovingly maintained old elevators and the dining room ceiling, which features a magnificently over-the-top painting, to the gold print wallpaper in the coffee shop, the place has an air of having survived past its time. You could wish for better-chosen carpeting upstairs or more furniture in the lobby (the place feels bare and somewhat empty, though maybe this is to show off the sheer expanse of the marble), but there's no denying that the place has presence. The double-wide roadway in front is a shame, but that's a problem shared by every hotel on the seafront. Rooms vary quite a bit but tend to be large and a bit chilly in the winter. Both service and room quality have been patchy in the past, so though things seem to have improved with a recent renovation, check out your room before you commit, and ask to see several if you're not happy.

17 Shohoda St. ⓒ 03/4808700. 63 units. LE658 ($120/£61) standard double; LE795 ($145/£74) deluxe double. AE, MC, V. **Amenities:** Restaurant; coffee shop; bar; Wi-Fi. *In room:* A/C, TV, minibar.

INEXPENSIVE

Le Crillon   This is probably the most charming of the Corniche pensions, and with a pleasant and efficient staff, it represents excellent value for money in both comfort and location. Simple rooms with high ceilings open onto the harbor with views of the crescent headlands of the harbor and the Qaitbey Fort. Each floor of rooms is built around an apartment-like sitting room. Most of the choice rooms have shared bathrooms (4 on each floor, 2 with large showers). The suites offer little added value, and rooms on the sixth floor should be avoided—they are windowless and reserved for overflow. Breakfast is served on the 2nd floor until 11:30am with coffee or tea, and for an extra 2 pounds, they offer a nice Spanish omelet.

5 Adib Ishak St. ⓒ 03/4800330. 28 units. LE80 ($15/£7.40) double. Rate includes breakfast. Cash only. *In room:* No phone.

Union Hotel   This is the classic Alexandria budget hotel. Long favored by archaeologists working on the North Coast and expats looking for a break from Cairo, it's on the fifth floor of an old building on the seafront. "Bare-bones" sums up the facilities, but the place is clean and the staff are friendly and helpful. The lobby and breakfast room areas face the sea and have a great view up and down the coast. The staff may try to describe the rooms, which are down the side of the building and look down quiet side streets, as having a sea view, but this stretching the truth: You *can* see the sea, but (especially toward the back of the hotel) you have to lean off the balcony and stretch your neck to get more than a thin sliver of blue. Once you hear the traffic noise at the front, mind you, you'll be happy with your room at the back. Breakfast here is as basic as the rooms. The upside of the Union, apart from the price, is the location; just meters from Saad Zagloul Square, it's an easy walk to several excellent coffee shops and lunch spots, The Graeco-Roman Museum, and shops and services. Taxis are plentiful for farther flung archaeological sites and restaurants.

164 26th of July St. ⓒ 03/4807771 or 03/4807312. 42 units. Double LE70 ($13/£6.50) double. Rate includes tax. Cash only. *In room:* No phone.

WHERE TO EAT
EXPENSIVE

Abu Ashraf FISH   Buried deep in the Anfousha district, this is the place to be if you find the Fish Market on the Corniche (below) a bit tame. You can take a taxi right to the entrance, but my recommendation is to get out of the cab at the parking lot at the end of Safar Basha Street on Ras el Tin Street and walk up Safar Basha and let the full effect of a crowded Alexandria backstreet wash over you.

As with other local fish places, there is an icebox display at the entrance of what's available for the day. Though the staff are friendly and helpful, they speak limited English, so ordering is going to be a sign-language process. My favorite dishes here are the *bouri bi ghada* (a small local fish lightly battered in bran), which I have after a heaping dish of grilled shrimp. Go with the flow and their recommendations with one vital exception: You want to specify that your fish is cooked *maftouah,* which means "open" (make like your hands are an open book in front of you to make sure they understand). Otherwise you risk getting a "closed" fish, which simply means it hasn't been gutted. I find this to be unpleasant.

28 Safar Basha St. ⓒ 03/4816597 or 03/4842850. Full fish meal (including salads, appetizers, bread, and entree) LE60–LE100 ($11–$18/£5.55–£9.25). AE, MC, V. Daily noon–2am.

Grand Café EGYPTIAN/EUROPEAN   This stylish, upmarket lunch cafe on the waterfront is one of the very few places in Alexandria that's directly on the water. In winter it fails to make the most of its location, and while the outdoor seating is pleasant, it actually doesn't have a view of the water itself. It's worth checking in the summer to see if the place is rearranged to make the most of where it is.

The food is simple but good. On a hot day, try the chicken Caesar salad, which comes with big chunks of chicken and a creamy dressing, or a seafood pizza. In the winter, this place is probably best for dessert after filling up with meat or fish next door at the Fish Market or Tikka Grill (below). Service is relaxed (read: slow) but pleasant and professional, and the profiteroles are the stickiest, most chocolaty dessert served in Egypt.

El Geish Road, Bahary. ⓒ 03/4805114. Main courses LE10–LE30 ($1.80–$5.45/95p–£2.75). AE, MC, V. Daily 9am–1am.

Fish Market ⭑⭑ ALEXANDRIAN   This is the best bet for a well-cooked fish meal in a town full of fish restaurants. Located directly on the water, the Fish Market's big windows offer a great, unobstructed view over the harbor toward the Qaitbey Fort. The atmosphere is casual and pleasant. Wood floors, white walls, wicker furniture, and grass-shaded lamps give the place a seaside feel, while bread being baked in the traditional oven fills it with a pleasant aroma. Like any self-respecting Alexandria fish restaurant, it sells fish by the kilo. You choose your meal from an ice-filled table near the door, and then retreat to your table while it's cooked. I recently had the *karous* (sea bream) grilled in olive oil and lemon juice accompanied by a pie of grilled vegetables and rice, and the white flaky fish was cooked to perfection.

El Geish Road, Bahary. ⓒ 03/4805114 or 03/4805119. Full meal (including appetizers, side salads, and bread) LE90–LE150 ($16–$27/£8.30–£14). AE, MC, V. Daily noon–1am.

Santa Lucia ⭑ EUROPEAN   When you're tired of fish (or if you never liked it in the first place), try Santa Lucia. A recent renovation to the interior brought in dark-wood paneling, heavy curtains, and a slightly eclectic mix of modern art and Indian handicrafts, resulting in a subdued and sophisticated atmosphere.

Menu options range from filet Madagascar and shrimp risotto to poached stingray and steak. The tiramisu finishes off the meal nicely, though it's not made with either mascarpone cheese or raw eggs (for which you should probably be grateful).

To get here, head up Safiya Zagloul Street from Saad Zagloul Square. After an 8-minute walk, you'll see it on the corner after the gas station. It's the place with frosted windows and the doorman outside. Elite (below) is across the street.

40 Safiya Zagloul St. ⓒ 03/4801706 or 03/4802054. Appetizers LE10–LE30 ($1.80–$5.45/95p–£2.75); main courses LE40–LE90 ($7.25–$16/£3.70–£8.30). AE, MC, V. Daily 1pm–midnight.

Tikka Grill INTERNATIONAL   Downstairs from the Fish Market, Tikka specializes in grilled meat. It has the same fantastic harbor view as its counterpart upstairs, but tries for a more sophisticated atmosphere. I don't think it succeeds, with its sherbet color scheme, but I like the open charcoal grill, which gives the whole place a warmth that can be very welcome on a chilly winter night.

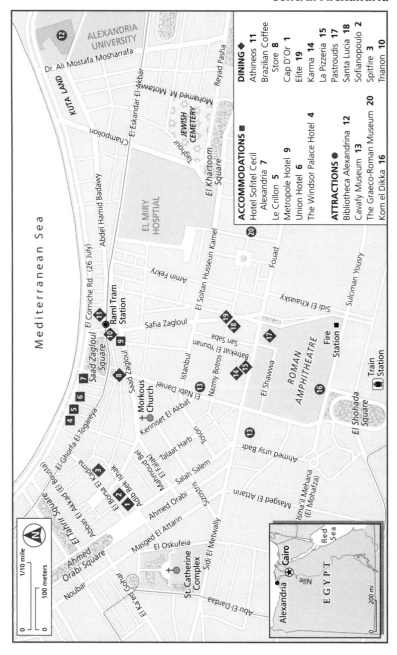

Central Alexandria

DINING ◆
Athineos **11**
Brazilian Coffee
Store **8**
Cap D'Or **1**
Elite **19**
Karma **14**
La Pizzeria **15**
Pastroudis **17**
Santa Lucia **18**
Sofianopoulo **2**
Spitfire **3**
Trianon **10**

ACCOMMODATIONS ■
Hotel Sofitel Cecil
Alexandria **7**
Le Crillon **5**
Metropole Hotel **9**
Union Hotel **6**
The Windsor Palace Hotel **4**

ATTRACTIONS ●
Bibliotheca Alexandrina **12**
Cavafy Museum **13**
The Graeco-Roman Museum **20**
Kom el Dikka **16**

Mediterranean Sea

ALEXANDRIA
UNIVERSITY
Dr. Ali Mostafa Mosharrafa

KUTA LAND

Champollion

El Eskandar El-Akbar

Mohamed M. Motawae

Reyad Pasha

JEWISH
CEMETERY

Taghour

El Khartoom
Square

Abdel Hamid Badawy

EL MIRY
HOSPTIAL

El Soltan Husseun Kamel

Fouad

Sulicman Yousry

El Corniche Rd. (26 July)

Amin Fekry

Raml Tram
Station

Safia Zagloul

Sidi El Khaiasky

Saad Zagloul
Square

Saad Zagloul

San Saba

Batrekiat El Younan

ROMAN
AMPHITHEATRE

Fire
Station ■

Morkous
Church

Istanbul

Nazmy Botros

El Shawa

Train
Station

El Nabi Daniel

Kenniset El Akbat

El Shohada
Square

El Ghorfa-El-Togareya

Tason

Talaat Harb

Salah Salem

Ahmed ursy Badr

Mahmoud Bel
El Falaki

Sizostris

Ahmed Orabi

Masged El Attarin

El Borsa El Kadima

Adib Bek Ishak

Abbes El Akked (El Bousta)

El Tahrir Square

Ahmed
Orabi Square

Noubar

El Ka'ed Gohar

Masged El Attarin

El Oskufeia

Sidi El Metwally

St. Catherine
Complex

Abu-El-Dardaa

Isma'il Mehana
(El Mohafza)

Red
Sea

Cairo

Nile

EGYPT

Alexandria

200 mi

1/10 mile
100 meters

N

Starters are collected from a salad bar, and the menu leans heavily toward Egyptian meat dishes such as rabbit with *molokheya,* grilled quail, and chicken *tikka.* Ultimately, the food isn't as good as it is upstairs—I tried the eponymous chicken *tikka* with some *aish bouri* (crispy fried bread) and found it to be a fine, but rather unimaginative, take on the theme of, well, barbecued chicken. Desserts, a fine looking selection of *mille-feuille,* fruit salads, and crème caramel, come along on a trolley, but you may want to go down to the Grand Café instead.

El Geish Road, Bahary. Ⓒ **03/4805114.** Main courses LE40–LE60 ($7.25–$11/£3.70–£5.55). AE, MC. Daily noon–1am.

MODERATE

Athineos EGYPTIAN/GREEK   In recent years, this waterfront hideout has turned to the tour bus trade, but it's managed to maintain its character. The main dining room is over the top, with crimson walls, a cream frieze depicting cavorting characters from Greek mythology, and loads of imitation gold leaf. The menu is a little United Nations, with salad niçoise alongside fish kebab, moussaka, and baba ghanouj. There's a bar just before the main dining room on the left, but you'll have to flag down a waiter when you need something—a small price to pay to avoid the large groups that pour into this place. The Alexandrian rice with seafood, an unlikely combination of calamari and fish with peanuts and raisins, is a bit heavy for summer, but it's a delicious and filling dish.

21 Saad Zagloul Square. ⒸⒸ **03/4868131.** Appetizers LE10–LE15 ($1.80–$2.70/95p–£1.40); main courses LE20–LE40 ($3.60–$7.25/£1.85–£3.70). Cash only. Daily 8:30am–12:30am.

Elite ALEXANDRIAN/EUROPEAN   There is one small problem with this classic Alexandrian fixture: The food, with the sole exception of the grilled calamari, has always been exceptionally bad during my visits (other people, however, report better experiences). If you're in the mood for squid, though, Elite is the perfect place to hole up on a rainy Alexandrian afternoon and people-watch. The staff are pleasant, the beer is cold, and the regulars who drift in and out are a subdued and jovial group.

43 Safiya Zagloul St. ⒸⒸ **03/4863592.** Main courses LE20–LE50 ($3.60–$9.10/£1.85–£4.60). Cash only. Daily noon–10pm.

Greek Maritime Club ALEXANDRIAN   Upstairs at the Greek Maritime Club, at the end of the breakwater close to the Qaitbey Fort, this place has a reputation for being a bit pricier than other fish restaurants (with the notable exception of the Fish Market, above), but considering the quality of its fish and cooking, I think it's worth it. It looks a little forbidding from the outside, but push through the doors and head upstairs, and you'll find that it has a great view across the bay. The menu is an odd mix of traditional Egyptian favorites (it has a wonderful, thick lentil soup) and Greek dishes such as moussaka and souvlakia. The meze (appetizer) servings are substantial, and you could easily make a light meal out of one with some soup on the side.

The atmosphere is lacking (the whole restaurant is one big room with a table of fish on ice near the door) and decorations are sparse, but it's certainly very clean. In summer, the long balcony along the sea side is the perfect place to sit with a cold beer and watch the sunset, taking in the fishing boats and the massive glass slope of the Bibliotheca.

Qaitbey Street. ⒸⒸ **03/4873245.** Appetizers LE10–LE20 ($1.80–$3.60/£95p–£1.85); main courses LE20–LE40 ($3.60–$7.25/£1.85–£3.70). Cash only. Daily noon–11pm.

Karma EUROPEAN   Down a quiet side street and upstairs in an old Alexandrian building, Karma's atmosphere is a mix of dimly lit civility and hip dance club. That's because, though it opens at 6pm to serve dinner amidst the period fittings and dark wood trim, by 11pm Karma transforms itself into a dance club. Nice touches, such as the gentle light that seeps from underneath the bar, contribute to the relaxed and pleasant dining experience here. The place is spacious, and you can choose between high tables in the bar area or a table in the adjoining room. The food (such as fried mushrooms and a pleasantly garlicky spaghetti *alio olio*) is excellent, and the service is informal, pleasant, and professional.

14 Horreya St. ℂ **03/4841881.** Appetizers LE15–LE25 ($2.70–$4.55/£1.40–£2.30); main courses LE30–LE70 ($5.45–$13/£2.75–£6.50). Cash only. Daily 7pm–3am.

Pastroudis GREEK/EUROPEAN   This classic Alexandrian restaurant opened in 1923, and though it's now sadly stranded beside a busy road, it's recently been renovated with plush red velvet that complements the old mirrors, curvaceous wood cabinets, brass railings, and marble bar. Despite the vicissitudes of the traffic engineers, I still recommend the outside area for an evening drink. My favorite part of Pastroudis remains the bar, however, tucked away behind the dining room. It has the feel of a discreet private drinking club (it can hold about a dozen drinkers), and the patrons tend to treat it as such. You won't feel particularly welcome in a T-shirt and jeans, let alone dragging a backpack (for which there is no room, in any case).

The food, unfortunately, isn't fantastic. Ordering is a bit of a crapshoot, as what ultimately arrives at your table tends to be only loosely related to the menu description. I recently had a *Salad Greque a la Pastroudis,* which arrived as an elegantly presented cucumber salad and some onion soup.

Intersection of Horreya and Fouad streets. ℂ **03/3929609.** Appetizers LE15–LE30 ($2.70–$5.45/£1.40–£2.75); main courses LE50–LE60 ($9.10–$11/£4.60–£5.55). Cash only. Daily 9am–midnight.

Qadoura FISH   Right on the Corniche, this Alexandria-style fish restaurant is popular with the local middle and upper-middle class. Staff are boisterous and friendly, and the whole place is decorated with a lively underwater theme that includes big underwater reliefs on the walls, faux-seaweed decorations, and ceiling mirrors. Staff speak some English and can help you choose your fish, calamari, or shrimp from the ice chest (though what you get might not be exactly what you ordered). As with many locally oriented places, no alcohol is served here, and it's customary to drink lemon juice with your food and have a soft drink afterward.

Corniche, Bahary. ℂ **03/3927634.** Full fish meal LE50–LE100 ($9.10–$18/£4.60–£9.25). Cash only. No alcohol. Daily noon–3am.

Trianon ⚜ EUROPEAN   Open since 1905, this is easily my favorite lunch place in Alexandria, with high ceilings and gleaming old paneling. Though it is licensed to serve alcohol, the old bar in the corner seems to be used mostly for blending excellent fresh juices. In recent years, management has managed to modernize, adding wireless Internet access and a breakfast menu, without losing any of its original charm.

For lunch, start with the creamy chicken or tomato soup, and then move on to one of the sandwiches; my favorite is the thick toasted club, stacked with roast beef, chicken, and cheese, but the smoked salmon with capers shouldn't be ignored, nor should the pizzas. Finish with a sampling of the pastries from the picturesque bakery outlet on the opposite side of the building. Service is sedate, and lunch will proceed at a dignified pace.

52 Saad Zagloul Square. ✆ **03/4860973**. Main courses LE20–LE40 ($3.60–$7.25/£1.85–£3.70). Cash only. Daily 7am–11pm.

INEXPENSIVE

La Pizzeria ITALIAN   Funky and fun, this little Italian restaurant is a smoky, friendly place to grab a quick bite or while away time with a disparate crowd of upscale locals and expats. Upstairs in an old building, the atmosphere is very casual, with simple furniture and not much space. Expect to be rubbing elbows with your neighbors, and probably talking to them as well. The pizza is great, and if you're lucky, Alex, the polyglot owner, will be holding forth behind the bar in the corner. An expert on all things Alexandrian, he is well worth listening to.

14 Horreya St. ✆ **03/4869197**. Main courses LE20–LE40 ($3.60–$7.25/£1.85–£3.70). Cash only. Daily 8pm–2am.

WHERE TO DRINK

Brazilian Coffee Store   Just off Midan Saad Zagloul, this is an updated version of the classic Alexandrian coffee shop. Renovated with new fittings and modern colors, it still has much of the atmosphere of the old places. Better yet, it serves a proper espresso and cappuccino. There's seating upstairs, but I prefer to stand downstairs and watch the coffee roasting and the people stopping in and walking by. In the morning, it has toast and pâté, as well as croissants, and later in the day it offers pastries.

44 Saad Zagloul St. ✆ **03/4865059**. Coffee and a croissant LE7 ($1.30/65p). Cash only. Daily 7am–1am.

Cap D'Or 🐟🐟   Tucked away on a quiet side street, this is the quintessential Alexandria bar, and no visit to the city is complete until you've popped in for a beer and a bite of *nishouga* (small, salty fish that's served as a bar snack). Presided over by the affable Ashraf, the atmosphere is warm, though rough enough to tell you that you're a little off the tourist circuit. The walls are hung with mementoes of long-forgotten advertising campaigns and other eclectic odds and ends. The food is famous, but I'm not sure why—it's fine, but nothing to intimidate would-be chefs. I tend to stick with a plate of grilled calamari with fries and a few cold beers.

4 Adib St. ✆ **03/4875177**. Main courses LE20–LE30 ($3.65–$5.45/£1.85–£2.80). Cash only. Daily noon–2am.

Karma   It may be a restaurant (p. 147), but from 11pm 'til dawn, Karma is a sophisticated nightclub. The music is mainly house, with some R&B and Asian pop, except for Fridays, which is karaoke night, and Saturday, when things heat up with salsa music.

55 Bab Sidra St. ✆ **03/3623069**. Cash only. Daily 11pm–late.

Malak al Mango   Malak al Mango (which literally means "King of Mango" in Arabic) is basically a juice stand on the side of the Corniche and is an example of the kind of place that explodes with business during the hot summer months. Piles of fruit, wacky decor (faux empire-style pillars), and plastic lawn furniture scattered about on the sidewalk mean it's probably best to get your drink and enjoy it on the beach across the street.

50 al Geish St. Juices LE3–LE10 (55¢–$1.80/30p–95p). Daily 10am–1am.

Sofianopoulo   A surviving relic of a more cosmopolitan yesteryear, Sofianopoulo points back to a time before the Greek exodus. Gleaming wood hoppers hold the coffee that is roasted in the back of the store, and the prices of each blend are written in

Arabic across their glass fronts. Though there's plenty of space to put in a few tables and chairs, there's nowhere to sit down, so sipping your coffee is strictly a matter of hunching over a little counter and watching the pedestrian traffic outside. The pastries in the glass box beside the espresso machine aren't as good as they look, but Sofianopoulo remains one of my favorite spots for a quick jolt of caffeine.

Corner of Saad Zaghloul and Adib streets. Coffee LE2–LE5 (35¢–90¢/20p–45p). Cash only. Daily 8:30am–11pm.

Spitfire   This is a straight-out dive bar with little pretence at anything else. Favored by the crews from visiting cruise ships and expats out for a raucous time, this is the kind of place you want to head when you're tired of drinking from glasses and minding your language. The music is even louder than the patrons, and when the boats are in, it can be extremely crowded. Keep an eye on your wallet, and be prepared for a good time.

7 Rue L'Ancienne Bourse. Cash only. Daily noon–1am.

SHOPPING

When the exodus began after 1952, many people didn't have the money or the time to take household goods with them and, as a result, Alexandria became the Egyptian hub for used European furniture. Most of the items left behind were unremarkable, but many were of high quality and quite a few were antiques. The trade in these items has long centered on **Attarine Street** (more properly, Al Masgid al Attarine Street), a disappointingly unromantic street that runs into the back of Ahmed Orabi Square. For antique furniture buffs, as well as those just looking to pick up an old postcard or some knickknacks, an hour or two spent strolling past the windows won't be wasted. Stores range from clean, well-organized emporiums of nicely polished Napoleonic chairs and 19th-century silver services to junk stores with moth-eaten crocodiles and piles of moldy school books from the 1920s. Take your pick—far better in my opinion to take home a battered piece of the real thing than a shiny factory-produced souvenir. If you're actually going to buy, though, remember that Alexandria (not to mention the city of nearby Damietta) is the Egyptian hub for furniture production, and much of what you see (and is offered as antique) was probably produced a couple of months ago in a shop around the corner.

DAY TRIPS
ROSETTA (RASHID)

This medium-size town is an easy day trip to the east of Alexandria. Rosetta (*Rashid* in Arabic) flourished after the Arab invasion of A.D. 640, which put an end to the Roman administration of Egypt and the dominance of Alexandria over the North Coast. The town did particularly well under the Ottoman Turks, who conquered Egypt in 1517. As the easiest Egyptian port to reach from Istanbul, it received a disproportionate benefit from the trade with Turkey.

GETTING THERE   BY CAR   This is the best way to visit the town because it allows you to get there on your own schedule and—more important—to leave when you want as well. See p. 134 about renting a car in Alexandria.

What to See & Do

The **Ottoman houses** in the old part of Rosetta are what make the town worth visiting. Efforts continue to restore and open some of these houses, of which only 22 remain. Unfortunately, work is sporadic, and though progress is being made, you can never quite tell what's going to be open for visits and what is not.

Amasyali House is one of the largest and best preserved, perhaps because the family of the original owner lived there until the early 1920s. One of the first buildings, along with Arab Killi, which has become the Rasheed National Museum, to be restored, it also has one of the most impressive exteriors (a small consolation if you can't get inside). It's five stories tall, and in the original design, the usual ground-floor well and cistern were displaced to a basement in favor of a reception hall. It's well worth going inside Amasyali if you can—it has some lovely examples of 18th-century wooden *mashrabeya* paneling and various secret rooms and byways that allowed the women of the house to move about unobserved.

Next door to Amasyali House is the **Mill of Abu Shahin,** where a grinding mill, originally used to grind flour and rice, has been fully rebuilt. Whether the wood mechanics of it are as fully functional as claimed is debatable, but they certainly move in all the right ways if you give them a push. The massive street doors of the mill are worth noting in passing.

The Rasheed National Museum ☆

On the far side of Gomhoreya Square from the Nile, this new museum is located in a restored 18th-century house. Some of the restoration work was unfortunately heavy-handed, but the collection of local coins and ceramic pieces is interesting. What you're really here for, however, is the building. Four stories high, it is typical of the tall, brick houses of wealthy Ottoman merchants. There is a replica of the Rosetta Stone near the entrance.

I recommend taking a guide from Alexandria. Ask first what is open, and make sure that they can give you a good rundown on what you can actually see. Avoid everything except the old part of town—the rest of the city is unprepossessing and is to be avoided in the rain, when the combination of garbage and mud in the streets will quickly sap the enthusiasm of even stoic and enthusiastic visitors.

Gomhoreya Square. ✆ **045/2921733.** Admission LE20 ($3.60/£1.85) adults, LE10 ($1.80/95p) students. Daily 9am–4pm.

AL ALAMEIN

Eighty kilometers (50 miles) west of Alexandria, the open desert is pinched to a relatively narrow strip of sand between the coast and the Qattara Depression. In early 1942, the Allied armies, retreating in front of a sustained Axis offensive that had already taken British-held Libya and was about to overrun their defenses at Marsa Matruh, threw up a defensive line here. Claude Auchinleck, who preceded the more famous Bernard "Monty" Montgomery as commander of the Allied armies, calculated that Axis commander Erwin Rommel, who had already proven himself a master of using his armor to flank defensive lines in the desert, would be held to frontal assaults by the impassable salt pan, ridges, and *fech fech* (a light sand that won't hold the weight of vehicles) to the south. He was proven correct, and his decision to hold the line at Al Alamein set the scene for one of the most famous and grueling encounters of the war. Pitting the combined Italian and German armies against an Allied force drawn from all over the world, it took 5 months of fighting and two major battles to reach a conclusion.

When you visit the area now, it seems a long way from Alexandria and a world away from Cairo. Though there is an increasing amount of seaside development, there is little in the way of towns.

GETTING THERE   BY CAR   A rented car or a taxi is the only way to get to Alamein that makes sense (see p. 134 for how to do this from Alexandria). The bus can drop you on the highway, but with no taxis there, you'll quickly find yourself stranded.

What to See & Do

Alamein Military Museum   This small museum, just up the road from the Commonwealth Cemetery, houses a collection of military equipment and artifacts from both the Allied and the Axis forces. Outside the main building there are field guns and tanks, as well as the remains of a crashed Spitfire. Inside, dioramas, photographs, and mannequins are used to re-create the history of conflict. It's certainly worth 30 minutes to an hour to visit.

Km 105, Alex. Matrouh Desert Rd. ✆ **046/4100031** or 046/4100021. Admission LE10 ($1.80/90p) adults, LE5 (90¢/45p) students. Daily 9am–3pm.

Commonwealth Cemetery   This is a somber, moving monument to the thousands of Allied troops who lost their lives in Al Alamein. As you walk down to the cemetery from the parking lot, the first thing you'll find is the Alamein Memorial. On its walls are panels that commemorate the 8,500 soldiers and 3,000 airmen who died in the Middle East and whose graves are unknown. Passing through the memorial, you come to the cemetery. Rows of white stones set in the sand mark the bodies buried here, and to the southeast there's a large memorial to more than 600 soldiers whose bodies were cremated. There are 7,240 graves in the cemetery, of which 815 are not identified.

The cemetery is well maintained, and its simplicity, as well as the desert setting—the wind whistling through the stones is about the only sound here—underscore both the drama and the tragedy of the battles that were fought here. There are no stairs, but wheelchair access would require some assistance.

The site is not visible from the main road and lies in a depression 130km (81 miles) west of Alexandria. If you're driving, turn left at the intersection 81km (50 miles) from the beginning of the coastal highway (at the Cairo–Alexander road) onto the old coast road. The turnoff is supposed to be marked by a sign, but at the time of writing there was nothing there. There is a second intersection about 1km (⅔ mile) later where a World War II tank is set in the median. You can also turn left here and loop back. If you take the first left, the cemetery will be on your left after a few hundred meters.

Key available 24/7 from the guard who lives on the edge of the cemetery. Daily dawn–dusk.

German Memorial   This massive edifice to the Germans who lost their lives in the North African campaign stands between the new coast road and the sea, 14km (8½ miles) west of the turnoff to the Commonwealth Cemetery. It stands on the brow of a small hill, from which you can see just how bleak and difficult the territory is. Its octagonal structure and lack of moat or drawbridge are reminiscent of another German military monument, the 13th century Castel del Monte in southeastern Italy. Inside, some 4,500 German bodies are interred under black basalt.

Daily dawn–dusk.

Italian Memorial   Though just 3km (1¾ miles) west of the German Memorial, the Italian Memorial is quite different: Its soaring 46m (150-ft.) white column with sharp, modernist lines stands against the bright blue sky. Inside the echoing interior, casualties from the Italian forces lie in walls of white-faced vaults. There's an altar inside the memorial backed by a large window that faces the sea. It's worth visiting this place when it's empty, simply because voices and footsteps echo loudly through the space.

Daily dawn–dusk.

Where to Stay

Alamein Hotel This is really the only place I recommend staying in the area, and it's several kilometers past the cemetery and the museum. Situated on a wide, lovely sweep of beach, it might seem a little overpriced, but if you look at the competition, you'll quickly be convinced that this is the only game in town. It's a long way from the main road, so it's nice and quiet, and the somewhat shabby gardens that surround it on three sides are clean if not very well kept up. The lobby is very 1970s, but is spacious and light, and the staff are quiet, relaxed, and friendly. Rooms are fairly standard midrange, and though the light isn't great, the view is fantastic and the ground-floor sea-view rooms have direct access to the beach.

Sidi abd al Rahman, Kilometer 129, Alexandria-Matrouh Road. © 046/4680140, 03/5856654 Alexandria office, or 02/23904701 Cairo office. Fax 046/4680341. 70 units. LE 764 ($139/£71) double. Rate includes half-board and taxes. **Amenities:** Restaurant; bar. *In room:* A/C, TV, fridge.

Where to Eat

There is a small restaurant just across the road from the Commonwealth Cemetery in the direction of the Military Museum, and another roadside place called **Rommel's** just before the turnoff for the Alamein Hotel. Rommel's looks the best of the two, but I would honestly avoid both and eat in the Alamein Hotel only.

MARSA MATRUH

You're probably not going to be in Matruh for anything but the diving, or perhaps to break a slow trip to Siwa. The Mediterranean here is a stunning and ever-changing shade of blue, and the beaches are of fine white sand. Just offshore there are a number of World War II wrecks, and the water is crystal clear. On the downside, however, the westward expansion of the local summer holiday market has been making itself felt here, and between June and September the town is packed. Perhaps more important, though, the standard of both food and lodging is low. The best hotel is budget-standard, and you'll quickly find yourself debating between bad local options and Pizza Hut. In the winter, the city rolls down the shutters, and the choices become even more restricted.

Orientation

Matruh (you can drop the official "Marsa" part of the name locally, and will get blank looks if you call the town "Marsa") is situated on a wide bay. The main "downtown" area is concentrated around Alexandria Street (Shara' Iskandreya), which is the main route from the train and bus stations and from the airport. Alexandria Street meets the Corniche at the eastern end of the bay near the Riviera Palace. The Beau Site is located at the other end. The beaches and the museum are located farther west.

GETTING THERE   **BY AIR**   During the summer months, there are three flights a week into Matruh. As they are scrubbed for the winter and then rescheduled in the spring, it is best to check the **EgyptAir** website (www.egyptair.com) or ask your travel agent. The taxi into town will set you back about LE20 ($3.60/£1.85).

BY BUS   The West Delta bus station is on the Matruh–Alexandria road about 2km (1¼ miles) from the seaside. There are usually plenty of blue-and-white taxis around. Five pounds (90¢/45p) will take you almost anywhere in town. Buses to Alexandria leave at 7:30am, 1:30pm, 4pm, 6:30pm, and 2am. Tickets are LE12 ($2.20/£1.10).

BY TRAIN   The train station is close to the bus station, and though taxis, in my experience, are more scarce here, you should have no problem picking up a blue-and-white to take you to your hotel for LE5 (90¢/45p). Trains arrive from Alexandria at about 1 and 8pm.

FAST FACTS   Getting online in Matruh is harder than most places in Egypt. The best place to go is a dank little store with no name in the "mall" at the very bottom of Iskandreya Street, across from the Riveria Palace Hotel.

What to See & Do

Beaches   There are a number of lovely beaches to the west of town. The water is a pristine, turquoise blue, and the jagged rocks that tumble to the shore set off the soft white sand beaches—everywhere you look, you see a postcard here. That said, however, bathing on the North Coast of Egypt is hardly for everyone, especially when it's busy (and Marsa beaches are pretty busy during the summer months).

Social mores have changed in Egypt, and though even 20 years ago Egyptians in Western-style swimsuits were quite comfortable on beaches here, this is no longer the case, and most women now find public beaches an uncomfortable experience. Foreign women may find a bit more leeway, but if there are Egyptian men present, you'll quickly become a celebrity, with your very own fan club of goggle-eyed admirers who will settle down to watch your every move. Men, meanwhile, can do as they wish.

Rommel's Beach (where Rommel supposedly unwound with a quick dip at the end of a hard day's strategizing) is just past Rommel's Cave and is the closest to town (except, of course, for the unbearably packed seashore of the town itself)—it's also uninspiring. It's best to keep heading west to **Cleopatra's Beach** or **Lover's Beach,** which are around the bay and about a 30-minute drive. At Cleopatra's Beach, you can splash about at a rock pool where Cleopatra and Anthony apparently bathed. Farther west, 25km (16 miles) from town, there's a lovely cove called **Miracle Beach,** which has a long, white sand beach between high rocky arms. Of these, your best bets for a good paddle or an outright swim are Cleopatra's Beach and Miracle Beach, with the edge going to Cleopatra's, as Miracle has been showing up on package-tour itineraries.

Diving 🐟🐟   For Marsa Matruh's share of the North Coast's diving options, which include a World War II submarine, a cargo ship cut open through the middle by the explosion that sank her, and a cluster of unexploded torpedoes. See p. 65 in chapter 4, "Active Vacation Planner," to learn more about accessing these sites.

Rommel's Cave 🐟   If you're a war or history buff, you're not going to want to miss the cave that Rommel used to plan the eastward offensive against the Allied forces that ultimately ground to a halt at Al Alamein. Though the military museum that now calls the place home comprises little more than some withering uniforms, including a coat that supposedly belonged to the Desert Fox himself, a clothing chest donated by his son, and some old photos, I think the quick trip outside town or on the way to one of the beaches is worth it for the location and the cave.

About 3km (1¾ miles) west of town. Admission LE20 ($3.60/£1.85) adults, LE10 ($1.80/95p) students. Daily 9am–4pm.

Where to Stay

Traffic noise, exacerbated by convoys of young Egyptians exuberantly honking their horns into the wee hours of the morning, is a problem in Matruh. The Corniche is dotted by flashing, red, NO HORNS signs, but there was no enforcement of the ban at the time of writing. Hopefully, this will change, but it would be wise to check the sound level of any room on the Corniche before committing yourself to spending the night. There are quite a number of hotels in town, particularly along the Corniche and in the first couple of blocks back from the sea just to the east of Iskandreya Street.

Arous Al Bahr   This basic beachfront accommodation is the best of the hotels that line the Corniche. Rooms are very basic, with hard beds and cheap furniture, but they're clean and cheap. Each has a small balcony where breakfast can be served and the sea breeze is nice. Try to get a room at the end of the hallways that run the length of the building—you want to be away from the TV noise (which probably goes on all night), and you don't want the teenagers tramping boisterously past your door while you're trying to sleep. There's a McDonald's, Pizza Hut, and Hardees nearby.

Corniche. ℂ 046/4934420. 32 units. LE80 ($15/£7.40). Cash only. **Amenities:** TV in lobby. *In room:* No phone.

Beau Site   This hotel is the best there is in Matruh. The lobby and restaurant have the look and feel of a low-end Western hotel, with clean white walls and windows that look down on the hotel's beach. Guest rooms are on the upper floors, and most have a view of the sea. Rooms are small—smaller than the Riveria Palace—but sufficient. Beds are a bit hard, but they're better than elsewhere. Bathrooms are small, with a shower surrounded only by a curtain—expect a wet bathroom floor after using it. Views of the sea are nice, and the private beach is right there. Though it doesn't rise above the requirements of basic accommodations, the Beau Site is clean and used to dealing with foreigners. It also offers at least three big advantages over everywhere else in town: If you're going to lay in the sun and swim, particularly if you're a woman, this is the only place to be in Matruh; it's away from the traffic noise of the Corniche; and the restaurant offers edible food.

Corniche. ℂ 046/4932066. LE437 ($79/£40) double. MC, V. **Amenities:** Restaurant; small bar; private beach. *In room:* A/C, TV, fridge.

Riveria Palace   This is the only competition for the Beau Site, and it's just a short walk from the public beach and closer to the shops and restaurants than the Beau. The decor is a bit cheap and gaudy (stuffed animal tigers), and it has the feel of a place that serves the high-end of the local tourism market during the summer. The basement restaurant and bar are bland but clean. The rooms are large and some of them have small balconies and garden views, so if you have a chance, look at a few before you settle on which one you're going to take. The air-conditioners are in good shape, and the bathrooms are better than anywhere else in town.

Iskandreya Street. ℂ 046/4933045 or 046/4930472. Fax 046/4930004. 41 units. LE400 ($73/£37) double. MC, V. **Amenities:** Restaurant; bar. *In room:* A/C, TV, fridge.

Where to Eat

Finding a meal in Marsa Matruh is a culinary adventure, though not necessarily in a good way. There are few options, and choosing is a matter of picking something acceptable rather than heading toward something you really want. All the places listed below are pretty down-market, and you may want to restrict yourself to eating at the restaurants in the Beau Site and Riveria Palace or at the cluster of fast-food places around the Arous al Bahr Hotel on the Corniche (which includes Pizza Hut, Hardees, KFC, and McDonald's). If you never head into downtown, you're not going to be missing anything special, and you may save yourself some stomach problems. During the summer months, keep an eye on the pizza places that crop up at the Beau Site end of the Corniche.

Hamed el Temsa FISH   This is a typical North Coast fish place, with enthusiastic paintings of fish on the windows, an open grill on the sidewalk, and boisterous staff. Choose your seafood from the wood market-style stalls, and wait while it's cooked to your specifications. Work out the price before you finalize the order—this restaurant is getting a bit of a reputation for hitting tourists with a ridiculous bill once they've finished the meal.

My favorite in these places is always the *bouri bi ghada* (mullet rolled in bran), but make sure that you specify *maftouah* (open) to make sure that it's cleaned before it gets cooked. Fish comes with rice on the side, and the usual range of *tahina* and salad-style appetizers are available.

Gala Street, 2 blocks east of Iskandreya Street. Fish meal (including salads, bread, and main dish) LE40–LE60 ($7.25–$11/£3.70–£5.55). Cash only. Daily 11am–2am.

New Alexandria Tourist Restaurant EGYPTIAN   Tuck into a pile of grilled *kofta* or kebab, or just go for the standard meal of grilled fish with a pile of rice on the side. The atmosphere is basic tourist-theme: white walls and white ceiling with a cooler for drinks and another for the fish so that you can see what's fresh. They do serve beer, and the staff will happily run down the street to make up for whatever the restaurant lacks.

Iskandreya Street, directly across the road from Panyotis. Main courses LE10–LE30 ($1.80–$5.45/95p–£2.75). Cash only. Daily noon–11pm.

Panyotis EGYPTIAN   This place is small and well established, and its narrow entrance makes it easy to miss. The food is the usual mix of Egyptian standards and local seafood, but the atmosphere is relaxed and jovial, and it serves alcohol. If you can't be in the water, relaxing at a seat near the door with a plate of grilled calamari and a cold beer is about the best way to pass a summer afternoon in Marsa Matruh. It's a couple of blocks up from the Riveria Paradise on the right side of the street.

Iskandreya Street, 1 block south of Riveria Palace Hotel. Main courses LE10–LE30 ($1.80–$5.45/95p–£2.75). Cash only. Daily 8am–11pm.

Sultana Hellwa PIZZA   Around the corner from the New Alexandria, this place does a busy local trade out of its open-to-the-street kitchen. I can't speak to the quality of the pasta, but the pizza is better than you would expect. An attempt has been made at decorating the place with a sort of maritime/beach theme, but it hasn't really worked out very well. If flies landing on your food bother you, go somewhere else.

Tahrir Street, just east of Iskanderya Street. Pizza LE7–LE25 ($1.25–$4.55/65p–£2.30). Cash only. Daily 2–11pm.

7

The Sinai Peninsula

For many years, the Sinai Peninsula was the kind of place that nobody went unless they had to. The Pharaohs sent expeditions to mine lapis here, and there were a few adventurous types (such as a young Ralph Bagnolds, later famous for his exploration of the Western Desert) who set out to see if it could be crossed. But mostly the area was for soldiers and the few resident Bedouin who mapped the mountains, valleys, and spectacular coastline of this massive empty land of rock and sand.

All this changed in the late 1970s and early 1980s with the withdrawal of the occupying Israeli forces that had captured the peninsula in the Six Day War of 1967. In their wake, a few adventurous Egyptians set out on their own to see what was on the eastern coast, and what they found were vast, pristine beaches and seemingly endless, untouched reefs of rich coral. Clustering around an abandoned Israeli settlement named Ophira (which was renamed Sharm el Sheikh) and a lovely palm-tree-lined beach at Dahab, they built grass-hut camps and simple restaurants.

Some of this early ethos can still be found, particularly around Dahab, a laid-back and funky resort town about two-thirds of the way down the coast between Taba in the north and Sharm el Sheikh in the south. For the most part, however, development has been quite high end, with walled compounds protecting the lush gardens and swimming pools of luxury resorts. If this is your thing, the eastern coastline of the Sinai beckons, and the lights of Sharm el Sheikh will burn brightly for you.

There is more to the Sinai, however, than the fun-and-sun developments along the coast. The very inaccessibility of the peninsula's interior mountains and plateaus make it perfect for trekking and adventure tourism, and there is a superb Bedouin-run ecolodge, Al Karm, in the center of the peninsula that's perfect as a base for trekking or a real getaway. There is also a beautifully preserved church and monastic compound at St. Catherine's Monastery. Even if you're not going to climb nearby Jebel Moussa (Mount Sinai), the area is worth a daylong visit.

The west coast of the peninsula, from Ras Mohamed up to the canal crossing near Port Suez, is less inviting. For a while it looked as though the beach resort industry around Ras Sudr might take off, and a lot of money was put into developments here, but today they stand mostly empty, victims both of the downturn that followed the incidents of 2004 and 2006 and a local climate that offers more wind than sun.

1 Taba Heights

The intention with Taba Heights is to eventually create another resort village along the lines of Gouna (p. 211), north of Hurghada on the Red Sea coast. In fact, many of the same developers involved in that project are also at work here. About 17km

The Sinai Peninsula

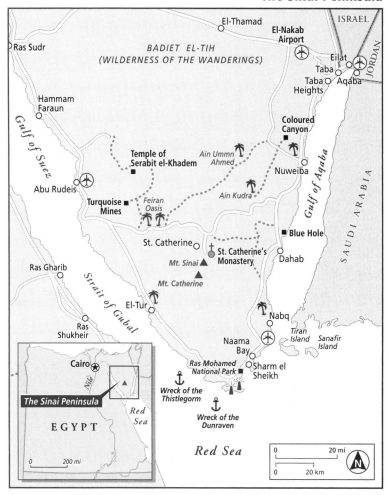

(a little more than 10 miles) south of Taba itself, the Taba Heights development spills down a long slope between a curve in the coastal highway and the sea.

Note: The Esso gas station across the road from the main entrance to Taba Heights has a small convenience store where you can buy water, soft drinks, and snacks for a fraction of the exorbitant cost inside the compound. You're almost certain to find someone who will sell you local beer and wine as well, but be discreet in asking, or the answer will never be "yes."

ORIENTATION
GETTING THERE
BY PLANE   Odds are, if you're staying at one of the big chain resorts in Taba Heights, you'll be flying in through Taba International Airport and then transfer from there to the hotel is included. The nearest airport that you could book a regular flight

---

⟮Warning⟯   **Terrorism on the Peninsula**

To most observers, the coordinated bombings that killed more than 30 tourists around Taba in the northeast corner of the Sinai in 2004 came as a bit of a surprise. After the attacks in Cairo and Upper Egypt in the 1990s, Egyptian security forces cracked down heavily and indiscriminately on Islamic organizations in the country, and seemed to have succeeded in killing or imprisoning its potential leaders. However, whoever was behind those bombings, or the subsequent attacks on Dahab and Sharm in 2005 and 2006, remains a bit of a mystery. Indications are that at least some of the attacks were carried out by indigenous groups whose support is bolstered by the glaring inequalities of opportunity and wealth exposed by the Red Sea tourist industry. Despite (or perhaps because of) getting free reign, security forces have struggled to deal with armed groups from north Sinai who may have been involved in the attacks. The risk to your personal safety while in Sinai remains extremely low, but as long as the basic issues remain unresolved, more attacks at some point seem inevitable.

A note on Taba to Nuweiba: The eastern coastline of the Sinai is at once bleak and beautiful, with high granite mountains that catch the light of the sun in morning and again just before dusk. If you're coming by road from Cairo, it's worth taking the time to watch the landscape pass. The coast here is filling up slowly with low-end tourist camps and resorts, most of which are aimed at either the local Egyptian market or the cross-border market with Israel. To an even greater extent than the rest of the coast, the market here is susceptible to the periodic threat of terrorism. The aftermath of bombings here in 2004, 2005, and 2006 are still evident in the number of building projects that you'll see along the coast highway that stand empty and half-finished, abandoned for lack of customers.

---

to is Sharm el Sheikh at the southern end of the peninsula, from which you would need to hire a taxi for the 3- to 4-hour drive up the coast. This is done easily enough—there are taxis at the airport that will take you for LE500 to LE800 ($90–$145/£46–£74)—but Dahab and Sharm are both closer and offer a greater range of hotels, so this doesn't really make much sense.

BY CAR   This is the best option if you're coming from Cairo independently. Expect the 5- to 6-hour drive across the desert to cost you LE800 to LE1,200 ($145–$218/£74–£111). You should also book your onward or return leg at the same time as you negotiate the ride there—there are few taxis on this stretch of the coast, and your negotiating position will not be good once you're at the resort.

BY BUS   It is possible to get a bus from the Turgoman Bus Terminal in Cairo to drop you on the highway by the gas station across from the main gates of the compound, but this isn't recommended. You'll arrive stiff and sore and then have to drag your bags down a long, hot driveway to the hotel.

WHERE TO STAY

Hyatt Regency Taba Heights   The Hyatt was designed by Michael Graves, who also did the Sheraton Miramar in Gouna (p. 212); you'll notice the similarities as soon as you walk through the front door to the lobby. The ambience here is tranquil, the gardens absorb other guests, and privacy comes easily and naturally because of the way the rooms and the landscape work together. Public areas thankfully lack the garish, over-the-top look of the Cairo Hyatt, and the rooms are designed around clean, modern lines and decorated with soothing earth tones. On the downside, the Hyatt doesn't make great use of its beachfront—you can lounge down there, of course, and there is the obligatory sea-view bar, but there's not much of a sea view from the rooms themselves.

Taba Heights. ✆ 069/3580234. Fax **069/3580235**. http://taba.regency.hyatt.com. 426 units. LE825 ($150/£76) double. AE, DC, MC, V. **Amenities:** 3 restaurants; 3 bars; 3 pools; gym; spa; dive center. *In room:* A/C, TV, minibar, safe, Internet.

Sofitel Taba Heights   If you're going to do a luxurious beachfront resort, you might as well go all out, and the Sofitel certainly does that. The central buildings are constructed in an attractive series of domes and arcades that surround the courtyard, and the pool area is designed to mimic an inlet with stepped "beaches" running down into the five swimming areas. My favorite aspect of this is the walk down to the long, sandy beach; paths lead over islands set in the middle of the swimming areas, so you never feel that you're very far from the water in this resort. Rooms are similarly opu-lent, with a bold mix of cream walls and dark wood, fabrics with traditional Asian pat-terns, and *mashrabeya*-style lattice work.

Taba Heights. ✆ **069/3580800**. Fax 069/3580808. 294 units. LE1,155 ($210/£107) double. AE, DC, MC, V. **Ameni-ties:** 3 restaurants; 3 bars; 5 pools; 4 tennis courts; fitness center; sailing. *In room:* A/C, TV, minibar, safe.

Taba Heights Marriot Beach Resort   This is the most fun of the resorts at Taba Heights. It's built on descending levels in an attempt to give the rooms in the back of the compound a clear view of the sea, and the low, Mediterranean-style buildings are surrounded by theme-park-style gardens where lagoon-shaped pools nestle among palm trees. The theme-park feel extends to the restaurants, with outlets such as the Grotto Restaurant, which is built in a fake-rock cave. Rooms are fine, lacking in char-acter, but spacious, clean, and comfortable.

Taba Heights. ✆ **069/3580100**. Fax 069/3580109. 394 units. LE770 ($140/£71) double. AE, DC, MC, V. **Amenities:** 4 restaurants; 4 bars; 2 pools (including kids' pool); 4 tennis courts; spa; dive center; Wi-Fi. *In room:* A/C, TV, minibar, safe, Internet.

2 Nuweiba

There are two very distinct sides to Nuweiba. At the southern end is the gritty port area, where you can catch a boat to Aqaba in Jordan. There's not much there, apart from the run-down dock facilities, some small stores, and a couple of hard-bitten fleabag hotels. Between here and the town itself, which is about 10km (6 miles) to the north, there are a number of hotels, many of which have been closed in the last few years or were never quite finished in the first place. The town is nothing special—it functions mainly to sell cheap T-shirts and beer to backpackers. Starting at its north-ern edge, there is a kilometer or so of beach that has turned into a strip of cheap hotels and camps known as Tarabin.

ORIENTATION
GETTING THERE
BY PLANE   The nearest airport is Taba International, which, at the time of writing, was not accepting regularly scheduled domestic flights.

BY BUS   The bus station is on the highway, directly across from the main entrance to the town. If you have (unwisely) arrived without setting up a car to your accommodations beforehand, you will probably be able to get a ride—for a price—from someone there. If not, try the nearby gas station.

GETTING AROUND

Transportation is a perennial problem on the coast. Staff at any of the hotels listed will be able to put you in contact with a private driver. Negotiate the price hard, and make sure that you explicitly nail down the specifics of time, destination, vehicle type, and air-conditioning (important during the summer). Unlike the rest of Egypt, ethical standards are pretty low among the drivers on this section of coast. You should pay around LE200 to LE250 a day ($36–$45/£19–£23) for a late-model, air-conditioned minivan.

WHERE TO STAY

The coastline on either side of Nuweiba is littered with little "camps" that fill in the holes between the half-finished resorts. Most are no more than a dozen woven-grass huts around a central shower and eating facility. I have listed one clean, basic place in Nuweiba and another to the south of the town. Tarabin, however, is one long strip of these camps for you to explore. The Petra is probably the first place I would try if Soft Beach (below) is full or doesn't appeal. *Warning:* A number of apparently more salubrious facilities exist around Nuweiba, but I strongly recommend not booking anything that is not listed here without first inspecting the premises—there are a string of half-finished and half-closed resorts in the area that will quickly turn a holiday into a nightmare.

EXPENSIVE

Hilton Nuweiba Coral Resort (Kids)   The Coral Resort has a lovely location, tucked into a long, sweeping curve of beach beneath a line of jagged granite mountains that catch the light of the setting sun. However, in terms of quality restaurants, bars, and entertainment, it might as well be at the end of the Earth. For this reason, almost all of its business is done in all-inclusive packages. Given the alternatives (or lack thereof), it's probably not a bad idea to pay for everything upfront (at a good discount to boot). Rooms are relatively small, though well appointed in a generic, beachfront resort kind of way. The difference between room grades is limited to a few square meters, so think about how much time you're actually going to spend in there before investing. The pools are fun and include quiet areas as well as more raucous kids' areas. The beach, of course, is a lovely great sweep of sand, perfect for sun-lounging, early morning jogs, or quiet evening walks to admire the sunset over the mountains.

Nuweiba. ✆ **069/3520320.** Fax 069/3520327. www1.hilton.com. 211 units. LE1,045 ($190/£97). AE, DC, MC, V. **Amenities:** 3 restaurants; 3 bars; kids' club; dive center; Internet. *In room:* A/C, TV, minibar, safe.

MODERATE

Nakhil Inn   This is a nice, fairly quiet place at the northern end of Tarabin. It has spacious, wood-paneled rooms and a cozy beach area out front. The atmosphere splits the difference nicely between the kind of laid-back attitude and closeness to the water and sand that you get at a camp and the creature comforts of a small hotel. The rooms open directly onto the beach area, which has plenty of seating areas, but is definitely too small for the kind of broad swathe of loungers that you get at a real beach resort. The restaurant, with its high ceilings and big windows that look in the direction of the beach, is a very pleasant place to linger over a long breakfast of pancakes and fruit salad.

Tarabin, Nuweiba. ✆ **069/3500879.** Fax 069/35000878. 38 units. LE231 ($42/£21) double. Rate includes breakfast. MC, V. **Amenities:** Restaurant. *In room:* TV, no phone.

Nuweiba Village Resort   This is a midrange place on the beach a little south of the town itself. The architecture of the main building will make you shudder—it looks like a cut-rate office building in an industrial park—but once you get to the grounds around the nicely sculpted pool, it's all holiday village, with lots of palm trees and sun loungers, and a long, beautiful beach. This is what you're here for, and the facilities are excellent. Rooms are small and have a bit of 1970s feel to them; the decor doesn't really make an effort to rise above generic, but they are spotlessly clean and comfortable. Even at the rack rate, what this place lacks in architectural style it makes up for in beach-lounging value for money.

Nuweiba. (©) **069/3500401-3.** Fax 069/3500407. www.nuweibavillageresort.com. 127 units. LE330 ($60/£31). **Amenities:** 2 restaurants; 2 bars; 2 pools (including kids' pool); 2 tennis courts; dive center. *In room:* A/C, TV, minifridge.

INEXPENSIVE
Basata   This is a simple but sophisticated beach camp run by a German-Egyptian couple. The name "Basata," which means "simplicity" in Arabic, is meant to sum up the camp's approach to vacationing. Accommodations are a mix of grass huts spaced out along the sandy beach and newer bungalows located at the very edge of where the beach runs into the desert. Unlike the uniform, and generally constricted and unpleasant, huts at other camps, Basata huts are spacious and comfortable, and each is unique. They are, to be sure, simple: grass-mat floors, simple beds made of the same material, and candles for light (there is no electricity in the huts). Toilet and washing facilities are shared. Only the bungalows (which I don't recommend—they are stiflingly hot in the summer, and offer no real advantage over the huts) have their own shower facilities. You can either cook your own meals (with food you bring in or purchase there) in the common kitchen or reserve a seat for the set meal each evening (LE40–LE50/$7.25–$9.10/£3.70–£4.60). Generally cooking your own is the best course (the set meals range from bland to unpleasant). Basata isn't for everyone: a tangle of rules, from no computers in the common areas to no snoozing on the beach, governs life here and may annoy some people.

25km (16 miles) north of Nuweiba. (©) **069/3500480** or 069/3500481. www.basata.com. 30 units. LE116 ($21/£11) per person in a beach hut; LE500 ($91/£46) chalet w/up to three occupants. MC, V. **Amenities:** Restaurant. *In room:* No phone.

Soft Beach   This is the best beach camp in Tarabin. Forty-five small huts are scattered about between the side road at the back and the wide, pleasant beach. Dining takes place in an open-sided area, with food coming through a little window from the clean kitchen area. The cabins are not the kind of place that you want to spend too much time, but then again, that's not what you're here for. The beach is superb, with (as advertised) very soft sand and a plethora of comfy lounging places.

Tarabin, Nuweiba. (©) **010/3647586.** www.softbeachcamp.com. LE60 ($11/£5.60). Cash only. **Amenities:** Restaurant. *In room:* No phone.

WHERE TO EAT
Between Taba and Dahab, there is almost nowhere to eat outside the major hotels. The truly desperate, and adventurous, may want to wander up the strip at Tarabin and try their luck with some of the beach-side places there.

The Castle Zaman   This is a really fun place to spend an evening or even a whole day. Built to resemble the ruins of a crusader castle on a ridge high above the sea, the place incorporates a commodious bar with open beams and rock-faced walls. A balcony along the front lets you enjoy the glorious view while eating dinner or just downing a few cold beers. There's a pool on a slightly lower level that also affords a stunning view out across the sea to Saudi Arabia, and even an underground cellar portion with "treasures" tucked into little niches. Food is excellent, but the portions are enormous—there is no way that anyone with a normal appetite will finish a serving. The slow-cooked lamb comes in a vast, traditional-style, earthenware dish, and the meat and the vegetables, which are cooked together, taste sublime. Keep in mind that you need to order your meal 2 to 3 hours in advance. If you're just stopping by for dinner, make sure that you phone ahead.

25km (16 miles) north of Nuweiba. ℂ 01/22140591. www.castlezaman.com. Dinner and use of all facilities LE292 ($53/£27). MC, V. Daily midday until the last guest leaves.

3 Dahab

With a laid-back atmosphere left over from the days when the only restaurant in town was a kiosk on the beach named the Hard Rock Cafe and the nicest hotel for miles had grass walls, Dahab is still the favorite vacation spot of expats and well-off Egyptians looking for something a little more low key than the sun and party scene in Sharm el Sheikh. Even 10 years ago, life was still a little rough around the edges here—unsophisticated food and hard beds were the price visitors paid for the spectacular scenery and even more spectacular diving. Nowadays, however, things are a little different. Not only have the attractions branched out into windsurfing and kitesurfing, but years of investment and some of the better urban planning on the Red Sea coast have paid off in making this town, if not elegant, at least pleasant to walk around. You can get some of the best food in the Sinai here, not to mention a very decent hotel at a good price, all with very little sacrifice in atmosphere and charm.

ORIENTATION

Dahab is divided into two main parts: new and old. The new part, now referred to as Dahab City, is to the south and is where the high-end hotels are. There is also a large lagoon that offers a range of conditions ideal for beginner and expert windsurfers.

The older part of Dahab is a kilometer or so north, connected by both a road and a seaside promenade for pedestrians and bikes. Known generally as Masbat, this older section of Dahab is more properly divided into Assala in the north, Masbat (the oldest section) in the middle, and Mashraba in the south. The length of the entire town is around 4km (2½ miles).

GETTING THERE

The East Delta bus arrives at the bus station in the new part of Dahab. From here it's usually possible to catch a taxi into Masbat for LE10 ($1.80/95p) or so, depending on your negotiating abilities. Beware of the friendly assistance of the boys in the jeeps—they'll demand an exorbitant amount when you get to your destination, and friendly negotiations will quickly turn to outright bullying.

GETTING AROUND

BY BIKE The long brick walkway along the edge of the water that links all three sections of old Dahab as well as the newer portion of Dahab City is fairly bicycle-friendly (though the pedestrians won't be if you don't take care and ride reasonably), and the traffic through the rest of town is pretty tame as well. The scale is perfect for biking, too. You can get anywhere in town in 15 or 20 minutes, and most places in 5.

Dahab

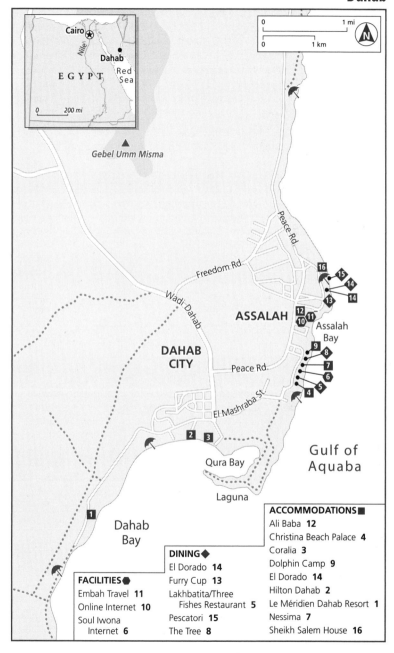

Cairo

Nile

EGYPT

Dahab

Red Sea

0   200 mi

0   1 mi

0   1 km

N

Gebel Umm Misma

Peace Rd.

Freedom Rd.

Wadi Dahab

ASSALAH

DAHAB CITY

Peace Rd.

El Mashraba St.

Assalah Bay

16
15
14
13   14
12 11
10

9
8
7
6
4   5

Gulf of Aquaba

Qura Bay

Laguna

Dahab Bay

FACILITIES ⬣
Embah Travel **11**
Online Internet **10**
Soul Iwona
   Internet **6**

DINING ◆
El Dorado **14**
Furry Cup **13**
Lakhbatita/Three
   Fishes Restaurant **5**
Pescatori **15**
The Tree **8**

ACCOMMODATIONS ■
Ali Baba **12**
Christina Beach Palace **4**
Coralia **3**
Dolphin Camp **9**
El Dorado **14**
Hilton Dahab **2**
Le Méridien Dahab Resort **1**
Nessima **7**
Sheikh Salem House **16**

Bikes can be rented at various places around town. None of them rises much above a rusted old clunker, and asking prices—LE10 to LE15 ($1.80–$2.75/95p–£1.40) per hour or LE80 to LE100 ($15–$18/£7.40–£9.25) per day—tend to be a little excessive. Bargain them down, though, and be happy with what you get. I like **Sam's,** below the Ali Baba hotel, or **Desert Divers** just around the corner.

BY FOOT   Most of Dahab, certainly if you stay in the old Masbat area, is eminently walkable. I recommend detouring around the town, in fact, and using the coastal walkway to get to where you're going.

BY TAXI   Taxis are available, but they tend to be exorbitant in their demands for money. Fortunately, you only need motorized transport to get outside town, to the Blue Hole for a day's snorkeling, for example. In this case, hire one of the jeeps that cruise about looking for passengers. Drivers of these vehicles, however, tend to be ethically disadvantaged—make sure to nail down every aspect of the ride before leaving. This includes not only the price but the drop-off point and whether he can pick up other passengers. Fail to specify these last two points, and you risk finding yourself jammed in with half a dozen new friends and dropped off somewhere only distantly related to your intended destination.

TOURIST INFORMATION

Increasing numbers of businesses offer Wi-Fi access, which means that road warriors who aren't afraid to tote the laptop to the beach will be able to lounge in the sun while staying in touch with the office, but Dahab hotels and restaurants on the whole remain behind the wired curve. Fortunately, there are several excellent **Internet** cafes right on the promenade. Expect to pay around LE5 to LE10 (90¢–$1.80/45p–95p) per hour.

Online Internet, Masbat (✆ 012/4017001), on the second floor of the building on your left about 10m (33 ft.) after you cross the bridge with the sea to your right, has eight Internet stations and good bandwidth. It's open daily from 10am to midnight; the rate is LE7 ($1.25/65p) per hour. **Soul Iwona,** Mashraba (✆ **069/ 3640987**), just past Lakhbatita heading north and right on the walkway, has six PCs, space for a laptop, and a whole lot of fresh air from the sea. It's open daily 10am to midnight; the rate is LE6 ($1.10/55p) per hour.

Dahab's not short on hole-in-the-wall **travel agencies** that can book your side trips to St. Catherine's or arrange for a few nights in the desert. **Embah,** Masbat (✆ **069/3641690;** www.embah.com), is an amazingly efficient full-service travel agency right in the middle of Dahab. They can book plane tickets, bus tickets (with 24-hour notice), and day trips, as well as more extensive diving and sightseeing trips. You can even pay by credit card (Visa only). Daily 9am to 7pm. See the "Active Vacation Planner" (p. 65) for other recommended companies in Dahab for diving, windsurfing and kitesurfing, and desert treks.

WHAT TO SEE & DO

Desert Treks   There are several locations within an easy day trip by jeep from Dahab that offer spectacular rock formations and perspectives on the desert. The top three locations for these trips are Colored Canyon, Ain Khudra, and White Canyon.

Diving   The combination of a laid-back attitude, stunning coral, and highly professional dive centers has long made Dahab a diver's heaven. Here's a selection of some dive sites within easy reach of the town:

Coral: Look but Don't Touch

Because of the year-round warmth of the water in the Red Sea, rich coral reefs abound. Everyone who visits the area should experience the richness of the life that teems just below the surface of the crystal-clear waters. At first sight, it's easy to imagine that these rocky outcroppings are tough and impervious to human touch, but this is far from the case. Touching the coral or walking on it will break and kill it, leaving behind a dead, gray wall and a hole in a complex ecosystem that can take decades or longer to heal. Most international resorts have opted to do the responsible thing and have built jetties that allow swimmers and divers to get into the water without damaging the coral. Unfortunately, there are many places on the coast—including Dahab—where the government and local entrepreneurs haven't found the foresight to protect this invaluable tourist resource, so it's the responsibility of individual tourists to look beyond the next few days of their holiday and think about the global environment. It's easy enough to do: Find a place where the water is deep enough to swim over the coral, never touch the coral with your hands or your feet, and never throw plastic bags or other refuse into the water.

Reef Island is a lovely concentration of brain and cabbage corals just off the shoulder of the bay that protects the lagoon in front of Dahab City. The aftermath of an earthquake has made some interesting passages through some of the corals.

Eel Garden is a colony of garden eels, which make their home in burrows on the sandy sea bed. Swimming above them, you see them extended vertically from their burrows like a little forest, bent a little into the current as they collect food from the passing water.

Ras Abu Galum is a popular spot to make a diving trek; arrive by camel or jeep, and spend a night or two at the Bedouin camp there. The reef has a variety of fire, brain, and table corals, and hosts a rich variety of sea life from emperor and puffer fish to turtles. What makes Abu Galum special, though, is the local population of sea cows, or manatee. Diving with these mammals, which can weigh up to 1,000kg (2,200 lbs.) is a truly special experience.

Snorkeling   Even if you're not ready to don tanks of air and bulky strapping stuffed with lead weights, you can experience the stunning underwater life around Dahab. The reef that runs parallel to Mashrab and Masbat is still worth snorkeling despite a decade of insensitive use, and the reef around Blue Hole is simply stunning. Many of the dive sites listed above are also accessible to snorkelers, depending on their level of fitness and swimming ability.

St. Catherine's Monastery   St. Catherine (see the "St. Catherine's" section later in this chapter) is a deeply significant site that is steeped in history and tradition and is a must-see for anyone with an interest in the history of the region or the church. Most hotels and any of the small tour operators in town can sell a tour up to St. Catherine's Monastery. Generally they leave late at night and arrive in time for the 2- to 3-hour climb to the top of Mount Moussa for the sunrise. Following is a tour of the monastery and a packed lunch before heading back to Dahab. Expect to pay about LE220 to LE330 ($40–$60/£20–£31). Think about whether you have time to overnight at the monastery and do the trek up the mountain, in addition to the tour of the church and its small but densely packed museum, in more comfort and less haste than these tours allow you.

WHERE TO STAY

Almost everywhere that's worth staying in Dahab fronts the sea. In the older parts of town, what was once a rough, unlit path along the foreshore has been replaced by an attractive and well-lit brick walkway that stretches the entire 3km (1¾-mile) length of the town.

EXPENSIVE

Coralia *(Kids)*   The Coralia has everything you need for a great loll-around vacation. The hotel is laid out in a series of buildings spread over a spacious compound that includes tennis courts, a big pool, and a lot of lawn. The beach, which looks out on the lagoon, is an equally great place for paddling and swimming or windsurfing and kiting. I particularly like the big, kid-friendly pool surrounded by comfy wicker furniture for relaxing and keeping an eye on things. The rooms are a mix of fairly standard, comfortable, resort-type offerings and some new, very stylish, Alain Jouen–designed rooms that feature bold colors and bolder angles. The super-modern fittings and sleek designs make me think that this is where the Jetsons would vacation if George won the lottery. Along with the Sofitel Tower in Cairo and the new Le Méridien in Dahab (below; coincidentally also designed by Jouen), these are some of my favorite hotel rooms in Egypt.

Dahab City, Dahab. ℂ 069/3640301. Fax 069/3640305. www.accorhotels.com. 139 units. LE715 ($130/£66) standard double; LE842 ($153/£78) deluxe double. AE, MC, V. **Amenities:** 3 restaurants; 4 bars; pool; kids' club; bank; dive center; Internet cafe. *In room:* A/C, TV, minibar, safe.

Hilton Dahab   This is a bit of a paint-by-numbers place, but it's none the worse for that. The architecture is generically Mediterranean, with high white walls and domes combined with touches of wood. The center of the compound is a wide lagoon, with a relatively modest pool set into a platform in the middle. Given the length of the beach available a 30-second walk away, however, it seems unlikely that there are too many complaints about the pool. Rooms are spacious and follow the stylistic lead of the rest of the hotel, with white walls, earth-tone curtains, and dark wood trim. Bathrooms are fitted with the kind of high-end fixtures you expect at this price, and beds, sofas, and chairs are as comfy as they are stylish. Do note, however, that the idea of "sea view" can be a little stretched at the Hilton—I asked where it was in one room and was told to "stand on the couch and look again."

Dahab City, Dahab. ℂ 069/3640310. Fax 069/3640424. 163 units. LE1,155 ($210/£107) standard double; LE1,238 ($225/£115) superior double; LE1,375 ($250/£127) suite. AE, MC, V. **Amenities:** 3 restaurants; 3 bars; pool; health club; gym; kids' club; dive center; Wi-Fi. *In room:* A/C, TV, minibar, safe Internet.

Le Méridien Dahab Resort   With the possible exception of the Sofitel Gezirah, this has got to be the sleekest, coolest, greatest looking big hotel in the country. Starting with the gorgeous, wide open lobby, this is a place that sets out to impress, and it doesn't let up until you've wandered by the series of cascading pools, each level with its own themed loungers; passed through the starkly beautiful garden landscaped with native plants and grasses; and collapsed into a sleek armchair in your bright orange and brown room. From dramatic angles to bold mixtures of textures and material, this is a hotel that keeps you on your toes and where the interior design will give you as much pleasure as the beach. Razzmatazz aside, rooms are spacious and everything from linens to the plasma TVs are the best quality.

Dahab Bay, Dahab. ℂ 069/3640425. www.starwoodhotels.com. 182 units. LE1,375 ($250/£127) standard double. AE, DC, MC, V. **Amenities:** 3 restaurants; 2 bars; 4 pools (including kids' pool); gym; spa; windsurfing; diving center. *In room:* A/C, TV, minibar, safe.

MODERATE

Ali Baba Tucked into the middle of Masbat in the older portion of Dahab, the Ali Baba may be fairly new, but it feels like an old regular. The entrance is down an alley and around the back, and the rooms then run in a line back in the direction of the foreshore walkway, at this point as wide as a two-lane road but pedestrianized. This is probably the most fun part of Dahab, with a host of shops, bars, and restaurants crowded into the immediate neighborhood, and a constant bustle of locals and tourists on their way somewhere (or, more likely, happily nowhere). The best rooms in the hotel are the "superior" rooms closer to the sea end of the building. These are large and nicely decorated with *mashrabeya* screens and comfortable arabesque furniture. They're worth the difference in price from the standard rooms. Compared to some of its competition—the super-clean Christina or the stylishly stark El Dorado—maintenance and upkeep aren't that great, but the funky factor is definitely higher.

Masbat, Dahab. © **069/3640504** or 010/1767970. 15 units. LE248 ($45/£23) standard double; LE330 ($60/£31) superior double. Cash only. **Amenities:** Restaurant. *In room:* A/C, TV, minifridge.

Christina Beach Palace The Christina is a moderately priced hotel that does a great job of combining laid-back Dahab funkiness with good old-fashioned quality such as soft beds, plenty of hot water, and extreme cleanliness. Laid out in several two-story white buildings, rooms are not very big, but they're exceptionally comfortable. Each one has a decent-size balcony with a sea view, and on the upper floor, ceilings are domed. Down on the other side of the walkway, meanwhile, the lounge area is all Dahab, all the time—the kind of place where time slips away between the late breakfast and the later lunch, and you only have time to squeeze in an hour of snorkeling on the reef before its time for a sunset drink and a stroll up the path to see what looks good for dinner.

Mashraba, Dahab. © **069/3640406** or 069/3640390. www.christinahotels.com. LE385 ($70/£36) double. MC, V. **Amenities:** 2 restaurants; bar. *In room:* A/C, TV.

Dolphin Camp "Run by nice people for nice people" may sound like a hollow slogan, but it seems to be true here. Management will give you a once-over as you come through the door of this midlevel camp on the foreshore walkway in Mashraba, and once you pass you'll be welcomed like a long lost family member. (I don't know what happens if you fail.) Accommodations range from traditional bamboo huts cooled with fans to simple domed rooms or full-on wooden cabins with en suite facilities and air-conditioning. At the budget end, I would take the fan-cooled bamboo hut over the non-A/C inside room any day of the week, but for a little more money, either the air-conditioned rooms or the air-conditioned cabins are definitely the way to go in the heat of the summer. The layout of the compound looks like it just sort of happened over the years; it's all very relaxed and friendly, and at the end of the day offers excellent value for money.

Mashraba, Dahab. © **069/3640081**. www.dolphincamp.net. 17 units. LE60 ($11/£5.50) double bamboo hut or room in main building w/fan only; LE105 ($19/£9.70) double in air-conditioned room or hut. Cash only. **Amenities:** Restaurant. *In room:* A/C or fan, no phone.

El Dorado This very compact, European hotel has the enviable advantage of being laid out around one of Dahab's best Italian restaurants (p. 168). Rooms are frugal and small—white walls and simple wooden furniture—but well proportioned, with comfortable beds and good-quality linens. Rooms vary from the very basic, toilet-down-the-hallway type, to somewhat more commodious (but still fairly slimmed-down) doubles with en suite. The central courtyard is mainly taken up by the restaurant, while on the other side of the walkway there is a beautifully designed graveled seashore area for sitting and watching the sunset or the sunrise. Most people are going to find the El Dorado substantially overpriced at the rack rate, but expect a good healthy discount.

Assala, Dahab. ✆ 069/3641027. 15 units (7 w/private bathrooms). LE413 ($75/£38) double w/private bathroom. MC, V. **Amenities:** Restaurant; bar. *In room:* A/C, no phone.

Nessima This is one of the first places in Dahab to move away from the purely beach-camp ethos that prevailed in the late 1980s and toward something a little more chic. The two-story buildings are nestled in a well maintained garden, and nice touches such as wooden latticework grills, which made the place the nicest in town when it was built, still stand in good stead today. There's a small-but-elegant pool in a courtyard that opens to the sea, which also means it's open to the public walkway; however, this doesn't detract from the facility. Rooms are not very large, but they're pleasantly designed with Nubian-style brick-domed ceilings and bathrooms that are a class above anything else in this price range. The "superior" rooms open directly onto the pool area, which is very nice, but I'm not sure that it's worth the difference in the price. The dive center attached to the hotel is one of the most competent in town, the restaurant is excellent, and the bar is great. This place is value for money.

Mashraba, Dahab. ✆ **069/3640320.** Fax 069/3640321. www.nesima-resort.com. 51 units. LE476 ($87/£44) double; LE652 ($119/£60) superior double. Rates include breakfast. MC, V. **Amenities:** 2 restaurants; bar; pool; dive center; Wi-Fi. *In room:* A/C, TV, minifridge.

Sheikh Salem House *(Kids)* This quiet little hotel at the northern end of Assala is one of the best budget options in Dahab, especially if you're traveling with kids. Rooms are large, particularly for their price range, and directly on the water. The decor is nothing fancy, but if you're looking to be away from the party zone and still on the sea, then the location is perfect. There are a range of rooms, from the small and very basic "economy" rooms to the "suites," which are really just large rooms with a niche for a kitchenette (complete except for the stove) that's sufficient to prepare snacks or store leftovers and cold drinks. They can also combine rooms to make apartments, so if you're traveling as a group, it makes sense to contact them by e-mail and plan well ahead. All the rooms are different; check the website before booking.

Assala, Dahab. ✆ **069/3641820.** www.sheikhsalemhouse.com. 16 units. LE60–LE90 ($11–$16/£5.50–£8) economy; LE220–LE280 ($40–$50/£20–£25) suite. Cash only. **Amenities:** Restaurant; Wi-Fi. *In room:* A/C, TV, kitchenette (in some).

WHERE TO EAT

Eating in Dahab used to be an adventure, a risky culinary crawl through beachside cafes that all offered the same menu of grilled calamari, *shish tawook,* and fries, and as often as not sent you away with a nasty case of funny-tummy. Nowadays, things are a little different. There are literally dozens of civilized restaurants along the seaside promenade, and a slow evening stroll checking them out is one of the pleasures of Dahab.

El Dorado ITALIAN Sophisticated European design and the best desserts in Egypt make El Dorado my number-one spot for Italian food in town and one of my favorite places to eat in the country. The roof is grass, and the tables are rough wood, but the walls are sleek and made mostly of glass, and the lighting is discreet. The gnocchi is perfectly formed and served in a tomato-and-basil sauce. On my last visit, I peeked at a neighbor's steak, which was nicely rare and served with a neat pile of tasty-looking grilled vegetables. Save room for dessert, which includes tiramisu and a stunningly rich panna cotta with Irish cream sauce.

Assala. ✆ **069/3641027.** Reservations recommended. Appetizers LE15–LE30 ($2.75–$5.45/£1.40–£2.80); main courses LE45–LE100 ($8.20–$18/£4.20–£9.25). MC, V. Daily 7–11pm.

⟨Warning⟩   No Belly Laugh

In a place such as Dahab, which still has quite a few backpacker places along the waterfront, you can still pick up stomach bugs that will put you in bed for a day or two, or worse. Stick with the midrange and upper-range restaurants—you won't pay that much more, and the cost in lost holiday time of making a mistake just isn't worth it. Outdoor grills are also a great way of ensuring that you're getting freshly cooked food, and avoid places with a low turnover or ones that seem to be bringing the food from another restaurant. Make sure that your chicken and fish is cooked all the way through, and it may be a little paranoid, but I almost never eat anything with ground meat in it.

Lakhbatita/Three Fishes Restaurant _Kids_ INTERNATIONAL   If you like Sam Cooke and the sound of waves, if you think that the sunset makes a nice backdrop for a dining room, and if you like fresh pasta and seafood, Lakhbatita is for you. The interior has funky seating, open wood, tiled walls, and braids of garlic hanging from the beams, while outside on the rock breakwater it's more sophisticated: Tables are arranged within a high, open-sided structure of large wooden beams, with a floor made of open-faced rock. The lighting has been carefully thought through (not that usual in Egypt) to enhance the mood and give enough light to eat by. When the tide is in, you're close enough to the water to have a spray-dampened tablecloth. The Milk Fish filet is simply cooked in olive oil with a light crusting of rock salt and spices and is served with grilled vegetables; it's the perfect complement to the atmosphere and the place. For those toting children, there's a small playground that's far enough away that the noise doesn't intrude, but close enough to keep an eye on what's going on.

Mashraba. ℂ **012/8284612.** www.lakhbatita.com. Appetizers LE20–LE40 ($3.65–$7.30/£1.85–£3.70); main courses LE30–LE80 ($5.45–$15/£2.80–£7.40). Cash only. Daily 7–11pm.

Pescatori ITALIAN   Down at the northern end of the seaside walkway in Assala, Pescatori offers tasty Italian cuisine made of organic ingredients and served in a funky, shaded, water-side dining area. The _risotto a frutti di mare_ has a creamy sauce and is full of shrimp and local fish; it goes great with a bottle of white wine. At the end of the walkway here, it's very quiet at night, and the only sound is the sea slapping against the rocks and the evening breeze coming through the trees.

Eel Garden. ℂ **012/7972361.** Appetizers LE20–LE45 ($3.65–$8.20/£1.85–£4.20); main courses LE45–LE70 ($8.20–$13/£4.20–£6.50). Cash only. Daily 6pm–midnight.

WHERE TO DRINK

Furry Cup   This oddly named place in Assala, toward the Eel Garden area at the northern end of the seaside walkway, is one of the nicest places to kick back for a few drinks or a cup of coffee, check your e-mail with the free Wi-Fi, chat with friends, or just contemplate life. It has high ceilings and a friendly staff, and it's about the only place in town where you can get imported liquor instead of the headache-inducing Egyptian brands.

Assala, in front of the Blue Beach Club. ℂ **069/3640411.** MC, V. Daily 10am to midnight; happy hour 6–8pm.

The Tree   Music videos, a couple of open-air pool tables, and a choice of indoor or beachfront seating make The Tree one of the classic beachfront hangouts in Dahab.

Oh, and the long bar backed up by a wall of liquor bottles doesn't hurt either. Ambience is laid-back and fun, and the staff are friendly and relaxed.

Masbat. ✆ 010/6466863. Cash only. Daily 11am–late.

4 St. Catherine's

St. Catherine's is smack in the middle of the Sinai Peninsula and has an end-of-the-Earth feel to it. The town is little more than a single loop of road that passes a few hotels and a couple of stores, and despite the enormous number of tourists and pilgrims who come here, it feels isolated and not particularly welcoming. Just a couple of kilometers outside town, however, is the beautifully preserved 6th-century monastery of St. Catherine, which is said to be built on the site where God spoke to Moses from the burning bush. Just behind the monastery is Mount Sinai, locally known as Jebel Moussa (Mount Moses), where he apparently received The Ten Commandments.

Apart from its religious significance, this area has some of the most spectacular, not to mention bleak and intimidating, topography in the country. For the most part, it's extremely arid (hot in the summer and cold in the winter), and the landscape is marked by low jagged mountains that conceal tiny valleys full of greenery. Hiking in this area is tough but rewarding. For those who wish to experience the area without the pain, or simply want a base for further exploration, there's a lovely ecolodge just outside the town of St. Catherine near the village of Sheikh Awad.

ORIENTATION
GETTING THERE
BY PLANE   There are strong rumors that the nearby Israeli-built airport may open soon, but there have always been rumors to this effect.

BY CAR   If you're coming up from Sharm el Sheikh, a rented car makes good sense. It may be more expensive than the bus, but the freedom of moving when you want and having transport around a taxi-less town is worth it. Moreover, thanks to a European Union aid package, the roads are exceptionally good here. See p. 178 for how to rent a car in Sharm.

BY BUS   There is a new and fairly pleasant bus station at the western end of town. The East Delta bus leaves for Cairo at around 6pm. There is an earlier bus that goes to Suez at 1pm, and a bus to Dahab and Nuweiba at the same time. Tickets cost LE40 ($7.30/£3.70) Cairo, LE30 ($5.45/£2.80) Suez, and LE16 ($2.90/£1.50) Dahab.

GETTING AROUND
If you've arrived by bus or taxi, you'll quickly find yourself stranded if you haven't made arrangements to be picked up (see the "Active Vacation Planner," p. 65, for help). With no public transport or taxis, getting around St. Catherine is a matter of prearranging transfers or hitching rides. The latter is surprisingly easy—there are usually foreigners staying in town who are heading up to the monastery in their own cars.

⌜ *Fun Fact* **In the Thick of It**

The walls of the St. Catherine's Monastery, which were built in the middle of the 6th century A.D., are 3m (more than 9 ft.) thick in some places.

The Catherine Wheel

A popular attraction, the Catherine Wheel, started out as a plain wooden-cart wheel that was put to ingenious use in a particularly nasty method of execution. The condemned was strapped to the wheel, and a bar was inserted between the spokes. As the wheel was turned, the changing angle of the lever snapped the arm and leg bones. The next step was to weave the mangled limbs of the still-living victim through the spokes and hoist the wheel up somewhere prominent so that the slow death that ensued could be enjoyed by all. It became known as the Catherine Wheel after St. Catherine of Alexandria apparently outdid the wheel to which she was strapped for execution, with the spokes breaking instead of her bones. Though she was subsequently beheaded, her short-lived triumph is still celebrated by children in Europe with a whirling shower of sparks.

TOURIST INFORMATION

There is a **Banque Misr** beside the gas station in town that's open 9am to 2pm and 5 to 7pm; it's a good place to change money. The Internet cafe **Desert Net** has six clunky PCs available for LE6 ($1.10/55p) an hour.

WHAT TO SEE & DO

Mount Sinai (Jebel Moussa) ⟨⟨   Most people start this walk about 3 or 4 hours before sunrise, timing it to arrive at the summit for the spectacular sunrise over the surrounding mountains. There are two ways up the 2,285m (7,500-ft.) mountain, both fairly easy to find from the base around the monastery. The first, which most people use for the ascent, is—initially, at least—a winding, gently sloped path that starts from behind the monastery. It's quite beautiful to see the thread of lights used by the walkers wending their way up the slope. A little more than about halfway up, at Elijah's Bowl, it turns to stairs (in fact, the last 750 of the Steps of Repentance), and if you're not in good shape, the final part of the climb on the narrow, crowded rock steps can be quite grueling. The other way, which many people use for the descent, is steeper and more direct. Known as the Steps of Repentance, it is comprised of 3,750 stone steps carved into the side of the mountain. It is sign-posted and easy to find, and from the top, it makes for a much quicker descent than going back the way you came up. Reckon on an hour for the descent this way.

A flashlight, plenty of water, a snack for the summit, and warm clothing are musts for this climb. Even in the summer, the nights are chilly, and in the winter it's downright cold. There are a good number of places on the way up to get a hot tea, mind you, and these places often have chocolate bars for sale. Keep in mind that the climb is pretty popular, and that the path as well as the summit itself can get pretty crowded in the hour leading up to dawn.

St. Catherine's Monastery ⟨⟨⟨   St. Catherine's Monastery, which was built in the 6th century by Byzantine Emperor Justinian I, is said to be the oldest continuously functioning Christian monastery in existence. It is still home to a community of the Greek Orthodox monks who guard the compound and its contents, and operate the nearby guesthouse and restaurant. It's built around the Chapel of the Burning Bush, which dates to the 4th century A.D. and is said to be built on the site of the original burning bush. Tradition holds that the bush growing there today is, in fact, the very

The Story of St. Catherine

St. Catherine of Alexandria, according to legend, started out as the daughter of a 4th-century governor of the Mediterranean city. Converted by a monk in an ecstatic, mystical rite, she made a reputation, and a powerful enemy, for herself by converting the wife of Roman Emperor Marcus Aurelius Valerius Maxentius. For her efforts, she was ultimately condemned to death on the wheel (p. 165), but when she was strapped down, it broke (hence her frequent depiction with a broken wheel), and she had to be beheaded instead. Her intact remains were discovered rather mysteriously several centuries later to the south of the monastery on the summit of what is now named Mount St. Catherine. You can climb the mountain and still see the indent where her body was found.

bush from which God spoke to Moses and told him that he was standing on holy ground. One of the things that makes this place special is the **collection of paintings and art** that was untouched by the iconoclastic hysteria that gripped the church in the 8th and 9th centuries. The second must-see within the compound is the **museum of relics and icons.** Entrance is LE50 ($9.10/£4.65), payable at the museum inside the walls of the monastery compound, which is more than reasonable considering the array of perfectly preserved early manuscripts, richly decorated reliquaries, painted icons, and embroidery. Finally, don't miss the **Church of St. Catherine** (more properly known as the Basilica of the Transfiguration), which includes a small sampling of the monastery's rich collection of icons, as well as one of the best preserved Byzantine mosaics in the world over the apse. Women and men should dress modestly.

© **069/3470343,** 069/3470677, or 069/3470740. Admission to monastery free; museum extra LE50 ($9.10/£4.65) 9am–noon.

Trekking   The mountainous topography around St. Catherine makes for spectacular trekking. The country is rugged, however, and it's all too easy to get lost if you set out on your own. Excellent trained local guides are available here (see the "Active Vacation Planner," p. 65), and it would be foolhardy not to take advantage of their services.

An easy walk from Al Karm ecolodge, **Nabatean Village** is the remains of a 3rd- or 4th-century village built by the ancient Nabatu people. It is a particularly striking walk from Karm because of the similarities in the stone work techniques between the old and the new. Make sure that you stop on the way by the rock leopard trap, out of use since the extermination of big cats in Egypt.

If you're lucky in **Wadi Farrah,** you may spot the remnants of the once considerably larger ibex herds that used to grace the peninsula. There is still a small resident population here, though hunting continues to pare down their numbers and threatens them with outright extinction. There are also a number of Byzantine buildings close by to visit.

A few kilometers to the south of the modern town, **Mount St. Catherine** is apparently where St. Catherine's uncorrupted remains appeared several centuries after her death. At more than 2,600m (8,500 ft.), it's actually the highest point on the peninsula and offers spectacular views of the surrounding mountains, as well as the small niche in the rock where the saint's corpse was laid by the angels.

St. Catherine's Monastery

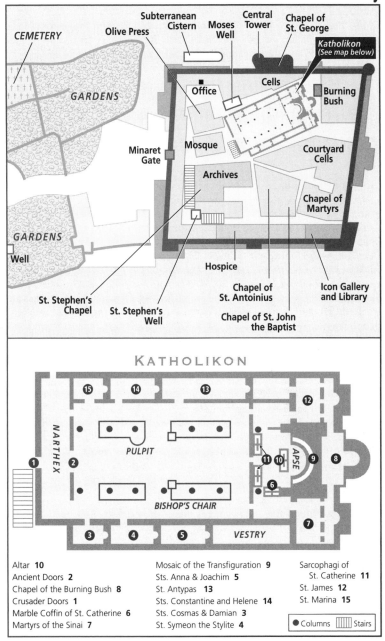

CEMETERY

Olive Press

Subterranean Cistern

Moses Well

Central Tower

Chapel of St. George

Katholikon
(See map below)

GARDENS

Office

Cells

Burning Bush

Minaret Gate

Mosque

Courtyard Cells

Archives

Chapel of Martyrs

GARDENS

Well

Hospice

Icon Gallery and Library

St. Stephen's Chapel

St. Stephen's Well

Chapel of St. Antoinius

Chapel of St. John the Baptist

KATHOLIKON

NARTHEX

PULPIT

BISHOP'S CHAIR

APSE

VESTRY

Altar **10**
Ancient Doors **2**
Chapel of the Burning Bush **8**
Crusader Doors **1**
Marble Coffin of St. Catherine **6**
Martyrs of the Sinai **7**

Mosaic of the Transfiguration **9**
Sts. Anna & Joachim **5**
St. Antypas **13**
Sts. Constantine and Helene **14**
Sts. Cosmas & Damian **3**
St. Symeon the Stylite **4**

Sarcophagi of
St. Catherine **11**
St. James **12**
St. Marina **15**

● Columns   Stairs

WHERE TO STAY

Catherine Plaza   This is the most modern of the three hotels in the town and is a favorite of pilgrimage groups who come to tour the monastery and climb the mountain. It is located on the loop road in St. Catherine itself, a 10- or 15-minute walk from the town and a 20-minute walk from the bus station. Rooms aren't large, but they're comfortable enough, with a bathroom and reasonable quality fixtures. Decor is pretty generic budget hotel, and there is a comfortable lobby-restaurant area. The pool is heated in the winter, when a dip would be, to say the least, bracing at the best of times.

St. Catherine. ℂ 069/3470289 or 069/3470298 St. Catherine's, or 02/24178928 or 02/4145141 Cairo. Fax 069/3470292 St. Catherine's or 02/24178928 or 02/4145141 Cairo. www.catherineplaza.com. 168 units. LE330 ($60/£31) double. MC, V. **Amenities:** 2 restaurants; bar; pool. *In room:* A/C, TV, minifridge.

El Karm   I am a huge fan of this Bedouin-owned and -operated ecolodge about 25km (15 miles) north of the town in the direction of Cairo. It was developed as part of the St. Catherine's Protectorate, and the buildings were built entirely by traditional methods using beautiful open-stone construction. Facilities are, in some ways, more basic than basic: There is absolutely no electricity, and beds are thin mattresses on stone shelves covered in camel blankets. But it's a very elegant simplicity, and the food, cooked by owner-manager Jamal Atteya, is superb. The last time I was there, he had rain-fed local olive oil to sample, and dinner was lake trout baked in the coals of an open fire. There's a dining room with handmade wood furniture, but most of the time you'll end up eating outside under the stars around the cooking fire. El Karm is hard to beat if you want to experience the desert culture, and my recommendation is to use it as a base for hiking the nearby canyons. Jamal and his associates are knowledgeable and considerate guides.

El Karm is up about 5km (3 miles) of track that is unpassable without a 4-wheel-drive. The best way to get there is to arrange with Jamal to meet in St. Catherine and ride out with, or follow (if you're traveling with your own 4×4), him or someone he recommends. If you're feeling adventurous, go to Sheikh Awad (the little village beside the turnoff to Al Karm), and ask around until you find someone willing to drive you up the road—you'll probably end up in the back of an old pickup truck for around LE50 ($9.10/£4.65). It is also possible to hike from St. Catherine.

ℂ 010/1324693 (if there is no answer, leave a message, including contact details, and keep trying—the network is patchy around St. Catherine). 12 units. LE100 ($18/£9.25) per person. Cash only. **Amenities:** Restaurant. *In room:* No phone.

El Wady El Mouqdous   This hotel is similar to its neighbor, the Catherine Plaza (above), but rooms are a little smaller and a little older, and bathroom fixtures a little more budget. There is an interestingly shaped pool in the central courtyard that's a great place to relax in the heat of the summer. Views of the low mountains around the town are pleasant, but nothing spectacular. This place is pretty good value for money if you're here for a purpose—to see the monastery, climb the mountain, or hike the surrounding countryside. It's not the kind of hotel that you would stay in just for fun.

St. Catherine. ℂ 069/3470225. 35 units. LE209 ($38/£19) double. MC, V. **Amenities:** Restaurant; bar; pool. *In room:* A/C, TV, minifridge.

Monastery Guest House   Nestled up against the monastery, this is the most convenient place to stay in St. Catherine if you're here to climb the mountain and tour the religious facilities. Fittingly, the rooms are almost monastically stark and small.

Decor is nonexistent, but the air-conditioning/heating units work well, and the bare-bones bathroom has an ample supply of hot water. Rooms are arranged in a row along a courtyard across from a coffee shop, a small store that sells snacks, and facilities that you will share with busloads of tourists who gather 2 to 4 hours before dawn to prepare for the climb up the mountain. Beside the convenience store is the dining hall, where the simple breakfasts and dinners are served to people staying at the guesthouse. Despite the large parking lot inside the compound, if you have a car with you, government security will make you leave it 500m (1,641 ft.) or so away from the compound.

St. Catherine. ⓒ **069/3470353**. Fax 069/3470543. 30 units. LE360 ($65/£33) double. Cash only. **Amenities:** Restaurant. *In room:* A/C, no phone.

WHERE TO EAT

Eating in St. Catherine is a problem that I have never solved. There is nowhere outside the hotels to eat, and the only one of them that serves a good meal is Al Karm, which is too far outside the town to go for dinner. My recommendation is to bring snacks or buy them in town.

5 Sharm el Sheikh

Up until the mid-1980s, the area that now holds Egypt's biggest resort city was virtually uninhabited. It wasn't unnoticed, however: Sharm el Sheikh overlooks the island of Tiran, and the narrow straits between the mainland and the island are a vital choke point for oil and other important supplies bound for Israel, and for many years it was actually held by the Israelis. Egyptian President Nasser's closure of the waterway in May 1967 was one of the triggers of the Six Day War, in which Egypt again lost control of the area to Israeli forces. It wasn't until after 1982, when the area was handed back to Egypt in exchange for a peace treaty under the Camp David Accords, that the town began to blossom as an international tourist destination. First came the divers, staying in rough-and-ready beach camps for the sake of the spectacular coral reefs just offshore and the profusion of wrecks in easy range of a day's boat trip. Today the majority of visitors are beach-holiday makers. Dozens of flights descend every day on Sharm International Airport, most direct from major European hubs.

Sharm is now plausibly claimed to contain one-third of all the hotels in Egypt, though a perhaps more telling statistic comes from the Egyptian government, which says that 86% of all the housing here is in the form of hotels, and only 3% houses the original Bedouin population of the area.

ORIENTATION

Sharm el Sheikh is divided into four distinct areas that are loosely strung out along the highway like close, but separate, towns. Arriving from the south, with the sea on your right, you come first to the Old Town. Then to your right, on a plateau that juts out into the sea, is Hadaba. Another 5 to 6km (3½ miles) up the highway is Naama Bay. The international airport is another 5km (3 miles) or so past Naama Bay, which puts it about halfway to the new, almost exclusively package holiday resort, area of Nabq (pronounced *Na*-bik).

The Old Town About as close to a "real town" as Sharm gets these days, the Old Town is a somewhat ramshackle collection of shops and restaurants. Tourist items such as *shishas* (water pipes), snorkels and fins for snorkeling, and T-shirts are

Sharm el Sheikh

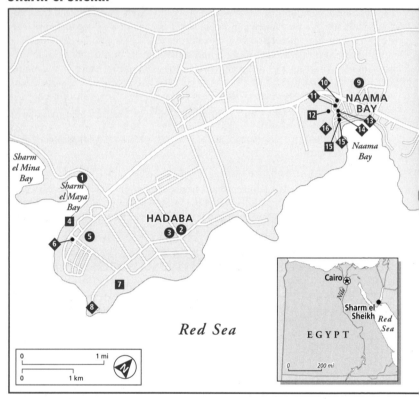

significantly cheaper here than in Naama Bay. Behind the Old Town, there's housing for the huge migrant tourism workforce that come to Sharm from all over Egypt.

Hadaba   An almost autonomous pocket of hotels and amusement facilities—there is a water park and two go-kart tracks—Habada is also relatively isolated from the goings on down in Naama Bay. Though there are one or two restaurants and a large open-air mall is being developed, this is mostly a neighborhood of high-end resorts.

Naama Bay   This intense cluster of restaurants, hotels, and a few bars around the bay is the "downtown core" of Sharm el Sheikh. It's the only part of Sharm where you can get out of your hotel and walk to a restaurant or a bar. For the most part boisterous and crowded, Naama Bay offers a pleasant almost-seaside promenade lined with restaurants where you can cruise for dinner. Many hotels that list themselves in Naama Bay, however, are well out of walking distance from the core.

Nabq   This is a newly developed area north of the airport. Big money has been spent supplying the place with shopping malls and facilities outside the walls of the big, all-inclusive resorts here, but it's still on an inhuman scale and ultimately a bleak and unpleasant place to walk around.

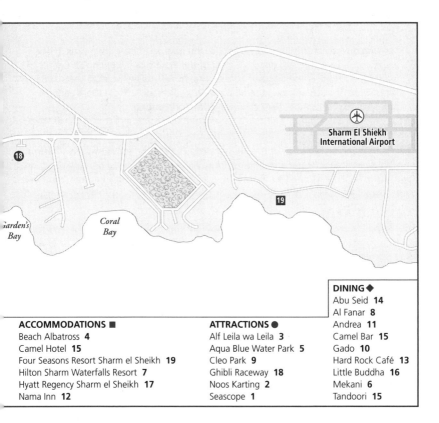

Sharm El Shiekh
International Airport

DINING ◆
Abu Seid **14**
Al Fanar **8**

ACCOMMODATIONS ■
Beach Albatross **4**
Camel Hotel **15**
Four Seasons Resort Sharm el Sheikh **19**
Hilton Sharm Waterfalls Resort **7**
Hyatt Regency Sharm el Sheikh **17**
Nama Inn **12**

ATTRACTIONS ●
Alf Leila wa Leila **3**
Aqua Blue Water Park **5**
Cleo Park **9**
Ghibli Raceway **18**
Noos Karting **2**
Seascope **1**

Andrea **11**
Camel Bar **15**
Gado **10**
Hard Rock Café **13**
Little Buddha **16**
Mekani **6**
Tandoori **15**

GETTING THERE

BY PLANE Sharm el Sheikh International Airport (which you will very occasionally still see listed by its Israeli name, "Ophira") is Egypt's second busiest airport. There are more than a dozen flights per day out of Cairo, and the cost of the 1-hour flight is around $150 return (which is actually less than the cost of the long, hot, and dangerous taxi ride). Despite its modern architecture, it's not one of the country's best—grit your teeth and remember you didn't come on holiday for the airport. It's also probably best to wait until you get to the hotel to use the toilet. There are always plenty of blue-and-white taxis around if you're not getting picked up by your hotel.

BY CAR You can get to Sharm el Sheikh by car, but it's really not worth it in anything less than urgent circumstances. Expect a car and driver for a one-way trip between Cairo and Sharm to cost around LE750 to LE1,000 ($136–$182/£70–£93).

BY BUS The bus station is in Hadaba. There are usually plenty of taxis around to take you to your hotel. Walking is not an option. **Super Jet** (© **069/3661622**) buses run back to Cairo regularly starting at 10:30am. There are more at 1, 3, and 5:30pm, and the last bus goes at 11:30pm. Tickets are LE70 or LE80 ($13–$15/£6.50–£7.40), depending on what type of bus it is.

Visas

Arriving directly at the Sinai from abroad, you have a choice of two visas. There is a free, 14-day visa that's good for most of the Peninsula (including St. Catherine's), and there is the regular 30-day visa for all of Egypt that costs LE83 ($15/£7.60). If in doubt, buy the all-Egypt visa; upgrading from the free Sinai-only visa can be tedious, time consuming, and frustrating.

BY FERRY The fast ferry from Hurghada comes in to the south of the Old Town. You'll have to walk across a wide parking lot to get out of the park and out to the street where the taxis are allowed to wait. This can be unpleasant if it's hot and you have heavy bags, and especially so if you're feeling a little queasy after a rough crossing.

GETTING AROUND

BY TAXI Taxis are an unfortunate necessity in Sharm el Sheikh, where hotels tend to be a good long way from each other and from the nightlife and eateries of Naama Bay. On the other hand, the fleet here is the newest and cleanest in the country (you're going to be blown away if you're coming from Cairo), and even at several times the price of anywhere else in Egypt, the fares are reasonable compared to the West. Expect to pay LE40 to LE50 ($7.30–$9.10/£3.70–£4.63) to get between areas of town (for example Hadaba to Naama Bay, Naama Bay to a hotel up the coast or around the airport). Negotiate the fare before getting in.

BY CAR If you're going to be running around between the different sections of Sharm, visiting Ras Mohamed National Park and maybe even taking a day trip up to Dahab, Colored Canyon, or St. Catherine's Monastery, you should think about renting a car. With a little bargaining, you should be able to rent something small but reliable for around LE165 to LE220 ($30–$40/£15–£20) per day.

CRC, Plaza Mall, Naama Bay (© **069/3601297**), is cheap, but the Peugeots they rent can be dirty and in rough shape. Rates start around LE165 ($30/£15) a day with about a LE1-per-kilometer (20¢/10p) charge after the first 100km (62 miles). It's open daily from 8am to 1pm and from 5 to 10pm.

Avis, Morgana Mall, Naama Bay (© **069/3600979**), is more expensive, but the cars are generally a little nicer. Rates start around LE248 ($45/£23) a day for a compact model with an extra LE1.35-per-kilometer (25¢/15p) charge. It's open daily from 8am to 1pm and from 5 to 10pm.

Traffic around Sharm is generally quite manageable for an experienced driver, but in the summer months take care of the Gulf Arabs playing testosterone-fueled racing games on the public streets.

TOURIST INFORMATION

Banks and change offices abound in Sharm, and most hotels accept major credit cards and will also accept payment in foreign currency (dollars and euros). You can also change money at the going rate at the airport.

Travco, Bank's Road, Ras Um El Sid (© **069/3660764** or 069/3660765; fax 069/3664256), is one of the few good **travel agents** that operates throughout the country and deals in international bookings as well. The friendly and knowledgeable staff at **Spring Tours,** Um El Sid Hill (© **069/3664427**), makes it my choice for booking local activities.

WHAT TO SEE & DO

From go-karts to quads and submarines to snorkeling, there's enough to fill quite a few days. With few exceptions, these activities are safe, and many are kid-friendly. There is a crocodile show in Hadaba that looks cheesy and potentially fun from the outside, but it's an unhygienic rip-off once you get inside, and the quad safari business is a largely unregulated, caveat emptor situation.

Alf Leila wa Leila If you're into the folklore shows that the activity leaders at your all-inclusive beach hotel's been putting on, you're going to love this—a whole theme park built around loud music, cheesy costumes, and scantily clad dancers shaking it in the name of cultural appreciation. Unless you're staying in Hadaba, it's going to be a bit of a trek, but you don't want to miss it.

Hadaba. Admission LE90 ($16/£8.35) adults, LE45 ($8.20/£4.20) kids 4–12. Cash only. Daily 8pm–1:30am.

Aqua Blue Water Park *(Kids* This big, brand-new, water-park facility in Hadaba is a great place to spend the day with the kids. There's not too much among the 32 slides to hold a teenager's attention, but those 13 and under should be in for all the slippery, speedy fun they can handle. To keep the grown-ups amused, there's a selection of five themed restaurants that range from Mexican to Italian. A long after-lunch float down the lazy river might be just the thing for a hot day in Sharm.

Hadaba. Admission LE165 ($30/£15) adults, LE110 ($20/£10) kids 4–12. Winter 10am–6pm; summer 10am–8pm.

Cleo Park *(Kids* This water park is located up the hill on the inland side of the highway as it runs past Naama Bay. The entry and, indeed, most of the park are gloriously and unashamedly cheesy, with a Pharaonic motif applied willy-nilly to everything from the pylon-style entry to the rides. My favorite is the one where the slide is a gigantic anaconda twisting its way down through the center of a mock pyramid. Managed by Hilton, the place is stuffed with lifeguards who seem attentive and alert, and there is a fast-food restaurant for sugary top-ups when the energy levels start to flag. Like Aqua Blue, there's not much here for adrenalin junkies, but a lot of noisy, good-natured fun for children and parents alike.

Naama Bay. (© 069/3604400. Admission LE165 ($30/£15) adults, LE105 ($19/£9.70) kids 4–12. Daily 10am–dusk.

Diving It's easy to forget in the midst of all the fun-and-sun hoopla that Sharm was—and still is—a diver's paradise. The range of reefs, corals, and undersea life is some of the best in the world, and there are two wrecks within easy day-trip range.

The wreck of the ***Thistlegorm*** (p. 204) and the ***Dunraven*** are both reachable from Sharm. The *Dunraven* was an iron sail and steam vessel on its way from Bombay loaded with spices and fabric that sank in the spring of 1876 after hitting a reef just inside what is now Ras Mohamed National Park. Its captain—ironically named Captain Care—was found at fault and had his license revoked over the incident, which ended with the ship upside down in about 25m (82 ft.) of water. It's possible to swim inside the wreck and look at the boilers.

Ras Mohamed, as famous for its near-vertical walls as it is for the enormous schools of fish that congregate there, is loaded with dive sites with names such as Jackfish Alley, the Shark Observatory, and Anemone City.

The **Straits of Tiran** are now better known for spectacular drift dives through the reefs named after 19th-century cartographers Gordon, Thomas, Woodhouse, and Jackson than for their strategic importance in regional politics.

Ghibli Raceway   The track here is huge, and facilities include a grandstand and a full-on pit lane with a row of garages. Though it offers a selection of smaller karts for more casual drivers, Ghibli is really aimed at the high-buck, high-thrill end of the market with a track that can be reconfigured to multiple lengths out to 1.3km (4¼ miles) for international races. "Arrive and drive" customers are limited, however, to about 570m (1,870 ft.).

Airport Road, Naama Bay. ℂ 069/3603939. www.ghibliraceway.com. LE127 ($23/£11) for 10 min. in a 6.5-horsepower kart 11am–5pm; LE165 ($30/£15) for 10 min. in a 6.5-horsepower kart 5pm–midnight; up to LE1,265 ($230/£117) for 15 min. in a "professional" Rotax-powered race kart in the evening hours. Daily 11am–midnight.

Go-Karts   With around a kilometer of track (it can actually be extended to a little more) and a variety of karts, **Noos Karting** can give the whole family all the speed it needs. While the kids putter about with the little 2.5-horsepower jobs, mom and dad can hit the track in anything from the fairly tame 6.5- and 9-horsepower karts to the outright scary 125cc, 150kmph (90-mph) race karts.

Hadaba. ℂ 069/3662539. www.nooskarting.com. LE66 ($12/£6.10) for 10 min. in 2.5-horsepower kids' kart; LE 110 ($20/£10) for 10 min. in 6.5-horsepower kart; LE165 ($30/£15) for 10 min. in 9-horsepower kart. Daily 10am–midnight.

Quad/Dirt Bike Safaris   A host of quad safari companies advertise their services in Sharm. Though one of them, **KTM** (p. 70), stands head and shoulders above the rest, it's easy enough to explore the competition with a quick browse through the offerings at your hotel's travel desk or a stroll around Naama Bay. Expect to pay around LE100 to LE150 ($18–$27/£9.25–£14) per person to ride double and LE200 to LE250 ($36–$45/£19–£23) to ride single along dirt tracks around the outskirts of Sharm for 2 hours. This should—but is highly unlikely to—include proper safety equipment such as a padded shirt and a European-specification (look for the tag at the back) helmet. It may also include a drink and a time-wasting stop at a store where your guides will receive a hefty commission on anything you decide to purchase.

Ras Mohamed National Park   This park is a slender peninsula that extends off the southern end of the Sinai. It's chiefly known for the spectacular diving and snorkeling afforded by the reef here, which marks the intersection of the relatively shallow Gulf of Suez and the depths of the Gulf of Aqaba. It's claimed that there are more than a 1,000 species of fish here, as well as more than 170 species of coral. It's easy to let hours slip by just floating on the surface watching the seemingly endless variety of the undersea world drift by underneath.

ℂ 069/3660668. Admission LE30 ($5/£2.50) per day. Daily 8am–5pm.

Submarines (Kids   Making like a fish and swimming about with a snorkel and fins, let alone air tanks and weights, isn't the only way to get up close to the corals and sea creatures. In fact, it's probably a lot simpler to head down to Sharm al Maya, the bay just past the Old Town of Sharm, and get onboard one of the **Seascope** fleet of "submarines." Unlike their counterparts in Hurghada, these don't submerge completely, but once you're downstairs and looking out the portholes at the sea life, you can't tell the difference. The trip, which visits the corals around the mouth of the bay, is very safe and takes about 90 minutes. Subs leave about every 30 minutes from the dock at the beach, and there are around 20 trips a day.

Sharm el Maya. ℂ 012/7784637, 010/0059502, 010/0059511, or 012/7784638. LE220 ($40/£20) adults, kids 6–12 half-price, under 6 free.

WHERE TO STAY

VERY EXPENSIVE

Four Seasons Resort Sharm el Sheikh   This is probably the best hotel in Sharm. It has that kind of casual perfection that makes the business of pampering guests look as easy as flipping burgers. The setting is lovely. The main building, where the lobby and the main restaurant are, sits at the edge of the plateau, and the rest of the buildings ramble gently down almost to the water. As you descend, either on the stairway or the small funicular railway, the landscape architecture is intimate without blocking the view over the sea. Service is warm, competent, and seamlessly unobtrusive. When you arrive, for example, you're simply shown to your room; the formalities of checking in are handled later. Rooms are big, sheets are high-thread-count Egyptian cotton, and your bathroom is a mini-spa. The decor manages to be at once traditional and modern, with clean lines, lovely light, and a view of the sea. There is, quite simply, nothing wrong here. On the other hand, there is precious little character either. The formula of quiet perfection that works so well in a densely packed urban setting leaves me a little cold in a resort setting. Though this is the perfect (and I mean *perfect*) place for a long weekend of relaxation or a romantic getaway, it is not the place to bring the kids.

1 Four Seasons Blvd., Sharm el Sheikh. ⓒ 069/3603555. Fax 069/3603550. www.fourseasons.com. 136 units. LE2,475 ($450/£229) superior double; LE5,775 ($1,050/£535) family suite; LE6,600 ($1,200/£611) 1-bedroom suite. AE, DC, MC, V. **Amenities:** 5 restaurants; 3 bars; pool; 4 tennis courts; spa; dive center. *In room:* TV, AC, minibar, safe, Internet.

EXPENSIVE

Hilton Sharm Waterfalls Resort   This is a big resort that sprawls over a big compound above the sea in Hadaba. Because of its size, it can offer something for everyone—the pools, for example, are divided into quiet pools, more boisterous pools, and pools with animation. The beach, which is linked to the main building by one of only two funicular railways in Sharm (in Egypt, as far as I know), is one of the nicest in town, with soft, warm sand enclosed in a small bay with a jetty to get prospective snorkelers out beyond the reef without damaging the coral. The spacious rooms hit just the right balance between beach and hotel, with tiled floors and colorful area rugs; the sea views are simply stunning. The location isn't ideal for getting into Naama Bay, but there is a regular hotel shuttle, and with these kinds of facilities inside the compound, you could very happily stay within the walls for your whole stay.

Hadaba, Sharm el Sheikh. ⓒ **069/3663232.** Fax 069/3663228. www1.hilton.com. 401 units. LE1,073 ($195/£99) double. AE, MC, V. **Amenities:** 5 restaurants; 8 bars; 6 pools; tennis court; health club; gym; dive center. *In room:* A/C, TV, minibar, safe, Internet.

Hyatt Regency Sharm el Sheikh *(Kids)*   This is one of my favorite big resort hotels in Egypt. It's a rare example of a resort with a genuine sense of fun that still manages to maintain very good service on all the serious fronts. Rooms are top-notch, with clean, modern lines and touches of tiles that remind you that you're at the beach. Bathrooms are fairly big, and balconies are big enough to lounge *and* dry your towels over the railing at the same time. The food is good, far better than you get from other hotel outlets, and my favorite is the Sala Thai restaurant, but the Beach House Grill isn't half-bad either. The fun part, though, happens in the middle of the resort, where the gardens cascade down to the short beach. There are pools, but there's also a lazy river tucked into the greenery and a small water slide that will keep the younger kids happy.

Naama Bay, Sharm el Sheikh. ⓒ **069/3601234.** Fax 069/3603600. http://sharmelsheikh.regency.hyatt.com. 439 units. LE1,375 ($250/£127) sea-view double; LE1,595 ($290/£147) sea-front double. AE, MC, V. **Amenities:** 4 restaurants; 3 bars; 3 pools; 4 tennis courts; gym; spa; dive center. *In room:* A/C, TV, minibar, safe.

MODERATE

Beach Albatross *(Kids* One of the oldest hotels in Sharm el Sheikh, the Albatross is located on the cliff overlooking the broad sandy sweep of the bay at Sharm al Maya, very close to the original Israeli settlement of Ophira. Parts of the hotel buildings, in fact, formed the officers' quarters for the Israeli forces stationed here. This is an all-inclusive facility, and even though it's a good one—maintenance has been kept up and the facilities are clean and freshly painted—it has that slightly downmarket feel to it. Rooms are comfortable, midrange, and spread out through low buildings that ring the low-key gardens and pool facilities. Though it doesn't make the most of the potential for a spectacular view off the cliff, the ambience is extremely pleasant and relaxed. My favorite part of the place, though, is the elevator that runs down the face of the cliff to the 1.2km (¾-mile) beach.

Ras Um el Sid, Hadaba. ℂ 069/3663923. Fax 069/3663921. 205 units. LE330 ($60/£31) per person. AE, MC, V. **Amenities:** 2 restaurants; 2 bars; 4 pools (including 2 kids' pools); tennis; health club; sailing; bank; Wi-Fi. *In room:* A/C, TV, minifridge.

Camel Hotel The Camel is an excellent, midrange hotel in the middle of Naama Bay with one of the best restaurants in town, Pomodora. It's also one of the few places in Sharm where you can really see the history—or maybe that should be prehistory—of the town. Some of the bare stone wall in the lobby is from the original camel station (hence, the name of the place) from which the current hotel and dive center developed. Rooms are basic with clean, white-tile floors and comfortable-but-plain beds and bathrooms, and eight of them are handicap accessible. There is no question of a sea view, and the central courtyard is nice, though nothing in comparison to the Hyatt's glorious garden playground. If you want to get out and try the restaurants and bars of Sharm, the location is perfect; from here, all of downtown Naama Bay is accessible by foot. Note that there is a sizeable discount available on room rates by booking in advance through the website.

Naama Bay, Sharm el Sheikh. ℂ 069/3600700. Fax 069/3600601. www.cameldive.com. 32 units. LE400 ($73/£37) double. MC, V. **Amenities:** 3 restaurants; bar; dive center. *In room:* A/C, TV, minifridge, safe.

Nama Inn This place doesn't look very nice from the outside, but it has been very pleasantly brought up to date inside. The lobby, set far enough back from the boisterous activity of downtown Naama Bay to be reasonably peaceful, is a mix of modern and traditional Egyptian furnishings and light fixtures. Though the rooms don't really keep up with the lobby in terms of style—the furniture is a little older and a little more budget—the beds are comfortable and the place is clean. Rooms vary quite a bit, so look at a few before deciding, or if you booked ahead and are unhappy, ask to see some others. Keep in mind that rooms near the front can get a fair bit of noise from the street, and this noise could go on very late into the night.

Naama Bay. ℂ 069/3600801 or 069/3600805. Fax 069/3600950. www.naamainn.com. 38 units. LE330 ($60/£31) double. Cash only. **Amenities:** 2 restaurants; bar; pool; dive center; Wi-Fi. *In room:* A/C, TV.

WHERE TO EAT

Naama Bay is really the only place to wander looking for a place to eat. When you get tired of the downtown core, which by dusk is thick with people looking for food and touts advising them on where to look, try a walk up the beach-side promenade from the bottom of Hussein Salem Street. It's quieter here, and you'll be left more or less in peace to contemplate the menus posted outside the many little eateries that line the beach.

EXPENSIVE

Abu Seid EGYPTIAN   Order a few appetizers—*sojok* (little beef sausages), *tahina,* stuffed vine leaves, baba ghanouj, or just go for the appetizer tray for a broad selection—because the service is leisurely here. Entrees are substantial, my favorite being the Circassian chicken (slices of chicken laid on a bed of rice and smothered in a walnut sauce). I also like the grilled veal chops and the *tagine* (a tomato-based stew). Decor is not up to the standards of the original Cairo location, but there are the same plush chairs and heavy round tables, traditional lamps hanging from the ceilings, and art prints of Umm Kalthoum and other prominent Egypt cultural figures on the wall. If you have any space left over after appetizers and your entree, which is doubtful, try one of their excellent sweet *fatirs* or the *om aly* for dessert.

Above the Hard Rock Cafe, Sultan Al Qaboos Street, Nama Bay. © 069/3603910. Appetizers LE20–LE40 ($3.65–$7.30/£1.85–£3.70); main courses LE40–LE120 ($7.30–$22/£3.70–£11). MC, V. Daily noon–2am.

MODERATE

Hard Rock Cafe INTERNATIONAL   I'm not a big fan of the Hard Rock restaurants in Cairo and Hurghada, but if you're in need of a burger and a beer, and like to eat in the company of signed guitars and various other pop music "collectibles," then this is the place in Sharm. The music is loud and familiar to anyone over 30, the service is good, and the food is a cut above what they're serving in the other outlets. (The pink Ford Fairlane parked outside the front entrance does it for me.)

Sultan Qaboos Street, Naama Bay. © 069/3602664. Main courses LE30–LE80 ($5.45–$15/£2.80–£7.40). MC, V. Daily 11am–1am.

Tandoori INDIAN   With no view over the sea, uninspiring decor, and no fancy art on the wall, the inner courtyard of the Camel Dive Club and Hotel isn't going to draw many people in off the street—unless they stop outside for a sniff. Walking in, the smell of roasting spices, that heady mix of cardamom, cinnamon, ginger, cloves, and turmeric that characterizes so much of north Indian cooking, will pick you up and carry you off. Used as a general lounging area and luggage dump during the daylight hours, this space is transformed after dark into one of my favorite eateries in Egypt. The food is simply exceptional, and on my last visit I stuffed myself with a tender and subtly spiced *murg malai* chicken kebab and an order of butter *naan* (bread). I finished with a syrupy sweet *gulab jamun* (deep-fried milk dumpling) for dessert. Nearly a third of the menu here is vegetarian, which is a rarity in Egypt, and it's all superb.

King of Bahrain Street, Naama Bay. © 069/3600700. Reservations recommended. Appetizers LE10–LE15 ($1.80–$2.75/95p–£1.40); main courses LE30–LE90 ($5.45–$16/£2.80–£8.35). MC, V. Daily 7–11pm.

BUDGET

Andrea EGYPTIAN   Boisterous street-side seating under flashing lights can make for a sociable meal here unless you sit at the quiet table toward the back. Meals are typical late-night Egyptian fare—a mix of kebab and *kofta* (ground meet on a skewer), vine leaves, and salads. The beef kebab is particularly juicy, and the traditional bread, fresh from the on-site oven, is the perfect way to soak it up.

Sultan Qaboos Street, Naama Bay. © 069/3600972. Appetizers LE15 ($2.75/£1.40); main courses LE20–LE40 ($3.60–$7.25/£1.85–£3.70). Cash only. Daily 11am–1am.

Gado EGYPTIAN   Good, cheap sandwiches are the name of the game at Gado. Decor is bare-bones, with white walls, but you can stuff yourself for LE10

($1.80/95p). I tend to stick to the *tameya* sandwiches (deep-fried balls of falafel stuffed into half-sections of pita bread with some salad and a dollop of *tahina* sauce), but the chicken *shish tawook* and beef kebab sandwiches are also tasty and safe if you feel the need for meat.

Sultan Qaboos Street, Naama Bay. ℂ 012/7997537. Sandwiches LE1.50–LE8 (30¢–$1.45/15p–75p). Cash only. Daily 11am–midnight.

Mekani SANDWICHES   Tucked away in the back of Hadaba, this is a great place for a quick lunch while you're out exploring the neighborhood. They specialize in fresh-baked pastries and bread, and you can have a fresh fruit juice with a variety of sandwiches while soaking up the early afternoon sun on their little deck. A recent pit stop included a zesty marinated chicken *tikka* sandwich in soft bread, a blended strawberry and orange drink, and a freshly made chocolate cinnamon role for the road.

Sheikh Abdullah Shopping Center, Hadaba. ℂ 012/3255897. Sandwiches LE15–LE20 ($2.75–$3.65/£1.40–£1.85). Daily 8am–midnight.

SHARM EL SHEIKH AFTER DARK

Al Fanar   The name, which means lighthouse, comes from this club's location at the end of Ras Um Sid in Hadaba. There is a dance floor right on the edge of the cliff overlooking the sea, a separate but similarly cliff-edge bar area, and a full-blown restaurant more safely located a few meters back. It's also a nice place to come during the day because you can make your way down to the water and use the place as a fully catered private beach. You can even buy snorkel gear from the ticket office for around LE70 ($13/£6.50). Dancing night is Wednesday, with the action starting around midnight and going till, well, very late. Admission is LE40 ($7.30/£3.70) for the beach, which includes a towel and a bottle of water; LE165 ($30/£15) for the dance club, which includes a drink. Happy hour at the bar is 5:30 to 7:30pm, when cocktails are three for the price of two. Daily 10am to midnight. Ras Um el Seid, Hadaba. ℂ 069/3662218.

Camel Bar   Two of my favorite Sharm bars are here. Inside there's your traditional bare-bones dive bar with signed memorabilia on the walls, cheap cold beer behind the bar, and endless bowls of unshelled peanuts on the tables. The place is noisy and friendly and just gets more so as the night progresses. Upstairs on the roof, the scene is no less fun and friendly, but the decor is a lot more sophisticated, with soft light from funky little lamps and simple-but-stylish furniture; the place is perfect for a casual night out in the middle of downtown Sharm. Daily 7pm to late. Naama Bay, Sharm el Sheikh. ℂ 069/3600700. MC, V.

Little Buddha   Modeled after the Parisian original, this place features an amber-colored bar that glows from inside and a massive Buddha statue on the ground floor that pokes its head up through an opening in the second. Stylishly lit and plushly furnished, there's a restaurant downstairs (around the base of the Buddha) and a bar/nightclub upstairs (at Buddha eye level) that plays a mix of Asian and progressive house music. It caters to the young tourist and wealthy local market—dress to impress, and get ready to dance a lot and make friends. It's definitely a good party place for the young and boisterous crowd, but even they should avoid the food—at any price it would be considered bad, but at Buddha prices it's offensive. Club hours 11:30pm to 4am. ℂ 069/3601030. Admission LE120 ($22/£11). Couples only.

Turquoise Souvenirs

Turquoise has been mined on the Sinai for at least the last 5,000 years and is sought after in the modern marketplace for its translucence and particular shade of green. You'll find it for sale in the shops and stores around Sharm. It's priced by the gram, and prices start around $25 per gram for small (1–2g) pieces and rise steeply for larger pieces.

SHOPPING

While there are shops littered about Sharm, the only place where shopping is much fun, and certainly the only place that you have any hope of getting a bargain, is down in "Old Sharm." Here in the free-wheeling souk, expect to pick up a *shisha* for between LE160 and LE600 ($29–$109/£15–£60), or a mask-and-snorkel set for LE30 to LE150 ($5.45–$27/£2.80–£14). There's also quite a lot of jewelry for sale, but keep in mind that there's nothing higher here than 18k gold, and this should cost you around LE220 to LE250 ($40–$45/£20–£23).

Catherine Jewelry   This is a recently opened branch of a family business that has been operating in Cairo's Khan el Khalili since before World War II. They sell a variety of semiprecious stones from all over the world, but they specialize in Sinai turquoise, the translucent variety of the stone that the Pharaohs began to mine on the peninsula millennia ago. They also have an interesting stock of Aswan jade and Upper Egyptian agate. Staff speak English, and prices are stable and generally fair. Daily 10am to 2pm and 4 to 8pm. MC and V accepted. Old Sharm. ℂ **069/3661022** or 069/3664964.

The Red Sea Coast

It wasn't so long ago that the stretch of coastline between the Red Sea end of the Suez Canal and Egypt's southern border with Sudan was just empty desert coast. Its few, small towns were largely forgotten by the guidebooks and known only to a hardcore fraternity of divers who kept the secrets of the spectacular reef sites and beaches near places such as Safaga, Quseir, and Marsa Alam closely guarded.

A decade of rapid development has transformed the coast, however, and nowadays the once pristine coast is thick with resorts and beach hotels. Development has had its unfortunate downsides—the once picturesque fishing village of Hurghada has become a concrete blight on the coastal landscape, and miles of coral reef are now threatened by overuse—but most of the facilities now being developed are world-class resorts that offer value for money to tourists. And, in partnering with foreign-aid schemes aimed at promoting sustainability, the new sites are minimizing their impact on local resources.

The newest star on what has become known as Egypt's "Red Sea Riveria" is the $1.2-billion Sun International–managed complex at Port Ghalib, close to the Marsa Alam airport. Built around a manmade lagoon, an international port facility, and three hotels that offer lush, luxurious accommodations at a variety of price levels, this promises to be the go-to place for a relaxing, high-end beach vacation for years to come. The only real competition in sight is the better-established resort-community of Gouna, north of Hurghada, which offers a funky low-key ambience combined with international-standard restaurant and hotel facilities.

Even with all the new resorts going up, however, the old Red Sea coast—a little remote, a little ramshackle—remains. El Quseir and Safaga have somehow retained the untouched, rough-edged, charm they had before the palm-shaded beachside restaurants and swim-up bars of the big resorts were even a gleam in the eye of the developers.

The best way to holiday on the Red Sea coast, whether you're looking to drift-dive the coral reefs, swim with the sea turtles, or just soak up sun and cocktails on the beach, is to fly in from Cairo or even direct from Europe. The two hub airports on the coast are Marsa Alam and Hurghada. If you haven't got a prearranged transfer, rent a car in Hurghada and make your way to your destination along the excellent coastal highway.

1 Marsa Alam

Once the exclusive preserve of divers willing to suffer the most basic accommodations for the sake of the spectacular diving opportunities (for more on this, see "Active Vacation Planner," p. 65), the coastline around Marsa Alam is now thick with high-walled luxury resorts. A few of the old dive hotels still exist, but more and more the

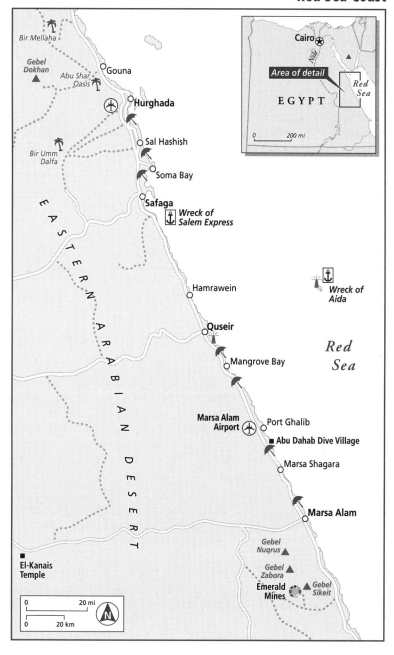

Red Sea Coast

Bir Mellaha

Gebel Dokhan

Abu Shar Oasis

Gouna

Hurghada

Sal Hashish

Bir Umm Dalfa

Soma Bay

Safaga

Wreck of Salem Express

E A S T E R N   A R A B I A N   D E S E R T

Hamrawein

Wreck of Aida

Quseir

Mangrove Bay

Red Sea

Marsa Alam Airport

Port Ghalib

Abu Dahab Dive Village

Marsa Shagara

Marsa Alam

Gebel Nuqrus

Gebel Zabora

El-Kanais Temple

Emerald Mines

Gebel Sikeit

0   20 mi

0   20 km

N

Area of detail

Cairo

Nile

Red Sea

EGYPT

0   200 mi

focus of the local tourist industry is on holiday makers who don't want to do anything more strenuous on their week's vacation than call for another cold beer.

The town of Marsa Alam itself is, to say the least, unprepossessing. The ambience is Mad Max, and the grittiness lacks romance. The locals aren't particularly friendly with non-Arabic speakers, and women without male accompaniment will not feel comfortable. That said, unless you're arriving by bus, there's no reason to go there.

ESSENTIALS
ORIENTATION

The Marsa Alam airport is some 65km (40 miles) north of the town of Marsa Alam itself, and it's connected to the little town by a fairly modern highway. All the hotels listed here are on that highway, either south of the airport in the direction of Marsa or north in the direction of Quseir. This highway is the only road around here—it runs north-south a kilometer or so from the actual water—and most of the hotels are between the water and the highway.

GETTING THERE

BY PLANE   This is definitely the best way to get to Marsa Alam. The airport is modern and relatively efficient, but a good distance—from 5km to 80km (3⅒–50 miles) or more—from most of the hotels. If you're arriving on a direct flight from outside the country, you'll have to buy a visa at the airport (p. 202). You'll be able to find a taxi at the airport if you need one, but all the hotels and resorts listed here will provide a transfer.

BY BUS   The best way to arrive by bus is to know exactly where you're going and get the bus driver to stop there for you. All the hotels and resorts listed have main gates and ample signage on the highway, and it's a rare bus driver in Egypt who won't stop to let someone off. The alternative is to arrive in the town of Marsa Alam itself. Unless you've made arrangements ahead of time, you'll then have to find yourself a ride to your next port of call. This may take some time.

GETTING AROUND

The question of getting around is mooted by the lack of places to go around Marsa Alam. Arrange off-site diving through the dive center at your hotel or one of the businesses listed in the "Active Vacation Planner" (p. 65). Cars for side trips to Quseir or Safaga can be arranged through the front desk of your hotel.

TOURIST INFORMATION

This was once a cash-only zone, but no more. Most of the hotels listed below are happy to take credit cards, and many have ATMs in their lobbies. It's probably still wise to arrive with some cash for emergencies and tips, however. There's an ATM in the airport if you've arrived with empty pockets.

There is a branch of the bank across the road from the Kahramana Resort to the south of the airport. It's open Sunday to Thursday 8am to 5pm for money changing and has an ATM. There is another, closer CIB across from Medinat Coraya to the north. It's open 9:30am to 3:30pm and 4:30 to 7:30pm Saturday to Thursday and Friday 5 to 8pm. It also has an ATM, which has a daily limit of LE6,000 ($1,091/£556). Piraeus Bank, which was not yet open at the time of writing, is by the entrance to the Cataract Resort about 20km (12½ miles) north of Marsa Alam.

WHERE TO STAY

When looking over the entries below, keep in mind that the rates listed have very little to do with the steeply discounted prices that are available through the big operators, and they aren't even a very good indication of quality. Also keep in mind that most of these places are miles from anywhere—the nearest small town is about 2 hours away by car, and even basic shopping will probably be out of the question without hiring a taxi. For this reason, a half-board or even an inclusive package may be worth considering.

SOUTH OF THE AIRPORT
EXPENSIVE

Abu Dabab Dive Lodge 🐾   As its name suggests, this place aims to accommodate the dive crowd. Accommodations are a little more basic than the big resorts and quite a bit cheaper, and service is more relaxed and rougher around the edges. Rooms are comfortable with high ceilings, and most have good light. They are spread out in single-story bungalows connected by wooden walkways. Unlike the green gardens of nearby resorts, here the grounds are sandy and sparsely planted with desert plants. The drawback of the Abu Dabab is that, for some reason, it's built on the wrong side of the highway between the airport and the town. To get to the beach (where there is a little restaurant, a bar, and a dive center), which is shared with several other facilities, you have to walk about 100m (328 ft.) across the road and through a parking lot.

Marsa Alam coast highway. ⓒ 010/2339271. Fax 065/3380010. res.aboudabab@balbaagroup.com. 63 units. LE600 ($109/£56) double. AE, MC, V. **Amenities:** Restaurant; bar; heated pool; massage. *In room:* A/C, TV.

Brayka Bay   Situated on a lovely bay with a sandy beach and a coral reef (usually you get one or the other), Brayka Bay is a popular place for all-inclusive European packagers. The facilities are great—the sun bed density on the beach isn't too high and there are enough palm trees for those who prefer natural shade. Rooms are above average, with a good amount of space and sleek, blonde-wood furnishings and nice bathrooms, though some people may find the beds a bit firm. The noise level around the public areas is generally subdued (piped-in music is kept low and fairly unobtrusive, and the activity leaders, most of whom seem to operate in Italian, are easy to escape). There are two downsides at Brayka Bay: First, all-inclusive customers can get the feeling that management is trying to save on the wine and beer by having small glasses and very slow service. Second, service is inconsistent and can be sloppy and unhelpful.

Marsa Alam coast highway. ⓒ 065/3380065 or 0121004401 Marsa Alam, or 32919419 Cairo. Fax 065/3380070 or 0121005811 Marsa Alam or 02/32918789 Cairo. www.braykabay.net. 465 units. LE880 ($160/£82) double. MC, V. **Amenities:** 3 restaurants; 3 bars; 5 pools (including kids' pool); 2 tennis courts; billiards and table tennis; gym; small spa; dive center (www.extra-divers.li); Internet. *In room:* A/C, TV, minibar, safe.

Elphinstone Resort   If you're looking for a quiet, snooze-by-the-pool vacation, this is not the place to stay. The resort is very popular with Italian sun seekers, and about the quietest place in the hotel is under the giant Nubian dome in the lobby—everywhere else the music is going, the activity leaders are at work whipping up the kids, and everybody's having a great, noisy time. The architecture and the ambience both reflect that people come here to have a good time. There is a pizza bar down at the beach and a health club offers a complicated menu of massages, facials, and scrubs. Rooms are big and a bit generic, with a definite package feel to them, but the beds are comfortable and the bathrooms are commodious.

37km (23 miles) south of Marsa Alam Airport. Cairo office, Osman Towers 7, Maadi, Cairo. ⓒ 065/3380031, 0122189203, or 0122189197 Marsa Alam; 02/25285770 or 02/25283321 Cairo. Fax 065/3380030 Marsa Alam,

02/25285771 Cairo. reservation@elphistone.com or dosm@elphistone.com. 270 units. LE990 ($180/£92) double. AE, MC, V. **Amenities:** 3 restaurants; 3 bars; disco; 2 pools (including children's pool); health club; kids' club; dive center; archery; canoes; horse and camel stables. *In room:* A/C, TV, minibar.

Amariya, Calimera, and Kahramana   These three hotels are grouped together in a complex about 40km (25 miles) from the airport. They share beach facilities, amenities, and restaurants, but have different pricing structures. There's an ATM in the lobby of the Kahramana and a CIB bank across the highway from the main gate. Their shared amenities include three restaurants, nine bars, three pools, two clay tennis courts, a health club, and a dive center. As with most of the resorts on the coast, you're better off booking online or through your travel agent, but you can also try booking directly through the Cairo office.

22 El Tahrir St., Dokki. (C) **02/27480883.** Fax 02/27604820.

Amariya   This is the low-end facility of the three, and despite the fact that it's some way from the beach and has no sea view, I actually like some parts of it better than anything at the other two. The pool is on the edge of the desert, and I like the inner courtyard with its pool and comfortable furniture. That said, the rooms are fairly basic and not as nice as the exterior might lead you to expect, and if you're here for a luxury stay, you're going to find the beach an inconveniently long walk away.

Marsa Alam coast highway. (C) **012/7458801.** Fax 012/458799. 96 units. LE352 ($64/£33) double. AE, MC, V. **Amenities:** Pool. *In room:* A/C, TV, minibar.

Calimera   This is certainly the liveliest of the three hotels. Rooms are in low buildings that surround a big swimming pool, where music and a bar keep guests in an upbeat mood. Interiors are a rare example of a beach resort that pulls off the contrast between traditional architectural cues such as brick domes and stone facing with simple, modern furniture. Staff are friendly and helpful, and the whole place has a warm and happy ambience, though it might be too boisterous for some. The beach is an easy walk down to the bottom of the gardens, but it has a lot of gravel.

Marsa Alam coast highway. (C) **012/7458801.** 300 units. LE715 ($130/£66) double. AE, MC, V. **Amenities:** 2 pools. *In room:* A/C, TV, minibar.

Kahramana   This is intended to be the quieter, more upscale facility at the other end of the beach from the Calimera, occupying its own hill so that it looks back on the Calimera and the sweep of the bay. The rooms are larger and a little nicer, and the view is lovely. Take care when booking a sea-view room here, as management might be stretching the point a little with some of them. The gardens are nice, with little stone paths winding around the two-story buildings. Staff are pleasant enough but, unlike their counterparts at Calimera and Amariya, almost completely clueless. The beach is a few minutes' walk down the hill.

Marsa Alam coast highway. (C) **019/5100261** or 012/7454105. Fax 019/5100259. 178 units. LE715 ($130/£66) double. AE, MC, V. *In room:* A/C, TV, minibar, safe (in some).

Port Ghalib 🏠🏠🏠   There are three main hotels in this integrated, self-contained resort village with an international port and marina, 18km (11 miles) of coastline, and a full village of shops and restaurants built around a large lagoon and a spectacular soft, sandy beach. It's the biggest and most luxurious resort operation on the Marsa Alam section of the coast, and certainly one of the best resorts in Egypt. Book through the Cairo office.

3 Mansour Mohamed St., Zamalek. (C) **02/27351962.** Fax 02/27351964. www.discoverportghalib.com.

The Palace ☆☆☆   The Palace is the premier destination in Port Ghalib and easily the most impressive hotel on this stretch of the coast. Public areas are designed to match a fantasy version of what a palace perched between the lush azure of the Red Sea and the rugged mountains of the Eastern Desert should look like. Vast halls are supported by ornate columns and adorned with hanging textiles and mosaic tiles. Rooms are everything that the rest of the place leads you to expect: big, lush, and beautiful, but at the same time surprisingly intimate and comfortable.

309 units. LE1,738 ($316/£161) garden-view double; LE1,975 ($359/£183) lagoon-view double; LE2,271 ($403/£206) sea-view double; LE4,417 ($803/£409) sea-view suite. Rates include breakfast. AE, DC, MC, V. **Amenities:** 2 restaurants; 2 bars; 2 pools (including kids' pool); 4 tennis courts; spa; kids' club; go-karts; kiting; mountain-bike rental; horse and camel stable; dive center. In room: A/C, TV, minibar, safe, Internet.

Sahara Sun Sands   The Sun Sands is a bit more casual and relaxed than the Palace and a bit closer to the beach, both literally and in terms of ambience. Rooms are designed to mirror traditional architecture, with rounded arches and niches and opulent bathrooms. Tiled floors and simple-but-comfortable furnishings remind you that you're at the beach, while the exterior of the buildings mimic the square silhouette and desert tones of a coastal village. Apart from easy access to the spectacular sweep of a beach, the Sun Sands embraces an enormous swimming pool on the inland side, offering a second option for lounging by the water or going for a quick dip.

347 units. LE1,117 ($203/£103) garden-view double; LE1,271 ($231/£118) lagoon-view double; LE1,425 ($259/£132) sea-view double; LE2,833 ($515/£262) sea-view suite. Rates include breakfast. AE, DC, MC, V. **Amenities:** 3 restaurants; 2 bars; 4 tennis courts; spa; bowling; bumper boats; go-karts; arcade; horse and camel stable; dive center. In room: A/C, TV, minibar, safe, Internet.

Sahara Sun Oasis (Kids)   This family-friendly alternative at Port Ghalib has big rooms that are a little less funky than over at Sun Sands but just as comfortable, and decor is a lot more fun here, with colorful murals in the lobby. The beach is close, but kids might prefer the water park with a slide and lazy river, and there are plenty of opportunities for adults to lounge while keeping an eye on the kids.

292 units. LE1,045 ($190/£97) lagoon-view double; LE1,337 ($243/£124) family room; LE2,624 ($477/£243) lagoon-view suite. **Amenities:** 3 restaurants; 2 bars; bowling; bumper boats; go-karts; arcade; horse and camel stable; dive center. In room: A/C, TV, minibar, safe, Internet.

Shagara Ecolodge Village   Despite the somewhat seedy, unpaved entrance, this is a nice midrange place to stay. The main clientele are divers, but with a very decent stretch of beach, this will do just fine for a pleasant sand-loll as well. There are three levels of accommodation—beach tents (best avoided), beach huts (check them out), and chalets. The latter have domed ceilings and comfortable beds. The bathrooms lower the tone a little and are more reminiscent of a budget hotel than somewhere charging these kinds of prices. The other drawback with the chalets is that they are sited well back from the beach and look out over a wide, gravel-filled area between them and the sea. The dining room is pleasant, and the food, while not gourmet, is definitely the kind of solid fare that will keep you going through a tough day underwater. Generally, you'll need to get a healthy reduction on the rack rate before this place is value for money, but at the right price it would be great.

Marsa Alam coast highway. ☎ 065/338002165. Fax 065/3380027. 120 units. LE814 ($148/£75) chalet double w/full board. **Amenities:** Restaurant; bar; dive center. In room: A/C, fridge, no phone.

Sol y Mar Abu Dabab   This is a real lie-on-the-beach place with a big, organically shaped pool, about a mile of beach, and a full range of activities to keep you from getting bored between meals. The rooms make up in size for what they lack in character, and they have nice soft beds. At the time of writing, the view in the direction of the sea from many of the pool-side rooms was being obstructed by new construction, so it might be worth looking for a room in the new wing if you want a sea view.

Marsa Alam coast highway. © 01/000960014. Fax 01/00096005. www.solymar-hotels.com. 160 units. LE1,480 ($269/£137). AE, DC, MC, V. **Amenities:** 2 restaurants; 4 bars; 2 pools (including kids' pool); 4 tennis courts; health club; gym; kids' club. *In room:* A/C, TV, minibar.

Sol y Mar Solitaire ⚓ This is a very nice facility, built bungalow-style around a pair of pools on a slope overlooking the sea. It has some of the nicest resort gardens in the area, a great view out to sea, and a professional dive center, all of which have made it popular with both divers and sun seekers. Rooms are spacious, with tiled floors and earth-tone furniture. All include nice touches such as Nubian rugs and wood fittings that, along with the high-quality bathrooms, make the Solitaire feel a little less like a package destination than some of its neighbors.

Marsa Alam coast highway. © 065/33801001/2/3. Fax 012/2493401. www.solymar-hotels.com. 127 units. LE825 ($150/£76) double. MC, V. **Amenities:** Restaurant; 3 bars; 2 pools; tennis court; health club; dive center; 2 ATMs. *In room:* A/C, TV, minibar, safe.

Tulip The rooms aren't very big at the Tulip, but they are nicely decorated and designed. Light-colored walls, dark furniture, and tile floors make you feel like you're at the beach. Most of the rooms face the pool area, which is embraced by the two arms of the main building. With a long beach, which includes a Bedouin tent, and a swim-up bar in the middle of the large main pool, the Tulip has plenty of options for those who want to lounge by the water. While the sand on the beach isn't the finest, it's pretty standard for this section of coast, and there's an easily accessible coral reef just offshore for snorkelers.

Pickup from the airport is a reasonable LE80 ($15/£7.40), and a ride into Quseir is LE121 ($22/£11).

Marsa Alam coast highway. © 02/24148001. Fax 02/24170852. www.flash-international.net. 246 units. LE1,100 ($200/£102) double. AE, MC, V. **Amenities:** 3 restaurants; 3 bars; 3 pools; gym; spa; kids' club; dive center; Internet. *In room:* A/C, TV, minibar, safe.

MODERATE

Cataract Marsa Alam This rundown package resort has a slightly offbeat charm to it, but you'd have to get a pretty good price for the evident lack of maintenance not to grate a little on your nerves. The rooms are better than you'd expect from the lobby. Fairly spacious, it has comfortable beds, most of which look out on the extensive artificial lagoon. The bathrooms, however, are more downmarket than the rooms themselves. The beach is a bit gravelly.

Marsa Alam coast highway. © 012/7343069 Marsa Alam or 02/37718060 Cairo. Fax 065/3380055 Marsa Alam or 02/37718073 Cairo. Cairo office, El Harraneya, Giza. www.cataractmarsaalamresort.com. 302 units. LE413 ($75/£38) double. AE, DC, MC, V. **Amenities:** 2 pools (including kids' pool); 2 tennis courts. *In room:* A/C, TV.

The Oasis Dive Resort ⚓ (Value) This is a good, small hotel about 20km (12 miles) north of the town of Marsa Alam that is eschewing the beach-vacation market for desert excursions and diving. Facilities are basic but comfortable, with rooms that are spacious, if unadorned. The cement floors are a bit of disappointment after the traditional exterior, but the split-level standard rooms are little cozier and nicer. Ask for no. 23; it has the best view. The grounds are sparse compared to the lush gardens of the beach resorts but appropriate to their desert surroundings. The pool has a great view over the sea and is definitely the best pool in this price range on the coast. There is a professional dive center on the ground floor of the main building, and a restaurant and bar with a fantastic view of the sea and the coastline on the upper floor. This isn't a good place for a beach lounging vacation, but there is a jetty that allows you to get into the water beyond the reef for snorkeling or diving.

Marsa Alam coast highway. (C) 01/05052855. www.oasis-marsaalam.com. 30 units. LE385 ($70/£36) double. MC, V. **Amenities:** Restaurant; pool; dive center. *In room:* Fan, no phone.

NORTH OF THE AIRPORT, TOWARD QUSEIR
EXPENSIVE
Akassia Swiss Resort 🐟🐟   This is a well-organized, well-run, and very clean hotel that caters mostly to Europeans on package tours. The main lobby and restaurant building is vast, built under a huge brick dome. Rooms are pleasant and fairly large, with domed brick ceilings that mirror the architecture of the lobby. Furniture is blonde-wood, the floors are tiled, and every room has a balcony. There are four different restaurants to choose from, including a beach barbecue. The "safari" tent is closer to something you would see at a European pop concert than anything you're likely to encounter in the desert, but the spa is nice. Dive or snorkel from the jetty, or go on a boat trip.

Marsa Alam coast highway. (C) 012/7455049 or 012/2307718 Marsa Alam, or 02/22733121 or 012/3150694 Cairo. Fax 0127429731 Marsa Alam or 02/22735451 Cairo. www.akassia.com. Cairo office, 95 Hafez Ramadan St., Nasr City. 477 units. LE935 ($170/£87) double. AE, MC, V. **Amenities:** 4 restaurants; 5 bars; 5 pools (including wave pool and kids' pool); beach; water slides; 2 tennis courts; playground and kids' club; travel desk; quad rental; Wi-Fi and small Internet cafe. *In room:* A/C, TV, minibar, safe.

Carnelia   This is a good midrange to budget-level resort choice, with basic rooms that, with domed ceilings and Nubian rugs, have some charm. It has all the usual facilities—a kids' pool next to the main pool, a tent on the beach for *shisha* smoking, and a beach with woven sunshades. The maintenance isn't the best, though, and it has the feel of a place that caters to the local market. One of the big upsides is that it is close enough to the town of Quseir to make a day trip for an afternoon touring the fort and poking about the old shops without a long drive and a big taxi bill. Expect to get a very healthy discount from the rates posted below, and expect a crowded, noisy, good time.

Marsa Alam coast highway. (C) 065/3395021. Fax 065/3395020. www.carnelia-redsea.com. 150 units. LE825 ($150/£76) double. MC, V. **Amenities:** 2 restaurants; 3 bars; 2 pools; fitness center; Internet. *In room:* A/C, TV, fridge.

Coraya Beach Resort   Just a little north of the Marsa Alam airport, the Coraya Beach is one of three resorts owned by Iberotel that share Coraya Bay. All three are nice, but the other two lean more heavily on the European package market, so this resort, the flagship operation of the three, is preferable. That said, all three are available on the same website and share many facilities including the long, pleasant beach, and if you can get a cheaper berth at the Lamaya or Somaya (there is an obscure logic behind the similar sounding names), go for it.

Rooms are a little on the generic side, lacking character, but they make up for this with large balconies with flowers. However, rooms feel a little down-market compared to the public areas. The resort is built around a sculpted pool and has an outdoor restaurant with live cooking stations and an 800m (½ mile) beach. The gym is a pleasant and well-lit place with basic, but good-quality, equipment, and the health club is spacious and inviting.

The usual proviso about the price applies here—at the posted rack rate, this place is far overpriced.

Madinat Coraya, Marsa Alam coast highway. (C) **065/3750000** Marsa Alam or 16416 or 02/27381125 Cairo. Fax 065/3750009 Marsa Alam or 02/27365305 Cairo. www.iberotel-eg.com. Cairo office 44 Mohamed Mazhar St., Zamalek. 364 units. LE1,023 ($186/£95) double; LE1,271 ($231/£118) sea-view double. AE, MC, V. **Amenities:** 3 restaurants; 3 bars; 2 pools; 2 tennis courts; gym; health center; kids' club; ATM; bank; dive center (www.coraya-divers.com). *In room:* A/C, TV, minibar, safe.

Dreams Beach   On the outskirts of Quseir, Dreams Beach is a low-end package place that would be fun at the right price (which would be considerably less than the rack rates quoted below). Its main claim to fame, other than its somewhat over-the-top theme-park-style main building and lobby (adorned with fake rock and Mamluke-style lamps), is that it has nine pools. This is a bit of a stretch, though, as the pools in question are long, narrow kids' pools lined with fake rock that run in front of the rooms. The theme-park feel continues with free pedal boats and waterslides for the kids. Rooms are big but a little on the budget side (the Tang offered as a welcome drink at check-in is a tip-off), and if you really want to be able to see the sea from your sea-view room, make sure they give you a place well away from the main building.

Marsa Alam. (C) **065/3395000-4.** Fax 065/3395009. www.dreamsresortsegypt.com. 230 units. LE1,100 ($200/£102) double. AE, MC, V. **Amenities:** 5 restaurants; 4 bars; 9 pools; tennis court; Internet. *In room:* A/C, TV, minibar, safe.

2 El Quseir

For centuries, El Quseir (which everybody just calls Quseir) was one of the most important ports in Egypt. Pharaohs sent trading fleets from this little town to the land of Punt to collect precious cargos of gold, ebony, and slaves. Later, after the Arab invasion, it became a vital stop on the hajj as well as a thriving commercial hub for the trade to India and the Gulf. The area slowly declined after the height of its importance in the 10th century, and though the Suez Canal brought back some life when it opened in 1869, today Quseir is a forgotten place. The only industry, a phosphorus mine set up by an Italian company in 1916, hasn't done much since the 1960s, when the deep-water port in Safaga to the north displaced Quseir's relatively small facilities. Nowadays, the old buildings slump a little lower each year as neglect takes its toll on mud-brick walls and the once-grand wooden facades along the waterfront. In a decade or two, the historic buildings will be gone, replaced as they have been almost everywhere else in the country by a mix of shoddy low-rise tenements and a sprawl of private homes.

Ten, or even 5, years ago, Quseir was still a word-of-mouth kind of place that the Cairo expat was just discovering, talking about the ruins of a fort, the gradually collapsing old buildings, and the lovely Hassan-Fathy–style Mövenpick on a bay north of the town. Now there are two more large hotels and a very nice basic hotel in a refurbished old house, and the fort has been extensively restored. There are even signs that perhaps tourism is beginning to perk up the town a little.

ESSENTIALS
ORIENTATION
There are two streets through Quseir—the main road, which runs past the old fort in the middle of town, and a loop that goes down to the waterfront. Between the two is the town, a pleasant jumble of run-down old buildings, a few small stores, and not much else. The nicer of the old buildings are on the water. All three of the big hotels are on the northern edge of town.

GETTING THERE

BY PLANE Quseir is more or less equidistant between the Marsa Alam and Hurghada airports. The greater frequency of flights into Hurghada means that coming from the north is cheaper and easier. All the hotels here can arrange a transfer from either airport. If you have to arrange your own transport (which may be cheaper, depending on your negotiation skills), you can do so with drivers at either airport or through **New Line Tours** (✆ **065/3366480;** www.newlinetour.com).

BY BUS You should get the bus driver to drop you off at the gates of the hotel if you're staying at one of the big three. If you're staying at the Al Quseir and you haven't arranged a transfer, it won't be a problem to rustle up a taxi at the bus "station" (✆ **065/3330033);** LE10 ($1.80/95p) will be enough to get you to your destination.

GETTING AROUND

Local transportation options are limited in Quseir. Most local activities, however, come with hotel pick-up included. If you want to move around independently, a car and driver are your best option, though the town is so small that unless you want to get out and see the surrounding desert, you'll probably only use them for the 10-minute ride into town and back.

BY CAR At the time of writing, there was no taxi company to recommend in Quseir, but Safaga is close enough that either Larose or Plus (p. 198) can send a car down for the day. Alternatively, check with the front desk of your hotel—the odds are that someone has a car and the time to take you around for a reasonable price. It should go without saying in this case that you should check the condition of the car before coming to a final agreement and settle on terms before you get in.

ON FOOT Once you're in the middle of Quseir in the area of the fort or the short beach area, everything is within easy walking distance.

BY BICYCLE The Mövenpick has mountain bikes that can be used to get into town. This is a great way to see Quseir, with one proviso: check the prevailing wind before you leave. A tailwind on the way into town can make for a long, hard pedal back home at the end of the day.

TOURIST INFORMATION

There are two **Internet** options in Quseir. Located in the modern, and very ugly, part of Quseir, **Spider Internet** is where the local kids go to play networked video games and chat with friends. It has 15 PCs and good bandwidth, and it's open daily 9am to 11pm. Rates are LE3 (55¢/30p) per hour. **Caspian Internet,** just around the corner from Spider, is not as new as the competition and has about half the number of computers. It's open daily 9am to 11pm and rates are LE3 (55¢/30p) per hour.

WHAT TO SEE & DO

Quseir Fort ✮ This fort was built by the Ottoman rulers of Egypt in the 16th century to defend the key harbor on the Red Sea coast from marauding Portuguese traders who were attempting to force entry to the lucrative trade with India and China in timber, pepper, and silk. Garrisoned until the 18th century, the fort seems to have been left to fall into disrepair ever since. These days a USAID project has restored and prepared the site for visitors. The entrance is on the main street side through a narrow tunnel, where you're sure to find some guys interested in being your unofficial guide. It's not a bad idea to have one of them along, if only to show you where the light switches are and to unlock doors. An LE5 (90¢/45p) tip at the end of the tour will suffice.

The surviving structure of the fort isn't tremendously elaborate, but a look at the displays of Bedouin cultural artifacts in the northern bastion and the trade goods in the west is worth 15 or 20 minutes. Climb the watchtower in the middle for a moderately good view of the surrounding town while the kids climb in and out of the old phosphate carts that are parked on a piece of old narrow-gauge railway line. Don't miss the pearl fishing boat or the old cannons. Expect to be out of here in less than an hour.

Admission LE10 ($1.80/95p). Daily 9am–5pm.

WHERE TO STAY

There are three big hotels in Quseir. If you're looking for a quiet, romantic weekend (or week) away from it all, the Mövenpick's the place to be. For a little more noise and action, try the Radisson or Flamenco. If you're looking for a little more connection to Quseir, try the Hotel Al Quseir in the old part of town. It may be right around the corner from the police station, but don't let that slow you down; rough wood floors and open-stone facing on the walls make this my favorite hotel in town (but it's also the most basic).

EXPENSIVE

Flamenco Beach Resort   The Flamenco is almost next door to the Mövenpick and has more of a beach-vacation resort tone. If you're looking for an active and fun-filled weekend, this should be your choice. The tall white buildings embrace the main pool, and there is a wide marble lobby. Rooms are spacious but a bit generic, with uninspiring but adequate bathroom facilities. The gardens around the hotel are lush, however, and there are plenty of activities to keep you busy when you don't feel like lolling on the beach. Diving and snorkeling on the spectacular reef is accommodated by a 150m (492 ft.) jetty, which means you don't even need to get wet to go feed the multicolored fish that bob and weave about the coral.

7km (4²/₁₀ miles) north of Quseir. ✆ 065/3350200. Fax 065/3350211. www.flamencohotels.com. 284 units. LE798 ($145/£74) double half-board. AE, DC, MC, V. **Amenities:** 4 restaurants; 3 bars; 3 pools; tennis court; gym; spa; bike rental; ATM; bank; Internet. *In room:* A/C, TV, minifridge, safe, Internet.

Mövenpick ★★ *Kids*   This great hotel, on the northern edge of Quseir, is situated on a little bay that was used in the Roman era as a port; my favorite aspect of the resort is the way it spills down almost to the edge of the water. Rooms are spread out through a series of single-story sandstone buildings that are built around 12 courtyards, and are designed to blend with the shape and color of the coastline. Inside, they are commodious, with domed ceilings and nice local touches.

The bay provides a 700m (½ mile) beach that curves away to the Subex Dive Center (p. 66) and has a relaxingly low sunshade quotient—no need to feel packed onto the sand like a bunch of beached sardines. The bay also accommodates diving and snorkeling of the nearby reef directly from the beach. The Top of the Rocks bar is built just above the spray line, and at night, with the lights turned low, it has to be one of the most romantic spots on the entire coast. At the opposite end of the romance scale, it's worth noting that babysitting and playground facilities are offered.

Sirena Beach, El Quadim Bay, Quseir. ✆ 065/3332100. Fax 065/3332129. www.moevenpick-quseir.com. 250 units. LE1,375 ($250/£127) garden-view double; LE1,793 ($326/£166) sea-view double; LE3,449 ($627/£319) suite. AE, DC, MC, V. **Amenities:** 5 restaurants; 2 bars; heated pool; 4 tennis courts; squash court; spa; kids' club; babysitting; quad and mountain-bike rental; desert tours; archery. *In room:* A/C, TV, minibar, hair dryer, Internet.

Radisson SAS Resort   Located between the old town and the other two big hotels, the Radisson does a good job of standardized service and amenities with some local touches. If there's one criticism to be made of the place, it's that it feels like it's working on a one-size-fits-all template here, and it doesn't quite fit with Quseir. That said, staff are friendly and professional, and the beach and jetty provide excellent swimming and diving. I particularly like the spa, which features Ayurvedic massage in Indian-themed treatment rooms and the two linked, outdoor pools that are heated in the winter. Rooms aren't huge, but they're nicely designed to give you a sense of where you are. Those obsessed with staying connected will be happy to note the free broadband and Wi-Fi Internet availability.

Quseir. ℂ 065/3350260. www.elquseir.radissonsas.com. 250 units. LE715 ($130/£66) double; LE770 ($140/£71) sea-view double. AE, MC, V. **Amenities:** 4 restaurants; 2 bars; 2 pools; spa; Internet. *In room:* A/C, TV, minibar, safe, Internet.

BUDGET

Hotel Al Quseir *Value*   Located in a restored historic stone building on the waterfront in the middle of Quseir, this hotel is best described as boutique on a budget. Considering the neighborhood—the old town is still pretty rundown, and even spiffed up will probably never compete with the picturesque European seaside towns—it's best that the hotel stayed small (there are only 6 rooms) rather than try to become an upscale, niche-marketed place. The fabric of the building is all there—restored, clean, and ready, with high ceilings and wooden floors—and it's tough not to stand at the bottom of the stairwell and look at the simple wooden staircase and rock facing of the walls and think, "What if some light fixtures were sourced out of an old villa and the money were spent to bring in some antique furnishings?" The bathrooms are fine—better than you would expect at the price—but they are shared. What could be a fantastic breakfast nook upstairs, surrounded by old *mashrabeya* screens and looking through a tree and out over the Red Sea, is apologetically presented by staff who don't seem to appreciate how close this place is to a being a diamond in the rough.

Bour Saied Street, Quseir. ℂ 065/3332301. 6 units. LE140 ($26/£13) double (bathroom across the hall). Cash only. **Amenities:** Restaurant. *In room:* Fan, no phone.

Simon Hotel   The only time you should consider the Simon is if you're stuck in Quseir with no credit card and just enough cash to get you home, and the Hotel Al Quseir is full. Buy a can of Raid from the kiosk on the other side of the road, spray the room, and get out quickly in the morning.

10th of Ramadan Street, Quseir. ℂ 065/3332625. 14 units. LE100 ($18/£9.25) double. Cash only. *In room:* No phone.

WHERE TO EAT

Looking for a decent meal in Quseir is a frustrating process. There are a number of very promising locations, but the best places to eat are in the hotels. Of these, **Seagull's** at the Mövenpick is probably the top choice. On the main street there is a pair of tourist-oriented fish restaurants, the **Admiral** and the **Citadel.** If you opt for one of these, check that the fish is fresh (you'll choose it from the cooler in the front) and bargain on the price.

Marianne SEAFOOD   This is the best place to eat in Quseir, located on the seafront in the old town. The grilled calamari is fresh and not overcooked. The setting is neat—the old building is pretty rickety, and the broad second-story veranda looks like it could collapse in the next couple of weeks. Toilets are not so great.

ℂ 01/09468198. Main courses LE20–LE100 ($3.60–$18/£1.85–£9.25). Daily 11am–10pm.

QUSEIR AFTER DARK

The Seventeenth Star   The Seventeenth Star is just off the highway about 5km (3 miles) north of the old town and aims to provide an alternative to the canned party facilities at the big hotels and the nonexistent party facilities in the town. Spaces are open-air or covered by a tent roof, with nice local stonework walls. This has the potential to be a really nice dance bar with the right crowd; big nights are Thursday through Saturday. Daily 10pm to late. (ℂ **01/26564188.** Cover LE70 ($13/£6.50).

3 Safaga

Like Marsa Alam to the south, Safaga is a divers' town slowly being won over by the indolence industry. Where roughing it was once the price to be paid for the spectacular diving and snorkeling, it's now possible to eat well, be waited on hand and foot, and sleep on high-quality sheets between dives.

ESSENTIALS

ORIENTATION

There's not much to Safaga. Unlike Quseir to the south, it is bypassed by the highway, but there is still a clearly identifiable road through the middle of the town. The bulk of Safaga is built around the port, which is used mainly for exporting phosphorus, but there is also a brisk ferry business running guest workers to and from Saudi Arabia. A little to the north of this is the old town. Most of the tourist services are in a little area close to the main roundabout, which features a giant mermaid on a pedestal, known as Maglis el Medina. On the highway out of town, there is a second area of tourist hotels and restaurants. Then, about another 5km (3 miles) up the road, is the resort compound of Soma Bay.

GETTING THERE

BY PLANE   Just 45km (28 miles) along a good highway from Hurghada airport, Safaga is easily reached by air from Cairo or even direct from a variety of European hubs. Arrange for a transfer through your hotel or one of the transport companies listed below.

BY BUS   The bus station is up on the highway. It's definitely wiser to arrange a ride to your destination before you get on the bus, as finding somebody once you get there is a very dicey proposition.

BY CAR   The intersections on the main highway are fairly well signposted. If you're headed into the old town, watch out for the giant mermaid traffic circle—when you see this, you're pretty close. Stopping at Ali Baba's (50m/164 ft. or so past the mermaid on the right) for directions should yield useful information.

GETTING AROUND

A number of companies in Safaga will provide vehicles and drivers to individuals or groups. Some are a little shady, so exercise judgment. Try **Larose Tours** (ℂ **010/ 3344222),** which maintains a small fleet of vehicles that range in size from compact cars to full-size buses; it can arrange airport transfers and sightseeing trips up and down the coast. **Plus Car** (ℂ **012/3676860** or 010/6146299) specializes in supplying cars with drivers for transfers or excursions.

WHAT TO SEE & DO

While most of the resorts have the "house reef" just off shore, there are literally dozens of spectacular sites for **diving** coral, animal life, or wrecks within a 30- to 90-minute boat ride. Consult the dive operators listed in the "Active Vacation Planner" (p. 65) for more specifics.

Tobya Hamra, also known as the **Coral Garden,** is a spectacular and multifaceted coral reef. At a depth of 5 to 30m (16–98 ft.), you'll see colorful formations as well as moray eels, octopus, stonefish, and sometimes eagle rays.

Panorama Reef is a big 400m (1,312 ft.) block of vibrantly colored reef that goes down almost 35m (115 ft.) at the southern end and offers the possibility to see eagle rays and the occasional white-tipped and hammerhead sharks. Turtles sometimes lurk at the northern end.

The 100m (328 ft.) **Wreck of the *Salam Express*** ferry sank in 1991, and the debris field and bridge are accessible to divers.

Just off the Sheraton Soma Bay beach, the eponymous **Seven Pillars** rise up from a depth of between 10 and 12m (33–39 ft.) and are usually surrounded by multicolored flora and fauna. There is a resident Napoleon fish here that is used to humans, as well as puffer, lizard, and lion fish.

Several companies around Safaga can arrange a day of **paintball.** Or, spend a full day or just an hour or two exploring the desert around Safaga on a **quad.** Destinations include a now-abandoned Bedouin village. See p. 65 in the "Active Vacation Planner."

Soma Bay (see "La Residence des Cascades" below) features an 18-hole par-72 **golf** course designed by South African golf legend Gary Player. The course has stunning views of the desert, the mountains, and the Red Sea, and, of course, a great bar on the 18th hole. Facilities also include a 9-hole "Golf Academy" practice course and a 60-bay driving range.

A combination of warm water and reliable, strong winds (on average one Beaufort stronger than off Hurghada to the north) combine to bring an increasing number of **windsurfers** and **kitesurfers** (p. 71) to Safaga. Not only do winds whip up exciting offshore waves, but the relatively sheltered bay means good flat water for beginners.

WHERE TO STAY

There are three areas to stay in Safaga. The old town has a handful of older, diver-oriented hotels. These are basic and relatively cheap, but for the most part lack beach facilities. Just to the north of town there is a line of older resort-style hotels, some of which have been spiffed up a bit in the last few years but are all still a bit musty and overpriced. Finally there is the Soma Bay compound a few kilometers farther north, which is more expensive, a lot nicer and, given that you can probably get a good package rate through your travel agent, better overall value for your fun-in-the-sun money.

EXPENSIVE

Intercontinental Abu Soma   This place is going to look familiar if you've been to the old Sidnaouwi's Department Store in downtown. The lobby is a fantastic, somewhat over-the-top imitation of the wide-open concourse style of the 19th-century department store, with wrought-iron railing and a domed ceiling. I like it—it's excessive and fun, like a good theme park. Inside, the excess continues, with brass railings and green leather. The cracks, if you care to look for them, begin to show in the stairwells and the hallways, where bad architecture leaves ceilings too low in places and cuts off your view unexpectedly. The rooms, however, are great, with the biggest balconies I've seen in an Egyptian hotel and spectacular views across the gardens and out to sea. Though there is no reef off the beach, it remains perfect for splashing about and lounging.

Safaga. ✆ **065/3260700.** Fax 065/3260749. 445 units. LE935 ($170/£87) double half-board. AE, DC, MC, V. **Amenities:** 4 restaurants; 2 bars; 2 pools; health club; kids' club; Wi-Fi. *In room:* A/C, TV, minibar, safe.

La Residence des Cascades ★★   In the middle of headland that defines Soma Bay, La Residence complements the Sheraton, which is just down the road, perfectly; where Sheraton is all about the beach and diving, this place is all about golf. Not only is it surrounded by an 18-hole par-72 golf course designed by Gary Player, it has bars with names such as Spikes and the Eagles Nest and a subdued, almost serious, feel to it that says, "We're here for a reason." Public areas are marbled and hung with traditional-style lamps, and the large pool is square and purposeful. Touches such as cotton hand towels in public-area toilets give the whole place a high-end feel. Rooms are large and have nice light, and the bathrooms are commodious. The health club facilities, which include a sauna, steam room, and gym, are well above average, even for a hotel in this price class, with a relaxed ambience and natural wood finishing.

Soma Bay, Safaga. ✆ 065/3542333. Fax 065/3542933. www.residencedescascades.com. 249 units. LE1,320 ($240/£122) golf-course- and pool-view double; LE1,375 ($250/£127) sea-view double; LE2,200 ($400/£204) Gary Player suite. AE, DC, MC, V. **Amenities:** Pool; 18-hole golf course; 60-bay driving range; 4 tennis courts; 2 squash courts; gym. *In room:* A/C, TV, minibar, safe.

Sheraton Soma Bay ★★★   The Sheraton Soma Bay is at the head of the class when it comes to beach-vacation facilities around Safaga, and it pulls off the role of ostentatious resort with confidence. The massive Pharaonic-themed lobby creates a stunning view across a fountain to the sea, framing the mountains perfectly. The beach and pool areas are designed to combine the sights and sounds of the seaside with just enough shade, and all without losing of sight of a bar. The beach, a 0.8km (½ mile) stretch of shimmering golden sand, is the nicest until you get to Port Ghalib down near Marsa Alam. If this isn't enough for you, there is great reef diving just off the beach, and plenty to see for snorkelers, too. The rooms, done up in pastel tones and light wood, are sumptuous, and there are groupings of suites arranged in beachfront bungalows for those who want to splurge a little.

Soma Bay, Safaga. ✆ 065/3545845. www.sheraton.com/somabay. 211 units. LE1,375 ($250/£127) resort-view double; LE1,513 ($275/£140) side sea-view double; LE2,283 ($415/£211) direct sea-view double. AE, DC, MC, V. **Amenities:** 4 restaurants; 5 bars; 2 pools; 4 tennis courts; squash court; gym; spa; sailing; kids' club; dive center. *In room:* A/C, TV, minibar, safe, Internet.

MODERATE

Holiday Inn Safaga Palace   Recently refurbished, the Holiday Inn is still a bit shabby and gloomy, with more of a budget feel than you would expect at this price. The pool, with its swim-up bar, is a nice place to spend an afternoon. The rooms are big and comfortable, and the staff are pleasant. For midlevel accommodation during a diving trip or on your way through town, the Holiday Inn will do just fine, but make sure that you get a healthy discount off the rack rate.

Safaga. ✆ 065/3260100. Fax 065/3260105. 327 units. LE550 ($100/£51) double. AE, MC, V. **Amenities:** 3 restaurants; 4 bars (including one swim-up); pool; health center; gym; playground; bank; ATM; Internet and Wi-Fi. *In room:* A/C, TV, minibar.

Lotus Bay Resort   This is an unassuming little resort on the main road just north of the old town. It's not the Sheraton, but it has nice gardens around low-rise buildings and a very big pool. It's built on much the same model as the Menaville (below) next door, with windsurfer and snorkel gear rental to complement the beach-lounging facilities and attract a broader range of customers. One of the nice things about this pair of hotels is that, between them, they offer quite a variety of reasonably priced restaurants, some not-so-reasonably priced but convenient shops, and at least one good Internet cafe. Rooms are basic, but fit and finish and general maintenance around the place is excellent.

Safaga. ℂ **065/3260005** Safaga or 02/27482639 Cairo. Fax 065/3251042 Safaga or 02/27482639 Cairo. www.lotus bay.com. Cairo office, 24 Fawakeh St., Mohandiseen. 224 units. LE473 ($86/£44) double. AE, MC, V. **Amenities:** 3 restaurants; 4 bars; 2 pools; windsurfing and snorkel gear rental; dive center. *In room:* A/C, TV.

Menaville 🐠🐠 This is the best all around hotel in Safaga, with a long, well-groomed beach and pleasant well-maintained gardens. Rooms are large and comfortable, though they have a bit more of a budget feel to the furnishings and maintenance than you would expect at this price. The "superior" rooms, which are only an extra $10, are worth paying for; they are larger, have a nicer view, and have decent balconies. The Menaville is a favorite among divers, but it's also a great place to go for windsurfing (p. 201). The pool is big and a great place to kick back after a busy day.

Safaga. ℂ **065/3260064-7** Safaga or 02/23620651 Cairo. Fax 065/3260068 or 02/23630431 Cairo. www.menaville. com. Cairo office, Methaf al Manial Street. 301 units. LE605 ($110/£56) double half-board. **Amenities:** 2 restaurants; 4 bars; 2 pools; dive center. *In room:* A/C, TV, minifridge.

Nemo This Dutch-run hotel and dive center near the seafront in Safaga is a good, solid, midrange facility. In keeping with the general no-nonsense ambience of the place, the rooms are nothing fancy, but they are clean and comfortable, and they have good-quality fittings and some nice local touches such as terracotta light covers. The bar downstairs is the best place for a drink in Safaga, and staff are friendly and professional. There is a beach across the street, but at the end of the day this is a great place to stay while you're diving, not a resort. Don't confuse the Nemo with its neighbor around the back, the best-avoided Toubia.

Maglis Medina, Safaga. ℂ **065/3256777**. www.nemodive.com. 33 units. LE413 ($75/£38) double. MC, V. **Amenities:** Restaurant; bar; beach; dive center. *In room:* A/C.

Sol y Mar Paradise Beach With rooms spread out through a series of low buildings, the Sol y Mar in Safaga has the look and feel of summer camp. In fact, it all seems to be aimed at that kind of slightly noisy, kid-oriented fun by the beach. There are a couple of tennis courts as a concession to the adults, but the kids' pool and the playground seem to be more important. The beach sand is a bit too coarse, and the sun beds are a bit too close together for my taste, but the atmosphere is jolly and nobody seems to mind. Rooms would be fine at about half the list price—these are budget rooms, with generic fittings, not much natural light, and cheap sheets.

Safaga. ℂ **065/3260017**. Fax 065/3260016. 236 units. LE440 ($80/£41) double. AE, MC, V. **Amenities:** 3 restaurants; 3 bars; 2 pools; gym. *In room:* A/C, TV, minibar.

BUDGET

El Yasmin 🐠 *Value* This basic, small hotel is tucked away on a quiet side street in the middle of Safaga. Rooms are modestly sized, with hard beds, and bathroom facilities are basic but spotlessly clean. Staff are extremely pleasant and helpful. Single rooms are a lot smaller than doubles, so if you're there alone, see if you can negotiate your way into the bigger room at the single price. The rooftop restaurant/bar is a lot of fun for sundown drinks or an early breakfast before heading out to the reef.

Maglis Medina, Safaga. ℂ **012/7430638.** Elyassminsafaga@hotmail.com. 15 units. LE193 ($35/£18) double. Cash only. **Amenities:** Restaurant; bar. *In room:* No phone.

WHERE TO EAT

Ali Baba EGYPTIAN   This might look like every other basic fish restaurant, but there's a difference: the food here's a lot better. Ali, the owner, is an affable guy who's usually found at one of the tables in either the original branch of the restaurant or the new one down by the Menaville hotel (above). Try the barracuda filet, which comes with an assortment of salads, hummus, *tahina*, bread, and Ali's secret sauce, and is cooked to succulent perfection.

Maglis Medina. ✆ 065/3250253. Main courses LE13–LE30 ($2.36–$5.45/£1.20–£2.80). Cash only. Daily 10am–midnight.

Hamada's SEAFOOD   Hamada Zarzor runs a cozy (*down-home* might be a better adjective), little (there are only 5 tables), back-alley place in Safaga where he prepares huge plates of seafood with surprising panache. On my last visit, he whipped up a heaping plate of delicious seafood featuring grilled lobster, a pile of grilled calamari, and a juicy fish and vegetable kebab. There were side dishes of rice, salad, and *tahina,* and dessert was fresh fruit. Clean dishes are neatly stacked on shelves beside the tables, and the plastic tablecloths have a tiger-stripe pattern. There is a TV in the corner and a model ship perched on top of an ancient stereo. It's not exactly fine dining, but the food's great.

Wust al Balad. ✆ 010/6123851. Set menu LE80 ($15/£7.40). Cash only. Daily 6pm–midnight.

4 Hurghada

The international airport in Hurghada has become the main hub for resort tourism on the northern end of the Red Sea coast. Not only are small towns such as Quseir and Safaga within easy reach, but a number of world-class resort compounds, such as Soma Bay, Sahl Hashish, and Gouna, are an easy transfer away.

The town itself, however, is another matter. In fact, when tourism experts get together to discuss development, it's usually only a matter of time before Hurghada comes up as an example of what to avoid. A gold-rush approach to building hotels has left this tourist town an ugly mess. The beaches have been divided between the resorts, and there is almost no public space from which you can see the water. Streets and squares are badly designed and hard to get around, and even if there were somewhere to go, it's all so spread out that you need a taxi for almost anything. To cap it all off, nobody really seems to want to be there—the locals have all come to make a quick buck off the tourists and would rather be back in their home villages, and the hassle-tired tourists you see on the streets generally look like they'd rather be back on the beach watching the palm trees.

ESSENTIALS

GETTING THERE

BY PLANE   Hurghada International Airport is connected to most of the capitals of Europe and the major cities of Russia by direct flights. Operated by Aéroports de Paris, its facilities are modern and relatively efficiently run. It has a full range of banking facilities, and taxis are easily available. If you are coming direct to Hurghada on an international flight, you will probably have to purchase a visa (hard currency only; $15/£7.40) here.

BY FERRY   The terminal for the fast ferry to and from Sharm el Sheikh is in a shabby end of town, and I recommend arranging a pickup before you arrive. Women traveling alone will not feel comfortable looking for a taxi here, particularly late at night.

You hear it everywhere you go in Egypt, recounted with the same wide-eyed wonderment with which Dick Whittington would have received the news that the streets of London were paved with gold: Foreign women come to Hurghada to meet and have sex with Egyptian men. To working-class men in Egypt, whose relations with the opposite sex are tightly circumscribed by tradition and who may not be able to get married until well into their 30s or even 40s, this is thrilling news, indeed. Whatever the merits of the story, the result is that female tourists in Hurghada, particularly those traveling alone, report a disturbing level of harassment. Keep in mind that what passes for banal conversation in the West may well be seen as an overt come-on when it takes place in the street or in a taxi in Egypt, and that the concept of consent is not as clearly defined in this context as it may be in your mind. Unless you wish to indicate a serious desire to move the relationship to an intimate plane, do not sit in the front seat of a taxi, do not let a man touch you anywhere (even shaking hands may be over the line, let alone accepting a hug or a kiss on the cheek), and do not go anywhere alone with a man whom you do not absolutely trust.

GETTING AROUND

BY TAXI   To get anywhere around Hurghada, you will need a car. There are orange-and-blue taxis everywhere, driven by men who have been drawn from all over Egypt by the rumors of quick and easy cash and women. Negotiate the price before setting out, and be prepared to pay substantially more than Cairo prices. Women should avoid solo taxi travel and understand that sitting in the front seat will be taken as an explicit sexual invitation.

BY FOOT   Hurghada isn't a good place to walk around. The main streets are shallow gullies running between the high walls of hotels or through messy unplanned shopping areas. The level of hassle is second only to Luxor, and, in many instances, a lot less friendly. Distances that would be walkable are turned into tedious treks by the unpleasant landscape and constant offers of cars, *shisha*, T-shirts, and drugs.

BY CAR   With or without a driver, a rented car is a good option for getting around Hurghada and moving up and down the coast. The roads are fairly good and the traffic, by Egyptian standards at least, is light and fairly sane. Car rental will cost LE165 to LE275 ($30–$50/£15–£25) per day and, in theory, requires an international license, a passport, and a major credit card. In practice, it's still worth trying if you have an American license (though not British or Canadian for some reason), your passport, and cash.

To rent a car, you can try **CRC** (© **065/3463366** or 01/06107387), apparently operated by Peugeot. It has a good size fleet of compact 206s and some of the bigger 306s and 406s. Prices start at LE165 ($30/£15) per day for the subcompact 206 and go up from there. A free allowance of 120km (75 miles) per day will get you around town and out to Gouna and back with a margin to spare. Extra distance is LE1 to LE3 (20¢–55¢/10p–25p) per kilometer.

Hertz has locations both at the airport (© **065/3444146**) and in downtown on Touristic Villages Road (© **065/3463176**). It's an excellent option for renting a car to get around the Red Sea coast. Expect to pay a little more than CRC, but you'll get a little more in terms of convenience and quality of car. Both locations are open daily 9am to 1pm and 6 to 8pm.

Easy Way, 18 Sheraton Road (© **065/3445246** or 01/22616349; fax 065/3445209; www.easyway-redsea.com), rents late-model Volkswagens. Prices start at LE50 ($9.10/£4.60) per day with the first 120km (75 miles) free and extra kilometers at LE1.35 (25¢/10p). A driver for the day is about LE85 ($15/£7.85) extra.

TOURIST INFORMATION

About the best things that can be said about the Hurghada **tourist information** office (© **065/3446513**) is that it's cool inside, and they usually have a photocopied map they can give you.

Most of the hotels around Hurghada now offer **Internet** access. At the lower end, you'll find a few PCs in the lobby (expect to pay LE10–LE15/$1.80–$2.70/95p–£1.40 per hour for access); at the higher end, expect an in-room access point for your laptop as well as PCs in the business center (expect to pay upward of LE80/$15/£7.40 per hour for these services in five-star hotels). Outside the hotels there are scores of small businesses offering better service for a lot less (LE3–LE8/55¢–$1.45/25p–75p an hour). The best place in town is the unfortunately named **Hooligan Club,** which has 20 PCs as well as a place to plug in your laptop. It's located down a side street next to the Albatross hotel and charges LE4 (70¢/35p) per hour.

WHAT TO SEE & DO

Loose environmental controls have meant off-beach **snorkeling** around Hurghada has been severely degraded in recent years, but dive sites within easy range of the daily boats remain some of the most spectacular in the world. Check out the "Active Vacation Planner" (p. 65) for a listing of well-established and accredited dive charter businesses.

The British cargo vessel *Thistlegorm* was only a year old when it was sunk by a pair of German planes in late 1941. The explosions blew a huge hole in her superstructure, making the inside of the boat accessible to divers. She lies in about 30m (98 ft.) of water, and a large quantity of cargo—including vintage BSA motorcycles, rifles, and locomotives—is still visible.

The large, bleak **Giftun Island,** just off the coast of Hurghada, is surrounded by coral reefs teeming with life. There are at least a dozen distinct dive and snorkeling sites around the rim of the island, and you'll see a huge variety of corals, moray eels, lion fish, lobster, parrotfish, angelfish, and more. Just south of the island is Abu **Rimata,** a reef nicknamed "the aquarium" for the enormous schools of fish that tend to congregate around it.

If you want to see the fish, but don't like the idea of joining them in their environment, check out the **Sinbad Club** submarines (© **065/3444688-90**) in Sekala. These 18m-long (59-ft.) crafts dive the reefs up and down the coast around Hurghada with up to 46 passengers onboard. With hotel pickup (at 9am) included, the whole tour takes around 2 hours, with about 50 minutes of that spent underwater. Tickets are LE385 ($70/£35) adults and LE220 ($40/£20) children.

WHERE TO STAY

Hurghada has seen a huge expansion in its hotel capacity in recent years, and the outskirts of the city are still a giant construction zone. Despite the pressure of increased competition and cut-throat pricing of packages, there are still some excellent high-end resorts in town and a little to the south in Sahl Hashish and to the north in Gouna. Though there are also some fine places to stay in town, they are the exception, and even some of the well-established hotels—such as the once respectable Grand Hotel—are now best avoided.

VERY EXPENSIVE

Hurghada Marriott Beach Resort The Hurghada Marriott has a nice location, with its own little beach tucked into a quiet part of town. Facilities may lack in character, but rooms are spacious and comfortable. Public areas are modern and elegant, and the view in most directions cannot be faulted. The small peninsula owned by the hotel offers particularly nice views of the sea and can be used for dining or just lounging about and enjoying the sea air. Unfortunately, the south side of the compound is overshadowed by a stalled construction project that shows no signs of proceeding in the immediate future. Spa and health-club facilities are very nice, though they cannot compete with the Steigenberger's (below) full-on Thalasso facilities.

El Corniche Road, Hurghada. ⓒ 065/3446950. Fax 065/3446970. www.marriott.com. 270 units. LE1,540 ($280/£143) double. AE, DC, MC, V. **Amenities:** 3 restaurants; 4 bars; pool; tennis court; squash court; health club. *In room:* A/C, TV, minibar, safe.

Oberoi Sahl Hashish 🏨🏨🏨 This is one of my favorite hotels in Egypt. If you're looking to wipe away the wrinkles and go home feeling a decade younger, you can't do much better than this. From the moment you're picked up at the airport, the Oberoi touches are clear: bits of *mashrabeya* adorn the car, and soft music plays on the stereo. The resort is a spread-out collection of low-domed buildings; one of the things that you're paying for here is a very low guest density. With only 102 rooms and suites spread out over the same size compound that other resorts use for many times this number, the grounds and facilities feel half-empty even when the resort is fully booked. Each room is a self-contained unit, and even the standard accommodations include a small living room and an outdoor dining area. The bathrooms are superb, with a huge bathtub and a shower that's built into a glass wall that opens into a small, jasmine-draped, private garden. Add to this the best horizon pool in Egypt, one of the nicest beaches on the coast, a snorkeling reef at the end of a graceful little jetty, and my favorite spa in Egypt, and you have an unbeatable recipe for relaxation.

Sahl Hashish, Hurghada. ⓒ 065/3440777. Fax 065/3440788. www.oberoihotels.com. 102 units. LE1,650 ($300/£153) double; LE2,475 ($370/£188) deluxe double; LE3,025 ($550/£280) deluxe suite. AE, DC, MC, V. **Amenities:** 3 restaurants; bar. *In room:* A/C, TV, minibar, safe.

EXPENSIVE

Hilton Hurghada Resort This is very much a middle-of-the-road, typical Hurghada beach resort. Rooms are big and comfortable, with enough beach-type touches, such as white-tile flooring and big sliding-glass windows that let out to the beach or around the pool. The lobby and buffet restaurants are a bit too noisy and crowded for my taste, especially when you're trying to relax, but the Lagouna restaurant at the end of the garden remains one of my favorite retreats in Hurghada. The beach is a great place to work on your tan, and the public pool areas heat up at night with an Asian-inspired show and disco.

Safaga Road, Hurghada. ⓒ 065/3465036. Fax 065/3465035. www.hiltonworldresorts.com. 311 units. LE1,073 ($195/£99) double. AE, DC, MC, V. **Amenities:** 4 restaurants; 5 bars; 2 pools; tennis court; squash court; playground; dive center. *In room:* A/C, TV, minibar, safe.

Steigenberger Al Dau   There are two Steigenbergers located across the road from one another. Avoid the overflow facilities (officially the Steigenberger Al Dau Club) that are cut off from the sea by the road—they are not only generic and bland, but sub-par considering the price. The facilities on the sea side of the road, on the other hand, are Steigenberger doing what it does best: a big, standardized hotel with lots of dark wood and chrome, a vast lobby, and friendly, responsive service. Rooms are huge, with big comfortable bathrooms and nice touches such as *mashrabeya* screens. The swimming pool is also vast, as is the sweep of the grounds down to the long beach of golden sand. Of course, the bill's not going to be tiny either, but in this case it might just be worth it.

About the only thing at the Steigenberger that's a little on the small side is the golf course, which is only 9 holes. On the other hand, you could literally toss a ball from many of the rooms down onto the greens, and then from the greens to the beach. It's hard to think of a more convenient package. There's also a full-on Thalasso Spa downstairs.

Yussif Afifi Road, Hurghada. (C) 065/3465400. www.steigenbergeraldauresort.com. 372 units. LE1,100 ($200/£102) double. AE, DC, MC, V. **Amenities:** 4 restaurants; 4 bars; 2 pools (including kid's pool); lazy river; 9-hole golf course; driving range; gym; Thalasso spa; dive club; Internet. *In room:* A/C, TV, minibar, safe.

MODERATE

Eiffel Hotel *Finds*   This may be the best midrange hotel in Hurghada. It's located close to some busy nightspots, such as Ministry of Sound, but it's quiet enough for sleeping in the morning after. It isn't directly on the beach, but it has beach facilities, as well as a rooftop bar and pool. Rooms are fairly basic but bigger and more comfortable than some of the truly low-end places, and staff are more professional, too. One of my favorite features at the Eiffel is the giant sea-themed cartoon that adorns the central courtyard. The dining room wouldn't be my choice for eating in, and I would think twice about paying for half-board options, but the Costa del Mar is just up the street, and beyond that are a host of other dining options within easy walking distance.

Sheraton Road, Sekala. (C) 065/3444570-1. Fax 065/3444572. www.eiffelhotel.org. LE220 ($40/£20) double. Rate includes breakfast. V. **Amenities:** Restaurant; bar; pool; Internet. *In room:* A/C, TV.

Geisum Village   This is a good budget beach getaway in the north end of town. Maintenance is a bit iffy in places, with some cracked plaster and peeling paint issues, but facilities on the whole are good enough, and important items—such as air-conditioners—are being kept up to date. Rooms are a bit on the small side, but the view (at least from the rooms closest to the beach) is decent and bathrooms are clean. The beach is short and the sand is a bit rougher and harder packed than you'll find it at higher-end places.

Dahar. (C) 065/3546692. Fax 065/3547994. 86 units. LE280 ($51/£26) double. Cash only. **Amenities:** Restaurant; 2 bars; pool; dive center. *In room:* A/C, TV.

Princess Palace Hotel   This is a budget resort on one of the main streets in Hurghada, close to several popular nightspots and with a nice beach for taking it easy and recovering from the night before. Rooms are small, but the white-tiled floors and wicker furniture aren't bad, and the sea view is across some villas. The wide (and very 1980s-style) lobby has Internet access and pool tables. Wildly overpriced at the rack rates quoted below, the Princess would be a good cheap-and-cheerful holiday option at the right rate.

Dahar. (C) 065/3465000-5. 324 units. LE572 ($104/£53) double. MC, V. **Amenities:** 4 restaurants; 4 bars; pool; Internet. *In room:* A/C, TV.

BUDGET

Cinderella Hotel   This budget accommodation doesn't pretend to be anything else. The Cinderella offers a bare-bones combination of a bed, bathroom, and some food. The beds are clean, but not the thickest in town, and the decor relies heavily on three-tone (all of them pastel) furniture and linoleum. The place is very clean, though, and staff are warm and friendly.

Dahar, Hurghada. ✆ 063/451675. 36 units. LE160 ($29/£15) double. Cash only. **Amenities:** Restaurant; bar; Internet. *In room:* A/C, TV, minifridge.

Seaview   This is another reasonably priced small hotel on the wrong side of the road, with the sea on the other side of a busy thoroughfare. Rooms are small and simply decorated with multicolored furniture, and while the place is clean and fairly well kept, fit and finish are second rate. Overall, there is little to distinguish the Seaview from its neighbors, except the pool, which is small and located in the dining room.

Dahar, Hurghada. ✆ 065/3545959. Fax 065/3546779. LE130 ($24/£12). Rate includes breakfast. Cash only. **Amenities:** Restaurant; bar; pool. *In room:* A/C, TV, minifridge.

White Albatros   The Albatros, in the middle of town, is probably the best deal for those who are looking for moderately priced basic accommodation and are willing to sacrifice staying at a beach-front hotel. Rooms are basic, with second-rate fit and finish, but they are clean, comfortable, and relatively large. The lobby is a little odd, as it's actually below street level, so you get a view of people's ankles as they walk past. The rooftop pool isn't something that you should take too seriously—it's just a little bigger than a whirlpool—and the "sea views" should also be taken with a grain of salt. All around, however, this is a friendly and pleasant place that offers rare value for money, and staff are friendly and competent (a bit of a rarity in Hurghada).

Sheraton Road, Sekkala, Hurghada. ✆ 065/3442519. www.albatros.com. 40 units. LE180 ($33/£17) double. Cash only. **Amenities:** 2 restaurants; pool. *In room:* A/C, TV, minibar.

WHERE TO EAT

Café del Mar ✿✿ INTERNATIONAL   This restaurant sits on the corner of a busy street close to the Ministry of Sound night club, but it's far enough away that the party beat doesn't intrude, and close enough that it's just a quick walk down to the beach after a light dinner for a night of dancing.

It has a nice selection of sandwiches and salads for lunch, but the place comes alive after dark with just the right balance of conversational hubbub and soft-but-upbeat music. Café del Mar is run by a pair of Swedish chefs who came here for the sun and the nightlife, and the steaks and pasta have an excellent reputation. The decor—a stylishly lit combination of red and orange walls hung with underwater photographs of brightly colored local fish—however, goes better with the fried noodles with shrimp, perfectly cooked with onion and peppers. The thin-but-tasty chocolate cake is the perfect finishing touch (though the pineapple pie with ice cream is also tempting).

Sekalla. ✆ 010/0716770 or 010/0716771. Appetizers LE16–LE30 ($2.90–$5.45/£1.50–£2.75); main courses LE30–LE100 ($5.45–$18/£2.75–£9.25). Cash only. Daily noon–midnight.

El Mina FISH   If you're feeling a little hemmed in by the walls of your resort, tired of eating in "outlets" instead of restaurants, and antsy to see a little bit of the "real" Hurghada, head to El Mina. The current owners claim family association with a local fisherman named Taha who discovered a particularly bountiful reef back in the 1950s. El Mina is now the best known and best established of the local eateries. Decorated in traditional Egyptian fish restaurant-style—which is to say over-the-top marine tableaux on the walls, aquariums, and bright colors—it offers guests a chance to choose their own fish from the ice-packed stand in front of the kitchen and practice their sign language in describing how it gets cooked. The only real choice you have to make is between grilled and fried (choose grilled), and everyone knows these words in English. It's one of the few places in Hurghada where you'll find the kind of easy-going, friendly welcome visitors get in less-touristy places around Cairo or the Delta.

Sakkala Square. ✆ **065/3556637** or 012/7320440. Main courses LE50–LE100 ($9.10–$18/£4.65–£9.25). Cash only. Daily noon–midnight.

Felfela EGYPTIAN   Despite a great location perched high above the sea with a stunning view over the water, this branch of the well-established Cairo restaurant used to have a questionable reputation. When I revisited the place recently, however, I found that it had improved. I had a light lunch of *shish tawook* (juicy chunks of chicken breast skewered with roasted peppers and onions) with a side of *tahina* and fresh-made bread from the on-site oven. The food, washed down with a cold local Stella beer, was excellent. The service wasn't great, but it was good enough by Hurghada standards.

Hadaba. ✆ **065/3442411**. Main courses LE15–LE50 ($2.75–$9.10/£1.40–£4.65). Cash only. Daily noon–midnight.

Hed Kandi INTERNATIONAL   Hed Kandi's better known as a nightclub (p. 209), but it's also worth a try for dinner. The influence of the German chef is obvious with offerings such as goulash and beef bordelaise in red wine sauce with a mound of roesti potatoes and crispy steamed veggies. They also serve excellent pizza and pasta and offer vegetarian alternatives at very reasonable prices. Atmosphere is more party than fine-dining, but the food holds its own with the best in town, with the advantage that the evening can move seamlessly to beachside dancing without the hassle of driving somewhere or finding a taxi.

Sekalla. ✆ **0167064452**. Appetizers LE18–LE35 ($3.30–$6.35/£1.70–£3.25); main courses LE50–LE70 ($9.10–$13/£4.60–£6.50). AE, MC, V. Daily 9am–3am.

Lagouna INTERNATIONAL   When the bright lights and disco beats are getting you down, retreat to the Lagouna at the Hilton Hurghada Resort, located beachside at the bottom of the garden. There's a small deck outside with a view across the bay, and though you may not be able to hear the wind in the palm trees inside, the lighting is soft and the atmosphere is intimate. I like the wooden ceiling beams and the wood floor, and I have a soft spot for aquariums at the best of times, and this one is small and nicely placed so that it sheds a soft light on the surrounding tables.

The menu is dominated by fish, and they have a variety of Egyptian and imported wines (running between LE200–LE400/$36–$73/£19–£37 per bottle) to go with your meal. You can go for the blackened sea bass filet or the stir-fried salmon, but I prefer the steak, seared and covered in peppercorn sauce with a side of sautéed vegetables and a neat stack of thick-cut French fries. The orange crème brûlée is a good way to end the meal.

Hilton Resort, Safaga Road. ✆ **065/3465036**. Appetizers LE15–LE40 ($2.75–$7.30/£1.40–£3.70); main courses LE40–LE110 ($7.30–$20/£3.70–£10). AE, MC, V. Daily noon–11pm.

Papa's II INTERNATIONAL   Good food, huge servings, and reasonable prices have made Papa's II one of the most popular and enduring restaurants in Hurghada. The setting is casual and friendly, and the food is excellent (they have a great midday breakfast).

If you're looking for a light meal, try the salad niçoise or a plate of meatballs. Entrees are more substantial, and I recommend heading straight for the burgers. Papa's has built its reputation around its enormous 750g (1.65 lb.) burger, and it's confident enough to offer a second one free to anyone who can finish one on their own. Why they offer desserts after such big entrees is anyone's guess, but I'm glad they do; the selection changes daily but tends to revolve around favorites such as chocolate fudge cake and strawberries and cream.

Downtown, next to the Shedwan Hotel. © 0123297530. Appetizers LE18–LE35 ($3.30–$6.35/£1.70–£3.25); main courses LE20–LE60 ($3.60–$11/£1.85–£5.55). AE, MC, V. Daily 1pm–2am.

HURGHADA AFTER DARK

The upside of being the cheap-package capital of Egypt is that Hurghada has an almost unparalleled party culture. Between European teenagers on term breaks, Russians breaking out of the winter blah, and Brits getting a bit of sun, there's no shortage of tourists who are ready, willing, and able to party all night, night after night. Below are a few of the alternatives, but improvisation is the name of the game here, and almost every hotel has some kind of disco. Meet up, make friends, and follow the crowd to where the party is happening.

Dutch Bar   There's a funky downmarket atmosphere going in this downstairs bar on the main street of Hurghada. The walls are hung with personal memorabilia—like a stuffed toy monkey—but are otherwise pretty bare. There is music all week, with Sunday night featuring a live band. Daily 10pm to 4am. Dahar © 065/3544381. Cover LE40 ($7.25/£3.70) per couple.

Hed Kandi   This is a beach-front lounge bar and dance club with a sophisticated atmosphere. With pink and blue lights glowing around the longest bar in town, designer benches and tables inside, funky beach furniture outside, and a big bimonthly party with the latest music from the London Hed Kandi label, it's easy to see how this place has become one of the hottest nightspots in Hurghada. The restaurant (p. 208) turns into a club at around 10:30pm. AE, MC, and V accepted. Sheraton Road, Sekala. © 0167064452. www.hedkandibeachbar.com. Tickets LE50 ($9.10/£4.60) in advance at the club; LE70 ($13/£6.50) at the door.

Matrix   Pool and beer, lots of beer, are what this place is all about. Located on the top floor of a building close to the seashore, it has an all-right view across a nearby hotel to the water. Best of all, it has a friendly crowd, substantial discounts if you can drink a lot of beer quickly, and Bob Marley posters hanging on the wall. Basic food, such as jacket potatoes and burgers (LE10–LE20/$1.80–$3.60/95p–£1.85; cash only), is also available. Daily noon to late. Sekalla. © 065/3576523.

Ministry of Sound   With a unique blend of a downbeat, laidback beach location and a distinctly upmarket rave party scene at night, Ministry of Sound brings London party know-how to the sands of Hurghada. Head down to the Ministry beach during the day for pub-style food and beach-style lounging, and stay late into the night for an international slate of DJs—which has included Judge Jules, Brandon Block, and Marco V—and plenty of dance-party action. Ministry of Sound is open daily 9am to 5am as a private beach, with pub-style food during the day, and as a club at 10:30pm. Sekalla. © 0127382442. Tickets LE70 ($13/£6.50).

Papa's I   Papa's I serves the same kind of hearty pub food as Papa's II (p. 208) but has a funky feel with dark wood that makes it a great place to hit for a cold beer on a hot afternoon. The view's nothing special, but if you've been looking at the sea all day, it could be the time to break from the beauty, kick back and watch the game, or play darts and do a bit of karaoke. Daily 1pm to 3am. Sheraton Road, Sekalla. ✆ **0123297530.**

DAY TRIPS FROM HURGHADA

While Hurghada is hardly an ideal location from which to see the rest of Egypt, it is easy enough to get to Luxor, Aswan, and even Cairo for a day trip. Most hotels offer a roster of possibilities through their travel desks. If they don't, you're never more than a 5-minute walk from a travel agency.

CAIRO

The capital is only an hour away by plane, and frequent flights throughout the day mean that a day trip to see the pyramids, walk through Islamic Cairo, or go shopping in Khan al Khalili is not only easy, but fairly cheap. Round-trip airfare, if you book it yourself with EgyptAir, is around LE825 ($150/£76).

LUXOR

The temples and tombs that are around the city of Luxor are also accessible as a day trip from Hurghada, and you'll find many companies that are prepared to sell you a single day round-trip bus excursion. Consider, however, that—what with waiting for the obligatory tourist convoy and inevitable traffic delay—it's going to take you between 4 and 5 hours each way. Ten hours on the bus is a steep price to pay for a day on the ground. The first option is to fly. Flights, unfortunately, go through Cairo, which means that even with a great connection you're looking at 2 to 3 hours each way. The second option, which I recommend, is overnighting in Luxor and taking two leisurely days to see the sites. See the "Upper Egypt" chapter (p. 215) for food, lodging, and transport.

MONASTERIES OF ST. ANTHONY AND ST. PAUL

A 3-hour drive north of Hurghada will take you to two ancient Coptic monasteries named for 3rd-century saints. Though you should confirm your visit with their Cairo office, both monasteries generally welcome visitors (the exception being during Lent), and you can even arrange an overnight stay.

The walled compound of the **Monastery of St. Anthony** lies about 45km (28 miles) inland from a slightly Mad Max junction town on the coast highway named Zafarana, which is about 270km (168 miles) from Hurghada. It was built at the foot of the mountain where St. Anthony lived from his youth until he died at the age of 105 in A.D. 356. Having been forbidden to come any closer to his cave, Anthony's followers settled on the site of the present-day buildings and buried him inside its walls in a chapel that is now called the **Church of St. Anthony.** On its walls are some of the most dramatic and important **Coptic murals** in Egypt. They were restored in the 1990s and are well worth a visit. You can also visit Anthony's cave, though it is a rather long climb—1,158 stairs. Reckon on about an hour and a good deal of water. The cave is worth a visit both for its original significance and for the scrawled annotations left by visitors over the last millennium and a half.

The **Monastery of St. Paul,** who was Paul the Anchorite, or Paul of Thebes, is about 35km (22 miles) southeast across the desert and mountains from the Monastery of St. Anthony. It was built on or near the site of the cave that St. Paul occupied for about 90 years, living on a half loaf of bread brought to him every day by a crow, until he died in about A.D. 345. It is reported that one day St. Anthony made the 2-day hike from his neighboring cave, and when he arrived Paul was expecting him because the crow had brought, instead of the usual half portion of bread, a full loaf. The monastery is reached by a road that leaves the highway about 25km (16 miles) south of Zafarana—the exit is not easy to spot from the northbound side of the highway, and you will have to go a few hundred meters past it to get across the median and then return to it. The monastery, which contains the intriguing Church of St. Paul and includes guesthouses and an olive press, is an imposing, almost military looking place, with a high wall around it. There is usually an English-speaking monk in the compound who can show you around.

It's possible to trek between the two monasteries, retracing St. Anthony's neighborly visit back in the 4th century. The trek takes 2 days and can be quite arduous during the summer. It's best to start at St. Anthony's, where they can supply a map of the route, and end at St. Paul's. Check with the office in Cairo (© 02/25900218) for local conditions before making firm plans.

EL QUSEIR

This is the most interesting place to visit on the coast south of Hurghada. The best way to get there is to drive yourself (p. 195) or to take a privately hired car. If you're hiring a car and driver, expect to pay LE300 to LE400 ($55–$73/£28–£37) for the day. If you're renting, reckon on driving about 300 to 350km (190–220 miles) round-trip.

5 Gouna

Only 20km (12 miles) up the road from Hurghada, Gouna might as well be on another planet. Where Hurghada was planned badly and implemented worse, Gouna is hard to fault on either front. Gouna is the brainchild of one of Egypt's biggest property developers and has gradually taken off as a real community with a sizeable residential population. Though it remains very much a resort village, it has the atmosphere of a town and is one of my favorite holiday spots in the country.

ESSENTIALS
ORIENTATION

From the moment you turn off the north-south coastal highway from Hurghada, you are in the world of Gouna, which is enmeshed in a confusing web of streets that curve and weave around the various little islands the town is built on. Every intersection has reasonably clear signposts pointing to the main hotels and the marina, however, and if they aren't enough, there always seems to be a cheerful security guard on hand to point the way. There are two main shopping and eating areas—Downtown, also known as Kafr Gouna, and the Marina. Downtown is larger, and resembles a proper town, with a grocery store and a good selection of restaurants and bars. The Marina, on the other hand, has a number of hotels and restaurants clustered around the boat docks.

GETTING THERE

BY PLANE   Gouna is less than 20km (12 miles) from Hurghada International Airport, which is served by half a dozen domestic flights a day from Cairo, and at least as many international flights. Fare for the 1-hour flight from Cairo is about LE880 ($160/£82). A transfer arranged through your hotel is the easiest way to complete the trip, but if you haven't arranged this, there are plenty of taxis at the airport. Bargain vigorously over the fare, but don't expect to get it below LE150 ($27/£14).

BY BUS   Gouna is easily reached from Cairo by bus. There are 12 buses every day from Turgoman Station to Gouna, which run from 7am to 2:15am for a fare of LE55 ($10/£5.10).

GETTING AROUND

Tok-toks (motor rickshaw taxis) abound. You can flag them down in the street, or you can have them pick you up at the hotel. Whichever you do, the fare is going to be LE5 (90¢/45p), so save those 5-pound notes whenever you get them.

TOURIST INFORMATION

The nice thing about Gouna is that there's no hassle about information. All hotels and many businesses have a well-designed map with a basic phone directory and a list of services that they hand out for free.

WHAT TO SEE & DO

Mangroovy Beach has acquired an international reputation for its facilities, beach, and wind, perfect for **wind- and kitesurfing.** The sand shelf extends several hundred meters offshore, making this an excellent place to learn because you can fall off the board and still stand on the bottom. On the other hand, a little bit out to sea there is a strong, consistent wind and good-size waves to keep experts amused. See the "Active Vacation Planner" (p. 65) for more details.

The **dive centers** and boats in Gouna all run trips to the same spectacular reefs and wrecks as the centers in Hurghada do—except at the end of the day, instead of bracing for Hurghada, you're relaxing into Gouna. See the "Active Vacation Planner" (p. 65) for more details.

Go-karting is also a lot of fun, and though Gouna doesn't have the biggest track in Egypt, or the fastest cars, the little 5-horsepower carts are in good shape and will give everyone in the family a much needed adrenalin rush after a day of relaxing by the pool and eating too much. Facilities include lap timers so that everyone gets printouts of their times at the end of the race. It's open daily from 10am to 10pm. Admission is LE50 ($9.10/£4.65) for 10 minutes or LE70 ($13/£6.50) for 15 minutes.

WHERE TO STAY
EXPENSIVE

Mövenpick Resort and Spa   The Gouna Mövenpick is a big resort, and it feels like it. The central pool space is vast, with loungers dotted around a series of pools. Rooms are typical of Mövenpick—large and comfortable with clean, sophisticated lines—and here in Gouna they're decorated in relaxing earth tones with tiled floors and area rugs. The high point of this Mövenpick is the large spa; treat yourself to a massage or a body scrub after that strenuous day by the pool, which will set you up nicely for a candlelit dinner by the sea.

Gouna. ℂ **065/3544501.** Fax 065/3545160. www.moevenpick-hotels.com. 554 units. LE1,265 ($230/£118) standard double; LE1,430 ($260/£132) deluxe double. AE, DC, MC, V. **Amenities:** 8 restaurants; 4 bars; 7 pools (including 3 kids' pools); 2 tennis courts; squash court; gym; spa; kids' club; dive center. *In room:* A/C, TV, minibar, safe, Internet.

Sheraton Miramar ⋘   The best word for the Miramar is **tranquil.** Spread out over nine small islands, the buildings are low and rounded, and ground lighting is used to good effect among the palm trees. The rooms, by contrast, are large and modern, decorated with bold colors and furnished in lushly comfortable style. Windows and verandas offer spectacular views out across the lagoons that surround the hotel on all sides. My favorite part of the Miramar is the little wooden bridges that connect restaurants and bars and the main building to the beach and dive center.

Gouna. (©) 065/3545606. www.starwoodhotels.com. 338 units. LE1,600 ($291/£148) standard double; LE1,760 ($320/£163) sea-view double. AE, MC, V. Amenities: 4 restaurants; 4 bars; 2 pools; bike rental; windsurfing; ATM; dive center. In room: A/C, TV, minibar, safe.

MODERATE

Captain Inn Hotel ☞   This moderately priced hotel close to the Marina is a favorite of windsurfers. From here you can access a wide selection of restaurants, and an easy *tok-tok* ride takes you to the go-karts (p. 212) and the beach. Rooms are cozy, with modern decor and a bit of flair, and they look over either the Marina or the sea; they also have a balcony from which you can watch what's going on in the pedestrian street below. The Captain Inn is excellent value for money and is in a great location.

Tig Marina. (©) 065/3580170. 41 units. LE 622 ($113/£58) **Amenities:** 2 restaurants; bar. *In room:* A/C, TV, minifridge.

WHERE TO EAT
EXPENSIVE

Kiki's ☞☞ ITALIAN   This is one of my favorite places to eat in Gouna. It's up two flights of stairs on the edge of the lagoon, so the view is superb, and the Italian menu is great as well. But what I really enjoy about the place is the little touches that make you feel like you're in a slightly nondescript restaurant somewhere in Italy. Leather-bound menus, checked tablecloths, Italian pop music coming out of the kitchen— these are all cues I'm going to enjoy dinner. On my last visit I had a fairly light meal of grilled chicken livers on arugula with balsamic vinegar followed by spaghetti *aglio olio,* which was a bit heavy on the pepper for me. The bill comes with a shot of home-made limoncello.

Kafr el Gouna. (©) 065/3580064. Appetizers LE10–LE25 ($1.80–$4.55/95p–£2.30); main courses LE25–LE75 ($4.55–$14/£2.30–£6.95). MC, V. Daily 6pm–midnight.

La Scala STEAK   This has to be just about the best place in Egypt to get your red-meat fill. Casual and bustling, La Scala features bare-bones decor and a long, open kitchen where you can watch your steak cooking on the grill. Service is brusque and businesslike. Staff don't mess around being too friendly, but they get the food to the table while it's hot and—unlike almost everywhere else in the country—they know how to pour a beer. I had a thick-cut filet grilled perfectly rare. It came with a pile of grilled zucchini, eggplant, and peppers, as well as fries.

Tig Marina. (©) 065/3541145. Appetizers LE15–LE25 ($2.75–$4.55/£1.40–£2.30); main courses LE25–LE65 ($4.55–$12/£2.30–£6). MC, V. Daily 6pm–midnight.

Le Deauville FRENCH   This restaurant on the waterfront in the Marina has the look of a small French bistro down pat. With white walls, simple furniture, and a few blue tiles thrown in for a Mediterranean touch, you could be anywhere in the south of France reading the menu off the blackboard. Service is a bit inept, but friendly enough (pretty well the opposite of what it would be in France), and the food is good. Those in the mood for seafood should try the *crevettes flambes au Pernod* (fresh shrimp expertly sautéed in anise-tinted liqueur). Otherwise, the *carre d'agneau* (rack of lamb) is cooked to perfection and comes with a simple-but-fresh side of vegetables. End with an espresso and the crepe caramel.

Abu Tig Marina. (©) 065/3541132. Appetizers LE15–LE30 ($2.75–$5.45/£1.40–£2.80); main courses LE60–LE140 ($11–$25/£5.60–£13). MC, V. Daily 6pm–midnight.

Pier 88 INTERNATIONAL   This is possibly the most romantic place in Gouna. The tiny restaurant floats in the marina and has no more than nine tables crammed around the central kitchen. Seating is upholstered in white, and the glass wind walls are hung with strings of blue lights. The Nordic toast with scrambled eggs and salmon make a delicious change from the run-of-the-mill hotel food, and the crêpes suzette is a fitting way to finish off.

Tig Marina. ✆ 065/3580032. Appetizers LE20–LE50 ($3.60–$9.10/£1.85–£4.60); main courses LE50–LE120 ($9.10–$22/£4.60–£11). MC, V. Daily 6pm–midnight.

Upstairs FRENCH   *Plush* is the word that will come to mind as you mount the eponymous staircase and enter this elegantly lit restaurant. There is a wine rack all the way up to the very high ceiling, and the curtains are gold in color. Try to get a table by the window (the view across the softly lit courtyard below is exquisite). The filet mignon with béarnaise and red wine sauce is exquisite and comes with roast mushrooms and vegetables. If you're not in the mood for meat, try the sole poached in white wine. There's a range of delicious desserts, but my favorite is the cheesecake with mango coulis.

Downtown. ✆ 065/3580052. Appetizers LE30–LE50 ($5.45–$9.10/£2.80–£4.65); main courses LE60–LE180 ($15–$33/£5.55–£17). MC, V. Daily 7pm–midnight.

MODERATE

Biergarden INTERNATIONAL   The Biergarden is a casual and friendly place for hanging out with good, filling food or, as the name suggests, meeting up for a few beers. Surprisingly, they also do an excellent breakfast that includes items such as scrambled eggs, pancakes, American-style filter coffee, and orange juice. If you're there in the evening, try the spicy and filling wiener schnitzel with *bratfkartoffeln* (essentially German home fries).

Downtown. ✆ 065/1132476. Main courses LE30–LE120 ($5.45–$22/£2.80–£11). MC, V. Daily noon–midnight.

Maison Thomas ☆ PIZZA   This branch of Cairo's Maison Thomas is one of my favorite pizza places in Egypt. It is a little more rustic than the original, with garlic hanging from the walls, rough wooden tables, and the trademark green hanging lamps, but the food is better. On a recent visit, I sat outside in the sun enjoying the fresh breeze off the sea and a Leonardo pizza—a mix of ham, artichoke, and red pepper. A medium is enough for one person for lunch.

Abou Tig Marina. ✆ 012/3611647. Pizzas LE20–LE60 ($3.65–$11/£1.85–£5.60). Cash only. Daily 11am–midnight.

Upper Egypt

Upper Egypt is, in fact, the part of the country that lies in the Nile Valley to the south of Cairo. Most of us think north when we think "up," and for this reason, the name seems counterintuitive. Remember, however, that the Nile flows downhill from its headwaters and the Ethiopian Highlands. As you go south from Cairo, you're literally going uphill into Upper Egypt.

The area, and specifically its biggest town, is the richest and most exciting part of the country for people with an interest in Egyptology and Ancient Egypt. Luxor, the biggest town in Upper Egypt, lies near the ancient city of Thebes, which was the religious and cultural capital of Ancient Egypt from the Middle Kingdom onward. The area around Luxor contains some of the best-known and most spectacular monuments of the ancient world including the Valley of the Kings, with its densely packed clusters of magnificent tombs that include the most famous of all ancient burials, the final resting place of Tutankhamun. It also includes Karnak Temple, the Temple of Hatshepsut, the Valley of the Queens, and the Valley of the Nobles—the list can go on and on, but words fail to capture the richness and variety of the ruins and sites here.

As you head south, you're not just heading into Egypt's past, but also away from her Mediterranean face and toward her African roots. South of Luxor, in Aswan, you'll find yourself in the ancient land of Nubia. This country, which had a history as long as Egypt itself, was first subsumed to the Egyptian state in antiquity and then all but obliterated by the construction of the Aswan High Dam in the 1960s and '70s. Apart from some magnificent monuments of its own, which include Abu Simbel and the Temples at Philae, Aswan is notable for its relaxed way of life. One of the high points of any trip to Egypt must be a few hours aimlessly crisscrossing the Nile at sunset near Aswan, where the dunes of the desert come almost to the water and the warm, fragrant air blows the scent of gardens across the valley.

The best way to access the sites of Upper Egypt is to fly from Cairo or, indeed, direct from Europe. If you're short on time, stick to Luxor and its immediate surroundings, as this is where the highest concentration of sites is. If you have a little more time, consider taking in Aswan and Abu Simbel by air or even taking a 4-day cruise between the two towns, which will open up the ancient sites along the riverbanks to you as well. One excellent option is to fly from Cairo all the way to Abu Simbel in the morning, and return to Aswan after a couple of hours at the lakeside monument. Planes go via Aswan, and it is possible to have your bags offloaded on your way through so that they're waiting for you on your return. From Aswan, the options are to stay a while or head back to Luxor by air or—my preference—cruise boat.

1 Luxor

Arriving in the modern town of Luxor by plane, you skim down over fertile fields that green all year round. If you're lucky, you'll see a farmer or two, their traditional *galle-beyas* pulled up around their knees as they tend to a water-buffalo-drawn plow. It's a scene that hasn't changed much since the first European tourists started arriving here a century ago. They found the local population living amongst the millennia-old ruins of Theban temples that they referred to in Arabic as Al Uqsor—"The Palaces"—which in time became Luxor.

Today, because it contains many of the biggest and most famous of the ancient monuments, Luxor is the center of gravity of the cultural tourism industry in Egypt. Most of the big sites are now open to the public and have, on the whole, been developed in a way that keeps damage to delicate ancient paintings and stonework to a minimum. The main downside of all this tourism is that the local economy has become completely dependent on foreigners, and tourists are subject to a higher level of hassle from touts, drivers, and salesmen than anywhere else in the country. For this reason, I recommend even independent travelers take advantage of tour operators here. It is, of course, quite possible to go individually from site to site, but joining a group for a day tour of the necropoli of the west bank or the temples of the east, cuts the annoyances to a minimum and lets you concentrate on the breathtaking array of ancient wonders that awaits you here.

When planning your campaign of sightseeing, keep a couple of basic facts in mind. Remember that the temples are mostly on the east bank (where the sun rises), and that the necropoli are on the west (where it sets). This has to do with how the ancient Egyptians saw the world, but more important for present purposes, it may determine how you set out your schedule: You'll need to do a lot of walking to see the tombs of the west bank, whereas temples afford you more opportunities to sit down and take a break. The other thing to remember is that, especially in the summer months (May–Sept), Upper Egypt is hot. In fact, it can be very hot. When confronted with the cost of private, air-conditioned transport, think of how much more you'll enjoy seeing monuments if you've just had a cool 15-minute break in a comfortable van.

ESSENTIALS
GETTING THERE

BY PLANE With a dozen flights a day out of Cairo, flying is the best way to get to Luxor. At time of writing, fares were less than LE1,100 ($200/£102) for the 1-hour flight, so though more expensive than the train, they're still fairly reasonable. The airport is a 15- to 20-minute ride from town, but taxis are available there. The easiest solution is to book a transfer through your hotel or travel company, but check on the price. Even if you pay the frankly extortionate LE100 ($18/£9.25) that airport drivers have been known to demand, this can be cheaper than the transfer.

The EgyptAir office, Corniche el Nil (© **095/23805803;** www.egyptair.com), is in front of the Old Winter Palace and is open Sunday to Thursday 8am to 8pm. Service is ostensibly controlled by an automated ticketing system, but the system is frequently down. When it is, don't hesitate to join the group at the counter to press your case. Better yet, book your ticket online.

BY TRAIN If you have time, or you want to save some cash, the train is a fine way to get to Luxor. The 9- to 10-hour ride from Cairo costs LE78 ($14/£7.20) for first class, LE40 ($7.30/£3.70) for second class in seats, and LE440 to LE660 ($80–$120/ £41–£61) for single/double accommodation on a sleeper train. **Note:** This must be paid in cash with U.S. dollars. With eight "tourist" trains a day (12:30, 1:15, and 7:40am, and 6:45, 7:15, 8:45, 9, and 10pm) and two sleeper trains (8 and 8:30pm), there's usually something to fit your schedule. The sleepers are comfortable (even if the 5am arrival in Luxor isn't), but take your own food—the stuff that comes on the trays as "dinner" should not be eaten no matter how hungry you are. If you're going to forego the sleeper, the night train is still a good option. Traveling up or down the Nile Valley during the day has some appeal, but even this scenery gets a little old after 5 or 6 hours. If you can stand to sleep in a seat, do so. The train station in Luxor is conveniently located downtown, and taxis are readily available to take you wherever you want to go. Expect to pay LE10 to LE20 ($1.80–$3.65/95p–£1.85).

BY BUS   As part of a downtown renewal plan, the bus station has been moved from its old, and very convenient, location behind the Luxor Temple to a new facility north of town near the airport. Twenty pounds ($3.60/£1.85) should be sufficient for the taxi ride into town, but settle on a price before you get in the car in order to avoid hassles at the other end.

Bus tickets to get back out of town can be purchased at either the Upper Egypt Buslines (© **095/2372118**) or Super Jet (© **095/2367732**) offices close to the train station. Of these, Super Jet is definitely preferable. Not only are its buses newer, cleaner, and air-conditioned, but it leaves from next to the train station, saving you the trek out to the bus station. All buses heading for Cairo, as well as Safaga, Quseir, and Marsa Alam on the Red Sea coast, go through Hurghada.

Upper Egypt Buslines buses leave frequently for Hurghada, but only the 7 and 8:30pm buses go straight on to Cairo after Hurghada; others require you to change in Hurghada. The 5pm goes on to Dahab. Fares are Cairo LE90 ($16/£8.30), Dahab LE120 ($22/ £11), and Hurghada between LE25 and LE32 ($4.55–$5.80/£2.30–£2.95).

There is only one Super Jet bus each day. It leaves at 7pm from beside the train station and goes straight through to Cairo via Hurghada. Tickets cost LE90 ($16/£8.30).

BY BOAT   The river route from Cairo to Luxor and Upper Egypt has been closed for several years and doesn't look set to open any time soon. It's a good idea to factor the cruise boats that shuttle between Luxor and Aswan into your transport plans. Cruises last from 3 days to a week (p. 236) and run frequently between the two cities. The northbound and southbound cruises are mirror images of each other, so take advantage of whichever one suits your priorities; a routing from Cairo to Aswan via Abu Simbel opens up the option of a 3- to 6-day cruise ending in Luxor.

GETTING AROUND
BY CAR   The best way to get around Luxor and its environs is to hire a car and a driver for the day through your hotel, a travel agent (see below for some options), or simply by negotiating a day rate with a taxi from the street. A reasonable fare would range from LE250 to LE350 ($45–$64/£23–£32) for the day.

BY TAXI   The blue-and-white cabs of Luxor tend to expect ludicrous fares, at least compared to anywhere else in Egypt. That said, they are also cleaner and newer than anywhere else in Egypt (with the possible exception of Sharm el Sheikh). Negotiate firmly for the fare before getting in. It's going to cost you LE10 to LE20 ($1.80–$3.65/ 90p–£1.85) for little jaunts up and down the Corniche.

Luxor

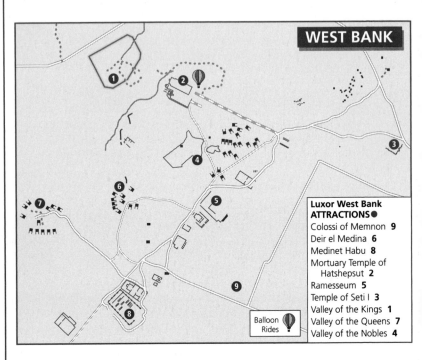

WEST BANK

**Luxor West Bank
ATTRACTIONS●**
Colossi of Memnon **9**
Deir el Medina **6**
Medinet Habu **8**
Mortuary Temple of
  Hatshepsut **2**
Ramesseum **5**
Temple of Seti I **3**
Valley of the Kings **1**
Valley of the Queens **7**
Valley of the Nobles **4**

Balloon
Rides

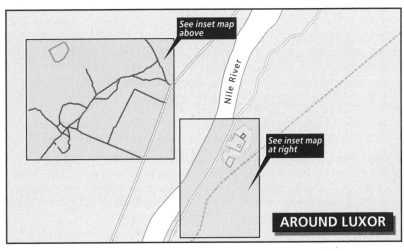

See inset map
above

Nile River

See inset map
at right

AROUND LUXOR

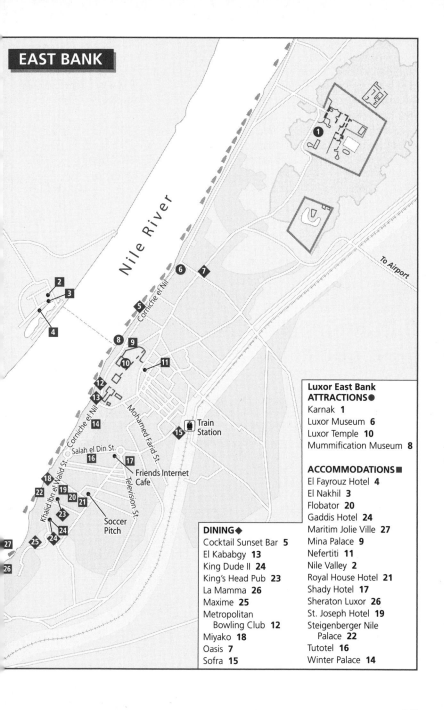

EAST BANK

Nile River

Corniche el Nil

Corniche el Nil

Mohamed Farid St.

Salah el Din St.

Khalid Ibn el Walid St.

Television St.

To Airport

Train Station

Friends Internet Cafe

Soccer Pitch

Luxor East Bank
ATTRACTIONS●
Karnak **1**
Luxor Museum **6**
Luxor Temple **10**
Mummification Museum **8**

ACCOMMODATIONS■
El Fayrouz Hotel **4**
El Nakhil **3**
Flobator **20**
Gaddis Hotel **24**
Maritim Jolie Ville **27**
Mina Palace **9**
Nefertiti **11**
Nile Valley **2**
Royal House Hotel **21**
Shady Hotel **17**
Sheraton Luxor **26**
St. Joseph Hotel **19**
Steigenberger Nile
   Palace **22**
Tutotel **16**
Winter Palace **14**

DINING◆
Cocktail Sunset Bar **5**
El Kababgy **13**
King Dude II **24**
King's Head Pub **23**
La Mamma **26**
Maxime **25**
Metropolitan
   Bowling Club **12**
Miyako **18**
Oasis **7**
Sofra **15**

BY BIKE Bicycles are a great way to get around the city if you can keep your nerve in the traffic. They can be hired from the numerous kiosks along the Khalid Ibn el Walid Street (my favorite is just outside the gates to the Luxor Hilton) for around LE10 to LE30 ($1.80–$5.45/90p–£2.80) per day. They are, without exception, clunky, one-speed junkers, but this somehow adds to the pleasure of the outing.

BY MOTORCYCLE Like the trade in their pedal-powered cousins, motorcycle rentals in Luxor are a slightly fly-by-night operation. Find them along Khalid Ibn el Walid Street (at the time of writing there was a kiosk just across from the Steigenberger), and expect to pay LE40 to LE60 ($7.30–$11/£3.70–£5.55) per hour, or around LE150 to LE200 ($27–$36/£14–£19) per day for a scrappy little 125cc model. Check closely that insurance and licenses are in order—there are plenty of fly-by-night operators around.

BY FOOT It's possible to walk around Luxor, but it's not very pleasant. Along the Corniche, the tout hassle is some of the worst in Egypt, and as you get away from the river, the view becomes unappealing and the traffic gets worse. The only walkable area is the immediate vicinity of the Luxor Temple and the souk, and between the ferry landing and the hotels on the West Bank.

BY CALECHE I'm no fan of carriages that cruise the streets of Luxor drawn by underfed horses, drivers aggressively touting their services to all and sundry. Prices depend very much on your bargaining skills and the state of the market, but expect to pay LE40 to LE70 ($7.25–$13/£3.70–£6.50) per hour.

ORIENTATION

The administrative, religious, and living areas of Thebes were all built on the eastern bank of the river, under the rising sun, with its symbolic associations with life and rebirth. The great necropoli of the Valley of the Kings, the Valley of the Nobles, and the Valley of the Queens, along with the associated mortuary temples, are located on the western side, the land of the setting sun, associated with death. Modern Luxor has developed in much the same fashion, with the main hotels, offices, and restaurants all on the east bank. The main street on the east bank is Corniche el Nil, or Khalid Ibn el Walid Street as it is known where it doesn't run directly on the water. This runs the length of the town from the Sheraton Luxor at the southern end to Karnak Temple and beyond at the northern. The most important point of reference is the Old Winter Palace on Corniche el Nil. This classic hotel is close to the souk, downtown (such as it is), and Luxor Temple, and is situated in the middle of a useful cluster of stores and travel agencies.

The West Bank is less commercially developed, a lot quieter, and a little less densely populated by annoying men who will pester you to buy something. You can get there on the ferry that leaves from just below Luxor Temple. It leaves about every 15 or 20 minutes (really, it just leaves when it leaves—buy your ticket, get on the boat, and enjoy the scenery), and costs LE1 (20¢/10p). Alternatively, hire one of the little motorized *falucas* from any of the docks along the river banks. If you go straight across from near Luxor Temple, the standard fare is LE5 (90¢/45p). You will be quoted substantially more at first, but stand your ground. From the ferry dock on the other side, there is one main street that runs directly west for about 5km (3 miles) to the necropoli, temples, and the ticket office. To the left of this street there is a dusty bundle of buildings wrapped in a tangle of narrow roads. This is where the hotels listed below are located.

FAST FACTS   The **tourist information office** in Luxor is located on the Corniche below Luxor Temple. There is little point in going, however, as they have almost no useful information and there doesn't seem to be anybody working there who speaks English. For **maps,** the best place to go is **Gaddis & Co.,** in the mall directly in front of the Winter Palace.

With most hotels now offering in-house **Internet,** the need for the Internet cafe has dwindled somewhat. If you're looking around, though, you'll have no problem finding one. Expect to pay LE10 ($1.80/95p) or less per hour. My favorite, Friends Internet Café, on Salah el Din Street (© **095/2367260**), is located behind the Old Winter Palace. It has eight reasonably new computers, good bandwidth, and a small coffee bar. Over on the West Bank, try **Europa,** on the main road near the ferry dock. It only has four PCs, but the service is extremely friendly, the bandwidth is great, and the price is right at LE5 (90¢/45p) per hour. It also has Wi-Fi and an extra Ethernet connection for laptops.

TOUR COMPANIES   There are numerous companies in Luxor that can arrange half-day, full-day, and longer sightseeing itineraries for you. The sheer number, however, means that there are quite a few shady operators on the market and several that will waste your time with tours of retail outlets that are paying them to bring in customers. If you use the right company, though, it can be a hassle-free and even cost-effective way of arranging your stay.

Before venturing out to find a company that can arrange your tours, however, your very first stop should be the lobby of your hotel—every hotel in Luxor will have a way of arranging for transport, tours, cruises, and balloon rides, and many will do just as good a job as one of the companies listed below. Odds are that you won't need to go any farther than your own front door.

If you do find that you need services that go beyond what's available in your hotel, the companies listed below have a proven track record of reliable, high-quality service. If you'd like to shop around further, there is a row of offices in front of the Old Winter Palace that houses a number of companies that have been there for a long time and may find you cheaper prices. That said, I found the services at the American Express office here and in Aswan to be consistently disappointing—with inaccurate information and bad service—and I would avoid both for any kind of local travel arrangements.

- **Karnak:** You won't be inspired by the demeanor of the staff or the look of the facilities at this little office on the Corniche, but they will get you where you're going, and do it for less than Thomas Cook (below). They have a long list of prepared tours and packages and can book cars and minivans. Corniche el Nil; © **095/2372360** or 0106082816 mobile.
- **Nobles:** Of the bigger local firms, this is also one of the best organized and highest profile. They run trips around Upper Egypt as well as offer day and overnight excursions to the Red Sea and Cairo. Khalid Ibn el Walid Street (Corniche just before first Midan after the Old Winter Palace); © **095/2373155;** fax 095/2376588; www.noblestour.com.
- **Thomas Cook:** With a couple of branch offices around town, I recommend going to the main one in front of the Old Winter Palace. They're a little more expensive than other agencies, but a little more efficient as well and generally deal in higher-quality products. Try Thomas Cook first for comfortable, low-hassle arrangements around Upper Egypt. Just don't expect them to answer e-mails. Corniche el Nil; © **095/2372402** or 095/2372196; fax: 095/2376808; www.thomascookegypt.com.

- **Thomson Tours:** This British company does a brisk trade here with British tourists. They can be trusted to use reputable, well-insured local companies to provide tours of the monuments, balloon rides, and day trips to Cairo. They keep a representative in Luxor, who can be found on a rotating basis in the lobbies of the following hotels: the St. Joseph, the Sheraton, the Steigenberger, the Sonesta St. George, the Maritim, Iberotel, Mercur, the Sofitel, and the Old Winter Palace. If you miss them, check the notice posted in the lobby for their schedule. ℭ **02/38510102** (this is a Cairo number, which will put you in touch with the local rep).

HOT-AIR BALLOONING   The idea of floating over the East Bank as the sun rises over Medinet Habu, the Valley of the Nobles, and the Colossus of Memnon has caught on with a vengeance. There are now dozens of companies vying for your business. The three below have been in business for several years, employ certified pilots, and carry insurance. That said, services vary little. They will all pick you up at your hotel very early (around 5am) and take you via boat to the other side of the river. A light picnic breakfast is served en route, and you're in the air a little after sunrise. Flights last 35 minutes to an hour and go where the wind blows. Check to make sure that you'll get a refund in the (highly unlikely) event of the flight being cancelled because of bad weather. Exactly which monuments you'll float over depends on the wind, but you're likely to get fantastic views of the temples of Hatshepsut, Mentuhotep I, and Thutmoses III as you rise up the Deir al Bahri escarpment that separates the valley from the desert. The village of Qurna, with its surrounding patchwork of green fields, will be spread out below, and you'll get a great view of the Nile as well.

Prices vary wildly by season. In season, expect to pay between LE500 and LE1,000 ($91–$182/£46–£93) per person for the flight. Out of season, you should expect to pay half of this with a bit of negotiating.

- If you book through a hotel or Thomas Cook, you may well find yourself flying with **Sinbad**, which is well established and heavily promoted. 37 Abdel Hamed al Omda St.; ℭ **095/2361960** or 095/2370437; fax 095/2365405; www.sindbad balloons.com.
- **Skycruise** maintains desks in the Sonesta St. George and Isis hotels at which you can pick up information and book flights. 110 Khalid Ibn el Walid St. (close to the Luxor Sheraton); ℭ **095/2360407,** 095/2370638, or in Cairo 02/27383751; fax 02/27383761.
- Part of a big transport company, **Viking** has a range of balloons for groups from 2 to 20. They also have desks in many hotels. 3 Ahmad Orabi St.; ℭ **095/2277212;** fax 095/2271211.
- A little more expensive than the others, **Hod Hod Soliman** has been in the business since it started, and once you've been featured on CNN, you can afford to charge a little more. Omar Ali Street (on the second floor close to the Golden Palace hotel); ℭ **095/2370116;** hodhodoffice@yahoo.co.uk.

WHAT TO SEE & DO

For some reason that nobody has ever been able to explain to me, temples and tombs tend to be open marginally shorter hours in the winter (officially Oct–Apr) than the summer. Keep this in mind when planning your itinerary.

Look, Don't Touch

It's the sad truth of mass tourism that our presence can damage the monuments that we come to admire. Despite massive foreign-aid investment in protecting sites, perspiration and even exhaled breath damage the delicate paintings in tombs; the lights thrown up around temples all too often heat and damage the ancient stone; and the exhaust from tour buses and cruise ships forms chemical compounds that destroy delicate relief carvings.

Fortunately, there is an easy and cheap way that we can reduce our impact on these irreplaceable artifacts—don't touch, or climb on, statues or buildings. Guards will often encourage you to climb under railings or get on top of walls or statues for a photo, but the 50¢ he'll take for this privilege doesn't pay for the damage you'll do to the 3,000-year-old masonry.

EAST BANK

Luxor Museum ⚶⚶   Though a lot smaller than the Egyptian Museum in Cairo, the Luxor Museum—which was designed by the Brooklyn Museum in New York—is a lot better put together and is worth at least an hour or two. It's hard to pick highlights from the stunning collection, but the 2.5m-tall (8-ft.) quartzite **statue of Amenhotep III,** found at Luxor Temple in 1989, shouldn't be missed (it's on your way to the exit), and I particularly enjoy the **Wall of Akhenaten** on the second floor. The wall is made up of small blocks known as *talatat* (which simply means "threes" in Arabic) that were used by Amenhotep III at Karnak Temple before he changed his name to Akhenaten and moved the capital away from Thebes (now Luxor) to Tel al Amarna. After his death, they were reduced to rubble, but they've been painstakingly pieced back together to form a tableaux that shows this rather odd Pharaoh and his wife. You should also see the pieces retrieved from Tutankhamun's tomb, which include three beautifully preserved chariots, some model boats, footwear, and a bow and arrows.

Corniche el Nil. ✆ **095/2380269** or 0106703638. Admission LE70 ($13/£6.50) adults, LE30 ($5.45/£2.75) students. Winter 9am–3pm and 4–9pm; summer 9am–3pm and 5–10pm. Guards are inconsistent on whether nonflash photography is permitted, but flashes are never acceptable.

Luxor Temple ⚶   You don't have to leave downtown to see one of the most spectacular sites in Upper Egypt. Luxor Temple was built in the middle of Thebes by Amenhotep III in the 14th century B.C. In describing the town, 19th-century visitors talked about houses clustered among the capitols of the buried columns (you'll see, approaching the temple, that it's now mostly below the level of the street).

Entering, you see the **Avenue of Sphinxes,** a road flanked by, well, a lot of sphinxes. If you find the sheer number of catlike creatures lined up to watch you pass a little unnerving, consider that this line of feline observers used to stretch all the way to Karnak Temple, 3km (2 miles) downriver. Some of the most spectacular aspects of the temple were actually built about a century after the death of its founder by Ramses II, who you see depicted on the first pylon killing the Hittites at the Battle of Kaddesh.

One of the most interesting sights at the temple is actually accessed from outside. The **Mosque of Abu Hagag,** which is named for a local holy man to whom an annual *moulid* is dedicated, was mostly built in the 19th century, but parts, such as the 11th-century northern minaret, are much older. It is all that remains of the village that was cleared away by 19th-century excavators. Look left and up once you're inside the first pylon, and you'll see it. Entrance is from Karnak Street behind the temple.

Beyond the mosque, there is a **colonnade.** The 14 columns here stand almost 20m (65 ft.) high. The area was finished by Amenhotep III's son, Tutankhamun. Beyond the colonnade is the **Court of Amenhotep III.** This part of the temple is a good place to end up around dusk, when the lights come on and bats swoop around the capitols looking for an evening meal.

Down the street from the Old Winter Palace Hotel (p. 233) and backing onto the main souk. Admission LE40 ($7.25/£3.70) adults, LE20 ($3.60/£1.85) students. Winter 6am–9pm; summer 6am–10pm.

Karnak Temple ✸✸✸   Karnak Temple is simply jaw dropping, and should not be missed under any circumstances. The temple is actually an enclosure containing a number of temples to Amun, and some parts of the eastern side of the complex may have been built as early as the 20th century B.C. It seems that almost every ruler who followed contributed to the site until it was a vast and spectacular collection of temples, halls, and statues. Now, since the entrance is on the western side, the general rule is that the farther you go into the complex, the older the surroundings become.

You'll enter through a massive pylon (it was never completed, but still stands 43m/141 ft. high) and find yourself fairly quickly in the famous **hypostyle hall.** There are 134 columns here, rising around you like the trees of a giant forest, dwarfing anything of human scale. If you've brought along a guide—probably a good idea for this massive, and massively complex, site—they'll stop you here and explain that the hall was planned by Amenhotep III (who built the older parts of Luxor Temple) but actually built by Seti I, with Ramses II (who contributed some spectacular additions to the Luxor Temple) adding relief work and decoration. They should point out the **reliefs on the northern wall** of the hall, which were done under Seti I and are of higher quality than those which were added by his successor. They should also add that the room was originally roofed, and that the columns and the walls were brightly painted.

From this point in the temple complex, you can continue east or you can head north. This second axis was added to the temple layout by Hatshepsut (1479–1456 B.C.). The east-west layout of the temple as it had developed to that point followed the track of the sun and represented celestial power, and this new direction, parallel to the Nile, symbolized terrestrial (and, by extension, royal) power.

Two Festivals, One Boat

If you're in Luxor the month before Ramadan, you may be lucky enough to catch the *moulid,* or festival, of Sheikh Abou Haggag. The festival, which lasts 2 days and draws participants from all over Egypt, commemorates the life of this 14th-century holy man with extravagant street parties and a parade that features floats populated by outrageously costumed men and boys, raucous music, and model boats that are held above the fray on polls. The festival is reflective of the scenes depicted on the walls of the colonnade at Luxor Temple, which show the ancient festival of Opet with the priests of Karnak carrying the boats of Amun, Mut, and Khonsu to the temple to mark the annual flood of the Nile.

Karnak Sound & Light Show

Gloriously over-the-top and cheesy, the sound-and-light show at Karnak is some of the best entertainment in Egypt. The 1-hour, heavily voiced-over show takes you through some of the history of the site and moves from the courtyard, through the hypostyle hall (which is absolutely magnificently lit and one of the very few examples of a modern improvement to an ancient site), and then to the sacred lake. Even if you don't like the loud music, it's really worth it for the walk through the temple at night. Make sure that you edge to the front of the crowd in the hall so that you get a good seat on the bleachers that are set up at the sacred lake. Admission LE50 ($9.10/£4.60). Winter shows 6:30, 7:45, 9, and 10:15pm; summer 8, 9:15, 10:30, and 11:45pm.

	First Show	Second Show	Third Show	Fourth Show
Saturday	French	English	German	X
Sunday	German	English	French	Italian
Monday	English	French	Spanish	X
Tuesday	Japanese	English	French	X
Wednesday	German	English	French	X
Thursday	English	French	Arabic	X
Friday	English	French	German	Spanish

Karnak can get very crowded. To avoid the squash, get here first thing in the morning. If you're going to go in the evening to catch the light, remember that because of the high walls, dusk comes 30 to 45 minutes earlier inside the complex than outside.

© 095/2380270. Admission LE50 ($9.10/£4.60) adults, LE25 ($4.55/£2.30) students. Winter 6am–4:30pm; summer 6am–5:30pm.

Mummification Museum *Kids*   Appropriately enough, it is Anubis (p. 226) who greets you when you visit the Mummification Museum. Displays include mummified animals as well as the mummy of Maserharti (a 21st-dynasty priest), but the tools of the trade—scrapers, scoopers, and hooks used to remove the internal organs and brains of the corpses—really make this place worth a visit.

Corniche el Nil. *©* 095/2387320 or 095/2370062. Admission LE40 ($7.25/£3.70) adults, LE20 ($3.60/£1.85) students. Winter 9am–7pm; summer 9am–10pm.

WEST BANK

You can easily arrange to do any, or all, of the sites on the West Bank with either private transport or an organized bus tour through any of the tour companies listed above. It is just as easy, though, to pay LE1 (20¢/10p) to cross the Nile on the public ferry that departs from below the Luxor Temple or LE5 (90¢/45p) to cross with a motorized *faluca* from any of the little docks along the edge of the river. Once on the other side, negotiate your itinerary with one of the many taxis that wait there.

Tickets for the sites below need to be bought at either the ticket office near the Valley of the Nobles or at the gate of the site itself; I have noted the former in the corresponding reviews.

Anubis

Long a favorite of the manufacturers of repro fake-basalt statuettes, Anubis was represented as a slender dog with tall pointed ears. You'll see him quite often at the entrance to a tomb, from where he guards the bodies of the interred from the depredations of the jackals he resembles. His color, black, is said to represent not only the color of decayed flesh (and, thus, death) but also the black, fertile earth of the Nile Valley (and, thus, life). It was Anubis who wrapped the body of the murdered Osiris and facilitated his resurrection, hence Anubis's association with mummification. He had many titles, among them *khentimentiu,* which meant "first among Westerners" and referred to his dominance over the necropolis of the West Bank.

Colossi of Memnon   These two statues of Amenhotep III are all that remain of a massive compound this Pharaoh built to house his mortuary temple. According to archaeologists, the site would have been bigger than Karnak, making it the biggest such complex in all of Thebes. Built on the actual flood plain of the Nile, however, it washed away, and all that remains now is this pair of headless, 18m-high (60-ft.) statues. From about the middle of the 1st century B.C. until the early 3rd century A.D., when a crack in it was fixed by Septimus Severus, the northern statue of the pair used to make a low wailing noise each morning. The Greek explanation associated the statue with the Homeric character Memnon and the noise with him singing a greeting to his mother Eos, the goddess of dawn. No ticket is required.

Deir el Medina—the Village of the Workmen   Deir el Medina is a fascinating site for anyone interested in how the ancient Egyptians actually lived. It's close to the Valley of the Queens, and incorporates a small Ptolemaic-era temple and the remains of a small walled village that housed the workers who built the temples and tombs of the West Bank. The village, which contained around 70 small houses, is still well enough defined that you can make out streets and the walls of individual buildings. The name of the area comes from the small 3rd-century B.C. temple to Hathor on the site, which was taken over by early Coptic priests and named Monastery of the Town, or "Deir el Medina."

Next to the village there is a small necropolis, which contains several tombs built for men who worked in the Valley of the Kings. Perhaps the most famous is the tomb of **Sennedjem,** himself a tomb builder in the 13th century B.C. The walls of his tomb are richly painted and well preserved, and include a rather chilling depiction of the jackal figure of the god Anubis preparing the mummy of the owner of the tomb. Much of the original contents of this tomb are now in the Egyptian Museum in Cairo. Another well-known tomb here contained the body of **Peshedu,** and while it is also decorated with Anubis, don't miss the touching painting of the owner himself by a palm tree near water. The tomb of **Inherkhau** is decorated with pictures of its owner from his quotidian life as well. Judging by the pictures, Inherkhau was not only bald, at least for part of his life, but an enthusiastic harp player.

Admission free at time of writing, but check with ticket office. Winter 7am–5pm; summer 6am–7pm.

Medinet Habu   Often passed over by tours and guidebooks, Medinet Habu is a great place for an afternoon visit. The complex seems to have been started by Hatshepsut in the 15th century B.C., but it was vastly expanded about 3 centuries later by

Ramses III. Over the millennia it was used for various purposes, and during the Ptolemaic period, the village of Djeme was built within the walls (hence the *medinet,* or "town," in the site's modern name), and for a while the room that precedes the hypostyle hall was used as a Christian church.

There are gory illustrations on the outer walls of Ramses III killing his enemies and subjugating their lands, but these become more religious as you progress inside. The columns of the inner hypostyle hall have unfortunately been reduced to stumps, but the vestibule and sanctuary farther in are worth a wander through. The reason that you should visit in the afternoon will become evident as the sun begins to set and the evening draws in on the surrounding village of Kom Lolah. Take a deep breath and let the calm settle into you before heading back to the hustle of the town.

Admission LE20 ($3.60/£1.85) at the ticket office. Winter 7am–5pm; summer 6am–7pm.

Mortuary Temple of Hatshepsut ✸   Much defaced over time, this spectacular temple is nonetheless worth a visit. It was built by Hatshepsut, who ruled Egypt as queen between about 1479 and 1458 B.C. Though she was a successful ruler, subsequent Pharaohs effaced her name where possible from her monuments, and her temple against the cliff of Deir al Bahri (named for the Coptic monastery that was installed on the site well after the temple had disappeared from view) is no exception.

Approaching the temple, you'll see that it rises in **three massive terraces.** The first two were originally covered in trees, and if you look around carefully you can still see stumps. If you pause at the colonnades between the first and second terraces, there are

My Name Is Ozymandias

Even among Pharaohs, whose careers were devoted to building monuments to themselves, Ramses II, whose name comes through Greek transliterations as Ozymandias, seems to have been a bit of an egomaniac. He left Egypt littered with massive tributes to his greatness, including the enormous Ramesseum on the West Bank of the Nile at Thebes, where he also had a 17.5m (57-ft.) statue of himself erected. It was this statue that inspired Percy Bysshe Shelley to write a beautifully metered poem that, more than two centuries later, still has a remarkable resonance in Egypt.

I met a traveler from an antique land
Who said: Two vast and trunkless legs of stone
Stand in the desert . . . Near them, on the sand,
Half sunk, a shattered visage lays, whose frown,
And wrinkled lip, and sneer of cold command,
Tell that its sculptor well those passions read,
Which yet survive, stamped on these life-less things,
The hand that mocked them, and the heart that fed:
And on the pedestal these words appear:
"My name is Ozymandias, king of kings:
Look upon my works, ye Mighty, and despair!"
Nothing beside remains. Round the decay
Of that colossal wreck, boundless and bare
The lone and level sands stretch far away.

Slow Boat to the Past

The last 10 years have seen a revival of a kind of river travel that was almost killed by "modern Egypt." In the 19th century, the *dahabeya* was the gentleman's way of traveling from Cairo to Upper Egypt. Part hotel, part transportation, they were comfortable, slow, and expensive—just about everything that Thomas Cook's mass-market steamboats weren't—and they were favored by anyone wealthy enough to hire on for the season. Today's *dahabeyas* go one better, with modern conveniences to match the stately comfort of traditional wind-driven travel. Prices include full board (excluding alcoholic beverages).

Nour el Nil runs five absolutely lovely custom-built *dahabeyas* on 6-day/5-night cruises between Luxor and Aswan. The big "panoramic" cabins at the back of the boat are some of the most attractive accommodations I've seen in Egypt. They're not huge, but they're fitted with period furnishings and a big picture window nearly at water-level. They're perfect for a fantasy vacation or a honeymoon. Rates range between LE8,580 ($1,560/£795) per person (based on double occupancy) in a standard cabin in regular season to more than LE17,160 ($3,120/£1,589) per person in the deluxe "panoramic" cabins during high season. ✆ **0106578322** or 0105705341. www.nourelnil.com.

Other options for sailing up the Nile are the ***Cenderella*** and the smaller ***Bab el Nil.*** Both boats rent out by the week, with the 10 to 12 passenger *Cenderella* going for LE42,900 ($7,800/£3,972) between May and September, and LE60,500 ($11,000/£5,602) for the rest of the year. The six-passenger Bab el Nil goes for LE25,850 ($4,700/£2,394) May through September and LE34,375 ($6,250/£3,183) the rest of the year. I find the fit and finish to be a little less appealing than the Nour el Nil boats, but the wooden-walled rooms are spacious, and the curvy steel railings are both romantic and functional. ✆ **0105272390.** beatrix.greco@free.fr.

Dahabieh runs converted cargo boats that may not have the sophisticated charm of some of the other *dahabeyas* on the river, but they are roomy, and the staff have a casual charm. At around LE12,100 ($2,200/£1,120) for a double cabin for a 6-day/5-night cruise, however, they are relatively economical without sacrificing comforts such as en suite toilets. None of the boats are particularly child-friendly, but these old cargo boats lack safety rails and are not recommended for young children. ✆ **0100062221.** www.dahabieh.net.ms.

some illustrations of boat building and the transportation of obelisks, but the most famous illustrations are at the back of the second terrace. Here, on the left-hand side, there are paintings that show a trading expedition to the land of Punt.

The other two must-see areas of the temple are the chapels of Hathor and Anubis, which are on the left and right, respectively, of the ramp leading up to the third terrace. The **Chapel of Hathor** bore the brunt of the defacement that followed Hatshepsut's death, but a colorful depiction of a massive naval parade remains, and the massive pillars are also intact. The **Chapel of Anubis,** however, with its 12 fluted columns and amazingly preserved colors, has a certain grace and, if you can find a moment when it's not jammed with camera-pointing tourists, tranquility.

Admission LE25 ($4.55/£2.30). Winter 7am–5pm; summer 6am–7pm.

Ramesseum ⟨★⟩ The mortuary temple of Ramses II isn't in the best condition now and may actually be best viewed from a balloon in the early morning. The unique feature of the place, besides its size, that might just make it worth a visit is the actual statue that inspired the 19th-century poet Percy Bysshe Shelley to write the poem (p. 227) later selected by high school teachers the world over as a beginner's exercise in exegesis. The original entrance would have been to the left as you walk in through the modern entrance, between two massive pylons that are worth checking out for their depictions of Ramses II's military triumphs. To the right, more than half the original columns of the hypostyle hall are still erect and, if you follow on beyond, there is a smaller hall with a portion of the original celestial decorations on the roof that are visible.

Admission LE25 ($4.55/£2.30) at the ticket office. Winter 7am–5pm; summer 6am–7pm.

Temple of Seti I This ruined temple is slightly odd in that it's dedicated not only to the ruler who started but did not finish it, Seti I, and the ruler who did finish it, Ramses II, but a third ruler who had nothing at all to do with it, Ramses I, whose rule predated Seti I's but was so short that he didn't have time to build his own facility. It has been sadly depleted, as much by the local habit of using it as a quarry as by weather and time. The walls of the ruined hypostyle hall have some excellent relief carvings, however, showing both Ramses II and Seti I with the gods.

Admission LE25 ($4.55/£2.30) at the ticket office. Winter 7am–5pm; summer 6am–7pm.

Valley of the Kings ⟨★★★⟩ The tombs of the Valley of the Kings are one of the many essential must-sees in Luxor. They are located on the edge of the river valley a 15-minute drive from the dock on the western bank of the Nile. It doesn't much matter how you get there—escaping the crowds and the feeling of being shuttled around just isn't going to happen. This is one place where (unless you want the flexibility to roam other West Bank sites) you might just as well take a bus tour. Take water and a hat—even in the relatively cool winter months, it can get hot. If you arrive at the bus parking lot without something to drink and headgear, head over to the mall to your left (facing the orientation center). Everyone will tell you that you're going the wrong way, but ignore them. You'll find a couple of stalls here that carry what you need. The prices are exorbitant, but it's better to part with a couple of extra pounds than dry out in the hot, dry valley above.

The orientation center at the bus parking lot is worth a 15-minute tour. I particularly enjoy the black-and-white footage of old excavation work, but there is also a good deal of very useful information on the placards on the walls. Before you head out the back to the ticket booth, be sure to check out the transparent topographical map of the valley—as you wander through the tombs, it's hard to form an idea of what the whole valley looks like unless you've seen this first.

Tickets for the tombs and for the little "train" (really just a converted airport baggage tractor) up to the valley are purchased separately from a booth around the back of the building. The train is definitely worth taking, at least for the inbound, uphill leg. The extra tickets for entering the Tomb of Tutankhamun aren't purchased here, but at the upper office where the train drops you off. Whether these tickets are worth it is subjective—the tombs are smaller and less colorful than the others, with a lot of fungus on the walls and ceilings. The price of getting in clearly reflects more of a desire to cash in on their fame than their actual interest value.

Keep in mind that your **ticket is good only for three of the tombs,** so choose wisely. The most spectacular three are those of **Horemheb, Seti I,** and **Ramses III,** but because tombs are closed on a rotating basis to protect them from the damaging effects of visitors, one or more of these may be shut when you get there. The least interesting in my opinion are Thawsert, Thuya, and Seti II. The tomb of Amenhotep should be avoided if you're already hot and tired—it is one of the deepest in the valley—as should the otherwise fascinating Tomb of Tuthmosis, which is only reached after a steep climb up a metal staircase.

Admission LE70 ($13/£6.50) adults, LE35 ($6.35/£3.25) students. Train tickets LE4 (75p/35p) per person. Tomb of Tutankhamun LE80 ($15/£7.40) adults, LE40 ($7.30/£3.70) students.

Valley of the Queens 𝒜𝒜   Effectively down the road and up the next valley from Valley of the Kings, the Valley of the Queens tends to be a little less crowded but no less interesting. It is slightly misleadingly named, for although there are a number of 19th- and 20th-dynasty queens buried here (previous to this, queens tended to be buried with their husbands), there are also other family members as well as some high officials.

At the time of writing, only three tombs were officially open, and only two of these were accessible to tourists. The **Tomb of Nefertari** is the crown jewel of the Valley of the Queens, and is both the largest the most elaborately decorated of the tombs here, with walls covered in stunning paintings commissioned by Ramses II to honor his favorite wife (he had four others). Though cash will open the door for a few minutes, the tomb is now effectively closed to most tourists. Though it was open between 1995 and 2003, only 150 tickets were sold a day and these sold out within minutes of the office opening at 6am, testimony to the effect of the multiple images of one of only two queens to be deified in her own lifetime.

The **Tomb of Khaemwaset** belongs to one of Ramses III's sons and is worth visiting for the reliefs showing his father introducing him to the gods. The **Tomb of Amunherkhepshef** was for another of Ramses III's sons, who died when he was 10. Note the touching scenes of the father introducing his son to the gods who will guide him through his afterlife, including a relief of the meeting with Anubis.

Admission LE25 ($4.55/£2.30). Winter 7am–5pm; summer 6am–7pm.

Valley of the Nobles

Between the Valley of the Queens and the Valley of the Kings lies another necropolis, this one for the use of the wealthy and the high officials who were not of royal blood. Not as intensely developed as a tourist site as the Valley of the Kings, the Valley of the Nobles is less crowded and also a little harder to access. Signage is poor, and it would be a good idea to have a flashlight with you. Of the 400 tombs that are known here, only about a dozen are open to tourists at any given time, including those below.

Khonsu, Userhet & Benia   These three colorful tombs don't match up to the Neferonpet, Nefersekheru, and Dhutmosi tombs (below).

Admission LE12 ($2.20/£1.10) at the ticket office. Winter 7am–5pm; summer 6am–7pm.

Nakht & Menna   If you're going to see one set of tombs in the Valley of the Nobles, this is the pair to see. Nakht was a high official in the court of Tuthmosis IV, and during his lifetime held the posts of astronomer, keeper of the king's vineyards, and chief of the granaries. Though some of the illustrations showing him and his wife (with whom he was buried) have been defaced, they retain a quotidian charm. There used to be a statue of the tomb's owner in the inner room, but this is now at the bottom of the Atlantic off Ireland; it was being transported to the United States in 1920 when the ship that was carrying it was sunk by a German submarine.

Menna, meanwhile, was a scribe of the fields, or agricultural inspector. My favorite illustrations are the pastoral scenes that feature quarreling girls and one who is pulling a thorn from her foot.

Admission LE20 ($3.60/£1.85) at the ticket office. Winter 7am–5pm; summer 6am–7pm.

Neferonpet, Nefersekheru & Dhutmosi   Neferonpet's tomb is probably the most interesting of the three for its depiction of its owner, who was a treasury official, weighing gold. If you're in here, Nefersekheru's tomb is also worth a visit. Dhutmosi's final resting place is not in good shape these days, however.

Admission LE20 ($3.60/£1.85) at the ticket office. Winter 7am–5pm; summer 6am–7pm.

Ramose, Userhet & Khaemet   The tomb of Ramose is unfinished because its owner, who began his career under Amenhotep III, ended it under Akhenaten, the ruler who moved the capital from Thebes to Armana, disrupting not only public religious and administrative functions, but the private arrangements of his functionaries as well. This tomb is highly significant because both its style and content bridge the two periods, with the western wall showing some of the earliest depictions of Akhenaten worshipping the new god. The relief work is also exceptionally fine.

Userhet was a royal scribe and tutor in the reign of Amenhotep II. His tomb has depictions of winemaking, gazelle hunting, and hair cutting on the walls. The heavy damage done to the scene of the funereal feast was done by early Coptic hermits. Khaemet was another royal scribe, though he served the subsequent Pharaoh, Amenhotep III. Though I prefer the tomb of Ramose, there is some stonework here as well.

Admission LE25 ($4.55/£2.30) at the ticket office. Winter 7am–5pm; summer 6am–7pm.

Rekhmire & Sennofer   Rekhmire was a governor under Tuthmosis III and Amenhotep II, and came from a long line of governors. I don't find that the paintings in his tomb have the same charm as those in Nakht's and Menna's (above), but the depictions of foreign tribute and various kinds of labor are probably more important to understanding the politics of ancient Egypt. Sennofer was an agricultural official and mayor of Thebes during Amenhotep II's reign. The lower area of his tomb is decorated with vines.

Admission LE20 ($3.65/£1.85) at the ticket office. Winter 7am–5pm; summer 6am–7pm.

SOUTH OF LUXOR

Temple of Horus at Edfu ★★   Because it was the last big temple to have been built (it was started under Ptolemy III in about 237 B.C. and finished under Ptolemy XII about 140 years later) and because it was built well above the Nile and escaped flood damage, the Temple of Horus at Edfu is one of the best preserved. The temple is actually a reconstruction of an older building on the same site, and was part of the Ptolemaic project to solidify their dynastic hold on Upper Egypt by identifying themselves with the Pharaohs. Not only is the design a copy of the old temple, so are the inscriptions on the walls.

The temple was actually buried, like the Luxor Temple, under the village when excavators started to dig it out in the middle of the 19th century. It took almost 40 years to clear it out entirely. The interior walls are covered in reliefs that tell the story of the birth of Horus and depict the Ptolemaic rulers of the country making offerings to the gods and destroying their enemies. Be sure to pause at the massive statues of Horus as a falcon that stand outside the main entrance and by the entrance to the first hypostyle hall.

About 110km (68 miles) south of Luxor, Edfu is best visited by car either as a day trip or on the way to, or from, Aswan. Though it's a healthy walk from the town to the temple, there are plenty of taxis around. The Upper Egypt bus stops conveniently close to the temple, too.

Admission LE20 ($3.60/£1.85). Winter 7am–4pm; summer 7am–5pm.

Temple of Kom Ombo   Like the surviving structures at Dendera and Edfu, this is a Ptolemaic construction but has an unusual symmetrically twinned architecture in which all rooms and doors are mirrored on the other side of the building. Once inside, you'll see that there are two sanctuaries in the middle of the temple, each a mirror image of the other.

Dedicated, at least in part, to the crocodile god Sobek, the temple was built on a bit of low land that juts out into the Nile. Real crocodiles, it is said, used to bask here, and mummified crocodiles were interred in crypts beneath the building. There is a small display of these just inside the main entrance.

While this structure hasn't stood the test of time as well as the Temple of Horus in Edfu, partly because it was built closer to the flood waters of the river, it has a particular charm. Apart from being the center of exalted rituals, it was also a place of healing, where ordinary people came to have their ailments tended to. If you look closely, you may still be able to find their graffiti scratched into the inside of the remains of the outer wall of the complex.

The unprepossessing town of Kom Ombo, which is about 4km (2½ miles) from the temple, is about 40km (25 miles) from Aswan to the south and 175km (110 miles) from Luxor to the north. If you're not arriving on a cruise boat, the next best way to be moving is by private car. Steer clear of eating or staying in town.

Admission LE20 ($3.60/£1.85). Winter 7am–4pm; summer 7am–5pm.

NORTH OF LUXOR

Temple of Hathor at Dendera   Located on the western bank of the Nile about 60km (37 miles) north of Luxor, this magnificently preserved temple of Hathor is a popular day-trip option and a standard river cruise stop. Though it has a passing resemblance to a lot of other monuments in Upper Egypt, the temple in Dendera is, in fact, a lot younger than most. It was founded in 54 B.C. by Cleopatra's father, Ptolemy XII. The hypostyle hall here is worth a visit in and of itself. Eighteen massive columns, with capitols representing Hathor, support a ceiling 18m (59 ft.) above the floor. Seek out the **Chapel of Osiris** and have a look at the famous Zodiac of Dendera on the ceiling. The disc is unique not only because it is the first known representation of the stars in the form of a zodiac in Egypt, but also because it shows a very detailed arrangement of the night sky that allowed for precise dating of the construction of the temple.

There are lots of ways to get to the temple, which is about 2km (1¼ miles) from the town of Dendera and about 8km (5 miles) from Qena. The two best ways are either to hire a taxi for the day from Luxor (LE200–LE400/$36–$73/£19–£37) or take a day cruise. The boats usually leave at 6am and return at 6pm. The round trip should cost LE220 to LE440 ($40–$80/£20–£41), depending on the class of the boat, and can be booked at any of the travel agents around the Old Winter Palace. It's also possible to take the train to Qena and take a taxi from there.

Admission LE20 ($3.60/£1.85). Winter 7am–5pm; summer 7am–6pm.

The Zodiac of Dendera

First observed by Napoleon's savants at the end of the 19th century, this massive map of the stars became the object of competition between the French and British in Egypt over the following two decades. It was ultimately nabbed by French antiquities dealer Sebastian-Louis Saulnier, who imported a master stonemason from France who used specially made tools, as well as a quantity of gunpowder, to remove a disc of stone about 2.5m (8 ft.) in diameter and almost a meter (more than 3 ft.) thick from the roof of the Osiris Chapel of the Temple of Hathor at Dendera. After being paid the at-the-time exorbitant sum of 150,000 francs for the piece, Saulnier handed it over to the French state, and today it is on display at the Louvre in Paris.

The disc is unique not only because it is the first known representation of the stars in the form of a zodiac in Egypt, but also because it shows a very detailed arrangement of the night sky that allowed for precise dating of the construction of the temple. Apart from its archaeological importance, it is also quietly beautiful and shows some particularly Egyptian twists on the standard signs of the zodiac, with Virgo represented by a figure that is probably Isis and Cancer's crab replaced by a scarab. There is now a plaster reproduction of the original in the Temple of Hathor at Dendera.

WHERE TO STAY
VERY EXPENSIVE

Old Winter Palace *(Overrated*   Dating back to the 19th century, the Old Winter Palace has some real atmosphere despite a number of soulless renovations. The corridors are wide enough to drive a horse and carriage down, and the high ceilings and period furniture contribute to making this Accor-managed hotel something different in Luxor. The gardens are neatly kept and extensive, and they're especially pleasant in the cool of the evening. This hotel is also more wheelchair accessible than most and has wheelchair-equipped rooms. Prices are too high for the sometimes lax service and unremarkable food, but you're paying for the past at the Old Winter Palace and not the present. I recommend dipping into its charms for an expensive tea or drink in the garden and staying somewhere else. Note that the charmless modern New Winter Palace addition to the back of the old facilities was thankfully slated for destruction in 2008 and so isn't included in this review.

Corniche al Nile, Luxor. © **095/23804225.** Fax 095/2374087. www.accor.com. 102 units. LE2,050 ($373/£190) garden-view double; LE 2,340 ($426/£217) Nile-view double. AE, DC, MC, V. **Amenities:** 3 restaurants; 3 bars; pool; Wi-Fi. *In room:* A/C, TV, minibar, safe.

EXPENSIVE

Al Moudira *ꞔꞔ*   This marvelous, one-of-a-kind boutique hotel on the quiet West Bank of the Nile is easily the best hotel in Luxor and certainly one of the 10 best in Egypt. Its traditional-style buildings are spread gracefully over extensive grounds, with domes, arches, and fountains fitting together in relaxing harmony. The construction has incorporated beautiful period pieces, including old doors, *mashrabeya* screens and stone basins, and each room is an individual creation decorated with paintings, carpets, and tiles. I love the carefully designed gardens, where jasmine hangs gracefully over the walled courtyards and palms whisper in the desert breeze, but fans of bowling-green-style lawns may be disappointed. The hotel is located far from the hubbub and tourist hassles of East Bank Luxor, but transport is easily arranged, and 30 minutes should be enough to put you back into the land of bright lights, loud music, and crowds. My advice on this one is if you can afford it, bite the bullet and go for it.

West Bank, Luxor. ✆ 095/2551440. Fax 0123220528. www.moudira.com. 54 units. LE1,470 ($267/£136) double; LE1,880 ($342/£174) deluxe double. Rates include breakfast and taxes. AE, MC, V. **Amenities:** Restaurant; bar; pool, spa; Turkish hammam; massage; Internet. *In room:* A/C, TV, minibar.

Maritim Jolie Ville *(Kids)*   If you're traveling with children, the Jolie Ville is *the* place to stay in Luxor. Located on an island 15 minutes by taxi south of the town, the hotel has a range of features to keep the kids occupied while you relax in the nicest Nileside horizon pool in Luxor or trek through the Valley of the Queens. The Maritim has pleasant rooms distributed in a series of shady bungalows surrounding the main building and connected to it with covered walkways. Each room has a small seating area out front, but Nile views are in the minority and fill up first, so book well in advance if this is a priority. Kid-friendly features include an all-day kids club with activities such as pottery painting and donkey races, a small zoo (some farm animals, but it does have monkeys and a crocodile), and a lifeguard at the pool. The sense of a family summer camp is sometimes reinforced by a slightly under-maintained feeling (particularly evident in the cracked tennis courts), and the food is nothing to write home about.

Note that at the time of writing the hotel was undergoing its transition from being operated by Mövenpick to Maritim management, which may change prices or services.

Crocodile Island, Luxor. ✆ **095/2374855.** Fax 095/2374936. www.jolieville-hotels.com. 332 units. LE825 ($150/£76) double. AE, MC, V. **Amenities:** 2 pools; 4 tennis courts; kids' club (daily 9am–4pm); free hourly shuttle to town; 3 shuttle boats per day; babysitting; zoo; Parcour course; ATM; Internet. *In room:* A/C, TV, minibar, safe, Wi-Fi (in half of rooms; full coverage planned for 2008).

Sheraton Luxor *(Value)*   At the low end of its class in terms of price, the Sheraton offers good value for money. One of its nicest features is its location—most of its competition either backs onto a busy road or looks over it, but the Sheraton is surrounded by gardens and fronts the Nile. The result is a quiet and very relaxing atmosphere. The architecture, which is supposed to mirror a cruise ship, isn't going to win any awards (frankly, it looks like it was built out of LEGO blocks), and though the fit and finish of the rooms aren't quite up to the Steigenberger standard, they're acceptable on the whole. The other thing that the Sheraton does well—and this goes for most of its facilities in Egypt—is friendly, relaxed service. If you're looking for a five-star chain hotel at a decent price, this would be my recommendation in Luxor.

Khalid Ibn el Walid Street. ✆ 095/2274544. www.sheraton.com/luxor. 290 units. LE505 ($92/£47). AE, MC, V. **Amenities:** 4 restaurants; 2 bars; 2 pools (including kids' pool); 2 tennis courts; croquet; ATM; bank; Wi-Fi. *In room:* TV, minibar, safe, Internet.

Steigenberger Nile Palace   This may be the quintessential cookie-cutter hotel, but it does it well. Rooms are spic and span, the food is inoffensive, and the view from the pool and barbecue area is one of the best in Luxor. Standard (as opposed to Nile-view) rooms look down into the enclosed central courtyard of the hotel, which is used at night for entertainment, so watch out for noise. The only facility that really lets the hotel down is the gym, which, while sufficient, is smaller and more basic than it should be.

Khalid Ibn el Walid Street, Luxor. ✆ 095/2366999. Fax 095/2365666. www.luxor.steigenberger.com. LE660 ($120/£61) standard double; LE1,045 ($190/(£97) Nile-view double. AE, MC, V. **Amenities:** 4 restaurants; 2 bars; 2 pools (including kids' pool); tennis court; gym; limo transport office; bank; Wi-Fi. *In room:* TV, minibar, safe, Internet.

MODERATE

El Nakhil ⚡ *(Finds* This is a little hotel that really punches above its weight. At the same price as several cheaper places, it offers substantially more than its competition. Rooms are spacious and feature nice Egyptian touches such as traditional *mashrabeya* screens and domed ceilings in some, and though these motifs (installed personally by the owner) can appear to clash to Western eyes, they have charm. The El Fayrouz (p. 238) has a nicer garden, but the Nakhil has a little more flair while offering the same quiet, village-like atmosphere. This is also the only hotel that I know of on the West Bank that's wheelchair accessible, with ramps from the street and to the ground-floor rooms. One room is wheelchair-equipped. They can also provide appropriate van transport from the airport.

Gezirat al Baraat, West Bank, Luxor. ℂ 095/2313922 or 0123821007 mobile. Fax 095/2311205. www.el-nakhil.com. 20 units. LE200 ($37/£19) double. Rate includes breakfast. Cash only. **Amenities:** Restaurant; Internet. *In room:* A/C, TV (in some), no phone (in some).

Flobator Down the same street as the St. Joseph, the Flobator is chasing the same formula: good basic rooms and a pleasant rooftop pool/bar area. The Flobator pool is bigger, mind you, but not as pleasant for lounging with beers and food. For those who want to stay connected, the free wireless (off and on though it is) may also be a deciding factor. Ask for a room in the new wing; they're a little bigger for the same price. Most rooms have a view across other buildings to the Nile.

Al Mahed el Deni St., Luxor. ℂ 095/2270418. Fax 095/2270618. 60 units. LE220 ($40/£21). Rate includes breakfast. MC, V. **Amenities:** 2 restaurants; bar; pool. *In room:* A/C (old, but functional), TV.

Gaddis Hotel With basic, clean rooms that front either the main street or the pool, the Gaddis is a definite possibility for a good midrange hotel once its renovation is done later in 2008. For now, however, the beds are hard and the rooms a little shabby, but the pool is pleasant and there are two restaurants in the hotel that, if you're looking for something a little different from the regular Luxor tourist fare, are worth trying.

Khalid Ibn el Walid Street, Luxor. ℂ 095/2382838. Fax 095/2382837. www.gaddishotel.com. 55 units. LE220 ($40/£20) double. Rate includes breakfast. MC, V. **Amenities:** 2 restaurants; bar; pool; Internet. *In room:* A/C, TV, minifridge.

Nour al Balad Nour al Balad is trying, with some success, to be a budget Al Moudira (above). Behind an unprepossessing facade lies a traditional-style building with high ceilings, arched doorways, and straw-thatched ceilings. Nour al Balad is located on the edge of the desert and doesn't have air-conditioning, so avoid it during the summer months (try mid- to late Oct, when the weather cools).

Two big rooms at the front of the hotel have an unobstructed sunset view of the rocky cliffs that edge the Nile Valley, and those at the back look over green fields and a small village. These front rooms will seem overpriced to those who aren't as taken with the charm of the large airy room with a four-poster bed, the desert view, and the colorfully tiled bathrooms as I am. Other rooms are better value for money, and since they vary in size and view as well as price, you would be wise to check out everything that's available before making a decision. It's possible to hike to many of the antiquities, including Valley of the Kings, in a couple of hours from the front door. The restaurant, however, is likely to disappoint those with anything more than basic expectations.

West Bank, Luxor. ℂ 095/2311430 or 0101295812 mobile. 14 units. LE150 ($27/£14) small double downstairs; LE250 ($45/£23) large double upstairs; LE500 ($91/£46) deluxe double. Rates include breakfast. Cash only. **Amenities:** Restaurant. *In room:* Fan, no phone.

A Nile Cruise: Set a Course for History

Life in Egypt has revolved around the Nile since the time of the Pharaohs. The waters have been the lifeblood of fields and the highway used to transport goods and people. During ancient times, the river was not only used for practical purposes, such as transporting the massive blocks of rock needed to build temples, but for the ceremonial movement of gods at festival times. It was even seen as the dividing line between the world of the living, on the east bank, and the land the dead, on the west side. There is no better way, then, to explore the history of Upper Egypt than from a cabin of one of the many cruise boats that ply the ancient waters of the river.

Cruises usually run from 3 to 6 days. You could see all the sites between Luxor and Aswan on the 3-day cruise, but I recommend taking at least 4 days to allow a little extra breathing room and time at each site. Unless life onboard the boat is the attraction, 6 days will probably be too many for most people. Some companies will cut Esna or an optional *faluca* ride out of the 3-day cruise, which is not much of a loss, as Esna takes up more time than it's worth in a tight itinerary, and a *faluca* ride can always be done at your leisure in Luxor, Aswan, or Cairo.

Keep in mind that these cruises shuttle back and forth between Luxor and Aswan, carrying passengers both ways; the upriver cruises are identical in all respects to the downriver. This opens up all kinds of possibilities for fitting boat travel into your itinerary. If you're looking to see as much as possible in a week or less without wearing yourself out, Luxor, with the preponderance of monuments and the most frequent flights to Cairo, makes the best endpoint. Start with an early morning flight to Abu Simbel, and you'll be back in Aswan in time to catch the northbound cruise boats. Kick back for a few days on the river before getting to Luxor for a couple of days of tomb tours and temple gazing, and then head back to Cairo for your return home.

The season is a very important consideration when deciding on a cruise. Winter is the best time to be stomping around monuments, but prices tend to be around a third higher between October and May. Before you jump at that summer bargain, however, see the temperature charts in chapter 2 (p. 16). The best bet is to try for something in mid- to late September or early April, when cheaper summer prices may overlap with the more bearable winter weather.

Abercrombie and Kent (© **800/554-7094;** www.abercrombiekent.com) is one of the best-established cruise-boat operators on the Nile, and it's comfortably positioned at the top of the field. The boats are small, well equipped, and intensely luxurious. Think floating boutique hotel with period furnishings and a swimming pool on the deck, and you're getting close. One of the best

Nile Valley *Kids*   It's not the greatest midrange hotel in Luxor, but the Nile Valley is probably the most kid-friendly place currently on the West Bank. The rooms are basic, clean doubles and triples with windows placed too high for good light, but most look down on the swimming pool. There is a kids' pool, and the restaurant is fun, moderately

things about A&K, aside from the first-class food, service, and lodging, is that it's flexible and has established the kind of local contacts that allow the company to tailor-make tours that include special access to many sites and facilities. Keep in mind that you're going to pay a premium for this kind of service, with the basics of a 4-day cruise running around LE11,000 ($2,000/£1,019) per person, and a full-on 10-day package that includes a 4-day cruise, five-star accommodation in Cairo, and first-class guides and experts going for about LE23,843 ($4,335/£2,208).

As you would expect, the **Oberoi** (© 02/33773222; www.oberoiphilae. com) is exceptionally equipped to make a cruise both relaxing and comfortable. Rooms are well appointed and big—in fact, they're fit with everything you would expect in a high-end hotel room. Whether you need a selection of movies and wireless Internet while cruising the Nile is debatable, but trust Oberoi to make sure that they're there for you anyway. Expect to pay about LE16,500 ($3,000/£1,528) in the high season, LE12,100 ($2,200/£1,120) in the low season, for a double on the 4-night cruises; LE24,750 ($4,500/£2,292) in the high season, LE18,150 ($3,300/£1,681) in the low season, for the 6-night cruise. For a real treat, check out the *Zahra,* Oberoi's luxury cruiser. The cruise takes a full, leisurely week, which gives you time to take advantage of the comprehensive spa facilities onboard. With only 27 suites, it's wise to book as far ahead as possible. Prices for a double range from a very reasonable LE13,475 ($2,450/£1,248) during the heat of the summer to a rather steep LE40,425 ($7,350/£3,743) over Christmas. Cruises can also be booked through your travel agent or the Mena House Oberoi (p. 109) in Giza.

On the other end of the scale, you'll see a lot of options moored along the riverbank between the Luxor Museum and the Old Winter Palace. These boats retail for between LE220 and LE550 ($40–$100/£20–£51) or more per night, all inclusive, depending on the class, and are sold in wholesale blocks to travel agents. You can reserve your place with your agent at home before you come to Egypt, or you can try your luck with a local agent when you arrive. (You can try to book ahead with a local agent, but even the branches of international firms such as Thomas Cook are notoriously slack when it comes to e-mail and fax queries.) I recommend using **Spring Tours** (© 02/27365972; info@springtours.com) in Cairo; they usually deal at the wholesale end of the market, but if you know what you want (they don't have the staff or resources to form itineraries for you, or give a lot of advice), they'll sell at a retail level, often at a far better price than an agent (who has to take his cut, after all).

priced, and has good food. There is one room with a kitchenette, and though it's pitched by the hotel as a family room, take note that it's simply a triple with three single beds.

West Bank, Luxor. © **095/2311477.** www.nilevalley.nl. 18 units. LE226 ($41/£21). Rate includes breakfast. Cash only. **Amenities:** Restaurant; bar; pool. *In room:* TV, minifridge.

Royal House Hotel   This is the third hotel along the street behind the St. Joseph, and once again follows the same concept as the nearby St. Joseph and Flobator hotels: pool (this time with a separate pool for kids) on the roof and basic air-conditioned rooms. The rooms feel a little smaller than those of its neighbors, but the whole place feels a little newer. The air-conditioning has done fewer summers, and the furniture has taken fewer hits. Like the Flobator (above), the poolside environment is a little bleak, and the hotel doesn't have Wi-Fi service like the St. Joseph. I would check the St. Joseph first, but I would be quite happy to end up here as well.

Al Mahed el Deni St., Luxor. ✆ 095/2280077. Fax 095/2270666. 40 units. LE150 ($27/£14) single; LE200 ($36/£19) double. Rates include breakfast. AE, MC, V. **Amenities:** Restaurant; bar; 2 pools. *In room:* A/C, TV, minifridge.

Shady Hotel   I would try other midrange hotels, like the St. Joseph or the Flobator first, but if you're looking to get away from the more heavily touristed areas, the Shady is an option. The hotel is located on a street 10 minutes' walk from the Nile but still convenient to the restaurants and stores along the Corniche. The hotel is clean and the staff are pleasant.

Television Street, Luxor. ✆ 095/2381377. 50 Units. LE210 ($38/£19) double. Rate includes breakfast. Cash only. **Amenities:** Restaurant; bar; pool; Internet. *In room:* TV.

St. Joseph Hotel ⭐ *Value*   This has long been a favorite of budget package holiday companies and is the best midrange choice on the East Bank. Rooms are spotlessly clean, spacious, and decorated with dark wood rooms and come with decent (but not spectacular) Nile views. That, combined with friendly, helpful owner/managers and modest rates, makes for exceptional value for money. The pool on the roof is not big, but if you're looking for a relaxing float in the afternoon or a place for a cold sunset beer, you don't have to look any farther.

Khalid Ibn el Walid Street, Luxor. ✆ 095/2381707. 75 units. LE193 ($35/£18) double. Rate includes breakfast and taxes. MC, V. **Amenities:** 2 restaurants; 2 bars; pool; Wi-Fi. *In room:* A/C, TV, fridge.

Tutotel   Tucked away beside the grounds of the Winter Palace, the Tutotel was built for a Spanish chain but has recently been bought up by an Egyptian company. The hotel is clean and tidy, though it lacks a view; rooms are modern, if not particularly spacious; and bathrooms are nicer than many hotels in the same range. At the moment, it's definitely worth the small price difference over the Shady.

Salah el Din Street, Luxor. ✆ 095/3777990. LE231 ($42/£21) double. Rate includes breakfast. MC, V. **Amenities:** Restaurant; bar; pool. *In room:* A/C, TV, minibar, Internet (though it wasn't working at the time of writing).

BUDGET
El Fayrouz Hotel   At the low end of the moderate price range, the Fayrouz is very accommodating and stacks up well against other locations costing substantially more. The building is new, and rooms are large and clean. There is a large, quiet garden restaurant with good shade. The other big plus of the Fayrouz is that it's located in an almost entirely hassle-free location on the West Bank. The road outside is unpaved and serves as a playground for children from the surrounding homes; the atmosphere is almost that of a tranquil village. Though the hotel is only 5 minutes' walk to the ferry, the only disturbance comes from the braying of donkeys and the periodic call to prayer.

Gezira al Bairat, West Bank, Luxor. ✆ 095/2312709 or 012/2770565. www.elfayrouz.com. 17 units. LE120 ($22/£11). Rate includes breakfast. Cash only. **Amenities:** Restaurant; Wi-Fi. *In room:* A/C (in some).

Mina Palace   This is a cheap hotel with a very expensive view and is directly on the Corniche close to the Luxor Temple. It doesn't have a garden (though there are signs of construction on the roof), but the views of the Nile are better than from the Old Winter Palace, a few hundred meters to the south. It is also conveniently close to the ferry and boat docks as well as the Mummification Museum. On the downside, the rooms are shabby and the public areas are unattractive. The restaurant is sufficient but at road level on a busy intersection. Keep in mind that there are two rooms on each floor that do not face the Nile. If you stay here, do it for the view and don't expect much more.

Corniche el Nile, Luxor. ℂ 095/2372074. Fax 095/2382194. 40 units. LE100 ($18/£9.25) double. Cash only. **Amenities:** Restaurant. *In room:* A/C, TV, minifridge.

Nefertiti Hotel ✦ *Value*   This is my personal favorite budget hotel in Luxor. A cramped lobby and narrow hallways tell you where you are on the star scale, and the rooms are modest, but the price is right, and the place is clean. The rooftop features a pool table, Internet stations, and Wi-Fi. What makes the place special in my mind, however, is the staff, who are forthright and cheerfully helpful, offering the kind of service that you expect, but rarely get, from places with a lot more glitter and higher prices. In fact, I have used the Nefertiti reception desk like a mini travel agency, acquiring everything from train tickets to a ride on a hot-air balloon, and all at a very reasonable price.

Al Sahab Street, Luxor. ℂ 095/2372386. 24 units. LE100 ($18/£9.25) double. Cash only. **Amenities:** Restaurant; Internet; Wi-Fi (LE10/$1.80/95p per day). *In room:* No phone.

WHERE TO EAT

El Kababgy EGYPTIAN/INTERNATIONAL   This is a great place for lunch, especially if you're staying on one of the cruise boats that dock below the Luxor Temple. Located below the Corniche, and between it and the Nile, the restaurant is quiet and more or less hassle-free. Better yet, it looks over a small *faluca* dock, so your view is unobstructed by the massive boats that blight much of the waterfront here. The outside seating has the best view and is protected from the sun by an awning; inside the atmosphere is pleasant with tiled floors, dark wood trim, and paintings of local scenes. The menu is an unremarkable mix of grilled chicken and pizza, but the grilled fish is excellent. They serve local beers and sunset cocktails, but if sundowners are what you're after, try the Cocktail Sunset Bar a couple of hundred meters to the north.

Corniche el Nil, just below the Winter Palace. Appetizers LE8–LE20 ($1.45–$3.60/75p–£1.85); main courses LE15–LE25 ($2.70–$4.55/£1.40–£2.30). Cash only. Daily 10am–midnight.

King Dude II *Kids* EGYPTIAN   Buried deep in the Gaddis Hotel (p. 235), the King Dude is the kind of place that will either make you smile or roll your eyes and walk out. Kids should love it; it's done up like a tomb under excavation. Suspended walkways carry tables a couple of meters in the air, and the walls are covered with spoof hieroglyphs featuring, I guess, King Dude himself (a Tutankhamun-esque figure with a cigarette hanging out of his mouth). The theme continues onto the menu, where the drink list includes lethal-looking items such as the Embalmers Special, a mix of ouza, rum, vodka, and fruit juices. The food is certainly not on a par with Sofra (below), but there's lots of it. Ordering is a matter of choosing between two or three set menus, which will take you through three or four courses of Egyptian favorites including lentil soup, vine leaves, *tagine*, or grilled pigeon.

Khalid Ibn el Walid Street. ℂ 095/2382838. Set menu LE25–LE80 ($4.55–$15/£2.30–£7.40). MC, V. Daily 6–11pm.

La Mamma ITALIAN   This Italian restaurant may not be a trattoria in Florence, but it's about as close as you're going to get in Luxor. The space is open on two sides to a courtyard with a fountain, and the decor is slightly downmarket, with big posters of the Colosseum and Tuscan girls in peasant dress, and wine barrels lined up over the bar. The staff are warm and friendly, and the wine list includes some Italian bottles (albeit at around LE400/$73/£37, due to exorbitant import duties). Start off with a plate of fresh buffalo mozzarella with basil and Egyptian olive oil and, unless you're very hungry (the dishes are not small), choose a pasta or a meat dish. The *fettucine alla carbonara* is a little heavy on the sauce, but it's tasty and the pasta nicely al dente. If you don't feel like pasta, try the *pollo alla panna* (the sauce is rich and flavorful and loaded with fresh mushrooms) or the rack of lamb in rosemary sauce. If you're still insufficiently stuffed at this point, try piling in a desert of sautéed apples on puff pastry with Pernod. You can work it off the next day trekking around some temples.

Sheraton Luxor. (①) 095/2274544. Appetizers LE32–LE60 ($5.80–$11/£2.95–£5.55); main courses LE65–LE120 ($12–$22/£6–£11). AE, DC, MC, V. Daily 5pm–midnight.

Maxime FRENCH/INTERNATIONAL   Maxime, tucked away on the upper floors of a building at the quiet end of town, has become a favorite tourist haunt and is almost always humming with activity. Spic-and-span white tablecloths, tightly packed tables, and the view of the street below give the place a pleasantly European feel, and the menu is a mix that reflects a mix of influences. Start with a creamy chicken or lentil soup, and then move on to the lamb cutlets with mint sauce or a filet with pepper sauce. Round it all off with an *um aly* or a fruit salad. Service is pleasantly businesslike and friendly.

Khalid Ibn el Walid Street. (①) 095/2386315. Appetizers LE5–LE12 (90¢–$2.20/45p–£1.10); main courses LE22–LE50 ($4–$9.10/£2.05–£4.60). Cash only. Daily 5–11pm.

Miyako JAPANESE   This restaurant is the only one offering Japanese food in Luxor and is a good choice when you're looking for something a little bit different. The quality of the food may not be what you would expect in New York, but they make a good attempt. If you're not in the mood for a slice of raw squid or a California roll, try the salmon filet from the teppanyaki menu. It comes with crispy, fresh vegetables and a side of slightly garlicky rice that sets off the sauce. The ambience is pleasant, if a little too "hotel," with windows that look onto a carefully tended garden. They even have a teppanyaki table where the chef will cook the food in front of you and put on an ostentatious display of knife- and pepper-grinder-flipping. There is a short but excellent list of desserts; I recommend the Sweet Tower, a simple fruit salad glued together with whipped cream and built into a little pyramid.

Sonesta St. George Hotel, Khalid Ibn el Walid Street. (①) 095/2382575. Teppanyaki LE28–LE138 ($5–$25/£2.55–£13). AE, DC, MC, V. Daily 5–11pm.

Oasis Café *(Finds)* EUROPEAN   This is a great little place for sandwiches, coffee, and dessert. American owned and located in a renovated old building with loads of character, high ceilings, and a unique collection of local art on the walls, it's a rare example of a place with a sense of history that offers modern service and excellent food.

Dr. Labib Habashi Street. (①) 095/2372914. Main courses LE20–LE40 ($7.25–$11/£3.70–£5.55). Cash only. Daily 8am–10pm.

Sofra *(Finds)* EGYPTIAN   Sofra not only has the best Egyptian food in Luxor but one of the nicest settings as well. The restaurant is located on a crowded and dusty back street in the al Manshiya district, close to the train station, and features *mashrabeya* screens, traditional lanterns hanging from the ceiling, and lovely period floor tiling. There's an air-conditioned, slightly more-formal area downstairs and a relaxed rooftop area that features low round tables, old chests, and little colored domes. Start your meal with plates of the best hummus, baba ghanouj, and *tahina* in Upper Egypt, served with baskets of fresh brown bread, before moving on to a veal or lamb *tagine* (a tomato-based stew). One taste of the veal with red peppers, garlic, and pearl onions, and you won't eat anywhere else in Luxor. The menu features enough variety to keep you busy for quite a few nights, and it includes a number of fish and some vegetarian dishes as well. Prices are far too low for the quality of the food. Service is extremely pleasant but very slow. Don't go to Sofra in a hurry, but go hungry—the wait is worth it.

90 Mohamed Farid St. ⓒ 095/2359752. Appetizers LE3–LE5 (55¢–90¢/30p–45p); main courses LE12–LE50 ($2.20–$9.10/£1.10–£4.60). Cash only. Daily 11am–midnight.

WHERE TO DRINK

There is no shortage of drinking places in Luxor, where every midrange and upper-range hotel has at least one place to hoist a cold one, but three establishments really stand out.

Cocktail Sunset Bar ⚡ *Finds*   There's no better way to round out your day in Luxor than having a long, cool cocktail on the Nile as the sun goes down, and the Cocktail Sunset bar, located on the upper floor of a 100-year-old houseboat moored on the Corniche, is the best place in town. All the liquor is imported, so no head-splitting hangover, but the prices are remarkably reasonable. Look for the swirling neon sign amongst the cruise boats just north of the Mummification Museum.

Corniche el Nil. ⓒ 095/2372180. Cash only. Daily 11am–midnight.

King's Head Pub   One of the rarest things to find outside England is a real pub. Big-budget hotel efforts and the experiments of expats alike seem to produce nothing better than gloomily lit, dark-paneled bars with little charm or appeal. The King's Head, on the other hand, somehow gets it right. The brainchild of a local entrepreneur, it is decorated with a unique mix of Princess Diana memorabilia and odds and ends from around Egypt. The effect is homey, a little down-market, and a bit odd, all in the right proportions. Oh, yes, and the food's not bad either.

Khalid Ibn el Walid Street. ⓒ 095/2380489 or 012/2140544 mobile. Cash only. Daily 11am–midnight.

Metropolitan Bowling Club   The name of this place does not mislead: The Metropolitan has the only bowling lanes in Luxor. Located on the banks of the Nile, just next door to El Kababgy (which supplies food here as needed), this place is outfitted with dark wood and plush furnishings, and the bar serves local and imported liquor and has a small espresso machine. The flip side of the place is a small disco with a large plasma-screen TV, so you'll have something to do while you wait for a lane (there are only two) to open up. Games are LE50 ($9.10/£4.60) each, and they have a limited selection of bowling shoes available.

Corniche el Nil, below Luxor Temple. ⓒ 095/2386543. Cash only. Daily 11am–2am.

SHOPPING

Unless you've been looking for a T-shirt with your name written in hieroglyphs, a stuffed toy camel, or a bag of overpriced saffron, the Luxor shopping scene is going to be a bit of a letdown. If you have, however, then you're in for a treat—the heavily touristy souk behind the Luxor Temple is bursting with stalls full of repro figurines, cheap water pipes, and souvenir shirts and hats. You shouldn't ignore the "tourist bazaar" next to the Winter Palace, however. Unlike the souk behind the temple, this dilapidated little mall hasn't been spiffed up recently (if ever) and contains a number of fake antiques and dusty curio stores that are fun to browse.

Aboudy   This small bookstore is crammed with English-language books about Upper Egypt. They also have a fine selection of postcards and some maps. Daily 8:30am to 9:30pm. Tourist Bazaar, Corniche el Nil. ℂ 095/2370753.

Akhmim Fabric Store   This store stocks a small but tasteful range of cloth from Akhmim, a Nile Valley town close to Sohag, renowned at least since the Roman era for the high quality of its cloth. Bolts of cotton and linen are arranged on the walls, ranging from heavy to light, and range in price from LE160 to LE320 ($29–$58/£15–£30) per meter. The proprietors provide a tailoring service if you'd like to have some cloth made into a *gallebeya* or just have your favorite shirt copied. Prices are negotiable, especially if you get into tailoring. Keep in mind when negotiating that, at a retail level, most tailors will make a shirt for LE50 ($9.10/£4.60; fabric extra), and that most other cloth on the market is a lot cheaper (and less desirable). A shirt requires about 3m (3⅓ yards) of single-width cloth, a *gallebeya* about 7m (7¾ yards). Don't pay for the garment upfront. Make an initial down payment and hold the balance until you're satisfied with the final product. Daily 9am to 10pm. Old Winter Palace, Corniche el Nil. ℂ 0183829677. Cash only.

Gaddis & Co.   A well-established store in front of the Old Winter Palace, Gaddis combines an excellent bookstore (which stocks maps) with a fair variety of tourist T-shirts, statues, and silver. The prize of the collection, however, is the stock of about 1,500 photographs taken by Attaya Gaddis around Luxor between 1907 and 1945. Depending on the size, prints of these historic pictures can be bought matted for LE60 to LE150 ($11–$27/£5.55–£14). Gaddis can also print photos from your camera's memory card (LE40/$7.25/£3.70), which includes a CD. Daily 9am to 10pm. In front of the Winter Palace. ℂ 095/2372142. www.gaddis-and-co.co.uk. AE, MC, V.

2 Aswan

Located at the strategically vital chokepoint of the first cataracts on the Nile, Aswan has long been a vital military and trade center and a border point of sorts. To the south, lies Nubia, and beyond Nubia, Sudan; Aswan has the feel of being somehow at the limit of Egypt—the place where Egypt ends and Africa begins.

The first cataract may be a bit disappointing if you're expecting white water rather than the sedate, smooth river. This is one of the most beautiful spots in Egypt, however. The band of verdant green that borders the Nile, narrowing from Luxor some 250km (155 miles) to the north, is just a few hundred meters wide in places around Aswan, and looking across the river, you can see the golden sand of the western desert sloping steeply down toward the sparkling blue of the water.

I find Aswan the perfect antidote to the hassle and pressure of Luxor. The people are extraordinarily laid-back, and life in Aswan slides by quietly. My advice is set a loose schedule and don't try to get too much done here. Visit the **Monastery of St. Simeon** and the **Nubian Museum,** stroll in the gardens around the **Aswan Museum,** and watch the boys in their toy boats catching a tow behind the ferries as they power up through the cataract. Above all, take a sail at sunset, trail your fingers in the water, and let the world slip past.

Aswan

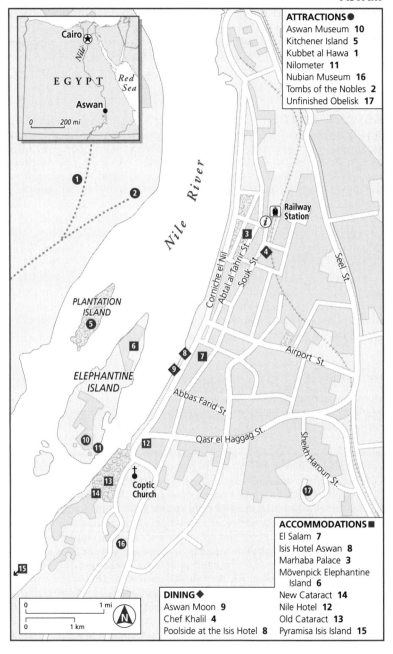

ATTRACTIONS●

Aswan Museum **10**
Kitchener Island **5**
Kubbet al Hawa **1**
Nilometer **11**
Nubian Museum **16**
Tombs of the Nobles **2**
Unfinished Obelisk **17**

ACCOMMODATIONS■

El Salam **7**
Isis Hotel Aswan **8**
Marhaba Palace **3**
Mövenpick Elephantine Island **6**
New Cataract **14**
Nile Hotel **12**
Old Cataract **13**
Pyramisa Isis Island **15**

DINING◆

Aswan Moon **9**
Chef Khalil **4**
Poolside at the Isis Hotel **8**

For many, the famous temple of Ramses II at Abu Simbel is a high point of their trip to Egypt. Aswan is the last staging post in getting to the temple's modern home on the shore of Lake Nasser south of the town. As the southern end of the cruise-boat route, it is also a great place to start a cruise that will take you back down the river to Luxor. For more ideas on how to fit Abu Simbel, Aswan, and Luxor together, see p. 59 or the Luxor and Aswan itineraries (p. 59).

ESSENTIALS
GETTING THERE
BY PLANE   Unless you're particularly fond of train travel, or on a tight budget that makes time less important than money, flying is the best way to get to Aswan. There are upwards of ten flights a day out of Cairo, and the 1-hour 25-minute flight costs about LE1,375 ($250/£127). The surprisingly pleasant and modern airport is some way outside town. If you haven't arranged a transfer with your hotel beforehand, negotiate the 25km (15-mile) ride with one of the waiting taxis. You may be able to do better, but I would expect to pay upward of LE50 ($9.10/£4.60).

BY TRAIN   The train is the most pleasant way to arrive in Aswan, which is only about 3 hours up the rails from Luxor. From Cairo, the fares are LE94 ($17/£8.70) for first-class seats and LE47 ($8.55/£4.35) for second-class seats. The sleeper is the same price as for Luxor, and departure times are the same as well (p. 216). Arrival is 3 hours later. As with any train travel in Egypt, take a warm sweater (even in the summer); the air-conditioning is always set to arctic. The train station is at the edge of the souk, and there are several hotels within an easy walk as well as plenty of taxis.

BY BOAT   Aswan is the southern terminal for the numerous cruise boats that shuttle between here and Luxor. The cruise from Luxor can be done in as little as 3 days, and usually includes enough discretionary time in Aswan to fit in a visit to Abu Simbel by air if you want. For more information on Nile cruise options, see p. 236.

BY BUS   The bus station is around 4km (2½ miles) from the middle of town. There are plenty of taxis around the station to negotiate your trip into town, which should cost you about LE20 ($3.60/£1.85).

Come Low Water

Coming in from the airport, or heading out to Abu Simbel, you will cross the Nile on a 2.5km (1½-mile) dam made of local granite. This is the original Aswan Dam, built by the British between 1898 and 1902. The house belonging to the lead engineer on the project is now the Aswan Museum on the southern end of Elephantine Island. The dam is an impressive feat of engineering when you consider that it was built more than a century ago and is still being used. Water flow through the dam was controlled by 180 sluice gates, which were raised and lowered with a crane that slid back and forth as needed.

It was originally built 30m (100 ft.) high, but it was raised twice after it became apparent that this was not enough, and ended up 42m (138 ft.) high at the outbreak of World War II. It almost overflowed during the 1946 inundation, but instead of a third phase of expansion, the British decided to build a second dam upstream.

GETTING AROUND

BY TAXI Aswan is stuffed with taxis, usually old Peugeot station wagons that can be guaranteed to wallow gently over the creased and pitted tarmac. Prices are on a par with Luxor, which is to say higher than Cairo, but drivers are a lot more mellow when it comes to negotiation. Expect to pay LE10 to LE20 ($1.80–$3.60/95p–£1.85) for longer distances within town and LE5 (90¢/45p) for shorter distances.

BY BIKE Biking is a great away to get around Aswan. There are rental places scattered about—look for clusters of bikes near a kiosk—but around the train station, heading up Souk Street toward downtown, is a good place to start. Expect to pay LE10 to LE30 ($1.80–$5.45/95p–£2.75) per day for the use of a rattling, squeaking single-speed with bad brakes.

BY FOOT If the weather is reasonably cool, Aswan is eminently walkable.

ORIENTATION

Aswan is pretty simple to get around. There are just three main streets, and they run parallel to the Nile on its eastern bank. Corniche el Nil, as the name suggests, runs along the water. Abtal al Tahrir Street, a mixed shopping and residential street, is the first street inland, and then there's Souk Street, which is where the shopping is. The famous Old Cataract Hotel could be considered the southern end of the town, while the train station is almost at its northern end.

A number of sites on the West Bank of the Nile across from the town are worth visiting, including the Valley of the Nobles, Deir St. Simeon, and the mausoleum of Aga Khan. Getting across to the sites by boat is somewhere between one-third and half the fun.

Around 5km (3½ miles) south of the city lies the original Aswan Dam, now more than 100 years old, and another 7km (4½ miles) south is the famous High Dam, built in the late 1960s with a combination of Soviet money and expertise and Egyptian muscle. Between the two dams lies the little island of Agilkia, site of the transplanted temples of Philae. Almost 300km (186 miles) farther south lies the famous Temple of Ramses II, lifted out of the Nile Valley and repositioned at Abu Simbel on the edge of Lake Nasser.

The **tourist information office** (© **097/2312811**) is immediately to your right as you emerge from the train station, or, if you prefer, directly ahead of you as you come out of Souk Street heading north into Midan Mahatta (Station Square). The affable and helpful manager, Hakeem Hussein, is a font of information about hotels and transport and speaks excellent English. The office is open daily 8:30am to 2pm and 6 to 8pm; Fridays it opens midmorning.

WHAT TO SEE & DO

When walking in the desert, and particularly if you're poking about in sandy, rarely visited tombs, you should keep an eye open for snakes. Although extremely rare and shy, there are a number of species of venomous snakes in Egypt, and you don't want to test the local supply of antivenin.

Aswan Museum ✦ On the northern end of Elephantine Island, the Aswan Museum lost much of the good stuff in its collection to the new Nubian Museum (below), and the few mummies and sculptures that are left are unremarkable. The building that houses the collection, which belonged to the architect of the Aswan Dam, Sir William Wilcocks, is worth a few minutes, however, and the new annex contains some interesting items dug up on the island itself.

Elephantine Island. ℂ **097/2313628.** Admission LE20 ($3.60/£1.85) adults, LE10 ($1.80/95p) students. Winter 8am–5pm; summer 8.30am–6pm.

Kitchener Island   This small island, between Elephantine Island and the west bank, was turned into a virtual botanical park by Lord Horatio Kitchener in the late 19th century. It's well worth a visit if you're in need of a quiet stroll along palm-lined walkways, though it's best avoided on Fridays when it can become quite noisy and crowded.
Admission LE5 (90¢/45p). Daily 8am–5pm.

Kubbet el Hawa   A brief scramble above the Tombs of the Nobles is the small tomb of a local sheikh, Sidi Ali. The structure itself is nothing to write home about, but the view from the edge of the desert back over Aswan is worth the climb.
West Bank.

The Mausoleum of Aga Khan   From the terrace of the Old Cataract, you can see what looks like a single isolated Fatimid tomb high up on the opposite bank. This, in fact, is the final resting place of the 48th leader of the Ismailies, Muhamed Shah Aga Khan III, and his French wife, Begum Aga Khan. He predeceased her by a considerable margin, dying in 1957. She kept a lonely vigil, placing a red rose on his sarcophagus every day until her death in 2000. Though it's a long walk up and the mausoleum itself was closed to visitors at the time of writing, the view from the top is stunning.

Monastery of St. Simeon ℱ   About a kilometer (½ mile) into the desert from the boat dock on the western bank, the ruins of the monastery of St. Simeon remain 8 centuries after it was officially destroyed by Salah el Din. What you see here, in fact, are the remains of a 10th century A.D. rebuilding of a 7th century A.D. monastery that was dedicated to St. Hadra, Bishop of Aswan. At the height of its power, this fortress-monastery (it was surrounded by a 10m/33-ft.-high wall) housed 300 monks and had guest accommodations for up to 100. Inside, there is a well-preserved church, and on the second floor you can visit the old cells with their rock-hard sleeping benches.

The walk up to the monastery from the dock takes about 30 minutes. On the other hand, you can usually hire a camel and guide at the boat dock and, because they work by the hour, the guides are perfectly happy to take you by various roundabout routes up to the monastery. Getting away from the water a little and approaching the monastery from the desert is a great experience.
West Bank. Admission LE12 ($2.20/£1.10). Daily 7am–5pm.

Nilometer   The Ptolemaic Nilometer of Satet is the more interesting of two such devices for measuring the level of the Nile on Elephantine Island. If you have a flashlight with you, descend the stairs from the Aswan Museum; otherwise, check it out from the boat on the way back. From there you can see the inscribed cartouches of Tutmoses III and Amenhotep III.

Nubian Museum ℱℱ   Built with the help of UNESCO and funding from the Japanese government, this large complex on the hill near the old granite quarries houses an enormous number of the artifacts that were saved from being inundated after the High Dam was finished in 1971. The exhibits are arranged chronologically, starting with prehistoric rock carvings and simple hand tools, and running through the successive dynasties of Egyptian domination, the arrival of the Ptolemies and the Romans, and finally the Islamic period, before coming to an abrupt halt with the construction of the dam. The "modern Nubia" section is particularly poignant, with a

Come High Water

Completed in 1971 with the help of the erstwhile Soviet Union, the High Dam was a nationalist dream for then-President Gamal Abdel Nasser, who died the previous year. The generating capacity of the massive dam doubled Egypt's supply of electricity, and its control of the floodwaters increased the cultivatable land by almost one-third. On the other hand, the medium-term downsides have been significant. Not only did it cut off the flow of nutrient-rich silt that came with the annual floods (forcing farmers to turn to chemical replacements that have had serious ecological consequences), but the reduction in water flow has led to stagnation throughout the extensive irrigation-canal system and resulted in the current endemic problem with bilharzia (schistosomiasis) that plagues the country.

lovely display of gold and silver jewelry that underscores the cultural sophistication of the land that has vanished.

It's worth visiting the Nubian Museum before doing anything else in the area, simply to give a context for everything that you see. Reckon spending an hour here for a thorough inspection without too much lingering over anything in particular.

© 097/2319222. Admission LE35 ($6.35/£3.25) adults, LE20 ($3.60/£1.85) students. Winter 9am–1pm and 5–9pm; summer 9am–1pm and 6–10pm.

Tombs of the Nobles *꘠꘠* Looking across the river from Aswan, just over to the right of the massive tower of the Mövenpick Elephantine Island, you should be able to make out little black specks in the face of the golden-brown cliff. These are the Tombs of the Nobles, the final resting place of the officials who ran Aswan and controlled the lucrative trade with Nubia and Sudan. In terms of execution and quality, the experts will tell you that these are inferior to those found to the north (they pale in comparison to the royal tombs of the Valley of the Kings). I think, however, that the setting adds a certain something here and that, after a trek up the steep slippery path from the dock, these tombs, not to mention the view back eastward to the land of the living, are a pretty rewarding experience.

Most of the tombs remain closed, and many have sanded up inside or collapsed. Of the open tombs, the most interesting is probably **Sirenput II.** The owner was a governor under the 12th-dynasty Pharaoh Amenemhat II. It's worth making your way to the burial chamber at the back of the tomb for illustrations of Sirenput with his family. The next tomb along is also a good one. The owner, named **Harkhuf,** was another governor who led several trading expeditions to the south and brought back what he described as a "dancing pygmy" to the delight of the Pharaoh. A letter from the Pharaoh is transcribed on the wall exhorting Harkhuf to hurry to the royal court with the pygmy, but to take care of him on his way and surround him with trusty men so that he wouldn't fall into the Nile or tumble from his hammock in the night. If the New Kingdom tomb of **Kakemkew** is open, it's worth a look as well. It was discovered by Howard Carter about 20 years before the opening of Tutankhamun's considerably more illustrious tomb at the Valley of the Kings, which made him famous, and there are notable illustrations of funerary rites and mourning family that adorn the walls.

West Bank. Admission LE21 ($3.80/£1.95) adults, LE11 ($2/£1) students. Winter 8am–4pm; summer 8am–5pm.

Unfinished Obelisk   This 42m (138-ft.) slab of granite partially cut from the rock of an ancient quarry was probably destined to become the biggest column in Karnak. Masons discovered a flaw in the stone, however, and the project was abandoned, leaving the obelisk-to-be still attached on one side. Maybe the most impressive aspect of it is that its makers were fully prepared to cut loose this massive rock (it would have weighed in at more 1,100 tons), drag it down to the water, and barge it several hundred kilometers down the river with nothing more than some levers, ropes, and a whole lot of manpower.

Admission LE20 ($3.60/£1.85) adults, LE10 ($1.80/95p) students. Winter 7am–5pm; summer 7am–6pm.

SOUTH OF ASWAN

Until the 1970s, there was a whole country between Aswan and Sudan. With the completion of the High Dam in 1971, however, and the subsequent flooding of the river valley, Nubia was inundated and submerged beneath more than 5,000 sq. km. (almost 2,000 sq. miles) of water that was named Lake Nasser. (Actually, only the Egyptian portion of the lake is named Lake Nasser. The Sudanese, with a fine sense of irony, named the portion that spilled southward over the border Lake Nubia.) Now there are just three major sites south of Aswan, one of which is the dam itself. The other two— the Temple of Ramses II and the temples of Philae—were rescued from the rising waters by the international community and transplanted to safe locations above the high-water mark.

Abu Simbel 𝕬𝕬𝕬   The temple of Ramses II is now one of the most famous monuments in the world. The Pharaoh carved it into the rock of the Nile Valley between 1274 and 1244 B.C., and it was saved from being flooded by the waters of Lake Nasser by a frantic international effort in the early 1960s. Three colossal (21m/69-ft.) statues of Ramses II guard the entrance to a temple dedicated to Re-Harakhty, Ptah, and Amun. Around his feet stand his family, including his wife Nefertari. Inside, the temple goes about 60m (200 ft.) back into the rock, passing eight smaller statues of Ramses II and some stunning reliefs proclaiming his military superiority on the way, to an inner sanctuary where there are statues of four seated gods—Amun, Re, Ptah, and Ramses II himself (who was deified). The whole facility is designed and oriented so that on every February 22 and October 22, the first light of the rising sun shines through the door all the way back to the sanctuary and onto the seated gods (though Ptah actually remains somewhat shadowed). Before the temple was raised up from its original location, this happened 1 day earlier.

There is actually a second temple in Abu Simbel, dedicated to Hathor and also built by Ramses II. It is a little to the north of its more famous counterpart, and about half the size. It is interesting, however, that, in this case, his wife Nefertari is shown the same size as her husband.

Abu Simbel will take a full day out of your schedule if you go by car. If your schedule is tight and this is on your must-see list, consider the flight from Aswan. Though it's expensive (around $150 per person from Aswan), it gets you there in 45 minutes instead of 3 hours. Leaving early from Aswan, the plane will get you back in time to catch many of the cruises out of Aswan that night. Airfare includes the 10-minute bus ride from the airport to the temples. There is a sound and light show at Abu Simbel, but to catch it you have to stay overnight in one of the expensive and bad hotels in the town, which isn't worth it. Spend the time, and money, taking in the show at Philae, and stay the night in Aswan.

Admission LE50 ($9.10/£4.60). Winter 6am–5pm; summer 6am–6pm.

High Dam *(Overrated*   The High Dam may be a popular tourist destination, but most visitors seem to come back wondering why they bothered. The views are interesting, if you're fascinated by dams, but not spectacular. There is a truly garish monument to Soviet-Egyptian friendship set in a small park at the western end of the dam. The permissibility of photography on the dam is a bit questionable. The theory seems to be that point-and-shoots are fine, but that big lenses and video are not. As with so many things in Egypt, it comes down to who's watching and what you can get away with. The best way to get here is by taxi.

About 15km (9 miles) south of Aswan. Admission LE8 ($1.45/75p). Daily 9am–5pm.

Kalabsha, Qirtassi & Beit al Wali ★★   These three temples were saved as part of the massive UNESCO effort to preserve as much of the legacy of ancient Egypt as possible from the waters rising behind the High Dam. Transplanted from their original locations, they are now located on an island just south of the High Dam.

Kalabsha was originally built on a stretch of narrow river about 35km (22 miles) to the south known as Bab al Kalabsha; this is the largest and best preserved of the three. It was moved here by a team of West German engineers. It is, like the Temple of Horus at Edfu, a Ptolemaic copy of an older structure.

Qirtassi is a single-room kiosk with little decoration that dates to either the Ptolemaic or the Roman period. It was originally on a site about 10km (6¼ miles) north of Bab al Kalabsha.

Beit al Wali is the only pre-Ptolemaic building here. This temple was dedicated to Ramses II, and the walls are covered with illustrations of the Pharaoh demonstrating his military superiority. The tribute of the Nubians, which includes leopards and giraffes, is particularly lovely.

To get to the island, you need to pick up a boat from the dock between the dam and the Soviet-Egyptian friendship monument. Expect to pay LE40 to LE50 ($7.25–$9.10/£3.70–£4.60).

Admission LE20 ($3.60/£1.85) adults, LE10 ($1.80/95p) students. Daily 7am–5pm.

Isis Temple Complex/Philae

Now trapped between the British-built Aswan dam and the High Dam 6km (3¾ miles) upstream, the stunning Ptolemaic monuments on Philae Island were already being flooded regularly well before they were moved by UNESCO in the 1970s to a site on nearby Agilkia Island, 20m (66 ft.) higher than their original location. They are a must-see for visitors to Upper Egypt.

Temple of Isis ★★   This is the largest structure on the island, covering about a quarter of the available space on the island. The boat dock is by the Hall of Nectambo, and you pass a colonnade (a Roman addition to the temple) on your way to enter through the Gate of Ptolemy II. I particularly like the forecourt of this temple, with its densely worked columns and scenes of offering incised into the massive pylon that separates it from the hypostyle hall inside.

Temple of Hathor ★   Though unfinished, the Temple of Hathor on the eastern side of the island is worth a look for the reliefs of musical entertainment that include Bes, the dwarf god of childbirth, playing a harp.

Kiosk of Trajan   This is not a kiosk in the sense of a small structure, but rather a massive structure on the riverbank illustrated with scenes of the Emperor Trajan making offerings to Isis.

Sound & Light Show at Philae

The show at Philae is perhaps a little more muted than its Karnak counterpart, but it follows the same formula: music, lights, and a voice-over that runs you through the history of the temples. Even if you're not a particular fan of sound-and-light shows, this one's worth it for the experience of being out on the river at night and seeing the temples lit up. There are three shows a night, and both the times and the languages vary, so it's wise to check with a travel agency in town or with the tourist information office rather than relying on the accuracy of the following times. Admission LE55 ($10/£5.10). Winter shows 6:30, 7:45, and 9pm; summer shows 8, 9:15, and 10:30pm.

	First Show	Second Show	Third Show
Saturday	English	Arabic	Arabic
Sunday	German	French	X
Monday	French	English	Arabic
Tuesday	English	French	X
Wednesday	English	French	Arabic
Thursday	Spanish	Italian	French
Friday	English	French	X

The best way to get to Philae is on your own, rather than with a crowd of other visitors who will set the pace for you. Take a taxi to Shellal, which is close to the Aswan Dam (the old one), and negotiate with a boatman at the dock. Expect to pay around LE50 to LE70 ($9.10–$13/£4.60–£6.50) for the taxi and another LE40 to LE50 ($7.25–$9.10/£3.70–£4.60) for the return trip by boat.

Admission LE35 ($6.35/£3.25) adults, LE20 ($3.60/£1.85) students. Winter 7am–5pm; summer 7am–4pm.

WHERE TO STAY

Aswan is a relatively expensive place to stay, certainly if you want to stay in any style. There's one good high-end place, however, and a couple of clean and decent budget places as well. The tricky part, as in most towns in Egypt, is finding a good, value-for-money, midrange hotel.

VERY EXPENSIVE

Mövenpick Elephantine Island   Locations don't get much better than this: The Mövenpick has the northern end of an island in the middle of the Nile all to itself. Cross from downtown on the hotel's free launch and stroll up from the picturesque little dock through the gardens. The hotel was extensively renovated in 2007, and the main building features huge windows and sleek modern decor in the large, light lobby. Some will find it a bit cookie-cutter and short on character, but the context makes up for any lack in this department. Standard rooms are large, well appointed, and comfortable, and are considerably cleaner than those at the New Cataract (below).

The pool area, which features a bar, kitchen, and barbecue, is commodious, but the highlight has to be the **Panorama Bar,** which perches atop a massive 14-story tower in the middle of the island. The view is spectacular, from tiny *falucas* flitting across the

Nile and the green of the island to the golden sands of the desert around the Tombs of the Nobles and the mausoleum of Aga Khan.

Elephantine Island, Aswan. ✆ 097/2303455. Fax 097/2313538. www.moevenpick-aswan.com. 234 units. LE1,650 ($300/£153) standard double; LE1,815 ($330/£168) superior double. Rates include taxes and breakfast. AE, DC, MC, V. **Amenities:** 3 restaurants; 2 bars; pool; gym, spa. *In room:* TV, minibar, safe, Internet.

Old Cataract *(Overrated* Though this hotel is scheduled to close in 2008 for renovation, the Old Cataract is a classic on the Egyptian scene, having housed Agatha Christie and formed part of the setting of her mystery novel *Death on the Nile.* Winston Churchill and Aga Khan were also guests here. With any luck, the expected relaunch of the hotel in 2009 as an all-suite facility will improve on food and service standards that have slumped badly in recent years.

Abtel al Tahrir Street. ✆ 097/2316000. 123 units. LE1,595 ($290/£148) standard double; LE2,992 ($544/£277) Nile-view double. AE, MC, V. **Amenities:** 2 restaurants; 3 bars; tennis court (at the time of writing, staff were using it for soccer). *In room:* A/C, TV, minibar, safe.

EXPENSIVE

New Cataract   Right next to the Old Cataract, the New Cataract has none of its counterpart's faded charm but few of the glaring faults, either. It, too, will be closing in 2008 for a much-needed overhaul, but the view on the Nile side will remain great: across the swimming pool to the first cataract and over the river to the golden sand of the desert. I wouldn't expect the view from the standard rooms to improve, however— the view across the back of Aswan is unappealing at the best of times, and particularly so at Cataract prices.

Abtal Tahrir Street, Aswan. ✆ 097/2316000. 144 units. LE1,007 ($183/£93) standard double; LE1,414 ($257/£131) Nile-view double. AE, DC, MC, V. **Amenities:** 2 restaurants; bar; pool; 2 tennis courts; travel agent in hotel (not recommended). *In room:* A/C, TV, minibar, safe.

Pyramisa Isis Island   This big pile of 1970s-style buildings occupies its own island just above the first cataract. Complete with tennis and squash courts, swimming pools, a waterfall, a health club, and its very own farm, the over-the-top architecture and generally cheesy feel to the whole complex may give you the feeling that it was designed by the villain of a James Bond movie. Rooms are spacious, but the color scheme—a combination of light maroon carpets with green walls and red trim in one wing—leaves a bit to be desired. It's a fun place to stay if the price is right, with the main drawback being the food, which is really bad.

Pyramisa Island, Luxor. ✆ 097/2317400. Fax 097/2317405. www.pyramisaegypt.com. 447 units. LE550 ($99/£51). AE, MC, V. **Amenities:** 6 restaurants; 2 bars; 2 pools; 4 tennis courts; squash court; gym; spa. *In room:* A/C, TV, minibar.

MODERATE

Isis Hotel Aswan   Located between the road and the river, the Isis is probably the best moderately priced option in town. The hotel is close to the Nile with a low-profile, one-story layout that puts the restaurant and 20 of the rooms directly on the water. The rooms are not particularly large, and the garden-view units can feel like rabbit hutches; both pool- and Nile-view rooms are very acceptable. A word of caution: There is at least one pool-view room at the end of the row that has a view of nothing but the registration desk, so be sure to ask whether your room really has a view of the pool.

Corniche el Nile, Aswan. ✆ 097/2315100. Fax 097/2315500. 102 units. LE440 ($80/£41) double. V. **Amenities:** 2 restaurants; bar; pool. *In room:* A/C, TV.

Marhaba Palace   The Marhaba is a newer hotel near the train station and has one of the most gloriously tasteless facades (an odd sort of neo-Pharaonic pastiche) in town. Once you're inside, though, everything follows suits for a fairly bland, midrange hotel. Rooms vary in size and design, so look at a few before deciding if possible. If not, try to avoid paying for a "side Nile view," as these really stretch the point of what constitutes a view. The health club is basic and quite small, and the pool area is cozy. Staff are well trained and very pleasant, and the Internet works very well. With a bit of a discount from the rack rates listed, the Marhaba is a good bet for a comfortable, midrange place to stay in Aswan. Note that the Marhaba is officially an alcohol-free zone, so don't expect any beer with dinner.

Corniche el Nil, Aswan. Ⓒ **097/23301024**. www.marhaba-aswan.com. 78 units. LE495 ($90/£46) double. MC, V. **Amenities:** Restaurant; pool; small health club; Internet. *In room:* A/C, TV, minibar.

Nile Hotel ⌘   This is probably the best value for money in Aswan. Rooms are basic but fairly large and very clean. Furnishings are modern and thoroughly innocuous. The rooms in the front of the building have a great view of the Nile, albeit across the wide and busy street. What really separates this place from the pack, apart from nice, new rooms at a decent price, is the staff, who are more friendly and helpful than those in more upmarket establishments.

15 Corniche al Nile, Aswan. Ⓒ **097/2314222** or 097/2332600. www.nilehotel-aswan.com. 30 units. LE193 ($35/£18) standard double; LE248 ($45/£23) deluxe double. Cash only. **Amenities:** Restaurant; bar; Internet; safe deposit boxes at reception. *In room:* A/C, TV.

BUDGET

El Salam   This is easily the best budget accommodation in Aswan. Rooms are very basic but clean, and all of them are air-conditioned. My favorite feature of the Salam, however, is the view. Granted, it comes with significant road noise (even on the fourth or fifth floor), but from the Nile-facing rooms you can see up and down the river for a long way. Oddly, these rooms with the premium view are also the ones that have the bathroom-down-the-hall option. Go figure. Breakfast (a roll, a boiled egg, and some Nescafé) is included in the price, and is served in a rather spartan atmosphere—if it weren't for the paucity of decent restaurants in Aswan, I would recommend skipping it and going elsewhere.

101 Corniche el Nil. Ⓒ **097/2302651**. 70 units. LE68 ($12/£6.30) Nile-view double (shared bathroom), LE80 ($15/£7.40) double. Rates include breakfast and tax. Cash only. **Amenities:** Breakfast restaurant. *In room:* A/C, no phone.

WHERE TO EAT

The safest course in Aswan is to keep it simple and stick to the fish. Don't expect to get a great steak or world-class tempura here, but do demand good-quality fresh Nile fish. Most of the big hotels here serve food that ranges from disappointing to overpriced. The exception is the Mövenpick; the restaurant has been completely renovated and hopefully that means better food. The Cleopatra Café, a few blocks south of the train station on Souk Street, is a great place to hang out and drink tea, smoke *shisha,* and people-watch.

Aswan Moon FISH   The Aswan Moon is the best of the floating Nile-side places and is just a couple of doors upstream from the Isis. Walk down through the landside building and sit on the float. The furniture is wicker and comfortable, the clientele is a mellow mixture of foreign and local, and most of the time the only soundtrack is the gentle gurgling of water underneath. Though the menu is a trove of malapropisms ("buck with orange" and "veal bane"), the fish is excellent—lightly battered and not overcooked—and the service is pleasant and efficient. There is an unfortunate lack of alcohol, however, so you'll have to wash down the fish with a soft drink or a bottle of water.

Corniche el Nil. Main courses LE15–LE30 ($2.70–$5.45/£1.40–£2.75). Cash only. Daily 11am–midnight.

Chef Khalil FISH   This little fish restaurant in the depths of the souks has a little more polish than the rest. The decor is a bit surreal, with a small water feature and a line of dolphins and turtles cavorting about the room, but the food is good. Either go to the back of the seating area to pick your own fish out of the cabinet or ask what's fresh. Much of the stock comes from the Mediterranean, but the tilapia, which is local, is great grilled and served with a side of rice. Service is both better and more businesslike than you're likely to find elsewhere in this laid-back town.

Souk Street, close to the train station end. Main courses LE25–LE40 ($4.55–$7.30/£2.30–£3.70). Cash only. Daily 11am–10pm.

Poolside at the Isis Hotel INTERNATIONAL   There are a dozen or so tables here lined up between the pool and the Nile. The menu's the same as in the main restaurant, but out here the waiters are relaxed, and instead of a stuffy dining room you have the breeze off the Nile, a view of *falucas* in the water below, and the open sky. The food's nothing special, so keep it simple and have the filet of Nile perch with rice and vegetables and a couple of bottles of the local Stella beer.

Isis Hotel, Corniche el Nil. Main courses LE40–LE60 ($7.30–$11/£3.70–£5.60). MC, V. Daily 8am–10pm.

SHOPPING

Though it has been drastically spiffed up in recent years, the souk in Aswan remains one of my favorites in all of Egypt. It is strung out along Souk Street, but excursions up the innumerable alleys and side streets are always rewarded with a new sight, sound, or shopping opportunity.

You'll find the usual range of T-shirts and bottles of colored sand layered into pictures of camels, but the **Aswan souk** is actually a good opportunity to pick up a few things. I particularly enjoy the dom-wood sculptures, which are usually reproductions of Pharaonic artifacts and are relatively rare to find farther north. If you search carefully among the mass-produced trinkets, you can also find some distinctively Nubian silver at the jewelry stalls. Visit the **Nubian Museum** (p. 246) first to get an idea of what you're after.

10

The Western Desert

No single name should really be applied to the vast area of desert that runs all the way from the Mediterranean coast of Egypt to the Sudanese border some 1,000km (600 miles) to the south. This massive area of sand and rock, in fact, contains many different deserts with different names, and topography that varies from smooth, windblown flats of sand to massive rocky escarpments to sinuous dunes of golden sand. Far from being empty wastelands, these deserts are rich in wildlife and contain several towns, some of which have been inhabited since Pharaonic times. Long ignored by all but the most adventurous tourists, the western desert is now becoming increasingly popular as facilities improve and word gets around about spectacular landscapes, hot springs, palm trees, and unexplored ruins.

One of the more surprising facts about this desert is just how much water it contains. Vast underwater aquifers fed by the North African water table well up into the dozen or so major depressions in the desert between the Nile Valley and the border with Libya. The most northerly of these, the Qattara Depression, comes within 80km (50 miles) of the Mediterranean coast near Al Alamein; it's also the deepest—at one point it's more than 130m (427 ft.) below sea level, which makes it the lowest point in Africa. The depression formed an impenetrable barrier to Rommel's tanks on their eastward thrust in World War II, preventing them from outflanking the Allies' 1942 defensive lines and setting up one of the biggest

and most dramatic confrontations of that war. Interestingly, there have been proposals since at least the 1920s to cut a trench to the sea to allow water to flow into the Qattara Depression in order to take advantage of the drop in level to generate electricity.

To the southwest of Qattara lies the Siwa Depression, walled to the west by the massive dunes of the Great Sand Sea and containing, incredibly, a wide, shimmering lake that perfectly reflects the bleak outlines of the mountains around it. Famous throughout antiquity as the site of the Oracle of Amun, Siwa has been visited by a remarkable range of celebrities including Alexander the Great and, more recently, Prince Charles.

Siwa is one of my favorite places in Egypt. Until recently very isolated, it now has several excellent hotels, stunning desert scenery and ruins, and—somewhat strangely—some of the best dining in the country.

A little farther south and well to the east of Siwa, the Bahareya Oasis contains a couple of towns. Bawaty, the main town of Bahareya, is connected to Cairo by a paved road and to Siwa by a track that is passable with a 4WD. South of Bahareya, and connected by a paved road, is the more sparsely populated Farafra Oasis.

Between Bahareya and Farafra lie the Black and the White deserts, two of the most spectacular desert topographies in the world. The Black Desert is marked by conical black mountains that rear out of the sand and provide an incredible view across the desert in all directions. The nearby White Desert, meanwhile, contains great chunks of white rock that have been carved by the wind into surreal, organic shapes. An overnight jeep safari into either of these deserts is an experience of a lifetime. Remains of Roman and Pharaonic sites also dot the area, as do hot springs where you can bathe at night amongst the palm trees.

From Farafra, the road continues to Dakhla Oasis, which is cradled by a relatively large depression in the desert and backed by a massive escarpment that looks from below like a range of mountains looming to the north. In fact, the top of this cliff marks the level of the desert, and its height above the little towns of the oasis is the depth at which they lie below their surroundings. Here the ancient town of Qasr, the numerous Roman ruins, as well as the gardens nestled into patches between the sand, can easily absorb a couple of days of wandering before setting out to see what lies beyond the edges of the settlements. To the east of Dakhla lies Kharga, the provincial capital, and then on to Luxor on the Nile in Upper Egypt.

1 Siwa

ESSENTIALS

GETTING THERE

In spite of persistent rumors that an airport will soon be built here, the best way to access Siwa remains the long drive across the North Coast to the town of Marsa Matruh, and then a 300km drive (180 miles) south on a paved road around the western end of the Qattara Depression.

BY CAR   Arriving by car in Siwa is very straightforward. There is only one road into town, and it will take you to the central square. You may wish to stop at the tourist information office on the way, in which case turn right at the bank. The office is directly in front of you after 20m (66 ft.).

BY BUS   Arriving by bus in Siwa is an entertainment in and of itself. The bus stops at a low, mud-plastered building about .4km (¼ mile) from the central square, which is called Midan el Souk, and is met by a gaggle of little boys with brightly painted donkey carts. Pile your bags into the back of one of these, clamber in behind, and you'll be delivered to your destination. Pay the boy LE5 (90¢/45p), and everyone will be happy. The system has a certain charm, but it's lacking a little in the suspension and upholstery department. The bus leaves Siwa at 7 and 10am and at 1, 5 and 10pm. Tickets to Matruh cost LE12 ($2.20/£1.10), and tickets to Alexandria cost LE27 ($4.90/£2.50). Check with the tourist office for the latest schedules and costs, and do not trust the signage at the bus station. Show up 30 minutes before the scheduled departure time to buy your ticket, and don't expect to leave on time.

GETTING AROUND

ON FOOT   The area around Siwa's central square is easily covered on foot. Hotels, shopping, and dining, as well as e-mail, museum, and tourist information facilities are all within a 10- or 15-minute stroll of each other.

BY BIKE   Though you don't need a bike to get around, you'll find that having one extends what you can do without hiring a car and guide. Besides, a day or two out on a bicycle amongst the palm trees is a great way to get the lay of the land around the oasis while getting some exercise.

The Western Desert

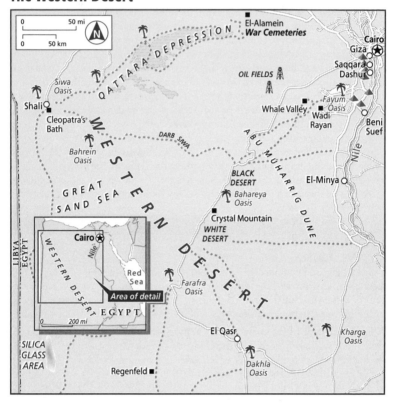

Several of the sites listed are bike-accessible. I suggest a slow tour out to **Cleopatra's Bath** via the Temple of Amun. There's a little restaurant beside the spring where you can pick up lemon juice and a pizza before circling back into town via Gebel Dakrour. The whole trip shouldn't take more than 2 hours, but note that the route is not always very clear and that you're probably going to need directions. Don't be shy about flagging down people in donkey carts or fellow cyclists, but keep in mind the rules of asking directions in Egypt. The following bike-rental places will rent you a single-speed clunker for LE10 ($1.80/95p) a day (I found the Magic Desert Safari bikes to be the best, but frankly there's not much to choose between them): Shalli Bicycles, next to the Bab Inshall Hotel; Magic Desert Safari, Midan al Souk; and Abu Redia, across from the gas station.

BY "TAXI"   Everywhere in Siwa you'll find boys with brightly painted donkey carts—these are the local taxis. Other than being a little hard on the backside, they're a great (if not especially speedy) way to get around. Negotiate your fare before setting out, and expect LE5 to LE10 (90¢–$1.80/45p–95p) to go a long way.

BY 4×4   You can see most of the oasis proper with a bike or a donkey cart, but for anything beyond the limits of the settlement, you'll need to hire a 4WD vehicle with a qualified driver (p. 256). Expect to pay around LE400 ($73/£37) per day.

A 4×4 also offers a good alternative to the bus when it comes time to get out of town and move on. Instead of going north from Siwa by bus to Matruh and Alexandria, you can simply head southeast to the oasis of Bahareya. The state of the road ranges from passable to nonexistent, however, and you need a 4WD vehicle and an experienced driver. The going rate is LE1,200 ($220/£111) for the 5-hour drive (which can be split between three people), and you need a permit from security. The permit can be arranged by the driver, but he will need three copies of your passport (which you can make across the street from the Bedouin Restaurant in Midan el Souk), and LE28 ($5/£2.50) and LE11 ($1.90/95p) for the various permits and stamps that make the trip possible.

Note: At the time of writing, security was insisting on sending an operative with the car. This is not only expensive (it means you can only split the fare three ways, and even this means squashing three passengers across the back seat), but irritating (the "officer" usually insists on taking the most comfortable seat with the best view and may refuse to let you stop for pictures or to eat) and unnecessary—there are no military facilities in the area and certainly no threat of terrorism or banditry. Hopefully, the Ministry of Tourism will be able to prevail on the security services to abandon this requirement.

ORIENTATION

The northernmost of the inhabited Western Desert oases, Siwa is located about 300km (186 miles) south of the coastal town of Marsa Matruh. Surrounded on all sides by a rugged desert, the town remained difficult to reach until the 1980s, when a paved road was built from Matruh. The road follows almost the same route that Alexander the Great took when coming to consult the Oracle of Amun and is relatively smooth going by bus or car.

The Bedouins of Siwa, who still speak a Berber dialect rather than Arabic in their homes, are culturally distinct from the Egyptians of the Nile Valley and retain, to this day, a fierce sense of their identity.

Siwa has undergone tremendous changes in the last 20 years, becoming something of a tourist destination as well as a base for desert trekking, but the place still has a frontier feel to it. Most of the roads remain unpaved, and the tallest buildings are four stories tall. Most important, there is very little tourist hassle. The center of the oasis is

Tribal Politics

The population of Siwa is divided into tribes *(kabila)*, with the broadest division between Easterners and Westerners. The Eastern families were the original builders of the Shali-fortified town, and the Westerners arrived later (local history has them as a mixed group of Berbers and Arabs who were brought in after the town was built). The Eastern tribe divided into three tribes, one of which (the Adadsa) then further subdivided into another three. The Western Tribe subdivided once, into three. Each of these tribes is headed by a hereditary leader (the *Sheikh al Kabila*) who is responsible for meting out justice, maintaining the peace, and negotiating on behalf of the tribe. He maintains land ownership records and adjudicates conflicts through meetings known as *meiyad*. In modern times, the Sheikh al Kabila has also become the intermediary between state institutions and the people of his tribe.

Siwa

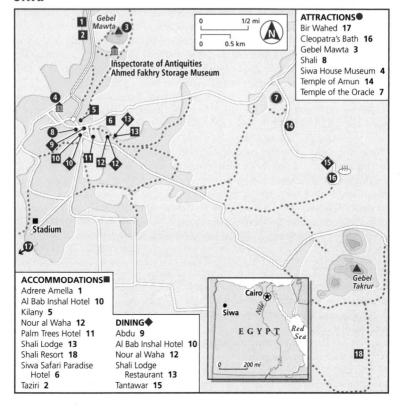

ATTRACTIONS●
Bir Wahed **17**
Cleopatra's Bath **16**
Gebel Mawta **3**
Shali **8**
Siwa House Museum **4**
Temple of Amun **14**
Temple of the Oracle **7**

ACCOMMODATIONS■
Adrere Amella **1**
Al Bab Inshal Hotel **10**
Kilany **5**
Nour al Waha **12**
Palm Trees Hotel **11**
Shali Lodge **13**
Shali Resort **18**
Siwa Safari Paradise
   Hotel **6**
Taziri **2**

DINING◆
Abdu **9**
Al Bab Inshal Hotel **10**
Nour al Waha **12**
Shali Lodge
   Restaurant **13**
Tantawar **15**

Shali, the old settlement, now abandoned, which rises above the new town of Siwa on a low hill. The walls of the old houses, shorn of their roofs and slowly disintegrating, look like shards of pottery stuck in a mound of sand, and at night they are lit up to spectacular effect. At the foot of the hill is Siwa's main square. This is where almost all the shops and restaurants are located. There are also a number of hotels close to the square.

It is worth noting that Siwa is more or less alcohol free—there is no beer, wine, or liquor for sale in the oasis either in stores or in restaurants, and there are no bars. You will need to bring with you anything that you'd like to consume while you're here, and this should be done in the privacy of your hotel room.

FAST FACTS The **tourist information office** (© **046/4601338**) is just across from the bus station in a traditional-style building. Friendly, helpful, and English-speaking, staff can supply updated bus schedule information and a serviceable map of the oasis. Hours are daily 9am to 2pm and 5 to 8pm, but note that evening hours are iffy—the rule is that if you see the lights on, someone's there. My advice is to go between 10am and 1pm.

There are four places to get connected to the **Internet**, all around the central square area, and rates are around LE10 ($1.80/95p) per hour. The connection is strictly dial-up, and though not blisteringly fast, it's stable and functional. There is little to choose between the four, but the nameless shop across the street from the Bedouin restaurant, which has only one computer, is the friendliest and most honest about times and rates.

There is a **Banque du Caire** close to the bus station, which is open 9am to 2pm. They change money and, more conveniently, there's an ATM on the outside of the building that accepts MasterCard, Maestro, and Cirrus cards. There is a daily withdrawal limit of LE2,000 ($364/£185).

WHAT TO SEE & DO

The landscape around Siwa is some of the most spectacular on Earth: The oasis sits on the very edge of the Great Sand Sea, and the area is literally littered with fossilized remnants of prehistoric life. There are several ruins to visit, and a number of hot springs and mini oases where you can soak yourself under the stars.

Bir Wahed ✦ If you've got time for nothing else in Siwa, visit Bir Wahed, located in a tiny oasis on the edge of the Great Sand Sea, around sunset. The quickest way here may be straight across the desert from Gebel Dakrour (where the Shali Resort is), but if you have a couple of hours, I recommend taking a longer route past Adrere Milal and through Bahai el Din. Stop along the way to take in the view across the lake and examine the fossilized remnants of the sea creatures deposited by the prehistoric sea that once covered this desert. Much depends on what the shifting sands choose to expose, but on a recent trip I saw an 8-inch section of sea snake and a perfectly formed and preserved mollusk sitting on a rock. It may be a dozen kilometers (7½ miles) away, but it's worth taking a couple of hours to get out there and back.

Any of the hotels can arrange this trip, as can the safari companies dotted around the main square in town. Though it's close to town, the trip to Bir Wahed (particularly if you go out through Behai el Din) involves getting through some sand dunes, and you'll be uncomfortable, and possibly unsafe unless you have an experienced guide behind the wheel. There are rudimentary changing facilities at the spring.

Cleopatra's Bath Whether or not it was ever visited by the eponymous queen, the spring will be something of a disappointment to a modern visitor hoping for romance. Enclosed in a circular wall, the pool is bound on both sides by a road. There's a nearby restaurant with good pizza and excellent fruit juice, however, and the location deep in the palms makes this a pleasant stop on a trip around the oasis.

Fatnas Island ✦ This is a palm-treed island in Siwa Lake with a spring for bathing amongst the trees. My preference, however, is to come here in the late afternoon, drink tea, and watch the spectacular colors of the sunset.

Gebel Mawta ✦ You'll see this easily accessible low mountain if you look to the left (east) of the road as you come into town. It's about 1.5km (a little less than a mile) from the market square. The name literally means "Mountain of the Dead," and this refers to the various tombs cut into the side of the rock. Over the centuries, the tombs have been used for living and as a refuge during invasions or storms, and the contents have been removed and most of the decorations stripped away. There is still enough wall painting (not to mention outright atmosphere) to make the trudge up here worthwhile, however.

Sandboarding ✦✦ To get the most of this activity, you really should have some snowboarding experience, but even if you don't, there are few things more exhilarating than strapping a truncated surfboard to your feet and skidding off the top of a 30m (98-ft.) dune. There was only one place to get a board at the time of writing

Oracle of Amun

Whether this temple was founded by two doves from the Temple of Amun in Thebes (now Luxor) or whether it was Dionysus, led out of the desert to safety by a ram, who built it out of gratitude, one thing is clear: This was one of the most important religious sites to the Greeks. When the Persian Emperor Cambyses conquered Egypt in 525 B.C., he sent an army across the desert to destroy it. Two centuries later, Alexander the Great wasted no time in paying a visit after conquering the country, arriving to ask the oracle whether he was, in fact, the son of Amun. The temple didn't fare so well under the Romans, who ignored it, thus undercutting its prestige and influence. By the time it was officially closed by Justinian in the 6th century A.D., it was already a shadow of the oracle it had once been.

(below), but I expect more to pop up fairly soon. You can arrange a half-day excursion, board included, for around LE400 ($73/£37) per person, but I recommend renting the boards separately and taking them with you when you head to one of the desert sites with your guide.

Note: The sand, which seems soft when you're struggling up the dune, is as hard as cement when you wipe out on the way back down. It's a 7-hour drive from Siwa to the nearest real medical facility.

Guide **Abdullah Baghri** (p. 69) has two purpose-made sandboards that are the best in the oasis, and will work out a sandboarding-and-sightseeing package. **Sahara Adventure Shop,** just around the corner from the Banque du Caire (✆ **010/2030215** or 012/4515394), has wooden boards with rudimentary foot straps for LE30 ($5.45/£2.75) per day and fiberglass snowboards for LE50 ($9.10/£4.60).

Shali ✦   Thanks to the written records kept in Siwa since the 7th century A.D., we know that the old fortress town was founded in about 1203 by the residents of the nearby town of Aghurmi (near to the Temple of Amun). Built on a hill, the town originally had only a single gate—the Bab Inshal (for which the hotel is named)—with a second gate added about a century later. In the evening, many of the town's sheep and farm animals were brought in through the gates before they were locked for the night. As the town developed within the confines of its walls, the limited amount of space meant that buildings grew upward and the streets became narrow and dark. By the 19th century, there were more than a dozen entrances to Shali, and its residents had seen off a number of determined attempts to invade the town. It was subjugated to central rule in 1820/1821 by Mohamed Ali, whose forces were able to take the town despite the residents flooding its approaches by diverting irrigation water.

Shali was finally abandoned not because of military conquest, however, but because of rain. The whole town was built of *kersheef,* a mixture of salt and mud, as well as blocks of rock salt. In 1926, a particularly severe storm occurred, and the destruction was such that most residents opted to abandon their homes and start fresh nearby.

These days, having suffered through a few more rains and decades of neglect, the town is in ruins but well worth a few hours of exploration. You can wander about freely on your own, but it's not a bad idea to have a guide—even just one of the donkey-taxi kids who hang around the market square—as some of the paths are treacherous. The view from the top at sunset is spectacular.

Siwa House Museum   This museum, in a recently renovated building close to the main square, is a great place to get perspective on traditional life in the oasis. Many of the items on display, such as the traditional wood bowls and the jewelry, are still in use today.

Admission LE1.50 (25¢/15p). Sat–Wed 10am–noon. Closed Thurs and Fri. It's possible that if you talk to the Antiquities Office (✆ **046/4600607**) or tourist information office (above), you'll be able to visit the museum outside these ridiculously restricted hours.

Temple of Amun (Temple of Umm Ubayda)   A pleasant 5-minute bike ride past the Temple of the Oracle up a quiet, palm-lined road (if you're coming by bike), the 30th-dynasty Temple of Amun is nothing more than a pile of rocks now. It stood fully intact until the beginning of the 19th century. The final blow was struck in 1897, apparently, by the local governor who used explosives to remove some rocks he wanted to incorporate into a stairway in his house. Walls and columns lie on their side in a clearing by the road. With no apparent guard or office nearby, visitors are free to clamber about and examine the hieroglyphs at their leisure.

Temple of the Oracle   This temple was once the main reason for coming to Siwa, but its remains now stand alone on a small hill. Built by the 26th-dynasty King Amasis, the temple constitutes some of the earliest evidence that the ancient Egyptians controlled the oasis (then called *Sekhet-imit,* Place of the Palm Trees). The oracle was an important and influential source of information to the Greeks, but it declined under the Romans.

A 10- to 15-minute ride from the middle of town, this site makes an excellent short bike excursion. Because it's situated on a small hill among the ruins of the abandoned town of Aghurmi, the view from the top gives you a good sense of where you are. Though the temple has been poorly restored, it's still worth a 30-minute visit.

Admission LE20 ($3.60/£1.85) adults, LE10 ($1.80/95p) students. Daily 9am–4pm.

WHERE TO STAY

Siwa doesn't have any cookie-cutter five-stars—yet. Hotels downtown (this remains a one-square town) and around the bus station tend to be down-market and not great, with two exceptions: the Shali Lodge and the Al Bab Inshal (below). Development outside the town aims at a higher-end market and looks to deliver a natural, Siwan experience. I suspect that there isn't a single panel of double glazing among them, and the nearest business center is at least 3 hours' drive from here; the more you pay, it seems, the more stripped down this experience becomes. Expect good (in some cases excellent) food, rough-edged but efficient service, and loads of atmosphere from these places, but minibars, satellite TV, and air-conditioning are simply not on the menu. If you're just getting off the bus and looking for somewhere to stay, avoid the first couple of hotels that you come to. If you're really stuck, the Cleopatra is probably the best of them, but it's only to be used as a last resort.

VERY EXPENSIVE

Adrere Amella ★★   Less is once again more, it seems, and at this stunning ecolodge, less is also a lot more expensive. It may not make sense at first—not only does this place have no TV, no phone, and no Internet, it doesn't even have electricity: you'll eat, drink, and read by the light of candles or oil lamps and be heated by hot coals in open braziers. Stay a while, however, and things will begin to drop into place.

The design, which is intended to blend the manmade seamlessly into the natural, is simply gorgeous. Nestled between the base of Gebel Gafa (Gafa Mountain) and the stunningly beautiful Lake Siwa, the buildings, made largely from traditional *kersheef,* are low and gracefully rounded. Exploring inside is an adventure of caves and oddly curved rooms, each one appointed in high-quality cotton cushions and furnished with painstakingly fashioned handmade wood tables and chairs. Modern fittings are kept to a minimum. My favorite items, though, are those carved out of solid blocks of local salt. These range from heavyset benches in the rooms to translucent blocks built into the walls, which let in sunshine during the day and light up from outside with the glow of lamps and candles at night. There is even a bar carved out of salt.

Eating is done in a number of different rooms throughout the lodge, some laid out as formal dining rooms, some carved into niches in the cliff walls and furnished with cushions and pillows. The bar facilities are similarly distributed. Each guestroom is unique, but most are very large and have high (5m/16 ft. high in some cases) ceilings. Bed linens and towels are extremely high quality, and the bathrooms are lovely, with natural fittings, deep bathtubs, and rock-salt benches.

Cairo office, 18 El Mansour Mohamed St., Zamalek. (℃ **02/27351924** or 02/27353797. www.eqi.com.eg. 41 units. LE2,462 ($448/£228) double. Rate is all-inclusive of meals, alcohol, and activities. AE, MC, V. **Amenities:** Restaurant; bar; pool. *In room:* No phone.

EXPENSIVE

Taziri   Built on a low escarpment over Siwa Lake, Taziri also looks at the back of Gebel Gafa. Like its neighbor, Adrere Amella, it bills itself as an ecolodge and eschews the use of electricity in favor of candles and oil lamps. Though it doesn't take the concept quite as far (there are some modern conveniences, including a generator), it does pursue the same concept of getting away from the loud noises and bright lights. There is a lovely spring-fed pool, and the whole place is built around a nicely laid out single-story restaurant and lounge building.

The rooms, which are separate from the main buildings, are pleasant and cool, with stone floors, palm-leaf ceilings, and Bedouin carpets. There is no air-conditioning, but windows have been carefully sited to provide cross-flow ventilation and cooling. Each room has a veranda that looks out over the mountain and the lake, which are about .8km (½ mile) away across the road and the desert. I recommend the second-floor rooms—they have the best view.

At the time of writing, Taziri was undergoing a significant expansion that will see a large increase in the number of rooms and possibly a second pool.

El Maraky Village. (℃ **046/4601981.** Cairo office, 1 Abdallah al Kateb St., Dokki. (℃ 02/37497818. Fax 02/37497818. 18 units. LE800 ($145/£74) double. MC, V. **Amenities:** Restaurant; pool. *In room:* No phone.

MODERATE

Al Bab Inshal Hotel ★★ *Finds*   Taking its name from the original gate that led into the fortress town of Shali in the 13th century, this is a wonderful hotel built in the traditional style. The whole building blends with its surroundings, giving guests a boutique version of the Siwan experience. Like the Shali Lodge (below), the rooms don't have air-conditioning but are kept cool in the summer by high ceilings, small windows, fans, and good ventilation. Touches such as exposed palm-tree beams and light covers carved from local rock salt accent the traditional feel, while at the same time you're pampered with quality cotton towels and bed covers. The restaurant offers very good food, and the room rate includes an excellent breakfast. In this price range, this and the Shali Lodge, which operates on the same basis, are two of my favorite small hotels in Egypt and offer very good value for money if you're looking for the real Siwan experience.

Midan el Souk. ℂ 046/4601499 or 046/4602266. Cairo office, 18 El Mansour Mohamed St. ℂ 02/27367879 or 2738/1327. Fax 02/27355489. 11 units. LE340 ($62/£31) double. Rate includes breakfast. Cash only. **Amenities:** Restaurant.

Nour al Waha   Just across the "street" (a quiet sandy track that leads through the palms) from Shali Lodge, the Nour al Waha is a tiny place—just two rooms tucked into the back of their somewhat sparse garden. It lacks the character and charm of its neighbor, as well as its swimming pool, but the rooms are large and clean, with a few local touches. Beds are large and of moderate quality, and linens are not as good as the competition's. Staff are friendly and helpful, and the restaurant is very pleasant.

El Seboukha Street. ℂ 046/4600293 or 012/545455. 2 units. LE150 ($27/£14) double. Cash only. **Amenities:** Restaurant; garden. *In room:* No phone.

Shali Lodge   This lovely little hotel, built in a style that matches the architectural curves in the old city, is situated down a quiet unpaved road that winds through palm trees, and is one of my favorite places in Egypt. A 3-minute walk from the tourist-dense central square of Siwa, here you feel alone in the oasis, with a palm grove all to yourself. The walls are rough, sandy plaster, and the lighting is subdued at night. Arched doorways, terra-cotta light shades, and simple-but-elegant furniture hand-carved with traditional motifs really make this place special. The rooms are large and follow the traditional motif of the rest of the hotel, with rounded shapes and handmade furnishings; they also have fans. For eating, choose between seating on the roof amidst the top of the palm trees, with a view across the grove, or downstairs on low cushions next to the fireplace. Staff are friendly and well trained, and the food is excellent.

El Seboukha Street. ℂ 046/4601299 or 046/4601395. Fax 046/4601799. Cairo office, 18 El Mansour Mohamed St., Zamalek. ℂ 02/27367879 or 02/27381327. Fax 02/27355487. info@eqi.com.eg. 16 units. LE340 ($62/£31) double. Rate includes breakfast. Cash only. **Amenities:** 2 restaurants; pool. *In room:* No phone.

Shali Resort 👣👣   Though it doesn't make the most of its great location between the golden sand of the desert and the dark green palm of the oasis, the Shali Resort (not to be confused with the Shali Lodge) offers a spacious layout and a pleasant garden with a pool and a canal running through the middle. Buildings are small and in traditional style to blend with the landscape. The sound of running water and the view of the dunes from the garden create a delicious ambience.

Rooms are basic but spacious, with only a few local touches such as handmade glass light covers and Bedouin rugs. I'm not thrilled by the cement floor, but at least it's neatly painted and clean. Don't bother with the suites, as the extra room they offer is wasted on a cramped and badly lit sitting area. The downside of the location is that you'll need some kind of vehicle to get into town to visit the museum, use the Internet, or eat at the restaurants there (the Shali has its own very adequate restaurant). A rented bicycle (see below) will get you there in about 20 minutes, but isn't very practical in the heat of the summer or after dark. A car is easily arranged through the hotel staff, however, and if the location doesn't bother you, the Shali Resort is a great base for day trips or a stopover on a longer safari.

Gebel Takrur. ℂ 046/9210064. www.siwashaliresort.com. 77 units. LE330 ($60/£31) double half-board. AE, DC, MC, V. (3% surcharge for AE and DC). **Amenities:** Restaurant; pool; hammam; billiard tables; massage. *In room:* A/C, TV.

Siwa Safari Paradise Hotel This hotel is a comfortable, if slightly ramshackle, place about 5 minutes' walk from the central square, giving the place a relaxed and quiet atmosphere and explains why it has long been a favorite of expats living in Cairo. The rooms are distributed throughout a cluster of small buildings surrounded by the garden, and the bathrooms are more modern than elsewhere around town. The furnishings are also fairly modern, and the domed ceilings of some rooms add charm. The hotel lacks the ambience of Shali Lodge or Al Bab Inshal, but on the other hand offers a range of modern accoutrements that these lack. The pool is a big plus after a hot day in the desert.

Midan el Souk. ⓒ 046/4601290 or 046/4601590. 90 units (70 w/A/C). LE280 ($50/£26) double, LE330 ($60/£31) double w/A/C. MC, V. **Amenities:** Restaurant; pool; laundry. *In room:* TV, minifridge.

INEXPENSIVE
Avoid the budget hotels around the bus station (they're not very clean). If you're desperate, your first stop should be the Alexander the Great. Take a can of Raid, and expect to pay LE20 to LE30 ($3.60–$5.45/£1.85–£2.75).

Kilany *(Value)* This is a decent, clean, budget hotel that's at the low end of this price range, and is the best place in town unless you're looking for super-cheap, super-basic. Several rooms have a view of the old town, which is spectacularly lit up after dusk, and the hustle and bustle on the street below is fun to watch. Bathrooms are very basic, with no shower stall, leaving you to mop the floor afterward, and mattresses are thin. A rooftop restaurant affords a good view of downtown and the old city. Look at a few different rooms before deciding which one you're going to take, and try to get as far from the entrance lobby and office as you can. Between the phone, the TV, and the socializing, it can get a little noisy down there.

Midan el Souk. ⓒ 046/4602052. 14 units. LE50 ($9.10/£4.60) double. Cash only. **Amenities:** Restaurant. *In room:* No phone.

Palm Trees Hotel Very much a budget place, the Palm Trees is just outside the main square, making it convenient to the town center with its unique Siwan atmosphere, shops, and businesses. A "chalet" is a better bet than the rooms in the main building. At the time of writing, the walled garden, which is this place's chief asset, was under construction, but once this is finished the place could be a good budget option.

Midan el Souk. ⓒ 046/4601703 or 012/1046652. m_s_siwa@yahoo.com. 25 units. LE15 ($2.70/£1.40) double with shared bathroom and no A/C; LE50 ($9.10/£4.60) double with garden view and bathroom. Cash only. **Amenities:** Restaurant. *In room:* No phone.

WHERE TO EAT
Abdu *(Value)* EGYPTIAN/INTERNATIONAL This is a very popular place on the quieter side of the main square, favored by locals and tourists alike. The street side of the restaurant is open, giving you a view of donkey taxis and dusty 4×4s piled with food and supplies. The menu is an eclectic mix of Western and Egyptian, and though there's pasta, I'd stick with items such as pizza and grilled chicken. The beef shish kebab is excellent, with a tasty and fresh side of French fries, and comes with tahina, fresh-cut cucumber, and Siwa olives.

Midan el Souk. Main courses LE15–LE25 ($2.70–$4.55/£1.40–£2.30). Cash only. Daily 8am–midnight.

Al Bab Inshal Hotel *(★★)* SIWAN The restaurant on the roof of this hotel is literally built into ruins on a hill above Siwa's old town and looks over the town's main square or the ruins, which are lit up spectacularly at night. Local specialties get a European twist, thanks to the French chef who was brought on to develop the menu and train the cooks. Dishes include a tasty mixed salad with crispy croutons, *shorbat maghrebi* (a vegetable soup with little piece of beef in it), and lamb *moza* (shank of lamb, braised and served with couscous and a side of vegetables in a light tomato-based sauce). Dessert includes *konafa* pastry with date sauce. I also highly recommend this place for breakfast, which, in addition to excellent a la carte options such as the date crepes, features a set menu of an omelet, *foul,* local bread, Siwa olives, and some of the best marmalade I've ever had.

Midan el Souk. ℭ **046/4601499.** Main courses LE15–LE40 ($2.70–$7.25/£1.40–£3.70). Cash only. Daily 8am–midnight.

Nour al Waha EGYPTIAN   Opposite Shali Lodge, nestled into its own walled palm garden with soft-lit ambience, Nour al Waha's open-air restaurant offers Egyptian staples such as *shish tawook* and *kofta,* as well as a small variety of Western dishes. The pizza, washed down with some fruit juice, makes an excellent lunch.

El Seboukha Street. ℭ **046/4600293.** Main courses LE15–LE25 ($2.70–$4.55/£1.40–£2.30). Cash only. Daily 8am–midnight.

Shali Lodge Restaurant ⚘ SIWAN   You can choose to eat on the roof of this hotel, the stars above you and the palm trees swaying in the night breeze or, if it's too chilly for alfresco dining, there's a cozier location downstairs that's equipped with low tables, cushion seating, and a fireplace.

Like the architecture, the food is a sophisticated version of traditional local fare, and it's some of the best hotel food in the country. Try the free-range chicken in a thick, rich sauce (made from local organic olives) with a big pile of rice on the side, or the lamb kebab with French fries. They also offer vegetarian dishes, which is almost unheard of in Egypt. All meals come with probably the best *tahina* in Egypt and fresh, warm bread, and the food is served on traditional clay plates. For dessert, choose from a selection of traditional pastries, or go for one of their crepes filled with date jam.

El Seboukha Street. ℭ **046/4601299.** Main courses LE15–LE40 ($2.70–$7.25/£1.40–£3.70). Cash only. Daily 8am–midnight.

Tantawar INTERNATIONAL   This basic restaurant is located in the palm trees next to Cleopatra's Bath. Seating is on cushions with your back to a palm log, and the structure is more reminiscent of a beach hut than a real restaurant. Both the pizzas and the sandwiches are good, however, and the fresh fruit juice is some of the best around.

Cleopatra's Bath. Main courses LE10–LE20 ($1.80–$3.60/95p–£1.85). Cash only. Daily noon–10pm.

SHOPPING

Siwa has long been Egypt's best source for traditional jewelry. Worn by local women on festive occasions, the simple silver designs have been attracting increasingly international attention. The oasis is also the source of beautiful, simple clay pots and tableware in unusual shapes, locally woven rugs, and embroidery. Unfortunately, much of the original household production has been bought up by unscrupulous collectors, and though an effort is now being made to keep these precious cultural artifacts in Siwa for the museum, you may still find them for sale. You can play a direct part in preserving a unique and special culture by leaving these in Siwa and taking away only newly produced pieces, which are just as genuine and just as beautiful.

Siwa Jewelry

The styles and patterns of Siwan jewelry owe more to the Berber heritage of the Siwan people than anything that you'll find in the far-off Nile Valley. Though beautiful and decorative, jewelry also served a number of social roles. Jewelry, in the days of bartering and in the absence of any kind of savings banks, served as a family's capital investment scheme, and a large proportion of savings could be literally hung around the necks of daughters and wives. Original work is scarce these days, but modern, locally made jewelry is just as nice, and buying it instead of the antiques ensures the dwindling heritage of Siwa stays where it belongs—in the hands of Siwans.

Visiting the stores and stalls of Siwa, you're sure to find a large selection of *aswira,* or bracelets. The narrow bands have a bird motif, the design that's most closely associated with the area and are usually worn in pairs by the women of the oasis. The elaborate headdresses of Siwa are also highly characteristic of the area. If you're lucky, you may spot a woman with an ornate headband across her forehead. This is a *lugaya* and is originally a Libyan style of orna-ment. The large, and quite heavy, crescent-shaped earrings that are hung with chains and bells are called *tilakin,* and if they look a bit much for your earlobes, don't worry: They are, in fact, hung from a strap that fits across the head.

The most interesting piece of jewelry in Siwa is a pair of pieces that are usu-ally worn together as a necklace by single women of marriageable age. The first piece is a hoop of silver, called *aghrou,* worn around the neck like the chain of a necklace. Tapered, it has a loop at the thicker end that's secured by nine windings of wire. The thinner end of the hoop has a hook, which fits into the loop and secures it around the woman's neck. It's said that the hook and loop represent the male and female reproductive organs, and the nine wind-ings of the wire refer to the 9 months of pregnancy. A medallion, decorated with a variety of motifs, is hung from the *aghrou.* When the woman wearing the *aghrou* gets engaged, part of her marriage ceremony involves handing this piece of jewelry to the next woman in her family to be married.

Midan el Souk, the main and only square in Siwa, is the place to go for shopping. The square is rung with small stores offering local weaving and embroidery and sim-ple jewelry. Browse and haggle are the rules.

Next to the Al Bab Inshal, which you can see at one end of the square, is the **Bab Inshal Concept Store,** open daily 8am to 5pm, offering a range of unexpected-but-delicious local food products. A jar of caramelized Siwa walnuts or a bottle of local orange salad dressing makes a good local gift.

2 Bahareya

From Cairo, Bahareya is the most accessible of the real desert oases. The main town of Bawiti (which is what most people mean when they talk about Bahareya) is an excel-lent base for trips into the White and Black deserts or to a range of sites around the oasis itself. However, the town isn't much of a destination in and of itself. This will hit home especially hard if you arrive by bus. The middle of town is a low, ugly sprawl of concrete buildings and ad hoc kiosks, and SUVs fresh from the desert, their roof-racks piled high with spare tires and boxes of water, churn up clouds of dust. If this place could talk, it'd say, "Let the adventure begin."

It wasn't always like this. During the Ptolemaic and subsequent Roman periods (around 2,000 years ago), the oasis was a rich and fertile agricultural center and may have had a population of up to half a million people. It was also the site of a massive necropolis, which was recently rediscovered by archaeologists in 1993 after a donkey fell in a hole. It has already yielded more than 100 mummies and is thought to contain as many as 10,000 more. The site of the necropolis hasn't yet been developed as a tourist site, but a few of the mummies are on display in Bawiti.

Note: There is no ATM in Bahareya, and no one at the time of writing was accepting credit cards, so you must carry cash. There is a place to change currency (and hotels should be happy to accept U.S. dollars and euros at the going rate), but that's it. Fortunately, Bahareya is also a low- to no-crime zone.

ESSENTIALS
GETTING THERE
I recommend organizing your transport from Cairo at the same time that you organize your hotel and desert tour. Most guides and travel companies can suggest a range of options, and many will simply pick you up from Cairo. You can get there easily enough on the bus (below), but it's not very comfortable, tends to run late, and takes longer than other options. If you're staying at the International Health Center (p. 272), they can arrange a nine-seater minivan to pick you up and take you back to Cairo for between LE800 and LE900 ($145–$164/£74–£83) depending on whether you need air-conditioning.

BY BUS   The "bus station" is a kiosk in the middle of the town. If you've been wise, you've already booked a hotel, and there should be someone there waiting for you. If not, walk down to the main square (to your left with your back to the kiosk) to the tourist information office and talk to Mohamed Abdel Kader. He can help find you a hotel and get you to it. Don't worry if you find yourself being met off the bus and escorted there by a member of the tourist police. He's just trying to be helpful.

You can buy tickets back to Cairo or on to Farafra at the bus-stop kiosk. Bus times to Cairo are 6:30am, 10am, and 3pm. There is at least one more bus, around noon, but it's not possible to make reservations, and catching it, according to the ticket seller, is "by luck." Tickets are LE27 ($4.90/£2.50). There are two buses to Farafra: one at noon, one at midnight. The ticket is LE20 ($3.64/£1.85).

When planning your arrival and exit by bus, keep in mind that you're in the desert—things happen when they happen. I recently took a noon bus out of town. It was nowhere in sight until 12:45pm and didn't leave town until well after 1pm.

BY CAR   Arriving in Bahareya by car couldn't be simpler: Turn right off the highway just past the signs for the perpetually-under-construction Oasis Panorama hotel, and you're on the main street of Bawiti. The main square, where the tourist information office is located, is directly ahead of you, and Bayoumi's Popular Restaurant (a likely point of reference if you're meeting anyone in Bahareya) is down the first big street to your right. There are two gas stations in Bawiti, one of which often has gasoline.

GETTING AROUND
BY FOOT   There are no taxis in Bawiti, but for the most part it's small enough to get around on foot when you're not in your guide's vehicle.

Bahareya

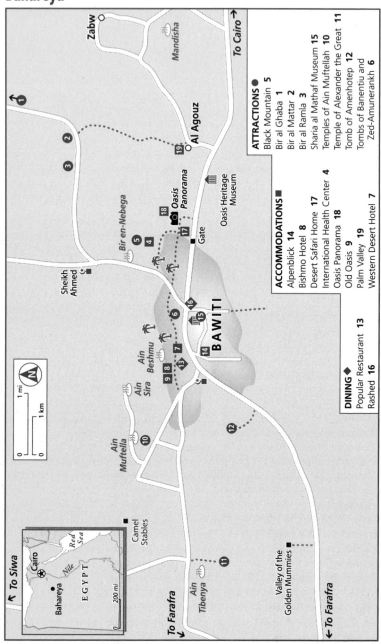

ATTRACTIONS ●
Black Mountain **5**
Bir al Ghaba **1**
Bir al Mattar **2**
Bir al Ramla **3**
Sharia al Mathaf Museum **15**
Temples of Ain Muftellah **10**
Temple of Alexander the Great **11**
Tomb of Amenhotep **12**
Tombs of Banentiu and
Zed-Amunerankh **6**

ACCOMMODATIONS ■
Alpenblick **14**
Bishmo Hotel **8**
Desert Safari Home **17**
International Health Center **4**
Oasis Panorama **18**
Old Oasis **9**
Palm Valley **19**
Western Desert Hotel **7**

DINING ◆
Popular Restaurant **13**
Rashed **16**

BY CAR   If you don't already have a guide and a 4×4 booked, ask at your hotel—there are plenty around. Expect to pay about LE250 to LE300 ($45–$55/£23–£28) for the day inside the oasis.

ORIENTATION

There is really only one main street in Bawiti, and it runs through a central square. The post office, tourist information office, bank, and bus station are all very close to this square. The town sprawls outward, becoming older, lower, and more ramshackle in all directions until it peters out into the desert. None of the hotels, services, and shops listed here is more than a 15-minute walk from the main square.

FAST FACTS   The **tourism office** (© 38473039) on the main square is run by the helpful Mohamed Abdel Kader. If you're coming down from the bus stop, it's the office on your left inside the large, gray government building. Mohamed can help you find a hotel and get you to it. He also has pamphlets in various languages that list local hotels. The office is open 8:30am to 2pm.

At the time of writing there was only one place in town to access the **Internet** (the kiosk across from the police station in the main square, on the Bayoumi side of the main road). A six-station Internet cafe was under construction at the Western Desert hotel across from the Popular Restaurant, however, and this should now be in operation. Expect to pay LE10 ($1.80/95p) an hour for a slow connection.

There is a **National Bank for Development,** just past the main square on the right, open 9am to 2pm. It doesn't have an ATM, and its services are limited to exchanging currency.

WHAT TO SEE & DO

Most visitors coming to Bahareya will be here at the beginning or the end of a desert safari. Below are the main sites within the oasis, but you can consult the "Active Vacation Planner" (p. 65) for features of the desert around Bahareya that you may want to consider as part of your safari.

Black Desert 👁   After about 30 minutes on the road heading south out of Bahareya, the desert begins to look dirty, like there's a dusting of black muck across the hitherto pristine sand—this is the Black Desert. The most interesting feature of the area, aside from its color, may be the large conical hills that rise straight up like rounded pyramids. The hike to the top of one of these is tough, but the view from even halfway up can be an ample reward.

Black Mountain   Quite close to town, Black Mountain was used during World War I by the British to keep a lookout for marauding Sanusi tribesmen (hence, its local name *Jebel Al Ingleez*). You can get to the top, check out the view and the ruins of the British outpost, and be back into town by foot easily in 1½ hours. Of course, if you're staying at the International Health Center, it's just out the back door.

Concert Bar   When you've had enough of dead rulers and their tombs, head out to the village of Al Agouz, about 5km (3 miles) from Bawiti. Here, recording artist Abdel Sadek el Badramany, who plays the *simsemeya* (a five-stringed lute), has created a place where you can settle by the fire and get a taste of Bedouin culture and music. If you don't have a guide to take you out there, head down to the Popular Restaurant and ask. Someone will be quite happy to take you out and bring you back for LE30 to LE50 ($5.45–$9.10/£2.75–£4.60).

Admission LE20 ($3.60/£1.85). Nightly around 9 or 10pm.

Hot Springs   Desert hot springs are rough-and-ready things, so don't expect changing facilities, wooden decking, and a swim-up bar. Sometimes the pool is just a natural depression, but most of the time it's actually a cement tank designed to collect irrigation water. There are a number of hot springs around Bahareya, and choosing the right one is a bit like Goldilocks choosing her porridge—Bir al Ramla's too hot (113°F/45°C) and Bir al Mattar is too cold (unless it's a really hot day), but for me, Bir al Ghaba's just right. Unlike several others, it's also a bit off the beaten track; about 15km (10 miles) northeast of town, past the International Health Center and past Bir al Mattar.

Etiquette demands that if you arrive to find it occupied, you wait your turn. Women should not go bathing alone, particularly after dark, and should bathe in at least a one-piece bathing suit and a T-shirt.

Something to keep in mind is that the temperature of these springs changes from time to time. It's not a bad idea to take the advice of a local on the matter of which spring is the best at the time of your visit.

26TH-DYNASTY & GRECO-ROMAN SITES

Before you head out to see any of the 26th-dynasty and Greco-Roman sites, stop by the kiosk by the museum to buy a ticket for all six sites (Tomb of Amenhotep, Tomb of Zed-Amunerankh, Tomb of Banentiu, Temple of Ain Muftellah, Temple of Alexander the Great, and the Golden Mummies). Hours 8am until 4pm. Six-site ticket LE35 ($6.35/£3.25) adults, LE20 ($3.60/£1.85) students.

Golden Mummies ⚑⚑   The Sharia al Mathaf Museum, just off the main road in the middle of Bawiti, houses 10 spectacular golden sarcophagi that were excavated in the early 1990s. They are Ptolemaic, rather than ancient Egyptian, so think "decorative coffin" rather than an artifact that was part of an elaborately well developed and sophisticated process of preservation. In practical terms, this means that the bodies inside did not last like those in earlier burials and, as you will see, decorative techniques were less sophisticated.

Temples of Ain Muftellah   These four temples, which were discovered in 1901, lie a little to the west of Bawiti. They are quite different both in layout and decoration from their Nile Valley counterparts. One seems to have been entirely dedicated to Bes, the dwarf god of musicians and dancers. Though the temples themselves were reburied in sand to preserve what was uncovered, you can admire some restored frescos.

Temple of Alexander the Great   This temple, built outside town but quite close to an old pass through which travelers from Siwa had to descend to get into Bahareya, presents a bit of a puzzle. When it was excavated by the well-known Egyptian architect and archaeologist Ahmed Fakry in the late 1930s, it was found to have Alexander the Great's effigy and cartouche inscribed in the wall. Both have since unfortunately been erased, literally sandblasted away by the wind, but the question remains of why, if the Macedonian never came farther south than Siwa, his image was engraved here.

Tomb of Amenhotep ⚑   This lovely 18th-dynasty tomb is full of inscribed reliefs showing the luscious afterlife experience of this former governor of the oasis: plenty of food, wine, and worship of the gods. It's the oldest tomb to be visited in the oasis, and the only one in which the ancient inscriptions have survived.

Tomb of Banentiu   This tomb, next to that of Zed-Amunerankh (below), is worth a visit for the pictures depicting gods and the owner of the tomb. Of particular interest is the panel depicting the journey of the moon god Khonsu; you'll see it to the right of the entrance to the main burial chamber; Khonsu is seated in the middle of the panel between the horns of the crescent moon. Worship of the moon god was particularly important in the oases, where the sun could be harsh, and both work and travel were often easier and safer than during the day. The four chains made of ankhs descending from the moon in this panel represent life.

Tomb of Zed-Amunerankh ★★   It's assumed that the original inhabitant of this tomb was a wealthy 26th-dynasty businessman, perhaps a trader in the wine for which the oasis was famous. It may have been robbed long before the archaeologists found it (though Ahmed Fakhry, who excavated the tomb in early 1938, was shown the tomb by the man who robbed it in 1918), but the rich wall paintings and oddly shaped doors make it well worth a visit.

WHERE TO STAY

I recommend staying at one of the hotels on the edge of town to take advantage of the space and the quiet there. All the hotels that I've listed will pick you up at the bus station if you let them know in advance when you're coming in. You might also want to try the Oasis Panorama (© 02/38473354). Located on a plateau at the edge of town. It was engulfed in construction chaos at the time of writing, but the rooms should be nice when it's complete.

Note that many of these hotels do not have air-conditioning in all their rooms. Read the listing information carefully, and specify clearly if you are booking ahead. At the same time keep in mind that you may not need it: temperatures in the desert drop substantially at night, and even during the heat of the summer, the nighttime temperatures can be quite bearable.

Alpenblick   Now under Swiss-Egyptian ownership, the Alpenblick has rooms on two levels facing a central garden. The single rooms are small enough to make you feel claustrophobic, and certainly too small for the price, but the doubles are standard budget-size rooms. There is a coffee shop on the roof, and all the rooms have air-conditioning. The place is very clean, and the staff are friendly and helpful. At the time of writing it doesn't offer the same value for money as some of the other places in town, but improvements are on the way, and it's worth checking out.

Close to the Egypt Telecom Building, Bawiti. © 02/38472184 or 010/2266599. alpenblick_hotel_oases@hotmail.com. 25 units. LE160 ($29/£15) double. Rate includes breakfast. Cash only. **Amenities:** Restaurant. *In room:* A/C, no phone.

Bishmo Hotel   If the Old Oasis (below) is full, try the Bishmo, which is right next door. I prefer the Old Oasis because it has a garden and pool, and the view across the desert isn't blocked. The Bishmo rooms are clean, however, with palm ceilings, stone walls, and scattered Bedu wall hangings. The best rooms are nos. 303 and 305—this is fairly well known, however, so you have to book well ahead to get them.

Bawiti. © 02/38473500. el_bishmo@hotmail.com. 18 units. LE160 ($29/£15) double. Cash only. **Amenities:** Restaurant; coffee shop. *In room:* No phone.

Desert Safari Home ★ *Value*   This great little budget place, tucked away from the center of town, is owned and run by Badri Khozam, who has been working as a guide in the area for more than 20 years (p. 69). The rooms are distributed around a central garden overflowing with jasmine and are fairly standard for the price range. They're not very big, but they're comfortable and very clean. Perhaps, most important, if you're ending a safari here, the showers are well-endowed with hot water. The little restaurant is basic, with a menu that tends heavily toward meat, rice, and okra. Staff are accommodating and helpful, and there's a motor rickshaw that they can use to run you around town if you need.

Bawiti, Bahareya. ② **02/38471321** or 012/7313908. www.desert-safari-home.com. 27 units (12 w/A/C). LE65 ($12/£6) double; LE100 ($18/£9.25) double w/A/C. Cash only. **Amenities:** Restaurant; Internet. *In room:* No phone.

International Health Center 🌴🌴   Run by a German-Japanese couple, this hotel is locally known as "Peter's Hotel" for its owner. Nestled into the foot of the Black Mountain about a kilometer (½ mile) from the middle of town, the main building incorporates a large hot-spring-fed soaking pool, with the rooms spread out in low, bungalow-style buildings around the gardens. The decor around the hotel is more evocative of a European spa (indicative perhaps of their market) than the Bedouin culture of the desert, and the wooden-floored rooms are spotlessly clean and fairly spacious. The restaurant has its own building with a thatched roof. Unless you're looking for something a lot more toward the budget end of the scale, the IHC offers good value for money and is a great place to base yourself for desert adventures.

Another good reason to stay at the IHC is that they can offer a one-stop shop for almost any conceivable safari need through their White Desert Tours company (p. 69). Pickup and transfer to Bahareya from Cairo is available for either LE750 ($136/£69; no air-conditioning) or LE950 ($173/£88; with air-conditioning).

Staff speak excellent English.

Bawiti. ② **02/38473014**, 012/3212179, or 012/7369493. Fax 02/38472322. www.whitedeserttours.com. 45 units. LE330 ($60/£31) double half-board. **Amenities:** Restaurant; bar; hot spring; gym; Internet. *In room:* TV, minifridge.

Old Oasis 🌴   Situated behind the main town of Bahareya, the Old Oasis literally sits on the edge of the desert. Though it doesn't make the best use of the location (the view of the desert is partially blocked by a fence), there's a pleasant garden and the whole place is very quiet and tranquil. The pool in the garden is a great place for a refreshing dip after a hot, dusty day of desert touring. Rooms are basic and vary quite a bit. The nicest are the newest, many of which have domed ceilings and local touches, but on balance I would request one of the older rooms that face the garden (and, thus, out to the desert as well). If possible, though, have a look at a few rooms before making a final decision. The restaurant, with its rock walls and palm ceiling, has some atmosphere. There is usually someone there who speaks English.

Bawiti. ② **02/28473028**, 02/28472177, or 012/2324425. Fax 02/8471855. www.oldoasissafari.com. 36 units (24 w/A/C). LE180 ($33/£17) double w/A/C. Cash only. **Amenities:** Restaurant; pool. *In room:* TV, no phone.

Palm Valley   Somewhat more plush than the International Health Center (above), the Palm Valley is a 15-minute drive outside Bawiti. Surrounded by palm trees and featuring a riding stable and a wide, low lobby with a billiard table, the Palm Valley claims proudly to be where Zahi Hawass, head of the Egyptian Antiquities Service, stays when he's in town. Rooms are fairly spacious, with tiled floors and wood roofs. Staff are very friendly and helpful, though on a recent visit there was nobody there who spoke English. This is a good place to spend the night if you're on your way through Bahareya with your own car, but I wouldn't recommend it over the International Health Center, at one end of the price range, or Desert Safari Home, at the other end, if you're looking for a base from which to see the area. If you do end up staying, make sure you ask for "Zahi's room."

Bahareya. ② **02/28478768**. 30 units. LE308 ($56/£29) double. Cash only. **Amenities:** Restaurant; stable. *In room:* A/C, TV, minifridge, no phone.

Western Desert Hotel   Smack in the middle of the town across from the Popular Restaurant, this is an attempt at a modern budget hotel. It doesn't have a garden, and the seating area on the roof of the building is a poor substitute, but the rooms, though basic, are clean. The Western Desert's advantage is its central location—it's literally around the corner from the bus station and the tourist information office. On the other hand, there's really nothing else in the town and no reason to be staying in the middle of it. Unless you're passing through in your own car and need an easy place to spend the night, you're better off somewhere farther away with more character.

At the time of writing, the hotel was installing a six-station Internet cafe in a room just off the lobby. If this is successfully completed, it will be the best place to get wired up in Bahareya.

Bawiti. ✆ 02/38471600 or 012/4336015. www.westerndeserthotel.com. 54 units (30 w/A/C). LE165 ($30/£15) double w/A/C. Cash only. **Amenities:** Restaurant. *In room:* TV, minifridge, no phone.

WHERE TO EAT

There are no restaurants in Bahareya that I actually recommend. When you get tired of the food at your hotel, try the International Health Center (assuming that you're not already staying there). The two below are strictly eat-at-your-own-risk affairs. Unlike Siwa, which is virtually dry, beer is available in Bahareya.

Popular Restaurant EGYPTIAN   This place has been here forever and has become the social center of gravity for the town. Hang out at Bayoumi's (as it's known locally) for long enough, and you'll see everybody in town. On the other hand, the food is bad and very overpriced, and the toilet is unpleasant. Unless the spirit of adventure is overwhelming, I recommend only using it as a point of reference.

Main courses LE15–LE40 ($2.70–$7.25/£1.40–£3.70). Cash only. Daily 9am–midnight.

Rashed EGYPTIAN   This basic restaurant, on your left after you pass the second gas station when coming into town, serves local food. It's perhaps a little better than Popular (above), but there's not much to differentiate the two except the social life.

Main courses LE10–LE20 ($1.80–$3.60/95p–£1.85). Daily 11am–midnight.

SHOPPING

In a short row of little shops across from the Popular Restaurant, the **Oases Bookstore** makes the most of a very limited stock. It stocks Cassandra Vivien's essential, if hard to follow, *Guide to the Western Desert,* Ahmed Fakry's book on Siwa, and Ahmed Hassan Bey's tales of turn-of-the-century exploration. They also carry maps, a few souvenirs, and T-shirts.

The **Girls Work Shop** sells local handicrafts made by the women of Bahareya. Wares include simple embroidery, some jewelry, and wool caps and scarves. Not only are prices very reasonable (wool scarves for LE30/$5.45/£2.75, for example), and fixed, but the money goes directly to the women who make the products. The store is in the corner of a schoolyard a couple of hundred meters from the main square. Don't be discouraged if the front door seems to be locked; just walk 20m (66 ft.) down the wall to your left, enter the yard through the gate, and go into the store from the back. Hours of operation are approximate, but they're usually 10am to 1pm and 4 to 8pm.

Ganoub is an attractively arranged place that sells handmade baskets and attractive camel-wool blankets, as well as locally made scarves, embroidery, and pottery. It's just off the main square near the bank, and is open daily 9:30am to 1pm and 4 to 8pm.

3 Farafra

Farafra is the smallest, yet one of the most prepossessing, of the main Western Desert oases. At first glance, the place doesn't seem like it's much more than a cluster of buildings on the side of the highway—a place to stop for gas, perhaps, and that's about it. Stick around for a while, though, and you'll find that the town has a very distinct character. A lot less touristy than Bahareya, and not so richly endowed with tombs and monuments, it nonetheless boasts two nice hotels, a spring that has been in use since the Romans were running the government, a surreal "museum," and some of the most spectacular desert scenery in the world.

ORIENTATION
GETTING THERE

BY BUS   Unless you ask to stop at the Badawiya, the bus stops on the side of the road in the middle of town. You will then have to walk back to the Badawiya. There are two buses a day in both directions, and in theory they run to Dakhla at 2pm and 6pm, and to Bahareya around 10am and 5pm. Tickets are LE27 ($4.90/£2.50) and LE20 ($3.60/£1.85), respectively, and can be purchased from the driver. Times and prices, however, are subject to desert vagaries, and it's absolutely necessary to check the day before if you want to avoid a long, and quite possibly fruitless, wait.

GETTING AROUND

BY CAR   The only way to get around the oasis is to hire a local car and driver by the hour or day. Ask at your hotel—there are plenty of both around. Expect to pay about LE250 to LE300 ($45–$55/£23–£28) for the day.

WHAT TO SEE & DO

In all honesty, there's very little to see in Farafra that would draw anyone here from Cairo. If you're here, though, it's likely on your way through the White Desert or on your way north to either the Black Desert or south toward the Gilf (p. 275). That said, a moment taken to look around and indulge yourself in random encounters with the accommodating and courteous residents of the town is a rare treat.

Ain Romani (Roman Spring)   This is touted as the last Roman spring in Egypt still to be in use. Tucked into the gardens behind the town itself, it's in need of a cleanup before it qualifies for much more than a 2-minute glance on your way somewhere else.

Badr's Museum   This is the creation of local painter Badr Abdel Moghny, who started by doing paintings of village scenes around town in a distinct, grippingly earthy, and detailed style. With success he branched out to off-the-wall sculpture and more commercially oriented techniques for his paintings. The museum is a constantly expanding building, with rooms and courtyards being added all the time to accommodate the fruits of Badr's latest artistic endeavors, and is worth a visit if only to liven up your day with something completely different.

© 092/7510091. Admission varies. Daily late morning to sometime in the evening.

Bir Sitta 🔆   A cement irrigation tank never looked so good—particularly in the dark. The name literally means "Well 6." One end of this utilitarian construction is an oblong tank big enough to accommodate 8 to 10 people in the steaming hot water, while the other end, where the water comes roaring in from the well head, is about the size of a Jacuzzi. A long, hot soak here under the stars at the end of a long day in a 4WD is heaven.

Crystal Mountain This is an enormous hunk of crystal (though nowhere near mountain sized) by the side of the road in the White Desert. It has a hole through the middle. It's not worth going out of your way to see, but it makes a good photo if you happen to be passing by.

White Desert ★★★ This is a surreal part of the Western Desert that begins around 50km (30 miles) north of Farafra in the Farafra Depression. At first, looking out the window, you think it's some kind of mirage. The ridges of the rocks seem to have a frost on them. Then you'll see a snowdrift, and pretty soon you're in a winter wonderland. In fact, what you're seeing is a combination of chalk and limestone. The effect is extraordinary, not only because of its unnervingly accurate impression of snow, but because the uneven hardness of the rocks has caused them to form massive, dramatically carved outcroppings known as *inselbergs*. Kids will delight in coming up with shape associations, and photographers will fill up their memory cards trying to capture the brilliant hues of the setting sun reflecting off the inselbergs' shiny surfaces. Waking up amongst them is one of the highlights of any camping trip into the desert.

WHERE TO STAY

There are a surprising number of hotels around the Farafra oasis, but only two I recommend. If you arrive in town and both are full (which would be surprising), try the Al Waha, over by Badr's Museum.

Aquasun This is a rather generic place out on the edge of Farafra. It does make an effort with wicker furniture and small, terra-cotta light covers in the rooms, but in the end, it's comfortable but lacking in the character department. The central courtyard is nice, however, and the pool, while a little small, is definitely the kind you want to be in on a hot desert afternoon. The other nice feature of the Aquasun is the hot

---

The Big One: Gilf Kebir

This massive plateau—in places it's more than 300m (980-ft.) high and has an area equivalent to that of Switzerland—rises out of the desert in the extreme southwestern corner of the Egyptian desert. One of the most remote places on Earth, it was also a strategic backdoor into Egypt during World War II and the centerpiece of a whole skein of narratives, including the story of the mysterious Austrian Count Almasy. Until the award-winning Canadian novel *The English Patient* wove a completely different story about the man, he was best known as a daring, even reckless, explorer of the Western Desert in the early years of the 20th century. He played a crucial part in mapping out the Gilf and used his knowledge with considerable bravery during the war, delivering a pair of German spies via his own route through the Gilf to Dakhla and down to the Nile Valley.

Nowadays, a number of companies regularly mount expeditions to the Gilf. For pure desert adventure, not to mention the dramatic scenery, the famous cave paintings, and the abandoned trucks and equipment that mark out the area's unique and colorful history, this trip's pretty hard to beat. See p. 68 for details.

Farafra

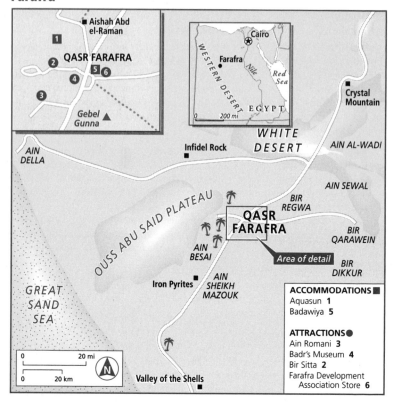

spring 50m (164 ft.) from the back step—just a walk down the slope to a hot soak under the stars.

Farafra. ☎ **0128139372** or 0101882808. 22 units. LE589 ($107/£55) double. V. **Amenities:** Restaurant; pool; hot spring. *In room:* A/C, no phone.

The Badawiya ★★ This is a great, comfortable hotel conveniently located at the northern entrance of Farafra (the bus will stop a 1-min. walk from the front gate). The whole facility is only one-story high, and the architecture of arches and domes blends into the desert background. Every room opens into a courtyard, and there is a village feel to the place that I find very comfortable. The food is not thrilling—the set menu is hearty, and all right—but nobody comes to Farafra for the gourmet experience, as far as I know. The rooms are comfortable but sparse, with clean plaster walls; local wood and terra-cotta touches abound. I recommend splurging on one of the suites in the new section—unlike so many "suites" that are just a regular room with an extra closet, Badawiya suites have full-on living rooms with fireplaces. The hotel also has a pool.

Qasr, Farafra. ☎ **092/7510060.** Fax 092/7510400. 33 units. LE176 ($32/£16) double in the old wing; LE275 ($50/£25) double in the new wing. V. **Amenities:** Restaurant; pool. *In room:* A/C, no phone.

SHOPPING

Farafra Development Association The name's not exactly exciting, but this is a great shopping opportunity if you want to pick up quality local handicrafts at excellent prices. Even if you're just passing through the oasis on your way to Dakhla or to Bahareya, it's worth pulling off to check out the wares being produced by the women of the village. The association is actually retraining local women in traditional crafts, so the slit-weave carpets, camel-hair scarves, and embroidered *gallebeyas* are not only handmade, but made to patterns that have been handed down over the centuries from generation to generation. Prices are fixed and reasonable. Daily 8am to 1pm. © **092/7510060.**

4 Dakhla

If you're coming from the north, the road into Dakhla is where you really begin to feel that you could see the end of the Earth with a good pair of binoculars. The road is a thin band of black that stretches out ahead of the car, snaking between shimmering mirages, while over to the right the massive, sinuous dunes of the Great Sand Sea appear and disappear on the horizon. Just outside town, you come to a place where the dunes seem to threaten the road itself, riding up the power poles until they're half-buried and sending fingers of sand across the tarmac.

Yet, like most places that seem to be in the middle of nowhere, Dakhla is very much the middle of where it is. It was an important town in the Pharaonic and up through the Roman and Islamic periods, and each successive era has left it monuments. For me, the real must-see places in the oasis are the medieval towns of Qasr and Balat. More or less abandoned these days, they are in remarkably good condition and some of the houses in Qasr are even in the process of being restored. From an archaeological perspective, I really enjoy Kellis, or Asmant al Gharab. It was a significant center under the Romans, and it seems to have housed a disproportionate number of Manicheans—a religious inclination frowned on by the Romans. This is particularly interesting in the context of how Kharga, the next oasis up the track, came to be used as a virtual penal colony for people who disagreed with their rulers. Far from being cut off from the world—or perhaps simply because, in a sense, it was—this section of the desert seems at one time to have been teeming with ideas. The other must-see in Dakhla is Deir al Hagar, a 1st-century Egyptian temple built by the Romans that was discovered in the 19th century and is now very nicely restored.

ESSENTIALS
GETTING THERE

As with the other New Valley oases, the best way to get here is by private car. The road in and out is good tarmac, so a 4×4 isn't necessary unless you're contemplating (as you should be) side trips into the desert along the way.

BY BUS The bus runs regularly (a relative term out here) from both Kharga to the southeast and Farafra to the north for LE24 ($4.35/£2.20) and LE27 ($4.89/£2.50), respectively. The main bus terminals (again, a relative term here—we're talking about a one-room kiosk on the side of the road) are both in Mut, but the bus will stop wherever you want en route and let you out.

BY PLANE The nearest airport is in Kharga, which is serviced by one flight a week. Contrary to appearances (a building in Mut with a large EGYPTAIR sign on top of it), there is no EgyptAir office in Dakhla.

Dakhla

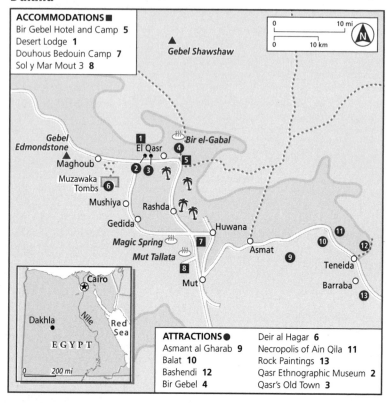

ACCOMMODATIONS ■
Bir Gebel Hotel and Camp **5**
Desert Lodge **1**
Douhous Bedouin Camp **7**
Sol y Mar Mout 3 **8**

Gebel Shawshaw

0 — 10 mi
0 — 10 km

Gebel Edmondstone
Maghoub
Muzawaka Tombs **6**
Mushiya
Gedida
Magic Spring
Mut Tallata
Mut

1 El Qasr
2 3
4 Bir el-Gabal
5
Rashda
Huwana
7
8
Asmat
9
10
11
12
Teneida
Barraba
13

Cairo
Dakhla
EGYPT
Nile
Red Sea
0 — 200 mi

ATTRACTIONS ●
Asmant al Gharab **9**
Balat **10**
Bashendi **12**
Bir Gebel **4**
Deir al Hagar **6**
Necropolis of Ain Qila **11**
Rock Paintings **13**
Qasr Ethnographic Museum **2**
Qasr's Old Town **3**

GETTING AROUND

BY BIKE There are a couple of places to rent bikes in Mut. The Abu Mohamed restaurant has a couple that they rent out for LE20 ($3.60/£1.85) a day, and so does the Garden Hotel (© **092/7821577**). Unless you want to cycle around to pick up bus tickets or see the Ethnographic Museum, however, you'll be wasting your time and energy. It makes far more sense to save your cycling for Qasr, where the Eco Desert Lodge will rent full-on Euro-spec 18-speed bikes for LE110 ($20/£10); the maintenance has been a bit dicey, but the bikes are fine. Fifteen minutes from the lodge has you winding your way down quiet tracks amidst the palm trees, with the sand dunes looming in the background. The Qasr Ethnographic Museum is 10 minutes by bike from the lodge, and if you're in a hurry, you can also tour the old town (just watch your head on the long, hanging arches).

BY CAR/MINIBUS The only way to get around the oasis is to hire a local car or minibus and driver by the hour or day. Ask at your hotel—there are plenty of air-conditioned cars and minibuses around. Expect to pay about LE250 to LE300 ($45–$55/£23–£28) for the day.

ORIENTATION

Dakhla, with more than a dozen small villages strung out over 80km (50 miles), each with its distinct patch of green, feels more like a series of oases than one big one. To the

---

> **Fun Fact** **Ancient Houses**
>
> The discovery of 200 round, Neolithic huts (in the same part of the oasis where rock paintings are still seen today) suggests that Dakhla may have been the site of the first major settlement in Egypt 7,000 years ago.

---

northeast and north (the valley curves like a banana) looms the escarpment that actually defines the edge of the desert, giving you a dramatic point of reference on how deep below the level of its surroundings the oasis lies. To the south there are great rolling dunes of golden sand. At some points, the patches of green disappear completely, with the desert cutting across the depression, but then around the next corner in the road you find a thin green field that widens into a whole farm and then a well-shaded village.

Mut (pronounced moot), the main town, is located in the middle of the oasis, and is where you'll find most of the hotels, Internet places, restaurants, the tourist information office, and the bank. Charmless and not very clean, Mut is probably best avoided as much as possible. Qasr, which is about 20km (12 miles) to the northwest of Mut and almost at the end of the oasis in that direction, is smaller, but has more charm. Between the two there are a number of smaller settlements such as Dohous and Budkhuli. East of Mut, the green thins out and is lost completely for several miles before reappearing around the ancient town of Balat.

The major sights are spread the length of the oasis starting in the northwest with Deir al Hagar and ending somewhere out near the eastern town of Bashhindi or a little beyond (depending on whether you consider the rock paintings near the highway a major sight). You could probably do the oasis in a day, but I recommend taking at least two, particularly if you're there in the heat of the summer.

The **tourist information office** (© **092/7821686** office, or 012/1796467 Omar's mobile; desertlord@hotmail.com) is on your left as you enter Mut. If you arrive at the first roundabout without seeing it, you've gone too far. Here the affable Omar Ahmed can answer general questions in very functional English, but you're better off checking on specifics such as bus schedules and opening times yourself. The office is open daily 9am to 2pm and 6 to 8pm.

Most of the hotels listed below have **Internet** connections in their offices that they'll let you use, but there are several Internet cafes with multiple computers. The best of them is Karmnet, in the old part of town directly below the Forsan Hotel on El Forsan Street. It has eight terminals and can deal with a laptop. Expect to pay LE4 to LE5 (70¢–90¢/35p–45p) per hour for a good connection. I would avoid accessing the Internet at Abu Mohamed's restaurant; not only is the connection the slowest in Mut, but the rate—LE20 ($3.60/£1.85) an hour—is around five times the going price.

There is a **Banque Misr** (daily 8am–2pm, closed Fri and Sat) just off Horreya Square that can change dollars and euros. There is no ATM.

WHAT TO SEE & DO

Asmant al Gharab ✿ East of the modern town of Asmant lies Ruined Asmant, or *Asmant al Gharab,* which is the site of a major Roman city that began to emerge from the sand in the last few years. Visible ruins include a Roman aqueduct and an amazingly well preserved 4th-century church. A wealth of documents—ranging from business documents to private correspondence to religious tracts—found at the site indicate that it was inhabited at least from the 1st century B.C. to the 5th century A.D., and reveal information about everyday life in the Roman era. Interestingly, they also indicate the presence of many Manicheans. Manichaeism was officially frowned on by the Romans, and the tracts found at Asmant al Gharab pose some puzzling questions about why it was apparently tolerated here and who the tracts were intended for.

There is no office or official facility for visitors, but the site is guarded. The resident guard will probably let you look around, however, for LE5 (90¢/45p).

Balat 🎯🎯   This little town on a hill about 30km (19 miles) east of Mut is one of my favorite sites in all of Egypt. Like the old town in Qasr, at the other end of the oasis, Balat has been abandoned relatively recently, with its younger generations moving to more modern dwellings that now ring the ancient site. Where the Ottoman houses of Qasr rise as much as five stories above the streets, Balat's are considerably more modest (but, in my opinion, more beautiful), and everything is low and rounded. Doors are ovoid, and sit in bowl-like sills. Many of the narrow streets are covered to protect residents from sun and sand, but also supposedly as a defensive measure to stop cavalry from penetrating the town. Though it was a vibrant community even 100 years ago, only a handful of residents remain in Balat and it's slowly disappearing. The mosque in the center of the town, though obviously in a state of collapse, is still used occasionally. If you're lucky, you'll slip into Balat without attracting the attention of the local children. If not, the best policy is to go with the flow and let them show you around.

Bashendi   At the eastern end of the oasis, the little town of Bashendi is, like most of the towns in the oasis, built on the site of a much more ancient town. For me, the town is worth a look for the unusual design of the houses, many of which have a covered front porch supported by square pillars. The design is said to be based on ancient Pharaonic patterns.

The tombs are at the back of the village. The domed one belongs to a medieval sheikh named Pasha Hindi (from which the name of the village is contracted), but Roman elements are still visible in the construction of the dome. The adjacent tomb, known as the Tomb of Kitinos, is from the 2nd century A.D. and was more recently used as a billet for Sanussi soldiers during World War I. There are six chambers inside, and the walls are decorated to show the original owner of the tomb meeting his makers.

Tombs: Admission LE20 ($3.60/£1.85). Daily 9am–5pm, or whenever the guard can be found.

Deir al Hagar 🎯🎯   This sandstone temple to the Egyptian gods Amun, Mut, Khonsu, and Seth was actually built by the Roman Emperor Nero (54–67 A.D.) and finished a few decades later by Domitian (81–96 A.D.). What makes it a real must-see for me is that it's covered with graffiti from the who's-who of early desert explorers. Names to be found include Sir Archibald Edmondstone, the first European to get to Dakhla (in 1819), Bernadino Drovetti (the French diplomat who accompanied Mohamed Ali's army to Siwa), and Gerhard Rolfs, who was the first European to cross North Africa. The temple itself is small but elegant and has been nicely restored.

Admission LE20 ($3.60/£1.85). Daily 9am–5pm.

Hot Springs   Soaking at night in one of the many hot springs in the oasis is a popular local pastime, and as soon as you try it, you'll see why: The stars shine, the breeze whispers, and the mineral-rich hot water undoes the knots and bows put there by the day's bumps. Mind you, most of these facilities are little more than irrigation tanks designed to catch well water and distribute it efficiently. Don't get your hopes up for a cabana and a cold drink (unless you bring it yourself), and be prepared to appreciate the rough-edged aesthetic for what it is. Your guide will whisk you off to his favorite spot, but here are some basic suggestions.

The best place for women to bathe in Dakhla is at the **Sol y Mar Mout 3** (p. 282). It may have the romance of an irrigation tank in the middle of a field, but this swimming-pool-like facility has the advantage of a high wall all the way around it. Entrance is LE5 (90¢/45p). There is another walled spring facility just east of Qasr, at Bir Jebel, next to the **Bir Gebel Hotel and Camp** (p. 284). Admission fees are flexible, but generally LE5 (90¢/45p) is about right. Food can be brought from the hotel and eaten in the garden, and though maintenance isn't what it could be (avoid the toilets), the color of the water is nothing to worry about: It's constantly running through the pool, and that's just the color it comes out of the aquifer. There's also a pretty good irrigation tank across the road from the Dohous Bedouin camp (p. 283), which is actually my favorite place for a dip in the oasis. You're going to have to change in the vehicle (if you brought one) or balanced on the edge of the tank—the ground around the spring is pretty muddy.

Mut Ethnographic Museum   On a sleepy side street on the western side of Mut, this museum doesn't look like much from the outside, but the inside is modeled on a traditional mud-walled house and is filled with domestic and agricultural artifacts from around the oasis. The building is usually locked up tight, so go to the grandly named Qasr al Sakafa (Palace of Culture) to find Ibrahim Kamel (or, alternately, give him a call on his mobile phone, listed below), and he'll bike over to let you in. Exhibits include a collection of old handmade clothing, a mortar and pestle for salt, and an ancient goat-skin churn. Ibrahim will guide you, and his narrative alone is worth the price of admission, let alone the shakedown for a tip after he's finished. But if you can keep a straight face as he describes, among other things, the "hangar for chickens" (a chicken coop), he's actually quite interesting and his comments on otherwise incomprehensible objects add a lot of value to the museum.

ⓒ 018/5740789 Ibrahim's mobile, 092/7821311 Palace of Culture, or 092/7871769 Ibrahim's house. Admission by arrangement with Ibrahim. I paid LE3 (55¢/28p), but you should negotiate that down if you're with a group.

Necropolis of Ain Qila   Just across the road from Balat, there's a site containing several ancient mastaba tombs, one of which—the 6th-dynasty tomb of a local governor—is open to visitors. The tombs are nothing to look at, but they're certainly historically significant, demonstrating the wealth and importance of the oasis more than 3,000 years ago. Bring your own refreshments; the new building by the ruins that looks like a good place for a cafeteria was locked up at the time of writing and didn't look like it was going to be opened any time soon.

Admission LE20 ($3.60/£1.85) adults, LE10 ($1.80/95p) students. Daily 9am–5pm.

Qasr Ethnographic Museum ⚘   This museum is located in an old mud-brick building on the edge of the ruins of the old town of Qasr, and the exhibits ramble through a series of rooms to the back of the building. Some of them are a bit cheesy, such as the mocked-up traditional oven, but there's quite a lot here that can give you insight to life in the oasis. My particular favorites are the land-tenure deeds. You don't have to be able to follow the complex swirl of the handwritten Arabic script to see how sophisticated the system of land usage is in the oasis, and, taken together with the toothed sluice board exhibit in the Ethnographic Museum in Mut, they begin to give a context for the complex interweaving of irrigation channels that you'll see on any excursion into the countryside.

Admission LE5 (90¢/45p). If the door's not open, check with the "office" behind the mosque. Daily 9am–5pm.

Qasr's Old Town ★★ Behind the rather unprepossessing new town of Qasr is a whole Ottoman village that's been gradually abandoned over the last two generations. Fortunately, residents have seen the value of their history in this instance, and the old mud-brick houses are being preserved. Reckon on at least an hour to wander through the narrow old streets among the four- and five-story buildings. The depths of the town are deeply shaded and cool even in the middle of summer. Don't miss the **tomb of Sheikh Nasr el Din,** the **Ayyubid mosque,** the **restored house of Abu Nafir,** or the **ancient olive press.** Keep your eyes open for the beautifully inscribed acacia wood lintels; 37 of them remain, and each bears the signature of the craftsman who made it. Though you can see much of what there is to be seen in Qasr on your own, this is one place where it's probably worth picking up one of the "guides" that you'll inevitably encounter around the entrance—not only is it extremely easy to get lost inside the old town (not that this is dangerous, but you simply won't be able to find the best parts), it also takes some nerve, and knowledge, to push into some of the old houses. An LE5 (90¢/45p) tip at the end of the tour is appropriate.

Rock Paintings The village of Teneida marks the end of the oasis, but if you head out about 8km (5 miles) farther, to the first bend in the road, you'll find a group of rocks, one of which looks like a camel and two others that are said to look like the sphinx. (The camel, viewed from the right angle, really does. The sphinx rocks, however, disappoint.) The real reason for coming out here—or stopping on the way to Kharga—is to check out the prehistoric rock paintings of giraffes and antelopes.

WHERE TO STAY
EXPENSIVE
Desert Lodge ★★ Perched on a plateau overlooking the village of Qasr, the Desert Lodge has become a favorite for European tour groups. Built mostly of local materials, it re-creates the look and feel of the old town of Qasr, which is spread out below, while maintaining modern standards of comfort. The rooms are large, comfortable, and clean, and the water is solar-heated. Doors and window blinds are handmade locally, and the walls are decorated by the same hand-lettered calligraphy that you'll encounter in the old town. The pool has a stunning mountain view, and I particularly recommend a dip at sunset, when the fading light of day washes the face of the escarpment in a warm, orange glow. This place may not fit everyone's budget, but it's certainly the nicest place in the oasis.

The lodge features a range of activities including biking, yoga, and safaris. Desert trips are organized by Pan Arab Tours (p. 69), which has extensive experience in running expeditions through the oases and all the way down to Gilf Kibeer.

The best way to book the Desert Lodge is to arrange dates and payments in advance through the Cairo office. Staff in Qasr are friendly and helpful, and they speak great English, but they aren't really set up for drop-in business.

Qasr. ⓒ 02/26905240 Cairo office. Fax 02/26905250. www.desertlodge.net. 32 units. LE490 ($89/£45) double. AE, MC, V. **Amenities:** Restaurant; pool; bike rental. *In room:* No phone.

Sol y Mar Mout 3 The odd name of this hotel is derived from the name of the Egyptian chain (Sol y Mar) combined with the name of the hot spring that's its main feature (*bir talata,* which literally means "well 3"). The hotel was developed in three parts: The first part, which has 10 rooms, is built around the swimming-pool-like hot spring. The second part is 50m (164 ft.) down the road and has 5 rooms (only one of which has its own bathroom). The third part is made up of a half-dozen small huts in a garden behind the second part. You want to be around the pool, which is pleasant though small, as the other rooms are only for the desperate. As a walk-in, you'll be charged the same for any of these, and prices are far too high for any of them except perhaps the two big air-conditioned rooms by the pool. For a better price, try booking through the Cairo office of Travco. The hotel is geared toward the local market, and you risk finding it crowded with a noisy group from Cairo, all of whom paid a fraction of what you're being charged. Check it out (there's a large sign on the road), but unless you get a good deal and it's empty, you're better off at the Desert Lodge in Qasr, the El Negoum in Mut, or, if you really want the hot spring and don't mind roughing it, the Bir Gebel.

Mut-Qasr Road. (©) 16416 Cairo, or 092/7929751, 092/7929752, 092/7929753 Kharga. Fax 27365305. Cairo office 44 Mohamed Mazhar St., Zamalek. 21 units. LE490 ($89/£45) double. Cash only. **Amenities:** Restaurant; hot spring. *In room:* A/C, TV, minifridge (these vary, however, from room to room).

MODERATE

Dohous Bedouin Camp   Perched on the edge of the oasis about halfway between Qasr and Mut, the Dohous camp (named for the nearest small village) has grown over the years. If you want to experience tourist accommodations as they were 10 years ago, you can stay in their original cluster of huts, though I don't recommend this. Better are the chalets built into the ridge below the building that houses the breakfast restaurant. The domed rooms are dark, tackily decorated, and very basic, but they're fairly clean and relatively cool even in the heat of the summer. There's also a new section, two stories high, with more standard rooms that have ceilings of woven palm fronds that let in some breeze. The beds have mosquito nets and the rooms have a fan. If you've been a week in the desert, this place is going to be fine, but if you're on a Sheraton-based tour, try the Desert Lodge in Qasr (best to arrange this in advance through its Cairo office). Proprietor Abdel Hamid (p. 70) also maintains a small fleet of 4×4s and a herd of 35 camels for desert expeditions.

Dohous village, 5km (3 miles) north of Mut. (©) 092/7850480 or 010/6221359. www.dakhlabedouins.com. 36 units. LE50 ($9.10/£4.60) double in a hut; LE120 ($22/£11) double in a chalet or the main building. Rates include breakfast. Cash only. **Amenities:** Restaurant; camel stables. *In room:* A/C, no phone.

El Negoum 👍   Possibly the friendliest hotel in the New Valley, the Negoum (which means "stars"), off the main street behind the tourist information office in Mut, has long been favored by archaeologists working in the oasis. From the outside, it looks like just another low-rise cement block, but inside, the lobby's decorated like an Egyptian living room, with mirrors, photos, and a long line of chairs. The rooms are very clean and spacious, and some of them have very good light. The restaurant is a little soulless, but functional. The staff are exceptionally welcoming.

Mut. (©) 092/7820014. Fax 092/7823084. 47 units (35 w/A/C). LE80 ($15/£7.40) double w/ A/C. Rate includes breakfast. Cash only. **Amenities:** Restaurant; satellite TV in lobby. *In room:* A/C, TV.

Mebrez   The Mebrez (pronounced Mu-*bar*-ez), a clean, basic budget hotel, is the first hotel that you come to as you enter Mut. The lobby and restaurant are both a little gloomy, with low ceilings and drab and uninspiring decor, but the hotel is an easy walk to a couple of small restaurants and an Internet cafe. Rooms are basic and maintenance has been moderate, but the view out of the rooms at the back is pleasant. Try the El Negoum first, but this will do if you find they're full.

Al Sawra al Khdra Street. ⓒ/fax 092/821524. 22 units (15 w/A/C). LE100 ($18/£9/25) single; LE165 ($30/£15) double half-board w/A/C. Cash only. **Amenities:** Restaurant. *In room:* TV, fridge.

BUDGET

Bir Gebel Hotel and Camp ⓕ *Value*   This is a simple little hotel close to the bottom of the escarpment and next-door to the hot spring after which it's named. Most of the very basic rooms are arranged in pairs that share a bathroom and a small common area between them, but there are four rooms with their own bathroom facilities. The restaurant is indoor, but the outside eating area around the barbecue pit is a lot nicer. The food is good, though only a little less basic than the rooms, and the kitchen area is clean. Staff are very pleasant—you'll probably end up chatting and playing dominos with them. The owner has invested in a well that should develop into a hot-spring pool over the next year or so; meanwhile, the eponymous hot spring is in a walled enclosure just a couple hundred meters away (p. 284).

El Qasr. ⓒ 092/7726600 or 012/1068227. Fax 092/7727122. elgabalcamp@hotmail.com. 12 units. LE80 ($15/£7.40) double w/shared bathroom; LE100 ($18/£9.25) double w/own bathroom. Cash only. **Amenities:** Restaurant. *In room:* No phone.

El Forsan   The Forsan is in an older, quiet part of town and backs onto a rather scraggy little garden where you can sit and take food from the restaurant. Rooms are a bit too small for the number of beds that they have in them, and the feeling of being cramped is made worse by the bad light, but they're clean. Staff are less casual and more polite than is usual in Egyptian budget hotels, but also more helpful.

Forsan Street, Mut. ⓒ 092/7821343. Fax 092/7821347. elforsan1@yahoo.com. 30 units. LE45 ($8.20/£4.15) double in the main building; LE55 ($10/£5.10) double in the "garden." Cash only. **Amenities:** Restaurant. *In room:* No phone.

WHERE TO EAT

Eating well is a bit of a problem in Dakhla, and I've found it's best to stick to the hotels. The food at the Desert Lodge in Qasr is an unexciting set menu of soup, meat, vegetables, and dessert, but the meal is substantial and the service is very pleasant. A few kilometers south, the Bir Gebel Hotel and Camp can supply a tastier, but rough-around-the-edges, meal of meat, rice, and a traditional dessert of *agwa*, a sticky, sweet mash of dates and olive oil that can serve as a meal in itself. In the central town of Mut, the Negoum and the Mebarez both serve passable food, and the restaurant at the Forsan is also decent. There are also several small local restaurants in the town. The cleanest are two on the main road into town from the north, close to the Mebarez hotel and across from the tourist information office, and they are explicitly aimed at the tourist market.

Abu Mohamed EGYPTIAN   Just down the street from Ahmed Hamdy's (below), Abu Mohamed serves up great plates of vegetable stew and rice, as well as the usual grilled chicken and meat fare. There's not much to distinguish this place from Ahmed Hamdy's except for the overpriced Internet service and some so-so desserts.

Main courses LE10–LE20 ($1.80–$3.60/95p–£1.85). Daily 9am–10pm.

Ahmed Hamdy's Restaurant EGYPTIAN   Next to the Mebarez Hotel, Ahmed Hamdy has a small, tree-shaded seating area out front with basic food and beer. Don't

Enjoy a Late-Night Dip in a Hot Spring

The whole length of Dakhla is dotted with hot springs. Almost any time a well is drilled for irrigation, the water comes out hot and mineral-rich from aquifers as much as 1km (⅔ mile) below the desert. Wherever it gushes from the pipe, a large pool inevitably forms. Generally, these days a cement tank is built, with a sluice system to control the flow of the water into the irrigation channels.

The experience of bathing in one of these, particularly at night, can be unforgettable. With no bright city lights to interfere with the view and only infrequent clouds, the stars shine exceptionally bright.

Etiquette demands that you wait your turn if the spring is occupied, and they frequently are. In fact, you may find yourself joining a queue. Women should bathe in a one-piece suit with a T-shirt on top and should certainly *not* bathe alone. Also, keep in mind that the minerals in the water can—and probably will—stain whatever they get on; consider it a free souvenir of a night to remember.

---

expect anything more elaborate than a *shish tawook* here, but dishes are substantial enough to keep you going and tasty enough to fill in the gaps.

Main courses LE10–LE20 ($1.80–$3.60/95p–£1.85). Daily 10am–10pm.

SHOPPING

There are a few shops around Mut, but they don't do much beyond the Khan al Khalili–style reproductions of Pharaonic carvings and cheap T-shirts. In Qasr, however, there's a small store with local handicrafts located just inside the entrance to the Ethnographic Museum. The prices aren't bad, and considering the options, you could do a lot worse than to acquire your Dakhla souvenirs here.

Some years ago, a few local women set up a stall selling local woven goods near the entrance to the old town of Qasr. Though a bit ad hoc, it's still there. Asking prices tend to be outrageous, but can be brought down to merely high with a bit of bargaining. All things considered, you're still only paying LE28–LE55 ($5–$10/£2.60–£5.10) for genuine local goods, and the money's going directly into some low-income households.

At the other end of the oasis, the women around the tomb of Pasha Hindi in Bashendi have been selling local jewelry to visitors for several years, and on my most recent visit their wares included some locally made clothes and a neat handmade wooden lock that you can see not only in the Ethnographic Museum in Mut, but in use around the orchards and pens of the oasis.

5 Kharga

Kharga has been a place of exile and banishment for at least 2,000 years. Roman satirist Juvenal (the man who came up with the phrase *bread and circuses*) is said to have been sent here at the ripe old age of 80 to end his life, and a number of other big names suffered the same fate. One of these, Bishop Nestorius of Constantinople—who gave his name to the kind of doctrinal innovation that gets you sent out into the desert—left behind bone-chilling accounts of 5th-century raids and plunder by Nile Valley tribes.

Kharga

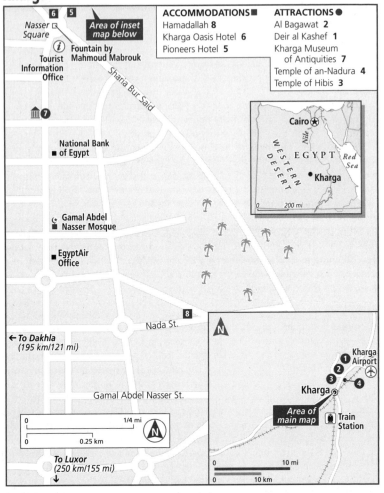

ACCOMMODATIONS ■
Hamadallah **8**
Kharga Oasis Hotel **6**
Pioneers Hotel **5**

ATTRACTIONS ●
Al Bagawat **2**
Deir al Kashef **1**
Kharga Museum of Antiquities **7**
Temple of an-Nadura **4**
Temple of Hibis **3**

Nasser Square **6** **5**
Area of inset map below
Tourist Information Office
Fountain by Mahmoud Mabrouk
Sharia Bur Said
National Bank of Egypt
Gamal Abdel Nasser Mosque
EgyptAir Office
Nada St.
← To Dakhla (195 km/121 mi)
Gamal Abdel Nasser St.
0   1/4 mi
0   0.25 km
To Luxor (250 km/155 mi)

Cairo
WESTERN DESERT
EGYPT
Red Sea
Kharga
0   200 mi

Kharga Airport
Kharga
Area of main map
Train Station
0   10 mi
0   10 km

The last 1,500 years have mellowed the place a little, but, in all honesty, Kharga (which has, in the meantime, become the provincial capital) remains a bit of a dump. Whatever was nice about this place has been ruined by badly planned attempts to modernize. Wide boulevards and cement blocks have been pinned onto lifeless traffic circles, and the two or three marginally decent hotels are a long walk from the slightly more interesting old town.

It's a pity the place isn't a little more hospitable, because apart from a small-but-excellent museum, Kharga has two world-class ancient sites that have been excellently preserved: a large 26th-dynasty temple, and a sprawling Christian necropolis from the 5th and 6th centuries A.D.

ESSENTIALS
GETTING THERE
BY PLANE   There is one plane a week into the airport, which is just outside town. Though this is officially a government flight, there are usually seats available for tourists for about LE413 ($75/£38). You'll probably have to pay in hard currency (dollars, euros, or pounds sterling). Flights depart from Cairo at 8am and leave Kharga at 3pm. Tickets can be booked with the very competent and English-speaking Mahmoud Shokri at the small EgyptAir office (© **092/7921695**) in the government building on Gamal Abdel Nasser Street, open Sunday to Thursday 9am to 5pm.

BY BUS   You can arrive and depart Kharga on an Upper Egypt bus. The station is in the old town, and the local green-and-white taxis, though scarce, can take you to a hotel for around LE5 (90¢/45p). Buses leave for Kharga at 2pm, 11pm, 1am, and 5am. Buses leave for Assiut on the Nile at 6, 7, 9, and 11am. Tickets (© **092/ 7934587**) for both trips cost LE12 ($2.20/£1.10).

BY CAR/MINIBUS   Coming from Luxur or Dakhla, you could consider hiring a car and driver. The journey from either town takes around 3 hours and will cost about LE400 to LE500 ($73–$91/£37–£46). When it's time to move on, you have further options if you're headed to Dakhla or to Assiut (a town on the Nile from which you can arrange onward transport to Luxor). You can save a lot of money by going to the bus station and taxi stand in the old city and buying a seat on a microbus or shared taxi (usually a big old Peugeot 504 station wagon). Vehicles don't travel according to a schedule, but instead leave when they're full. Seats cost LE10 ($1.80/95p) to Assiut, LE9 ($1.60/80p) to Dakhla, and LE4 (70¢/40p) to Baris. The only way to get to Luxor directly is to hire a vehicle for yourself. The cost of the 3-hour trip will depend on your negotiating skills, but you should have no problem finding a minibus (7–9 seats) or taxi (3–5 seats) to take you to Luxor for LE400 ($73/£37), which is a little more than if you're going to Dakhla, which will set you back about LE300 ($55/£28). You'll notice that prices for traveling the same stretch of road seem to vary depending on which direction you're going. This is because fewer cars and more tourists in Dakhla mean that drivers can charge more for getting to Kharga than away, and the same applies in Luxor.

GETTING AROUND
BY TAXI   The green-and-white taxis are the only option for getting around Kharga. Unless you're staying in the old town (which I don't recommend), it's not a walkable place. Prices are cheaper than Cairo, but almost no English is spoken.

ORIENTATION
The main street in Kharga is the north–south Gamal Abdel Nasser Street. At the northern end is Nasser Square, and at the southern end is Saha Square. The museum, tourist information office, EgyptAir office, and banks are all along this street. The

---

⌜Fun Fact Traffic Stopper
The fountain in the middle of the Nasser Square traffic circle was completed in 3 days by local sculptor Mahmoud Mabrouk. The buxom woman represents Egypt, dragging her reluctant people into the modern world.

Darb al Arbein

Kharga was once a major stop on one of the most important major trade routes between Sudan and Egypt. Today, the highway south of the city follows almost exactly the route of what was known as Darb al Arbein, or the "Forty-Day Road." For more than 700 years, this was the conduit of the untold wealth in ostrich feathers, gold, ivory, and slaves that Sudan sent to Egypt in return for weapons, cloth, and metal goods.

Nowadays the old route is abandoned, and though the name is still in use, it actually refers to quite a different route: a camel-trading track that starts in Omdurman, across the river from Khartoum, and makes its way to Daraw, near Aswan in Upper Egypt. The new route sticks close to the Nile and, being a little shorter and easier than the old one, only takes about 30 days.

Back in the heyday of the big trading caravan, staying so close to the Nile would have invited attack and robbery, and so the route looped far out into the relative safety of the open desert. The Sudanese town of Dongola, on the Nile between the third and fourth cataracts, was the major southern terminal back then, and the caravans, which were made up of more than 10,000 camels, bore due north across some of the most arid and inhospitable territory on Earth. After a pause in Kharga, they would angle northeast, reentering the Nile Valley around Assiut, where the riches could be unloaded and sold to merchants from Cairo.

Kharga Oasis Hotel and the Pioneers Hotel are just beyond Nasser Square. The old town lies to the east of its axis.

Tourist information (② **092/7921206**) is run out of a shabby office just off Midan Nasser. Ferahat Shera is there, officially, from 8am until 2pm and then again between 3 and 8pm. He speaks good English and is very pleasant and helpful, but there's really not much to tell. He has a map of the town that is almost entirely useless, but he's probably a good place to start if you have a problem or an emergency situation.

There are two **banks** that can change money in Kharga. The National Bank of Egypt is right across from the museum on Gamal Abdel Nasser Street, and there's a Banque du Caire on the next traffic circle south. They're both open 8:30am to 2pm.

The **El Salam Hospital,** across from the museum, should only be used in emergency situations. Take cash, and leave as soon as possible. There is a pharmacy next door in the same building. The **El Shiffa Pharmacy,** on Midan Shoban Musleem (② **092/7921676**), has a better range of supplies, but the owner doesn't speak enough English to be very helpful.

There are two places to check your **e-mail** in Kharga. The Pioneer Hotel (below) has one terminal available for guests and outside customers; the connection is a slow dial-up. Prices are relatively exorbitant at LE15 ($2.70/£1.40) an hour, but factor in the taxi ride to the other end of town to old town, where the only other Internet cafe is, and back, and they begin to seem more reasonable. If you have anything heavier than a few words to send or receive, head for Al Nasiah, just around the corner from the Dar al Bida hotel and a 2-minute walk from the service bus station. The sign is in Arabic, but look for the computer parts in the window. The last time I was there, the place was being run by a child of 10 who seemed to know everything, bandwidth was more than sufficient, and the charge per hour was LE1.50 (27¢/14p).

WHAT TO SEE & DO

Al Bagawat 🗸 Built during the exile of Nestorius to the oasis, Bagawat is today one of the best-preserved Christian cemeteries from its era in the world. There are more than 260 domed mausoleums still standing, and several still have intact wall paintings. Two of the tombs stand out and shouldn't be missed. The first, the **Chapel of the Exodus,** gets its name from the scenes of Moses and his followers on their journey out of Egypt. Other scenes include Noah's Ark, Daniel in the lion's den, the suffering of Job, and Jonah and the whale. The other must-see is the **Chapel of Peace,** where vines, peacocks, and biblical figures in their allegorical settings adorn the walls.

A bit like the old city of Qasr in Dakhla, Bagawat is one of those sites where it's probably worth accepting the attentions of one of the "guides" who'll approach you there. For a tip of about LE5 (90¢/45p), they will ensure that you get to see the nooks and the crannies of this large site that you would otherwise miss.

Admission LE20 ($3.60/£1.85) adults, LE10 ($1.80/95p) students. Daily 8am–5pm.

Deir al Kashef On the cliffs north of Bagawat looms the ruins of an old building named for the Mamluke governor Mostafa al Kashef (which literally means "Mostafa the tax collector"). It is very much a ruin, but the remains of a 5th-century church can still be identified inside it, and there are some inscriptions there that are fast being eroded out of sight.

Admission and hours are unregulated.

Kharga Museum of Antiquities 🗸 Just across from the tourist information office, in an ugly modern edifice, the Kharga Museum of Antiquities is well stocked and worth a serious visit. Located in the provincial capital, it has benefited from excavations in several significant sites, including a number that you can visit in the Dakhla (p. 279) and Bahareya oases. It has a collection of prehistoric tools, but I found the Greco-Roman hand tools, some of which you can still see in use virtually unchanged around villages in the New Valley, more interesting and relevant. The second floor is well worth the climb up the stairs, not only for the 4th-century embroidered fabrics and a small selection of lovely 18th-century tiles, but for a peculiar collection of 19th-century tableware from the Manial Palace in Cairo (p. 91).

Note that if security at the front gate wants to put your bag through the shiny new X-ray machine just inside the door, supervise carefully. At the time of writing, it was incorrectly set up and liable to dump the contents of your bag on the floor.

Admission LE25 ($4.55/£2.30). May–Sept daily 8:30am–5pm, Oct–Apr daily 8am–5pm. Photography is allowed.

Temple of an-Nadura Between the town and the Bagawat cemetery, this 2nd-century temple-cum-fortress looms over the road and is impossible to miss. Inside, there are still some faded hieroglyphs to be seen, but the main reason to climb up here would be the view of the oasis and, if you don't mind trudging back down in the dark, the sunset.

Hours and admission are unregulated.

Temple of Hibis ☆ This well-preserved 26th-dynasty temple was almost completely buried under farmland until it was discovered and excavated by a team from the Metropolitan Museum of Art in 1909. At the time of writing, it was still undergoing restoration, but a friendly smile and a small tip were sufficient to gain enough access to appreciate it. The temple actually sits in the middle of a much bigger site but is by far the most interesting location to visit. Stop to examine the Roman gate as you approach the temple—the inscriptions there have proven to be a fruitful source of information on the oasis during the 1st-century A.D. Just past that is a gate decorated by Darius I. It is an extremely rare example of work done for the Persian king in Egypt. A line of sphinxes then ushers you into a colonnade and ultimately to the sanctuary. As you look around, watch for the signed graffiti left behind by 19th-century explorers such as Drovetti, Houghton, and Rohlfs.

Officially closed, but a friendly smile and a LE10 ($1.80/95p) tip to the guard will get you in. Daily dawn–dusk.

WHERE TO STAY

Dar al Bayda If you're desperately in need of a place to stay and have a can of Raid with you, this place is about the best hotel in the old town. The paint is peeling off the crumbling walls, there are motorbikes parked in the lobby (seriously), and the rooms are cramped, but it's fairly clean and very cheap. The best reason to stay here, unless you really like to keep your motorbike close, is that it's a minute to the service bus station and taxi stand in one direction, and a minute in the other direction to a good Internet connection. Other than that, the Kharga Oasis Hotel (below) offers better value for money and a more comfortable stay.

Shoala Square. ℂ 092/9211717. 18 units. LE50 ($9.10/£4.60) double. Cash only. Motorcycle parking. *In room:* A/C (in some), no phone.

Hamadallah Only stay here if the Kharga Oasis is full (which I can't imagine happening). The building is a crumbling cement block, and inside is dark and, at least during my visit, echoingly empty. That said, the staff are very pleasant, the rooms are fairly clean, and the air-conditioners work well. Bathrooms were clean enough, but maintenance doesn't seem to be as good as at the Kharga. Peeling paint and crumbling plaster are not hard to spot.

Just off Nada Street. ℂ **092/7920638**. 32 units. LE85 ($15/£7.85) double. Cash only. **Amenities:** Restaurant. *In room:* A/C, TV.

Kharga Oasis Hotel Unprepossessing from the outside, with its run-down courtyard now serving as a goat pasture, the Kharga improves a little inside, with high ceilings and good light. The rooms are spacious, clean, and comfortable for the price, which is low. The garden in the back is cleaner than the one in front, and is pleasant enough to look at from your balcony. The staff are friendly and helpful. The dining room is joyless and the food is bad; skip dinner and eat up the street at the Pioneer.

Nasser Square. ℂ **092/7924940**. Fax 092/7921500. 36 units. LE94 ($17/£8.70). Cash only. **Amenities:** Restaurant; bar (closed at the time of writing). *In room:* TV, no phone.

Pioneers Hotel ☆ This is part of the Egyptian-run Sol y Mar chain, and is definitely the best place to stay in town (though whether it represents value for the money is another question). It has a vast lobby with an appropriately large wall hanging depicting the president (which you can sometimes buy at Omar Effendi in Cairo, by the way). Rooms are generic but clean and comfortable. If you can get one at the back, the view across a palm-lined field to the desert is very nice. There is a pleasant if unimaginative coffee shop, bar, and restaurant setup, and the central garden is clean. A cold beer by the pool could be the ticket after a few days in the hot, dusty desert, but on the other hand, LE50 ($9.10/£4.60) will get you into the pool as an outside guest if you want to save some money by staying down the street at the Kharga Oasis.

If you're having problems finding the place, it's locally known as *al rou-ad.*

Gamal Abdel Nasser Street. Ⓒ **092/7929751,** 092/7929752, or 092/7929753 in Kharga; 16416 in Cairo. Fax 092/ 7927983 in Kharga, or 02/27365305 in Cairo. Cairo office, 44 Mohamed Mazhar St., Zamalek. reservations@ solymar.com. 102 units. LE605 ($110/£56) double; LE743 ($135/£69) double w/half-board. AE, MC, V. **Amenities:** 2 restaurants; bar; pool; Internet; ATM. *In room:* TV, minibar.

WHERE TO EAT

There is the usual concentration of kebab and *fuul* places in the old town, particularly around the service station, but I recommend eating at your hotel. The restaurant at the Pioneers, serving a mix of generic European dishes and Egyptian food, is as good as it gets in Kharga. The *shish-tawook* is edible, but the desserts are surprisingly fresh and tasty. Avoid eating at the Kharga Oasis unless you're truly desperate.

Appendix A:
Egypt in Depth

Egypt has fascinated Europe since it was "discovered" at the end of the 18th century by French savants traveling with Napoleon Bonaparte on his short-lived and ill-fated adventure along the Nile. Long acquaintance, however, has led to surprisingly little understanding on either side. For many, Egypt remains a country of Pharaohs and pyramids, a romantic haze jolted by the occasional explosion. This may well be true, but the pyramids are not always where you expect them to be, and the Pharaohs are not all buried under the shifting sands of the West Bank.

1 History 101

THE ANCIENT PHARAOHS The traditional starting point for ancient Egyptian history is around 3,000 B.C. Documentary evidence isn't very good this far back, and what there is tends to be subject to periodic academic reinterpretation. What we do have, however, is a tablet known as the Narmer Palette (which is now on display in room no. 43 on the ground floor of the **Egyptian Museum;** p. 89), which shows a Pharaoh (Narmer) wearing the crowns of Upper and Lower Egypt and pondering a stack of headless prisoners. Dug up in 1894 and dated to about 3,000 B.C., this palette was long thought to represent the moment at which the two kingdoms were united under a single ruler, whose capital was Memphis. Academics being what they are, this view has fallen out of fashion in the last 20 years, and the unification is now thought to have happened some time earlier.

The Pharaohs subsequently ruled Egypt for an enormous period of time—more than 2,700 years—and devised precise theories for predicting the motion of the stars and planets; developed systems of taxation and government that gave them the power to construct enormous temples, complexes, and monuments that have survived until modern times, and built sophisticated irrigation systems.

Their years are divided, according to their own system, into the regnal years of their rulers, and these in turn are grouped into dynasties, which are divided into three kingdoms—Old, Middle, and New—divided by intermediate periods.

The Old Kingdom saw the construction of some of the most enduring and best known symbols of ancient Egypt, including the great pyramid of Khufu (Cheops) on the Giza Plateau. Khufu (who reigned from 2589–2566 B.C.) was only the second ruler of the 4th dynasty (which was, a little confusingly, the first dynasty of the Old Kingdom), but building pyramids already ran in the family: His father, Sneferu, built the Bent and Red pyramids in Saqqara. Only one, very small sculpture in Khufu's likeness has ever been found. It is on display in room no. 37 of the Egyptian Museum, and the location of his mummy, if it still exists, has never been discovered. Khufu represents the height of Old Kingdom power—subsequent rulers appear to have had less concentrated control of the country. By the 7th and 8th dynasties (2181–2125 B.C.), centralized control of Egypt had broken down, ushering in what is now called the First Intermediate Period, which separates the Old Kingdom from the Middle Kingdom.

The Middle Kingdom was characterized by the expansion of Egyptian territory to include Nubia (now sunk beneath the waters of Lake Nasser behind the Aswan High Dam) and the development of a vast and sophisticated bureaucracy that was able to exert influence over most aspects of life in the country. It is the New Kingdom, however, with which most people associate the glories of ancient Egypt. While Memphis retained its ancient administrative role, Thebes, with its chief god Amoun, became the religious center of an extraordinary period in human history. Modern-day Luxor is a feast of their monuments.

Hatshepsut, who reigned between 1473 and 1458 B.C., was one of the most successful rulers of the New Kingdom, and doubly notable for having been a woman. Her spectacular mortuary temple on the West Bank of the Nile is one of the must-visits for anyone with an interest in the Pharaohs. Akhenaten is also notable, though you'll find little evidence of his reign (1352–1336 B.C.) during your tour of Luxor. This is because after only 5 years on the throne, he abruptly abandoned Thebes and its gods and attempted to found a new capital near modern Al Amarna in Middle Egypt dedicated to the worship of Aten, the sun disk. Room no. 3 of the Egyptian Museum has some of the most extraordinary, stylized depictions of

this unusual man. The most famous of the Pharaohs, however, is the New Kingdom Ramses II, who reigned an incredible 66 years between 1279 and 1213 B.C. A good candidate for the position of the Old Testament Pharaoh, Ramses II also built some very well-known monuments including the temple at Abu Simbel.

ALEXANDER THE GREAT & THE PTOLEMAIC PERIOD

Timelines have it that the Pharaonic Period ended in 332 B.C. with the successful invasion of Egypt by Alexander the Great, a Macedonian with a brilliant, but rather short, career. He visited Siwa, where he consulted the Oracle of Amoun and was declared to be the son of the God, founded the city of Alexandria on the coast, and promptly left Egypt. He left behind one of his bodyguards, a general named Ptolemy, to run the country. The reality, of course, is a little fuzzier. The Egypt that Alexander invaded was already under occupation by the Persians, for one thing, and Alexander, rather than defeating any kind of Egyptian resistance, was welcomed as a liberator. At the same time, he made an obeisance to Egyptian deities and left local administrative structures intact (though overseen by his own, notoriously rapacious and flagrantly dishonest, tax collector). One wonders

Dateline

- **3100–2686 B.C. Early Dynastic Period.** For the first time Egypt unites under a single ruler, with his capital in Memphis.
- **3100 B.C.** Pharaoh Narmer depicted in the Narmer Palette wearing the crowns of Upper and Lower Egypt.
- **2686–2181 B.C. Old Kingdom Period.** The Giza

Pyramids and the necropolis in Saqqara are built.

- **2613–2589 B.C.** Reign of Sneferu; he builds the Bent Pyramids at Dashur.
- **2589–2566 B.C.** The biggest of the three pyramids in Giza is built under the reign of Khufu.
- **2181–2025 B.C. First Intermediate Period.** The country is fragmented, and the power of the rulers in

Memphis barely extends beyond the city.

- **2125–1750 B.C. Middle Kingdom Period** spans the 11th and 12th dynasties; both are ruled from Thebes.
- **1750–1550 B.C. Second Intermediate Period.** Government is fractured, with lengthy periods in which a large part of the country is ruled from the Delta city of Xois.

continues

whether ordinary Egyptians noticed that anything had changed.

After Alexander's death in 323 B.C., there was a dispute over his body, which Ptolemy won. This was a vital battle, because the burial of a predecessor was a crucial rite of succession in Macedonian tradition. By burying Alexander's body in Egypt (quite where remains a mystery, mind you), Ptolemy was able to lay claim to legitimacy, name himself Ptolemy Soter (savior), and found a dynasty that would rule Egypt for the next 3 centuries until 30 B.C., when Gaius Octavius Thurinus, recently crowned Emperor Augustus of Rome, effectively took over control and Egypt became a province of the Roman Empire.

HAIL CAESAR The transition from Ptolemaic to Roman rule was similarly a matter of a slow fade rather than dramatic change. The Ptolemies had gone to some lengths to publicly integrate their regime into Egyptian society, adapting Greek religious figures to match local morays, building or rebuilding temples in the southern parts of the country, and even going so far as to follow the Pharoanic practice of marrying their siblings. As inbreeding took its inevitable toll and Roman pressure mounted on the militarily and politically weaker Ptolemaic dynasty, it was inevitable that their politics become intertwined. Cleopatra VII (69 B.C.–A.D. 30), the famous Cleopatra of the Hollywood screen, played Roman politics with verve but lost in the end. She bore a son for Gaius Julius Caesar (the famous Caesar of the Shakespearean stage) before he was knifed by his opposition, and she shifted her allegiance, and favors, to Mark Antony. When he, too, was defeated, she killed herself, allegedly by allowing a pet asp (snake) to bite her. Her son, and Caesar's, ruled, briefly and nominally, before being executed by the victorious Roman Emperor Augustus, inaugurating Roman rule over Egypt.

The centuries of Roman rule in Egypt were characterized by gradually stricter and heavier military control of the country, combined with an ever more efficient bureaucracy (at least until the 3rd century A.D.), designed to squeeze more taxes from it. It was, perhaps more important, also characterized by the rise of Christianity. At first persecuted and suppressed by the Romans but generally accepted by Egyptians, Christianity was well established here by around A.D. 200. Most Egyptians date the formal origin of the religion to the founding of the Patriarch of Alexandria in A.D. 33, but sources and evidence are fairly sketchy on this period. What is clear, however, is that the situation eased up significantly once the Christian Constantine

---

- **1550–1069 B.C. New Kingdom Period** in which many of the most spectacular monuments, such as Karnak Temple and many of the Valley of the Kings tombs, of Upper Egypt are built.
- **1473–1458 B.C.** Hatshepsut rules; her mortuary temple is in Luxor.
- **1352–1336 B.C.** Akhenaten, who started as Amenhotep

IV, starts a new religion in a new city miles from home.
- **1336–1327 B.C.** Tutankhamun, son of Akhenaken, oversees the reinstatement of more traditional worship, and became famous very late in life.
- **1279–1213 B.C.** Ramses II's longevity allows him to leave several huge monuments to himself, including the

world-famous temple in Abu Simbel.
- **1069–747 B.C. Third Intermediate Period,** characterized by overlapping family lines and regional disputes.
- **747–332 B.C. Late Period.** Egypt struggles to regain the unity and stability of the New Kingdom and is invaded and successfully divided during this period.

(known as Constantine the Great, or even St. Constantine) was declared emperor in A.D. 306, and the Edict of Milan (which made Christianity legal) was circulated in A.D. 313. Constantine, of course, was also the point at which the center of imperial gravity—at least for Egypt—shifted eastward from Rome to the newly named city of Constantinople. By the 5th century A.D., Egypt had not only largely made the transition from 4,000-year-old deities of Pharoanic Egypt to a relatively new (at least officially) monotheistic cosmology, but also from a country ruled by Egyptians from Egypt to a province of empires.

There were flies in the religious ointment, however, and the chief one was that the church in Egypt was on the wrong side of the Council of Chalcedon, which in A.D. 451 ruled on what now seems a rather abstruse religious question concerning the physical and spiritual nature of Christ. Suffice it to say that the Egyptian Church professed a belief in the monophysite nature of Christ (that his essential being was at once divine and human) and refused to alter its view despite having been ruled out of bounds by a Byzantine council that had declared itself infallible. It is an amusing twist on the debate that the most vehement of the monophysites opponents, Nestorius, was himself subsequently exiled from his comfortable position in Antioch (now Antakya in southern Turkey) to the thoroughly unpleasant Egyptian desert outpost of Kharga for falling afoul of the same need for doctrinal uniformity. In any event, the rifts caused by these disputes were never properly closed, and by the 7th century, Christian Egypt was in no position to close ranks with the Byzantine Empire and present a unified front against a small army that arrived from the Arabian peninsular under the banner of a new prophet: Mohamed.

In late 639, a small army crossed the Sinai Peninsula under Amr ibn al 'As, a Muslim convert from a tribe near Mecca in what is now Saudi Arabia. Fresh from victories in Palestine and Syria, the men had little difficulty reaching massive fortifications of Babylon (now in Coptic Cairo) by the fall of the next year. By the spring, the country was theirs. There are different perspectives on the ease with which this band of 4,000 men, which even with reinforcements only reached about 15,000 by the end of the campaign, managed to conquer one of the richest provinces of the Byzantine Empire. But, a population that was not inimical to the invaders (who seemed to offer the Monophysite Copts a greater degree of religious tolerance than their nominal co-religionists had) combined

---

- **332 B.C.** Alexander the Great arrives, establishes a coastal city in his name, consults the Oracle of Amoun in Siwa, and leaves.
- **332 B.C.–A.D. 30 Ptolemaic Period.** Egypt is under the control of a Macedonian dynasty, with its capital in the city of Alexandria.
- **305–85 B.C.** Ptolemy I is left to run Egypt in Alexander's absence, makes himself ruler,

and establishes a dynasty after Alexander's death.
- **51–30 B.C.** Cleopatra VII takes part in Roman politics and one of the most famous affairs of all time before committing suicide.
- **A.D. 30–640** During the **Roman Period,** Egypt is the breadbasket of Rome; Christianity flourishes.
- **640–969 First Islamic Period.** Egypt invaded and

held by Muslim forces. Governed from Damascus, Fustat (near Cairo), and Baghdad.
- **969–1071 Fatimid Dynasty.** The country is ruled from the new city of Al Qahira by Shia invaders from the west.
- **1074–1252** Ayyubid dynasty, founded by a Syrian Kurd named Salah al Din, saw off the European invaders of the Crusades.

continues

with general fatigue on the part of the Byzantines after centuries of conflict frames the most likely explanation.

THE ARAB INVASION   In 639, Babylon was a strategic and well-fortified, but provincial, town on the Nile. The fortress there guarded important port facilities and the entrance to an ancient system of waterways that, at its height, enabled navigation between Cairo and the Red Sea. To the invaders from the Gulf, the site must have looked a lot more comfortable and secure than the soon-to-be conquered capital of Alexandria ever would. After all, they may have handily defeated the Byzantine land forces, but they were still a long way from being able to challenge the empire for naval supremacy of the Mediterranean. The new capital of Egypt—known as Fustat—was founded on the banks of the Nile near the ancient capital of Memphis and not far from the pyramids at Giza, and here it remained as control of Mohamed's legacy passed from Saudi Arabia to the Baghdad Caliphate. The two most dramatic monuments left from this period are the 9th-century **Nilometer** (p. 92) on the southern tip of Rawda Island and the **Mosque of Ibn Tulun** (p. 98).

At the very foundation of Islamic history is a schism between two groups— Shi'a and Sunni—that is still present today. Understanding a little of the religious soap opera that surrounds this fracture is essential to understanding what happened next in Egypt.

When Mohamed died in A.D. 632, leadership of his rapidly expanding movement passed first to the father of his wife, Aisha (a man named Abu Bakr), and subsequently to three more Caliphs. These four became known as the *Rashidun,* or Right-Guided, and they came from a tight tribal circle that supported Mohamed from the beginning. The last of these men, Ali ibn Ali Talib, was not only Mohamed's cousin, but married to his daughter, Fatima. Ali lost a power struggle to a man named Mu'awiya Abi Sufyan, who had been appointed governor of Syria by his predecessor. It was, as the participants recognized, something of a sea change—the moment that Islam outgrew its humble origins and became an empire, it went big-time. The schism occurred because some of the followers of Ali would not accept this new succession and began to develop an alternative, independent line of theology and political structures to go with it. One group, ultimately the most important, called themselves the "Supporters of Ali" or *shi'at Ali,* to differentiate themselves from the supporters of the new Damascus-based Umayyad dynasty founded by Mu'awiya,

---

- **1252–1517** Egypt is ruled by a military caste known as the Mamlukes, whose roots are in the Ayyubid practice of importing slaves to serve in the army.
- **1517–1798 Ottoman Rule.** Run nominally from Istanbul; Egypt enjoys a great deal of independence from the empire.
- **1798–1802 Napoleonic Interlude.** Bonaparte's occupation thwarted by the combined efforts of the Ottomans and the British, but it had a big impact.
- **1805–1848** Mohamed Ali reasserts Ottoman rule and establishes a dynasty that spends ruinously on attempts to modernize the country.
- **1882–1954** British occupation sees two world wars and the development of modern tourism.
- **1899–1902** Construction of the first Aswan Dam by the British.
- **1952–present** Modern Egypt run under military rule.
- **1952** Free Officers Movement, led by Gamal Abdel Nasser, seizes power, taking control of the government and exiling the king.
- **1954–1970** Nasser's presidency.

who associated themselves with the *sunna,* or way of the Prophet.

For Egypt, this might have all been irrelevant, except that as the Muslim empire expanded across North Africa and ultimately into Spain, the neighboring territory of Tunisia was taken over by a Shi'a group who were originally supporters of Isma'il bin Ja'far and were known, as a result, as Isma'lis. Because they traced their parentage back to Fatima, daughter of Mohamed and wife of Ali, they also came to be known as the Fatimids. By the time the Fatimids were established in North Africa, around 3 centuries had passed since the original dispute and the capital of the Muslim empire had moved from Damascus to Baghdad. No matter—the first obstacle on their march remained the same: Egypt.

After a number of failed invasions, they finally succeeded in taking the country from the local allies of Baghdad in A.D. 969. The first thing they did was build a new city outside Fustat, which they named Al Qahira (The Victorious); the massive walls of their city define much of what we now know as Islamic Cairo.

There was at least one precedence for this, the city of Al Qatai, built by breakaway Abassid ruler Ahmad ibn Tulun in the late 9th century. Unlike the Fatimid city, however, Al Qatai was completely razed, and today all that remains of it is the Mosque of Ibn Tulun.

As outsiders, the Fatimids trod lightly when it came to religion. Though they were prodigious in their construction of monuments (which include Al Azhar Mosque and Bab Zuweila), there was little pressure on the mass of Sunnis to conform to Shi'a practice (though there was at times heavy promotion of Shi'a festivals), and Christians and Jews alike (despite a few notable and violent exceptions) were allowed to go about their lives. Indeed, on the whole, the Fatimids presided over a period of stability and relative prosperity in which education and the spread of knowledge (they endowed several large public libraries and countless schools) were high priorities. Moreover, they inherited holdings built up by two strong and capable mini-dynasties, the Tulunid and the Ikhshids, and had the resources not only of North Africa to draw upon, but Syria and Sicily as well.

The first three Fatimid rulers were strong and competent, but the government began to fall apart after that with a series of young and incompetent Caliphs who allowed the government to slip into the hands of military commanders. Inevitably, the economy slipped into shambles, and the political legitimacy of the government was undermined. Even at

- **1956** Suez Crisis is prompted by Nasser's threat to nationalize the canal and close the Straits of Tiran; Great Britain, France, and Israel invade the canal zone.
- **1967** The Six-Day War. Preceded by a military and rhetorical buildup, Egypt and Israel fight a brief war on the Sinai; Israel wins.

- **1970** Aswan High Dam completed.
- **1970–1981** Sadat's presidency.
- **1973** October War results in brokered peace and Egypt is able to reclaim the Sinai.
- **1978** Camp David Accords lay out the terms under which Israeli forces returned the Sinai Peninsula to Egypt.

- **1981–present** Mubarak's presidency.
- **1991** In exchange for a reported $20 billion, Egypt takes part in the operation to drive Iraqi forces from Kuwait.
- **1997** Sixty-three people are killed in an attack by terrorists in Luxor.

continues

their height, however, the Fatimids had their quirks. It may be unfair to single out the third Caliph, Al Hakim, as typical, because though he was a reasonably competent administrator in many regards, he was also palpably crazy. Amongst his better-known edicts were bans on *molakheya,* a staple dish in Egypt, and shoes. He was also notorious for touring the city in the company of a slave whose job was to publicly sodomize shopkeepers caught cheating on measures or prices. Personally abstemious, he was in the habit of taking long walks during the night with little or no guard, and on one of these walks he disappeared and was probably murdered, quite possibly with the collusion of his sister. He was formally succeeded by his nephew who, still a minor, ruled with the help of his aunt, the sister who probably had something to do with Al Hakim's mysterious disappearance.

The slide of the Fatimid Empire was arrested by a series of ministers, who initially trimmed back the encroachments on government by the military with a broad-ranging policy of assassination. The last of these ministers was a Sunni Syrian Kurd by the name of Salah al Din Yusuf Ayyub, who took the post in 1169. By this point, the dynasty was in the hands of a scattering of querulous, epigenous siblings who were not up to the challenge of running

Cairo, let alone a whole country under attack from a wearying succession of heavily armed invaders from the still undeveloped northern regions of Europe. The credibility of the last of their line—Caliph Al Adid—was severely undermined by his making an alliance with the Christian invaders against co-religionists in Damascus. Salah al Din effectively took over when Al Adid died in 1171, and 3 years later was able to have himself declared ruler of Egypt (as well as North Africa, Nubia, and Syria) by the reigning Caliph in Baghdad.

Salah al Din immediately set about modernizing the defenses of Cairo, which included the construction of the Citadel that now overlooks the old Fatimid city and the completion of expanded walls. He then set about using his rule of both Syria and Egypt to shove the plundering hordes of Christian Europeans back to their miserable chilly climes, and in the process founded the Ayyubid dynasty.

A short-lived dynasty, the Ayyubids controlled Egypt until 1250, sowing the seeds of their own destruction with one of the keystones of their military successes against the Europeans.

Mamluke literally means "the owned," and under Salah Ayyub, the sixth and second-to-last Ayyubid ruler, the use of these imported slaves was key to the military.

- **2003** Riots erupt in Cairo in protest of the U.S. invasion of Iraq, despite Egypt's nonparticipation.
- **Aug 2004** Wrestler Karim Ibrahim wins Egypt's first Olympic gold medal since 1948.
- **Mar 2007** Amendments to the constitution are designed to preserve security forces' power and restrain the Mus-

lim Brotherhood's political advances.
- **2008** Egypt's national football team wins the Africa cup for the sixth time.

In the Beginning: The Story of Egyptian Cosmology

A lot can change and evolve over 2,500 years, and the story of Egyptian cosmology is mind-bendingly complex. At its root, however, there is a story of creation that is as elegantly simple as it is intriguingly evocative.

In the beginning, there was chaos, and all was filled with the primordial, unformed, and unconscious waters known as Nun. From these waters, a god, Ra, willed himself into physical existence. This god was alone and contained both male and female principles. Ra spat from his mouth two children: Shu, who became God of Air and was shown in paintings wearing an ostrich feather on his head, and Tefnut, who was the Goddess of Mist and depicted as a woman with the head of a lioness. As a result, the world was ordered, and the chaos abated.

You will often see Ra in a solar barque, which he used to traverse the sky each day. On his head, he has a rearing cobra. It seems that early in the story he had to send out his eye—at that moment he was still incompletely formed and had only the one—in search of his children. When the eye returned, it found that, while it had been gone, Ra had grown a second one, which angered it. In order to calm the situation, Ra gave his first eye, the sun, greater power than his second, the moon. The first he also expressed as the rearing cobra that you will see on his head, and which you will also see as a protective headdress worn subsequently by the Pharaohs.

Once he had eyes and children, Ra wept, and his tears became humans. Meanwhile, Shu and Tefnut had been busy procreating, and the results of their union were Geb, the God of the Earth, and Nut, the Goddess of the Sky. Geb was depicted with a goose on his head, and is often referenced with a picture of a goose alone. Nut, on the other hand, was frequently depicted as a naked woman arched over the world. It is in this capacity that she was thought to give birth to the Sun each morning and then eat it in evening.

It was Geb and Nut who ultimately gave birth to most of the rest of the gods who figured in ancient Egyptian cosmology, but first there was a problem that had to be overcome. It seems that Ra himself, the most powerful god, was in love with Nut, and when he found out that she and Geb were involved (so to speak), he cursed her, saying that she would not be able to give birth on any day of the month. The cosmos was evolving, however, and soon enough a loophole opened up. Thoth, the God of Wisdom, who was also associated with the moon, somehow wrested from the moon 5 extra days (my favorite account has them playing a board game for time, with the moon losing badly).

The connection to the mundane world is clear: The ancient Egyptian calendar added 5 days to the end of the year to make up for the shortcomings of the lunar year. The cosmological significance, however, was even more profound. During these days—which belonged to no month—Nut rapidly began to have children. In short succession, she gave birth to Osiris, Horus, Seth, Isis, and Nephthys. With these, the basic cosmological population of ancient Egypt was complete, and the long drama of their conflicts and loves could begin in earnest.

Forming ruthless and highly effective corps of soldiers without particular ties to soil or family, they quickly seized control, marrying into the royal lineage when Shagarat al-Durr (for whom a street in Zamalek is still named) became queen in 1249.

Mamluke rule lasted until 1517, when the Turks once again took control, at least nominally, of Egypt and reduced it again to the status of an imperial province ruled by a *pasha* (you will still hear *ya basha* on the streets of Egypt as a term of respect) appointed by Istanbul. In reality, however, the Mamlukes retained most of their local authority (at least until Napoleon's catastrophic invasion of 1798 demonstrated the powerlessness of their outmoded cavalry against modern arms), and the political history of Egypt became the story of their incremental victories over a series of Turkish administrators.

THE FRENCH INTERLUDE Though brief, Napoleon's occupation of Egypt marks a key moment in European relations with Egypt. Previous invasions from Europe had been beaten back, if not easily then at least effectively. Not so this time. At the Battle of the Pyramids (named by the French more for effect than geographic accuracy—the pyramids of Giza were only distantly visible from the site of the actual clash) in July 1798, Napoleon's infantry made hamburger of the Mamluke cavalry, killing perhaps 3,000 of them (along with a similar number of infantry) for a reported loss of 29 French soldiers.

Despite this crushing tactical triumph, the strategic situation was about to get dramatically worse. Unfortunately for Napoleon, a British fleet under Horatio Nelson was already stalking the naval forces that he had left near Alexandria to guarantee his supply lines. Ten days later, the French boats were found and destroyed (and have only recently been rediscovered and opened as a recreational dive site) in what has become known as the Battle of the Nile. So, doomed from the get-go, Napoleon's occupation was brief, but its significance went beyond the dramatic proof of the superiority of European arms and tactics.

Along with his army, Napoleon imported a team of more than 150 civilian scholars, as well as around 2,000 engravers and artists. They spent their time cataloguing everything that they could get their hands and eyes on. Eventually they were able to produce the *Description of Egypt*, a mammoth (some of the volumes are nearly 1m/3⅓-ft. squares) 20- or 37-volume (depending on the edition) set of plates and texts on just about everything in Egypt, including some dramatically large monuments and a good number of Pharoanic artifacts decorated with a mixture of pictorial symbols that remained undecipherable until the Rosetta Stone—also unearthed by the French—was translated 30 years later. Apart from their academic value, the illustrations of massive ruined temples would define Egypt for many decades in the European mind as the seat of a mysterious and powerful lost civilization.

Sensing the inevitability of embarrassing failure, Napoleon got out of Egypt in 1799, leaving his army to struggle against a combination of Ottoman and British forces. Decimated by disease and conflict, the remnants of the army he left behind were shipped back to France 2 years later.

TURNING TO EUROPE In the wake of the French retreat from Egypt, the Ottoman administration in Istanbul appointed an Albanian, Mohamed Ali, viceroy of the reclaimed province. The new ruler took power in 1805, and 6 years later liquidated what remained of the Mamlukes in a classic piece of ruthless treachery. Having invited them to dine at the Citadel, he allowed them to leave together through Bab al Azab, the gate that now lets out onto Midan al Qala, below the Citadel and in front of the

Madrasa of Sultan Hassan. Though the gate is unfortunately now sealed, you can see from the walls above that between the top and the lower gates there is a narrow defile enclosed by high walls. Once his guests were in this chute, Mohamed Ali simply had both gates closed, and from there it was a simple enough matter to have his Albanian loyalists shoot the well-fed and probably tipsy Mamlukes. Having thus eliminated the possibility of serious opposition, Mohamed Ali could set about pursuing a remarkably energetic policy of reform aimed at bringing Egypt up to military and economic parity with Europe. Though he succeeded to a great extent, building a navy and an army that was the most effective in the region and forcing the Ottoman Sultan to establish his family as the hereditary rulers of Egypt, he also spent ruinously and converted much of Egyptian agriculture to the production of cotton for sale in Europe to pay for his reforms.

Mohamed Ali died in 1849, and his successors continued the path of reform, much of it carried out by European experts, to the best of their sometimes limited abilities. Old canals were repaired and new ones dug, a postal service was founded, bridges were built across the Nile, and a magnificent opera house was built. One particular reform, however, was to have unforeseen consequences: Opening Egypt to Western expertise and investment also made it possible to start borrowing money in large quantities. Initially, harsh taxation and manipulating the cotton market had been sufficient to make ends meet, if not actually balance the budget, but soon enough the practice of borrowing money to make up for domestic shortfalls became common-place. Debts driven by the expense of modernization, a profligate elite, and 1875 Egypt's financial situation were so precarious that the country's share of the Suez Canal was sold to the British.

THE BRITISH INVASION The British seizure of power was more like a bank sending in the bailiffs to secure the assets of a failed business than a military conquest. A small force of British soldiers landed in Ismailia in the fall of 1882, ostensibly to put down an army mutiny. They were to stay in Egypt until the mid-1950s, propping up a series of rulers who were little more than facades maintained to provide local legitimacy to colonial rule.

The major development in Egypt under the British occupation was commercialized tourism. Fueled by images of ancient ruins brought back by the French expedition, Egypt quickly became a required stop on any grand tour. At first, the reserve of the wealthy few, by the end of the 19th century, with British troops on the ground in Cairo to guarantee the safety of Her Majesty's middle classes, Egypt had become open to anybody with time for a vacation and the money for passage on one of the regular liners.

Parallel to the opening of the tourist market ran the development of archaeology. This, too, began as a pastime for those wealthy enough to winter at the aptly named **Winter Palace** (p. 233) in Luxor and fund a crew of locals to dig about in what became known as the **Valley of the Kings** (p. 229). The British attempted to control the process by forming a professional antiquities service that supervised the digging and tried to ensure that the most significant pieces stayed in Egypt, but local dealers and diggers, delighted at this sudden cash market for buried leftovers, went to work, and soon enough, between local supply and foreign demand, a roaring export trade in everything from pottery to mummies had developed. It was to be after World War I before the professionals started to get a grip on the situation and qualified, institutional projects began to be favored over the efforts of the financially gifted amateurs.

Who's Who: A Guide to the Key Gods & Pharaohs

Akhenaten (1390–1352 B.C.): Though he started his reign as Amenhotep IV, this Pharaoh veered suddenly into a dramatic religious and political shift about 5 years into his reign, changing his name and establishing a new capital city at Amarna in Middle Egypt. With the new capital came a new religion, the worship of Aten. The upheaval ultimately came to nothing, as after his death, Thebes and Memphis were restored to their former positions, and religious life returned to normal.

Amun (Amun-Ra): Though worshipped as early as the 5th dynasty, it wasn't until the 11th dynasty that this god had temples dedicated to him. His importance was linked with the shift of power from the north to the Upper Egyptian city of Thebes, where he became the King of Gods. His temple at Karnak is one of the most impressive monuments in Egypt. He was usually shown as a human with a double crown, with a staff in one hand and an ankh in the other.

Anubis: The God of Mummification and Death is usually depicted as a human figure with the head of a dog or as a long-eared dog. You will see him frequently around tombs, where he protected the contents against the depredations of jackals and tomb robbers. His black coloration associates him both with the color of decaying bodies (death) and the black, fertile soil of the Nile Valley (rebirth).

Hathor: The Goddess of Joy, Music, and Love is depicted as a woman with the head of a cow, the ears of a cow, or simply with cow horns (and a sun disc) perched above her head. She was understood to be the divine mother of the reigning Pharaoh. One of her jobs was to greet and protect arrivals (the recently dead) on the West Bank of the Nile.

Hatshepsut (1473–1458 B.C.): Apparently a strong-willed and wily woman, Hatshepsut found herself widowed early and took over as regent while the heir to the throne—her dead husband's son by a concubine—was still too young to rule. She extended her power by having herself declared king and asserting her divine birth. She left behind a magnificent mortuary temple in Luxor and a reputation for fearsome independence that has made her a heroic figure in some modern feminist circles.

Horus: Horus was a multifaceted and almost ubiquitous god, of whom there were more than a dozen manifestations. One of these is the winged sun-disc that you will see over the doorways of many temples, which signifies that you are under the protection of the gods. Horus was also the falcon, and in this form you will see him all over the place, including on the EgyptAir logo.

Khufu (2589–2566 B.C.): The son of Sneferu, who had both the pyramids in Dahshur built, and the father of Khafre, for whom the second biggest pyramid on the Giza Plateau was built, Khufu (whom you may also see as Cheops) acquired a reputation for cruelty from a number of historians (including Herodotus), but he doesn't seem to have deserved it. As the builder of the largest of the pyramids, he is thought to have presided over a period of exceptional organization and centralized political power.

Nun: The God of the Primeval Waters, which were Ra's pre-creation dwelling. After order was imposed by Ra's act of spitting out Shu and Tefnut, Nun did not vanish but receded to the edge of being and became the abode of liminal beings. If you can spot the wavy-patterned paving at the edges of Karnak Temple, you will have found the realm of Nun surrounding the well-ordered and safe home of the god. If you see Nun depicted as a man bearing a solar boat laden with human figures, he is representing the underworld.

Nut: The Goddess of the Sky is seen arched over other figures, depicted as a naked woman. She was the protector of the gods and the mother of Osiris, Horus, Seth, Isis, and Nephthys.

Osiris: A god of wide-ranging powers over death and resurrection, as well as the underworld, Osiris was also the first king of humans. He is often shown as a mummy whose hands stick out through the white cloth wrapping his body and wearing a distinctive crown with twin plumes.

Ra: Ra is the god who gave birth to the first two other gods, Shu and Tefnut, and brought order to the original chaos. One of his main functions was to pilot the solar boat across the sky each day, and you will often see him seated in a boat with the rearing cobra of the sun on his head.

Ramses II (1279–1213 B.C.): This extraordinarily long-lived Pharaoh is commonly identified as the Pharaoh responsible for the plight of the Jews in the Old Testament. He left Egypt scattered with monuments to himself, including the colossal temple at Abu Simbel, the Ramesseum, and large parts of both Luxor and Karnak temples, and outlived a series of heirs.

Seth: One of the children of Geb and Nut, Seth was the God of Violence, Darkness, and Chaos. He was driven to the desert by Horus, his nephew, after he murdered his brother Osiris.

Thoth: Depicted with the head of an ibis, or sometimes just as an ibis, Thoth was the God of Wisdom and Science. It was Thoth who helped Osiris to bring civilization to mankind, and who helped Anubis with the first rites of mummification that led to Osiris's resurrection.

Tutankhamun (1336–1327 B.C.): It is one of those little historical ironies that this little-known Pharaoh, who probably ascended to the throne as a boy of about 8 years old, is now one of the most famous of all rulers of ancient Egypt. His (almost) immediate predecessor was Akhenaten, who attempted to overthrow the established political and religious order of Egypt, and Tutankhamun's reign saw its rapid reestablishment. Though he was born in Amarna, there is some doubt as to whether he was Akhenaten's son, or perhaps his brother.

The Cruelest Cut: The Tale of Two Brothers

One of the most dramatic conflicts of Egyptian mythology took place between Osiris, the god of the Underworld, and his brother Seth, the red-headed god of violence and darkness. The story developed over centuries, adding some aspects and altering others, but one of the more complete versions goes like this:

Osiris, in his human form, was a good and wise king of the humans, bringing them civilization, agriculture, and wine with the assistance of Thoth, god of wisdom. He was so popular and successful, in fact, that he aroused the jealousy of his brother Seth, who one day tricked him into laying down in an elaborately decorated coffin. Seth then sealed the coffin with hot lead so that his brother would asphyxiate, and threw it into the Nile. When Osiris's wife Isis found out about the murder, she set out to find the coffin. The first thing she found, however, was that her husband had had a brief affair with her sister, Seth's wife, and that a child had been born as a result. Fearing Seth's anger, Isis's sister had abandoned the child in the forest. Isis immediately went out and found the boy, who had (in a manner typical of the abandoned progeny of gods) been protected by wild dogs and took him in, naming him Anubis.

Eventually the coffin was found on the shores of a distant land (one account has this as the coast of Syria) and brought back to Egypt. The unremittingly vengeful Seth, however, tracked it down, and this time tore Osiris's corpse into between 14 and 42 pieces (sources vary on this point). He threw the pieces, once again, into the river.

Isis set out untiringly once again to find the body, this time traveling the length of Egypt to retrieve the pieces. Whenever she found a piece, she engaged in an elaborate ruse to conceal from Seth what she was up to. She pretended to bury the body part on the spot, but actually concealed it about her person and transported it to her home, where Anubis, with the help of Thoth, was gradually putting his uncle back together again. In the end, she found almost all the pieces—unfortunately Osiris's phallus had been eaten by a Nile carp and a fake one had to be substituted. Even so, the story had a happy ending: The reassembled Osiris was revived and was able to father Horus before ascending to heaven. Horus subsequently vanquished Seth in a series of trials and banished him to the desert.

WORLD WAR II   World War II was marked in Cairo primarily by the occupiers' need to halt the Axis drive across North Africa and the ambivalence of the support afforded them by the occupied Egyptians. The struggle came to a head in 1942 at El Alamein, a virtually empty stretch of desert on the north coast some 80km (50 miles) west of Alexandria. German and Italian tank and infantry had been making rapid eastward progress that, had it not been halted, would have resulted in them capturing strategically vital supply routes and oil supplies and dealing the Allied war effort in Europe a serious blow. Ultimately victorious at Al Alamein, however, the Allies were then able to reverse the defeats of the previous months and put an end to German and Italian ambitions in the Middle East.

THE MODERN PHARAOHS   By the end of World War II, it was clear that the era of direct colonial rule in the region was over. The process of a negotiated British withdrawal from Egypt had actually started in the mid-1930s, with treaties such as the 1936 Anglo–Egyptian Treaty, which provided for the withdrawal of British troops from the country. How the process was affected by the humiliating defeat of the Egyptian army in 1948 (assisted by the armies of Lebanon, Jordan, and Syria) in the first of several wars against the newly created neighbor state of Israel, is unclear. But, within 3 years of its retreat from the Negev Desert, a group of officers known as the Free Officers Movement, led by Gamal Abdel Nasser, were to overthrow the British-protected government of King Farouk and assume control of the country.

Nasser's group of officers, nominally headed by General Mohamed Naguib, who they initially installed as president on July 26, 1952, arrived under the banner of reform. Though numerous histories have since claimed that the coup was a reaction to the incompetence and corruption of the royal government propped up by British arms, this merely begs the question of why revolutions haven't taken place far more frequently in Egypt. Apart from a general desire to rule Egypt, and to do so unfettered by colonial interference from the British, Nasser and his followers did not arrive in office with a specific program for the country. Most of their initial moves were aimed at consolidating control, and over the next 4 years political parties were banned, foreign companies were nationalized, the Muslim Brotherhood was made illegal, and a new constitution was promulgated that gave President Nasser (who took the post from Naguib, whom he had placed under house arrest, in 1954) broad powers over government.

One of Nasser's first moves on the international stage marked a significant turning point in Egypt's relations with the West. When the World Bank backed out of a tentative agreement to fund the building of the Aswan High Dam, Nasser announced that he would nationalize the Suez Canal and use the revenues to pay for the dam. The canal was still jointly owned by the British (who had purchased Egypt's share of the waterway 80 years before) and the French, who had acquired the original concession to build it. At the same time, Egypt closed the straits of Tiran (now a prime diving spot off the coastal resort area of Sharm el Sheikh) to Israeli shipping, choking off a key supply route.

The announcement and the closure of a vital shipping lane prompted a joint British, French, and Israeli operation to attack Egyptian forces in the canal zone in the fall of 1956. They were quickly forced to withdraw by the United States, which had initially acquiesced to the plan, but not before the Egyptian military had blocked the waterway by sinking a number of ships in it. Once the forces had withdrawn, Egypt seized not only the canal but other British- and French-held businesses in the rest of the country. Nevertheless, the United Nations went in to clear the ships that had been scuttled in the canal, and the USSR subsequently funded the construction of the dam.

Nasser's apparent victory over the former colonial powers made him enormously popular in Egypt and throughout the Middle East, and made him a major force in regional politics and a leader of the pan-Arab movement. It was a reputation that took a heavy blow in 1967, however, with a second resounding Egyptian military defeat at the hands of Israel during the Six-Day War. In the wake of the loss of the entire Sinai Peninsula, Nasser tendered his resignation but stayed on after massive demonstrations of support. He died in 1970 of a heart attack.

Nasser was succeeded by his vice president, Anwar Sadat. Sadat, though expected initially to be a transitional figure, maintained his control and consolidated his position against his rivals and became a power in his own right. He reversed a number of Nasser's positions, reopening Egypt to the West and ultimately even making peace with Israel. The high point of his presidency, in the eyes of many Egyptians, came in October 1973, when Egyptian forces launched an imaginative and boldly executed attack on the well-fortified Israeli defensives on the east bank of the Suez Canal. The attack, which coincided with a massed Syrian attack on the Golan Heights, opened what came to be known as the Yom Kippur War, or the October War.

It is said that the plan for the war was the brainchild of then-president of Syria, Hafez al Assad (an extraordinarily competent politician who had been given refuge early in his career in Egypt by Nasser) and Sadat. The idea apparently was to press home a surprise attack from two sides, with Syria entering Israel from the Golan and Egyptian Forces crossing the Sinai Peninsula to retake the Negev Desert, from which they had been so ignominiously driven in 1949. What happened next is open to questions—just not the kind of questions you want to bring up with Syrians and Egyptians in the same room. To Syrian dismay, the Egyptian Army halted its advance once it had crossed the canal, unwilling to move beyond the cover of its surface-to-air missiles. The pause allowed the Israelis to stabilize new defensive lines on the peninsula and concentrate their reserves on the Syrian front, where they were hugely outnumbered. Once the Syrian advances had been reversed (the Israeli army, the IDF, got within artillery range of Damascus), their Sinai forces were able to counterattack, and by October 23 forces under Ariel Sharon had crossed the canal, encircled the Egyptian Army, and effectively had Cairo at their mercy before the UN could make a ceasefire stick.

The end-state of the 1976 war gave the Americans, as the state with the most leverage on Israel, the power to broker a peace on their terms. The result was the Camp David Accords, under which the Sinai Peninsula was largely demilitarized and the Egyptian government was handed an annual aid package second in size only to Israel's.

Sadat's presidency was abruptly cut short in 1981. He was assassinated by members of an Islamic organization that opposed his peace with Israel while reviewing troops at the annual 6th of October military parade. Lead assassin Khalid Islambouli is said to have cried "Death to the Pharaoh!" as the attack was launched from the back of a truck as Mirage jets swooped overhead. Air Force General and Vice President Hosni Mubarak then became president.

Mubarak's subsequent tenure as president has been marked mainly by holding patterns with regard to regional politics and a drift away from the socialism of the past and toward a more open economy. The state of emergency that was declared in 1981 has never been lifted, effectively freezing the interplay between legislative and judicial bodies into rigid patterns enforced by executive diktat. The result has been a general political stagnation in Egypt for 26 years, with security forces playing a steadily increasing political role as the regime has come to rely on them to stifle dissenting voices that have been denied parliamentary expression. Recent constitutional amendments appear to be aimed at further consolidating the status quo by giving legal cover to the enforcement mechanisms that support it.

2 Egypt Today

Looking at it on a map, Egypt seems vast and spread out, but, in fact, almost the whole population is concentrated in a thin green band of arable land that stretches down the Nile Valley from the High Dam to Cairo and on to Alexandria.

It broadens dramatically into the Nile Delta just below Cairo, but even so the strip of land never gets to be more than about 300km (200 miles) wide. The result is that most of the 76 million Egyptians live on about 33,000 square kilometers (13,000 sq. miles) of land, or an area only marginally bigger than the state of Maryland. With 13 times the population, however, Egypt is significantly more crowded.

DOLLARS & SENSE Economically and socially, the country struggles with deep-seated problems, most of which stem from poor planning and corruption. Looking purely at broad statistics, the economy has been doing well in recent years, with annual growth rates around 5% to 7%. What the growth numbers mask, however, is that cronyism steers just about all of that extra cash into the pockets of the wealthiest 10% of the country, while the economic policies that are driving the growth—privatization and liberalization—are meanwhile driving the cost of living for the poorest 50% of the population steadily upward. Egypt, once a huge exporter of wheat, has become the world's biggest importer, spending around $2.7 billion dollars in 2007 buying grain on the international market. Despite subsidies, anecdotal evidence suggests that the price of many staples has as much as quadrupled in the last 2 years, forcing families already at subsistence level to cut back on food purchases. There is a very real possibility that, following this path, where the rich get richer and the poor get progressively hungrier, will have a destabilizing effect on the country. It is an accepted journalistic practice at this point to balance that possibility against the immense capacity of Egyptians to get along peacefully despite the absurdities that have been foisted on them by generation after generation of corrupt and incompetent rulers. It doesn't take most people very long in the country to start scratching their heads, however, and start asking just how much more these people can take.

The good news is that the growth rate of the population seems to be leveling off. Projections indicate that by the second decade of the 21st century, there will be fewer babies than children in Egypt. Though this indicates that the population may be retreating from the disastrously explosive growth that followed World War II, it leaves the thorny question of what to do with the vast numbers of unskilled workers that the overwhelmed and underfunded public education system continues to pour into the labor pool every spring. A study a few years ago estimated that the economy would have to grow by 44% per year—an obviously unattainable number—in order to accommodate them all and make any meaningful dent in the current levels of unemployment.

Tourism continues to be the biggest earner and highest-profile employer in the Egyptian economy. The government boasts of more than 43 million "tourist nights" (1 tourist for 1 night; 2 people a week would thus count as 14, give or take), bringing in around $9 billion in 2007. The industry is heavily underwritten by foreign aid, with the United States and the European Union investing particularly heavily in the preservation of tourist-drawing monuments in Upper Egypt, attempting to protect sensitive ecosystems in tourist areas, and building infrastructure on the Sinai Peninsula. The next biggest source of money for the country is remittances by Egyptians living abroad sending their earnings home. In 2006, these amounted to more than $5 billion, much of it coming from the Gulf countries, where large numbers of Egyptians work in low-status jobs. The third source of money here is the Suez Canal, seized from the British and French by the Egyptian government in 1956. The fees paid by ships for traversing the

163km (101-mile) artificial waterway topped $4 billion in 2007.

POLITICS Politically, the country is at a point of transition, though it is unclear what comes next. The army, which seized power in 1952 and has run the country ever since, has lost much of its credibility as the engine of modernity and nationalism over decades of economic mismanagement and the loss of two wars with Israel. The current regime of Hosni Mubarak is widely unpopular and, with the president in his late 70s, the question of succession is openly raised.

Apart from the military itself, there are only two political organizations in Egypt that are capable of making a serious bid for power. The first is the National Democratic Party (NDP), usually referred to in the press as the "ruling NDP party" because it is the parliamentary arm of the Mubarak military regime. Despite substantial internal debate, it would appear that the NDP is preparing to line up behind Mubarak's son Gamal as his anointed successor. The electoral position of the NDP is shored by the security forces, which collude openly in fixing elections by beating and detaining members of the opposition and closing polling stations to their supporters.

The other viable political force in Egypt is the Muslim Brotherhood. Founded in 1928 by Hassan al Banna, the Brotherhood has been through various stages and incarnations in its 80 years of activity. Its claims to have moved beyond violence as a means of gaining power have some credibility, while its claims to having moved into a modern and democratic framework have less. It is clear that it remains a party based on Islamic principles, calling for *sharia* law to be the source of secular law and the standard by which it should be judged legitimate. It is also clear that as an organization as well as a set of principles, the Brotherhood in Egypt has widespread and deeply committed support in the population.

In order to maintain control of the country through the coming succession, the NDP needs to retain the support of the foreign community, reinvent itself as the competent custodian of Egypt's modernization, and throw off its aura of corruption and incompetence. The Brotherhood, meanwhile, will continue to present itself as a modernized, moderate party capable of taking over a secular government that can work with regional realities that it has opposed—at times violently—in the past. Their relative success will determine the course of Egyptian politics for decades to come.

THE ISLAMIC MOVEMENT Though the 1980s and 1990s saw a number of successful attacks by Islamic groups, including the assassination in 1981 of then-President Anwar Sadat, the end of the 1990s also saw Egypt put the era of homegrown Islamic-inspired terrorism, at least on a scale that could threaten the stability of the state, behind it. This was due to two factors: first, a heavy crackdown in which internal security forces killed most of the leadership and potential leadership of any remaining cells, and second, a loss of credibility and legitimacy in the economically disastrous aftermath of the Luxor attacks in 1997. Seeing the virtual disappearance of tourist revenues, very few people in Egypt were willing to support a violent solution. Those who did were easily enough picked off.

What is left now is an essentially peaceable Islamic movement, followed by broad swathes of the middle and upper-middle classes and led by the Muslim Brotherhood, but also bringing in major Islamic institutions such as Al Azhar University. The Mubarak regime continues to talk and act as though it were still facing the threat of violent terrorist groups, but this is largely political maneuvering designed to discredit the opposition and to maintain its position as the second-largest recipient of U.S. foreign aid in the world. This rhetoric represents a policy of hiding its head in the sand when it comes to the threat represented by a moderate, modernized, and politically astute Islamic movement, and points to a brighter political future for the Islamist groups than for the old-guard military.

3 Recommended Reading

These books are a good starting point to give you insight and some different perspectives on Egypt, old and new. I have tried to stick mostly with books that are available at **Diwan** or the **American University in Cairo Bookstore** (p. 117), but most should also be widely available elsewhere and online. Egyptian literature is a rich but little-known field, and the American University in Cairo Press has made its home in this niche. Serious readers will find a morning browsing the shelves of the downtown branch of its bookstore time well spent.

- Ahmed Fakhry, *Bahariyah and Farafra* (American University in Cairo Press, 2003): It's worth getting the second edition of this classic by this multi-faceted archaeologist/architect (rather than the 1974 edition) for its brief but informative introduction by Tony Mills.

- Alaa Al Aswany, *Yacoubian Building* (Harper, 2006): This book, and the film made of it, kicked up some dust in Egypt for its frank look at the lives of a cross-section of contemporary Cairene society.

- André Raymond, *Cairo: City of History* (American University in Cairo Press, 2001): One of the classic histories of the city—a must-read if you have the time and are going to be doing any walking through Cairo. Originally published in French in 1993, Willard Wood's translation is extremely readable.

- Christian Jacq, *The Battle of Kadesh* (Grand Central Publishing, 1998): This is a ripping yarn of a tale, and the middle of a five-book series about Ramses II, a Pharaoh for whom this French Egyptologist seems to have a particular penchant.

- Edward Said, *Out of Place* (Vintage Books, 1999): This is a little slice of life from 1940s Cairo—the recollections of an oddly privileged childhood from one of the more interesting commentators on the colonial and post-colonial experience.

- E. M. Forster, *Alexandria: A History and a Guide* (American University in Cairo Press, 2004): What better travel companion than the great E. M. Forster? Travel back in time without leaving your armchair and listen as he awards "the palm of gentility" to Rosetta Street for the "refined monotony of its architecture." A great book, but be prepared for disappointment if you read it before you go to the city.

- Fathi Malim, *Siwa: From the Inside* (Katan Books, 2001): This is a short-but-fascinating look at Siwa by a resident. You're not going to read this stuff anywhere else.

- Maria Golia, *Cairo: City of Sand* (Reaktion Books, 2004): Golia's engaging and incisive writing describes the experience of living in modern Cairo. This is a great airplane read and a gentle introduction to what Cairo is really about.

- Max Rodenbeck, *Cairo: The City Victorious* (Vintage, 2000): Sweeping, amusing, and intimate, Rodenbeck's highly readable volume on Cairo gets under the skin of the city like no other.

- Nabil Shawkat, *Breakfast with the Infidels* (Dar Merit, 2006): The lightly off-the-wall observations of an ex-national columnist, screen writer, and bon vivant offer a new perspective on the Egyptian experience.

- Naguib Mahfouz, *The Cairo Trilogy: Palace Walk, Palace of Desire,* and *Sugar Street* (American University in Cairo Press, 2001): Mahfouz, who won the Nobel Prize in Literature in 1988, traces the lives of three generations of an early-20th-century family. A classic, and indispensable, read for anyone seriously interested in Cairo.

- Naguib Mahfouz, *Adrift on the Nile* (American University in Cairo Press, 1999): If you don't have the time to get through a thick tome, this is one of the slimmest and most readable of Mahfouz's *oeuvre*. It tells the tale of a group of louche Bohemian wannabes and their drug-addled evenings on a Nile houseboat.

- Nawal Saadawi, *The Hidden Face of Eve* (Zed Books, 2007): Saadawi, a medical doctor from a large, rural, Egyptian family, is uniquely positioned to offer not-always-cheerful insights into the position of women in Egypt.

- Neil Hewison, *The Fayoum: History and Guide* (American University in Cairo Press, 2001): A short-but-solid guide to the Fayoum by a long-term resident of Egypt.

- Nesreen Khashan, *Encounters with the Middle East* (Travelers' Tales, 2007): This will give you a bit more of a regional perspective, and the sections on Cairo and Egypt are good and readable. Excellent for some pre-departure perspective.

- Nicholas Warner, *Guide to the Gayer-Anderson Museum* (American University in Cairo Press, 2006): An in-depth look at this extraordinary collection, and an indispensable companion on your tour.

- Ralph Bagnold, *Libyan Sands: Travel in a Dead World* (Immel, 1987): Originally published in 1935, Bagnold's accounts of his early adventures on the Sinai and later exploration of the Western Desert are the perfect read for anyone who has caught the desert bug, and it may infect those who haven't.

- Robert Armour, *Gods and Myths of Ancient Egypt* (American University in Cairo Press, 1986): This is a handy guide that you can shove in your backpack and use as a who's-who as you wander through tombs.

- Salima Ikram, *Divine Creatures* (American University in Cairo Press, 2005): Everything that you ever wanted to know about mummies (and then some), with a twist: These are mummified animals, buried with their owners or just on their own.

- Samir Raafat, *Cairo, the Glory Years* (Harpocrates, 2003): Really the only book out there on the villas of 19th-century Cairo; Raafat knows his stuff.

- Sonallah Ibrahim, *Zaat* (American University in Cairo Press, 2004): Deliciously biting satire from my favorite living Egyptian novelist. Not only is it more readable than most of his competitors, it will give you a distinct sense of the ironies and perplexities of life in this country.

- T. G. H. James, *Howard Carter: The Path to Tutankhamun* (Tauris, 1992): This is far more of a tour through the world of 19th- and early-20th-century archaeology—the people, the places, and the things—than the title suggests. Not a quick read, but well worth some time.

4 Egyptian Food & Drink

ETIQUETTE

Egyptians are incredibly sociable on the whole and fantastic hosts. In fact, in order to survive an invitation to eat in an Egyptian house, you need to keep in mind a couple of vital self-defense tips.

First, it's your host's duty to see that you're well-fed, and well-fed people do not leave an empty plate in front of them. It is fatal, therefore, to try to do as you were told as a child and clean your plate. However much you protest, it will be filled again. Rule number one: When you don't want any more food, leave your plate half-full and push it away. Rule number two, then, is only eat half the food on your plate—make a space and refill it. This allows you to control the supply.

Egyptians tend not to drink while they eat, but they'll often finish off with something sweet, like a soft drink. If you need to wash down your food, you may well have to alert your host. Don't be afraid to ask. Guests who ask will receive, and receive copiously.

Being on time isn't very important. In fact, showing up at least 15 minutes after the appointed time is expected. Be sensitive to the fact, however, that because you're a foreigner, an effort will probably be made to start at the appointed time. Double-guessing like this is inevitable and causes great confusion and hilarity.

Showing up with a gift is important. Flowers are perfect, chocolates are great, and even a bottle of wine is fine, but only if you're visiting a Christian household.

FOOD

Egypt's best-known foods are drawn from a peasant menu, a heavy carbohydrate diet emphasizing economical but tasty and filling ingredients such as beans, pasta, and rice. Even wealthy Egyptian families, while eating meat dishes, will serve some of these with most meals.

Koshari, a distinctly Cairene specialty, is typical: a pile of rice and macaroni topped with lentils and garnished with hot sauce and fried onions. A big bowl of this will keep you going all day long. Every truly Egyptian breakfast, meanwhile, includes a bowl of simmered fava beans. Known as *fuul,* these come cooked in a variety of ways, including spicy Alexandrian and the blander Cairene, but they should always be accompanied by fresh-baked loafs of flat **aish baladi** bread. *Molakheya,* unlike the generally well-liked *koshari* or *fuul* dishes, is an acquired taste. A green, gluey, soup-like dish made of Jew's mallow, it is usually served with rabbit or chicken and a side of rice. If you're lucky enough to be in Egypt in the spring around the time of *Shem el Nessim,* you may find yourself invited to try **fessikh,** a cured fish dish made of raw-but-aged salt mullet. Prepared correctly, it is palatable. Prepared incorrectly, however, it is dangerously poisonous and can be fatal. There's no way to test it other than trial and error. On a happier note, be sure to try **hamaam** (pigeon) or the somewhat meatier **samaan** (quail); they're delicious grilled and sprinkled with fresh lime, the same way they've been eaten since the time of the Pharaohs.

Um Ali, a flavorful mix of pastry, cream, coconut, raisins, and nuts, is the best-known Egyptian dessert. The origins of the name are subject to much friendly dispute. My favorites include an Irish nurse named O'Malley who, allegedly a mistress of Khedive Ismael, cooked him an Egyptian bread pudding.

DRINKS

Inevitably, you'll find yourself invited for a cup of tea or coffee in Egypt. Basic courtesy demands it from anyone who sits down with you, not to mention shopkeepers and businesspeople at meetings.

You may well be served before or after meals.

Coffee, or **ahwa,** is drunk all day and all night long from little cups and is thick, black, and strong. Milk is not an option, and it comes at four main sweetness levels. No sugar at all is *sada; wasat,* which means "medium," will get you something moderately sweet; *hellwa,* which means "sweet," will get you a sweet dessert of a coffee; and *zee-yada,* which simply means "extra," will result in something that, for most people, is unbearably syrupy.

Tea, or **shai,** comes in an even greater variety. As a foreigner and a guest, you will generally be treated to *shai fetla,* which literally means "thread tea" but refers to the tea bag (which hangs from a thread). *Shai kosheri* is a rougher variant with a spoonful of loose tea at the bottom of the glass. You will be asked how many sugars you want in it. There may also be mint on offer. Tea with mint *(shai bi-nana)* is a popular variant, or you can have just straight mint in hot water *(nana)* if you want to avoid caffeine. Another good decaf option is *yansoon,* which is anise, or *urfa,* cinnamon. You are also sure at some point to be offered *kirkadeh,* which comes either hot or cold. This is a bright red drink made from hibiscus. It has a pleasingly tart taste when left unsweetened and is said to lower blood pressure, so don't stand up too quickly after a few glasses on a hot day.

Finally, there is the ubiquitous *haga sa',* which just means "something cold" and refers to cans or bottles of refrigerated soft drinks.

5 Architecture

As you drive into Cairo from the airport, you may wonder whether there is anything beautiful left in Cairo. The last 60 years in Egypt have seen the flowering of what can only be described as the architecture of corruption: With planning permission for anything easily bought, and the pressure of explosive population growth driving builders to put up the cheapest and biggest buildings as quickly as possible, the city has almost vanished underneath shoddily built cement highrises that are stained with pollution and that flake and crumble starting the day after they're built. Look a little more carefully, however, and you will start to see that, amongst the jumble and collapse, there are 1,000-year-old domes and minarets that have stood since before the days of Charlemagne.

The best way to begin to make sense of the welter of styles around the city is to take a brief skim through the history of the city as it's told by a few significant buildings. By picking out the details that make them unique and tying them with buildings from other periods, you can have a richer Cairo experience.

ANCIENT EGYPT Any architectural tour of Egypt should start with the great pyramid of Khufu on the Giza plateau. Pause for a moment to consider it not as simply a gigantic heap of rock, or a historical monument so photographed it has been familiar to you since childhood, but as a very large public work of art. The symmetry and proportions are a stunning combination of grandiosity and simplicity and make much that followed seem somewhat overweening by comparison.

Some of the most impressive artifacts of later Pharoanic periods are the temples. You'll notice after visiting a few that they tend to follow a standard pattern. Remember as you enter that you are being led on a symbolic journey from the mundane world of the living, a world of space and light, to the realm of the gods. Notice how spaces become more cramped, with ceilings lowering and sometimes the floor coming up as well, and the light is more restricted as you penetrate toward the core of the temple. The main entrance is through the middle of a massive wall, called a *pylon*. When the temple was in use, the pylon would have been topped by a row of colorful flags that snapped and waved in the breeze. Inside, you'll find yourself in a courtyard. Beyond the courtyard, a densely columned *hypostyle* (a Greek term that simply means "supported by pillars"—it refers to the roof of the hall) hall that was originally roofed and only dimly lit by small, high windows. At the back of the hall there is the *barque* of the god, the place his or her representation was set for ceremonies. Beyond the *barque* is the *naos,* an enclosed cabinet—the smallest and darkest place in the whole temple—where the representation of the god was kept.

You will find these patterns played out over and over again, at places such as Luxor Temple, Karnak (though keep in mind here that it was built and enlarged by successive rulers), and Edfu.

The people who built the temples, meanwhile, weren't living in them, of course. It should come as no surprise, however, that a society as sophisticated as the Egyptians', and with as much engineering knowledge and architectural finesse, developed very comfortable domestic housing. By the Middle Kingdom, three- and even four-story urban houses were common, with amenities that would not be developed in Europe for more than 3,000 years. Ruins show that a central courtyard, or large room with a high, column-supported ceiling, was common, as well as stairwells to contain internal staircases, comfortable bedrooms, and tiled bathrooms with running water.

ISLAMIC ARCHITECTURE
Cairo has one of the richest collections of Islamic architecture in the world, with major examples of architecture from the earliest days of the Muslim Empire. As you wander through their courtyards and admire the arches, towers, and decorations that make these magnificent structures some of the greatest religious monuments in the world, noticing a few simple aspects will help you locate yourself in a sometimes-confusing mass of historical details.

The single easiest feature to pick out when you look at a mosque are its minarets—the towers from which the call to prayer is issued five times a day. Almost every mosque has at least one. Interestingly, the first mosque in Egypt (in Africa, for that matter), the mosque of Amr Ibn al As (named for the leader of the army that successfully defeated the Byzantine defenders of Egypt in 640), was built without minarets. They were added some 30 years after the mosque was first built and have been rebuilt several times since. The design of the minarets that you will see, however, changes quite clearly over time. They start with the simple, square Ayyubid tower with a veranda, on top of which there is a second, slightly more elaborate stage with a simple dome on top. The Mamlukes elaborated on this with two, or even three, separate stages above the first veranda. The pencil-shaped Ottoman minarets, meanwhile, represent a visually striking contrast with their predecessors. Know your minarets, then, and you'll know the period of the mosque you're looking at.

The other fairly easy and reliable clues can be had by looking at the shape of the door and window arches. Pointed arches, which you will see in many periods, came into use early, but the "keel arch" that you see in the porticos at Al Azhar was a distinctly Fatimid innovation. With Mamluke designs, however, you begin to see square windows, and windows picked out with bands of different-colored stones.

One of my favorite mosques anywhere is the Ibn Tulun mosque in Cairo. This is pretty much all that remains of a whole city that was built by the short-lived Tulu-nid dynasty (868–902). Its character is derivative of what was going on in Mesopotamia, the seat of the Abbasid rule and center of the Islamic world at the time, and it's often referred to as being in "Iraqi-style." There are a few things to notice as you enter. First is the *ziyada*. This literally means "extra"—you'll hear it used when people order coffee; it means "extra sugar"—but in this case it refers to the extra land that lies like a moat around the mosque. This separates the mosque, as a holy place, from the hassle and noise of the marketplace, and gives the whole building a tranquil quietness.

The next item to note is the plaster decoration—the arches are crusted with carved stucco. These touches are directly imported from Samarra in Mesopotamia, now modern Iraq. Finally, check out the minaret. The design, with its outside staircase, is another distinctly Samarran touch, and it's unlikely that you'll see another like it in the city.

You can also get a good idea of many of these features if you visit the Mosque of Al Hakim, which is next to the Bab al Futuh. Both the gate and the mosque are Fatimid, which is to say they were built around a century later than the Mosque of Ibn Tulun; the latter was built between 876 and 879, while the former was built between 990 and 1013. Al Hakim was known as "The Mad" because of some of the edicts he issued, which included banning *molakheya* and shoes. His mosque fell into disuse after his death and was used as a prison and a stable, among other things, until the early 1980s, when it was subjected to an unfortunately heavy-handed restoration. Like Ibn Tulun, but few mosques after this time, it was "con-gregational," which means it enclosed a large central courtyard that was intended to hold the whole population of the surrounding town. Note particularly the minaret with an internal staircase.

Though the Mosque of Ibn Tulun has distinct features, it also has similarities with other mosques, such as the *mihrab,* the niche in the wall that indicates the direction of Mecca. Originally there was a single *mihrab,* above which is written the standard Muslim opening to prayer, "There is no god but God, and Mohamed is the messenger of God," but over the years, several more have been added. Note also the *minbar,* or wooden pulpit, reached by a set of stairs, from which the Friday sermon was delivered. The central courtyard is also a feature of some later mosques, such as Al Hakim, but they gradually disappeared over time.

Al Azhar is probably the most famous of Cairo's Fatimid mosques, though it has been added to and reworked so much that it's unfair to credit any particular dynasty now with the whole. The entrance is typically Mamluke, but the central courtyard is all Fatimid. Note par-ticularly how the "keel arch" of the porti-cos contrast with the pointed Mamluke arches.

When it comes to Mamluke- and Ottoman-style architecture, Cairo pro-vides a lovely juxtaposition in the Madrasa of Sultan Hassan and the Mosque of Mohamed Ali. The massive *madrasa* is located immediately below the Citadel where, almost 5 centuries later, Mohamed Ali would build his mosque.

The *madrasa* is a great example of Mamluke architecture. Not only does it have typical minarets, with multiple upper stages, but the sheer mass of it shows the Mamluke tendency to overawe with size. Inside, the big difference from the earlier buildings is that the congrega-tional layout had been left far behind in favor of a cruciform plan in which the central courtyard opens into four enor-mous *liwans,* covered spaces that are enclosed on three sides. Each *liwan* was devoted to one of the four *madrasas* that existed here, and the doors on the back walls lead to student accommodations. Decorative glass lamps would have hung for illumination, and the stone paneling is also fairly typical of Mamluke buildings.

The Mosque of Mohamed Ali, meanwhile, is immediately identifiable from any angle as an Ottoman mosque, and will look familiar to anyone who has visited Istanbul. Even from below you can see its large dome and tall, thin minarets. If you do visit the Citadel, and go inside the mosque, check out the distinctly Turkish ablution area in the middle of the courtyard. Inside the huge dome of the mosque (supposedly it can take 6,500 people), you will also note the total absence of the *liwan*. This feature, which creates a lovely space to lounge in the cool of the evening or have your packed breakfast, was instead absorbed into Ottoman domestic architecture. You will note fine examples of this if you visit the **Gayer-Anderson Museum** (p. 96) next to the Ibn Tulun mosque, or Beit Harrawi behind Al Azhar Mosque.

MODERN ARCHITECTURE Modern architecture in Egypt has been more a search for direction than the practice of an established art. Initially, there was a wistful riffling through the centuries, exemplified in the pastiche of Manial Palace or the confused eclecticism of Sakakini Palace. After World War II, however, a kind of defensive nationalism seems to have gripped the government planners. Despite the presence of promising themes such as the simple and effective forms used by Hassan Fathy in his projects around Luxor, the result in the end was either gigantic Soviet-inspired monoliths such as the Mugama that dominates Tahrir Square or a kind of neo-Pharaonic revivalism that never made it past theme-park caricature, embodied by the new Constitutional Court near Maadi.

One of the most depressing aspects of modern Egyptian buildings is that, in the search for modern forms, building practices have also abandoned millennia-old designs that combined carefully calibrated airflows and evaporative cooling to regulate the temperature. You would be forgiven for elevating your eyes on your way out of town to the pyramids at Giza, and forgiven for looking over and above the slums that now ring the city and toward the desert where the pristine forms of the pyramids hang in the dirty air as though suspended over the unfortunate sprawl that constitutes most of Cairo. Here, cheap, high-density concrete buildings have been built willy-nilly, and with their big flat sides and sunbaked roofs catching the heat of the sun, they need the air-conditioners that hang from every possible window. The burden that the air-conditioners alone place on an already overstretched electricity grid is bad enough, without considering that, thousands of years ago, these same lands held simple, sustainable housing sufficient to the needs of the workers and artisans who built monuments that combined sophisticated engineering and elegant design in a way that is about as close to timeless as anything that mankind has built.

6 Arts & Crafts

BLOWN GLASS Glass making was a craft raised to an art during the Mamluke period. Nowadays, there are only a few people left doing the work, and their products are limited to simple tableware. Made with recycled glass bought from the rubbish collectors and mixed to produce browns, white, and greens, most of the pieces are bubbled and fragile but quite charming. Take care when you pack them or they won't survive the trip home. On the other hand, you may well be handed a lot finer glass (usually little perfume bottles), along with a tale about its being the genuine handmade Egyptian article; this is not true.

CARPETS   Egypt's not a great place for a carpet aficionado to be digging around for the real deal, but the carpet factories around the city produce some fine stuff from imported New Zealand wool if you just want a souvenir to throw on the floor back home. You'll see three basic types. First, there are copies of traditional Afghani, Iranian, and Turkish patterns; these can be of reasonable quality, but be aware that they are not real, so don't be bilked into paying real prices for them. Then there are cheesy scenes, usually from a generic Mamluke-esque period past involving layabouts, ruffians, and farm animals. Finally, you'll see flat-weave rugs done in a deliberately "naïve" style, usually depicting a Nilotic scene. Just about the only "genuine" rugs and wall hangings that you'll see are the Bedouin-woven camel's-hair blankets and rugs; designs are extremely simple, often no more than strips of beige or brown, and the texture is very hard.

INLAID WOOD   The production of little inlaid boxes, once the field of highly skilled artisans, has been raised to a semi-industrial level in Cairo to serve the tourist trade. All around Khan al Khalili the Al Hussein district is dense with shops employing a handful of workers churning out piles of them. That said, many are beautiful and they certainly have a long heritage. Check carefully when you buy to make sure that what you think is bone or mother-of-pearl inlay is not actually plastic, however.

JEWELRY   When you go shopping in Cairo, keep in mind that there are several different markets for jewelry in Egypt, each with its own clientele and price range. The biggest local market is for fairly simple gold jewelry that is bought by, or for, women as a secure and portable saving instrument that they can take into (and out of) marriage. These are the pieces that you will see being sold by the gram in local jewelry stores around town. Then there are the smaller, and considerably higher-end, boutique markets in Egyptian jewelry by local designers such as Azza Fahmy and Suzanne al Masry, who are gaining an international reputation for work that draws on and modernizes traditional forms. Their pieces are sold through discreet stores in Cairo to an international clientele. Then again, the ancient Egyptians produced some startlingly refined gold work that included colorful enamels and inlays, and in the tourist souks, such as Khan al Khalili, you'll find some first-rate imitations of these. Like the simpler gold work for the local market, these pieces are sold by the gram and should be stamped with the purity of the gold. Finally, there is some very attractive Bedouin jewelry for sale. Don't believe what you're told about age—the old stuff has pretty well all been bought up now—or about the purity of the metal, but appreciate the designs.

KHAMEYA   Many of the souks and handicraft stores in Egypt sell this traditional appliqué work. Historically it was used to decorate tents used in marriage and festival gatherings, but it is now made for the tourist market in the form of cushion covers, bedspreads, and quilts. The source of much of the work is the Tentmakers' Souk (p. 99) across from Bab Zuweila. Traditional and nontraditional designs are fairly easy to pick out. Traditional colors include vivid red, yellow, green, blue, black, and white. Geometric Islamic designs have been used for centuries, while something with Nefertiti's head on it was probably made purely for the tourist market. Examine the stitching carefully if the difference between machine and handwork is important to you: Hand-stitching may be impressively regular, but keep in mind that the length of the thread is limited by the length of the sewer's arm; look for knots, not necessarily irregular work.

MASHRABEYA   Keep a sharp eye out in Cairo, and you'll see these screens made of turned wood covering windows and dividing rooms. Traditionally, it was used as part of a natural air-conditioning system: The wood screen at once blocked the heat of the sun and allowed the breeze to flow through the window to an unglazed pottery container of water. The water seeping out through the walls of the vessel and evaporating kept the contents cool and lowered the temperature of the air that then blew through the house. Though its usefulness has obviously dwindled with the introduction of glass windows, it continues to be made into screens, picture frames, trays, and a variety of other decorative items. If you think you can fit it in your bag, it makes a great souvenir.

METALWORK   This is one trade that seems to have been practiced uninterruptedly since Pharaonic times in Egypt. There is a great show made of the industry in Khan al Khalili, with artisans banging away at huge copper trays etched with scenes of Cairo life. You will also find a huge variety of water jugs and coffee pots, lamps, braziers, candlesticks, and vases for sale. Exercise caution if you're thinking of buying anything "antique": The Cairene expertise in metalwork is matched by their expertise in aging metal to make something produced the week before look as though it's been in the family since Sultan Hassan the Mad was Caliph.

PAPRYUS   Apparently the ancient art of making this course, paper-like material out of pounded stems was lost until it was revived by Hassan Ragab in the 1960s. It is now for sale almost everywhere you look in downtown Cairo and Luxor, painted with an amazing variety of scenes copied, with greater and lesser verisimilitude, from the walls of temples and tombs. Easy and light to pack or ship, attractive and reasonably priced, these make great gifts and souvenirs. Beware the banana leaf imitations; these are coarser, darker, less supple, and a lot cheaper.

PERFUME & INCENSE   This is an industry that goes back to the days of the Pharaohs but is now unfortunately best avoided unless you really know your stuff. Someone will inevitably try to usher you into a store with hundreds of rows of dusty little bottles lining the walls. There you will drink tea and hear the story of the sun-drenched herb garden owned by the shopkeeper's grandfather. While granddad may have had a garden, the products on the shelf are more likely to be cheap imports thinned out with glycerin.

A better bet is the incense that's sold in any spice store or souk. Though you can find modern manufactured sticks, the more traditional kind, which are sprinkled on hot coals, make for more interesting souvenirs. These are made of a mix of myrrh, frankincense, sandalwood, and ambergris and smell absolutely delicious.

Appendix B:
Useful Terms & Phrases

The official language of Egypt is Arabic, though many people, especially if they work in the tourist industry, speak enough English to get by. The social rewards of learning even just a few words, however, are enormous, and you'll find yourself embraced (literally quite a lot of the time) for your efforts.

Egyptian Arabic is a national dialect that is significantly different from the Arabic of Lebanon, Syria, Tunisia, or any of the other neighboring countries. Complicating matters is that there are a number of registers: the classical Arabic of the Koran, the transnational Modern Standard Arabic (MSA) of the educated upper classes and written work, and the *amaya* Arabic of everyday use. The three share grammar, but vocabulary is a matter as much of difference as it is overlap. Then, of course, there are differences stemming from area and socio-economic grouping. Bedouins on the Sinai, for example, will pronounce the letter "jeem" (as it is known in MSA) as a short *j*, while a resident of the Delta will pronounce it as a soft *g*. Meanwhile, a resident of Upper Egypt will pronounce the MSA letter "qaf" (a sort of heavy *k*) as *g*, while residents of Cairo will replace it with a glottal stop.

One of the oddest things you'll notice if you speak the slightest bit of Arabic in Egypt is that locals will often switch into whatever level of MSA they can muster. The result is instant confusion on all sides. A few notes on pronunciation:

- "A" is pronounced like the *a* in *art*.
- "Aa" is a longer sound and is pronounced like the *a* in *ma'am*.
- "A'"–or "ain," is a short, hard but strangled "*a*."
- "Kh" is pronounced like the *ch* in *loch*.
- "Hh" is an unvoiced *h* and comes out as a puff of air.
- ' is a glottal stop; imagine somebody poking a finger into your esophagus.
- "S" is pronounced like the *s* in *soft*, not like in *is*.

What Goes Around . . .

European languages, particularly Spanish, and Arabic have a huge number of cognates. Many words that begin with "al" or "el," for example, come from Arabic (alcohol, alchemy, algebra, almanac, elixir), but there are some odder examples as well. The word *hazard* was picked up and brought back by crusaders who learned to say *"haza!"* for luck as they threw their die. Crusaders also brought back a variety of essential words for luxuries, including *sugar* (from *sukr*), *sherbet* (from *shorba*), and *gauze* (which came from Gaza). My own favorites include *admiral,* which comes from either *emir al bahr* (commander of the sea) or *emir al rahl* (commander of transport), and *floozy,* which came back with the British soldiers who frequently came across Egyptian women offering their favors in return for *falous,* or money.

Hieroglyphs: An Ancient Mystery

When Napoleon invaded Egypt in 1798, he arrived as well prepared to deal with a foreign culture as any invader has ever been. Apart from his soldiers and planners, he brought along 167 experts on just about everything that Europe had expertise in at that point: There were linguists, mathematicians, astronomers, surveyors, doctors, Arabists—the list could go on. One thing they found, however, stumped them entirely: the strange picture-script known as hieroglyphs, found all over the tombs and ancient temples.

The French experts weren't the first to try to figure out the language. For at least 2 centuries, Europeans had been scratching their heads over the code, and though some progress had been made—by the time of the invasion, a German named Carsten Niebhur was correctly postulating that the signs had alphabetic value and that the Coptic language might be the key to unlock their meaning—the end was nowhere in sight. A major part of the problem was that nobody had used the signs for a long time. Hieroglyphs had gradually slipped out of use during the Roman era, and the last inscription that we know of that made use of them was made at the Temple of Isis near Aswan (p. 249) in A.D. 394, so there was nobody around to help.

In the end, the break came with the discovery of the Rosetta Stone, a large slab of black stone on which the same text was repeated in three different scripts, including hieroglyphs, by French soldiers refurbishing a fort in the coastal town of El Rashid. Its final decipherment is now generally credited to a French prodigy named Jean-Francois Champollion, who realized, by cross-referencing the Greek text and hieroglyphs of the Rosetta Stone, that each ancient symbol must have a dual meaning—both a sound and thing. On September 14, 1822, he managed to decipher the name "Ramses" in a cartouche, whereupon he is supposed to have yelled, "I've got it!" and fainted.

1 Basic Vocabulary

ENGLISH-ARABIC PHRASES

A lot of social interaction takes the form of standard greeting and response patterns. Just saying a casual hello takes a lot longer, culturally, in Egypt than it does in the West. You'll find that Egyptians will appreciate your taking the time to say hello properly. This not only means saying hello, but enquiring after everyone's health and well-being.

English	Arabic
Yes	Ay-wa/naam
No	La'
Thank you	Shokran
No thanks	La' shokran
Sorry	Assif/assfa (M/F)
Go away	Imshi

English	Arabic
God willing	In-sha-la
Hello	**Salam alaykoom**
Response	**Wa alaykoom salam**
Good morning	**Sabahh el kheer**
Good morning (response)	the same or **Sabah el foll**
Good evening	**Massa' el kheer**
Good evening (response)	the same or **Massa' el foll**
Welcome	**Ahhlan wa sahhlan**
Response	**Ahh-lan beek/beeki** (M/F)
Greetings	**Marhaba**
How are you?	**Izayak/izayik?** (M/F)
Good	**Quie-iss**
Praise God	**Al hum-duleh-la**
Great	**Zay al foll**
What's new?	**Akhbarak eh?/akhbarik eh?** (M/F)
What's your name?	**Is-mak eh?/is-mik eh?** (M/F)
What's his name?/What's it called?	**Is-mo eh?**
My name is	**Is-mee** [your name]
No problem	Mish-mishkella
Where are you from?	**Inta min-ayn/Inti min-ayn?** (M/F)
I'm from	**Ana min** [country]
It's a pleasure to have met you	**Forsa sai-eeda**
I'm honored (response)	**Ana as-ad**
Good-bye	**Ma-salama**

NUMBERS

0	**sifr**	16	**sittaasher**
1	**wahed**	17	**sabataasher**
2	**itnain**	18	**tamantaasher**
3	**talaata**	19	**tissataasher**
4	**arbaa'**	20	**ashreen**
5	**khamsa**	30	**tala-teen**
6	**sitta**	40	**arba-een**
7	**saba'**	50	**khamseen**
8	**tamanya**	60	**sitteen**
9	**tissa**	70	**saba-een**
10	**ashera**	80	**tamaneen**
11	**hadaasher**	90	**tissa-een**
12	**itnaasher**	100	**mia**
13	**talataasher**	200	**mee-tain**
14	**arabataasher**	1,000	**alf**
15	**khamsataasher**	2,000	**alfayn**

DAYS OF THE WEEK, PERIODS OF TIME
The week starts on Sunday, and the weekend is Friday and Saturday. You'll notice if you compare the names of the days to the numbers (above) that they are simply numbered sequentially. Days of the week are usually preceded by the word *yom*, meaning "day."

Sunday	**yom al had**
Monday	**yom al it*nayn***
Tuesday	**yom al tal*aat***
Wednesday	**yom al arba'**
Thursday	**yom al khamees**
Friday	**yom al goma'**
Saturday	**yom as-sebt**
Day/days	**yom/ayam**
Week/weeks	**isbu- a'/asabee-a'**
Month/months	**shahr/shahour**
Today	**an-nahar-da**
Yesterday	**imber-ihh**
Tomorrow	**boukra**
Now	**dil-wa'atee/al-an**
Later	**badayn**

STATEMENTS OF FACT
I don't understand	**ana mish fa-him/ana mish fahhma** (M/F)
I'm sick	**Ana ay-*yan*/Ana ay-*yana***
I like	**Ana beheb**
I don't like	**Ana mabeh-bish**
I am allergic	**Ana andee hasasiya**
to nuts	**min mukassarat**
to penicillin	**min benisilin**
to aspirin	**min asbirin**

ASKING QUESTIONS
What?	**eh?**
Who?	**meen?**
When?	**imta?**
Where?	**fayn?**
How?	**zay?**
Excuse me (asking for attention)	**lo sa*maht*?/lo sa*mahti*?** (M/F)
I want/I would like	**ana a'iz/a'iza** (M/F) [thing]
I'm looking for	**ana badowar** [thing]
the Four Seasons Hotel	**al fundu' Four Seasons**
a taxi	**taks**

Where is	**wayn al** [thing]
the grocery store	**ba'ala**
the gas station	**benzeena**
What does that mean?	**yanni eh?**
How?	**Zey?** (also a mild expression of disbelief)
How do I get to	**ana unzil** [place] **zay?**
the Corniche	**corniche zay?**
What time is it?	**sa' kam?**
It is . . .	**sa'** [number]

INSULTS

You may find yourself on the receiving end of derogatory comments, delivered with a smile on the assumption that you will not understand. Knowing a few will help you understand what's going on and gauge the atmosphere around you. All the words listed here are derogatory in Egypt.

'assal   honey, an easy woman
homar/hameer   donkey/donkeys
kelb/kelab   dog/dogs
khawaga   foreigner
khawal   homosexual, feminine, weak
ghabee/aghbiya   idiot/idiots
sharmuta/sharameet   prostitute/prostitutes

2 Menu Terms

English	Arabic
breakfast	**iftar**
check/bill	**hisab**
dinner	**asha**
enough	**kifaya**
more	**kamaan**

DISHES

kosheri   a mix of macaroni, lentils, and fried onions topped with hot sauce

mashi   usually *wara ainab* (below), but the outer wrapping of this stuffed vegetable dish can be made with cabbage *(croom)* or baby zucchini *(kosa)* as well

molokheya   gluey, green soup-like sauce made from Jew's Mallow; served with chicken or rabbit

ta-gine   a traditional oven-baked, tomato-based casserole, often with meat and sometimes with fish

tameya   fava beans mashed and deep-fried in balls; similar to falafel

wara ainab   literally "grape leaves," these are like Greek dolmades, stuffed with a combination of rice, onion, and (often but not always) a little meat

ACCOMPANIMENTS

butter	*zib*da
cheese	*gib*na
chickpea paste	*ho*mous
flat bread	a'ish
white	a'ish shami
whole wheat	a'ish baladi
French fries	pa*ta*tas
yogurt	za*bad*i
sesame seed paste	ta*hi*na

FRUIT & VEGETABLES

apple	tefah
apricot	mish-mish
banana	moez
date	*ba*lahh
eggplant puree	baba*ganou*
fava beans	fuul
fig	teen
lemon	lay*moon*
orange	bar*tuaan*
peach	kokh
pineapple	ana*nas*
pomegranate	ru*maan*
strawberry	fir*aula*
watermelon	ba*teekh*

MEAT

chicken	fir-*akh*
egg	bayd
fish	samak
meat	*lahh*-ma
grilled meat on a skewer	ke*bab*
ground meat shaped around a skewer	kofta
chunks of chicken grilled on a skewer	shish ta*wook*

DRINKS

anise drink	yansoon
beer	bira
locally produced non-alcoholic beer; tastes like the real thing	Birrel

coffee (Turkish)	**ahhwa**
sweet coffee	**ahhwa helwa**
medium-sweet coffee	**ahhwa wasat**
coffee with no sugar	**ahhwa saada**
hibiscus drink	**kerkaday**
juice	**a'seer**
milk	**leban**
soft drink	**haga saa'**
tea	**shai**
w/tea bag	**shai fetla**
w/tea leaves	**shai kosheri**
mint tea	**nana**
water	**maiya**
bottled water	**maiya madeneya**
wine	**na*beeth***
red wine	**na*beeth* ahh**mar
white wine	**na*beeth* abiyad**

3 Travel Terms

DIRECTIONS

ala yameen   to the right

ala shi-mel/ala yassar   to the left

fo'   up or above

wara'   behind

wara es-shams   middle of nowhere

uddam al   in front of [thing]

khush   go

ala tool   straight

henna   here

khush yameen min henna   go right here

HOTEL ROOMS

fundu'   hotel

ghurfa   room

Andak/andik [thing]? (M/F)   Do you have . . . ?

ghurfa fadya?   an empty room?

Bikam?   How much?

tareekh   date

an na-harda   today

Mumkin at*farag*-ha?   Can I see it?

takif/mukae-yif   air-conditioning/air-conditioned

. . . Comes Around

Though for centuries Europeans absorbed Arabic into their languages, the flow now goes the other way. *Televizeon, otobus,* and *batatis* (potato) are all fairly obvious. My favorites though are *firen-geh* (which you don't hear in Egyptian, mind you), a now archaic word referring to the Franks, which came to refer generically to foreigners. The word recently got recycled into popular culture as the womanizing traders of *Star Trek: the Next Generation.* Another good one is something you'll hear every day on the streets of Zamalek. It is the cry of the junk and used clothing dealer as he pushes his cart along, announcing his wares: "Roba vecchia! Roba vecchia!" (from Italian, meaning "old clothes").

ghurfa mukae-yifa   air-conditioned room

marwaha   fan

hamam   toilet

leila *wah*ada   one night

DESCRIPTORS

Simply tack these adjectives after nouns (for example, cheap room = *fundu' arkhees*)

arkhees   cheap

ghalee   expensive

Ghalee giddan!   That's expensive!

hali   free

faadi   empty

kabeer   big

sagheer   small

OTHER USEFUL NOUNS

mataar   airport

sareer   bed

beera   beer

agala   bike

arabeya   car

hes-*sab*   restaurant check/bill

bab   door

bab al reisi   main door/entrance

saffara   embassy

   saffarat Amrikeya   American embassy

   saffarat Canadeya   Canadian embassy

   saffarat Britaneya   British embassy

benzene   gas/petrol

benzeena   gas station

moustashfa   hospital

fallous   money

methaf   museum

sayidalaya   pharmacy

mat'am   restaurant

ughfa/ghurfa (plural)   room/rooms

mahata   station

mahatet otobees   bus station

mahatet al 'atr   train station

taks   taxi

haga   thing

walla haga   nothing

maiya   water

maiya madaneya   mineral water

Index

See also Accommodations and Restaurant indexes, below.

GENERAL INDEX

ACCOMMODATIONS

Restaurants

Explore over 3,500 destinations.

Frommers.com makes it easy.

Find a destination. ✓ Book a trip. ✓ Get hot travel deals.
✓ a guidebook. ✓ Enter to win vacations. ✓ Listen to podcasts. ✓ Check out
e latest travel news. ✓ Share trip photos and memories. ✓ And much more.

Frommers.com

The new way to get AROUND town.

Make the most of your stay. Go Day by Day!

The all-new Day by Day series shows you the best places to visit and the best way to see them.

- Full-color throughout, with hundreds of photos and maps
- Packed with 1–to–3–day itineraries, neighborhood walks, and thematic tours
- Museums, literary haunts, offbeat places, and more
- Star-rated hotel and restaurant listings
- Sturdy foldout map in reclosable plastic wallet
- Foldout front covers with at-a-glance maps and info

The best trips start here.   ***Frommer's***®

A Branded Imprint of ⓦ**WILEY**
Now you know.

A Guide for Every Type of Traveler

Frommer's Complete Guides

For those who value complete coverage, candid advice, and lots of choices in all price ranges.

Pauline Frommer's Guides

For those who want to experience a culture, meet locals, and save money along the way.

MTV Guides

For hip, youthful travelers who want a fresh perspective on today's hottest cities and destinations.

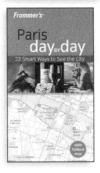

Day by Day Guides

For leisure or business travelers who want to organize their time to get the most out of a trip.

Frommer's With Kids Guides

For families traveling with children ages 2 to 14 seeking kid-friendly hotels, restaurants, and activities.

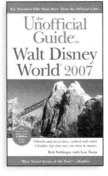

Unofficial Guides

For honeymooners, families, business travelers, and others who value no-nonsense, *Consumer Reports*–style advice.

For Dummies Travel Guides

For curious, independent travelers looking for a fun and easy way to plan a trip.

Visit Frommers.com

WILEY
Now you know.

Now hear this!

FREE download of Frommer's Top Travel Secrets at
www.audible.com/frommers*

Download **Frommer's Audio Tours**
into your MP3 player and let **Pauline Frommer**
be your personal guide to the best sights in
cities around the world.

Get your Frommer's Audio Tours plus Frommer's
recommended language lessons and other great
audiobooks for the trip ahead at:
www.audible.com/frommers

The One-Stop Travel Audio Solution.

audible.com®
*Offer valid through May 2009

Frommer's®
A Branded Imprint of ⊛**WILEY**
Now you know.

FROMMER'S® COMPLETE TRAVEL GUIDES

Alaska
Amalfi Coast
American Southwest
Amsterdam
Argentina
Arizona
Atlanta
Australia
Austria
Bahamas
Barcelona
Beijing
Belgium, Holland & Luxembourg
Belize
Bermuda
Boston
Brazil
British Columbia & the Canadian
 Rockies
Brussels & Bruges
Budapest & the Best of Hungary
Buenos Aires
Calgary
California
Canada
Cancún, Cozumel & the Yucatán
Cape Cod, Nantucket & Martha's
 Vineyard
Caribbean
Caribbean Ports of Call
Carolinas & Georgia
Chicago
Chile & Easter Island
China
Colorado
Costa Rica
Croatia
Cuba
Denmark
Denver, Boulder & Colorado Springs
Eastern Europe
Ecuador & the Galapagos Islands
Edinburgh & Glasgow
England
Europe
Europe by Rail

Florence, Tuscany & Umbria
Florida
France
Germany
Greece
Greek Islands
Guatemala
Hawaii
Hong Kong
Honolulu, Waikiki & Oahu
India
Ireland
Israel
Italy
Jamaica
Japan
Kauai
Las Vegas
London
Los Angeles
Los Cabos & Baja
Madrid
Maine Coast
Maryland & Delaware
Maui
Mexico
Montana & Wyoming
Montréal & Québec City
Morocco
Moscow & St. Petersburg
Munich & the Bavarian Alps
Nashville & Memphis
New England
Newfoundland & Labrador
New Mexico
New Orleans
New York City
New York State
New Zealand
Northern Italy
Norway
Nova Scotia, New Brunswick &
 Prince Edward Island
Oregon
Paris
Peru

Philadelphia & the Amish Country
Portugal
Prague & the Best of the Czech
 Republic
Provence & the Riviera
Puerto Rico
Rome
San Antonio & Austin
San Diego
San Francisco
Santa Fe, Taos & Albuquerque
Scandinavia
Scotland
Seattle
Seville, Granada & the Best of
 Andalusia
Shanghai
Sicily
Singapore & Malaysia
South Africa
South America
South Florida
South Korea
South Pacific
Southeast Asia
Spain
Sweden
Switzerland
Tahiti & French Polynesia
Texas
Thailand
Tokyo
Toronto
Turkey
USA
Utah
Vancouver & Victoria
Vermont, New Hampshire & Maine
Vienna & the Danube Valley
Vietnam
Virgin Islands
Virginia
Walt Disney World® & Orlando
Washington, D.C.
Washington State

FROMMER'S® DAY BY DAY GUIDES

Amsterdam
Barcelona
Beijing
Boston
Cancun & the Yucatan
Chicago
Florence & Tuscany

Hong Kong
Honolulu & Oahu
London
Maui
Montréal
Napa & Sonoma
New York City

Paris
Provence & the Riviera
Rome
San Francisco
Venice
Washington D.C.

PAULINE FROMMER'S GUIDES: SEE MORE. SPEND LESS.

Alaska
Hawaii
Italy

Las Vegas
London
New York City

Paris
Walt Disney World®
Washington D.C.

FROMMER'S® PORTABLE GUIDES

Acapulco, Ixtapa & Zihuatanejo
Amsterdam
Aruba, Bonaire & Curacao
Australia's Great Barrier Reef
Bahamas
Big Island of Hawaii
Boston
California Wine Country
Cancún
Cayman Islands
Charleston
Chicago
Dominican Republic

Florence
Las Vegas
Las Vegas for Non-Gamblers
London
Maui
Nantucket & Martha's Vineyard
New Orleans
New York City
Paris
Portland
Puerto Rico
Puerto Vallarta, Manzanillo & Guadalajara

Rio de Janeiro
San Diego
San Francisco
Savannah
St. Martin, Sint Maarten, Anguila & St. Bart's
Turks & Caicos
Vancouver
Venice
Virgin Islands
Washington, D.C.
Whistler

FROMMER'S® CRUISE GUIDES

Alaska Cruises & Ports of Call

Cruises & Ports of Call

European Cruises & Ports of Call

FROMMER'S® NATIONAL PARK GUIDES

Algonquin Provincial Park
Banff & Jasper
Grand Canyon

National Parks of the American West
Rocky Mountain
Yellowstone & Grand Teton

Yosemite and Sequoia & Kings Canyon
Zion & Bryce Canyon

FROMMER'S® WITH KIDS GUIDES

Chicago
Hawaii
Las Vegas
London

National Parks
New York City
San Francisco

Toronto
Walt Disney World® & Orlando
Washington, D.C.

FROMMER'S® PHRASEFINDER DICTIONARY GUIDES

WITHDRAWN

Chinese
French

German
Italian

Japanese
Spanish

SUZY GERSHMAN'S BORN TO SHOP GUIDES

France
Hong Kong, Shanghai & Beijing
Italy

London
New York
Paris

San Francisco
Where to Buy the Best of Everything

FROMMER'S® BEST-LOVED DRIVING TOURS

Britain
California
France
Germany

Ireland
Italy
New England
Northern Italy

Scotland
Spain
Tuscany & Umbria

THE UNOFFICIAL GUIDES®

Adventure Travel in Alaska
Beyond Disney
California with Kids
Central Italy
Chicago
Cruises
Disneyland®
England
Hawaii

Ireland
Las Vegas
London
Maui
Mexico's Best Beach Resorts
Mini Mickey
New Orleans
New York City
Paris

San Francisco
South Florida including Miami & the Keys
Walt Disney World®
Walt Disney World® for Grown-ups
Walt Disney World® with Kids
Washington, D.C.

SPECIAL-INTEREST TITLES

Athens Past & Present
Best Places to Raise Your Family
Cities Ranked & Rated
500 Places to Take Your Kids Before They Grow Up
Frommer's Best Day Trips from London
Frommer's Best RV & Tent Campgrounds in the U.S.A.

Frommer's Exploring America by RV
Frommer's NYC Free & Dirt Cheap
Frommer's Road Atlas Europe
Frommer's Road Atlas Ireland
Retirement Places Rated